ALSO BY KURT EICHENWALD

Conspiracy of Fools

The Informant

Serpent on the Rock

500 DAYS

SECRETS AND LIES
IN THE
TERROR WARS

KURT EICHENWALD

A TOUCHSTONE BOOK
PUBLISHED BY SIMON & SCHUSTER

NEW YORK LONDON TORONTO SYDNEY NEW DELHI

Touchstone
A Division of Simon & Schuster, Inc.
1230 Avenue of the Americas
New York, NY 10020

First Touchstone hardcover edition September 2012

TOUCHSTONE and colophon are registered trademarks of Simon & Schuster, Inc.

For information about special discounts for bulk purchases, please contact
Simon & Schuster Special Sales at 1-866-506-1949 or business@simonandschuster.com.

The Simon & Schuster Speakers Bureau can bring authors to your live event.
For more information or to book an event contact the Simon & Schuster Speakers Bureau
at 866-248-3049 or visit our website at www.simonspeakers.com.

Designed by Ruth Lee-Mui

Manufactured in the United States of America

10   9   8   7   6   5   4   3   2   1

Library of Congress Cataloging-in-Publication Data

Eichenwald, Kurt, 1961–
    500 days : secrets and lies in the terror wars / by Kurt Eichenwald.
      p. cm.
    1. September 11 Terrorist Attacks, 2001.   2. War on Terrorism, 2001–2009.
3. Terrorism—Prevention.   4. World politics—21st century.   I. Title.
II. Title: 500 days : secrets and lies in the terror wars.
    HV6432.7.E445 2012
    973.931—dc23   2012001214

ISBN 978-1-4516-6938-1
ISBN 978-1-4516-7413-2 (ebook)

To Frank Jordan
Teacher, mentor, friend and role model
to untold numbers of boys and men,
including me.

The interval between the decay of the old and the formation and the establishment of the new constitutes a period of transition which must always be one of uncertainty, confusion, error and wild and fierce fanaticism.

—JOHN C. CALHOUN,
A Disquisition on Government

500
DAYS

SECRETS AND LIES
IN THE
TERROR WARS

INTRODUCTION

This is not the book I set out to write. Originally, I had planned to chronicle the Bush administration's response to terrorism from the day of the September 11 attacks through the end of the president's second term in January 2009. The deeper I dug, though, the more I came to realize that my original strategy was off base. Instead, I concluded that every aspect of the terror wars flowed from judgments made in little more than five hundred days after 9/11—554 to be exact. Everything—the wars in Afghanistan and Iraq, warrantless wiretapping, detainee treatment, CIA tactics, and more—could be traced to those eighteen months. What followed in the nearly six years afterward was little more than reactions to those early decisions.

Equally important, I found that the strategy cobbled together in those initial days was not the creation of a single group of politicians or even of a single government. The Bush administration was important, but America did not hold a monopoly on shaping the multipronged assault on terrorists.

So, I changed directions. By concentrating my research on the rush of events over those 554 days, I would be able to lay bare the essence of a trauma that haunts the world to this day. I later decided that the full story could not be understood simply from a depiction of events in the corridors of power; this history was also shaped by the experiences of the powerless. Extraordinary rendition was not simply a policy adopted in government conference rooms—it played out in real ways on real people's lives, as did decisions about the application of the Geneva Conventions, the use of secret prisons, and the like. These experiences, sometimes horrendous, helped shape directions of international policies in profound and often unseen ways. I would be remiss in ignoring those individual consequences.

As with most histories, this endeavor entailed covering some now-familiar paths, although I was surprised by how often the accepted version of events proved to be inaccurate. A trove of additional evidence—derived from years of conducting interviews, reviewing documents, and listening to secret recordings—exposed a vast array of previously unknown details that make the narrative of this era clearer and, in some cases, more shocking. Woven together, I believe these elements of the story—the known and unknown, the domestic and the international, the great and the small—reveal the heart of an epochal upheaval that historians will continue to examine for decades to come.

Readers looking in these pages for my view of these events will no doubt be disappointed. I have little faith in opinion, even my own. Instead, this book is meant to be a dispassionate history of this crucial time. And I have found there is little in these tales that is black-and-white. While there have no doubt been horrible decisions, there are few villains; the Bush administration and its allies did not want to impose a police state and its critics did not want to coddle terrorists. Few on either side acted with disregard to the concerns of the other; instead, each wrestled with finding the proper balance, as they saw it. I leave it to the readers to decide who, if anyone, was right.

KURT EICHENWALD
(June, 2012)

THE CHARACTERS

The White House

George W. Bush	President of the United States
Dick Cheney	Vice President

On the White House Staff

Andy Card	Chief of Staff
Josh Bolten	Deputy Chief of Staff
Karl Rove	Advisor
Richard Clarke	Special Advisor on Cybersecurity
Stuart Bowen	Deputy Staff Secretary

In the National Security Council

Condoleezza Rice	National Security Advisor
Stephen Hadley	Deputy National Security Advisor
John Bellinger III	Senior Associate Counsel

In the White House Counsel's Office

Alberto Gonzales	White House Counsel
Tim Flanigan	Deputy Counsel
Bradford Berenson	Associate Counsel

In the Office of the Vice President

David Addington   Senior Counsel

The Central Intelligence Agency

George Tenet   Director
John McLaughlin   Acting Deputy Director
John Rizzo   Acting General Counsel

In the Counterterrorist Center

Cofer Black   Director
Ben Bonk   Deputy Director
Hank Crumpton   Special Operations

Station Chief

Robert Lady, Milan

Field Officers

Gary Schroen
Gary Berntsen
Johnny Michael Spann
Dave Tyson
Jeffrey Castelli
John Kiriakou
Deuce Martinez

Consultants

James Mitchell   Retired SERE psychologist
Bruce Jessen   Retired SERE psychologist

The Pentagon

Donald Rumsfeld   Secretary of Defense
Paul Wolfowitz   Deputy Secretary
William "Jim" Haynes   General Counsel

Whit Cobb   Deputy General Counsel
Richard Shiffrin   Deputy General Counsel, Intelligence
Alberto Mora   General Counsel, U.S. Navy
Douglas Feith   Undersecretary for Policy
Steve Cambone   Principal Deputy Undersecretary
                                               for Policy

United States Central Command

Tommy Franks   Commander

With the Joint Chiefs of Staff

Richard Myers   Chairman (from October 1, 2001)
Hugh Shelton   Chairman (until October 1, 2001)
Peter Pace   Vice Chairman
Jane Dalton   Legal Advisor

With the Naval Criminal Investigative Service

David Brant   Director
Michael Gelles   Chief Psychologist

With Survival, Evasion, Resistance, and Escape Program

Lt. Col. Morgan Banks   Chief Psychologist
Joseph Witsch   Instructor

At USAMIIRD

Bruce Ivins   Anthrax Specialist
John Ezzell   Anthrax Specialist

At Guantanamo Bay

Maj. Gen. Michael Dunlavey   Commander
Brig. Gen. Michael Lehnert   Commander
Maj. Gen. Geoffrey Miller   Commander
Lt. Col. Diane Beaver   Legal Advisor
Maj. John Leso   Psychologist

Col. Larry James	Psychologist
Britt Mallow	Commander, Criminal Investigation Task Force (CITF)
Mark Fallon	Director, CITF
Blaine Thomas	Assistant Special Agent in Charge, CITF

The Department of Justice

John Ashcroft	Attorney General
Larry Thompson	Deputy Attorney General
Theodore Olson	Solicitor General
Paul Clement	Deputy Solicitor General
Gregory Garre	Assistant Solicitor General

In the Criminal Division

| Michael Chertoff | Director |

In the Office of Legal Counsel

Jay Bybee	Assistant Attorney General
John Yoo	Deputy Assistant Attorney General
Patrick Philbin	Deputy Assistant Attorney General
John Delahunty	Special Counsel

With the Federal Bureau of Investigation

Bob Mueller	Director
Tom Pickard	Acting Director
Dale Watson	Assistant Director
Pasquale D'Amuro	Assistant Director
Ali Soufan	Special Agent
Harry Samit	Special Agent
Russell Fincher	Special Agent
Craig Donnachie	Special Agent
Robert Fuller	Special Agent
Greg Jones	Supervisory Special Agent
Michael Maltbie	Supervisory Special Agent

With the Immigration and Naturalization Service

James Ziglar	Commissioner
José Meléndez-Pérez	Customs Inspector
John Weess	Special Agent

Department of Transportation

Norm Mineta	Secretary

With the Federal Aviation Administration

Monte Belger	Acting Deputy Administrator
Dave Canoles	Manager, Air Traffic Evaluations and Investigations
Ben Sliney	Manager, National Operations

Department of State

Colin Powell	Secretary
Richard Armitage	Deputy Secretary
William Taft IV	General Counsel
Pierre-Richard Prosper	Ambassador-at-Large
Christopher Hoh	Deputy Ambassador Sarajevo
Gary Edson	Deputy Assistant

The National Security Agency

Michael Hayden	Director

The Centers for Disease Control

Sherif Zaki	Chief, Infectious Disease Pathology

The United States Senate

Joe Biden	Delaware Democrat
Robert Byrd	West Virginia Democrat
Tom Daschle	South Dakota Democrat
Patrick Leahy	Vermont Democrat

Joseph Lieberman	Connecticut Democrat
Ted Kennedy	Massachusetts Democrat
Don Nickles	Nevada Republican
Harry Reid	Nevada Democrat
Arlen Specter	Pennsylvania Republican

Federal Courts

Robert Doumar	District Judge
T. S. Ellis 3d	District Judge
Colleen Kollar-Kotelly	District Judge
Michael Mukasey	District Judge
J. Harvis Wilkinson 3d	Appellate Judge
Tommy Miller	Magistrate Judge

In Great Britain

Tony Blair	Prime Minister
Jack Straw	Foreign Secretary
David Manning	Foreign Policy Advisor
Geoff Hoon	Defense Secretary
Alastair Campbell	Director of Communications
Jonathan Powell	Chief of Staff
Christopher Meyer	Ambassador to the United States
Lt. Gen. Anthony Pigott	Coordinator, Afghanistan campaign

The Tipton Three

Shafiq Rasul
Ruhal Ahmed
Asif Iqbal

In Canada

Bill Graham	Foreign Minister
Ahmad El-Maati	Terrorist suspect (exonerated)
Abdullah Almalki	Terrorist suspect (exonerated)
Maher Arar	Terrorist suspect (exonerated)

Monia Mazigh	Arar's wife
Patrick Callaghan	Staff Sargeant, Mounties
Randy Buffam	Corporal, Mounties
Rick Flewelling	Corporal, Mounties
Alexander Gelvan	CSIS agent
Theresa Sullivan	CSIS agent

In Bosnia

Alija Behmen	Prime Minister
Muhamed Bešić	Interior Minister
Belkacem Bensayah	Terrorist suspect (exonerated)
Anela Kobilica	Bensayah's wife
Lakhdar Boumediene	Terrorist suspect (exonerated)

In Italy

Silvio Berlusconi	Prime Minister
Gianfranco Battelli	Director, SISMI
Nicolò Pollari	Director, SISMI
Gustavo Pignero	Director of Counter-Espionage, SISMI
Stefano D'Ambrosio	SISMI officer
Luciano Pironi	Carabinieri officer
Abu Omar	Terrorist suspect, uncharged

In Afghanistan

Hamid Karzai	Chair, Transitional Administration

With the American Military

John Bolduc	Master Sergeant
Mark Nutsch	Captain, Special Forces
Henry Smith	Army Major

With the Northern Alliance

Ahmad Shah Massoud
Rashid Dostum

Masood Khalili
Muhammed Aref Sawari

With the Taliban

John Walker Lindh
Yaser Esam Hamdi

In France

Jacques Chirac   President

In Russia

Vladmir Putin   President

In Germany

Gerhard Schröder   Chancellor

In Syria

George Salloum   Head of Interrogations

In Libya

Moussa Koussa   Former Deputy Director of Intelligence

In Australia

John Howard   Prime Minister

In Indonesia

General I Made Mangku Pastika   Commissioner, General Police

At the United Nations

Kofi Annan   Secretary General
Hans Blix   Chairman, UNMOVIC

At the International Atomic Energy Agency

Mohamed ElBaradei   Director General

With al-Qaeda

Osama bin Laden
Khalid Sheikh Mohammed
Abu Zubaydah
Ibn al-Shaykh al-Libi
Muhammad Salah

Assistants

Salim Hamdan
Nasser al-Bhari

Operatives

Mohammed al-Qahtani
Ramzi bin al-Shibh
Zacarias Moussaoui
Richard Reid
José Padilla

With Jemaah Islamiyah

Riduan Isamuddin (Hambali)
Yazid Sufaat   Head of Biological Research

Operatives

Amrozi bin Nurhasyim
Imam Samudra
Ali Imron
"Iqbel"
"Jimi"

Journalists

At NBC News

Tom Brokaw	News Anchor
Erin O'Connor	Assistant to Brokaw
Casey Chamberlain	Assistant to Brokaw

At the Middle East Broadcasting Company

Baker Atyani	Reporter

At al Jazeera

Yosri Fouda	Reporter

At the British Broadcasting Corporation

David Frost	Talk Show Host

At The Sun

Robert Stevens	Photo Editor

At the Sunday Times of London

Matthew Campbell	Reporter

At Newsweek

Colin Soloway	Reporter, freelance

Lawyers

Frank Dunham Jr.	Federal Public Defender
Neal Katyal	Visiting Professor, Yale Law School
Tom Wilner	Partner, Shearman & Sterling
Clive Stafford Smith	Founder, Reprieve
Michael Ratner	Director, Center for Constitutional Rights

Others

Dr. Ayman Batarfi	Physician, Guantanamo detainee
Hermis Moutardier	Flight Attendant, American Airlines
Cristina Jones	Flight Attendant, American Airlines
Gail Jawahir	Customer Service Representative, United Airlines
Dr. Martin E. P. Seligman	Psychiatric Researcher

PROLOGUE

Crawford, Texas
Twelve Months

With the flick of a switch, the electronic timer on a concealed briefcase bomb flashed red, its digits counting down from five minutes. A small fan quietly whirred, generating a breath of air that could disperse enough sarin gas to kill everyone within several yards.

A few feet away, George W. Bush set a plate of cookies on a table, shooting a glance outside as he dropped into an overstuffed chair. His beloved ranch was as tranquil as he had ever seen, with sunlight pouring through the trees in streaks of blazing heat. A cow lumbered past, attracting the fleeting attention of the grim-faced visitors who were there to reveal some of the nation's most sensitive secrets to the Texas governor.

Thirty days earlier, Bush had been selected at the Republican National Convention in Philadelphia as the party's candidate for the 2000 presidential election. By tradition, the Central Intelligence Agency provides a broad-ranging intelligence briefing during the presidential campaign to both the Republican and the Democratic nominees, preparing them for the responsibilities of the White House. On this day, September 2, 2000, four agency officials—led by John McLaughlin, the acting deputy director—had traveled to Bush's ranch outside of Waco to present him and three of his senior advisors—Condoleezza Rice, Paul Wolfowitz, and Josh Bolten—with classified information from the most closely guarded sanctums of American power.

For three hours, the conversation roamed the globe—from Russia to China, from the Middle East to Latin America. Ben Bonk, the deputy director of the

CIA's Counterterrorist Center, kept his silence, biding his time as he took the measure of America's would-be commander in chief.

Bush struck him as intriguingly quirky; here was an aspirant to the highest office in the land attending his first intelligence briefing decked out in full Marlboro Man regalia—cowboy boots, jeans with a big buckle, and a checked short-sleeved work shirt. He was unpretentious, a presidential candidate willing to fetch food from the kitchen for his guests. Just as strikingly, the walls were plastered with tacky memorabilia, like a rubberized bass that could turn its head and break into song—a peculiar choice for a man seeking to become leader of the free world. But Bush's down-home veneer, Bonk thought, disguised a keen mind. He had expected to be dealing with an intellectual lightweight, reliant on his aides for guidance in the subtleties of statecraft. Instead, it was Bush who peppered the briefers with frequent and often insightful questions, while his subordinates stayed quiet.

Bonk's plan for this day was itself a testament to the effectiveness of Bush's aw-shucks folksiness. Because of that reputation, Bonk had overcome his hesitance about sneaking the briefcase bomb into the house, providing Bush a vivid exhibit of the terrorist threat. Even though it contained no poison gas, the device was real enough—the CIA had built it based on a design seized from a Japanese terrorist cult that had used the bomb to kill thirteen commuters in attacks on Tokyo subway stations.

He had let the Secret Service in on the ruse, of course—otherwise, the security detail would probably have arrested him at the door—but the governor had been left in the dark about it. Once inside, Bonk set the briefcase on the floor next to his chair and had now, just before it was his turn to speak, activated the bomb with the switch on the briefcase handle.

The governor's eyes shifted to Bonk.

"All right, Ben," he said. "You're up."

Bonk looked down at his briefing book. His colleagues had all opened their presentations with a joke—some were even funny—but terrorism didn't lend itself to laughter. So Bonk had chosen a more attention-grabbing tack: shock.

"Governor Bush, everything you've heard today about future events has been qualified as probable or likely things," he said. "But I can say one thing for sure without any qualification: Sometime in the next four years, Americans will die as a result of a terrorist incident."

Bush furrowed his brow as the slightest wisps of joviality were sucked out of the room. Bonk paused to let his audience absorb the import of his statement.

Numerous terrorist organizations were on the move, he continued, but the most dangerous were the Islamic extremist groups. Al-Qaeda, Hamas, Hezbollah, Islamic Jihad—the names varied but their recipe for mayhem was the same: suicide and truck bombings, kidnappings, torture, executions.

Still, the bloody toll from those tactics was nothing compared to what lay in store for America and its allies if the terrorists succeeded in their quest for chemical, biological, radiological, nuclear weapons, collectively known as CBRN. Al-Qaeda, led by Osama bin Laden, was the group most likely to succeed, Bonk said; it had the deepest pockets and the most far-flung operational networks. Its deadly shopping list was long—sodium cyanide, anthrax, radiological disbursal devices, improvised nuclear arms. If al-Qaeda or another terrorist group got its hands on any of them, it would show no hesitation in using the weapons immediately to murder as many Americans as possible. America's nuclear arsenal, which had kept an uneasy peace with the Soviet empire in the decades of the Cold War, wouldn't deter Islamic extremists.

These weapons of mass destruction did not have to be large or cumbersome to transport, Bonk explained. Terrorists could easily slip compact bombs into a crowd without raising suspicion.

Bonk reached for his briefcase, stood, and walked toward Bush. As he approached, he popped it open, then tilted the case forward. Bush saw the red digits counting down.

"Don't worry," Bonk said. "This is harmless. But it is exactly the kind of chemical device that people can bring into a room and kill everybody."

He glanced down at the timer. "And this one would be going off in two minutes."

Bush looked at Josh Bolten. "You've got one and a half minutes to get that thing out of here," he said.

Outside of Kandahar, Afghanistan
Three Months

The dilapidated minibus kicked up a cloud of dust as it rumbled over a wasteland of sand and rock. Inside, a Pakistani journalist named Baker Atyani rode in silence, occasionally glancing at the Arab fighter beside him. The man cut an imposing—even frightening—figure, with grenades hung from his belt and a machine gun clutched in his hands. Atyani's seat had been installed facing the rear, and the windows on all sides were darkened, leaving him unable to see where they were or where they were headed. He knew better than to ask.

For three hours, the rattletrap bounced and shuddered until it finally arrived in front of the towering walls of a compound. The main gate swung open and the bus passed through, heading toward a nondescript mud house. A group of heavily armed men approached; their alert eyes flickered about, looking for signs of danger.

The man in the passenger seat—whom Atyani knew as Osman—rolled down his window. "This is the guy who is supposed to meet the sheikh," he said.

Okay, a guard replied. But they still needed to search the newcomer.

Atyani stepped out of the bus. Dust stung his eyes and heat baked the air. The security team patted him down for weapons, riffled through his bag, and confiscated his watch, promising to return it later. Then they escorted Atyani and Osman into the house and made them wait for five minutes. Finally, the guard led them to an unimposing room. As they entered, Atyani spotted several men wearing head coverings and dressed in long white robes. Among them was Osama bin Laden, the most wanted man in the world.

Bin Laden approached Atyani, greeting him with a handshake and customary hug. "You are welcome here in Afghanistan, and in my place," he said.

The moment was dreamlike. As he looked around the room, Atyani could not help but wonder if the house might be bombed while he was there. Yet, it had never crossed his mind to refuse the offer to travel to this remote spot for an interview with a man shaping history, an Islamic radical whose global influence exceeded that of some nations.

Bin Laden preached a philosophy of endless battle, of international conspiracies seeking to destroy Islam by attracting Muslims to the material comforts of *jahiliyya*, an evil rejection of divine guidance. This was a battle between God and Satan, bin Laden declared, requiring Muslims to wage war against the purveyors of *jahiliyya*—be they Westerners, Jews, or fellow Muslims. Defending Islam, he said, justified any action—even mass killing.

The army that would scatter the enemy and drive Western nations out of the Middle East was al-Qaeda, a group bin Laden cofounded in 1989 to lead a religious purification of the Muslim world. By 2001, he had transformed al-Qaeda into a formidable fighting force, trained at camps like Tarnak Farms near the Kandahar airport. He and his followers established hideaways and safe houses: Mujama' 6 in Kandahar; Bayt al-Ruman, a religious institute inside an old Afghani school; Khan Gulan Patsheh, a Kabul guesthouse that was previously part of the palace for the king of Afghanistan; and four mountain military bases named for "martyrs" who killed themselves in battles against the West.

Al-Qaeda had also set up a sophisticated communications system. The solar-powered technology relied on Casio FX-795P computers and handheld Yaesu radios. When a computer operator typed in a message, the Casio system encrypted it into a series of numbers. The operator would then read them over the radio. A second operator would enter the numbers into another computer, which would decrypt the message. The al-Qaeda members used a set radio frequency, but knew to switch to another if someone in the conversation called out a code name.

The true power of al-Qaeda flowed from its arsenal of deadly weapons: SA-7 Grail surface-to-air missile systems, Stinger missiles, self-propelled antiaircraft systems, ZIL-130 vehicles with mounted SA-6 missiles, cluster bombs, RKG-3 antitank grenades, Sagger antitank guided missiles, 30mm automatic grenade launchers, AKSU-74 assault rifles, Uzi 9mm, and scores of other armaments. Most were kept safely stashed in a four-and-a-half-mile tunnel in the vicinity of the Sharsiab camp near Kabul.

While al-Qaeda had yet to obtain chemical, nuclear, or biological weapons, bin Laden's top deputies had their sights set on a radioactive waste storage site in the Turkmenistan city of Ashkhabad. There, they believed, al-Qaeda could obtain the fissionable material it needed for an atomic bomb or a dirty bomb that would use conventional explosives to spread radiation over a wide area. The group had come close; in March 2000, some of its members had tried to spirit a load of strontium 90 from Uzbekistan to Kazakhstan, but it was seized at the border.

Even without weapons of mass destruction, bin Laden and al-Qaeda had orchestrated large-scale assaults on Americans. They bombed U.S. embassies in Kenya and Tanzania in 1998, slaughtering 224 people; in 2000, they crippled the USS *Cole,* a navy destroyer, killing 17 sailors. The attacks were a triumph for al-Qaeda, yielding a bonanza of recruits eager to wage jihad.

Al-Qaeda rarely varied its basic plan for carrying out its lethal missions. The group would spend years planning an attack, then, before it was launched, bin Laden would issue a public warning that a strike was in the offing. Atyani had traveled to this terrorist enclave anticipating that he would hear just such a proclamation of calamity to come. It would be the biggest scoop of his career.

His voice quiet and measured, bin Laden invited Atyani to sit. The men settled down on flowered throw cushions and started talking. There was the usual delicate choreography of an interview, until Atyani shifted the conversation away from pleasantries to the matter at hand.

"Now, I need to do my job," he said.

Bin Laden nodded gravely. "We will bring the camera," he said. But circumstances had changed since his followers had last contacted the reporter.

"I know we agreed for you to come here for an interview with me," bin Laden said. "In fact, I cannot give interviews myself."

He was a guest of Afghanistan's ruling government, the Taliban, bin Laden said, and he had promised them that he would no longer speak with reporters. Speaking on camera would be too egregious a violation of his word.

"But we will give you something better. There is some footage we are going to give to you, and some news."

"What footage?"

"Have you watched CNN or Al Jazeera in the last few days?" bin Laden asked. There had been some video of al-Qaeda members training, images from the heart of the group's operations.

"I will give you that film and more," bin Laden said. "We will give you better than what's already been shown, so you can use it in your story."

Amazing. Bin Laden knew the rules of television broadcasting—a video already shown on another network was old news. To generate a new report, there needed to be fresh footage. And apparently, bin Laden had saved some film for Atyani. He might live like a nomad, Atyani thought, but bin Laden was pretty media-savvy.

Bin Laden played one videocassette and one DVD for Atyani. It was standard propaganda, showing al-Qaeda fighters training and bin Laden praising jihadists who killed Americans. Once the screening finished, bin Laden told Atyani that he could have the videos.

At that point a man limped into the room carrying a television camera and began setting it up. Bin Laden invited senior al-Qaeda leaders Ayman al-Zawahiri and Abu Hafs to sit beside him. Zawahiri stepped forward, while Hafs stood back.

"I don't want to be on camera," he said.

After less than a minute of filming, bin Laden went silent, deferring to Hafs for the first time since the meeting began.

"Just wait," Hafs said. "In the coming weeks there will be a big surprise."

"What do you mean by 'a big surprise'?" Atyani asked.

"We will strike American and Israeli interests."

There it was. The threat of an attack, the news they had brought Atyani into Afghanistan to hear.

Atyani turned to bin Laden. "How much of this is correct? What are you planning?"

Bin Laden smiled but said nothing. Another man in the room, an African, confirmed Hafs's statement.

"Okay," Atyani said. "Then I am putting this on the news that you are preparing a surprise."

Bin Laden nodded. "You can carry the news," he said. "And you can quote al-Qaeda as saying that the coffin business in the United States is going to increase."

CIA Headquarters, Langley, Virginia
Two Months

Frustration was building inside the Counterterrorist Center. For months, credible intelligence had been flowing in that al-Qaeda was preparing another spectacular attack. Electronic intercepts, informants, details from foreign intelligence services—everything pointed toward something big on the way. Topping it off, bin Laden had practically announced the plans to a Pakistani journalist. But the administration wasn't responding.

The CIA officers had hit a wall. They could gather all of the information possible about the nature and severity of a threat, but it was the political leaders who decided whether and when to take action. Sometimes, the two sides worked well together—when a drumbeat of intelligence in 1999 alerted the CIA that al-Qaeda was planning significant strikes on the first day of the new millennium, the government sprang into action. George Tenet, the CIA director, had ordered the Counterterrorist Center to throw everything it had into thwarting any attacks. From the White House down through the executive branch, the mobilization of forces was astonishing and had succeeded in foiling multiple plots around the globe, including one operation to bomb Los Angeles International Airport.

That was just one of an almost endless series of planned terrorist operations over the years, many of which the CIA prevented. In 1998, the CIA learned that al-Qaeda was set to launch a new attack against an American embassy, this time in Tirana, Albania; the plotters were identified and snatched up. That same year, the agency disrupted terrorist plans by Turkish extremists connected to bin Laden; the men, who were arrested, had hoped to crash an airplane filled with explosives into the tomb of Mustafa Kemal Atatürk, the leader of the Turkish war of independence, during a government ceremony marking his death. Still, counterterrorism officials knew the odds were not with them. There was always too much worrisome information flooding in too fast. To stop al-Qaeda's relentless operations, the intelligence community had to be successful every time. The terrorists had to be successful only once.

Now the evidence of a potential attack was as stark as it had ever been. Cofer Black, the chief of the Counterterrorist Center, had already accompanied Tenet and other CIA officers to the White House to sound the alarm. The Federal Bureau of Investigation had detected the emerging threats; the National Security Agency was picking up a disturbing increase in the amount of "chatter" among terrorists and their sympathizers. But the warnings engendered no coordinated, government-wide response, no sense of urgency to match the reaction to the millennium threat. No orders to strain budgets to the limit. No instructions to step up support for the Northern Alliance, the American-backed fighting force in Afghanistan that was battling al-Qaeda and the Taliban for control of the country. A gathering danger to the homeland was being met with a collective yawn.

On July 9, a Monday, the center's top officials gathered in a basement conference room at headquarters to gauge the hopelessness of their dilemma. They knew the awful reality of what was coming—a massive terrorist attack, potentially on American soil. They knew, too, that they had a shield against the outcry that was bound to be hurled their way in the aftermath of a terrorist onslaught. Critics might rail that the Counterterrorist Center had fallen asleep at the switch, but the group's records would prove otherwise—Cofer Black had retained a trove of classified PowerPoints that his team had presented in repeated briefings to senior government officials, all of them warning in dire terms of the impending disaster. His people were putting together another one at that moment, in a last attempt to get the message across that the administration was slumbering though an emergency.

Yet they knew, despite that proof of their diligence, the politicians would still make them the scapegoats if the worst happened. Not so much for their failure to collect intelligence, but for their failure to persuade the White House to listen.

As the meeting unfolded, one official offered a suggestion. "You know, if we were smart, we would rotate out of here and they can bring some new guys in to ride this thing down. 'Cause it's going to be really, really bad."

From the head of the table, Black waved away the idea. "Sorry, I don't think we can do that," he said. "First of all, we'd have to find somebody that's capable of coming in here quickly, and I don't think that's likely."

He flashed a smile. "Nobody's more qualified than us to ride this thing down."

Everyone laughed uneasily.

FBI Headquarters, Washington, D.C.
Two months

"You're not going to believe this!"

Tom Pickard, the acting director of the FBI, was fuming as he stormed into the office of Dale Watson, the top FBI official in charge of counterterrorism. It was about one o'clock on the afternoon of July 12 and Pickard had just returned from briefing the new attorney general, John Ashcroft, on the status of the FBI's most pressing items.

The opinion within the FBI of Ashcroft had rapidly soured, and every few days brought another "you're not going to believe this" story. He refused to allow security agents to check the locks and alarms in his house, or even to lay their eyes on his family members, whom they were duty-bound to protect. Then, in May, as the CIA was warning of a potential attack, Ashcroft had released a department-wide statement of his top priorities, and it hadn't even mentioned terrorism. Pickard and Watson had been flabbergasted.

Despite Ashcroft's apparent indifference, Pickard tried to hammer home the magnitude of the terrorist threat almost every time they met. But at this latest briefing, Pickard told Watson, the attorney general had gone off the rails.

"I was telling him about the high level of chatter, and how it suggested something big was about to happen," Pickard told Watson. "And then he interrupted me and said, 'I don't want to hear about that anymore.' "

"*What?*"

"He didn't want me to talk to him about al-Qaeda or the threats. He said there was nothing he could do about that."

At that point the analysis indicated that any attack would occur overseas, but *still*. Investigating a strike on American interests, anywhere, would fall to the FBI. Americans would certainly die. All of the law enforcement machinery in the Justice Department—the FBI, the INS, the Border Patrol, the Marshals Service—needed to be oiled and ready. Why couldn't Ashcroft grasp the obvious?

"I told him he should sit down right now and talk to George Tenet so he could hear from him right away about what was happening," Pickard told Watson.

He had tried getting in Ashcroft's face, and pushing back as much as he could. "But it didn't work," Pickard said. "He doesn't want to hear about it."

Orlando, Florida
One Month

The customs agent was at a loss. Since the Saudi had come to her booth minutes before, nothing had gone right.

The traveler had arrived that day, August 4, at Terminal A of the Orlando International Airport aboard Virgin Airlines flight 15 from London. He walked to customs and, after a short wait, presented his passport, declaration, and arrival-departure form.

But the documents had been filled out incorrectly, and the agent was struggling to solve the problem. The visitor, Mohammed al-Qahtani, didn't speak English and was combative. The agent decided to refer him to another inspector, who could bring in a translator.

Just past 5:30 that afternoon, Qahtani was sent for further questioning to José Meléndez-Pérez, a twelve-year veteran. He'd often dealt with Saudi travelers and was accustomed to helping them straighten out problems with entry forms. This, he figured, wouldn't be difficult.

Quickly, he realized how wrong he was. Qahtani's dark, angry eyes frightened him. His body language conveyed pure arrogance. He seemed consumed by hate.

Before working as a customs agent, Meléndez-Pérez had spent twenty-six years in the military, and to him, Qahtani looked like a soldier. He was dressed in black, with short hair and a thin mustache. He appeared to be very strong.

Meléndez-Pérez shuffled through Qahtani's paperwork and saw more problems—there was no return airline ticket, and no listed hotel reservation. This was suspicious. The agent requested an Arabic interpreter, and was soon questioning Qahtani.

"Mr. Qahtani, why are you not in possession of a return airline ticket?"

"I don't know where I'm going when I leave the United States," he snapped in Arabic as he jabbed his finger toward the agent's face.

Meléndez-Pérez stepped back. *Is this guy a hit man?* Such hired guns often improvised their travel plans as they went along. On the other hand, Meléndez-Pérez thought, maybe he had watched too many gangster movies. Either way, Qahtani's answer wasn't reassuring. The agent tried again.

"A friend of mine is arriving in the United States at a later date," Qahtani said. *"He knows where I'm going. He is going to make the arrangements for my departure."*

"Do you know when your friend is arriving?"

"Three or four days," Qahtani said with a sneer.

Moving on.

"What's the purpose of your trip?" the agent asked. "And how long are you staying?"

"I'll be vacationing and traveling through the United States for six days."

"Why would you be vacationing for only six days, and spend half the time waiting for your friend?"

Qahtani threw out a dismissive response. Meléndez-Pérez changed subjects.

"Where are you going to be staying?"

"Hotel."

Again, nonsense. "With you not speaking English, and without a reservation, you're going to have a lot of trouble getting around Orlando."

"I have a friend waiting for me upstairs."

"All right," Meléndez-Pérez said. "What's the name of your friend?"

Qahtani thrust his chin forward in defiance. *"No one is meeting me."*

A contradiction—in a matter of seconds.

"So, this goes back to what I asked before," Meléndez Pérez said. "How are you getting around Orlando?"

"I have to call my friend. Then he'll pick me up."

Meléndez-Pérez tried to show no reaction to what he knew was a stream of lies. "All right, give me your friend's name and number."

"No!" Qahtani barked. *"It is none of your business!"*

The interview went on for an hour and a half. A search turned up $2,800, hardly enough for a six-day vacation plus a hotel room and return airfare. Qahtani said a friend was bringing him more money—a friend he hadn't known long.

Meléndez-Pérez suppressed a smile. Someone this guy barely knew was going to shell out hundreds of dollars for his airline ticket? Another lie. The agent asked if Qahtani would consent to being placed under oath. The Saudi agreed.

Meléndez-Pérez swore in Qahtani and asked his first question.

"I won't answer," he replied brusquely.

The interpreter translated the words, then looked Meléndez-Pérez in the eye. "Something's wrong here."

The agent nodded. That was clear. He would not allow Qahtani into the country.

Meléndez-Pérez explained his decision to his bosses. They authorized him to put the man on a plane back to London. The agent returned to Qahtani and told him that he was being turned away and advised that he voluntarily withdraw his application for admission.

Qahtani responded in fury. *"I am* not *about to pay for a return ticket!"*

Meléndez-Pérez nodded. "No problem," he said. "We'll place you in a detention facility overnight and tomorrow we will make the necessary arrangement to get you a plane ticket so you can go back where you came from."

When the words were translated into Arabic, Qahtani's face fell. *All right.* He would withdraw his application.

Arrangements were made for the return flight. Just before departure time, Meléndez-Pérez summoned another inspector, and the two of them escorted the Saudi to his gate. As he was about to board, Qahtani turned and glared at the two inspectors.

"I'll be back," he growled, his first English words since his arrival.

Qahtani, an al-Qaeda operative assigned to help fellow terrorists seize and crash commercial airliners, stormed onto the plane. Outside the terminal, Mohammed Atta, the leader of the plot, waited in vain for the arrival of the twentieth hijacker. But Qahtani would never return.

Bloomington, Minnesota
Twenty-six days

The air was stale and warm inside the interrogation room at the St. Paul field office of the Immigration and Naturalization Service. Two rumpled federal agents—Harry Samit of the FBI and John Weess of the INS—sat across from a moonfaced, heavyset French citizen named Zacarias Moussaoui. He had been arrested the previous day for overstaying his visa, but the charge was mostly a pretext for holding him; the agents believed he might be a terrorist.

An official at the Pan Am International Flight Academy in Eagan had called the FBI to report suspicious behavior by Moussaoui. He had never made a solo flight but wanted to be trained to fly 747s. He paid wads of cash just to use a flight simulator. And he was Muslim.

When they arrested Moussaoui, the agents questioned his roommate, Hussein al-Attas, who told a frightening story: Their suspect had talked about killing civilians for jihad and proclaimed his willingness to become a martyr for Islam. Then, when the agents first questioned Moussaoui, he had played the fool, claiming not to know where he worked, what he did for a living, or how much he was paid. He was carrying thousands of dollars in cash that he said had been given to him by associates whose names he didn't know. And even as he was being questioned, he begged the agents to let him finish his flight lessons.

This time, the pleading had resumed as soon as Samit and Weess walked into the interrogation room. Moussaoui promised to answer all of their questions, but only if they allowed him to continue his training. Once he finished, he would gladly come back for deportation.

"Not now," Samit replied. "Too many questions still need to be resolved."

Let's discuss the money again, he said. How was it that Moussaoui couldn't identify the people who sent him so much cash?

"I've told you about that!" Moussaoui shouted.

He spluttered angrily that he was being treated unfairly. Then he tossed out the name of the men who had financed him—Ahmed Atif and someone named Habib from Germany. Weeks would pass before the agents proved Moussaoui was lying about his supposed benefactors.

There was something else, Samit said. During his initial interview, Moussaoui had mentioned conducting Internet searches for flight schools. A laptop computer had been recovered among Moussaoui's things. "Would you allow us to search that computer?" Samit asked.

"No. I won't permit that."

That was his right, Samit responded. But now, he said, he wanted to tell Moussaoui a few things.

"Your story doesn't add up," Samit said. "You haven't given us a satisfactory explanation for why you're in the United States, or why you came here for flight training. The reasons you give don't make any sense."

He leaned in. "We know you're an Islamic extremist, Mr. Moussaoui. We know you talked about violence before. We know you're planning something. I want you to tell us what your plot is and who you're working with."

Moussaoui stiffened. "My training is just for fun. I am not a terrorist. I'm not part of a terrorist group. I don't have any contact with terrorists."

Samit's gaze bored in. "Mr. Moussaoui, we know you're involved in a plot, a plot involving airlines," he said.

"I want to remind you, you are in custody. And if anything happens, you will be held accountable by the United States, by the American people."

Moussaoui stared at Samit in silence.

Minneapolis, Minnesota
Fifteen days

FBI supervisors in Washington wouldn't authorize an investigation of Moussaoui. There wasn't enough information to justify a search warrant, they said, or to push through an application under the Foreign Intelligence Surveillance Act—FISA. Finally, Samit's boss, Greg Jones, called Michael Maltbie, the supervisory special agent in Washington who was blocking the case. Tempers flared.

The FISA application—in fact, the whole case—was built on air, Maltbie argued. "What you have done is couched it in such a way that people get spun up."

"Good!" Jones replied. "We want to make sure he doesn't get control of an airplane and crash it into the World Trade Center or something like that."

Ridiculous, Maltbie scoffed. "That's not going to happen."

Takhar Province, Afghanistan
Two Days

As the first cool nights of fall approached, the American-backed Northern Alliance was struggling in its fight against the Taliban and al-Qaeda. The change of weather punctuated the end of a failed summer offensive by the force led by Ahmad Shah Massoud, the alliance's most important commander and Afghanistan's only credible threat to bin Laden. An attempt to capture the city of Taloqan, lost to the Taliban in 2000, had flopped. American support was inadequate, but Massoud still made a show of bravado, promising his fighters that they would soon take Kabul.

Amid the strategic planning, a phone call came in that puzzled Massoud. The Taliban and al-Qaeda were building up forces on the front line, he was told, but were not pushing forward to the north. Then Massoud learned that Taliban communications had been intercepted, instructing the units not to attack yet. It was as if the Taliban and al-Qaeda knew that something big was about to happen.

As this turn of events was unfolding, two journalists—Karim Touzani and Kacem Bakkali, who both carried Belgian passports—were pestering Massoud's top officers to arrange for an interview with the military leader. They said that they had traveled from London to document Islam in Afghanistan. After three weeks of waiting, on the night of September 8, the men begged for the meeting to take place within the next twenty-four hours. After that, they would have to leave for Kabul.

Just before lunch the next day, Massoud agreed to get together with the men for their interview. He motioned to his friend Masood Khalili.

"I want you to sit with me, and translate," he said.

The visitors, who had turned unusually quiet, set up their camera on a table in front of Massoud. "I want to know your questions before you start recording," he said.

The men agreed, but their words had to be translated from French. Touzani brought out a blue pen and started scribbling: *Why are you against Osama bin Laden? Why do you call him a killer? If you take Kabul what will you do with him?*

After writing down fifteen questions, Touzani handed the notes to Khalili, who translated; eight of the queries were about bin Laden. That struck Khalili as odd, and he glanced over at Massoud. There were five worry lines on his forehead, instead of the usual one.

"Okay," Massoud said. "Let's film."

One of the men asked something—no one would remember what—and Khalili started interpreting.

Then, an explosion. A bomb hidden inside the video camera detonated; Touzani set off explosives that were strapped around his waist, blowing him to bits. Amid the chaos, Massoud's guards started shooting, killing the other man.

Massoud, critically injured by the attack, was rushed to a helicopter, which flew to a hospital in Tajikistan. But it was too late. When the chopper landed, he was dead.

The most important challenger to al-Qaeda and the Taliban, the man most likely to help the Americans hunt down bin Laden, had been taken out of the equation.

Boston, Massachusetts
September 11, 2001

By 7:00 A.M., only a smattering of passengers had arrived for United Airlines flight 175 at Boston Logan International Airport. Gail Jawahir, a United customer service representative for thirteen years, had been at work for two hours and was surprised that the flow of passengers was so sluggish.

Two well-dressed Arabic men approached the ticket counter, and Jawahir greeted them. They were Hamza and Ahmed al-Ghamdi, men assigned by al-Qaeda to join in a murderous hijacking plot. They had just checked out of the Days Hotel after performing their ritual cleansing, including dousing themselves with cologne, in anticipation of their own deaths. The fragrance was still heavy, almost overwhelming. They had arrived at the airport by a Bay State Taxi, angering the driver with just a fifteen-cent tip. From there, they had entered into Terminal C and walked directly to Jawahir's station.

"I wish purchase ticket," Ahmed said.

Already, Jawahir knew this was going to be difficult—the man's English was terrible.

"Checking in or buying a ticket?" she asked.

"Purchase ticket."

Jawahir noticed that the man was holding a United Airlines envelope with an itinerary. He had an e-ticket.

"Sir, you don't need to buy a ticket. You already have a ticket. You can head right over to the check-in area."

The two walked off to another line. They were sent back, apparently still confused.

"I need buy ticket," Ahmed again said to Jawahir.

She decided to guide the two men through the check-in process and asked for their itinerary. They were booked for United 175. She saw they were both named al-Ghamdi and were seated next to each other in row nine.

Jawahir requested their identification; Ahmed handed her a Florida driver's license, while Hamza gave her one from Virginia. She asked the usual security questions—*Did you pack your own baggage? Has it been out of your sight?*—but had to keep repeating them until the men could answer.

Each checked a bag and had a carry-on. Jawahir printed out their boarding passes.

"Would it be okay if I put both of these in one envelope?" she asked. The men seemed uncertain what she meant, but agreed anyway.

Jawahir circled the gate number to make sure that they could figure out where to go. Then she slid the boarding passes into the envelope and handed it to them.

"Now, you need to go through security," she said, pointing them in the proper direction.

The two men took the envelope without a word. They walked calmly through security, then headed toward Gate 19 to board the awaiting plane.

• • •

The attacks were over in less than three hours. But it was the eighteen months after 9/11 that set America on the course that it pursued for more than a decade.

Decisions that only weeks before the hijackings would have been inconceivable tore through the White House in a desperate race to armor the United States against unseen enemies. Each perceived threat—al-Qaeda, the Taliban, Iraq, biological attacks, and other weapons of mass destruction—fueled revisions in the long-held philosophies of America's leaders.

Secret relationships were established with foes like Syria and Libya; past disputes with any nation, any organization, and any individual were set aside in search of supporters for the new American cause. Suspected terrorists were delivered into the hands of foreign torturers, allies were threatened with devastation, wars were fought by unprecedented means. Detention, intelligence collection, the treatment of citizens—each piece of the national security puzzle was reexamined and revised, at times setting American against American in a furious debate about what was right, what was pragmatic, what was counterproductive, and what was wrong.

The struggle during that period of just over five hundred days played out on a global stage, from the White House to the Kremlin, from the grandeur of the British Parliament to the dusty caves of Afghanistan. Decisions emanating from every level of the American government rippled around the world, transforming the nature not only of allies and enemies, but of the United States itself.

This, then, is more than a recounting of events in an age of terror. Rather, it is the narrative of a wrenching transformation of international allies and enemies in a period of unprecedented tumult. It is a tale of triumph and fiasco, of choices born from necessity, fear, and misplaced conviction. In the end, it is a portrait of an America struggling to find its way, torn between the needs for security and the hopes for an uncertain future.

BOOK ONE

A WAR OF
UNKNOWN WARRIORS

1

Crowds poured out of the White House and raced down the driveway toward Lafayette Park. The exodus had erupted at 9:22, nineteen minutes after a hijacked plane smashed into the World Trade Center, the second to hit the towers that morning. No evacuation had been ordered; rather, staff members, fearful that a third plane might crash into the executive mansion, had spontaneously dropped what they were doing and rushed for the exits.

From a limousine driving on West Executive Avenue alongside the White House fence, Norm Mineta, the secretary of transportation, uneasily watched the crush of fleeing workers. He had been summoned to the White House just after the second airliner had hit, and now saw evidence of the panic rippling through the nation's capital. Mineta turned to a security agent beside him.

"Is there something wrong with this picture?" he asked. "We're driving in and everybody else is running away."

After being cleared through the northwest gate, the limousine eased past the swelling mob and pulled to the portico at the West Wing entrance. The secretary emerged from the car and walked through the lobby, where another member of the administration greeted him. He should go to the Situation Room, the official said. Dick Clarke, until recently the longtime counterterrorism czar in the White House, was there and would brief him. Mineta headed to the basement and strode into the intelligence management center.

Clarke sat at the head of a conference table, opposite a series of screens showing the video hookup connecting administration officials from around the city. Mineta approached, and Clarke turned toward him.

"Norm, let me give you a rundown of what we know," he said. He spelled out the details of the attacks, said they were the work of terrorists with probable al-Qaeda connections, and expressed the fear that more hijacked planes might be in the air. The president apparently was safe; he was in Sarasota, where he had been scheduled to attend a few events highlighting his education plans.

The briefing lasted five minutes. Then, just past 9:30, it was time for Mineta to move again. Senior administration officials had already established an open line with the FAA Operations Center, and Mineta needed to take over the call.

"You've got to go to the PEOC," Clarke said.

"What's the PEOC?" Mineta responded.

"The Presidential Emergency Operations Center." The secure bunker where other senior officials were waiting.

"I don't know where that is or what it is," Mineta said sheepishly.

A Secret Service agent standing against the wall spoke up. "I'll take you."

On the third floor of the Pentagon, senior Defense Department officials raced past a staircase toward a military guard behind bulletproof glass. They turned left into a small alcove, reaching a heavy door that was supposed to unlock with hand-scan identification. As usual, the technology wasn't working, so a soldier inside, recognizing the group on camera, buzzed them in. They piled into the Executive Support Center, better known inside the Pentagon as "Cables."

The group ran down a hall to a large conference room. Steve Cambone, the undersecretary for defense policy and the senior-most person in the room, sat at the head of the table. The idea of evacuating the Pentagon was batted about, then rejected.

As information flowed in, the events of the day took on a surreal air. Torie Clarke, the Pentagon's head of public affairs, picked up a pen and reached over to her right where Jim Haynes, the general counsel, was sitting. She scribbled some words on Haynes's notepad.

Tell me this is a dream.

Two floors belowground at the White House, Dick Cheney—flanked by his security detail and Scooter Libby, his chief of staff—rushed down a long tunnel toward the PEOC. In his hand, the vice president carried a copy of the *Economist* that he had grabbed off a table upstairs. He paused in a section of the tunnel that had been sealed on both ends, providing a measure of safety. Surrounding him were a television, a bench, and a secure phone.

Cheney watched a news report on CNN showing smoke and flames at the World Trade Center. He already knew from the Secret Service that at least one more plane was heading toward the White House.

Washington's going to be hit.

After a pause, Cheney turned to an aide. "Get the president on the line."

Zacarias Moussaoui abruptly stopped exercising.

He was walking with other prisoners on an upper section of the Sherburne County Jail, listening to a small radio that he kept with him at all times. He knew what was coming and couldn't wait to hear news broadcasts about the destruction.

Then, the bulletin. There was a fire in the World Trade Center, the reporter intoned. Nothing about a hijacking or a plane, but perhaps, Moussaoui thought, the day of reckoning had finally arrived.

Word spread among the prisoners that something big had happened in New York. Moussaoui and a number of others headed downstairs to a recreation area, where the television was turned to ABC News.

On the screen, Moussaoui saw flames at the Twin Towers, the buildings enveloped in smoke against a blue sky. And he knew. The attacks on the Americans, so foolish and blind, had begun.

He closed his eyes and spoke under his breath. *"Allahu Akbar."*

God is great.

Stephen Hadley, the deputy national security advisor, stepped into the Situation Room carrying a pile of papers. As the senior official in the room, he walked toward the principal's chair, where Clarke sat.

"Okay, let's get this going," he said.

Clarke hunkered down, ignoring Hadley. His body language was clear—he wasn't giving up the seat at the head of the table. Minutes before, Rice had named him the lead crisis manager, and he had no intention of relinquishing that assignment. Hadley hesitated, then walked to the other side of the table. Tension filled the air; staffers were unsure who was in charge.

Hadley turned to Tim Flanigan, the deputy White House counsel who was standing nearby. "Tim, get hold of Justice. We need everything they've got."

Nodding, Flanigan reached for a phone and called the Justice Department's command center. At that point, Ashcroft was on a plane heading back to Washington. Larry Thompson, the deputy attorney general and a good friend of Flanigan's, was holding the fort.

A retired FBI agent who helped run the command center answered.

"This is Tim Flanigan. I need to speak to the deputy AG right away."

"Hold one," the agent said.

Deep inside the J. Edgar Hoover Building, charcoal-suited legions of lawyers, agents, and supervisors buzzed about the FBI Strategic Information Operations Center, a windowless high-security information room. Bob Mueller, who had assumed the job of Bureau director just one week earlier, was monitoring information about the Trade Center attacks that was being collected by the burgeoning ranks of New York agents.

Thompson burst into the room, having just arrived from the command center at the Justice Department. A phone rang, and someone shouted out that the Situation Room wanted to talk to him. He picked up the receiver.

"Larry Thompson."

Flanigan could tell that his call had been forwarded from the Justice Department to the FBI. Just as well—the Bureau's command center was more state-of-the-art.

"Larry, it's Tim. I'm sorry to jog your elbow on this, but I need to know as much as we can about what's going on. There's a real thirst for information over here."

"Just a minute. I'll check."

Thompson put the call on hold and turned to Mueller.

"The White House wants an update on what we've got," he said.

Everything was in motion, Mueller said. Criminal investigators were already at the attack site.

Thompson thanked him, and pressed the hold button.

Flanigan stared at a television in the Situation Room, watching the horror unfolding at the Trade Center, when he heard Thompson click back on the line.

"The FBI is at the scene and is treating it as a crime scene," he said.

A pause. Flanigan glanced again at the television.

A crime scene? That's absurd. This wasn't some bank robbery. What he saw on the screen was a war zone.

"We have no information about possible perpetrators," Thompson continued. "And no info about casualties at this point."

"Okay, thanks."

Flanigan hung up and turned to Hadley.

"The FBI's on the scene, and they're treating it . . ."

He stopped speaking, unwilling to finish the sentence. The idea that the Bureau considered this a criminal case was beyond ludicrous.

"The FBI's there," he said. "And we'll be getting reports from the scene."

About half a mile away at FAA headquarters, Dave Canoles was working like a desperate juggler, struggling to keep up with each new development. Information was scattered and confused. Thousands of planes were still airborne, every one a potential weapon of mass destruction. There were murmurs at some air traffic centers about evacuating. Canoles, a senior manager supervising six hundred of those centers nationwide, was connected to them by conference call and told the workers to stay at their posts. If ever there was a time when the country needed them at work, he said, it was today.

An official at a radarscope was tracking the jet headed toward Washington. Canoles instructed a member of his staff to go into another office and look out the window in search of the airliner.

The tracking on the radarscope continued. "Six miles from the White House," a calm voice said.

Inside the PEOC, Mineta was holding a phone to each ear, connected to his office and the FAA Operations Center, where he spoke with Monte Belger, the agency's second in command.

Word came in confirming rumors that another aircraft was headed toward Washington. No one knew what flight it was. Mineta needed more information.

"Monte, what do you have on radar on this plane coming in?" he asked.

"Well, the transponder's been turned off," Belger replied. "So we don't know who it is and we don't know the altitude and speed."

"Where is it?"

Beyond Great Falls, Virginia, Belger said. Then the plane disappeared from the screen.

"Uh-oh," Belger said. "I lost the bogey."

"Well, where is it?"

"Somewhere between Rosslyn and National Airport."

The Pentagon loomed through the cockpit window of American Airlines flight 77. Traveling at 780 feet per second, the plane was so low to the ground that it severed light posts on an adjacent road as it barreled forward.

In a yellow building nestled on a hill west of the Pentagon, Michael Cifrino, general counsel of the Missile Defense Agency, was working in his fifth-floor office. His window in the Navy Annex faced the Potomac, but the view was obstructed by the Pentagon's western façade, about a mile away.

At 9:37, he heard a roar and glanced outside.

The scene lasted about a second. A large jet, a 757, thundered past; Cifrino watched the back of the plane as it exploded into the west wall of the Pentagon.

Flight 77 slammed through at the first floor, inside Wedge One, leaving a trail of destruction as it raced at a forty-two-degree angle toward the fifth corridor. A huge fireball exploded upward more than two hundred feet above the Pentagon as the front of the fuselage crumpled and disintegrated. The plane essentially reversed itself, the tail end crushing the remaining body and plowing the greatest distance into the building.

In the vaulted SVTS on the second floor of the Pentagon, Defense Department officials were continuing the teleconference with other senior members of the administration.

A sound jolted the room. It was muffled, strange. To feel it in a room so full of metal, so insulated, they knew it had to be something big.

Steve Cambone was the first to speak.

"Wow," he said. "That was loud."

The skies are filled with guided missiles.

Ben Sliney—the FAA's national operations manager at the command center in Herndon, Virginia—had anguished for more than half an hour about the possibility that other planes had been hijacked. Now, with the attack on the Pentagon, his fears were confirmed.

It was his first day on the job, but Sliney had to make a command decision. There was no time to contact his supervisors in Washington. Well, if people wanted to fire him afterward, he could always find another job. The airspace over the United States had to be cleared.

"Order everyone to land, regardless of destination!" he shouted. "Let's get them on the ground."

Minutes later, Mineta arrived at the same conclusion. "Monte, bring them all down!" he shouted.

That effort was already in motion, Belger said. Of course, the pilots would still have some discretion, he said—regulations allowed pilots to make independent decisions in the case of an onboard emergency.

"Screw pilot discretion!" Mineta snapped. "Get those goddamn planes down!"

The order went out to the 4,646 commercial jets still in the sky: Head to an airport and land, immediately.

At 9:42 inside the PEOC tunnel, Cheney was still waiting to be connected to Bush by phone when he noticed CNN was reporting that a huge fire had broken out at the Pentagon just minutes before.

Donald Rumsfeld had disappeared.

Starting just minutes after the attack on the Pentagon, officials throughout Washington had begun searching for him. No one knew if the attacks had ended, and other than Bush, no one was more important than Rumsfeld in defending the nation against that threat. But he was nowhere to be found. Was he dead? Had the terrorists succeeded in crippling the civilian leadership at the Pentagon? Who could take charge?

But Rumsfeld was safe. At that moment he was running down an inside corridor at the Mall side of the Pentagon, trying to reach the crash site—much to the dismay of the security detail rushing alongside him.

"Sir, we have to turn back!" protested Aubrey Davis, Rumsfeld's personal bodyguard.

No response. Rumsfeld kept running.

The group hustled down two flights of stairs; darkness and smoke surrounded them. They saw a door to the outside hanging open, and struggled their way through.

The western side of the Pentagon was a mass of fire and flame, bits of twisted debris, concrete wreckage, body parts, and injured people. A mangled eighteen-inch piece of metal that was lying in the grass caught Rumsfeld's eye. He leaned down to pick it up.

"Sir, we shouldn't be disturbing a crime scene," Davis said.

Rumsfeld ignored him. He turned the metal over in his hand.

"American Airlines," he mumbled.

Rumsfeld was quiet for a moment as he surveyed the scene; there was a fire to fight and people to rescue. Someone called out—a group of rescuers were trying to move an injured man on a gurney away from danger. Rumsfeld ran over and helped push it across the road toward the emergency crews.

Back inside the Pentagon, Steve Cambone was close to panic; officials from the PEOC wanted Rumsfeld, and Cambone still couldn't reach him. He sent out an urgent appeal over the radio for someone to find the secretary.

Davis, the bodyguard, heard the plea. "We've got him," he answered into his walkie-talkie.

No luck. The babble of other frightened voices on the same frequency drowned out Davis's response.

The billows of smoke pouring from the upper floors of the Twin Towers grew thicker and darker as the stage was set for an even more deadly spectacle.

The pressure on the exterior supports was growing rapidly. When the planes smashed into the towers, they ripped apart the internal core; those reinforcements of five-inch concrete fill on metal deck were used to distribute the buildings' weight from the external box column, significantly reducing the downward pressure on the supports that ringed the structures.

With the core mostly gone on several floors—the ninety-fourth to the ninety-eighth in the North Tower, and the seventy-eighth to eighty-fourth floors in the South Tower—pressure shifted back to the external columns. The weight on those supports in the South Tower was far higher—the plane had been traveling faster, knocking out more floors, and the impact was lower, meaning the surviving reinforcements held more weight from the greater number of floors above them.

The wreckage put particular stress on the surviving external columns on either side of the gaping hole in each building. With the supports cut apart at the points of impact, the load normally held by those reinforcements shifted to a small number of neighboring columns. If those gave way, the buildings couldn't stand.

• • •

Connecting Cheney and Bush by phone had been a nightmare, with calls dropped or drowned out by static. Finally, a clear line came though while Bush was in the back of a limousine, racing toward the Sarasota Airport.

"We're at war, Dick," Bush said. "And we're going to find out who did this and we're going to kick their ass."

The danger wasn't over, Cheney said. A number of commercial flights were missing and might be aimed at vital centers of the federal government. With the vice president, the leaders of Congress, and many members of the cabinet all in Washington, the ability of government to continue in the aftermath of an attack was threatened. America needed to keep its commander in chief safe.

"Mr. President, I strongly recommend that you do not return to Washington at this time," Cheney said. "I believe we are a target."

Bush said that he wanted to reach the White House as soon as possible, but agreed to proceed carefully.

At about that moment Bush's motorcade was pulling off U.S. Route 301 onto Desoto Road, then into the airport. The vehicles rolled onto the tarmac, coming to a stop just yards away from Jones Aviation—a school where two of the terrorist hijackers had learned how to fly.

A small stream of molten aluminum flowed out of a window at the northeast corner of the South Tower's eightieth floor. No one could see this omen of the horror that was just seconds away.

A mass of officers hustled about the National Military Control Center. The smoke filling the room from the attack didn't distract from the business at hand.

On one of the large screens in the front of the room, the South Tower buckled. It fell in a sudden, horrifying moment, crushing down in a swirl of smoke and debris.

The NMCC went silent. The hard-edged military officers all stared at the screen, motionless.

Cheney and Libby made their way into the PEOC conference room just before ten o'clock. The bunker was unremarkable, just a sparse and cramped tubular space. Voices stopped flat, with no acoustic echo, muffled by the hardened structure surrounding the room that was designed to withstand the shock waves from a nuclear blast.

Cheney walked down one side of the oak conference table and sat at the center, the presidential seal hanging on the wall behind him. To his right was a bank of television sets; in front, the faces of senior officials throughout the Capitol appeared on the large projection screen used for secure video.

Just before 10:02, the Secret Service reported that, based on FAA information, another aircraft was heading toward Washington. Cheney told an aide to get Bush back on the phone.

At the same moment, passengers on that aircraft—United 93—were fighting to break into the cockpit. The lead hijacker, Ziad Jarrah, had been maneuvering the plane violently, rocking it side to side, then up and down, attempting to throw the counterattackers off balance. But to no avail—they kept coming.

"Is that it?" he asked another hijacker. "I mean, shall we put it down?"

"Yes. Put it in it and pull it down."

For a moment Jarrah delayed the final act, as the sounds of the passengers' battle grew louder. Finally, he pushed the control wheel forward and turned it hard to the right.

Just below, in Shanksville, Pennsylvania, Bob Blair was riding in a coal truck down Route 30 alongside a friend, Doug Miller. The two were making small talk when they heard a roar overhead.

Blair looked up and gaped as a huge, upside-down plane flew past. It headed over the treetops, spiraling down at 580 miles per hour into an empty field. A deafening explosion rocked their truck.

"My God," Blair said. They pulled to a stop, grabbed fire extinguishers, and ran toward the crash site.

But there was nothing to be done for the passengers on United 93. The plane and everybody on it virtually disintegrated on impact.

Air Force One had reached cruising altitude but was still circling while the pilots and the Secret Service debated where to go. An aide told Bush that the vice president was calling again. This time, the connection was clear.

Cheney explained that additional hijacked planes appeared to be headed for the capital. A defense had been readied; Combat Air Patrols were flying over both New York and Washington but had not yet been given authority to act if they encountered an airliner posing a threat.

"Sir, they're going to want to know what to do."

Bush's response was quick. "Well, if they don't land," he said, "we'll have to shoot them down."

"Yes, sir," Cheney replied.

Rules were set. A fighter would give a passenger plane three chances to change course or land. If it did neither, the military jet would destroy the commercial airliner with a missile.

On the third floor of the Pentagon, the armored door of the secure video teleconference room depressurized with the push of a white button. Rumsfeld stepped inside and saw a group of his top lieutenants talking to officials across Washington.

Rumsfeld had just come from his office, where he had updated the president on the status of the Combat Air Patrols. Now Rumsfeld was pacing, trying to gather his thoughts. He scribbled notes to himself on a small yellow pad, speaking out loud as each idea occurred to him.

He reminded everyone that he had been appointed in 1983 as a special Middle East envoy after terrorists used a truck bomb to kill 241 American marines in Beirut. The reaction then, he said, had been too timid; a planned air assault had been scuttled, and in just four months, all of the remaining marines were withdrawn from the country. Islamic extremists had perceived that pullout as evidence of American military impotence.

"The country can't react this time the way we reacted last time," Rumsfeld said. "We have to go and root these guys out. We can't just hunker down again."

This was not a time to be out of Washington, Bush decided. He understood why Cheney and his others advisors wanted him to stay away—the most senior people in the line of succession for the presidency were in the capital. An attack that killed them all, including Bush, would leave the government rudderless. But the American people, Bush thought, needed to see that their president was in charge.

He called Rice to let her know his decision. "I'm coming back," he said.

"You cannot come back," she replied, her voice stiff. "The United States of America is under attack. You have to go to safety. We don't know what's going on here."

Not her decision. "I'm coming back."

Rice exploded. "You can't!" she shouted.

Then she hung up on the president of the United States.

• • •

No one in Washington knew that United 93 was gone.

Radar was no longer reliable. So many planes had been disappearing—transponders turned off, flying through uncovered areas—that the FAA was tracking flight 93 on a display that provided only route projections, based on speed and altitude. Even when the plane fell from the sky, the estimates showed it still headed toward Washington.

Shortly after Cheney received the shoot-down order from Bush, a military aide entered the room.

"Sir," he said, "there is a plane eighty miles out coming toward D.C., and there's a fighter near there. Should we engage?"

"Yes. Engage."

The military aide returned several times. The plane was seventy miles out, then sixty miles out, speeding toward the capital at hundreds of miles an hour.

"Do the orders still stand?" he asked.

Cheney whipped his head around and glared at the aide. "Of course the order still stands!" he snapped. "Have you heard anything to the contrary?"

A few seats away, Josh Bolten, the White House deputy chief of staff, observed the exchange with growing alarm. He had not heard the earlier call between Bush and Cheney; for all he knew, the vice president was acting on his own. If the Bush administration was going to issue an order to shoot down a commercial airliner, if it was going to authorize the killing of untold numbers of Americans, then everyone in the room had better be damned sure that the president was certain.

Bolten hesitated, then spoke up.

"Mr. Vice President, I'd like to suggest that you contact the president to confirm the engage order."

Cheney nodded, and another call went through to *Air Force One*. He again described the situation, and asked Bush to reaffirm his earlier decision.

"I authorized a shoot-down of an aircraft if necessary," he said, his voice steady and without emotion.

The call ended. Cheney looked up. The engage order stood, he told the group.

Hezbollah did it.

The Shia Islamist terrorist group was the culprit behind the hijackings. Or so a preliminary CIA review concluded.

From the moment of the second attack on the World Trade Center, analysts with the Counterterrorist Center had been poring through an ocean of intelligence, seeking anything that might shed light on the identity of the perpetrators.

One raw file revealed a clue: an earlier report indicating that Hezbollah had been seeking to recruit certified pilots. The information wasn't much and hadn't been viewed as significant when it was received. But now, with planes slamming liked guided missiles into some of America's most symbolic buildings, it took on a more sinister cast, throwing suspicion on the militant group based in Lebanon. The CIA analysts conferred with their counterparts at the FBI; everyone agreed—the deduction made sense.

One analyst rushed to Ben Bonk, the center's deputy chief, to report their finding. Maybe, Bonk thought. Hezbollah must at least be placed on the list of likely conspirators in the attack.

Less than an hour later, Richard Blee from the bin Laden unit walked into Bonk's office, carrying a piece of paper.

"We've got something important," he said.

An FAA analyst had obtained the manifest for American 77, the flight that had crashed into the Pentagon. The names of two of the passengers—Khalid al-Mihdhar and Nawaf al-Hazmi—showed up in a number of intelligence reports. These were two men tied to al-Qaeda.

Forget Hezbollah. Bin Laden did it.

General Richard Myers, the vice chairman of the Joint Chiefs of Staff, was running up the stairs to the third floor of the Pentagon. He was the senior-most officer working in the National Military Command Center—the chairman, Hugh Shelton, was out of the country—and was responsible for keeping Rumsfeld up-to-date on how the military was responding to the attacks.

The deputy director of operations at the command center had decided immediately after the second strike on the Trade Center that the United States was under terrorist attack. With their responsibility for establishing communications along the chain of command during an emergency, the officers and staff in the center had been working at full throttle since then; their first all-purpose conference had been held almost an hour earlier to put together an action plan.

Myers briefed Rumsfeld in a voice that was steady and admirably mechanical; he was a soldier, trained to remain calm in the most chaotic situation. He told Rumsfeld that the North American Aerospace Defense Command—

NORAD—had been tracking Delta 1989, which military officials believed had been hijacked. The NORAD commander had ordered aircraft to battle stations, fully armed. The White House had requested fighter escorts for *Air Force One.*

Keeping Rumsfeld informed was tiring business. Myers had to run up the stairs to the defense secretary every few minutes with the latest details from the military command center, then head back down to gather additional information. Rumsfeld threw out more questions to Myers each time—what's happening in other parts of the world, what's the posture of the Russians, what are different combatant commanders doing?

At close to 10:30, Myers walked out of the secure videoconference room toward the stairs. Rumsfeld followed the general with his eyes, a look of distaste on his face. He didn't like the military mind-set in the Pentagon; during the Clinton administration, he believed, the generals had taken control from the civilian leadership, and Rumsfeld had dedicated himself to reversing that. Now, he realized, at a time of national crisis, he was being forced to depend on the officers who made him so wary.

He glanced down the conference table. "I don't trust those guys," he said with a shake of his head. "I'm going down there."

Rumsfeld barreled out the door, followed by the other officials in the meeting. They raced downstairs, crossing the C-ring of the building, then through a secure door into the command center, the inner sanctum of the Pentagon. Large screens showing television news programs and details of military deployments loomed over a crush of officers in the room.

Rumsfeld and his team swept into the center's secure videoconference room, normally used by the Joint Chiefs of Staff. The place was packed, with officials seated at a large table and lined up against the wall.

Then, a problem. Despite being a central communications system at the heart of the military operations center, the equipment in the SVTS didn't work. Two officers tried to fix it, with no success.

Frustrated, Rumsfeld stormed away, crossing the NMCC toward a white telephone—known for historical reasons as the "red switch"—which would allow him to reach Cheney.

The call went through instantly.

"There's been at least three instances here where we've had reports of aircraft approaching Washington, a couple were confirmed hijacks," Cheney said. "Pursuant to the president's instructions, I gave authorization for them to be taken out."

Rumsfeld didn't respond. "Hello?" Cheney said.

"Yes, I understand," Rumsfeld replied. "Who did you give that direction to?"

"It was passed from here to the center at the White House, from the PEOC."

Apparently, orders were going out to military fighters without Rumsfeld's knowledge. "Okay, let me ask a question here," he said. "Has the directive been transmitted to the aircraft?"

"Yes, it has," Cheney answered.

"So we have a couple of aircraft up there that have those instructions at this present time?"

"That is correct. And it's my understanding that they've already taken a couple of aircraft out."

A couple? "We can't confirm that," Rumsfeld said. "We're told that one aircraft is down, but we do not have a pilot report that we did it."

While Bush had ordered the military to shoot down a passenger plane that posed a threat, no one had yet asked the question: Was it legal, whatever the reason, for a president to authorize the killing of innocent citizens?

Tim Flanigan, the deputy White House counsel, had heard about Bush's decision while still in the Situation Room. The reasons for the directive were clear, but no one had determined what law gave a president such power.

Flanigan approached John Bellinger III, the legal advisor to the National Security Council, who was standing near some television monitors. He mentioned the shoot-down order.

"Do we have the legal authority nailed down for this?"

Bellinger was holding a copy of a transcription from a short conversation between Bush and Cheney, and tossed it to Flanigan. "Here's the authority," he said.

The president had given the order. He was commander in chief. It was a time of national emergency. That was that.

As Flanigan read the half-page transcript, he grew increasingly uncomfortable. *What if we shoot down a Lufthansa airliner? Could the German government construe that as an act of war? Was there a domestic and international legal basis for that?*

This was a military question, and Flanigan knew the right person to ask about it. He walked over to a young officer manning the communications equipment and told him to track down Jim Haynes, the Pentagon general counsel. In no time, Haynes was on the phone.

Flanigan explained what he had just read in the transcript; Haynes already knew about the shoot-down order.

"Jim, we need the best possible rational legal basis for this," Flanigan said. "We've got commander-in-chief authority. But what else have we got?"

"I'll look into it," Haynes replied.

There wasn't much time to think; events were unfolding too fast. Rumsfeld and Haynes had already discussed the legal issues surrounding an order to fire on a commercial airliner. They had checked the standing rules of engagement—the standards on self-defense would probably apply.

Haynes knew that whatever legal conclusion he came up with would be tantamount to a rationalization: The president had given the order; someone had to say why he had the authority.

The most obvious issue was constitutional. Under the Fourteenth Amendment, the passengers on those planes could not be deprived of their rights to life, liberty, and property without due process of law. Certainly shooting them out of the sky didn't meet that standard. Then there was the Fourth Amendment prohibition against unreasonable search and seizure; this would be quite a dramatic seizure of those citizens.

Still, the preamble of the Constitution spoke of providing for a common defense and promoting the general welfare. Under Article 2, the president was the commander in chief of the military.

This was a matter of self-defense, of protecting the citizenry, balanced against the rights of the passengers. An order could be lawfully issued, Haynes concluded, but only by the president.

Word came into the Situation Room confirming that another plane was headed toward Washington. This time, it was a Northwest Airlines flight from Portugal to Philadelphia. It was squawking a hijack code and not responding to radio calls. Clarke barked some orders for someone to come up with more information. Where was the plane? What was its fuel capacity? What assets did the military have available to intercept it at the coast?

No one had a clue, but the assembled group was doing its best to find out. Officials scrambled to reach Northwest as the FAA riffled through its own data in search of information about the flight.

Standing by a wall, Flanigan watched as the participants in the videoconference grew ever more anxious. No orders about the mysterious Northwest flight could be issued until *someone* dug up some details.

A brainstorm. Without a word, Flanigan walked out of the conference room and found an unsecure computer. Calling up travel sites, he scanned the records for details of the Portugal flight. Perplexed, he searched again on the Northwest Airlines Web site.

Nothing.

Flanigan grabbed a piece of paper from the desk and scribbled down whatever he could learn about every Northwest flight from Europe. Then he headed back to the conference room, where Clarke was still struggling to find out more about the plane, and took a seat at the conference table.

"Dick," Flanigan said. "I've checked, and there's no such flight."

Clarke turned away from the microphone in front of him, muting it as he stared at Flanigan with a stunned expression.

"How did you check?" he asked.

"I looked on their Web site."

A pause. Clarke clicked the audio back on.

"I have information that there is no such flight," he said calmly. "Check that again."

Computers. The analysts at the CIA were being impeded in their work by a shortage of computers.

The frequent budgetary shortfalls at the Counterterrorist Center had left the unit without all of the technology it needed to deal with the attacks that morning. Congress and the White House had consistently financed the CTC with an on-again, off-again approach—after a terrorist strike, the money came flooding in. Then, when the strike faded from memory, cash dried up. Managers at the center had been forced to cut back on equipment and operations in order to stay afloat. On this horrific morning, no one in the unit doubted that a new and huge injection of funds would soon be on the way. But that prospect was no help in navigating the crisis now.

Then a supervisor had an idea. Almost all of CIA headquarters had been evacuated; the CTC was the only unit that remained fully staffed, despite concerns that those who stayed might be killed in a subsequent attack. There were computers everywhere in the building—some packed for delivery, others on people's desks. There was a way to close the equipment gap after all.

The CTC could start stealing.

Staffers were sent out to track down whatever equipment they could find at other CIA divisions. Over the next twenty minutes, they returned carrying tens of thousands of dollars' worth of computers.

At the Justice Department command center, a young lawyer named John Yoo sat at a tacky wood-laminated table, fielding questions from officials all over Washington.

Two months before, Yoo had joined the Office of Legal Counsel, a little-known unit of the department that provides legal advice to the executive branch, a responsibility that earned it the nickname "the president's law firm." To take the post, Yoo had gone on leave from his job as a professor at the University of California's Berkeley School of Law, where he had gained a reputation as an expert on international law, American foreign policy, and separation of powers under the Constitution. For years, he had written articles for law reviews about the scope of presidential authority, arguing that in a time of war, the executive had a sweeping claim to act independently from the other branches of government.

His first months at Justice had been quiet and his assignments pedestrian, like analyzing a treaty about polar bears. But now, in the aftermath of the terrorist attacks, Yoo's legal expertise was suddenly a gold mine.

The questions were momentous. *Are we at war? Had the terrorists just fired the first shot? Can we use force in response? What level of force? If we know that the terrorist group behind this is in Afghanistan, can we attack there?*

Calmly, Yoo recited the same answers over and over. "We've been attacked," he said. "We're in a state of war and can use force in response."

But, he added, there were conventions governing the tactics. Any action would have to be proportionate, and anyone targeted must be a combatant.

There were also rules, he said, that applied to how to treat captured enemies. "You can't use force just to interrogate."

Air Force One leveled off at forty-five thousand feet, far higher than most commercial jets could fly. Inside, television monitors were turned to a local Fox news broadcast; the signal stayed strong because the aircraft was circling over the Sarasota area, its pilots unsure where to go and fearful that the president's plane might be attacked.

That concern was sparked by an anonymous phone call that morning to the Secret Service claiming that *Air Force One* was the terrorists' next target. Officials who heard about the threat considered it credible because, they were told, the caller had used the code word for the president's plane—Angel. But that proved to be false; the reporting agent, in relaying the message about the call to his superiors, had spoken the code word. The caller hadn't.

In response, a group of F-16 fighters were scrambled, under orders to escort *Air Force One*. The first of the military jets reached the 757 just before 11:30. Air traffic control radioed the president's pilot, Colonel Mark Tillman, to let him know.

"You've got two F-16s at about your—say, your ten o'clock position," the controller said.

Tillman looked to his left and saw one of the jets. Back in the cabins, passengers gathered at the windows, watching in amazement as the F-16s appeared, flying so close off *Air Force One*'s wings that they could see the pilots' heads. Bush walked out of his private office and peered through the window. He caught the eyes of one pilot and snapped a salute.

Bush told his staff that he wanted to land so that he could make a public statement and speak with his top lieutenants in Washington. The security team chose Barksdale Air Force Base near Shreveport as the first stop.

At 11:45, *Air Force One* was seconds from touching down when a report from CBS appeared on one of the televisions in the main cabin—the number of casualties in New York was in the thousands. The reporters and White House staff members fell silent.

On the tarmac, air force personnel in full combat gear and carrying drawn M-16 rifles surrounded the plane. In the flurry of activity, one airman ran to the wrong spot, angering a nearby officer.

"Hey, hey!" the officer barked. "Get to that wingtip! Move to that wingtip *now!*"

Instantly, the younger man dashed under the right wing, holding a rifle across his chest.

The internal stairs on the lower portion of the plane opened, and White House staffers and reporters piled out. The sky was cloudless, the temperature roasting. A dark blue Dodge Caravan drove across the tarmac, coming to a stop beside the stairs. Seconds later, it pulled back to be inspected by dogs.

When the Dodge returned, Bush bounded off the plane, saluting an air force officer before climbing into the van. A small motorcade drove to the General Dougherty Conference Center; Bush got out and headed inside to call his national security team.

Shortly after 12:30, Bush strode into the Center's main conference room, where the White House press corps waited. His eyes were red-rimmed and his face was grim as he stepped behind a podium. Sketches of sixteen Medal of Honor winners from the Eighth Air Force were on the wall behind him. The red light on a television camera blinked on.

"Freedom, itself, was attacked this morning by a faceless coward," he said. "And freedom will be defended."

The 443-foot-tall London Eye Ferris wheel stood motionless on the bank of the Thames, shut down out of fear that terrorists might soon strike the popular tourist attraction. Across the river, a convoy of police vehicles and black vans raced down Parliament Street. Inside a sedan, Prime Minister Tony Blair sat with one of his chief aides, Alastair Campbell; both men had just returned from Brighton, where news of the attacks on the Twin Towers had aborted Blair's plan to deliver a speech to the Trades Union Congress.

The motorcade arrived in front of the tall black gates at the entrance to Downing Street, a barrier erected during the premiership of Margaret Thatcher to protect prime ministers from terrorists. Blair's car stopped in front of Number 10; he and Campbell stepped out and hurried into the residence.

Some of Britain's top intelligence officials were waiting to brief them on what they had learned about the events in America. First, the precautions in London—the Department for Transport had closed the airspace over the city, special security details had been placed around the stock exchange and Canary Wharf, and the general security alert had been raised.

As for the attacks that morning, the intelligence agencies were already certain of the culprit's identity. "Bin Laden and his people are the only ones with the capability to do this," said John Scarlett, chairman of the Joint Intelligence Committee for the British Cabinet Office.

Moreover, he and his al-Qaeda terrorists had probably acted alone, Scarlett said, without the connivance of a sovereign state. Agreed, said Stephen Lander, the director general of Security Service, known better as MI5. Bin Laden just didn't work with governments in his operations—he was too much of an egomaniac to place himself as subordinate to anyone.

"We need a command paper immediately on who al-Qaeda is, why they exist, what they do, and how they do it," Blair said.

Britain, Blair said, was going to have to move deftly to influence the Bush administration's response to the attacks in hopes of preventing the president from doing anything rash. It would be a delicate diplomatic challenge.

"The U.S. is going to feel beleaguered and angry because there is so much anti-Americanism around," he said.

"The pressure on the Americans to respond quickly, even immediately, is going to be enormous," Lander added.

Afghanistan, which had harbored al-Qaeda for years, would most likely be the immediate object of America's wrath. But the Blair government couldn't exclude the possibility that the United States might turn its guns on hostile nations like Iraq, Libya, and Iran if it uncovered evidence that they were complicit in the attacks—however unlikely that might be.

There was a general agreement on two points: The Bush administration should demand that the Taliban government in Afghanistan serve up bin Laden, and Britain should aid in appealing to the international community to support the United States in its inevitable quest to take down al-Qaeda.

It was also important not to overstate the terrorists' capability to inflict further damage on the West, at least based on that morning's attack. "This was less about technology than it was about skill and nerve," Scarlett said.

Lander jumped in. "It's the next logical step up from a car bomb," he said. "Turning a plane into a bomb and destroying a symbol of America takes some doing, but it could be done by al-Qaeda because there are so many terrorists willing to kill themselves."

All that was beside the point for now. The critical issue, Blair repeated, was how Bush would react to these events. He had been president for less than a year and was largely untested. He might flail out against America's enemies in ways that could be unpredictable, or even counterproductive.

"He could be under enormous pressure to do something irresponsible," Blair said—especially if the international community didn't unite behind the United States.

"If America hears that the world view is that this happened because Bush is more isolationist," Blair said, "there is going to be a reaction."

Massoud. Scooter Libby tossed the name over in his mind. Islamists posing as news reporters had just assassinated the Northern Alliance leader. The strongest fighting force battling al-Qaeda and the Taliban had lost its most important leader. Then, in less than forty-eight hours, America was attacked. The United States had been deprived of an ally who could have been counted on to join in any military operation against bin Laden and his cohort. An unlikely coincidence, or perhaps more proof that bin Laden's hand was behind the hijackings.

Libby reached for a pen and wrote a note.

Did Massoud's assassination pave the way for the attack in the United States?

He slipped the piece of paper to Cheney. The vice president skimmed it, turned to Libby, and nodded.

At 3:00 P.M. in Toronto, a truck driver named Ahmad El-Maati unlocked the door to his apartment, went inside, and greeted his mother.

El-Maati looked exhausted; it had been a day of enormous strain. Early that morning, he had quit the long-haul trucking business, returning his rig's keys to his employer, Highland Transport. He had enjoyed the work until a month before, when he was stopped at the American border and searched. On that day, he had been driving a loaner because his truck was in the shop, and the inspection turned up a few items that weren't his, including a map. It was a black-and-white photocopy, only slightly better than hand-drawn, and it depicted Tunney's Pasture, an area in Ottawa developed exclusively for federal government buildings. A few of the facilities were labeled with names like H&W VIRUS LABS, ELDORADO NUCLEAR LTD, and ATOMIC ENERGY OF CANADA. The agents had interrogated El-Maati extensively about the map, demanding to know why he was carrying it. He could only reply that the paper wasn't his.

The border confrontation had left El-Maati jittery for weeks, despite the efforts of his supervisors at Highland to assure him of their support. The company had investigated and concluded that one of the truck's previous drivers had picked up the map while on a delivery in Ottawa. Ann Armstrong, a manager at Highland, had given El-Maati a letter stating that he had reported the incident to his superiors and that he should be commended for his professionalism in dealing with the matter. But he still felt too frightened to keep crossing the border. Better, El-Maati decided, to give up transporting items thousands of miles and drive shorter—if less profitable—routes in Canada.

Then came the terrorist attack that morning in the United States. Shortly after he returned his keys, he saw the news of the second plane crash on a television in the drivers' lounge. The sight had made El-Maati nauseated, and he wanted to vomit. His emotional turmoil continued all the way back home as he grappled with the images of death that he had just witnessed.

Now, at his apartment, he was ready to sit down and take a moment to gather his thoughts. Before he could, a knock came at the door. Odd, since no one had buzzed from downstairs to be allowed into the building.

El-Maati answered. Two men in suits stood in the hallway. Both flipped open leather cases, showing their identification. They were with the Canadian Security Intelligence Service—CSIS.

One of the men identified himself as Adrian White. "We need to speak with you," he said.

"Okay," El-Maati replied.

"Can we come in?"

El-Maati shook his head. "No. Let's talk outside."

He turned toward his mother and saw terror in her face. Then he left, leading the men to the elevator.

Back in the apartment, his mother reached for the phone and called El-Maati's father. "Some people came and took Ahmad!" she said.

Downstairs, El-Maati and the two agents crossed the street and sat on a bench. White explained that, given the attacks in the United States, CSIS was visiting people whose names had come up in the past—known as a "knock-and-talk" in the intelligence service.

"We heard about the map and what happened at the border," White said. "Tell us about the map."

The map! How could he get them to understand that he didn't know anything about it?

El-Maati brought out the letter written by Ann Armstrong. He always carried it in his shirt pocket for moments like this.

The two agents read the letter, then gave it back.

"Okay," White said, "let's talk about your background and about your travels."

El-Maati suggested that they continue the conversation at a coffee shop in a nearby plaza. The three men walked there and sat at a table on a patio.

The questions were boilerplate—where was El-Maati born, where had he gone to school, what had he studied. He answered for a while, but grew increasingly worried.

"Look, I want to have a lawyer present to make sure nothing I'm saying gets misinterpreted," he said. "So we can continue this same conversation any way you like and anywhere you like, but with a lawyer present so I can preserve my rights."

White looked annoyed. "We're not a court here. You don't need a lawyer."

El-Maati insisted. White mentioned that CSIS knew that he was trying to sponsor a woman he planned to marry so that she could move to Canada. The file for that type of request went through the intelligence service, which had to give its approval. Maybe, the agent suggested, that application might be stopped if he refused to cooperate.

"You know, Ahmad, we are *mukhabarat*," White said.

El-Maati recoiled backward as if he had been slapped in the face. In Arabic, *mukhabarat* generally referred to government units involved in gathering intelligence. Perhaps White was attempting to make clear that he was not part of a criminal prosecution.

But, El-Maati feared, perhaps not—in the popular parlance of the Middle East, *mukhabarat* had come to mean something more sinister. It referred to the secret police departments in Egypt, Iraq, Jordan, and Syria that imposed state controls over their citizens; the *mukhabarat* were renowned for snatching up people and making them disappear into prisons where they were tortured while under interrogation.

El-Maati wasn't sure how to respond. "You speak Arabic?" he asked.

"Well, a little bit."

El-Maati let out a breath.

"You know how the *mukhabarat* here in Canada deals with its citizens," White said. "We're soft on our citizens. There are laws that control what we do. And you know how the *mukhabarat* deals with people back in the Middle East."

Hesitation. El-Maati believed they were telling him that if he didn't speak now, he would have to deal with the *mukhabarat* in his home country of Egypt.

"Are you threatening me?" he said.

White held up his hands. "No, no. Absolutely not. We just want you to cooperate."

No chance. "I think you are threatening me, and I insist that I have a lawyer."

White asked something else. *I want a lawyer* came the response. Then another question. *I want a lawyer.* Again and again El-Maati responded with the same words; it became almost laughable, with the agents joining El-Maati in saying *I want a lawyer* after their last query.

The interview ended. El-Maati asked for the men's names again. White wrote them on a piece of paper and handed it over.

As he watched the agents depart, El-Maati took a deep breath. *The map.* He was terrified.

Years would pass before El-Maati learned the truth about the map. It was a decade old. The sensitive buildings it depicted had not existed for years before El-Maati crossed the border. It had been drawn not by terrorists, but by the government of Canada, a visitors' guide printed up by the hundreds.

But by the time that was discovered, it would be too late to stop the terrible events caused by unfounded suspicions about a meaningless piece of paper.

At Offutt Air Force Base, just outside Omaha, Bush hurried into an underground command post that resembled a Hollywood depiction of a crisis center, a vast room with high-tech wizardry of astonishing diversity. The president took a seat in front of a screen projecting the videoconference; the chair was a particularly comfortable one.

He listened for several minutes as Cheney, Rice, Hadley, and other officials gave him the latest news. The potential number of casualties was as many as ten thousand, he was told. But for now, it appeared the attacks were over. Government agencies had set up defenses. The FAA had successfully grounded all commercial airliners. A carrier battle group had put to sea. The Coast Guard was boarding ships. Immigration was locking down the border.

"At this point, Mr. President, I think it's safe to come back to the White House," Cheney said. "And that's probably the wisest course of action."

"I agree," Bush replied. He wanted to speak to the nation again, this time from the Oval Office.

Deputies from the State Department—the secretary, Colin Powell, was en route home from South America, so couldn't be on the call himself—gave a rundown of contacts they had received from foreign governments, both to express condolences and to offer help.

The president jumped in. The Russian president, Vladimir Putin, had already called. "He understands that, if this can happen to us, it can happen to him as well," Bush said.

On to the intelligence. Tenet reported that the first indications suggested that al-Qaeda was almost certainly the group behind the strike. Known associates of the terrorist group had turned up on the passenger manifests for American 77. The attacks displayed both al-Qaeda's trademark meticulousness and its practice of launching multiple, simultaneous strikes against related targets.

Bush ended the call with the message he had been delivering by phone to his subordinates all day.

"Somebody has declared war on America," he said. "We are at war."

This would entail a lot of actions and decisions by officials throughout the administrations. It would be demanding and involve taking a lot of risks.

"And if it comes a cropper," he said, "I'll be behind you."

John Ashcroft had arrived in Washington a few hours earlier aboard a Cessna Citation V. An armored SUV had attempted to drive him away from downtown to a secure classified site but was blocked by a traffic jam. The attorney general told the driver to turn around and take him instead to FBI headquarters, where he could join other top law enforcement officials in the command center.

By the time Ashcroft arrived, the FBI had culled data on the hijackers and their connections to al-Qaeda. A senior agent briefed Ashcroft; Mueller, the FBI director; Michael Chertoff, the head of the criminal division; and other officials of the findings. As part of the presentation, photographs of the hijackers were shown on a television screen. By the end, no one in the room harbored any lingering doubts that these attacks had been acts of Islamic terrorism.

Evidence usually led to decisions. But they needed to be coordinated, and a number of Justice officials were across the street at headquarters, so an order from Ashcroft went out: Everyone was to drop whatever he was doing and report to the FBI command center.

Attorneys from the Office of Legal Counsel walked over to the Hoover Building together and took an elevator upstairs. As the group headed into the complex, John Yoo glanced into an adjoining office. He saw one of Ashcroft's top aides sitting in a chair and reading a book.

The Complete Idiot's Guide to Understanding Islam.

Omigod. *That's not a good sign.*

Alberto Gonzales's mind was racing.

The White House counsel had flown to Washington by helicopter an hour earlier from Norfolk, Virginia, where he had given a speech to government ethics advisors. His return had taken a little longer than it might have; he overruled his pilot's suggestion that they land on the White House lawn. That, he said, was the prerogative of the president. Instead, they flew to Andrews Air Force Base, a twenty-minute drive away in good traffic.

A van picked him up and ferried him straight to the White House, where he was rushed to the PEOC. SWAT teams armed with pistols and machine guns lined the tunnel, the highest level of security at the bunker since the crisis began. The conference room was in an uproar, with phone calls, videoconferences, and individual meetings. Things were bad but not out of control.

There wasn't much for him to do at the PEOC, Gonzales decided, but there were certainly legal matters that he and his lieutenants needed to tackle. He called his deputy, Flanigan, who was still in the Situation Room.

Flanigan saw the caller ID. "Hey, Al."

"Timmy," Gonzales said, "let's go upstairs."

They headed to the west lobby and met in front of the elevator. From there, they hiked upstairs to Gonzales's office. Flanigan dropped onto a couch beside a coffee table. Gonzales sat in his usual wing chair.

"Okay, what else needs to be done?" Gonzales asked.

The two men discussed what were emerging as the key legal issues—*Was this a war? How could the country respond?*—and decided that they needed to bring in someone with more expertise.

"I'm going to call John Yoo," Flanigan said.

Yoo picked up the line at his new work space in the FBI command center.

"John, Al and I are going through some issues here and were hoping you could help us. We're not even sure how to phrase the right questions."

"Okay," Yoo said. "Where do you want to start?"

Over the next forty-five minutes, the three men laid out the legal framework for policies that would govern the coming war on terror.

First, logistics. Bush needed to declare a state of emergency; Gonzales instructed Flanigan to handle that. The markets were reeling and trading had stopped—should there be a bank holiday, to let the financial centers of the country regroup? Then, what about the victims? Could the president throw money to New York, without a specific appropriation by Congress? What was the scope of his power? The answer to that was easy, Yoo assured his colleagues, repeating what he had told other officials throughout the morning: In a time of military conflict, the president's authority was sweeping.

In fact, Bush could take just about any action he wished. A war was certain, and legal. But this wasn't a standard confrontation, they agreed. The combatants were not part of any country; they were not soldiers whose rights were dictated by the rules of war under the Geneva Conventions. These enemies were renegades, Yoo said, like the pirates of the late nineteenth century. Their rights would be far more limited than those of a soldier fighting on behalf of an established government.

The lawyers recognized they were venturing into areas dealing directly with personal freedoms and rights of individuals. Nothing was clear-cut.

"These are the scary things," Flanigan said.

Could the president block captured terrorists from the courts, suspending habeas corpus? The Constitution allowed for such an action only in cases of rebellion or invasion, but neither word quite fit the attacks on the Trade Center and the Pentagon. Still, if the United States declared the terrorist operation an act of war, the president should have that authority, Yoo said.

Once the United States had terrorists in custody, they had to be locked up someplace. But they couldn't be taken into American prisons, under the authority of the courts, and then told they had no rights. The combatants, the lawyers agreed, needed to be someplace beyond the reach of the judicial system. They began batting around ideas about possible locations.

Then, a suggestion. What about Guantanamo Bay?

About an hour later, Karen Hughes hurried through the West Wing. The top communications advisor for Bush, Hughes had heard that the helicopter carrying the president from Andrews Air Force Base was about to land on the South Lawn and wanted to be there to greet him.

On her way toward the Oval Office, Hughes ran into Gonzales, who had left the planning meeting after receiving a call that Bush was arriving.

The two walked onto the portico outside the Oval Office, watching the touchdown of *Marine One,* a twin turbine-engine VH-3D flown by HMX-1, an elite marine squadron. Usually, a crowd would greet Bush, but this time it was only Hughes and Gonzales. Bush stepped out, his face grim as he headed toward the Oval Office. His helicopter had just flown over the Pentagon, and the devastation he saw still haunted him.

"Welcome back, Mr. President," Hughes said. "How are you?"

Bush nodded curtly at his aides and kept walking. The floor of the Oval Office was lined with planks of plywood, set up to hold the camera and other video equipment that would be used for his speech to the nation that night.

With his two aides in tow, Bush strode past his desk and into a small study. Over the next few minutes, Andy Card and Ari Fleischer, his chief spokesman, came in; both had flown back with Bush on *Marine One*. Then Rice arrived from the Roosevelt Room.

The group huddled around a table, reviewing a draft of Bush's address. Speechwriters had been at work much of the day attempting to massage the thoughts conveyed by Bush into inspiring prose. Their work had been forwarded to Hughes, who did her own rewrite.

The key position Bush had expressed was that his administration would hold accountable any country that aided terrorists. As he read through the speech, he came upon the words intended to express that point.

"We will make no distinction between those who planned these acts and those who permitted or tolerated or encouraged them."

Bush didn't like it. "That's way too vague," he said. All those past-tense verbs at the end of the sentence were unnecessary. "Just use the word 'harbor.' "

The phrase was rewritten. *"We will make no distinction between the terrorists who committed these acts and those who harbor them."*

Those few words transformed America's counterterrorism policy into the most robust in its history. By holding accountable any governments that supported terrorism, Bush was rejecting the notion of launching only targeted strikes against criminal groups and instead was committing his administration to a worldwide campaign to eradicate the apparatus of terror.

Rice wondered whether the first Oval Office speech, coming at a time when the nation was still reeling from the attacks, was the place to proclaim this aggressive policy.

"You can say it now, or you'll have other opportunities to say it," she said.

"What do you think?" Bush replied.

Rice paused. *First words matter more than almost anything else.*

"I favor including it."

Bush gave her a brisk nod. "We've got to get it out there now."

The head of the television crew in the Oval Office gave the final countdown, dropping a finger with each second. Behind the desk, Bush waited, looking at the teleprompter where his speech was keyed up.

Just off camera, several of his aides—including Card, Hughes, Gonzales, and Rice—stood in silence. At zero, the director pointed at Bush. His image appeared on millions of screens around the world.

"Good evening," he said. "Today, our fellow citizens, our way of life, our very freedom came under attack in a series of deliberate and deadly terrorist acts."

The victims were friends and neighbors, moms and dads, businesspeople, secretaries, members of the military—a cross section of America. They had been killed in an evil act of terror, a mass murder that was meant to panic the country. But America would stand strong. Its great people would defend their great nation.

"I've directed the full resources of our intelligence and law enforcement communities to find those responsible and to bring them to justice," Bush said.

Then, the line in the sand. "We will make no distinction between the terrorists who committed these acts and those who harbor them."

He spoke for eight minutes. Once the camera was turned off, Gonzales approached him.

"Good job, Mr. President."

Bush looked Gonzales in the eyes. "I'm glad you're here," he said.

Almost two hours later, Bush was in the presidential bunker beneath the White House with a small group of his closest advisors. They had just wrapped up a meeting of the National Security Council, the first Bush had attended in person that day. Now he wanted to restate his new policies.

"This is a time for self-defense," Bush said. "We have made the decision to punish whoever harbors terrorists, not just the terrorists themselves."

Tenet and Mueller, the FBI director, briefed the group. Bin Laden's fingerprints were all over this operation, but other actors may have played a supporting role. He wouldn't be surprised, Tenet said, to find Iran or Iraq wrapped into this somehow.

Colin Powell—who had made it back from Peru—jumped in. The first diplomatic task was to confront both the Taliban and Pakistan, he said. The reasons were obvious: The Taliban was giving shelter to bin Laden, and among all nations, Pakistan had the closest relationship with them.

"We have to make it clear to Pakistan and Afghanistan this is showtime," Powell said.

Tenet agreed. In particular, it was imperative to hammer the Taliban hard for allowing al-Qaeda to transform Afghanistan into an incubator for terrorism worldwide. The administration had to make it clear that the United States was through with them, he said.

The foreign policy implications were far broader than that, Bush said. "This is a great opportunity. We can change and improve our relations with countries around the world."

The United States, he said, could use this terrible episode to rebuild its relationships with the nations of the Middle East, to add another dimension to its dealings with the Russians, and to realign its approach to Pakistan.

Taking too hard a line with Pakistan could backfire, one advisor warned. Its president, Pervez Musharraf, had assumed the post in June, following two years as the country's de facto leader in the aftermath of a bloodless coup. But his government had an uncertain hold over a fractious nation that was rife with Islamic extremist groups; Musharraf had done nothing to curb the activities of the Taliban. Quite the contrary—Pakistan actively backed the group.

No matter, Bush said. The United States was at war with a merciless enemy, and governments around the world would have to choose sides. "This is an opportunity beyond Afghanistan," he said "We have to shake terror loose in places like Syria, and Iran, and Iraq."

He surveyed the room with calm eyes. "This is an opportunity to rout out terror wherever it might exist."

A blanket of stars flickered in a clear Afghan sky, bathing the al-Qaeda campsite at Logar Province in a soothing spectral glow. The jihadists had come here, thirty miles from Kabul, to hide out in the aftermath of what they called the "planes operation."

Bin Laden was both delighted by and disappointed in the results. The damage in New York shocked him. He had expected that, at most, 1,500 people would be killed. He praised Allah that the attack inflicted far more casualties. But he regretted that the second plane heading to Washington had crashed before it could hit the Capitol Building; he had been looking forward, he told an associate, to seeing the Dome destroyed.

Still, the al-Qaeda faithful at the military camp were giddy about the attacks. Sounds of singing and dancing broke through the still night; nearly everyone gathered in a single house to share in the celebration.

Outside, one man stood alone, staring at the sky. He had heard of the attacks on the radio and had been stunned that someone would launch an assault on such a powerful country. It hadn't take long for the man, Salim Hamdan, a driver for bin Laden, to realize that his boss had orchestrated this foolish mass murder.

Hamdan thought of his house in Yemen. Like many of his countrymen, he

could afford to build only one floor at a time. That's why the height of each Yemeni house reflects the owner's wealth—a single floor meant he was just getting
by, while three trumpeted success.

He had been proud when he built his bottom floor, had recently begun his
second, and was already dreaming of his third. But the attacks changed everything. His hopes were dashed. His second floor would never be finished. His
life, his house, had been torn apart. Hamdan's anger rose. The attack had been
reckless, worthless.

Bin Laden, he thought, had destroyed them all.

2

Deep beneath the Cabinet Office in Whitehall, Tony Blair stepped into a windowless, soundproof room where senior members of his government had already gathered. They were there as members of the national crisis council known as COBRA—a James Bondian acronym that stood for the far more mundane term *Conference Briefing Room A,* where the meeting was taking place.

It was the morning after the attack, September 12. This was only the fourth time that Blair had chaired a COBRA meeting, and the third had taken place the previous day. As he approached his seat, he glanced up at the bank of screens that filled one side of the room; they could be used for secure videoconferences with other members of his government, or simply as a means of watching the television news.

Sitting at the center of the table, Blair called the meeting to order. The committee first turned its attention to domestic issues. Quashing a dissenting voice, Blair declared that both City Airport and the flight path over London would stay closed. He reported that he had spoken with the governor of the Bank of England about strategies to maintain confidence in the financial system.

Blair was only now beginning to absorb the full magnitude and meaning of the terrorist operation. This, he told his aides, was a transformative moment in history, a turning point that would roil international relations in every corner of the globe. He ordered his team to gather every scrap of intelligence about the attacks and report back to him. He wanted to see the evidence that he had been told put the responsibility squarely on the shoulders of Osama bin Laden.

Next, international challenges. The most pressing diplomatic issue that COBRA had to address, of course, continued to be how to deal with the

Americans. Members of the crisis committee had watched Bush's address to the nation—at about 2:00 A.M. British time—and he had said pretty much what they had expected. True, he had appeared a little shaky and uncertain, but that could be forgiven. What government leader wouldn't struggle when addressing his country about the deaths of thousands of its citizens?

There was a delicate point that the British must not forget, remarked Jack Straw, the foreign secretary.

"We have to be careful not to get ahead of the U.S. in terms of what we say," he said. This was America's tragedy, whatever the international repercussions might be.

The smart thing to do, the officials agreed, was for every nation to proceed with caution, waiting several weeks to see how things played out in America before taking action. Blair agreed, but still feared events might spin out of control.

"Things are likely to move much more quickly than that," Blair said, particularly if the Americans became as convinced as British intelligence officials were that the attacks had been orchestrated by bin Laden.

There was one other piece of the puzzle to be considered: Russia. Blair had spoken to Russian president Vladimir Putin the day before and had been put off by his almost smug I-told-you-so attitude, given his warnings in the past about the danger of Islamic fundamentalists. The conversation worried Blair, he said. Putin could try to exploit this tragedy to justify Russia's brutal assault on Chechnya and its largely Muslim population.

Blair needed to discuss all of these issues with Bush; he wanted a report, he told aides, spelling out the president's options for action. "I have to get inside his mind, if I can," he said.

A few hours later, a message arrived—Bush wanted to consult with Blair. The call was placed, and for the first time since the attacks, the British prime minister and the American president spoke. Blair expressed his deep condolences and the unwavering support of the British people for the Americans as they grappled with the horrors of the previous day. Bush thanked him; it was important for the two countries to collaborate closely in bringing the perpetrators to justice, he said.

"I would very much value staying in close touch," Bush said.

"Of course," Blair replied.

There would be no immediate response to the attacks by the United States, Bush said. "The American people are going to give me a bit of time."

Perhaps, Blair suggested, Bush should solidify international support by reaching out to the Group of Eight, an organization of allies that included both the British and the Americans and that dealt with issues of global significance. Bush thanked him, then brushed the topic aside.

That response worried Blair. *They're looking inward, when they should be looking outward.* This was the time to seek cooperation from America's friends and allies, to coax even the sometimes prickly French and obstreperous Russians into an alliance against a ruthless enemy that threatened them all. To let that opportunity slip away would be an epic miscalculation.

Blair spent a few minutes summarizing the points brought up at the COBRA meeting. Bush replied that he was grateful for the information and asked if it could be sent to him in writing.

"These people are going to have to come out of their holes sometime," Bush said. "And we'll be ready to hit them."

The demands on a president at a time of such a national trauma were incalculable, Blair said, and his heart went out to the president.

"I know what I've got to do," Bush replied. "I'm not a good mourner. I'm a weeper. I'll weep for the country and then act, but I don't want to just hit cruise missiles into the sand."

Shafts of sunlight streamed into the White House Cabinet Room, illuminating walls adorned with paintings of former presidents. Walking in from the Oval Office, Bush glanced through the French doors that lined the east side of the room. Fall flowers bloomed in the Rose Garden, an image of tranquillity that all but mocked the horror of the moment.

It was four o'clock on the afternoon of September 12, a few hours after Bush's conversation with Blair. Members of the National Security Council and their aides stood as the president approached his usual seat at the center of the table.

"All right," he said. "Let's see what we've got."

Bush flipped open a folder that had been placed in front of his chair. Inside was a short document—a draft of National Security Presidential Directive number nine—that was written after an NSC meeting earlier that day. Bush had told his aides that he wanted the wording to frame the overall strategy for America's response to the previous day's attacks.

Peering through his reading glasses, Bush considered the statement his team had composed, describing the goal of his single-minded campaign: *"Eliminate terrorism as a threat to our way of life,"* the draft said. That would entail destroying terrorist organizations, shutting down their networks, disrupting their finances, and cutting off any potential access they might have to weapons of mass destruction.

Bush set the paper on the conference table. "It's not just us," he said. "This has to be a cause on behalf of all of our friends and allies around the world. How do we capture that?"

Perhaps, one cabinet officer suggested, the statement of principles should describe terrorists as being both threats to the American way of life as well as to the country's global interests.

Bush shook his head. "That doesn't quite get it."

He paused. "How about '. . . and to all nations that love freedom.' "

No one questioned that phrase; it would be included in the final draft.

Tenet took the floor.

"There is no doubt in my mind this was al-Qaeda," he said. Not only had there been the spike over the summer, but over the last thirty hours, the agency had listened in on al-Qaeda operatives taking credit for the attack as well as for the assassination of Massoud.

The United States would be able to move against al-Qaeda quickly, Tenet said. For years, the CIA had been working with tribal leaders in Afghanistan in their pursuit of bin Laden. These were battle-tested men, warriors and leaders from the Northern Alliance. They could serve as intelligence contacts and even fighting forces.

"We have people in place," Tenet said. "I think we can handle this thing."

Rumsfeld jumped in. "This needs to be a military operation," he said decisively. And that meant it had to be run by the Pentagon, not by the CIA.

"I'm not even sure that Afghanistan is the right place to start," he said. "What if Iraq is involved?

There were lots of pieces here, Bush said. "But let's not make the target so broad that it misses the point and fails to draw support from normal Americans. What normal Americans feel is that we're suffering from al-Qaeda."

Once bin Laden was out of the way, Bush said, they could turn to Iraq and any other supporter of terrorism.

The CIA team responsible for operating the Predator aerial surveillance drone wasn't sure how to proceed. The technology had been developed to weaponize the bird, so that it could not only broadcast images of terrorists, but shoot missiles at them as well. Yet the White House had held off on granting the agency the authority to deploy the armed Predator; days before the terrorist attacks, members of the Counterterrorist Center had been told to go ahead and ship the Predator into the field. Just don't arm it or send missles with it.

Surely, that restriction would now be swept aside—wouldn't it? A specialist on the Predator team went to see Bonk, the deputy director of the center, to find out. His team was ready to send out the advanced technology drones to where they could be used in Afghanistan, he said.

"But what do you want us to do in terms of missiles?" the specialist asked.

Bonk smiled. "Buy and load every one you can get your hands on," he said. "By the time we get there and are set up to go, we'll have the authorization."

This wasn't a time for wait-and-see. Bonk had no doubt the CIA was about to receive everything it had been seeking for the fight against terrorism. It wasn't as if the White House was going to hold back the permission to use the armed Predator—or the money for whatever other operations the agency wanted to undertake.

"Judge is back."

Tim Flanigan looked up from his desk. Libby Camp, the executive assistant for Al Gonzales, was at the door, giving him the heads-up that their boss—a former judge on the Texas Supreme Court—had just returned from a meeting with the war cabinet.

Grabbing a notepad, Flanigan walked through the staff area and into Gonzales's office. He sat on the couch as Gonzales flipped open his ever-present brown notepad portfolio.

Straight to work. "Timmy," Gonzales said, "you need to focus on the congressional resolution."

Already that morning, numerous assignments had been divvied up among the office's lawyers to determine legal issues dealing with the airlines, the financial markets, the insurance companies. But the resolution was the most important. The administration wanted congressional authorization to use force in response to the terrorist attacks.

Flanigan knew what the White House needed in the resolution, so his discussion with Gonzales was brief. Then, after a staff meeting, he walked back to his office to prepare the document defining the scope of the president's powers during a time of crisis.

At his computer, Flanigan called up the Web site for the Legal Information Institute at Cornell University Law School, a resource he often used to conduct research. From the site's search engine, he found the joint resolution that authorized deploying the military against Iraq in 1991. With a few keystrokes, he copied the document and pasted it onto a blank page for word processing.

He stared at the screen for a moment. It struck him that he might be a bit out of his depth—for the eight years before joining the administration, he had specialized in white-collar criminal and civil litigation, not laws governing the use of force. He picked up the phone; there was another lawyer in the administration, Flanigan knew, who was renowned for his dazzling intellect and a seemingly unmatched knowledge of national security law: David Addington, the vice president's chief counsel, a man dubbed Cheney's Cheney.

It could be argued that Cheney's relationship with Addington was born of scandal. In the mid-1980s, Cheney was a congressman from Wyoming and the ranking Republican on a House select committee investigating Iran-Contra, the affair that exposed how members of the Reagan administration had been secretly selling weapons to forces in Iran and funneling the profits to the anti-Sandinista fighters in Nicaragua.

Cheney considered the matter within the president's foreign policy authority, something that should remain immune from congressional meddling, and ordered up a minority report that largely endorsed Reagan's actions. Among those contributing to the report was a young staffer named David Addington.

While Cheney had a strong understanding of the mechanics and policies of national security, Addington brought an unmatched knowledge of the laws governing intelligence collection and presidential powers. A sober figure, Addington had started his career as assistant general counsel at the CIA before joining the staff of the House Intelligence Committee.

His encyclopedic knowledge and almost manic work ethic were the stuff of legend—and even awe—among his colleagues. They whispered that Addington seemed to have read *everything*, from the latest best seller to arcane articles and court decisions on intelligence matters to the texts of national security laws. He had collected an extensive archive of legal documents at his home in Alexandria, and was devastated when it was destroyed in a fire. For years he carried a copy of the Constitution in his pocket; on the back, he had taped statutes that laid out the procedures for presidential succession in a time of national emergency.

In his discussions with colleagues, Addington often underscored the tensions between protecting the country and protecting the rights of its citizens. Security, he believed, was the first requirement for freedom. A strong defense of the country gave rise to the rights it bestowed.

Those conversations, however, weren't always collegial. Methodical and meticulous in his analysis, Addington had no patience for others who advanced what he considered soft or lazy thinking. While he was open to debates with those he respected, he had no qualms about antagonistically shooting down arguments he saw as sloppy. His approach could be so aggressive that he was often described as a bureaucratic infighter more likely to use a knife than persuasion to advance his position.

Now, with the 9/11 attacks, Addington had become indispensable. He knew more about the issues involved than the White House counsel, the attorney general, the director of the CIA, and the vice president himself. Even now, just one day after the attack, other administration lawyers were speculating that Addington's influence on the course of American policy would grow exponentially in the years ahead.

Flanigan placed the call.

"David Addington."

"David, it's Tim. I'm drafting the resolution on the use of force, and wanted to get your input."

"Okay."

"I'm going to use the '91 resolution as a starting point."

Good idea, Addington replied. No need to reinvent the wheel.

"But," he added, speaking rapidly, "we need to be sure that we give the president all of the authority he needs to do this, because we don't know what this conflict is going to look like."

That made sense. Flanigan had skimmed the 1991 resolution, and had seen it was constrained by numerous specifics—the president could use force only to implement United Nations resolutions against Iraq, for example, and only after exhausting all diplomatic measures. Such restrictions simply couldn't be applied in a war against a nebulous enemy—or network of enemies.

No, this resolution would have to give Bush almost unfettered power to pursue terrorism anywhere, for any length of time, using any legal authority he deemed necessary.

Flanigan went back to his computer. He read the opening words from Section 2 of the 1991 resolution.

The President is authorized, subject to subsection (b) . . .

Subsection (b). That had required the first President Bush to assure Congress that his administration had used all appropriate peaceful means to resolve the dispute with Iraq.

Flanigan tapped on two keys, control and delete. A black line edited out the words *subject to subsection (b)*. The subsection would have to come out, too. How could the administration engage in diplomatic efforts with al-Qaeda?

He returned to the opening sentence of Section 2, with the new edit.

The President is authorized, ~~subject to subsection (b),~~ to use United States Armed Forces . . .

That wouldn't do. Too restrictive. This battle would range to other components of American power beyond just the military. To the Treasury, for example, which was engaged in efforts to interdict terrorist financing. To the CIA, of course, which not only would be gathering intelligence but would almost certainly be playing a large role when boots hit the ground in Afghanistan. The National Security Agency was already conducting signals surveillance. The State Department was scouring the globe to enlist allies in the fight. There were certain to be more initiatives that no one in the administration yet imagined.

Flanigan tapped control-delete again, then thought about a new phrase, one that would allow the White House to wield broader powers. He typed a few words, then read the sentence again.

The President is authorized, ~~subject to subsection (b),~~ to use ~~United States Armed Forces~~ all necessary and appropriate force . . .

Flanigan hesitated. There was no explanation of *what* constituted "all necessary and appropriate force." If Congress voted for this, it was essentially giving Bush carte blanche to act as he saw fit in fighting terrorists.

In for a dime, in for a dollar. The use of force in the 1991 document was limited solely to enforcing United Nations resolutions calling for Iraq to leave Kuwait. Out went those words. The U.N. would have nothing to say about the administration's response, and there would be no detailed definition of who or what could be the target of American force.

Then there was the problem of terrorist cells inside the United States; there had to be words taking into account the need for domestic action. For a minute, Flanigan typed. He cleaned up the edit, and read the sentence again.

The President is authorized to use all necessary and appropriate force in the United States and against those nations, organizations, or persons he determines planned, authorized, committed, or aided the terrorist attacks that occurred on September 11, 2001, or harbored such organizations or persons, in order to prevent any future acts of international terrorism against the United States by such nations, organizations or persons.

That was about as broad a grant of power as Flanigan could write. He wasn't sure if it went too far, or if the language was clear. He reached for the phone again. This time, he wanted to speak with John Yoo.

In a matter of minutes, Yoo came to the White House from the Eisenhower Executive Office Building across the street. He passed by the secretaries in the main room, offering a quick greeting, then walked into Flanigan's office.

"Thanks for coming over," Flanigan said. "We've got some important work to do with this resolution. I already took a stab at drafting something."

He picked up a white binder on his desk and handed it to Yoo. Inside were the 1991 resolution and the new draft. Yoo sat on the sofa and started reading. He reached the words *necessary and appropriate force*. The draft, he saw, went far beyond the terms in the authorization on Iraq.

He looked up. "You realize this is quite different."

Flanigan nodded. "Yeah."

They discussed the implications. The casual reader might not realize it, but this document could be used to authorize the use of military force inside the country. Not long ago, it would have been unthinkable that a war could be carried out on American soil. But, Flanigan noted, there was already a precedent, established the previous day: Bush had been called upon to approve shooting down a civilian plane, and the Pentagon had ruled that he had the statutory authority to do so.

That was true, Yoo said. This document, no matter how obliquely, merely spelled out that new reality.

Yoo returned to parsing the words of the full order and began to wonder if it was too sweeping. It was one thing for administration staffers to proclaim an open-ended doctrine on the scope of the president's authority. It was quite another for Congress to endorse it.

"I don't know if they're going to let us get away with this," You said. Congress and presidents had long tussled about who had the authority to decide to go to war, and this revision of the 1991 resolution went the heart of that dispute.

Flanigan shrugged. "Why don't we try and put it in?"

Cofer Black and his deputy, Ben Bonk, were taking a breather.

The analysts in the Counterterrorist Center had been running themselves ragged since the attacks, with no chance to relax and often no desire to do so. Black had watched a longtime analyst pull on her coat and head for the door after almost forty-eight hours on the job; in the hallway, she had stopped by a table loaded with food and glanced at a wall already filled with children's letters and drawings that thanked those in the government who were working so hard to keep their families safe. The analyst had blinked, turned, and slid off her coat as she walked back to her desk to take up the next assignment.

Black and Bonk spoke with pride of these people who had sacrificed so much, struggling in anonymity with too few resources, too many leads, and not much pay as they worked to protect their countrymen. Their dedication was no secret inside the agency—the CIA Office of Inspector General had just spent six months conducting a review of the Counterterrorist Center, and the report issued just a few weeks ago was nothing short of a rave. The staffers were highly dedicated and knew they were working to save American lives, the report said. But the center's funding was unreliable, leaving the group shorthanded. That, the report said, meant the existing crew was turning in its superb performance while operating pedal-to-the-floor almost all of the time, as crisis after crisis emerged.

With the attacks in New York and Washington, money, equipment, and people would soon be flowing in, which was certain to give the staffers a morale boost as they hit their stride. But Black and Bonk recognized they wouldn't be around to watch the reinvigoration of their beloved division.

"You know, we're finished here," Black said.

Neither had to put the reason into words. It didn't matter how effusive the recent praise of their work had been, or how many times they had warned the White House of an impending slaughter. It didn't matter that they had retained all of the PowerPoint presentations in their files that proved their diligence. Someone would have to be held accountable. Fighting terrorism was their business. They were about to be shown the door.

"That's true," Bonk replied. "Let's not worry about it for now."

"Yeah, we're finished," Black repeated. "So while we're here let's just focus on doing what needs to be done."

A moment passed. Then they returned to work.

In Kabul, Khalid Sheikh Mohammed, the mastermind of the 9/11 attacks, arrived at the home of Muhammad Salah, eager to describe the events of the previous day. Some of al-Qaeda's top leadership, including bin Laden, had been on the move and for now had taken refuge with Salah, a terrorist operations planner.

Sheikh Mohammed walked into the room where everyone waited. The men called out his code name—Mukhtar—and greeted him with blessings, hugs, and kisses.

This was the kind of adulation that Sheikh Mohammed had craved ever since his nephew, Ramzi Yousef, gained worldwide recognition for detonating a truck bomb at the World Trade Center in 1993. Three years later, Sheikh Mohammed came to bin Laden with a proposed plot that was as daring as it was grandiose. Ten commercial airliners would be hijacked by teams of Muslims, with nine of them crashing into targets on both the East and West Coasts—the World Trade Center, the Pentagon, the CIA, the FBI, nuclear power plants, the Library Tower in California, and others. Then, exposing his egotism and desire for fame, Sheikh Mohammed announced he would pilot the tenth plane, land at an American airport, kill all of the male passengers, and deliver a speech condemning the Americans.

Bin Laden had responded coolly to the idea. Sheikh Mohammed's proposal seemed too ambitious, too impractical. Other, less complicated ideas, like the plot for the embassy bombings, were already in the works. But by 1999, bin Laden considered Sheikh Mohammed's plan once again, deciding it might work if it was pared back to a more manageable size—four planes rather than ten.

Now Sheikh Mohammed's vision had come to pass. He took a seat beside bin Laden and offered up details of the successful operation. Each attack had been planned to take place twenty to thirty minutes apart, he said, and that had played out perfectly.

He showed bin Laden three publications he had brought with him—two newspapers in Arabic and one magazine in English. Photographs of explosions and flames at the World Trade Center filled the first pages. Flipping inside, Sheikh Mohammed showed bin Laden pictures of some of the hijackers that had already been publicly distributed by the FBI. Bin Laden smiled, praising the men by name.

"Thanks be to God for the success of the operation," bin Laden said. "God willing, accept these men as martyrs."

He looked toward Sheikh Mohammed. "May God reward Mukhtar for this work."

Bush and the war cabinet met on the morning of September 13 in the White House Situation Room. Plans to chase down al-Qaeda were starting to gel, but the details weren't set.

"This is not business as usual," Cheney said. "Six weeks to figure out what to do is six weeks too long."

The administration needed to be aggressive in its retaliation by inflicting pain on the terrorists and their supporters, he said. Anyone, any group, any nation that did business with al-Qaeda would be hurt—in finances, in logistical capabilities, in everything.

"We've got to cast the net broadly," he said. "A state that provides support for terrorism in any way will be a target for U.S. pain."

Tenet had come to the meeting ready to lay out details of the CIA proposals. Long before, the agency had drawn up two blueprints—one called "Going to War," which centered exclusively on fighting in Afghanistan; and the other, "Worldwide Attack Matrix," which detailed covert operations against the entire global spectrum of groups and individuals affiliated with al-Qaeda. These were set to go and could be used as the foundation of a comprehensive battle against bin Laden's organization, starting in Afghanistan.

"We're prepared to launch an aggressive covert action program that will carry the fight to the enemy," he said. To do that, CIA paramilitary teams would be sent into Afghanistan to work with the Northern Alliance and others battling the Taliban; that would pave the way for American military forces.

Tenet turned to Cofer Black. Using a PowerPoint presentation, Black described his group's capabilities for covert action, the projected deployments of paramilitary forces, and the lethal potential of the armed Predator that, as expected, had just been approved for combat.

"Now, we will not just be taking on al-Qaeda in Afghanistan," Black said. "We'll be taking on the Taliban, too. They're inseparable."

"How quickly could we deploy the CIA teams?" Bush asked.

"In short order."

"How quickly, then, could we defeat the Taliban and al-Qaeda?"

"A matter of weeks, once we are fully deployed on the ground countrywide."

Tenet listened with unease to Black's confident prediction. A matter of weeks? Tenet doubted that was possible. It would take time to find the enemy, and as Black had just acknowledged, these terrorists were tenacious and fearless fighters.

Bush harbored no such doubts. For the first time, he believed that he understood how America was going to win this war.

Two black sedans motored up Pennsylvania Avenue, flashing winks of sunlight as they moved. The air was clear, the sky virtually cloudless—the same surreal beauty that had bathed the Northeast on the morning of the attacks two days earlier.

Inside the cars, a small phalanx of White House lawyers were heading to Capitol Hill for the first negotiations over the resolution granting Bush new powers to fight terrorists. Flanigan had sent his latest draft to Senate staff members the night before and was now ready to wrestle with them about it.

"What are they going to want to change?" Flanigan asked Yoo, who was sitting in the front seat.

"They're certainly going to want to add more War Powers language to it," Yoo replied.

That was something the lawyers had already agreed to fight. Since the War Powers Resolution was adopted in 1973, Congress had maintained that a president could commit American armed forces overseas only with its approval. Successive administrations had rejected that claim as an attempt to usurp the president's constitutional authority to wage war. The proposed resolution put that issue front and center. But the challenges, the lawyers knew, wouldn't end there.

"They're definitely going to go after the 'necessary and appropriate' language," Flanigan said.

Not so, Nancy Dorn, Cheney's head of legislative affairs, said from the backseat. The country was too traumatized and emotions were too raw. No member of Congress would want to be castigated as the stumbling block to Bush's initiative for shielding the homeland against terrorists.

"In the end," she said, "they're going to give the president what he wants."

The sedans arrived at a checkpoint that had been set up to stop car bombers from getting near the Capitol. The lawyers spilled out and strolled the last fifty yards to the building. A tiled staircase led to an ornate high-ceilinged conference room where filament bulbs cast a weak glow over portraits of some of Congress's great history makers.

More than a dozen congressional aides were already gathered around the conference table when the White House officials arrived. There were handshakes and pleasantries all around; then everyone got to work.

The first item for discussion: War Powers language. The dance opened with a traditional step—the congressional staffers argued for inclusion of phrases from that decades-old resolution to ensure that Bush didn't veer off into an open-ended commitment of military forces without consulting legislators.

Not applicable here, the administration lawyers responded. Beyond the fact that the executive branch maintained that the War Powers Resolution was an unconstitutional encroachment on presidential authority, this was not like any previous conflict. No one, at this point, could say where this campaign would lead; the White House would be hampered by requirements that might come into play each time there was new information identifying culprits in the attacks.

An aide to Senator Edward Kennedy was studying the draft, her face pinched with concern. "This grant of power to the president is scary," she said.

"But," Yoo replied, "it's perfectly appropriate under the circumstances where we don't know what the threat is."

The Kennedy aide held up a copy of the 1991 Iraq resolution. "This one has some specificity," she said. "We've got to have something in this new one to sort of cabin the president's power. This grant is just too broad."

Several of the staffers focused on the words *in the United States,* which followed the phrase granting the president the authority to use *all necessary and appropriate force.* Use of force inside the country? That was unprecedented. The congressional side dug in, and the four words were cut.

Round and round the dancers circled, with the Senate aides trying to lead the discussion into restrictions on Bush's authority and the White House staffers pushing back.

After several hours, an aide to Senator Joe Biden, the Delaware Democrat, suggested adding a few words to modify an element of the resolution. The revision struck Flanigan as reasonable.

"Okay," he said, weariness in his voice. "I think we can live with that."

A jolt of excitement crackled among the staffers for the Democratic senators. Before anyone else could speak, Yoo grabbed Flanigan's elbow.

"Let's talk about this," he said, almost lifting Flanigan from his seat. The two men walked outside the room. Yoo showed Flanigan how the proposed words changed meanings in the draft.

"This would really eviscerate the language of the resolution," Yoo said.

Flanigan took a deep breath. His exhaustion, the strain of maintaining a mood of cordiality—something had blinded him. He had almost single-handedly made a fatal concession that would have constrained the president's power to wage war on terrorists.

"Okay, John, I get it," Flanigan said. "I lost focus."

The two men walked back into the room.

"We can't accept that language," Flanigan said.

And the dance resumed.

At 9:00 A.M. on September 14, Andy Card stood at the front of Room 450 in the Eisenhower Executive Office Building, his eyes roving over the contingent of somber White House aides who had been summoned to discuss how to stay alive.

"I want to thank you all for coming here," he began. "Obviously, we're all facing unprecedented and difficult challenges. You have the opportunity but also the burden of serving your country in a time of real crisis and emergency."

Card paused. "I know this is not what any of you signed up for when you joined the White House staff," he said, his voice steely. "And nobody here will blame you—not me, not the president—if under these circumstances and conditions you do want to leave. If that's the case, tell someone and you can leave, with no recrimination or dishonor or bad feeling."

The reassurance was no mere formality—real fear gripped those who were listening. Word had circulated about one official who was so frightened at the thought of an attack on the White House that she repeatedly threw up in her trash can. But, like most of her colleagues, she would dismiss Card's offer and continue working in the executive mansion.

Card assured everyone that there was no reason to be concerned about Bush. "The president is doing enormously well," he said. "I've been amazed at how calm and centered and decisive he has been. He has been a pillar of strength, and you all would be very, very proud of him."

In a moment, Card said, he would be turning the meeting over to the Secret Service and Bush's doctor, Colonel Richard Tubb, who would discuss ways for the members of the White House staff to protect themselves from terrorists. But first, he wanted everyone to understand that their access to Bush would become severely limited.

The president's circle of advisors had to shrink dramatically, Card said, to a handful of players who would stay in near-constant contact with him.

"So if you *want* to see the president in the coming weeks and months, you will not see the president," Card said. "But if you *need* to see the president, you will see the president."

Next, a Secret Service official briefed the staff on precautions they should take each day—varying their routes to and from work, keeping an eye open for any cars that might be following them, and going to different restaurants for lunch.

Out in the audience, Bradford Berenson, an associate counsel for the White House, knew he would be spurning the advice.

That's ridiculous, he thought. Like most of the others in the room, his name was listed in the phone book. If terrorists wanted him dead, all they had to do was wait outside his house and shoot him as he walked to his car.

The safety lesson over, Dr. Tubb gave a brief tutorial on biological and chemical arms. Years before, a Japanese group had demonstrated it was possible for terrorists to kill using sarin gas, one of the most toxic chemicals available.

Biological weapons that used disease and natural poisons to incapacitate and kill had the potential to be even more deadly; viruses and bacteria could spread before anyone knew an attack had occurred. Infectious agents such as smallpox had been used in the past.

But these days, Tubb said, the most likely pathogen for a biological weapon was a parasite that has a natural life cycle in hoofed animals and could cause an infectious disease—anthrax.

About that same time, legislators milled about the Senate floor discussing the pending vote on the White House resolution to grant Bush new powers for fighting terrorists.

Some senators were expressing nervousness about the open-ended authority that the vague wording appeared to give to the president. But a leading member of each party—Harry Reid, the Nevada Democrat; and Don Nickles, a Republican from Nevada—were making the rounds to tamp down those fears, assuring their colleagues that Congress could always revisit the issue if members came to believe the president was going too far. For now, they argued, it was imperative for them to set aside their differences and speak in one voice by approving the resolution unanimously.

Just minutes before the morning session began, the White House contacted Senator Tom Daschle, the South Dakota Democrat and majority leader. There were some words that should be added to the resolution, the administration official said—after "appropriate force," the phrase "in the United States and" should appear. That same language had been removed in the earlier negotiations with Senate staffers.

Daschle was appalled. The White House was seeking a revision of unprecedented import and asking for it so late in the game that senators would have no chance to even think about the implications. He was not going to negotiate whether the president would be allowed to take military action inside the country, potentially against American citizens.

"I don't see any reason for the Congress to accede to such an extraordinary request for additional authority," Daschle said. That was that.

By 10:16, the clamor in the chamber had barely abated when Senator Evan Bayh, the Indiana Democrat serving as the presiding officer, banged a gavel, calling the Senate into session. He gazed out at those colleagues who were still in earnest discussion.

"The senators will take their conversations to the cloakroom and clear the aisles," he said.

Among the senators stepping out of the chamber was Arlen Specter, the Pennsylvania Republican. Even though his own party occupied the White House, Specter could not shake his discomfort about the resolution's phrasing. The senator spoke to an aide—get someone from the White House on the phone who knows about the language in the authorization, he said.

Minutes later, a phone in the cloakroom rang for Specter. Tim Flanigan was on the line.

"Senator, I understand you have some concerns."

"Well now, Tim, this language is very broad—very broad—and you know that this gives the president a lot of authority. We shouldn't be doing this and we should be limiting this."

Perhaps, Specter suggested, the administration should seek a declaration of war instead. "I've spoken with Joe Biden, and he agrees that this language is very broad."

There wasn't much for Flanigan to say. The White House had the votes to get the resolution passed. Would Specter and Biden really want to publicly oppose the president's request for the power he needed to fight terrorists? There wasn't a chance that everyone would run back on the field so that Specter could call the play over again.

"Senator," Flanigan said, "this is the language that was negotiated with staff."

"Well, I know you've negotiated it, but we ought to rethink this."

For a minute Specter parsed specific wording in the resolution. What was the meaning of "necessary and appropriate"? What *kind* of force was the resolution authorizing? The language didn't make that clear. What standards would be used in declaring which countries or organizations aided in the 9/11 attacks?

Flanigan gave a few perfunctory answers, but there really wasn't much to discuss. "Senator, this is what the president feels he needs to do," he said, his voice quiet. "This is how he will be able to respond to the attacks on the United States."

Specter sighed. "I just think you ought to think about this," he said. "I know you'll talk to the president about this."

Yeah, right. "Senator, I understand your points. We just disagree."

A pause. "I think you're making a big mistake."

With that, Specter hung up. Frustrated and angered, he returned to the floor. The clerk had been running down the roll for senators' votes for several minutes and had just called for the decision of Olympia Snow, Republican from Maine. She said aye.

"Mr. Specter?" the clerk said.

A few seconds ticked by. Finally, Specter swallowed his worries and voted yes. The resolution passed unanimously.

Several Democratic senators had cast their votes with unease, including Biden. The best way to deal with those concerns, he decided, was to address the chamber and clearly state what he had just approved—and what he had not.

Biden walked to the lectern on the Democrats' side of the chamber. The presiding senator recognized him to speak.

"My mom has an expression," he began. " 'Out of every tragedy some good will come.' "

What the Senate had just done, he said, was something that would likely not occur in any other country in the world. They had followed the principles enshrined in the law, despite the anger and hatred spawned throughout the United States and inside the Senate chamber by the terrorist attacks.

"We didn't pell-mell just say 'Go, do anything, anytime, anyplace, Mr. President, you've got to just go.' "

Instead, Biden said, they had honored America's founders by holding fast to the dictates of the Constitution.

"We said, 'What does it call for here?' And what it called for was for the United States Congress to meet its constitutional responsibility to say, 'Mr. President, we authorize you, we authorize you in the name of the American people, to take action and we define the action in generic terms.' "

Biden turned toward Robert Byrd, the West Virginia Democrat who was the second-longest-serving senator in American history and who jealously guarded Congress's authority. Byrd was nodding forcefully.

Gesticulating to emphasize his message, Biden faced front again. "We gave the president today, as we should have and as is our responsibility, all of the authority he needs to prosecute these individuals or countries, without yielding our constitutional right to retain the judgment in the future as to whether or not force could, would, or should be used."

For Biden, the record was clear; Congress was not granting the president a blank check and was not ceding any of its inherent powers to the White House.

He glanced back at Byrd. The elderly senator pursed his lips as he proudly nodded again.

Bush sat at his desk in the Oval Office speaking by phone to Tony Blair in London. The United States, Bush said, was nailing down its plans for attacking its terrorist enemies.

"We're going to be using conventional forces to fight a guerrilla war," he said. "We're going to be matching that up with the full force of the U.S. military, with bombers coming from all directions."

The first phase of the conflict, Bush said, was not going to be limited to combat in Afghanistan. "We're cutting off money, we're rounding up people, we've gotten people to go after them."

Each step, Bush said, would set in motion events that would eat away at the entire terrorist infrastructure. "It'll be like circles coming from a pebble dropped in the water."

Blair listened with growing alarm about Bush's words. There was no mention of a multinational response. Instead, there was an echo of the president's apparent disdain for consulting the Group of Eight. America, Blair feared, might be turning inward, in its anger developing a go-it-alone mentality. Such an approach would only isolate the country. It would be a strategic blunder that could blunt or even derail America's fight against terrorists.

Afghanistan was only the beginning, Bush continued. If the United States took out al-Qaeda and stopped there, the war would reach an inconclusive stalemate. Other terrorists would simply take al-Qaeda's place. There had to be a strategy to starve, disrupt, and destroy all terrorist groups.

"The next step is to look at other countries, including Iraq," Bush said. "I think there might be evidence that there might be a connection between Saddam Hussein and Osama bin Laden."

Time to reel this in. "The evidence would have to be very compelling indeed to justify taking any action against Iraq," Blair said. "I would strongly advise dealing with Afghanistan very distinctively. To go after Iraq would be certain to lose Russia and France."

Bush listened politely, and thanked Blair for his thoughts. But the United States would be following the terrorist threat wherever it went, and his administration had little doubt that the trail would lead to Iraq.

Blair hung up the phone and glanced around the room at his aides. They could see that the prime minister was quite troubled.

They had to do something. Bush was going in the wrong direction. "We have to think of a way of getting to the U.S. for a face-to-face meeting," he said. "I need to see Bush in a room, and look in his eyes, not do all this in phone calls with fifteen people listening in."

He summarized the conversation, then looked over at David Manning, a foreign policy advisor. "David," Blair said, "I want you to stay in permanent contact with Condi, and make sure they do nothing too rash."

The group spent a few minutes mulling over the military strategies that Bush had laid out. When Blair mentioned Bush's plans for Iraq, Geoff Hoon, the defense secretary, spoke up.

"Rumsfeld has been looking for reasons to hit Iraq," he said. "They definitely want regime change, and that has been the channel of advice Bush has been getting since the election."

Jack Straw, the foreign secretary, broke in. "They would be mad to do Iraq without justification!" he said. "They'll lose world opinion."

Nodding, Blair took a deep breath. "My job," he said, "is to steer them in a sensible path."

High atop the bucolic Catoctin Mountains in Maryland sits Camp David, a 180-acre compound ringed by three fences and obscured from public view.

Presidents and their families have often described the retreat as a rustic, wilderness getaway where ordinary Americans would feel at home. But in truth, it is far from modest; with its heated pool, skeet range, bowling alley, and movie theater, Camp David is a sumptuous spread more akin to a five-star resort than a backwoods campsite.

On the morning of September 15, a Saturday, Camp David was alive with activity as top administration officials—guarded by a beefed-up contingent of the elite Marine Security Company—plotted the final details for America's retaliation to the terrorist attacks.

Bush, dressed in a blue shirt and a bomber jacket to ward off the chilly mountain air, left his Camp David residence early and walked to Laurel Lodge, a building in the compound. He made his way into a narrow, wood-paneled conference room and took a seat directly across from George Tenet, who was accompanied by his deputy, John McLaughlin, and Cofer Black.

After a brief presentation by Paul O'Neill, the treasury secretary, Tenet distributed copies of a briefing packet that had been compiled by the counterterrorism unit. The title projected its ambitions: "Destroying International Terrorism."

The actions that the paper proposed were the same ones that the CIA had been advocating for more than a year. Elite agency paramilitary units would sneak into Afghanistan and link up with the Northern Alliance. Later this would be joined by Special Forces from the military.

The initial goal, Tenet said, was to close off Afghanistan from the outside world, which would require engaging its neighbors—Iran, Turkey, Tajikistan, Uzbekistan, and Pakistan. At that point, Tenet said, America's only strong relationship was with the Uzbeks; they had been secretly aiding the United States to conduct surveillance flights over Afghanistan by granting permission for the CIA to launch the Predator from their country.

First the Americans would demand that officials with Afghanistan's Taliban government turn over bin Laden. If they refused, the CIA would demolish the regime. Agency operatives would step up their contacts with Pashtun leaders and Taliban commanders who they believed would turn on their leader, the inarticulate village cleric, Mullah Mohammed Omar.

The now-familiar elements of a full-frontal assault on al-Qaeda were part of the presentation—a covert attack on the terrorists' finances, tracking down al-Qaeda cells in the United States, using mullahs on the agency payroll for propaganda efforts, employing the Predator to track down and kill bin Laden or his top lieutenants. Agency operatives would need the authority to unilaterally detain the terrorists anywhere in the world. And the efforts would require a huge infusion of cash.

To accomplish this, the president would have to clear away bureaucratic hurdles by signing a Memorandum of Notification granting the agency the authority to conduct operations, including the use of deadly force, without having to return time and again for approval. Al-Qaeda operated out of ninety-two countries, Tenet said, but if the president signed off on the proposals, the CIA would be ready to go; already, the agency had allies in scores of countries, disrupting terrorist plots.

"That's great!" Bush exclaimed.

Now it was the military's turn. General Hugh Shelton, chairman of the Joint Chiefs of Staff, laid out three options. If the president wanted to move quickly, he could follow in Clinton's footsteps by launching cruise missiles into Afghanistan and obliterating al-Qaeda camps—which, unfortunately, had emptied out just before the 9/11 attacks. Bush dismissed the idea. A more aggressive approach, Shelton said, would be to rain down destruction on military targets with sustained attacks, lasting about ten days, with both cruise missiles and bomber aircraft—B-1s, B-2s, and B-52s.

The third alternative was the most ambitious of all: an assault using every offensive force at the military's disposal. Missiles, bombers, Special Forces commando units, perhaps army soldiers and marines, could all be part of the mix. This, he said, was being called the "boots on the ground" option. It would take time to get the first forces there—perhaps as long as twelve days—but after that point they would be ready to go.

As Bush listened to Shelton expound the military plans, he felt a rising sense of disappointment. None of this seemed imaginative—it was as unimpressive as the CIA strategy had been electrifying. He was in a hurry for a strategy, and it was growing increasingly clear that the military couldn't put a viable one together quickly.

The discussions became free-floating, almost unmoored. Officials brought up old ideas and new challenges—a report by the United States Agency for International Development was raised, showing that the northern part of Afghanistan was on the cusp of a drought-induced famine. Unless specific attention was given to that threat, any war effort could lead to mass starvation.

As the talks wore on throughout the day, the core strategic elements of the war against terrorism crystallized. The path ahead was clear. But before the meeting ended, Cheney raised a question.

"Suppose this doesn't work?" he asked. "Then what do we do?"

Just past 4:30 on the next afternoon, Donald Henderson, called "D.A." by everyone who knew him, was sitting in an easy chair in the den of his Baltimore home. It was a lazy Sunday afternoon, and Henderson was taking in the calming view of his nearby Japanese garden.

A renowned epidemiologist, Henderson in the 1960s had led an international team of scientists in what eventually proved to be a successful effort to eradicate smallpox. Following thirteen years as dean of the Johns Hopkins School of Public Health, Henderson had served as a senior government advisor with expertise in communicable disease. While he had returned to academia in 1995, he was still seen by senior government officials as one of the country's best minds on the use of microbes to create biological weapons. Now, at seventy-three years old, Henderson was planning to retire, to slow down, to travel, and to enjoy life with his wife, Nana.

As Henderson lounged in his upholstered chair, his home telephone rang. On the line was an aide to Tommy Thompson, the secretary of health and human services with the Bush administration.

"Can you come to a meeting in Washington?" the aide asked.

"When?"

"Tonight at seven. We're asking 'What's next?' We'd like you to be there."

Henderson understood. Administration officials weren't just wrestling over how to deal with the September 11 attacks, but were preparing for future strikes, including those that might involve bioterrorism.

After telling his wife about the call, Henderson climbed into his silver Volvo and drove off for Washington.

Inside the Roosevelt Room at the White House, the topic was smallpox.

Bush, Cheney, and the war cabinet were sitting at the conference table as Michael Brown, the director of the Federal Emergency Management Agency, briefed them on the horrendous power of biological weapons. The meeting had been called at the vice president's request and a number of the country's top epidemiological experts had been invited to attend. As the secretary of defense during the Persian Gulf War in 1991, the vice president knew about the stores of anthrax, botulism toxins, and VX nerve agents that Saddam Hussein had stockpiled. Deadly in even small quantities, any of these substances could be transported across national borders with little risk of detection; at this very moment one of them might be in the hands of terrorists somewhere.

Bush and Cheney both fervently believed another wave of attacks was imminent—most likely involving a biological weapon, with anthrax or smallpox the prime candidates. The Secret Service had already begun monitoring the air inside and outside the White House for contaminants, and Cheney had taken to traveling with a full biohazard suit at the ready. As for Bush, he still could not shake what he had learned in his first intelligence briefing almost a year before, when Ben Bonk of the CIA had sneaked a functional biological bomb into a meeting; anyone in the country, the president understood, was in danger of being killed by such a weapon. Al-Qaeda, Saddam, any terrorist group could launch an attack with viruses and bacteria. The smallpox virus made an almost perfect weapon, Bush and his aides were told. The incubation period for the illness was long—about twelve days, enough time for the pathogen to spread widely before anyone showed symptoms. Smallpox attacks skin cells, causing lesions to erupt on the faces and bodies of the infected. In its most malignant form, it can trigger severe bleeding in the skin, mucous membranes, and stomach, leading to an agonizing death for one of every three victims.

While a decades-long global campaign led by Donald Henderson had eradicated the disease by the late 1970s, the virus itself still existed. But nobody knew how much of it there was or where, exactly, it was stored. About a decade before, a Russian defector had confirmed to American officials that, over many years, Moscow had overseen the production of as much as twenty tons of weaponized smallpox. In 1997, the Russians confirmed that they possessed a smallpox repository and promised to move it to a virology research center in Koltsovo. But there were reasons to fear that some of it had escaped the custody of Russian officials. The breakup of the Soviet Union had left many biological weapons experts looking for work. Conceivably, terrorists could have exploited the economic turbulence in Russia and bribed their way into obtaining the virus, the technology, and the know-how they would need to launch a biological attack anywhere in the world.

The president listened quietly. Most of the questions came from Cheney and Rice.

The presentation ended. Bush, looking shaken, stood as the other officials gathered their notes. Before he reached the door, he stopped and turned, facing his advisors.

"God help us all," he said.

Nassau Street, the central spine of downtown Princeton, New Jersey, was alive with its usual assortment of cars and pedestrians. Outside the Coldwell Banker office at the intersection of Bank Street, people ambled past an unremarkable blue postal service mailbox, one of four on the town's main thoroughfare.

A man, largely unnoticed, walked near a grouping of small bank branches that served students at Princeton University across the street. He approached the mailbox, which had been set up sixty feet from a building that housed offices for Kappa Kappa Gamma, the national sorority. He carried several envelopes, each prestamped with postage of thirty-four cents and addressed to members of the news media. Multiple pieces of tape had been applied across the back, an attempt to seal small openings where the edges of the paper had been glued together.

Inside, the letters had been irregularly cut, allowing for them to be wrapped in a "pharmaceutical fold," used for centuries to dispense small quantities of medicinal powder. This time, the fold was not holding medication, but a small amount of a brown granular substance—the bacteria that cause anthrax. The biological agent was called RMR-1029, which had been created in laboratory B-313 at the Army Research Facility at Fort Detrick. Only researchers trusted by the government to work with the lethal spores could gain access to them.

The man reached for the handle on the mailbox and pulled it open, placing the envelopes inside. The tray slammed shut, dropping the letters on top of other mail set for pickup at eleven o'clock on the morning of September 18.

The anthrax attacks had begun.

3

"It starts today."

As he spoke the words, Bush glanced around the table at the members of his National Security Council. The days of planning and discussion were over. Now, early on the morning of September 17, the first pieces of the plans for the American attack on worldwide terrorism were ready.

He ordered Ashcroft to develop a legislative package that would grant expanded powers to federal law enforcement for combating terrorists. Tenet was instructed to act on the CIA plan to destroy al-Qaeda that had been presented two days before. The State Department, he told Powell, was to issue an ultimatum to the Taliban—either turn over bin Laden or face the consequences. The Treasury Department was to launch an immediate assault on terrorist financial networks. Finally, the Pentagon was directed to develop military plans for a massive attack, using missiles, bombers, and troops, including Special Forces.

"I want to signal a change from the past," Bush said. "I want to cause countries like Iran and Syria to get scared and change their views."

"It will take about four days to establish an air bridge," said General Shelton, the chairman of the Joint Chiefs. No large-scale military deployment could occur without first setting up a route and the means of delivering equipment and supplies. That would entail bringing in the support of other nations.

"That's fine," Bush said. "I want you to explore the possibility of getting some Muslim nations involved."

A document describing the broad directives of the new strategy was ready for Bush's signature; Rice had remained at Camp David after the strategy session two days before and had composed a short memo. That was then compiled into a Memorandum of Notification, which would be used to inform congressional intelligence committees of changes in counterterrorism policies.

The memorandum included no new presidential findings about the threat posed by al-Qaeda, but sharply toughened the operational authority and resources available for the CIA and other agencies. Among the powers assigned under the memorandum, the agency could now, without seeking prior approval, use lethal force against terrorists or render them to countries that had not requested their extradition. To spell out the new mission in detail, administration officials immediately began work on a more specific, twelve-page authorization—called National Security Presidential Directive number nine, "Combating Terrorism"—that listed the new duties of every agency and department playing a role in the country's national security system.

Attached to the directive were annexes, dividing up the strategy by region. In Annex A was Afghanistan. In Annex B, Iraq.

At 11:45 that morning, Bush had just finished being briefed at the Pentagon about plans to call up military reserves. He stepped into the Joint Staff corridor, where reporters awaited him. He gave a short statement, then invited questions.

The journalists asked about the prospects for war, whether the administration could keep the country out of a recession in the event of armed conflict, and the health of the airline industry.

"Do you want bin Laden dead?" a reporter asked.

Bush paused. "I want him held—I want justice," he said. "There's an old poster out west, as I recall, that said 'Wanted: Dead or Alive.' "

Wanted: Dead or Alive.

As he heard the president's words, John Bellinger almost fell out of his chair. As senior associate counsel to the president and advisor to the National Security Council, Bellinger was responsible for helping Bush and his administration wade through the legal thickets of international affairs. With his new statement, Bellinger feared, the president may have gone too far.

He composed an e-mail to Gonzales. The lawyers needed to warn Bush not to say things like "dead or alive." Such a reckless remark could be interpreted as an instigation for assassination, and that would cross the legal line. Bellinger finished composing his e-mail and hit the send button.

• • •

David Addington fumed as he met with Gonzales and Flanigan.

"Al, you've got to get control of Bellinger," he said. "You've got to rein him in. Is he working for you? Because he's going to be trouble eventually."

The three men had seen Bellinger's e-mail and had been astonished. He was criticizing a statement that the president *had already made* and suggesting that Bush might have violated the law. Hell, Flanigan said, some political opponent could argue that Bellinger was accusing the president of essentially committing a war crime. Maybe he thought he was simply making a lawyerly point intended to warn Bush about potential land mines, but the way he said it—*in writing*—infuriated the attorneys.

Flanigan shot an e-mail back to Bellinger stating that he should not create White House records defining a statute and applying it to Bush's comments, since clearly any claim of illegality would be based solely on a misinterpretation of what the president meant. There was no response.

For Addington, Bellinger's e-mail was the last straw. The man, he declared, could not be trusted.

The planned aerial assault against Taliban targets in Afghanistan was hitting some snags.

Efforts to secure regional bases for the military campaign were faltering. President Musharraf of Pakistan had immediately, and quietly, offered the United States use of several airfields—including the strategically important Shahbaz Air Base in Jacobabad—which could be used as a staging site for the air force, Special Operations Forces, and Combat Search and Rescue units. But Shahbaz and the other fields were too far from the European bases where air force cargo planes loaded equipment for the military operation. The planners at Central Command needed to find a base closer to Europe, but still within Central Asia.

They turned to Uzbekistan, a country on Afghanistan's northern border that had been helping American intelligence efforts for a year. Quickly, the Uzbeks signaled a willingness to cooperate in the full military assault. There were several former Soviet air bases available, the most suitable at Samarkand, but the Uzbeks refused to allow the Americans to set up there. Instead, they offered a dilapidated base at Karshi-Khanabad, a name that military planners shortened to K2.

Problems abounded there. The crumbling Soviet-built runways were too short to handle the air force's C-5 Galaxy transport planes. Few buildings were intact. Old jet fuel had seeped through the ground, emitting dangerous vapors.

Worst of all, after making a show of cooperation, the Uzbeks began dragging their feet on reaching a final agreement.

A more daunting challenge to the emerging war raised its head back in Washington: micromanagement. Before the first missiles could be fired, someone needed to select the targets. That meant each option had to be examined in excruciating detail by Central Command, the Combined Air Operations Center, and commanders on navy aircraft carriers. Then their proposals went to the Pentagon and the White House, to be picked over by the lawyers.

In the Kremlin, teams of American and Russian officials gathered around a large conference table as they discussed the destruction of al-Qaeda and the Taliban.

For some time, relations between Washington and Moscow had been chilly at best; Kremlin officials had felt marginalized by the United States and Europe in recent years, and in response had turned eastward, bolstering their ties with China as a counterweight. President Vladimir Putin had also been long frustrated with Western criticism of his war against Islamic separatists in Chechnya, whom he had labeled terrorists. But with the 9/11 attacks, the Russians believed that Washington was finally coming to understand the brutality and danger of Muslim extremists. Now they could work together against a common enemy.

The officials at the meeting were part of a standing partnership, the U.S.-Russia Working Group on Counterterrorism, but this time, the Americans were controlling the agenda. The head of the delegation, Richard Armitage, was the number two at the State Department and led the discussion. The longest presentation, however, was given by Cofer Black of the CIA, who shared intelligence obtained about the 9/11 attacks and al-Qaeda and then discussed the American plans to strike back hard. The Russians were slack-jawed by the information they received and had not anticipated its detail or fervor. The United States, they were shocked to find, had come full tilt.

At a break, the officials stood and chatted among themselves. Some Russian military officers walked around the table to where Black was still sitting, gathering his papers.

"We just wanted to say hello, wanted to talk to you," one of the officers said. There was a pause.

"Mr. Black," the officer said. "*Finally* the Americans are acting like a superpower."

Black smiled. Apparently, the Russians had been waiting a long time for America to get tough. This, he thought, was great.

• • •

A group of Pentagon lawyers studied the piles of charts and photographs showing strategic bombing targets in Kabul and Kandahar. Each option had its own
page complete with a classified photograph—some taken by satellite, some from
the air, and a few from the ground. Superimposed on each image was a group
of concentric ovals along with a color chart and a series of numbers. The ovals
showed possible blast effects, with the range based on different assumptions—
what time of day the attack might occur, whether there was a stone wall
nearby—so that calculations could be made to limit collateral damage.

Bush had indirectly compelled the extensive review when he publicly stated
that this was not a war against religion; if, he said, any of the bombs or missiles struck a mosque—or even damaged one from a distance—Muslims might
believe they were witnessing an attack on their faith. So any potential bombing
sites that smacked of having a religious connection received extra scrutiny.

Some appropriate targets were equally troublesome. Antiaircraft placements
could normally be destroyed without hesitation, but the Taliban had placed
some in centuries-old forts, the types of historic locations that the president had
declared could not be bombed.

Rumsfeld grumbled about the legal somersaults, comparing them to his
experience in 1975 when the Khmer Rouge government seized an American
container ship, the SS *Mayaguez*. A decision was made to use F-111As to sink
some of the Cambodian gunships near the *Mayaguez*. As White House chief of
staff for President Ford, Rumsfeld watched as a group of men in the Oval Office
gave orders to navy pilots flying in Southeast Asia. He reviled the exercise now
unfolding in Washington as a horrible repetition of that absurd event.

Absurd or not, though, the legal review had been required by his boss's orders. So lawyers lumbered along on the bombing plans, day after day after day,
one target at a time.

What if the United States captured bin Laden?
The problem dawned almost simultaneously on administration officials
across Washington—from the White House to the Pentagon to the Justice Department. The United States was preparing to launch a war in Afghanistan. The
military was going to hunt for bin Laden and, in the process, was sure to turn
up a number of other top al-Qaeda leaders. Then what?

This would not be some criminal case—it was war. Bin Laden and his ilk
couldn't simply be snapped up in Kabul and hustled off to Manhattan for trial.

The questions would surface immediately: Could war crimes be charged as civilian offenses? What would the procedures be? What would be the standards of evidence? How could intelligence about al-Qaeda and bin Laden be used without public disclosure? Then there was the danger—the threat of terrorist attacks on judges, jurors, even people living near the courthouse, would be tremendous.

In America's past wars, enemy troops were captured and held until hostilities ended, then returned to their home countries. But terrorists were not soldiers. They didn't fight under the authority of any nation. Hostilities might never end. And if they did, there was no place to seal the terrorists off from the civilized world.

There had to be some form of justice system, outside of the criminal courts, for determining whether terrorists could be lawfully held forever, or even executed. Someone just had to figure out what it was.

This was a matter, Gonzales decided, that should involve the best minds from across the administration. He approached Pierre-Richard Prosper, a former war crimes prosecutor with the United Nations who now served as ambassador-at-large with the State Department's Office of War Crimes Issues. Gonzales had respect for Prosper and considered him a diplomat who would carefully weigh the options in a calm and broad manner. He would be a counterbalance, Gonzales thought, to Addington's hard-charging approach.

At a meeting with Prosper and Addington, Gonzales laid out the issues. "What we need," he said, "is to understand our alternatives here." Would Prosper be willing, he asked, to study the issues and make a recommendation for the president?

Absolutely, Prosper replied.

Cheney and Addington weren't about to just wait around for Pierre Prosper. This, they agreed, was not a time for the chin-stroking contemplations of a study group.

The CIA was already heading into Afghanistan; the military would be joining it quickly. Scores, if not hundreds, of terrorists would soon be in American custody. If Washington dawdled, relying on bureaucracies or interagency committees to devise plans for bringing the enemy to justice, the decision might be determined by circumstance. The Justice Department could well start demanding that the Pentagon turn over its captives for criminal prosecution—a disastrous outcome, both men thought.

Addington came up with what he considered the ideal solution. The next morning, he attended a staff meeting with Gonzales, then afterward wandered into Flanigan's office.

"We ought to take a look at the military commission set up by Roosevelt," he said.

Addington launched into a history lesson. Franklin Roosevelt convened a commission in 1942. It was charged with trying eight German saboteurs who had sneaked into the United States as part of a Nazi plan to stage attacks on economic targets. The infiltrators were not soldiers, so could not be held as prisoners of war. But criminal courts would be slow and couldn't guarantee the sentences that Roosevelt and his attorney general wanted—death, or at least life in prison. Plus, since the saboteurs had plotted to attack civilian locations on behalf of the Nazis, they were not criminals. They were, Roosevelt declared, unlawful combatants.

After the military tribunal began its work, the German prisoners filed a brief arguing that their prosecution should be held in civilian court, where they would enjoy constitutional rights. Their case, called *Ex Parte Quirin,* went to the Supreme Court, which upheld Roosevelt's order as constitutional. After the ruling, commission hearings were held, convictions handed down, and sentences imposed. Six of the Germans were executed; two were jailed. The whole procedure—including the trip to the Supreme Court—lasted four weeks.

"This may be the perfect solution," Addington said.

The terrifying classified information was passed from American intelligence officials to their counterparts in Canada. To avoid a panic, the details could not be publicly released—indeed, they would still be secret more than a decade after 9/11.

Additional weapons had been discovered on commercial airliners—box cutters, knives, and the like. The planes where they had been stashed had been grounded after the attacks began. And blades weren't just hidden on aircraft in the United States—some had also been found on commercial jets at Canadian airports. But by the time the weaponry had been located, the passengers on each flight were long gone.

On September 18, a Canadian intelligence unit issued a classified report to government officials, warning of the danger.

"Weapons, similar to those identified on the hijacked planes have been found aboard other aircraft in Canada and the United States in the last few days," the report read. "These weapons may have been intended for additional attacks or were backups in case the other attacks failed."

Controls on the border between the United States and Canada had been beefed up after the attacks. But, with the knowledge that more hijackers might be lying in wait, both governments tightened the restrictions even more. Then, the desperate search began. Intelligence operatives dug through their files looking for the names of jihadists residing in either country who might be part of the next wave of attacks.

Just past 8:30 that same night, Abdullah Almalki was in his Ottawa apartment watching television with his family when the doorbell rang. Almalki couldn't quite decide if he should be annoyed or just surprised—with small children at home, this was awfully late for an unannounced visit.

He opened the door. In the hallway was a man in a suit.

"Mr. Almalki, my name is Alexander Gelvan. I'm with CSIS."

Gelvan handed over an identity card. Almalki studied it—*Canadian Security Intelligence Service*. Canada's CIA.

This wasn't the first time that CSIS had dropped by. Three years earlier, another agent, Theresa Sullivan, had asked to speak with him. Back then, Almalki saw no reason to refuse. Instead, he gave her his life story. He had moved to Canada from Syria in 1987, when he was sixteen. He had attended Canadian schools and became an electrical engineer. In the summer of 1993, he had traveled to Afghanistan for two months to help on a reconstruction project that had been awarded to a Canadian agency, Human Concern International. Ahmed Said Khadr operated that group, but Almalki hadn't liked the man's management style, he had told Sullivan.

Sullivan's ears had pricked up. Khadr was a name she knew—he was suspected of having close ties to militant mujahideen, as well as to bin Laden himself. She had pressed Almalki for more information. Had he received military training in Afghanistan? Did he know any mujahideen?

Absolutely not, he had responded. He was a businessman, an engineer who had started his own electronics export business, Dawn Services. His company served as a middleman in acquiring, repacking, and selling equipment like handheld radios to Microelectronics International, a Pakistani behemoth that supplied technology to that country's military. Had he ever sold equipment to the Taliban? Sullivan had asked. Again, no.

In the intervening years, Almalki had heard from Sullivan one more time. Then he noticed some oddities. All of his company's shipments were being searched by customs. He was stopped at an airport and intensively interrogated about his business dealings. He was asked to meet with other CSIS agents, who questioned him about a trip he had taken to Hong Kong.

Almalki felt harassed and eventually hired a lawyer to keep the intelligence operatives off his back. So on this night, just a week after the 9/11 attacks, he was hardly in the mood to speak with Gelvan, the CSIS agent who had just popped up on his doorstep.

"I want to ask you some questions," Gelvan said.

"No," Almalki replied. "If you want to talk to me, I have to have my lawyer present."

That wasn't necessary, Gelvan replied. He just wanted to get some information. Almalki had a Muslim friend in Montreal, Ibrahym Adam, who possessed both a pilot's license and his own single-engine Cessna airplane. No one had seen Adam for a week, Gelvan said, and CSIS wanted to locate him. Almalki thought he understood what Gelvan was implying—Adam was one of the 9/11 hijackers.

"Ibrahym would never do anything like that," Almalki said. "If you look at Islamic law, you cannot do such things. Those attacks totally go against the teachings of Islam."

Gelvan persisted, but Almalki repeated that he did not know where his friend was and had nothing else to say. When the CSIS agent left, Almalki went straight for the telephone and called Adam. His friend was not there, and Almalki left a message.

The next day, Adam called back. Almalki told him about the strange visit from Gelvan, and the CSIS agent's statement that Adam was missing.

"No, I'm not missing," Adam responded, sounding perplexed. "And CSIS knows that. They've been questioning me, too."

Almalki put down the phone, his mind racing. He was—scared? Angry? Confused? Whatever his emotions, he knew that he would have to be careful. Somehow, CSIS agents must believe they had suspicious information about him. And he had no idea what it might be.

It was a morning of threes in the basement of the CIA on September 19. There were three unmarked cardboard boxes, sealed up with tape, looking like something a homeowner might toss into an attic. Inside them, there were three hundred bundles of cash. The money totaled $3 million.

The currency was one of the first, and most important, weapons for seven intelligence agents about to be secretly inserted into Afghanistan, something that would allow them to grease some palms to earn the cooperation of indigenous fighters. Code-named "Jawbreaker," the group was responsible for laying the groundwork in the war on al-Qaeda and the Taliban.

Gary Schroen, a thirty-five-year CIA veteran tapped to lead Jawbreaker, arrived about 10:30 at the Counterterrorist Center to take charge of the cash. Cofer Black had asked him just two days after the terrorist attacks to accept the assignment, and Schroen had moved into place quickly—after a matter of days, his team was ready to be deployed. Moving the boxes was not easy; he found that so much cash, in hundred-dollar bills, is awfully heavy. He needed a cart to get the money where it needed to be.

About fifteen minutes later, he caught up with the other team members in a parking area who were standing beside piles of luggage. A Chevy Suburban arrived, and the men loaded it up.

Schroen headed back inside and walked to Black's office for one last briefing. Black looked up when Schroen arrived. "Hey!"

The men sat at a table, discussing the travel plans.

"Gary," he said, "I want to give you your marching orders."

He had discussed everything he was about to say with Bush, who was in full agreement. Jawbreaker was to project into Afghanistan and meet with the Northern Alliance. Then, the agents would have to determine what the needs of the alliance were in order to facilitate the arrival of the American military, allowing the troops to use the Panjshir Valley as a staging area so that they could engage and destroy al-Qaeda.

"On the battlefield, if you see bin Laden killed, we need DNA evidence of his death, which would require bringing back part of his body," Cofer said. "We cannot just accept that the target has been taken out."

And if there was a choice of body parts to bring, Black said, the head would be better than hands. He paused.

"Have I made myself clear?"

At Rockefeller Center, the New York offices for NBC News were in near chaos, with an army of reporters and producers chasing leads about the 9/11 attacks.

In an outer portion of the newsroom, Casey Chamberlain was sorting through the mail for Tom Brokaw, the anchor of the *NBC Nightly News*. She came across a hand-printed envelope with no return address—probably another ranting letter of the sort Brokaw received every day.

She opened the envelope, and a brown, granular substance spilled out. She brushed it into the wastebasket, then opened the letter. The paper was cut on some of its sides, as if the author was trying to shape it. Chamberlain read the message. No surprise—typical crackpot fare.

9-11-01

THIS IS NEX**T**

TAKE PEN**A**CILIN NOW

DE**A**TH **T**O AMERICA

DEATH **T**O ISRAEL

ALLAH IS GREA**T**

The misspelling of *penicillin* and the darkening of some of the *As* and *Ts* struck her as odd. That, plus the threatening tone, made her think that someone else needed to see the letter. She sent it on to Erin O'Connor, Brokaw's assistant.

O'Connor read it but decided not to bother her boss, who had been working almost nonstop since the attacks. This new letter wasn't much different from other off-the-wall missives that had been arriving since 9/11; it wasn't even the first one with some sort of substance inside. Weeks before, O'Connor had opened a letter for Brokaw and a white powder had spilled out. Just to be cautious, she had sent that material to NBC security so it could be examined.

This time, O'Connor decided not to alert anyone; Chamberlain had already tossed out most of the material. But she was still a bit suspicious. Rather than just throwing the letter away, O'Connor set it on the side of her desk.

Brokaw was walking past O'Connor's desk the next day when he noticed the letter. He picked it up and read it.

"Well," he said, "you'd think if he's going to threaten my life, he could at least be grammatical."

He put down the letter and went back to work.

• • •

Perhaps the American military should strike a country in South America. Or maybe Southeast Asia. Or, of course, Iraq. That, Douglas Feith argued, would surprise terrorists worldwide. None of them would expect it.

Feith, the undersecretary of defense for policy, crafted the proposal in a memo to Rumsfeld. Bush wanted a global war on terror, but Rumsfeld had been grousing that Afghanistan didn't offer good bombing targets or suitable terrain for a ground operation. Hitting terrorists in another country, Feith maintained, would put fanatics everywhere on notice that the Bush doctrine had placed them all in America's crosshairs.

Already, the early rumblings about launching a war against Iraq were strong. But South America? Southeast Asia? Those ideas were shelved.

The retired four-star general stepped briskly through the halls of the Pentagon, dozens of medals and service ribbons gleaming on his chest. Wesley Clark had left the military a year and a half earlier, but was dropping by to see how his old friends and colleagues were holding up.

After meeting with Rumsfeld and Wolfowitz, Clark went to visit some officers who were working with the Joint Chiefs of Staff. He passed the office of a senior general.

The general called out to Clark. "Sir, you've got to come in and talk to me for a second."

"Well," Clark responded, "you're too busy."

No, the general said, ushering Clark into his office.

Once they were alone, the general blurted out the news. "We're going to war with Iraq."

Clark was perplexed. Bin Laden, the fundamentalist, was a sworn enemy of Saddam Hussein, the secular leader. *What did Iraq have to do with this?*

"Did they find more information connecting Saddam to al-Qaeda?" Clark asked.

No, the general replied. "There's nothing new that way," he said. "They just made the decision to go to war with Iraq."

The whole idea seemed to have been born of uncertainty, he said. "I guess it's like we don't know what to do about terrorists, but we've got a good military and we can take down governments," the general said.

Remember that old cliché, he said. "If the only tool you have is a hammer, then every problem has to look like a nail."

• • •

A tuxedo-clad butler stepped into the president's private dining room. With-out a word, he placed a white china plate on an octagonal place mat. Then he walked around the table and served the president's guest, Tony Blair.

It was the evening of September 20; the British prime minister had come to Washington to meet Bush face-to-face for the first time since the attacks. The president was scheduled to address a joint session of Congress at nine o'clock that night and had asked Blair to attend in a show of solidarity.

Blair and his aides met earlier that day with Bush, Rice, and Powell in the upstairs residence. There, Blair and Bush had huddled together in a corner for a few minutes. The attacks, Bush had said, had been horrendous, but he now believed that something good would come out of them.

"When I speak to Congress tonight, the focus is going to be on bin Laden and the Taliban," Bush had said. "I'm going to deliver the ultimatum."

Blair was concerned about how far Bush would push his threat to the Taliban if they spurned his demand to hand over bin Laden; he counseled a measured response.

From there, it was on to dinner—a gourmet meal of salad, veal, and scallops. Bush directed the conversation.

"I'm grateful for your support," he said to Blair. "Britain is a true friend and we are going to win."

He leaned his arms on the table. "Anyone can join our coalition, provided they understand the doctrine," Bush said. "We are going after terrorists and all those who harbor them. Obviously, the broader the coalition the better, but either way, we're going after them."

Blair gave a tight smile. Bush's ambitions were so broad—hunting down all terrorists wherever they might be found *and* going after any country, organiza-tion, or person supporting those criminals—that they risked collapsing in hu-miliating failure. He was going to have to keep trying to rein Bush in.

The waiter returned and set a plate in front of the president—scallops, with a ring of pastry on top. Bush looked down at the ring and made a face.

"God dang," he said. "What on earth is that?"

"It's a scallop, Mr. President," the waiter replied.

Bush smiled. "Well, it looks like a halo and you're the angel."

Everyone at the table laughed. No one quite got the joke.

The conversation veered into an assessment of how other world leaders were behaving.

"It was interesting that Putin himself made sure the Russians didn't react that week," Bush said. "That's a clear sign the Cold War is over."

Then there was Pakistan. While Musharraf had shown some signs of cooperation, neither Bush nor Powell had a clear idea of how he would handle future American demands. The president asked Blair if he would provide recommendations for how the United States would deal with the Pakistanis; the prime minister agreed to do so.

"We're going for the Taliban after the ultimatum," Bush said. "They're a bunch of nuts, and we need to get a new government in there."

That was going to require keeping all allies on the same page about the goal of the American campaigns, something that was already raising hackles among other world leaders. His conversations with Ariel Sharon, the recently elected Israeli prime minister, had been particularly tense, Bush said.

"I had to really beat up on him. Sharon was clearly trying to use this to go after Arafat. I said, 'Arafat is not bin Laden, and you do nothing.' "

There could be no distractions in the effort to cripple al-Qaeda, Bush continued, because the group was already putting together its new round of deadly plans. His administration feared that Hollywood would be the next target, he said, not only because of its high profile, but also because of the terrorists' perception that it was decadent and controlled by Jews. It also possessed intelligence, he said, that the terrorists had targeted *Air Force One.*

Blair saw an opening to push for caution.

"You need to be sure of your ground," he said. "We have to have public opinion with us at all times."

"Yes," Bush replied. "But when I'm speaking tough, I'm speaking to Middle America."

Most ordinary citizens had never heard of bin Laden before, he said. All they knew was that he and his al-Qaeda followers were behind the attack that killed thousands of their fellow citizens.

"And they're saying, 'Hey, Mr. President, go get someone. And why ain't you done it the day before yesterday?' "

The next day at a Long Island church, a wedding ceremony dragged on. In one pew, Johanna Huden, an editorial assistant at the *New York Post,* looked at her hand, where a blister had appeared the day before on her right middle finger. At first she figured it was a bug bite, and now it was starting to itch.

She rubbed it against the coarse linen of her dress. A white liquid bubbled across the cloth. "Ee-yew," Huden said to herself quietly. "That is just really bizarre."

Weeks would pass before Huden would learn that she was the first victim of the anthrax attack.

That night, stage lights cast sparkles across a painted lake on the stage at the Kennedy Center Opera House. The soprano Ainhoa Arteta, playing a saucer-eyed Fiordiligi in Mozart's *Così fan tutte,* walked past an archway as her voice soared in the perilous aria "Per pietà."

Sitting beside his wife amid oceans of red velvet that decorated the auditorium, Bradford Berenson, a lawyer in the White House counsel's office, felt awed by the music's splendor. It was September 22, a Saturday, and Berenson could finally relax on one of his first nights off since 9/11.

He had been working almost nonstop on an initiative to freeze the assets of individuals and groups that had been sending money to terrorists, a new topic for him. Just after he was assigned to the job, he had been escorted to a secure room so that he could review classified information. He had been astonished to see folder after folder containing names linked to terrorism by volumes of intelligence, from powerful Middle Easterners to little-known charities. The data had been collected over many years and apparently were just left in filing cabinets gathering dust.

The immersion into that ugly world had given him a new perspective about the terrorists, their philosophies, and their goals. Now, as the orchestra played and the music soared, Berenson began to see connections between this magnificent moment and the emerging battle of cultures.

Bin Laden, al-Qaeda, the Taliban—they wanted to remake the world based on their beliefs, to purge the beauty of Mozart, Shakespeare, Picasso, everything that exalted human civilization. The Taliban had already destroyed the Buddhas of Bamiyan, two giant statues from the sixth century that had been carved into the side of a cliff near Kabul. This heritage of incalculable beauty and grandeur had survived 1,500 years, only to be demolished in a matter of weeks by fanatics who declared the statues to be anti-Islamic. Taliban members rejoiced as they tore down the historic works of art with hammers, spades, and explosives; they used dynamite to blow off the face of the smaller statue and then fired rockets into its groin.

Berenson glanced around the opera house. These mindless extremists would gleefully demolish everything his eyes and ears devoured. Without a second's thought, they would reduce the architectural treasures of America's capital to rubble; they would outlaw dance and music and paintings and sculpture. They were monsters, really, who cared for nothing that didn't fall into the orbit of their beliefs—not the lives of the innocent, not the beauty of artistic creation, not the accomplishments of man.

And Middle Easterners supported them, quietly sending money to finance their atrocities. This battle was about more than the security of American citizens, Berenson realized. It was about the protection of civilization itself.

The conference room on the second floor of the Eisenhower Executive Office Building was tinted in red, white, and blue from sunlight pouring through a giant flag outside the window. The table was crowded with officials from the CIA, the White House, the State Department, and the Treasury, all working on the plans to block asset transfers by individuals and organizations connected to bin Laden's financial network.

Gary Edson, the reedy, professorial, and ruthlessly efficient White House deputy assistant for international economic affairs, chaired the meeting. The officials sifted through the intelligence establishing the connection of each entity to terrorists, then reviewed drafts of the executive order that would freeze its bank accounts.

On one list of names were people close to the Saudi royal family. A rumpled State Department official spoke up.

"Whatever we do has to be handled with great delicacy and care," he said. "We don't want to upset the royal family."

The official continued speaking for a few more moments, laying out details of the problems that the State Department feared would unfold if the administration alienated the Saudis. Edson listened in silence, waiting for the presentation to end. Then he nodded his head and paused for a moment.

"I understand," he said, a friendly expression on his face. "But everybody knows you guys are a bunch of weenies anyway."

No one in the room spoke or moved. With a smile, Edson had just cut the legs out from under the official. He spoke for the president, and his message was brutally clear: Bush didn't care if diplomats came down with a case of the vapors. All those aiding al-Qaeda, regardless of who they were, would be crushed—if not militarily, then financially.

The discussion resumed. One Treasury official mentioned that, under normal circumstances, it would have taken ten months for his department to assemble and vet the names on the list. Now the same thing would be accomplished in about thirteen days.

Part of the reason the effort usually took so long was banal: Arabic names were complicated. Transliterating them into the Roman alphabet was an inexact process, resulting in the same name being spelled different ways. That increased the chance that the wrong person might turn up on the asset freeze order.

As the group struggled with a particular name shared by many people, one official chuckled.

"Well," he said, laughing, "How many Osamas can there be?"

From one end of the table, Buzzy Krongard, the executive director of the CIA, spoke. The number was huge, he said—and the CIA had already counted them up. He tossed out the answer, one that shocked the assembled group.

"And you want to know the scary thing?" Krongard said.

He paused.

"Most of them are under the age of five."

Everyone understood—to their horror. Arabic children had been named to honor Osama bin Laden. The magnitude of the challenge in defeating al-Qaeda suddenly loomed much larger.

The correspondent from *Ummat*, an Urdu-language newspaper based in Karachi, sat beside bin Laden, a tape recorder rolling.

"You have been accused of involvement in the attacks in New York and Washington," the reporter said. "What do you want to say about this? If you are not involved, who might be?"

Bin Laden gave praise to God and thanked *Ummat* for speaking with him. "I have already said that I am not involved in the 11 September attacks," he said. "As a Muslim, I try my best to avoid telling a lie."

He had no knowledge of the strikes before they occurred, he said. "Islam strictly forbids causing harm to innocent women, children, and other people," he said. "Such a practice is forbidden even in the course of battle."

While he was uninvolved, he added, he had learned secrets that the United States was trying to keep hidden. "According to my information, the death toll is much higher than what the U.S. government has stated, but the Bush administration does not want the panic to spread."

To identify the perpetrators, the Americans needed to look inside its own country at the scores of armed groups capable of the operation. Or at Russia. Or Israel. Or India. Or Serbia.

"Then you cannot forget the American Jews," he said, "who are annoyed with President Bush ever since the elections in Florida and want revenge."

Of course, he went on, the attacks could also have been launched by the country's own intelligence agencies, which had been seeking new adversaries since the fall of the Soviet Union. Orchestrating such murderous violence would help them get more money from the administration.

Whoever the culprit might be, he said, it wasn't al-Qaeda.

"We are not hostile to the United States," he said. "We are against the system."

The reporter asked about the efforts to block al-Qaeda's bank accounts.

"Freezing of accounts will not make any difference," bin Laden replied. "With the grace of Allah, al Qaeda has more than three such alternative financial systems, which are all separate and totally independent from each other."

Once the *Ummat* interview with bin Laden was published, a unit at the CIA obtained and rapidly translated it. The statements were bizarre. Bin Laden says that he has access to secret information about the death toll from the strike? That al-Qaeda was not hostile to the United States? And most astonishing, that Islam would have forbidden the 9/11 operation? Bin Laden had orchestrated this assault; at some point, probably soon, he would have to confess al-Qaeda's role, if only to demonstrate the group's power. After proclaiming that the Koran forbade the attack? What would he say then?

There could be no doubt. Bin Laden did not just have a psychopathic personality. He was insane.

A group of lawyers gathered for a briefing from the Pentagon in the sitting area of Alberto Gonzalez's office. Jim Haynes, the Defense Department's general counsel, described elements of the military's capabilities that would be available for the coming war.

Haynes looked across the coffee table, where Gonzales sat in silence in his wing chair. It was a Gonzales trademark—listening sphinxlike to a presentation and voicing his opinion only after the speaker finished. On either side of Haynes were Addington and Flanigan, who had emerged as the key team in dealing with the legal issues of the administration's antiterror strategy.

There were complexities limiting the NSA's ability to intercept and report communications among radical Islamists, including rules involving mobile phones and calls into the United States, Haynes said. That was serious, since the intelligence agencies already knew that sleeper cells were inside the country, even if all of them could not yet be identified.

For several minutes, Addington and Flanigan quizzed Haynes about the technical abilities for electronic surveillance.

"If we know these conversations are taking place, why can't we just listen to them?" Flanigan asked. "Why can't the NSA 'big ear' be turned to follow the individuals we can identify as al-Qaeda operatives, regardless of where they are, regardless of whether these conversations are occurring within the U.S. or across international borders?"

These people were the enemy, Flanigan said, and they were hiding among the country's own citizens. There was intelligence that a second wave of attacks was coming. Why couldn't the government use every resource at its disposal to hunt them down, rather than just waiting for the next bloodletting?

Neither Haynes nor Gonzales responded. Addington sat back in his chair, a faraway look on his face. After months of working together, his colleagues knew that this was Addington's body language signaling he was deep in thought.

Finally, Addington looked at Flanigan.

"You may have hit on something that's worth thinking about," he said.

The idea rocketed through Washington's corridors of power.

Addington approached Cheney with the concept—the NSA's authority had to be beefed up to help find terrorists in the United States. Sure, under the present rules, applications for electronic surveillance could be filed to secret courts that handled national security issues, set up under the Foreign Intelligence Surveillance Act—FISA.

But that law was from 1978, long before cell and satellite phones, the Internet, and e-mail. Al-Qaeda operatives were using those technologies, Addington said, in ways that moved faster than FISA could keep up.

The terrorists purchased disposable cell phones, made calls, then tossed them out. They signed up for e-mail services with Web-based providers like Yahoo! and Hotmail, sent a few messages, then deleted the accounts. The calls and e-mails flowed into the United States unimpeded and, too often, unknown. There was no wire to tap—killers were exploiting a virtual world of communications, and the government wasn't using its best resources to stop them. FISA was not flexible or nimble enough to deal with the change. The law, Addington argued, had become a suicide pact.

It struck Cheney as inconceivable that al-Qaeda had not already placed other terrorists inside the country to launch a second—and perhaps a third or fourth—wave of attacks. He had recently heard about the al-Qaeda operative named Moussaoui who had been arrested in Minnesota. Was he supposed to join in the 9/11 hijackings, or was he part of the next strike?

Cheney contacted Tenet. Could the NSA, he asked, do more against terrorism? Tenet said he would run the question by Michael Hayden, director of the intelligence agency.

Hayden's reply was brief: Under current law, the NSA's hands were tied. The agency was doing all it could.

"What might you do with more authority?" Tenet asked.

"Let me put together some information on what would be operationally useful and technologically feasible," Hayden said.

The security agency assembled the material, and Hayden shared it with Tenet. Then they traveled to the White House to present Cheney with the new, classified proposals.

The NSA plan was elegant in its theoretical simplicity, awesome in its technological cunning, and terrifying in its potential for abuse. At its essence, the ambitious new blueprint would give the agency unprecedented surveillance powers in the hunt for terrorists.

Already, enormous volumes of data about al-Qaeda were sprinkled throughout the government—names of operatives and sympathizers plus their relatives and friends, locations where they hid, phone numbers they called, as well as contributors and organizations in the group's financial network. Webs of interconnections—some obvious, some almost undetectable—linked these bits of data in ways that allowed intelligence analysts to perceive the skeletal framework of al-Qaeda's operations. That was how American intelligence had learned about a terrorist summit in Kuala Lumpur the previous year, by listening in on a phone in Sana'a that had been monitored since 1998. The tiniest morsel of information—records of just two calls, placed from East Africa to a number in Yemen before and after the embassy bombings—had been culled from a flood of data flowing through the NSA, establishing a slender but unmistakable tie between the phone and al-Qaeda.

Sometimes, though, the effort to pursue those leads hit legal roadblocks. The NSA was barred from domestic spying; it could not use its technology to track down someone inside the country who was known to be preparing to bomb Los Angeles. Even if the agency was listening to bin Laden himself in Canada, it had to shut down its monitoring if he crossed the bridge into Buffalo. At that point, the FBI took over. To continue electronic surveillance inside the United States, the bureau had to obtain a FISA warrant from a special national security court and could do so only for intelligence-gathering purposes. Investigators also had to establish in their warrant application that the people to be monitored were agents of a foreign power, a term that had been traditionally interpreted as another government. Members of the administration were painfully aware that none of those standards would have applied to the hijackers—or most other al-Qaeda members.

The new plan could change everything, constituting the most dramatic expansion of the NSA's power and authority in the agency's forty-nine-year history.

Tracking calls from what NSA analysts called "dirty numbers" could be conducted without triggering a warrant requirement, regardless of whether they were placed to people in the United States. The agency, the CIA, and the FBI had obtained an array of such numbers, both independently and from foreign intelligence services, including those of Middle Eastern countries such as Saudi Arabia, Jordan, Egypt, and even Yemen. All of those were entered into one massive data set at NSA.

If a call from a dirty number went to one phone, then another, then another before finally reaching the United States, the NSA could monitor the conversations at each point. With the agency in hot pursuit, it could continue listening to calls from the American phones connected to the dirty numbers, even if they were placed to others in the United States. At that point the FBI could be brought in to seek a FISA warrant so that the assorted American phone lines linked to the original number could be monitored.

The standards for what constituted "an American person" under FISA would be changed, removing some investigative impediments to the NSA's work. A suspected terrorist—or someone tied to a terrorist—could no longer trigger a warrant requirement simply by standing on American soil. Monitoring United States citizens or resident aliens overseas would no longer—if they could be linked to terrorism—require a warrant. Charities or companies based in the United States and suspected of terrorist ties would no longer be defined as "an American person" and afforded Fourth Amendment protections.

Moreover, a previously forbidden tactic known as "reverse targeting" would be allowed in certain circumstances. In the past, relatives or friends of a known terrorist could not be monitored if they lived in the United States unless evidence had been discovered showing their own involvement with groups like al-Qaeda. So, if the terrorist telephoned them from another country, the NSA would have to intercept the call from his side. As part of the new plan, the NSA could conduct electronic surveillance of the family or friends in the United States, in hopes of picking up an overseas call from the call from the terrorist.

The techniques and abilities to monitor e-mails would change, too. For years, there was a perceived difficulty in e-mail interception—digital data flowing through the Internet is broken up into smaller packets of information, which then can be routed anywhere in the world. An al-Qaeda member in Kabul could e-mail another in Kandahar, but the packets might travel through Internet connections in America. That posed a theoretical problem under FISA: the data racing through American Internet systems could be deemed as being within the United States, setting off the need to go to a FISA court. The proposed NSA plan of action would ignore these technical intricacies and instead focus solely on the location of the sender and recipient of the e-mail.

There were two methods of e-mail monitoring. The most simplistic involved the direct interception of a message to and from an account linked by other intelligence to an al-Qaeda member. The second method involved deeper scrutiny. Connections between a suspect e-mail address and others—accounts that both sent and received messages there, whether in the United States or not— would be examined. At that point, a more detailed level of analysis would be applied, creating something of a ripple effect. The suspect e-mail address would lead to a second, the second to the accounts it contacted.

It was largely impossible to analyze so much information—upward of six petabytes, or six quadrillion bytes, of digital records every month—on a message-by-message basis. Instead, the NSA had to conduct broader analysis of a massive data set pulled together from an array of sources, starting with almost four billion public documents collected from thousands of easily accessed databases: property and airplane ownership records; boat and car registrations; phone numbers throughout the country; terrorist watch lists, and more. All those details would be melded with certain data from commercial sources; other government information, such as flight information from the FAA, could potentially be thrown into the mix.

This would be added to other materials that were not readily available, such as communications records held by telephone and broadband companies. The NSA would urge the corporations to share logs showing all calls to and from phones, including the time and length of the conversation, as well as details of e-mails showing when they were sent, to what accounts, and subject lines; for the most part, the contents would not be reviewed without a warrant.

This data set posed its own set of risks. It would not be composed solely of records from terrorists; rather, details of the activities of millions of Americans would be included. Rules would be in place to ensure that no one snooped on individual information contained in this vast data bank. The NSA would have no authority to pull up, say, some American's e-mail account out of curiosity. Anyone violating this ban could potentially be committing a crime, just as an unauthorized IRS employee sneaking a peek at an individual tax return could be cited for wrongdoing. But the stricture was largely theoretical; sifting through the metadata to isolate a single individual's records would be an almost impossible—and pointless—undertaking.

Instead, the NSA would use a larger process known as "Knowledge Discovery in Databases"—or KDD—to clean, select, integrate, and analyze the data. In essence, the ocean of information could be mined, not for the purpose of spying on any individual American but for creating a model the NSA could analyze to discern anomalies that could in turn reveal the path to a terrorist cell.

Whatever the intent, the proposal was explosive. If the public learned of it, administration officials might be slammed for violating the Fourth Amendment as a result of having listened in on calls to people inside the country and collecting so much personal data. Still, the proposed program intrigued Cheney. Granting the NSA authority to track phone calls and e-mails of a specific terrorist and to develop a massive data model might give the government the power to stop the next attack. He told Hayden and Tenet to assemble a presentation for the president.

The new program needed a code name. It would be called Stellar Wind.

The trip to North Carolina had been a delight. Robert Stevens and his wife, Maureen, had driven from their home in South Florida on September 27 to visit their daughter Casey in Charlotte. On a crisp day, they hiked the trails at Chimney Rock State Park, watching as hawks flew overhead.

Now it was October 1, and the Stevenses were packing their car to head home. Robert, sixty-three, needed to get back to work. He had recently landed a job as a photo editor at the *Sun*, a supermarket tabloid published in Boca Raton, and didn't want to get off on the wrong foot by spending too much time away from the office.

As the couple prepared to leave, Robert told Maureen that he wasn't feeling well. Driving home, he became nauseated. By the next day, he was running a high fever and became incoherent. At 2:00 A.M. on October 3, with his condition worsening, Maureen took him to John F. Kennedy Medical Center in Palm Beach County. In the emergency room, the doctor on duty theorized that Robert was suffering from meningitis. Then, five hours after he arrived, Robert began to shake with violent seizures. The doctor decided that a spinal tap was needed to help make a diagnosis.

The spinal fluid was cloudy, a sign of a possible virus or bacteria. An infectious disease specialist, Dr. Larry Bush, examined the substance under a microscope and saw rod-shaped, meshlike cells. A Gram stain, used to differentiate bacterial species into two large groups, turned the sample a bluish-purple color; they were gram-positive. The shape of the bacteria, the stain results—these microbes were part of the genus *Bacillus*.

Dr. Bush's mind raced. He had already read that some of the 9/11 terrorists had lived in South Florida and attended flight school there. There had been reports that one of the men had scouted around for a crop duster, a plane that could be used to scatter disease-causing bacteria over a wide area.

He put the pieces of the puzzle together. He knew what he was seeing. *Anthrax.*

In the days to come, more tests would prove Dr. Bush to be right. Stevens was suffering from inhalation anthrax. He soon fell into a coma and died on Friday, five days after the symptoms first appeared.

On October 2, the urgent request from Ottawa scrolled out of fax machines at diplomatic and intelligence agencies around the globe. The Canadians, it read, needed help taking down a terrorist cell inside their country.

The national police—the Mounties—had assumed control over the investigations of domestic threats from the Canadian intelligence agency, CSIS. Now those officers were ready to arrest al-Qaeda members living in Canada—all they needed was evidence to prove their suspects' guilt.

Since the 9/11 attacks, CSIS had already contacted two men on the list, Ahmad El-Maati and Abdullah Almalki, but the interviews hadn't gone far; the men had demanded lawyers before they would answer many questions. Still, the Canadians thought there was no time to waste—both men, officials concluded, were extremely dangerous.

El-Maati, the Mounties believed, could well be planning an attack. He had been stopped in his truck at the border weeks before carrying a map of Canadian federal buildings. He also had spent time in Afghanistan and had come in contact with suspicious people.

A CSIS agent had dropped by Almalki's home late in the evening a few nights before. The intelligence agency believed it had good reasons for their wariness of him—Almalki had traveled to Afghanistan, too, spending two months there seven years before; he also came into contact with one suspicious person. And then there were those shipments of field radios from his company, Dawn Services, to Microelectronics International, which supplied the Pakistani military. Before shipping the radios, Almalki's company removed them from their original boxes and repacked them into new ones labeled with the Dawn Services name. Standard fare for the exporting business, but to law enforcement it was proof of something devious—Almalki, they concluded, was a procurement officer for bin Laden.

Somewhere in the world, the Mounties felt sure, was evidence to prove their suspicions. And so they launched their dragnet by fax, asking counterparts worldwide to search their files for information. Responses were needed quickly, the fax said—both Almalki and El-Maati constituted "imminent threats" to Canada and were working with al-Qaeda.

Despite the certainty of their message, the Mounties didn't know if any of what they had written was true. They hadn't started investigating either man, and had obtained only skimpy records from CSIS. Other than the map, they had next to nothing on El-Maati. There was some information in the files about Almalki, purportedly provided by an outside source. But the records were wrong—the source had given evidence about someone else, not Almalki.

None of the recipients could know that the statements in the fax were fiction. Instead, the countries that received the document—including Syria, where both men were born—now listed these two Canadian citizens as dangerous terrorists.

Brad Berenson strolled from the Eisenhower Executive Office Building to the White House. As an associate counsel in Gonzales's office, Berenson made the short trek almost every day from his office in the beautifully monstrous structure to the executive mansion, where his boss worked.

This time, Berenson was coming over with an important purpose. He had been thinking about how the terrorists would be brought to justice after they were captured; he didn't know that very question was already being explored.

Berenson reached the White House counsel's suite and spotted Flanigan in his office. "Tim," he said, "I've been thinking about a problem, and I'm not sure what the answer is, but what are we going to do legally when we capture these terrorists?"

There was going to be a need to interrogate them for intelligence, to help wage the war and protect the country from other attacks. But that couldn't be done in a criminal case; prosecutors can't talk to defendants represented by counsel unless the lawyer is present. Treating terrorists like criminals would be a colossal blunder, Berenson said. The government couldn't kill them, couldn't let them go, and couldn't indict them.

"So how do we finally dispose of these guys as a legal matter?" he asked.

Flanigan gave a fleeting smile. "You know, it's interesting. You're not the only one who's been thinking about that."

He told Berenson to look up an old Supreme Court decision, *Ex Parte Quirin*, the case that Addington had told him about recently involving some captured Nazi saboteurs who were tried before a special military commission.

There was also, Flanigan mentioned, an interagency group headed by Pierre Prosper that had been trying to resolve this issue. "You should go ahead and start attending those meetings, be our representative there."

Berenson agreed to read *Quirin* and to find out more about the Prosper group. But from his short conversation with his boss, he already suspected that Flanigan had decided on military commissions as the answer.

The interviewer held a digital camera in his hands, trying with little success to keep it steady. The automatic lens rotated, focusing on a bearded, turbaned man sitting in front of a concrete wall. The man was subdued in every way, his languid face expressionless. He seemed shy and withdrawn, averting his eyes as he stroked his beard.

But his appearance belied his reputation. This man, Abu Zubaydah, had been deemed by the United States to be one of the world's most dangerous terrorists. Intelligence operatives had linked Zubaydah to devastating al-Qaeda attacks, including the bombings of the USS *Cole* and American embassies in eastern Africa.

Zubaydah had been slow to commit to the extremists. In his youth, he had considered himself to be a bad Muslim but was inspired in the early 1990s by the Palestinian cause. He traveled to Afghanistan for military training, much to his parents' dismay. At the time, his brother had journeyed to Kandahar, where he tried to persuade Zubaydah to come home to Saudi Arabia. Zubaydah had refused, instead unsuccessfully urging his brother to join him in jihad. Still, he had doubts about his decision. Sometimes he considered leaving Afghanistan and abandoning the Islamist life for college; maybe, he thought, he could become a computer expert or an engineer, marry, and raise a family. For a while he felt homesick, but over time, those feelings had diminished. Eventually, he began to think that any activity outside of jihad was silly.

On this day, Zubaydah had reluctantly agreed to be interviewed for an al-Qaeda recruiting video. He considered the exercise relatively pointless—he didn't think the recordings provided any benefit. Their enemies knew why al-Qaeda was fighting and knew that the Islamist cause was righteous. But Zubaydah's superiors had persuaded him to take part. They wanted him to speak of al-Qaeda's past successes and praise the 9/11 attacks—even though, at this point, bin Laden was still asserting the terrorist group had not been involved.

Zubaydah opened by offering prayers to God. "We follow Allah and the messenger has said regarding killing the enemies of Allah—Jews or Christians or apostates or Hindus or atheists—all those, all enemies of Islam they are our enemies," he said, fumbling his words.

He glanced toward the ground. "Allah almighty said, 'Strike the terror into the enemies of Allah for they are our enemies.' Therefore when we terrorize them, we implement accordance that what Allah has commanded to us."

Averting his eyes to the right, Zubaydah began listing several attacks launched by al-Qaeda since 1990.

"Then the operations set up by the sheikh Bin Laden in Kenya and Tanzania, then the Cole operation, truly magnificent operations at the Trade Center on Manhattan Island and in areas around Washington and in New York," he said. "Truthfully, I am one of the people who support the most such an operation wholeheartedly."

Jihadists would champion further attacks, he said, as martyrs, financiers, or coordinators. "Enemies of Allah shall not rest," he said. "Allah is willing."

Nighttime on October 3. Bush was sitting behind the desk in his private office at the White House residence when a handful of administration officials arrived to discuss Stellar Wind. Their scant numbers were no accident; Bush had earlier ordered that only a select group would be allowed to know about the NSA program. If it leaked, he told his advisors, it wouldn't work. They couldn't secretly monitor al-Qaeda if the terrorists knew how it was done.

The final shape of the program had been worked out. Only the mechanics of the formal approval remained, such as briefing a select group of cabinet officers, seeking their involvement, and obtaining their signatures. But before Bush's aides went through those machinations—with the potential of setting off disclosures to the press—they needed to check one last time with the president.

There was good reason for caution. Lawyers from both the NSA and the CIA had already expressed reservations about the plan in conversations with the White House. This was a very bold idea, the lawyers said; while they didn't contend it was illegal, they feared it was so close to the line that the NSA could easily shift from legitimate intelligence collection into improper overreaching. There was a strong argument, they said, that tapping calls coming into the United States or collecting a massive database of personal information about Americans might constitute domestic surveillance in violation of FISA.

White House lawyers assured Bush that Stellar Wind was within the law. But at this meeting in his office, they again reviewed the legal implications. Was the president, Gonzales asked, comfortable with setting the initiative in motion?

"Everyone understand, I know this is a big deal," Bush replied. "We are undertaking something that I know may be unprecedented." Sometime in the future, others may question the legality of Stellar Wind. But he was convinced that it met the dictates of the law and, more important, was necessary to keep America safe.

That was that. He told his entourage to produce the final directive for his signature the next day.

The document Bush approved was just a few pages. But the amount of paper that Stellar Wind required could have filled a library.

Under the standards developed over the next few weeks, a new authorization had to be signed by Bush every forty-five days. Each time, Tenet's chief of staff directed analysts at the terrorism center to write an appraisal of the current threats, with particular focus on domestic dangers. Specific intelligence had to be provided in support of the evaluation. At first, none of the analysts knew why they were preparing the assessments—they had not been told about the NSA program.

After their handiwork was completed, Tenet's aides would then add a boilerplate paragraph written by Addington that described the individuals and groups with the capability to launch new terrorist attacks inside the United States.

In the paragraph was a sentence stating that the circumstances "constitute an urgent and compelling government interest." As such, it said, the CIA director recommended renewing the NSA's authority to conduct surveillance activities under Stellar Wind. CIA lawyers would then review the document; if they felt it lacked sufficient evidence to present a strong case in support of reauthorizing the program, it would be sent back to the analysts for more details. Once it was completed, Tenet or the deputy director, John McLaughlin, would sign the memo.

From there, the responsibilities were handed off to the Office of Legal Counsel at the Justice Department. There, more lawyers would review the material, and another document would be attached to the memo stating that there was "sufficient factual basis demonstrating a threat of terrorist attacks in the United States for it to continue to be reasonable under the Fourth Amendment" for Bush to continue to "authorize the warrantless searches."

Each of the reauthorizations included a requirement that everyone who knew of Stellar Wind keep mum about it. And, when the program was inaugurated, Bush's secret written statement specified that the appropriate members of Congress would be notified only "as soon as I judge that it can be done consistently with the national defense needs."

All of those steps in the approval process fell into place in the program's early stages. But the first authorization was managed almost offhandedly. Ashcroft was informed about Stellar Wind after Bush had okayed it and was only then asked to attest that the initiative complied with the law.

Ashcroft gave his after-the-fact certification of the program's legality on the same day he learned of it. He conducted no legal research to verify his conclusion.

Gonzales and Addington were behind closed doors in the White House counsel's office. Stellar Wind was in place, and the question now was who else could be told about it.

"Can we get Timmy read in on this?" Gonzales asked. It might be useful if Flanigan knew the secret.

"No," Addington replied. "The president has been very clear about keeping the circle very, very small on this."

Gonzales nodded. "Yeah, that's what he said." Flanigan would not be told.

Later, Flanigan joined them. While he couldn't know any details, there was no harm, Addington decided, in letting him know that *something* was up.

"That idea you had, it's going to bear fruit," he said.

Flanigan was puzzled. What did that mean?

"It's the greatest favor anyone is ever going to do for you that you're not going to be read into this program," Addington said.

He smiled. "This is the one they're going to come and try to chop everybody's heads off for."

That was all Flanigan had to hear. Probably this was about granting the NSA more power. Whatever the details, Flanigan was happy to be in the dark.

A member of NBC security saw Tom Brokaw walking down the hallway and stopped him.

"You know, that white powder that we tested for you, it's negative."

"What white powder?" Brokaw asked.

"Your assistant gave us this white powder, and it's totally negative."

Brokaw said thanks and headed on his way. He would have to speak to his assistant, O'Connor, to find out what was going on. But she wasn't feeling well that day. She was experiencing flulike symptoms and had begun to develop a skin rash. And the young assistant who usually opened his mail, Casey Chamberlain, had also called in sick.

Probably just some infection going around.

The chartered plane from Atlanta touched down on Runway 10R/28L at the Palm Beach International Airport. The pilot taxied toward a hangar where the passengers—a team of pathologists from the Centers for Disease Control and Prevention in Atlanta—climbed down to the tarmac.

It was the morning of October 6, a day after the death of Robert Stevens. One of the doctors involved in the case almost immediately called the CDC with the news, speaking with Sherif Zaki, the chief of infectious disease pathology. Facing a potential case of anthrax—and possibly an epidemic—Zaki and his team decided to fly to Florida right away, then head to the Palm Beach County Medical Examiner's Office for Stevens's autopsy.

After arriving, the team members made their way into the autopsy suite in the center of one of the county buildings. Examiners working on two other bodies paused to glance up as the CDC scientists arrived.

"We're here to assist you," Zaki said softly.

Stevens's body was brought out from a morgue refrigerator and lifted onto a metal gurney. The county's medical examiner, Dr. Lisa Flannagan, would handle the initial incisions, while the CDC would examine the organs.

After everyone donned biohazard suits and masks, the autopsy began. Flannagan sliced the skin over the chest, then peeled it away. Using a large pair of shears, she cut through ribs. Then she slid her fingers under the front of the rib cage and lifted.

A surge of blood-filled liquid burst out of the chest cavity, cascading from the body onto the gurney and from there spilling to the floor. It was unlike anything the pathologists had ever seen before; Zaki had studied photographs of autopsies from an outbreak of anthrax in the Soviet Union, but had been completely unprepared for the flood of bloody fluid gushing around them.

There had been only eighteen cases involving inhaled anthrax in the past century. The most recent incident had been in 1979, when an accident at a bioweapons facility released anthrax dust, killing sixty-six people. That disaster from more than twenty years before was explainable. This was different. An American had died from the same rare disease, triggered by a microbe of uncertain origin—but one that was known to be coveted by terrorists as a weapon for mass murder.

About eight hours later, outside of high-security laboratory B-313 at Fort Detrick, a psychologically troubled microbiologist named Bruce Ivins was stripping off his clothes, preparing to enter the "hot suite" where deadly bacteria were stored.

The army base in Frederick, Maryland, was the military's primary site for studying agents that cause infectious disease. The research institute maintained labs rated at Biosafety Levels 3 and 4, a designation for facilities that handled and examined the most hazardous and exotic bacteria, parasites, and viruses.

Among the dangerous agents maintained in B-313—a Biosafety Level 3 lab—was *Bacillus anthracis,* the bacterium that causes anthrax. And few researchers were more trusted with those spores than Ivins, who had secured a reputation in the scientific community as one of the top experts on the microbe and the vaccines against it. He had created large batches of the microorganisms for research, among them one he labeled RMR-1029, which he kept in a walk-in cold room in his laboratory.

Ivins had worked in B-313 every night that weekend—a highly unusual deviation from his typical Monday-through-Friday schedule of the past three years. He kept no notes in his lab books the previous two nights and would not write any entries this time either—another change from his normal procedure.

He had increased his off-hours over the last few weeks, although there were no significant experiments taking place that would account for the change. But it was a period when Ivins was feeling particularly troubled about his work. He had learned recently that the army facility was down to its last approved lot of the anthrax vaccine, meaning that, without new production, the antitoxin would quickly be depleted. That would be devastating for Ivins. He soon wouldn't have a vaccine to study and would no longer be allowed to enter B-313, since his inoculations would not be up-to-date. His research would be dramatically slowed, if not irreparably damaged.

Ivins did not have the psychological strength to handle that kind of pressure. At times, he feared he was insane. Paranoia, delusions, thoughts of violence— all of these pathologies tortured him during cycles of mental instability. And he seemed to understand how dangerous it was for someone with his mental problems to be working with a biological weapon—he joked with one of his psychiatrists that someday he might be featured on the cover of the *National Enquirer,* under the headline PARANOID MAN WORKS WITH DEADLY ANTHRAX.

Some of his problems, he told his therapists, stemmed from his own troubled childhood. He suspected that his mother, Mary, was a schizophrenic. She beat her husband, Randall, relentlessly, once to the point that she thought she had killed him. Ivins did not escape the abuse, having often been whipped with a razor strop. Meanwhile, Randall brutalized him emotionally with severe public cruelty. He told his son that he had been unwanted and that both of his parents were disappointed he had not been born a girl. Despite Ivins's strong academic performance in high school, Randall relentlessly berated him as being doomed to failure. Ivins feared his father had been proved right—he wanted to attend Randall's alma mater, Princeton University, but was rejected.

By his adulthood, there was no hiding that Ivins suffered from a severe mental illness. One psychiatrist diagnosed manic depression; another said the symptoms were from a paranoid personality disorder. Whatever the cause, Ivins recognized that his thoughts could be psychotic, but his realization came only after the episode passed.

When the mental breaks were at their worst, Ivins would refuse to share his thoughts, sometimes even with the doctors who were supposed to treat him. He had told his counselor the previous year that he planned to travel out of town to watch a young woman play soccer; if her team failed to win the game, Ivins said, he would poison her. The counselor called the police, but no action was taken.

His obsessions with particular women haunted him. As an undergraduate, he asked a young student who had pledged Kappa Kappa Gamma for a date. She turned him down, a rejection that set off a forty-year fixation with the sorority.

In graduate school, he began stalking a female colleague when he learned that she not only had joined Kappa as an undergraduate but still held an advisory role with the sorority. Years after receiving his doctorate, Ivins used directory assistance to track down the address of the woman, a microbiologist, then went to her home and spray-painted KKG on the sidewalk near her car. Many times over the years, he drove three hours or more to visit Kappa sorority houses; after staring at the buildings for about ten minutes, he would then drive back. He had even burglarized two of the sorority's houses and stole a cipher used to translate the instructions and sayings for the rituals; the document contributed to his fascination with codes.

Ivins's mania about Kappa drove him to try to damage its reputation. He raged about hazing by sororities, devouring every article and book he could find on the topic. Then in 1983, posing as the Kappa member he had met in graduate school, he sent her local newspaper a letter that strongly defended hazing. The letter was printed along with the woman's name and address. Three weeks later, he contacted the mother of a college student who had died in a 1978 hazing incident and gave her a copy of the bogus letter. Ivins had first learned of that mother's loss when she was interviewed by Tom Brokaw, a host of the *Today* show; in that segment, Brokaw noted that his cohost, Jane Pauley, was an alumnus of Kappa. Brokaw and Pauley became a new focus for him.

His life was an endless series of secrets and oddities. As a boy of five or six, he had developed a strange fascination with blindfolds, wrapping them across the eyes of his stuffed animals and teddy bears. As Ivins matured, that fixation snowballed and took on a sexual focus; scores of images of blindfolded women filled his computer. He used assumed names to open post office boxes, including one he chose as the address for trading letters about sadomasochism and for receiving bondage equipment and magazines. He became fixated on women's underwear and began cross-dressing.

With Ivins's mental state deteriorating even more in the fall of 2001, his doctor had doubled his prescribed dosage of the antidepressant Celexa, but little changed. The attacks of 9/11 bothered him, though only because he found it curious that the events anguished his colleagues while stirring no reactions or emotions in him. He felt alone and anxious that he could not reveal the full truth about his spiraling problems. And he believed his colleagues would never find out—Ivins had long before passed a background check that allowed him to work with the deadly bacteria. The investigators hadn't discovered anything about his psychiatric history.

Just before eight o'clock that night, Ivins finished changing into his lab attire. With the swipe of a security card, the mentally unbalanced and embittered scientist walked into the hot suite, surrounded by the deadly biological agents that caused anthrax infections.

David Addington's face hardened in rage.

"What are they *doing*?" he snapped. "This is the *worst* of the Clinton administration's national security apparatus being visited on us."

The bombing campaign in Afghanistan was set to begin; the targets had been selected and approved at the Pentagon. But Addington had just learned that another set of lawyers had been brought in to review the targeting once again. This time, it was people without *any* connection to the military: White House lawyers.

Both Gonzales and Bellinger, the principal legal advisor to the National Security Council, had somehow gotten wrapped up in debating about what to bomb. Addington could only shake his head in dismay—lawyers piled on lawyers were all taking turns playing war.

Addington got the news from Flanigan, who had just overheard Gonzales and Bellinger lamenting the moral burden of the task and the complexities of studying photos and charts and maps in reviews of proposed targets.

After recounting what he knew to Addington, Flanigan paid a visit to Gonzales to warn him of the treacherous waters he was treading.

"Al, are you sure you want to get involved in this?" Flanigan asked. "I mean, since when is the counsel to the president an expert on either the laws of war or tactical imperatives?"

Gonzales paused. "Well, I have to be involved in this," he said, sounding defensive. "This is important."

Flanigan soon realized that he couldn't coax his boss into reconsidering his position with soft words. It was time for the sledgehammer. He called in Addington and asked for help. The vice president's counsel went straight to Gonzales's office.

"Al, this is stupid," he said.

Gonzales opened his mouth to protest. Addington spoke first.

"What do you know about this, Al?" he asked. "What makes you an expert in these decisions?"

Gonzales pushed back, but Addington slapped down every argument he mustered. It took a few days, but finally Addington and Flanigan pulled the White House legal team out of the business of targeting missiles and bombs.

4

A three-quarter moon lit up a clear night, casting muted shadows over Kabul. The air was crisp, the city calm and quiet.

There was no warning, no sound of a plane overhead, no screams or combat fire. Tomahawk guided missiles sliced through the air, slamming into the city's electrical grid. Kabul plunged into darkness as more missiles and then bombs rained down from the sky.

It was just before 9:30 on October 7. The air campaign against the Taliban and al-Qaeda had begun. This opening round of attacks involved an array of weaponry, including B-2 "Spirit" Stealth bombers from Whiteman Air Force Base, B-1B and B-52 bombers from Diego Garcia, Navy F-14 and F/A fighters, cruisers, destroyers, and SSGN submarines.

As the assault continued, the skies over Kabul lit up with white flashes and the city shuddered with thunderous explosions. The Taliban raced to their military positions, shooting antiaircraft guns toward bombers they could not see, their tracers streaking up into the night.

About an hour later, the bombing came to Kandahar. Hundreds of armed residents and Taliban soldiers ran into the street, firing weapons haphazardly in an attempt to hold off an imagined attack by ground troops. Deafening explosions ripped apart Kandahar Airport and its radar facilities, the Taliban military headquarters, and a guesthouse used by the Taliban leader, Mohammed Omar.

Despite the appearance of a massive assault, the first night was far from impressive. A modest thirty-one targets were struck; in addition to Kabul and Kandahar, the bombs hit Shindand, Herat, Mazar-e Sharif, and Sheberghan. None of the Taliban frontline positions were destroyed—or even targeted. It dawned on members of the Northern Alliance that the Taliban fighters who most threatened them were, for the most part, unscathed.

This was the best the Americans could do?

Inside the Treaty Room at the White House, technicians were adjusting lights and checking an audio feed as Bush sat nearby, reviewing his speech. At 1:00 p.m., the camera rolled, showing Bush at a desk.

"Good afternoon. On my orders, the United States military has begun strikes against al-Qaeda terrorist training camps and military installations in Afghanistan."

The campaign was carefully targeted, Bush said, designed to disrupt terrorists' use of that country as a base. He lauded Great Britain for aiding in the attack, and listed allies that were pledging forces for the operation.

"This military action is part of our campaign against terrorism," he said. "Today we focus on Afghanistan. But the battle is broader." Other countries that sponsor terrorists would be considered outlaws and murderers. Those nations, he suggested, risked being subjected to the full force and fury of the United States.

"The battle is now joined on many fronts," Bush said. "We will not waver, we will not tire, we will not falter and we will not fail."

Thirty minutes later, an image of Osama bin Laden, clad in fatigues and sitting in a rocky outcrop, appeared on the Arab television network, Al Jazeera. The video had been prerecorded, although no one could say precisely when. The timing of its broadcast, coming so soon after the bombing began, hardly seemed a coincidence.

Bin Laden held a black microphone in his right hand and, as he spoke, wagged his index finger up and down. "God Almighty hit the United States at its most vulnerable spot, he destroyed one of its great buildings," he said. "Here is the United States. It was filled with terror from north to south, from east to west, praise be to God."

Less than two weeks had passed since bin Laden proclaimed the attacks were the work of Jews or enemies of the United States, that such an act was forbidden by the Koran, that al-Qaeda was not the enemy of America—comments that CIA analysts saw as the ravings of a madman. As expected, he was contradicting himself by proclaiming the horror as an act of God—on behalf of Muslims.

This was divine retribution, bin Laden said, an infliction of the same pain felt by Islamic nations for decades. America was a nation of hypocrites, he intoned, killing hundreds of thousands of innocent civilians with the atomic bomb dropped on Hiroshima while bemoaning as terrorism the deaths of far fewer people. All Muslims had to rise up in defense of their religion and join the fight to drive evil from Saudi Arabia.

Finally, bin Laden had a few words for the American people. If peace did not come to Palestine, if infidels did not leave the land of Mohammed, the threat would never end.

"I swear by Almighty God," he said. "America will not live in peace."

The anthrax killer was back in Princeton, walking toward the mailbox.

Government health experts had already revealed news that someone had died from inhalation anthrax, but there was no real panic. The officials had told the public that there was nothing to fear, saying they did not believe this single case was the result of terrorism.

Despite the number of letters that the killer sent to the news media almost two weeks before, no one seemed to have found them. There had been no announcement of anthrax discovered at NBC or the *New York Post;* no letter had been located at the *Sun,* where Stevens worked. There was a distinct possibility that the attacks might slip by without anyone's ever knowing they had occurred.

Soon, there would be no doubt that the country was again facing a terrorist threat. The killer arrived at the mailbox on Nassau Street carrying new letters. One was addressed to the Senate majority leader, Tom Daschle, and the other to Senator Patrick Leahy.

Both men played a role in the nation's anthrax efforts. Months before, Daschle had sent a letter to the Pentagon expressing concern about the safety of anthrax vaccines administered to soldiers. Shortly afterward, the Defense Department announced it was curtailing the program; the vaccine was running out, threatening the life's work of researchers like Dr. Bruce Ivins.

Daschle's political influence on anthrax research was perhaps exceeded only by Leahy's financial role. He was the former chairman of and now a senior Democrat on the Agriculture, Nutrition, and Forestry Committee. That Senate body oversaw funding for biosafety animal research facilities, such as the anthrax lab at Fort Detrick.

These two men were among the most important politicians in Washington when it came to the future of the anthrax vaccine program. And they had just been targeted for exposure to the deadly bacteria.

• • •

Several sedans came to a stop at a mansion in the northwestern section of central London. A group of American intelligence and diplomatic officials climbed out and headed toward the front door, where a well-dressed servant awaited to escort them inside.

The home was owned by Prince Bandar bin Sultan, a member of the Saudi royal family who had served as ambassador to the United States since 1983. In those eighteen years, Bandar had become known internationally as an indispensable operator, a dominant diplomatic figure who served as a bridge between the Middle East and Washington.

On this day in mid-October, Bandar was hosting a secret summit between government officials with both the United States and Libya, two countries that had not had formal diplomatic ties for twenty-two years. Libya had been on the State Department's annual list of state sponsors of terrorism since 1979, and the country's leader, Muammar al-Gaddafi, had been quietly pushing for a détente with the West. Bandar brokered earlier meetings between the Americans and the Libyans—at his London home, at his British country house, and in Geneva—as part of the opening steps in a potential diplomatic thaw.

Until now, the discussions had focused on the role of Libyan officials in the 1988 bombing of Pan Am flight 103 over Lockerbie, Scotland; there could be no progress, the Americans said, until Libya accepted its responsibility and agreed to a settlement with victims' families.

The meeting today would be quite different. The entourage of American officials walked through the first floor of Bandar's home, passing an indoor swimming pool, before heading downstairs to a large, windowless room. There, they met with Moussa Koussa, who had worked as a deputy director of Libyan intelligence and had been linked to both the Lockerbie bombing and the downing of a French airliner a year later.

The first rounds of meetings were handled by William Burns, the assistant secretary of state for Near East affairs, with the talks focusing on the Libyans' admitting their role in the Pan Am 103 attacks and agreeing to surrender their weapons of mass destruction.

Ben Bonk, the deputy director of the Counterterrorist Center at the CIA, listened to the discussion without offering much input. He had attended several of these meeting with Koussa but arrived today with a new agenda.

After a break, Bonk and Koussa headed upstairs to a parlor filled with elegant sofas and matching chairs. Although his English was excellent, Koussa brought along a translator; a CIA official accompanied Bonk from the Near East division. Everyone sat down around a coffee table. Bonk looked Koussa in the eyes.

"I don't care about the past anymore," he said. "Forget about it, this is the past, ended, done with. All I care about is what happens from now on."

Bush had been clear about the new administration position, Bonk said—countries had to choose. They would be either with the United States, or against it. There was no longer a middle ground.

"You know these are serious problems. If you're going to work with us, we want to work with you," Bonk said.

A moment passed. "You go after them, you have to go after all of them," Koussa said. "You can't just go after bin Laden and expect this to go away. If you don't get them all, they're not going to stop."

"That's fine with us," Bonk replied. "We're going after everybody."

Koussa's voice dropped. "You know, of course, that your biggest problem is the Saudis and what they're doing with the spread of their philosophy."

Amazing. They were meeting in the home of the Saudi ambassador. This was no place to talk about the role of Wahhabism—the austere form of Islam promoted by the royal family and practiced by bin Laden and other extremists—in the growth of al-Qaeda.

I'll bet this room is bugged. Bonk stayed silent, not disagreeing, not nodding. The conversation moved on.

After about half an hour, Bonk handed Koussa a small pile of documents containing information about the hijackers—nothing earth-shattering, but enough to signal that the administration was willing to cooperate and provide intelligence to Libya on terrorists. In return, Koussa brought out sheets of paper covered with a matrix of telephone numbers.

"We think al-Qaeda is contacting these phones," Koussa said. "We've picked these up from our people in Afghanistan."

The meeting ended, and Bonk walked away feeling pleased with the progress. Tentative steps, to be sure, but the American and Libyan intelligence agencies were starting to work together in confronting the al-Qaeda threat.

At his first opportunity, Bonk studied the papers that Koussa had provided him. The telephone numbers could be helpful; Bonk planned to turn them over to the NSA as soon as he returned home. As he scanned the numbers, one almost jumped off the page.

Area code 202.

Then he saw the prefix, 456. Bonk's eyes widened in disbelief. Someone at that prefix had been calling a phone number in Afghanistan linked by Libyan intelligence to al-Qaeda.

It was a number that Bonk knew well, a prefix used at only one building in Washington.

The White House.

Shortly after 10:30 on the morning of October 8, a red Volkswagen Golf parked in front of an apartment building in Zenica, north of Sarajevo. Two Bosnian police officers stepped out and approached the ground-floor residences. A knock on the door, and Anela Kobilica answered.

"Is Belkacem Bensayah available?" one of the officers asked. "We need to speak with him."

Kobilica hesitated. Bensayah, her husband, was an Algerian Arab who did not understand Bosnian well. Meeting with the police would be difficult for him.

"Why do you wish to speak with him?" she asked.

"We want to check on the status of his citizenship."

This was bad news. Kobilica was aware that a number of Arab men had been expelled from Bosnia recently and feared this would now be her husband's fate. She grew upset, but one of the officers told her not to worry.

"We're just here to conduct a check," he said. "Ask him to collect his identity papers and come with us."

Kobilica went inside to fetch her husband. Minutes later, Bensayah was heading out to the street with the police, his immigration papers in hand.

Before Kobilica could close the door, two more uniformed officers appeared. They instructed her to stay at home with her daughters until Bensayah returned. She agreed. The two men took up positions in front of the apartment building, standing sentry.

The plan to question Bensayah had been set in motion days before. Since the 9/11 attacks, authorities in Bosnia-Herzegovina had been working with the Americans to root out terrorist sympathizers. During the Bosnian War, the country had become a magnet for jihadists, as large numbers of them joined the battle in defense of fellow Muslims. After hostilities ended, many remained, often taking jobs with Muslim charities that American intelligence believed were fronts used to funnel cash to terrorists.

For six years, the Bosnians had looked the other way as their country emerged as a haven for Islamic fundamentalists. But Bush's "with us or against us" edict had shaken the Federation government into action. A new counterterrorist unit was formed, which immediately launched a headlong assault on the terrorist threat in Bosnia. Over the previous few weeks, a coterie of law enforcement officials had pulled up in SUVs every few days at homes and offices around the country, quietly conducting arrests and searches. That had culminated two weeks earlier with a significant raid on Visoko airfield, northwest of Sarajevo; armored fighting vehicles, Humvee jeeps, and attack helicopters descended on the landing strip that American intelligence had identified as a hub for organizations providing support to al-Qaeda. Calls intercepted at a listening post in neighboring Croatia had fueled concern that Visoko was about to be used as a launch site for another airborne attack, this time against the American embassy or military bases in Sarajevo.

In the crackdown, information emerged about an Algerian known to law enforcement only by the nickname "Abu Maali." The intelligence suggested that this man—a veteran of conflicts in Algeria, Afghanistan, and the Balkans—worked closely with al-Qaeda. Bensayah was the prime suspect; the Americans had evidence that he had placed as many as seventy calls to Abu Zubaydah, identified by the CIA as a top al-Qaeda operative. In one intercepted conversation with Zubaydah after 9/11, the Americans told the Bosnians, Bensayah had discussed passport procurement. But the Bosnians had only the assurances of United States embassy officials that Bensayah associated with terrorists. If they were going to arrest him, they needed their own evidence.

The police returned Bensayah to his home just before 1:30 P.M., this time with a show of force. Almost forty officers arrived, parking their vehicles haphazardly around the street, then milling about for ten minutes until one of them informed Bensayah and Kobilica that they had come to search the apartment. There was no Arab interpreter present, so Kobilica did all the talking.

"Can we observe?" she asked.

"Yes," one of the officers replied. "But don't talk to each other."

The police began by searching a small room with a couch. There wasn't much to examine there, so they moved on to the bedroom. They checked the floor, opened all of the drawers and closets, and dug through the couple's clothes.

The telephone rang. On the line was a friend of Kobilica, sounding distressed. "I just heard on the news that Belkacem was arrested!" the friend said.

That was odd. He was home, and this was about immigration. Why was any of that newsworthy?

"There are just some questions about his citizenship papers," Kobilica said.

"That's not what they said on the news. They said that Belkacem was connected to terrorism!"

Kobilica thanked her friend, hung up, and approached the nearest officer. "They are saying on the news that this has something to do with terrorism," she said. "What is all this about?"

"It has nothing to do with terrorism," the officer replied. "This is just an investigation relating to your husband's citizenship."

Just before 3:30, the couple asked if the search could be interrupted to allow for afternoon prayers. The police agreed. The prayers lasted longer than usual; the two had missed the noon session, so they doubled up on their devotions this time. The search resumed as soon as they were finished.

The police returned to the bedroom closet. About twenty books were stacked inside, and an officer inspected each one. A number of boxes were also stored there, and those were moved into the bedroom. An officer prepared to look inside the first.

"No!" Bensayah blurted out in Arabic. "Do not open that box. It contains items that are not mine. They belong to other men who have left the country. They asked me to keep their things safe for them until they returned."

Ignoring the protests, the officer opened the box and pulled out a fax machine. When she saw it, Kobilica whipped around on her husband, furious. This device communicated by *telephone*. Who knew what calls the men who owned it may have made?

"What are you doing with this?" she barked. "Why would you store something like that from someone you don't know?"

"Don't talk to him!" one officer snapped. Kobilica was escorted into the living room, away from Bensayah.

Searching through more boxes, an officer found about seventy books. While flipping through the pages of one, he saw a slip of paper with numbers on it. He pulled it out of the book and held it aloft.

Soon after, the police emerged from the bedroom and turned their attention to the living room. An officer saw the remote control for the television, picked it up, and held it out to Kobilica.

"What's this?" he said, suspicion in his voice.

Kobilica blinked. "It's the television remote control."

The officer nodded. "All right," he said.

One of the searchers standing near the television noticed a book entitled *The Tragedy of Immorality*. He opened it and saw handwriting on the pages.

"Whose book is this?" he asked.

"It's mine," Kobilica responded.

"What's all this writing?"

"It's mine. It's the answers to scores of personality tests that I saw in the newspaper."

The officer continued to look through the book. Kobilica thought nothing of it.

As each belonging was seized, the police recorded it on a receipt for the couple. The paper with the numbers on it was listed as the ninth item. The book, *The Tragedy of Immorality*, was thirteenth. The description of that entry said that it included two sheets of paper with Arabic letters. There was no mention of numbers. None of the officers could read Arabic.

About that same time, Muhamed Bešić, the interior minister for the Federation government, was standing before a group of reporters in Sarajevo.

A man named Belkacem Bensayah had been arrested in nearby Zenica on terrorism charges, Bešić said. Police had discovered a slip of paper at his home with the phone number of Abu Zubaydah, a senior al-Qaeda member.

The evidence, though, was curious. In court, the government would identify item thirteen on the receipt list—*The Tragedy of Immorality* and the two sheets of paper—as the one containing the Zubaydah phone number. But none of those papers had numbers on them. The one that did, number nine, was never identified as suspicious.

Erin O'Connor stayed home sick from her job at NBC for a few more days.

Her flulike symptoms and rashes had grown worse the week before. She had been unable to shake the fear that she had been exposed to anthrax from the powder-laced letter addressed to her boss, Tom Brokaw. So, she had called the FBI and the New York City Police Department, and had gone to see a doctor, asking repeatedly, "Could this be anthrax?" Each time, the answer was no. A bite from a brown recluse spider maybe, but not anthrax.

She returned to work on Monday, October 8, and Brokaw asked her how she was doing. "I'm actually feeling quite a bit better," she replied.

Soon after, O'Connor went to the restroom with two coworkers. When they came out, one of the employees immediately tracked down Brokaw. They had just seen O'Connor's skin, she told him.

"It's a scabrous mess," she said.

Brokaw approached O'Connor. "We've got to get additional medical care for this."

He needed to find Kevin Cahill, Brokaw decided, his family's doctor and an expert in infectious disease. Cahill would know what to do.

The crowd of administration officials took their seats around a conference table in Room 6320 at the State Department.

It was the first meeting of the interagency group formed to devise a system of justice for captured terrorists. The room was filled with lawyers from the State Department, the White House counsel's office, the National Security Council, the Pentagon, and all the other departments involved in national security policy.

Pierre-Richard Prosper, the ambassador-at-large who headed the group, opened the meeting at 9:30 A.M.

"Thank you all for coming here," he said. "I really appreciate your time and attention to this important subject. I've been asked to convene this group so we can consider what the right way to try these war criminals might be. We want to look at all the options and eventually make a recommendation to the White House."

The questions to be resolved were myriad, Prosper said. How would they deal with the terrorists? How would they prosecute them? For what? And where were the terrorists going to be detained?

Prosper described his experience working with an international war crimes tribunal, suggesting that model might offer some idea for how to proceed. Another option, of course, was the criminal courts, but Prosper said he was skeptical.

"From a logistical standpoint, can the federal courts in New York handle this?" he asked. "There are potentially hundreds of cases involved. And do we want to put judges and juries in harm's way?"

The other officials around the table chimed in, at first asking more rhetorical questions than providing answers. One mentioned that the Office of Legal Counsel at the Justice Department needed to craft an opinion about the president's authority in this area, particularly when it came to the possibility of convening military commissions. That job was handed to Pat Philbin, an old friend of John Yoo's who had been hired in the Justice Department office days before September 11.

After about an hour of discussion, the meeting broke up. There was a lot of work to be done, Prosper said.

At the CIA, relief. There wasn't some terrorist spy in the White House.

The calls in the Libyan records handed to Bonk by Moussa Koussa had been placed by an NSC staffer from the Middle East who knew people in Afghanistan. There was no reason to investigate, officials decided; lots of people in the White House had known about the calls.

The issue was shelved. But the lesson remained—a call to a suspicious number might be perfectly innocent.

With the war under way, retired general Wesley Clark wanted to return to the Pentagon for a visit. Two weeks earlier, a general with the Joint Chiefs of Staff had told him that the administration was planning to attack Iraq after hitting Afghanistan. Clark wanted an update.

He arrived at the general's office. "So," he asked, "are we still going to war with Iraq?"

"Oh, it's worse than that." The general grabbed a piece of paper off his desk. He had just received the document from the office of the secretary of defense.

"This is a memo about how we're going to take out seven countries in five years," he said, "Starting with Iraq, Lebanon, Libya, Somalia, Sudan, and finishing off, Iran."

Amazing. "Is it classified?"

"Yes, sir."

"Well," Clark said, "don't show it to me."

"It could be anthrax. It looks like what I've seen in Africa before."

The words from his doctor, Kevin Cahill, were the first confirmation to Tom Brokaw that his assistant could have been the victim of a biological attack. Cahill said that he was sending O'Connor for some biopsies. Then they might know for sure if she had been exposed to the deadly pathogen.

The news terrified O'Connor. She had a toddler at home and had been with the child day after day, possibly carrying anthrax—on her skin, on her clothing, anywhere. Could she have infected the youngster? There had to be *someone* who could tell her what to do to help keep her family safe.

Brokaw grew tired of waiting. He knew where to find anthrax experts and decided to open a back channel to them. He called Fort Detrick in Maryland and spoke with two officials there, giving a short description of what was happening to his secretary.

"I need some help," he said. "We're not getting any straight answers. You're supposed to be the leading authorities in this country on biological warfare and weaponry. Could you talk to my secretary?"

Yes, one of the officials said, they would love to talk to her. Brokaw put O'Connor on the phone. The scientists asked her about where she had been the week before, what her skin looked like, and how she was feeling. Then Brokaw got back on the phone.

"You know," one of the officials said, "we don't think it's anthrax. We think it's a brown recluse spider. It has the same characteristics."

"Well, do me an additional favor," Brokaw replied. "If I can get a biopsy, will you test it for me?"

"That's not the business we're in. We work for the army."

"I understand. But these are extraordinary circumstances and you'll be protected."

There was a moment's pause. "Okay, get us a biopsy."

The scientist provided some short instructions on how to perform two biopsies. That information was forwarded to a dermatologist, who conducted the procedure on O'Connor. The biopsies were sent to Brokaw, who arranged for them to be flown to Washington. A motorcycle courier met the plane at the Reagan National Airport and rushed the samples out to Fort Detrick.

From there, the biopsies were taken for testing to Building 1425, the work site for Dr. Bruce Ivins, the anthrax expert who was struggling with his deteriorating mental condition. When the O'Connor samples arrived, Ivins wasn't there. He'd missed a lot of work the last two days. No one knew where he was or what he was doing.

Brokaw heard the results the day after O'Connor's biopsies reached Fort Detrick: No anthrax. His assistant was safe.

Relieved, Brokaw thanked the scientists. Not everything was finished yet, he was told. Samples had also gone to the CDC in Atlanta, but the lab there hadn't been able to conduct tests yet. The scientists at Fort Detrick had worked through the night.

O'Connor was not reassured by the news.

A misting rain fell in Ottawa on the afternoon of October 12, sprinkling a light sheen on the Kamlo Plaza strip mall in the northeast section of the city. About four o'clock, Abdullah Almalki turned onto the parking lot and maneuvered his car into a space at the south end, near a carousel-shaped restaurant called Mango's Café.

Almalki popped open the driver's side door and headed down the sidewalk to the glass-enclosed eatery. He had been invited to meet at Mango's by Maher Arar, a man he knew in passing. Both of their families were from Syria and had become part of that immigrant community in Canada. Arar obtained a master's degree in computer engineering and had worked alongside one of Almalki's brothers at a high-tech company. Because of his friendship with the brother, Arar crossed paths with Almalki occasionally; once, when the brother was unavailable, Almalki agreed to allow Arar to list him as an emergency contact on an apartment lease.

Earlier that year, Arar had opened a home-based technology consulting business. The company was thriving, leaving him burning rapidly through printer cartridges. Ink became one of his largest expenses.

Then he heard that Almalki might be able to get him a deal on cartridges through a contact at Future Shop, Canada's largest consumer electronics retailer. So, the previous day, Arar had called, asking for help in obtaining a good price for printer ink. He offered to treat Almalki to a late lunch at Mango's, which featured Middle Eastern delicacies.

They met inside the restaurant, where Arar shook Almalki's hand. "It's good to see you again," he said.

Almalki ordered a large lunch of shawarma chicken and fruit cocktail, and the two spent an hour chitchatting. Arar mentioned that his wife was pregnant, Almalki recommended a midwife he knew; then the conversation veered into a wide-ranging discussion about everything from children to ink cartridges.

After an hour, they left the restaurant. It was still misting, but neither man got particularly wet; Almalki did not even have to remove his glasses. They walked to a local Islamic center for afternoon prayers, and from there to Future Shop, where Arar purchased ink supplies.

As the men parted ways, three surveillance teams—two from the Mounties and one from the Ottawa police—were watching. They had followed Almalki to the meeting at Mango's, parking nearby as he dined with Arar.

The investigators came away deeply suspicious. Almalki was a terrorist, they were sure of that. But why was he meeting with Arar? Why had they walked outside together in the bad weather? That must be a sign that they were trying to hide something. And when an officer standing nearby tried to listen in on their conversation, he couldn't hear them. Why were they leaning close to each other while talking? Perhaps Arar was a terrorist and had been plotting something with Almalki.

With the surveillance completed, the Mounties headed back to the office. They wrote their reports, specifically noting that their suspicions had been heightened because the two men walked in the pouring rain—an exaggeration of the weather that would prove critical in the years to come.

With that, the investigators believed the evidence had piled up—the meeting with Almalki, the rain walk, the soft speaking. They opened a formal inquiry of Maher Arar and his possible ties to terrorists.

After the days of tension, Tom Brokaw was relaxing, jogging with his dogs and feeling pretty good about life. The fear of a biological attack at NBC had subsided. The nightmare that had upended the lives of his staff seemed finally to be over.

When he returned home, the phone rang. It was a colleague from the NBC news desk. The New York City police commissioner, the colleague said, is trying to find you.

The words from the day before shot through Brokaw's mind. The CDC hadn't done their tests. By now, they should have been completed.

Oh my God, he thought. *It's anthrax.*

The two intelligence officials met alone at the Rome headquarters of Italy's military intelligence service, known as SISMI.

The older man, Admiral Gianfranco Battelli, had been appointed as SISMI's director five years before and now was on the verge of retirement. Across from him sat Jeffrey Castelli, the CIA station chief in Rome. Since 9/11, the two had been in frequent contact; Castelli had been asking top officials at both SISMI and its domestic counterpart, SISDE, for any information they had on al-Qaeda. But on this day, Castelli had arrived to sound out Battelli about assisting the CIA with one of its new initiatives.

"What would be your opinion of performing renditions in Italy?" he asked.

Battelli understood. He had already heard that Bush had granted the CIA greater powers to snatch terrorists around the world without seeking an extradition order or any of the other legal niceties. The authority was not new; the CIA had been rendering Islamic radicals and criminals for years, picking them up in one country and moving them elsewhere. But now the scale was larger, abductions could take place on the soil of allies, and the targets could be shipped to countries with reputations of brutalizing prisoners. No one would be officially informed of what had happened to the suspects. They would simply disappear.

The CIA had someone specific in mind whom it wanted to render, Castelli said. "We might be picking up a suspected terrorist, taking him to the airport, and sending him to a foreign country."

Battelli leaned forward, elbows on the table, his face blank. This was an extraordinary and delicate moment. The Americans were planning to spirit an Italian resident—maybe even an Italian citizen—out of the country, and then do God-knows-what with him. And they wanted Battelli to give a thumbs-up.

"If you make a formal request for assistance," Battelli said, "I would have to inform the prime minister or other political authorities."

Plus, Battelli said, Italian intelligence would not give Castelli a go-ahead without first checking to be sure he wasn't undertaking some autonomous cowboy operation. The request would have to come from George Tenet himself.

Still, Battelli thought, this wasn't his problem. His retirement would begin in a few days. "I'll also refer this conversation to my successor," he said. "You'll have to speak to him."

Castelli thanked him and left the office. Battelli breathed a sigh of relief—he didn't want anything to do with this new American initiative. But he had little doubt that, sometime soon, someone in Italy would be kidnapped.

Panic set in at NBC headquarters. The results were definitive: Brokaw's assistant had contracted anthrax. The newsroom had been a target of a biological attack.

An emergency meeting was called, held in a conference room on the fifty-second floor. Jeffrey Immelt, the newly appointed head of NBC's parent company, General Electric, was the most senior executive taking part in the meeting, followed by Bob Wright, the network's president. Brokaw was there, and the head of the CDC was on the line from Atlanta.

Before discussions began, the door burst open, and Rudy Giuliani, the mayor of New York, stormed in. Until that day, he had not heard about the suspected case of anthrax at NBC. He was angry that he had been kept in the dark, and now he wanted to help manage what was sure to be a new episode of terror for the already battered city.

News of the anthrax infection at NBC crackled throughout offices and homes around the country. Other terrifying developments poured in—more infections had appeared at American Media Incorporated, where Robert Stevens had worked. An envelope containing a suspicious powder had been mailed to the *New York Times*, requiring an evacuation of the building. Then the FBI came out with a public announcement—additional terrorist attacks might be unleashed over the next few days.

To confuse matters, Ashcroft seemed to promptly contradict the Bureau, announcing that there was no evidence yet linking the multiple cases to terrorism.

Cheney thought Ashcroft was being overly cautious. He had been bracing Bush and other senior members of the administration for the biological attack that he felt sure would be part of the second wave of assaults. Bin Laden had for years been trying to obtain weapons of mass destruction and had launched an anthrax development program. Saddam Hussein had been found with tons of poisonous bacterial agents after the first Gulf War, and some of that arsenal could easily have been sneaked to any of America's enemies. The timing of the anthrax mailings, Cheney felt certain, was not happenstance.

He appeared on PBS television and delivered a very different message from Ashcroft. Bin Laden, he averred, might well be the culprit.

"We know that he's trained people in his camps in Afghanistan. For example, we have copies of the manuals that they've actually used to train people with respect to how to deploy and use these kinds of substances."*

---

*Cheney was mistaken. While the document he is referencing, known as the Manchester Manual, includes information about the use of poisons, it describes only how to make simple toxins out of natural substances, like spoiled food. While the poisons mentioned, such as ricin, can be deadly, there is no discussion in the manual of anthrax or of how to "deploy and use" any bacterial agent. Moreover, contrary to the determinations of the American and British governments, the Manchester Manual was not an al-Qaeda document. See Notes and Sources for pages 193–195.

Could it be a coincidence? "I'm a skeptic," Cheney said. The only responsible thing to do, he added, was to proceed on the basis that the anthrax and September 11 attacks were related.

The message coming from the administration to the American people was, at best, ambiguous.

The president did not share any sense of uncertainty.

The anthrax attack was the second terrorist strike in a matter of weeks. Both occurred on his watch. From his first intelligence briefing as the Republican nominee for president, he had been warned that jihadists were seeking biological and chemical weapons and were prepared to use them. The CIA had since reported to him about the almost incomprehensible danger posed by weaponized viruses and bacteria—as well as about stockpiles of microbes that it believed were still held by Saddam, an arsenal that would undoubtedly attract terrorists hell-bent on killing Americans.

The assaults on the World Trade Center and the Pentagon had been searing for Bush. But it was the anthrax attack that shook him to his core. Years later, some of his aides would say that the delivery of those contaminated letters had a far greater impact on Bush than anyone outside the White House imagined. His resolve grew unshakable—he would do whatever it took to protect civilians from another anonymous attack. No more Americans would be killed, he swore, by the murderous plotting of the evildoers.

On the afternoon of October 13, Ahmad El-Maati was at his Toronto apartment watching CTV Network news with his mother. He was listening to the anchor when he glanced at the news crawl running along the bottom of the screen.

He gasped.

Los Angeles Times reports 36-year-old Kuwaiti man
caught crossing border with map of nuclear site.

"Oh my God!" El-Maati shrieked. "This is me!"

His mother blinked, her mouth agape. "Yes," she said. "I think you're right."

El-Maati went out to search for a copy of the *Globe and Mail,* Toronto's largest newspaper. He saw the story on the front page.

Kuwaiti Found with Papers on Sensitive Ottawa Sites

He dropped into a chair.

This is bad, he thought. *This is very, very sinister.*

His fears intensified as he read the article. American agents had been briefed about the man with the map. A spokesman for the Mounties stated that this was part of a criminal investigation. The document that had been discovered by customs agents identified an atomic energy building and a virus-and-disease control laboratory.

Suddenly everything made sense. He had suspected that he was being followed. At first, he had figured it was just his imagination, but now he was sure that his wariness had been justified.

El-Maati decided to call a lawyer. Since 9/11, one attorney, Rocco Galati, had been speaking with Muslims at local mosques, suggesting that they call him if they were contacted by Canadian intelligence or law enforcement. This was the person to hire, El-Maati decided.

He telephoned Galati, explained what was going on, and set up an appointment. El-Maati's parents accompanied him to the law office, listening as he spilled out the story of the map and the recent articles.

"I think, one hundred percent, the newspapers are talking about me," he sighed. "So, please, call them. Let's make a meeting and see what they want."

Holding up a hand, Galati signaled for El-Maati to be calm. "Okay, no problem, don't worry," he said. "I know the CSIS people. I know how to contact them. We'll take care of this."

Sometime after the meeting ended, Galati called a CSIS investigator, leaving a message that he represented El-Maati and wanted to arrange a meeting to clear things up. The investigator received the request, but decided he didn't have the authority to return the call.

Three days later, El-Maati checked in with his lawyer.

"I've left several messages," Galati said. "The guy never called back."

El-Maati asked a few questions and then hung up, terrified. The Canadian government was after him, and there was nothing he could do about it.

The news reports about the Kuwaiti man with the map appeared on the Internet and were published in newspapers worldwide. A day later, a Middle Eastern intelligence service wrote a letter to CSIS, asking for more information as well as for the name of the man being investigated.

The Canadian agency reported back, identifying El-Maati. The map he had been carrying, the response said, was about ten years old. But the Canadians didn't think that made any difference. El-Maati, they were convinced, was part of an al-Qaeda sleeper cell.

On Monday, October 15, an intern in the office of Senator Tom Daschle picked up a letter from a pile of mail that had remained unsorted for days.

The lettering on the envelope was a scrawl of blue ink, the words hand-printed and uneven, as if written by a child—not surprisingly, since the return address was a fourth-grade class from Greendale School in Franklin Park, New Jersey, at zip code 08852. It was tightly sealed with an excessive amount of cellophane tape adhered to all sides.

Sitting in the sixth-floor mail room, the intern slit open the envelope and removed the letter. White powder floated out, curling upward like a wisp of smoke. The paper was an odd shape, with a trimmed edge. The intern unfolded it.

09-11-01

YOU CAN NOT STOP US.

WE HAVE THIS ANTHRAX.

YOU DIE NOW.

ARE YOU AFRAID?

DEATH TO AMERICA.

DEATH TO ISRAEL.

ALLAH IS GREAT.

The Daschle letter was not just deadly. It was baffling.

The return address on the envelope made no sense. There *was* a Greendale School, but it was in Wisconsin, not New Jersey. There *was* a Franklin Park, but not at zip code 08852; that number corresponded with Monmouth Junction, New Jersey. And why did the killer go to the trouble of identifying the sender as being the fourth grade?

The FBI would spend years trying to solve the puzzle.

Investigators could have found the clues they needed in a clutter of magazines piled up in the "hot" suite used by Ivins at the military's anthrax research lab.

Ivins subscribed to *American Family Association Journal* and stacked issues going back months and years in the lab. The October 1999 edition contained an article about a lawsuit filed by the association on behalf of the parents of a

fourth-grade student at Greendale Baptist Academy in Wisconsin. The litigation related to corporal punishment at the school, a hot-button issue that had
engrossed Ivins for years, perhaps because of his own abuse as a child. He discussed the Greendale case with at least one colleague, and just one month after
the article was published, he and his wife sent their first contribution to the
association in about two years.

Franklin Park, the community listed in the return address, is about nine
miles from Princeton, where the letter was mailed. Monmouth Junction, the
unincorporated area designated by the zip code on the envelope, had distinct
links to Ivins. His family's American roots went back to seventeenth-century
New Jersey; specifically, Ivins's great-great-grandfather Thomas Ivins was born
in Monmouth. Ivins knew this and considered it significant—stuffed away in
a file where he kept his most important papers was an August 26, 1986, letter
explaining the genealogical connection between him and Monmouth.

Moreover, Ivins obsessed on the word *Monmouth* for reasons having nothing
to do with his family history—not only was Thomas Ivins born in a place called
Monmouth, but so was Kappa Kappa Gamma, the focus of Ivins's most intense
and decades-long obsession. The sorority was founded at Monmouth College
in Monmouth, Illinois, a fact mentioned by Ivins in some of his many diatribes
about the group that he posted, using aliases, on the Internet.

For Ivins, an increasingly unhinged loner with a fixation for codes, the return
address was virtually his signature.

The same day as the Daschle letter was discovered, Italian prime minister Silvio
Berlusconi arrived at the White House for a private meeting with Bush. Just a
few days had passed since Admiral Battelli, the head of Italian military intelligence, had brushed aside a CIA appeal to support a plan to abduct a suspected
terrorist in Milan. Such a request, he had said, would have to go through political authorities, perhaps even the prime minister himself.

Minutes before, Bush had done just that. Over a lunch in the Oval Office,
Bush had described the multiple fronts in the war on terrorism. The prime
minister agreed to share intelligence and help disrupt al-Qaeda's financial
network.

Then, Bush brought up the CIA's request—would Berlusconi's government
allow American intelligence to snatch a suspected terrorist in Italy and take him
out of the country? After asking a number of questions, Berlusconi said that he
would consult with others but gave his tentative approval.

When their discussion ended, Bush and Berlusconi walked out on the colonnade that led to the Oval Office. Reporters were waiting outside. The two men stood side by side, each clasping his hands at his waist. Bush said that he was honored to host the prime minister, mentioning that they had eaten lunch together—one of the best meals, he said, since he had assumed the presidency.

"We had a long discussion about our mutual desire to rout out terrorism," Bush said. "We're making progress. One reason we're making progress is because we've got good, strong friends such as the Italians."

Berlusconi turned to thank Bush, then looked back at the reporters.

"I am here, first of all, to express our great pain and sadness for the attack on September the eleventh," the Italian president said. "And also I'm here to express to you our desire to be as close as possible and to provide both moral and material support."

Now, Bush said, they would answer a couple of questions.

"These anthrax attacks, sir, do you believe that there is any connection to bin Laden's organization? Your vice president on Friday seemed to suggest there may be a possible link."

"There may be some possible link," Bush replied. "We have no hard data yet, but it's clear that Mr. bin Laden is a man who is an evil man."

With bin Laden bragging about inflicting more pain on the United States, Bush said, there was reason to closely monitor the evidence for a connection.

"We have to find out who's doing this," Bush said. "I wouldn't put it past him."

Agents with the FBI's Hazardous Materials Response Unit pulled into a parking lot near building 1425 at Fort Detrick. In the trunk, they carried the Daschle letter and envelope, sealed with evidence tape inside biohazard containers. The agents took them out and handed them off to John Ezzell, an anthrax specialist at the USAMRIID, the army's infectious disease center.

Ezzell carried the containers to a BSL-3 lab—the second-highest biosafety level. After putting on surgical scrubs, gloves, and a respirator, he brought the containers inside the suite. He cut the evidence tape, opened the containers, and removed the bags and tinfoil holding the letter and envelope. He slid a metal spatula inside the envelope and removed some of the sample.

A small amount of powder floated away. It was light and airy; the spores had likely been purified, the kind that would be used in a biological weapon.

"Oh my God," he said out loud.

• • •

At about that same time, NSA analysts were listening in on a telephone call from Sarajevo that had been picked up from a Croatian listening post.

The discussion between the two men on the line focused on the bombing in Afghanistan. What should be the response in Bosnia? They bantered about American and British targets, then wrapped up their conversation.

"Tomorrow we will start," one of the men said.

The Daschle letter, the envelope, and the powder were processed over the next few hours. Multiple researchers worked with the material, and at least one scientist began to fear sloppy handling had contaminated the office. An investigator left a hot room wearing a single glove—it must have been carrying the microbes that cause anthrax, the scientist feared.

Seventeen people—all of them working on the anthrax attack project, code-named Operation Noble Eagle—had been exposed to the deadly bacteria. The researcher and his colleagues would need to be treated with the antibiotic ciprofloxacin as a precaution.

New orders went out strengthening the safety procedures for researchers at the infectious disease center. Afterward, the Daschle letter was turned over to another scientist for analysis. He was given the letter inside of two ziplock bags. He weighed an empty vial and then placed the Daschle letter through a pass box into the BSL-3 lab. He scraped some of the powder into the vial. Then, violating the rules, he passed the vial with the spores back out and took it for weighing to a BSL-2 lab. The room had a lower safety rating, but he considered the scale to be more accurate.

The next day, he wrote a report on his findings. "The nature of the spore preparation suggests very highly that professional manufacturing techniques were used in the preparation and production."

Then at the bottom of the report, this scientist who had dangerously mishandled the sample typed his name.

Bruce E. Ivins.

The next morning in Sarajevo, the American and British embassies closed. Between the intercepted telephone call from the previous day and earlier intelligence about plots to attack embassies and military bases from a nearby airfield, both countries concluded that their ambassadors and staff were in mortal danger.

Prime Minister Alija Behmen of the Federation government was deeply disappointed in the decision. Both embassies had never shut down during the Bosnian War, a time when buildings all over Sarajevo were being bombed. That certainly was a more threatening time. Closing them now could devastate the international reputation of his struggling country. If Bosnia-Herzegovina was perceived as incapable of guaranteeing the safety of its friends' diplomatic representatives, other nations would certainly be hard-pressed to trust the government.

Worse, both the United States and Britain were key members of the United Nations' military units inside Bosnia-Herzegovina that had been put in place at the end of the war. They had successfully kept control of the bubbling ethnic and nationalistic tensions that might fuel a resumption of hostilities. If the commitment of the Americans and the British waned, the very survival of Bosnia-Herzegovina could be in doubt.

Behmen agreed to an urgent meeting with officials from the American embassy. The senior representative at the meeting, Christopher Hoh, the deputy ambassador, took charge of the discussion.

There were five men who needed to be arrested, Hoh said. They were all Algerians and lived in or around Sarajevo. These people were behind the threats to the embassies, he said, and neither the Americans nor the British would feel secure until the Bosnians put them away.

Behmen assured Hoh that his government was eager to cooperate. If the Americans could just turn over some evidence, the Bosnians would arrest the men immediately.

"We have reasons for having justified suspicions regarding members of this Algerian group as perpetrators of these threats," Hoh said. But he refused to explain why.

Evidence would help, Behmen said. The men could be arrested on suspicion, but couldn't be held forever without proof. Was there *anything* the Americans could provide?

No, Hoh said. But the Federation government should not underestimate the level of American resolve on this issue.

"Unless the authorities arrest these men, the United States will withdraw all embassy personnel and stop any further U.S. support to this country," Hoh said.

He fixed his eyes sternly on Behmen.

"And then let God protect Bosnia-Herzegovina," he said.

5

Brad Berenson was sitting on the couch in Gonzales's office, briefing his bosses about the progress of the Prosper interagency group.

It was 6:00 P.M. on October 18. Weeks had passed since the first meeting had been held at the State Department to devise a plan for trying captured terrorists. A large matrix of options was still under consideration—international war crimes tribunals sponsored by the United Nations, courts-martial, military commissions, federal criminal prosecution. Each choice presented a range of issues that needed to be resolved, such as the crimes that could be charged, standards of evidence, presidential authority to convene hearings, and the rights of suspects.

For fifteen minutes, Berenson described the debate in the Prosper group, laying out how each topic had been considered. The same questions were being mulled over three or four times. It didn't feel as if the discussion was narrowing. In fact, Berenson said, it was expanding.

As he spoke, Flanigan and Addington exchanged glances. This didn't sound good. They had hoped Prosper would wrap up the job quickly, and that certainly wasn't happening.

They're still deciding what kind of corners their conference table should have, Addington thought.

Berenson shrugged. "This thing's going slow," he said. "At this rate, you won't see an order until after Thanksgiving."

The room was silent for a moment. Gonzales gave a half smile, then dropped his head to his chest. Flanigan brought his hand up to his forehead.

"This is ridiculous!" he snapped. "This is starting to be like the damn NSC!"

Things weren't going to get much better, Berenson said. "Look, if you want to keep your hands off this, it's just going to roll along at its own pace," he said. "But then it's going to be a long time before you have the answers you want and, more importantly, before the president has the authority you think he needs."

The discussion ended and Berenson headed back to his office. The other three lawyers stayed behind.

Addington was shaking his head. "We're never going to get there with these guys," he said.

"No," Flanigan replied. "We're not."

They needed other options, the three men agreed. Maybe the best idea would be to forget about the Prosper group and just put together a presidential order on their own, without worrying about other agencies' opinions.

Addington returned to his office. On his computer, he searched for a copy of Roosevelt's original order to convene a military commission.

Tony Blair was frustrated. He had deployed British Special Forces to the fight in Afghanistan but worried that the Bush administration wasn't throwing its complete support behind any particular strategy.

General Franks was a good leader, Blair thought, and the right man to head the military's effort in Afghanistan. Rumsfeld was another issue—the prime minister considered him erratic, wrapped up in bureaucratic turf battles when he should be focusing on winning the war.

Blair was astonished that no one was stepping in to compensate for Rumsfeld's inadequacies. There was no clear political direction coming out of the White House; critical decisions were being shoved off. The Americans had only a halfhearted commitment to the Northern Alliance—a consequence of the Pentagon's sniping at the CIA plan.

The moment had come, the prime minister told his aides, to take a stand— the Americans needed to fully back the Afghani fighters or not. He wanted to plow ahead, but there wasn't much time. They couldn't afford for Washington to keep dithering.

"The Northern Alliance must be sitting there thinking the Americans are just scared of suffering casualties," Blair told an aide.

At 2:00 P.M. On October 17, he reached the president and explained his concern that the administration had not signaled unwavering support to the Northern Alliance.

"We have to go for the Northern Alliance, let them do what they can, put them on a leash if need be, and hold them back later," Blair said.

"You're right, as always," Bush replied. "The Northern Alliance are the best people to help us, but they have to be willing to share power later."

Blair got off the phone feeling cautiously relieved. Bush seemed to have understood his message—the Taliban were not going to fold unless the militias drove them out.

Soldiers with Operational Detachment Alpha 585—an "A-team"—stood before their leader, Master Sergeant John Bolduc. The group, stationed at Fort Campbell, was one of the first Army Special Forces teams in Afghanistan for the battle against the Taliban and al-Qaeda. Today, Bolduc wanted his soldiers to understand that the coming fight to protect their fellow countrymen could well be a suicide mission.

"We might not survive," he told them. "But I want you to fight to the death rather than surrender or be taken prisoner." The enemy was not like any other they had encountered—they honored no military code and would certainly kill anyone they captured in the most brutal and gruesome way they could conceive.

A-Team Detachments 555 and 595 arrived in Afghanistan on October 19. Eleven members of 555 traveled by MH-47 Chinook helicopters to the Panjshir Valley, landing late in the evening at the Jawbreaker camp in Astaneh. There, they received their initial briefing from the CIA operatives.

Meanwhile, twelve members of 595 made it to Darya Suf Valley, linking up with a Northern Alliance force led by General Rashid Dostum. The plan was for the Americans and Afghanis to launch an assault on the strategically important town of Mazar-e Sharif, a Taliban stronghold.

The operation would be difficult. The only means of transportation was horses, which would have to travel some seventy miles to Mazar-e Sharif. The Afghan saddles were too small, and the stirrups too short, but the soldiers managed to keep up with Dostum and his men. The Special Forces commander, Captain Mark Nutsch, was particularly skilled at riding; he had been a rodeo rider and calf-roping champion before joining the army.

Relying on horses created some strategic issues—how, for example, would the animals be fed? Bales of hay would simply be too heavy to lug into battle. Instead, cargo planes flew over Afghanistan, dropping parachutes loaded with hay at prearranged sites.

This band of American and Afghani soldiers proved inordinately superior to the Taliban. Two days after reaching Afghanistan, the fighters located Taliban positions in the Beshcam area, about eight miles from Dostum's headquarters. Nutsch got on the radio and called in airstrikes. Delighted that the enemy would soon be bombed, Dostum radioed the commander of the Taliban unit.

"This is General Dostum speaking," he said. "I am here, and I have brought the Americans with me."

The airstrikes continued as the convoy moved relentlessly toward Mazar-e Sharif. On the journey, they drove enemy forces from more than fifty towns and cities, killing and capturing thousands of Taliban and al-Qaeda soldiers, while destroying vehicles, bunkers, and weapons.

The soldiers were stunned at their success. "We are doing amazingly well with what we have," Captain Nutsch wrote in his first field report. "Frankly, I am surprised that we have not been slaughtered."

Weeks after being rebuffed in Congress, the administration was still ruminating about an unprecedented question: Could the president order the armed forces to conduct military operations inside the United States?

Despite the new powers granted to law enforcement and intelligence agencies since 9/11, there still were no guidelines on the limits of the president's power to pursue terrorist cells already operating inside the country.

As the rules seemed to stand now, the FBI would be in charge. Then all of the rules for a criminal case would come into play—warrants, indictments, lawyers, standard rules of evidence. Afterward, there would have to be trials in federal courts, which the White House lawyers had already decided would put judges and juries in jeopardy.

While the president hadn't yet signed any order, the lawyers knew that captured al-Qaeda members were going to be tried through military commissions. To make sure that terrorists caught in the United States were subjected to those rules, the FBI couldn't arrest them.

But a law had been on the books for more than one hundred years—the Posse Comitatus Act—that specifically prohibited the use of the military for domestic law enforcement operations. Perhaps, Pentagon and White House officials suggested, there was an argument to be made that the law did not apply at a time of war.

The question went to John Yoo in the Office of Legal Counsel. Working with

Robert Delahunty, special counsel in the unit, Yoo reached a definitive conclusion: The century-old law could be ignored.

"We conclude that the President has ample constitutional and statutory authority to deploy the military against international or foreign terrorists operating within the United States," the lawyers wrote in a memo to Gonzales and Haynes.

In undertaking an operation against terrorists inside the country, the military would not be bound by the same constitutional restrictions faced by law enforcement—there would be no need to establish probable cause or to obtain a warrant. Soldiers could raid any domestic location—a house, an office building, a meeting center—and capture any suspect. All they would need was an order from Bush or any other high-ranking administration official.

The White House mess is a group of three small dining areas adjacent to the Situation Room in the basement of the executive mansion. They were elegant, but without pretension—beige linens draped circular and smaller rectangular tables amid wood paneling. The food was tasty, but not what anyone would call gourmet.

Flanigan was there at a junior staff table enjoying his lunch when Addington arrived and dropped into a seat beside him. He held out a few pieces of paper.

"This is my draft of the military commissions order," Addington said. "It's carefully modeled on the Roosevelt order. I'd like you to take a look at it, and give me your thoughts."

Flanigan took the draft and gave it a once-over. After lunch, he went back to his office and reviewed the document more carefully. He marked it up with a pen; there were some issues about how suspected terrorists would be designated for a commission trial and also some problems with timing. But all in all, he thought, Addington had nailed it.

American ground forces were preparing for their first operation in southern Afghanistan. The plan was to launch a parachute assault with about two hundred Rangers from the Third Battalion, Seventy-fifth Ranger Regiment. Their goal: to capture a small desert airfield about fifty miles southwest of Kandahar, a target dubbed Objective RHINO. With the airfield under American control, it could then be used as an arming and refueling point for helicopters carrying Special Operations Forces for the next wave of attacks.

First, the target had to be cleared of Taliban fighters by the Third Battalion's A and C Companies. Then air force B-2 Stealth bombers hit various areas around RHINO, followed by strafing runs by an A-130 gunship.

But the clearing operations missed a particularly grave Taliban position protected by a ZSU-23 antiaircraft gun. It was set on a mountaintop, overlooking the drop zone where the parachuting Rangers would soon be landing.

Just as the transports were carrying the Rangers to the location for their assault, an armed Predator captured the image of the Taliban gun, transmitting it in real time back to CIA headquarters seven thousand miles away.

The video showing the antiaircraft gun appeared on a screen in the agency's Global Response Center in McLean, Virginia. An agency staffer turned to Cofer Black.

"What are we going to do?"

"You're armed?" Black asked.

"Yes."

Black didn't hesitate. "Shoot the thing."

Seconds later, the Predator launched an AGM-114 Hellfire missile. It struck the antiaircraft gun, obliterating the Taliban position. Soon after, the Ranger paratroopers began landing at Objective RHINO. The airfield was secured that same night. Only one Taliban fighter defended it.

John Ashcroft was sitting at his desk, facing the wall, when John Yoo arrived. He swiveled around in his chair, facing the lawyer. Ashcroft was pleased. He had summoned Yoo only minutes before and didn't tolerate dawdling.

The attorney general stood and asked Yoo to follow him to the nearby Sensitive Compartmented Information Facility—the SCIF—where they could conduct a classified discussion. After setting the proper entrance codes and heading inside, Ashcroft went to one of the SCIF's five safes that were used to hold highly classified material. He brought out a document, just a few pages in length.

"What I'm about to talk to you about is extremely sensitive," Ashcroft said. "No one else in the department is allowed to know about it. You are only allowed to talk to me about it."

Yoo was intrigued but still thought the restrictions were odd. He listened without comment.

"This involves surveillance by the NSA," Ashcroft continued. "You've been working on these matters, so you've been brought in on this to offer a legal opinion."

The attorney general held out his hand. "Take this. Let me know when you're finished."

The discussion ended. Ashcroft had told him nothing, no background, no details of the program's operation—Yoo was just supposed to figure it out from the presidential order he had just been handed by the attorney general.

The NSA program had been in operation for about three weeks. Only now was someone going to do the analysis to make sure that the administration wasn't breaking the law.

On the afternoon of October 24, Jack Straw, the British foreign secretary, settled onto a couch in Cheney's ceremonial office. He and some aides had arrived in Washington earlier that day and had proceeded through a series of meetings to discuss the progress in the Afghanistan war.

Cheney was bullish. "The military campaign is going extremely well," he told Straw. "Everything is unfolding the way we planned. We are going to be victorious."

"Yes," Straw said. "But what's the strategy?"

The question was blunt, almost designed to be insulting. The air campaign had begun three weeks before, the British Special Forces teams were deep inside Afghanistan engaged in brutal firefights with Taliban forces, and the Blair government was the Americans' strongest ally in the war. Yet, Straw was suggesting, the Bush administration hadn't yet explained the details of its military plan.

Cheney paused, as if he were thinking through his answer. There was no life in his face; he struck Straw as cold, with slightly menacing body language.

"The Northern Alliance should be taking Mazar soon," Cheney replied. Then he laid out what might follow with the American drive to capture Taliban and al-Qaeda fighters.

Straw listened, unsatisfied.

What is the military strategy? Cheney was talking, but he wasn't answering the question. The words of prediction—"We're going to take this city and we're going to capture that terrorist"—told Straw nothing about how the administration was going to accomplish those goals.

Straw eased around the same question. What was the strategy?

Cheney never answered.

• • •

Little girls' dresses. That was the focus of the next classified mission for the battle in Afghanistan.

The war plan was beginning to show progress. Jawbreaker and the A-teams were advancing, working with the Northern Alliance and American bombers to rout the Taliban from city after city, village after village.

The key tactic now was gaining allies. Local warlords had no particular allegiance to the Taliban. Each of them who could be persuaded to side with the Northern Alliance and the Americans became another wall closing in on the Taliban and, more important, a source of intelligence to help locate, capture, or kill members of al-Qaeda.

Winning them over became a practiced skill. The warlords wanted to support the likely victor, and sometimes that meant demonstrating the overwhelming power of the American military. One warlord questioned a member of a CIA team how, if the Taliban won, he and his people would be kept safe. The intelligence operative pointed at a nearby radio tower.

"Watch that," he said. The operative got on the radio and said a few words.

Minutes passed. Then, an explosion. The tower was gone, destroyed by a missile launched from far away. The tribal leader agreed to oppose the Taliban.

Others wanted to prove to their people that they could provide for them. Power was always in flux in Afghanistan, and each leader sought to keep his villagers as eager supporters. That meant gifts or other benefits.

When the CIA agents arrived at one location, they met with the commander. They explained what they were doing, and that the Taliban were about to fall. What, the warlord was asked, would he need to support the effort?

The answer—little girls' dresses. Nice clothing for the children in his village was a rarity. The boys could make do, but parents hated to see their young daughters dressed so poorly. If the American military could arrange to bring girls' dresses to the warlord, he could distribute them; that would gain him renewed support among his people.

The message was relayed from the field, then back to Ramstein Air Base in Germany. An officer ordered a shopping mission. The dresses were purchased, loaded onto the next cargo plane, then parachuted into an agreed spot in Afghanistan. The CIA delivered the clothes to the warlord.

With that, a new ally was won.

• • •

John Yoo was walking down Pennsylvania Avenue for a meeting at the White House. Shortly before, he had received a call from Flanigan to come over for an important discussion, but he didn't feel the need to rush.

He arrived at the South Gate in about fifteen minutes and, after being cleared through security, headed to the main entry for the West Wing, then upstairs to the White House counsel's suite.

Gonzales and Flanigan were waiting for him. Everyone took a seat around the coffee table. Addington was the last to arrive.

Yoo nodded to him. "Hi, David."

Flanigan held out a piece of paper. "Look at this," he said. "Do you have any thoughts on it?"

Yoo glanced over the document. It was a draft presidential order, setting up military commissions to try terrorists. The wording was familiar.

"This is very similar to the FDR order," he said.

Addington agreed. They had used Roosevelt's order as a template, he explained, making very few changes, since it had already been challenged in the Supreme Court and ruled constitutional.

"Well, it's been sixty years," Yoo said. "A lot has changed since then."

Yoo spent another minute reading.

"This is a huge step," he said. "If the president issues this, it's going to be a big deal."

"We know," Addington replied. "But we think things are going too slowly. We've got to make a decision."

Yoo noticed some wording that suggested that the White House lawyers wanted to exclude the courts from having the authority to review anything related to the commissions. Not a good idea—the Supreme Court had already considered military commissions in the *Quirin* case. That precedent established the authority of the judiciary. The justices wouldn't agree to give that up just because a presidential order said they should.

"Well," Flanigan said, "what, if anything, in here might be considered unconstitutional?"

Before Yoo responded, Addington broke in. "Why *would* any of it be unconstitutional?" he asked. "Tell me if I'm wrong. This is FDR's order. The Supreme Court upheld it. Why would anything in it be unconstitutional?"

Because the court had changed, Yoo replied. "Look, there is a political portion that you're overlooking," he said. "We've got a very divided court. Look at the *Bush v. Gore* lineup. The court is made up of politicians, they're political actors. So just because FDR's court upheld this sixty years ago doesn't mean the court will do the same thing."

Politicians? The other lawyers chuckled. "That's pretty cynical," Flanigan said.

No, thinking otherwise was naive. "I clerked at this court before," Yoo said. "I've seen how the sausage is made. I wish they were like a machine that would do the law in a predictable way, and I think most of the people in this country think they're like that. But they're not."

"I don't buy your explanation of the court," Addington replied. "The court said this in *Ex Parte Quirin,* and that's the law. They're not going to change it."

Yoo shrugged. "They change the law all the time."

There was another issue, Yoo said—nothing legal, just political. The order said that the secretary of defense would have the power to decide who should be tried before a commission. That meant the Justice Department would play no role in dealing with captured terrorists. A criminal prosecution of the 9/11 plotters would never take place. Ashcroft was not going to be happy about that.

Bush and Cheney were eating lunch in the president's private dining room, down a corridor from the Oval Office. This was their usual get-together where they could discuss pressing issues in confidence.

About twenty minutes into the meal, Cheney produced the draft order on military commissions. "This is something my people have been working on," he said, "and I think it deserves serious consideration."

Bush read the short document. He asked no questions and returned it to Cheney.

"This is good," he said. "Let's keep going on this."

"Do you want to bring it to the NSC?" Cheney asked, without mentioning that he opposed doing so. If the members of the National Security Council got their hooks into this, the bureaucratic debate would delay everything.

Bush agreed. Taking the order to the NSC was unnecessary.

"Let's just keep this thing moving," he said.

Ahmed El-Maati had become engaged in the spring to a Syrian woman and had agreed with his fiancée to marry during Ramadan. Now, with the Islamic holy month fast approaching, he and his mother were preparing to travel to Damascus for the wedding.

The timing was perfect. Government agents had not let up on shadowing him—as he walked down the street, when he drove. They made little effort to keep it secret, once tailing him with multiple cars that followed him when he took side streets in relatively untraveled areas. Between the news reports, the surveillance, and the government's refusal to return his lawyer's calls, El-Maati was glad to be getting out of Canada for the month.

As he readied himself, he spent a few days purchasing gifts for his fiancée and her family. He wanted to impress them—marriage was important in his culture, and he had been searching for a wife for more than four years. When he met her months before, he knew that this was the woman he wanted to spend his life with.

As he happily dreamed of his wedding that day, El-Maati couldn't have guessed that he would never see his fiancée again.

Rumsfeld pulled no punches.

"The Northern Alliance is not going to overcome the Taliban," he said. "The CIA's plan is failing."

The militias would not seize strategically important cities, Rumsfeld argued, particularly Mazar-e Sharif. The Afghani capital, Kabul, would not be captured before the brutal winter arrived, and the alliance—even working with the CIA and the A-teams—would be incapable of encircling the city.

To prove his point, Rumsfeld produced an analysis from the Defense Intelligence Agency, handing it out at a meeting of the National Security Council. The report's conclusions were equally stark.

"The Northern Alliance will not secure any major gains before winter," it read.

There was no real option, Rumsfeld argued. The CIA needed to surrender its independent authority and start reporting to General Tommy Franks. The armed forces should take over.

Tenet argued that Rumsfeld was wrong. "We are closing in on our objectives," he said. All they needed was a little more time.

Other members of the National Security Council were skeptical; less than three weeks after the bombings began, there were news articles that proclaimed that the United States was sinking into a quagmire, another Vietnam.

Tenet was steadfast. The plan was going to work.

The battle for Mazar-e Sharif began at dawn on November 5. In the opening salvo, a group of MC-130 aircraft dropped two BLU-82 "Daisy Cutters" on Taliban locations at the city of Aq Kupruk.

American A-Team 595 moved toward enemy positions, but the Taliban counterattacked in an effort to trap the soldiers. Using satellite radios, the Americans called for air support. F-14 jets flew in, strafing the Taliban.

The bombing, followed by Northern Alliance attacks, was relentless. Taliban commanders were killed. An attack on the Taliban forces by an F-18 Hornet aircraft pushed most of the enemy back; on horseback, the Northern Alliance launched a cavalry charge immediately after the explosion. The remaining Taliban retreated to the north.

A Middle Eastern country passed on the intelligence—another al-Qaeda hijacking was in the works, with at least one terrorist planning to divert a Canadian flight to strike a new, high-profile American target.

The information reached CSIS on November 8, and this was something the intelligence services could act on. The country that had developed the intelligence knew the name of a hijacker: Amer El-Maati, the brother of Ahmad, the man with the map.

Amer had long been suspected of being an al-Qaeda member, and the new intelligence said that he had already arrived in Canada to prepare for the hijacking. CSIS provided multiple agencies with the information, but there was no record of Amer having traveled there.

The next morning, Canadian law enforcement dug up another frightening scrap of evidence. Ahmad El-Maati was planning to fly from Canada to Syria, supposedly for an impending wedding. Investigators considered that to be nothing more than a ruse—El-Maati, they feared, might instead be planning to fulfill his brother's hijacking plan.

An official with a division of the Mounties took steps to make sure El-Maati was not allowed to fly. But, unknown to the official, another unit was planning to let him board the plane and place him under surveillance.

The Canadians decided to tell the Syrians nothing about El-Maati's itinerary; there was no threat to their country, and letting them know that a suspected terrorist was arriving in Damascus might put him at personal risk. The CIA, on the other hand, needed to know, since the threat involved the United States.

El-Maati's travel plans were passed to the Americans. They, in turn, notified Syrian intelligence.

• • •

A group of lawyers arrived in Ashcroft's office. Bush had instructed Gonzales to inform the Justice Department about the plans for military commissions, and the attorney general was not pleased with what he heard.

He was particularly angered to find out that two of his *subordinates*—John Yoo and Pat Philbin in the Office of Legal Counsel—had not only known about the proposed order but had even helped the White House write it. And neither of them had said a thing about it to Ashcroft.

Yoo and Philbin were told to come to the meeting, and they were the last to arrive. They already knew this was about the White House plan.

"Tell me why you two are involved in this and why didn't I know about it?" Ashcroft asked.

Philbin answered, explaining that Yoo had been called over to the White House counsel's office and given the draft order without any warning. Yoo had brought it back to the office and discussed it with Philbin. Then the two of them came up with the preliminary thinking about the legality and took that to the White House. Philbin mentioned their research on the *Quirin* case and another Supreme Court decision.

Ashcroft broke in. "Why does Rumsfeld get to decide who's going to be designated for the commissions? Why isn't it me?"

This was weird. They had been in Ashcroft's office for five minutes, and every question had been about turf. Nothing about constitutionality, nothing about how the commissions would work, nothing about their history. Many department lawyers whispered that Ashcroft had no interest in law, only politics, and Yoo had seen that for himself. But on a matter of such import, he thought the attorney general would ask *something* about the law. No such luck.

"We look on that as a legal issue," Philbin said. "This is all going to be reviewed by the courts someday, and it's more likely to be upheld if it's the military deciding who goes to the military courts, because that's a function of fighting war."

On the other hand, Philbin continued, if the attorney general made that decision, it would seem more of a law enforcement effort than a function of a military campaign. That had far less probability of winning court approval.

Ashcroft fumed. The answer wasn't good enough. He wouldn't stand for being cut out. He was going to have to take on Rumsfeld, and win back his turf.

• • •

At a National Security Council meeting that day, Rumsfeld picked up his now-familiar refrain: The CIA plan was a failure. The Northern Alliance would not capture Mazar-e Sharif. The military needed to take over.

On the other side of the table, Tenet was sitting with Hank Crumpton, a legendary CIA operative who led the new Special Operations branch at the Counterterrorist Center. It was Crumpton who crafted the CIA strategy for Afghanistan, and he remained unwavering in his certainty that it would succeed.

The Pentagon was wrong, he argued. "Mazar will fall in the next twenty-four to forty-eight hours," he said.

Not many in the room believed him.

Mazar-e Sharif fell the next day.

The final battle was being waged even as the meeting of the National Security Council was taking place. Taliban fighters, driven back to the north, had dug in on a ridge outside the city, giving them cover as they launched a rocket assault. A-Team 595 called in strikes by B-52 bombers, hitting the Taliban. By late afternoon, the Northern Alliance fought off the Taliban counterattacks and, led by the Special Forces team on horseback, seized the ridge.

The fight came to an end when General Dostum and his Northern Alliance forces seized the city's airport and rode into Mazar-e Sharif. Afghanis poured out of their homes, celebrating and kissing the fighters who had routed the Taliban.

Afterward, General Dostum spoke to Captain Nutsch and his fighters in A-Team 595, expressing his gratitude.

"I asked for a few Americans," he said. "They brought with them the courage of a whole army."

While the fight for Mazar-e Sharif raged, a less deadly war for turf unfolded in the Roosevelt Room at the White House.

The previous day, Ashcroft had demanded a meeting with Gonzales to hash over the military commissions order. It was wrong for the Justice Department to be cut out of this new process, he had groused. This was a dispute that had to be resolved immediately, before the president signed.

Even though it was a Saturday, there was no casual dress; everyone arrived in dark suits. Gonzales came into the room with Addington, Flanigan, and a few others. Ashcroft was accompanied by two of his top aides.

The discussion began abruptly. "You've been going behind our back," Ashcroft snapped, looking at Gonzales. "We wouldn't be in this situation, at this level of disagreement, if you had done the right thing and just involved us in the first place."

While he made no accusation, Ashcroft glanced at Addington as he continued fuming about his sense of betrayal.

Addington leaned in. "This is not something I did on my own. The vice president of the United States asked me to do this."

"Yes, and I'm sure you had nothing to do with that," Ashcroft said, his tone dripping with sarcasm.

"There really isn't an issue here for DOJ, except as to form and legality of the presidential order," Addington continued. "This is an issue with respect to the president exercising his commander-in-chief power, which, Mr. Attorney General, is not your area."

Ashcroft looked at Gonzales. "I don't think this is appropriate unless the attorney general of the United States decides who's in and who's out of this military system," he said. "Otherwise, you're creating a system that stands outside the justice system."

"That's the point," Addington said.

"*You* created this mischief!" Ashcroft barked at Addington, pointing a finger at him. "You created this havoc by not bringing DOJ in!"

"I'll bring in who I'm asked to bring in by the vice president of the United States."

Ashcroft turned away from Addington. He would no longer acknowledge that the vice president's lawyer was in the room.

He stared at Gonzales. "The person who did this is the spawn of the devil!" Ashcroft boomed.

The room went silent. Addington was Satan's son? No one knew how to respond. Gonzales let the comment pass.

"We'll have to tee this up for further discussion," he said. There would have to be another meeting, this time with Cheney.

Bin Laden closed his grip around an AK-74 Kalakov assault rifle as he crossed a basement banquet hall at the Jalalabad Islamic studies center. A crowd of about one thousand tribal leaders had just feasted on lamb kabobs, rice, and hummus, and now awaited the al-Qaeda leader's words.

It was the afternoon of that same day. The Saudi-funded Islamic institute where the crowd gathered had been converted to an al-Qaeda intelligence outpost in the days after 9/11, but with the Americans and the Northern Alliance moving relentlessly toward Jalalabad, bin Laden had decided that it was time to fall back.

As bin Laden approached a podium, the people in the room grew silent; the only sounds were of American bombs exploding nearby. The al-Qaeda leader, dressed in a long shirt and camouflage jacket, praised God before launching into a fiery speech.

"The Americans had a plan to invade," he said, "But if we are united and believe in Allah, we will teach them a lesson, the same one we taught the Russians!"

As he spoke, there were shouts from the crowd. *God is great! Down with America! Down with Israel!*

"God is with us, and we will win the war," bin Laden said. "Your Arab brothers will lead the way. We have the weapons and the technology. What we need most is your moral support. And may God grant me the opportunity to see you and meet you again on the front lines."

Bin Laden stepped away from the podium. The crowd rose to their feet and began to chant. *Long live Osama! Long live Osama!*

The al-Qaeda leader placed his right hand over his heart as envelopes of cash were dispensed to the tribal leaders. Then fifteen guards surrounded bin Laden and whisked him out the door.

The lines were drawn for the meeting the next day: the attorney general versus the vice president. And Andy Card, the White House chief of staff, would referee.

A large group of officials, including both Ashcroft and Rumsfeld, arrived early in the Roosevelt Room. Ashcroft was jovial, and everyone engaged in lighthearted banter. Cheney walked in and took a seat at the center of the table. He said a few pleasant words to Ashcroft.

"All right," Cheney began. "There are some issues we need to resolve. What are they?"

Addington spoke up. "Well, Mr. Vice President, the issues are—"

Ashcroft interrupted. "What we need to discuss is what's the role of DOJ going to be in making designations for military commissions."

"Well," Cheney began, "from what I understand from the lawyers, we need to be concerned about how the courts—"

"No, we don't need to be concerned about that," Ashcroft said, interrupting again.

Cheney stopped speaking and lowered his head. Some of the people watching thought he was counting to ten, trying to avoid getting angry.

The door opened and Card stepped into the room, looking cheerful. "All right," he said as he took a chair beside Cheney. "What do we need to resolve here?"

Ashcroft spoke. "We've got to make sure that this order preserves the DOJ's role in these prosecutions. I am the president's top law enforcement official. We need to have some role in deciding whether or not we take these cases before a grand jury."

"Well," Cheney began, "I understand if we had that role for the DOJ, it will open it up for attack—"

"No, I don't think that's true," Ashcroft said, speaking over Cheney.

The two kept talking simultaneously with Cheney expecting the attorney general to stop. When Ashcroft kept going, Cheney went silent.

On another side of the table, Rumsfeld watched without speaking a word. He wasn't eager to be the one choosing which suspects would be tried by the commissions, but he was perfectly happy to allow Ashcroft to undermine his own argument by making a fool of himself.

The debate continued for another few minutes, getting nowhere. Card wrapped it up. "I'm going to talk to the president about this," he said. With passions running this high, Bush was going to have to play peacemaker.

Ashcroft returned to his office, certain he had lost out to Rumsfeld. "Chalk up another win for the rock star," he said to an aide.

The dispute was presented to Bush. No matter which department he chose to make the designations, Bush was told, somebody was going to walk away furious.

He gave it a moment's thought. Maybe he just needed to take both the Pentagon *and* the Justice Department out of the mix. Hell, he was the commander in chief.

"I'll do it," he said.

Ahmad El-Maati and his mother had just obtained boarding passes for their flight out of Toronto Pearson International Airport. They joined the security line; it was moving slowly, but El-Maati was comfortable that they had enough time to make their flight.

Two officers approached.

"Sir, could you please step out of line?"

El-Maati blinked. "Is there a problem?"

"Sir, I just need you to step out of line, please."

His mother was escorted away, and El-Maati was taken downstairs by two detective sergeants. They asked him a series of questions—why was he traveling, when had he planned his trip? They removed the gifts he was carrying in a bag and asked him why he had them. Meanwhile, in another part of the airport, other police officers were interviewing his mother about the itinerary.

The questioning dragged on, and the two missed their flight. Finally, El-Maati and his mother were escorted through security to the boarding gate for the next plane. Two undercover officers monitored them on the first leg of their trip, from Toronto to Vienna, but stopped there. The plane to Damascus, they decided, was Syria's problem.

El-Maati was shaken, but by the time the plane landed the following day, he had put the experience behind him. He was excited about seeing his fiancée and her family, who were waiting inside the terminal. At immigration, he presented his documents to an agent, who punched his name into the computer.

The agent looked up from the screen and asked El-Maati to come to a nearby office. There, Syrian officials checked his papers, then escorted him to his luggage, leaving his mother behind.

"Follow us outside," one of the officials said.

El-Maati stepped through the airport doors. Without a word, someone grabbed his arms and handcuffed him. A car drove up, a door flung open, and El-Maati was shoved inside.

As the car pulled away, someone slipped a black hood over his head.

The four-page military commissions order was finished the following day. Cheney brought it in a folder to his weekly lunch with Bush and passed it over the table.

The president put on his glasses and silently read. "That's it," he said. "Ready to go."

Lunch ended and Cheney took the order with him. Even though Bush had given his oral approval, the document still had to go through a final processing before it was ready to sign. Cheney handed it over to Addington, who in turn brought it to the White House counsel's office. Once Flanigan took charge of the paperwork, he called Brad Berenson over from the Eisenhower Executive Office Building.

"This is the order," Flanigan told him. "It's ready for the president's signature."

Bush had already reviewed the document, Flanigan said, and it should be taken to him right away. Since the president was about to leave for his ranch in Crawford, he said, forget about the usual, detailed process that preceded the signing of an order. Berenson took the document and headed to the White House basement. Before the order could be presented to Bush, it had to be logged with the office of the staff secretary, Harriet Miers.

When Berenson arrived, he found Miers's second in command, Stuart Bowen. Berenson told him that he had an order for Bush's signature. Bowen was dumbstruck—there was a procedure for reviewing and coordinating the presentation of documents to the president. It wasn't some rapid-fire undertaking.

This had to go through the staff, Bowen protested. Every assistant or advisor with a stake in the new rules had to sign off. That was fundamental. The president needed a full range of advice to avoid making a mistake.

"Brad, there's a process for this," he said. "I've handled thousands of documents, and I've never bypassed that procedure."

"It's urgent," Berenson replied. "the president is waiting to sign this. As I understand it, somebody already briefed the president, and he's already approved it."

After some more back-and-forth, Bowen reluctantly gave in. He knew Bush's schedule; the president would be leaving for Crawford in a matter of minutes. If Bush was going to sign the order, Bowen said, they had to hurry.

The two men rushed up the stairs. Outside the window of the Oval Office, they could see *Marine One* landing on the helipad. The president would be leaving momentarily.

Bush glanced up. "Hey, Brad, Stuart, how you doing?"

"Fine sir, thank you," Bowen said. "Mr. President, there's a document that requires your signature before you leave. It's the military order authorizing the secretary of defense to establish military commissions."

Bush walked from behind his desk toward the sitting area. Bowen opened up the blue portfolio containing the order. Bush scanned it impassively.

He signed with a felt-tip marker.

6

How can he do that?

Neal Katyal, a visiting professor at Yale Law School, watched CNN in disbelief. A news crawl at the bottom of the screen read that Bush had just issued an order creating military commissions to try suspected terrorists. Katyal jumped up off the couch where he had been sitting with his wife, Joanna Rosen, and strode to the computer. The news report couldn't be accurate.

This was not a new issue for Katyal. Years before, as a lawyer in the Clinton Justice Department, he had researched a similar proposal, concluding that the president could not construct his own legal system: Congress had to approve legislation establishing the arrangement, the president had to sign it, and the courts had to uphold the new rules from certain challenge. That was basic constitutional law out of a seventh-grade civics class. But from the sound of it, Bush had decided to skip a few steps and instead rule by presidential decree.

Katyal sat at the computer and saw he could access the Internet only by phone; he and his wife had just moved to New Haven and were staying at the home of another professor who apparently didn't want to pay for broadband.

The modem connected to the dial-up service provider with the usual squeaks and squawks. Katyal opened a browser and typed in the address for the White House Web site.

Slowly, the page loaded, and Katyal found the order. As he read it, he chuckled. This had to be a joke. Some hacker was playing around and had set up a fake Internet page designed to look like the White House site. The release was too preposterous to be true.

Checking the address, Katyal felt his heart drop. This was no fake. Bush had engaged in an unconstitutional power grab.

Katyal's sense of alarm grew as he kept reading. Bush proclaimed that he could set up a trial system on his own, then determine what constituted a crime and what rights would be afforded the defendants. He would handpick the prosecutors, the defense attorneys, and the judge. He declared that a suspect could be convicted based on the votes of just two-thirds of the panel. His administration was going to determine the punishments, including life imprisonment and death.

Katyal read down to the last lines of the order.

"The individual shall not be privileged to seek any remedy . . . in any court of the United States, or any State thereof."

Amazing. Bush believed that he could establish a new legal system, and then declared his order exempt from judicial review? Had anyone in the White House even *read* the Constitution?

Less than half an hour after the announcement, Stephen Hadley, the deputy national security advisor, knocked on Flanigan's door. Inside he found Addington hunkered down, trying to avoid the backlash from officials who had been cut out of the debate that led to the commissions decision.

Hadley was slow to anger, but his face was etched with disappointment. He fixed his gaze on Cheney's counsel.

"You should have trusted me on this," he said, an edge to his voice. "You know how the process works."

Everyone heard the unspoken message. Hadley wasn't there just for himself. He was an emissary of Rice. The national security advisor was fuming, too.

"David, you know Dick has to have his papers managed," Hadley said. Cheney often wanted to sidestep usual procedures. Bush needed to be protected from premature, poorly briefed decisions.

Addington shrugged. "The vice president and the president wanted to do it this way," he said. "They're in charge, so that's how it got done."

As Hadley spoke, Flanigan thought of another run-in he'd had minutes before, that time with Harriet Miers, the staff secretary. She would never raise her voice or hurl accusations—she was too nice for that—but she had also bitterly criticized the way the commissions order had been handled. Flanigan, she said, should have made sure that things were done the right way.

Flanigan had nodded sympathetically, biting his tongue. Was she kidding? Was Hadley? Cheney wanted something to go straight to Bush, and *the staff* was supposed to stop that runaway train?

Jim Haynes was in his office at the Pentagon when the call came in from John Bellinger, the legal advisor to the National Security Council.

There were no pleasantries.

"Did you know about this?" Bellinger asked.

"Yes," Haynes replied. "I knew about it."

Bellinger said nothing.

"Go talk to Judge Gonzales if you have a complaint," Haynes said.

As soon as Hadley left, Bellinger stormed into the White House Counsel's suite and through the open door to Gonzales's office.

"What is going on?" he barked. "Why wasn't I informed? Why weren't we brought in?"

Gonzales stood and closed the door.

"It's very serious that the NSC staff was not involved," Bellinger said, his voice raised. "We should have been part of this. *I* should have been part of this."

As Bellinger's steady drumbeat of criticism mounted, Gonzales reverted to type, nodding his head without saying a word.

They couldn't hear what was being said in Gonzales's office, but Flanigan and Addington understood the message. Bellinger's tone and volume were enough to communicate his wrath.

Addington turned to Flanigan and smiled. "Hey," he said. "I hope he offers to resign."

Bellinger took a breath. "Judge, you always say there is one team. So is there one team? Or two?"

"Well, John," Gonzales said, "we have one team, but there are certain matters where it's important to have smaller meetings."

Bellinger circled back, explaining that the National Security Council couldn't do its job if it was left in the dark on policy development. Gonzales listened, nodded, and told Bellinger he appreciated his thoughts.

As Bellinger left the office, the White House counsel took a seat. While

Gonzales had been willing to allow the new policy to be developed outside the normal channels, Bellinger had persuaded him that adopting the unusual process had been a mistake. The National Security Council should have been included in the discussion. But there was nothing that could have been done about it—Bush and Cheney had wanted to keep the commissions order secret from most of the senior staff until it was too late to stop.

In the heart of downtown Damascus, blocks from the lush Sheraton Hotel, stands an unassuming group of three unattractive concrete buildings. There, behind thick concrete walls patrolled by heavily armed guards, reside the damned—prisoners held by Syrian military intelligence at Far' Falastin, or the Palestine Branch.

This place would now be the home of Ahmad El-Maati, who had just been snatched from the Damascus Airport. After he arrived, El-Maati was hustled inside and up a flight of stairs to an office. There, Syrian officials opened his suitcases, tossing his clothes and personal items to the floor and pocketing the gifts he brought for his in-laws. But they wanted something else.

"Where are the documents?" one asked. "Where is the map?"

El-Maati asked them to explain. In response, they punched and kicked him, then led him to a dark hallway in the basement. Along the wall were narrow doors, like small closets. Number five was opened, and the Syrians threw him inside.

The cell had no window, no light, no toilet, and reeked of urine and feces. It was only about three feet wide, and his head almost reached the ceiling. El-Maati felt as if he were standing in his own coffin.

The door slammed shut and El-Maati stood alone in the darkness, perplexed and terrified. From upstairs, he heard screaming.

At nine o'clock that night, an elongated Toyota Corolla came to a stop in Jalalabad, about the sixth car in a convoy of hundreds. The back door opened, and bin Laden emerged, gripping a machine gun. As he barked orders at his men, he seemed nervous; he was heading to an al-Qaeda base at Tora Bora, trying to stay ahead of the American bombers and the advancing Northern Alliance troops.

Bin Laden stood under a tree beside a mosque, flanked by dozens of guards. He met with the governor of Jalalabad, then both men spoke with the son of the city's patriarch, who had ties to both al-Qaeda and the Taliban.

The discussions ended, and bin Laden returned to his car. Then he and his al-Qaeda fighters fled town, taking a rocky dirt road toward Tora Bora.

Just before dawn, the Northern Alliance began its wild dash for Kabul.

Military leaders in the Pentagon had been planning for a calculated assault, fearful that the Taliban would brutally repel a direct attack by the Northern Alliance on the capital city. General Franks wanted plans drawn up for paratroopers to drop somewhere near Kabul, hoping to lure the enemy away from the front lines north of the capital and opening the way for the Northern Alliance to storm into the city.

But with the Taliban rapidly falling apart, Northern Alliance leaders didn't want to wait. Instead, General Mohammed Fahim, defense minister of the Northern Alliance, moved his forces ahead of schedule across the Shomali Plain. Taliban resistance evaporated. Thousands of fighters advanced twelve miles in record time. Near the city, the roads were littered with the bodies of former Northern Alliance supporters who had switched sides to the Taliban in what proved to be a fatal gamble.

The leaders of the American coalition feared a hasty influx of fighters into Kabul, and Fahim agreed. Quickly pouring into the city might threaten—and frighten—some of its Pashtun tribal leaders; the situation called for a more measured approach. To ensure that his troops didn't succumb to the thrill of the chase, Fahim ordered armored vehicles into position to block the advance.

Hours later, the Northern Alliance reached Kabul in orderly fashion. People rushed into the street, arms raised in exultation. A chant arose from the crowd.

Kill the Taliban! Kill the Taliban!

About 6:30 that same morning at his West Village home in Manhattan, Michael Ratner poured himself a cup of coffee and lay down on his couch. Following his morning routine, he picked up that day's *New York Times* and scanned the front page. A headline caught his eye.

Bush Sets Option of Military Trials in Terrorist Cases

That immediately captured his interest. As president of the Center for Constitutional Rights, a public interest law firm that used the courts to defend civil liberties, he spent much of his time fighting what his organization deemed as inequities in the justice system. But this sounded as if the Bush administration was planning to abandon that system entirely.

As he read on, Ratner's dismay grew. Inside the paper, the *Times* had printed the text of the order, and it was worse than he feared. The *president* would decide who was a terrorist, personally designating defendants for the commissions. The government could put anyone—picked up anywhere—on trial. The prosecution would not have to prove guilt beyond a reasonable doubt. There would be no strict rules of evidence. No one would be able to challenge his incarceration in the courts. The administration could hold anyone it chose, forever, without having to prove a damn thing.

This is unbelievable, he thought.

He went for the phone and called Bill Goodman, the center's legal director.

"Bill, go pick up the *Times* right now," Ratner said. "You will be completely floored by what you see."

He summarized the details of Bush's gambit. "Essentially, the president is taking over the country," Ratner said. "And we have to figure out what to do about it."

"Okay, I'll look at this," Goodman said.

They agreed to meet at the office immediately. There, they reviewed the order line by line. The more they understood it, the worse it seemed.

"This idea that you can hold people forever is unbelievable," Ratner said.

"Michael, I agree with you. We're going to have to do something."

In a matter of seconds, they decided. They would wait until the first defendants were moved into the military commissions system. And then they would run immediately to court to fight the administration.

His classroom was filling up with law students when Neal Katyal arrived carrying copies of Bush's military commissions order.

The discussion this day, he thought, was sure to surprise his students. For weeks, Katyal had given lectures about presidential authority, advancing his views that the clout of the executive branch increased markedly at a time of war. He had argued that a president could order the rendition of a suspected terrorist from another country. He had voiced his support for the Patriot Act, the controversial, recently passed statute granting law enforcement new muscle in dealing with terrorists. Katyal's support of executive power during a national threat was so consistent that students often joked that the government could do nothing he would deem outside the law.

Today, he would prove them wrong.

"Okay," he announced as he handed the document around. "Here is something that I think is *really* unconstitutional."

Katyal spoke passionately, criticizing Bush for ignoring Congress and the courts in making this declaration. Under the process used by Bush, he said, a president could declare laws independently, with no checks or balances.

As one student listened, she had a thought. She had once worked for Senator Leahy, who sat on the Judiciary Committee. Katyal would make a perfect witness for a hearing on the military commissions order. Maybe that was something she could arrange.

Two guards brought El-Maati into a poorly lit room. George Salloum, the head of interrogations, waited inside. He smiled as he approached his new prisoner.

"There is no point hiding information," Salloum said. "I already know so much about you."

In a calm voice, Salloum ticked off El-Maati's address in Toronto, plus the make, color, and license-plate number of his car. The moment was terrifying—the Canadians, El-Maati thought, had to be working with the Syrians.

Salloum leaned in and spoke slowly. "Tell me about the map."

El-Maati blurted out the now-familiar story. It wasn't his truck with the map. He had borrowed it. He had done nothing wrong.

A pause. Then someone hit him in the face. Then again. And again. El-Maati was on the ground, and the guards kicked him in the head, in the torso, in the groin.

The days of torture ran together. El-Maati was blindfolded and told to strip to his shorts. His hands were cuffed behind his back and to his legs, and he was forced onto his stomach. Ice water was poured over him. He was whipped with the splayed metal wires from an industrial electric cable on the bottoms of his feet, his thighs, his knees, his back. Pain seared through his body; blood blinded his eyes.

These people are not human! Maybe some kinds of devils from hell!

"Please!" El-Maati begged. "Tell me! Tell me what you want me to say!"

Salloum smiled. "No. It isn't time yet."

The torture resumed. El-Maati could hear nothing but the sounds of his own screams.

A cloth was swabbed over a keyboard in Building 1425 at the military's infectious disease center. It was evening, and the offices were empty. Bruce Ivins, the anthrax researcher, walked from place to place in a "cold area"—a work space that was supposed to be free of bacteria and viruses. He wiped about twenty areas—desks, telephones, computers—and stored the samples for testing.

The next day, the results came in. The office area contained colonies of anthrax bacteria. Ivins destroyed the samples he had gathered.

That evening, he worked alone again. He went to the spots he had tested and cleansed them with bleach. If done correctly, that would kill the microbes.

Under the strict rules for the lab, Ivins was not supposed to test for bacteria or try to kill them without the direct involvement and approval of a supervisor. But he told no one of his effort to hide the contamination.

The interests of the Americans and the Northern Alliance had diverged. Having marched unimpeded into Kabul, the Afghanis now focused on consolidating their power in the capital city; crushing the surviving al-Qaeda forces and the Taliban army remained a distant second on their priorities list. They had no interest in pursuing the terrorists as they fled farther into eastern Afghanistan.

With the strong fighting forces unavailable, the Americans turned to the ragtag ones. The job of cobbling together Afghani militias for the continuing battles fell to Gary Berntsen, commander of the CIA's Jawbreaker forces in the eastern region. With commanders in eastern Afghanistan mostly aligned with the Taliban, Berntsen was able to win over only four groups of fighters, totaling about 2,500 troops. The two largest were led by bitter enemies, Commanders Hazrat Ali and Mohammed Zaman Ghun Shareef, whose factions would soon be shooting at each other rather than at Taliban or al-Qaeda fighters.

But these bands were willing to join with the Americans—for Berntsen, a distasteful choice but the only one available. The combined militias were dubbed the Eastern Alliance and immediately joined the hunt for bin Laden in Afghanistan.

The torture of Ahmad El-Maati continued, without interrogation, for two days. Finally, bloodied and raw, El-Maati again pleaded with his tormentors to let him talk and at last they said yes.

"Tell me what you know about some of these Arabs living in Canada," Salloum said.

He listed names. Some of them El-Maati recognized. Others he didn't.

"Tell me about Abdullah Almalki."

"I know him in passing," El-Maati replied. Their contact was minimal—he knew nothing about Almalki's business of repacking radios for a Pakistani company. He also didn't know how the Syrians got his name.

"What about Maher Arar?"

The man who had eaten at Mango's with Almalki, who raised suspicions because investigators believed he had walked in the rain.

"I know him," El-Maati said. "But only in passing."

The questioning stopped, and one of the Syrians pulled a bag over El-Maati's head. They began to beat him again, without asking any questions. The new round of torture lasted for a week, maybe more. He lost track of time.

For the Northern Alliance, the best intelligence about Kabul came from the city's residents. They pointed out Taliban and al-Qaeda members who were trying desperately to hide among the crowds. They led soldiers to Taliban safe houses, weapons caches, and supply sites. They turned over locals who had chosen to help the Taliban, unless the townspeople decided to kill the collaborators themselves.

Northern Alliance troops showed up at one of the buildings that citizens had identified as an al-Qaeda safe house, kicked in the door, and swept through the building. No one was there, but the place was littered with intelligence materials, including computers, documents, manuals, and other records.

One soldier looked on the floor and found some papers issued in Canada—a patient card for Toronto General Hospital and a letter from a government agency in Ottawa. Both were for the same man, Amer El-Maati, the brother of Ahmad El-Maati. In a matter of days, the United States informed the Syrians about the newly found link between al-Qaeda and the brother of their recently arrived prisoner.

Lower Manhattan was on the verge of ruin.

For weeks, as work and rescue crews dug through the rubble at Ground Zero, pressure had been building on the retaining walls that held back the Hudson River. Now surrounding debris had caused the barriers to become unstable. Water flowed through a growing number of cracks and the engineers feared the structure could soon collapse.

The ensuing deluge would expose the already battered city to a new tragedy of almost incomprehensible proportions. The Hudson would flood lower Manhattan. Water would pour into the subways; anyone riding on them in those neighborhoods would surely drown. The workers at Ground Zero would be buffeted by the torrent, and some would die. While it was impossible to tell how far the river would flow into the city, there was no question that a good portion of Manhattan would be underwater.

Representatives from a handful of structural engineering and construction firms traveled to the White House to brief officials on the situation and to ask for help. These contractors—including AMEC, Bovis Lend Lease, Tulley, Turner/Plaza, LZA Thornton Tomasetti, and others—had been unsung heroes of 9/11, bringing equipment, workers, and other resources to Ground Zero almost immediately after the towers collapsed. They arrived on-site without contracts or guarantee of payment and they had taken on the dangerous engineering jobs with no protection from liability if another tragedy struck.

The contractors brought the sobering message to the White House domestic policy office in the West Wing. One construction manager gave a presentation about the growing instability of the walls.

"We're shoring them up as best we can," the executive said. "But it's obviously a very chaotic, messy situation."

One official asked: What would be the impact if the walls collapsed? While the potential death toll could not even be estimated, other outcomes were predictable. The flooding of the subways would shut down New York's transportation system. The New York Stock Exchange, the investment banks, and the brokerage firms—hell, all of Wall Street—would shutter. The global economic impact could well be epic.

Fighting the catastrophe once it began would be a significant challenge, the executives warned, since there might not be any contractors to handle the work. The engineering and construction firms already on-site would lose their equipment, their people—everything. Even if the businesses survived the devastation, they would be financially wrecked; their insurance policies wouldn't come close to covering the damages, if they paid off at all.

"We really need to get some help getting a contractual indemnity in place," the executives said. "Ours are very big companies, and their survival is at risk. If there's a flood, we will all go bankrupt."

The White House officials pledged to research ways that they could lawfully protect the companies in the event that the walls collapsed. But they could make no promises about whether the government would be able to help.

Before the meeting ended, everyone in the room struck a pact—word of the potential disaster would not be disclosed, not even to workers at Ground Zero. New York was still shell-shocked from 9/11 and the anthrax attacks; this news about a chance—just a chance—of calamity would cause a new panic and probably shut the city for months.

Instead, the engineering firms would monitor the retaining walls closely. If they found that disaster was inevitable, the government would launch a rescue operation to save the residents and workers in downtown Manhattan.

Slowly, over a matter of days, the Syrians told El-Maati what they wanted him to say. Admit to attending a terrorist camp in Afghanistan, admit that Arar and Almalki were there, too. It was a script, El-Maati knew, but one that might lessen the daily infliction of agonizing pain. His resistance crumbled. Yes, he said, it was true. He had received military training from al-Qaeda in 1993. Almalki and Arar had joined him at the same camp.

Next, his brother. The guards demanded that he confess to having attended flight school at his brother's instruction so that he could prepare for a suicide mission similar to the 9/11 attacks. El-Maati acknowledged that he took a few flying lessons, but quit long ago; the "plot" made no sense, he told his captors. The Syrians accepted El-Maati's logic and revised the script. It wasn't a plane, it was a truck bomb. Their suggested target: the American embassy in Ottawa. That, one interrogator said, was why El-Maati had been carrying the map of federal facilities—except the embassy was not on it.

Suddenly El-Maati understood. The Syrians were torturing him so that he would invent a story that they could dangle in front of the Americans. They wanted to show that they had caught a big fish and were working to protect the United States. The Syrians and the CIA had already begun swapping intelligence about al-Qaeda. This new information might solidify their budding relationship.

El-Maati's mind raced. He didn't want to confess to planning an attack on the American embassy—then he might be sent to prison in the United States instead of Canada. He had to change the story.

"No, no!" he shrieked. "It's not the U.S. embassy! It's the Canadian Parliament!"

As he confessed to the horrific, yet imaginary, crime, El-Maati saw a broad smile split Salloum's face, an image that would haunt him for years to come.

In Karachi, a scientist named Yazid Sufaat was speaking to Khalid Sheikh Mohammed about lethal bacteria.

Sufaat was a member of Jemaah Islamiyah, the Southeast Asian Islamic terrorist group affiliated with bin Laden. But in recent months, he had assumed a more important role as al-Qaeda's top bioweapons expert, charged with growing deadly anthrax spores that could be used to kill thousands.

Sheikh Mohammed, the 9/11 mastermind, had been told about the anthrax program months before by Mohammed Atef, al-Qaeda's military chief. He had assumed that the special laboratory in Kandahar was being used to develop the microorganisms—suspicions largely confirmed over the summer when he had helped move multiple crates containing biological lab equipment from Karachi to the secret site.

But Sufaat would no longer be conducting anthrax research in Afghanistan. With al-Qaeda fleeing the country, he had decided to move his lab to Pakistan, and was spending six days there at Sheikh Mohammed's house as he prepared to resume his work.

During a lengthy conversation, Sufaat told Sheikh Mohammed for the first time about details of his role as the head of the anthrax program.

"I'm very happy with my work," Sufaat said.

He particularly enjoyed mentoring younger al-Qaeda members who were helping with the program. He had been giving biology lessons to two young terrorist operatives, Sufaat said, and they had proved to be very able assistants.

"Do you worry about the danger of your research?" Sheikh Mohammed asked.

"No," Sufaat replied. "There's nothing to worry about."

He and his assistants had all received anthrax inoculations, Sufaat said, and there was no reason to doubt their effectiveness.

Through myriad go-betweens that disguised the real customer, Sufaat had obtained the drugs from the Bioport Corporation, the same company that supplied the vaccines for American soldiers. To ensure effectiveness, Bioport had turned to an integrated product team, a group of top experts in the field—including Bruce Ivins, the psychologically troubled anthrax researcher.

A silver Toyota hatchback tore down Highway 4 past Takteh Pol, just south of Kandahar. The village wasn't much of a village at all, just adobe huts sprinkled around a few dilapidated structures that might once have been buildings.

It was November 24. The fighting in Kandahar was reaching a fever pitch, with the Northern Alliance about to overrun the city. The car's driver, Salim

Hamdan, was fleeing the raging combat, trying to make his way to Pakistan, where his wife and daughter were waiting.

Taliban 107-millimeter artillery rockets struck the ground nearby, sending up clouds of dirt with each explosion. A roadblock loomed ahead amid the chaos, and Hamdan slowed down. As he rolled to a halt, he saw Pashtun troops stopping cars and searching passengers.

The fighters blocked a van directly ahead of Hamdan. Two men emerged from the vehicle and were swarmed by angry troops. As that drama unfolded, another soldier opened Hamdan's door and ordered him out. The soldier barked at him to stay still and fired a gun at his feet. Hamdan was terrified; he knew there were two AK-47s inside a bag in the car.

Suddenly, up by the van, a scuffle. The driver had grabbed a grenade and pulled the pin. The soldiers jumped him, scrambling to snatch the explosive, but there was no need—it failed to detonate. Angered by the attempt, the Pashtun combatants leveled their guns at the two men and fired. Even when both had collapsed in bloody heaps, the troops continued to pump bullets into their lifeless bodies.

Hamdan saw only the shooting; he knew nothing of the grenade. He believed that the Pashtun could be frighteningly brutal—he had heard stories about some of their fighters playing soccer with the head of a Russian soldier during the war against the Soviets. They had just searched his car, and now they would be coming for him. He couldn't stay. He didn't want to die.

Hamdan ran up a ridge alongside the road and slid into a gully, illogically hoping that the Pashtun soldiers would be unable to find him. Within seconds, the fighters yanked him out and dragged him back to the road. They hit him, knocked him to his knees. They were going to kill him, one soldier snarled as he pointed a gun at Hamdan's head.

Major Henry Smith of the army heard the commotion.

He and his soldiers were fighting alongside the Northern Alliance in the battle for Kandahar and had just survived a Taliban ambush the previous night at Takteh Pol. Now, as his team was preparing for the next leg of the attack, the shouting and gunfire erupted. Some Afghanis ran to Smith, stuttering that something important had happened. He walked to the checkpoint, where angry Pashtun were milling around. He glanced to the right and saw fighters pulling a man who was struggling to get away.

A Pashtun soldier approached, motioning to the back of the Toyota. "Take a look at this," he said.

The hatchback was open. Inside, Smith saw two SA-7 antiaircraft rockets. He realized that this was the car of the man he had just seen being dragged off. He walked over and heard the Afghans saying they were about to kill him. Smith stepped in.

"No, no, no," he said, his hands raised.

He called out to some of his guys. "Take positive control of this man," he said, pointing at Hamdan.

The American soldiers took Hamdan away and secured him under guard to ensure that the Afghanis had no opportunity to murder him. He was taken to an empty building where he was restrained with a hood over his head. A medic examined him, and the soldiers gave him food and water.

Hamdan understood that Smith had saved his life. And soon, the major would learn that his quick actions had led to the capture of a critical source of intelligence—Salim Hamdan was Osama bin Laden's personal driver.

That same day, hundreds of Taliban fighters gathered on a dusty desert road near Mazar-e Sharif. It was a hazy, cold Saturday, and the soldiers had just fled Kunduz, the latest target of the American air assault. They had come to meet the Northern Alliance. And surrender.

General Dostum, who had led the Northern Alliance in capturing Mazar-e Sharif weeks before, handled the negotiations. He offered the Taliban representatives a deal: If the native Afghanis laid down their weapons, they could go home. But the foreigners fighting alongside them would have to be turned over to Dostum. The Afghanis agreed and returned to their men.

"Surrender your gun in the name of the Koran," a Taliban leader called out, explaining nothing about the terms of the agreement with Dostum.

The weapons were taken from the fighters by Dostum's men and laid on the ground. As promised, the Afghanis were released; the foreigners were told to climb into the back of flatbed trucks. Uncertain if they were to be killed or imprisoned, the men hid guns and grenades in their clothing. The Northern Alliance failed to search them.

"Take them to Qala-i-Jangi," Dostum called out.

His forces knew the location well—it was a sprawling, nineteenth-century fortress that served as their commander's headquarters. Hundred-foot pale yellow walls surrounded the two compounds inside, sealing them off from entry or escape.

As the sun set, the convoy reached the main gate on the east side of the stronghold. The trucks pulled to a stop, and Northern Alliance soldiers unloaded the enemy fighters.

A prisoner hid a grenade in his hand as Nadir Ali, one of Dostum's senior commanders, approached. When Ali was a few feet away, the Taliban fighter pulled the pin and waited. Seconds later, the abrupt explosion pierced the sounds in the courtyard, tearing both men apart. Later that night, another grenade, another Northern Alliance leader killed. Soldiers herded the surviving prisoners to cells in the basement of a pink building. But even with the two attacks, there was no reinforcement of the guards.

The plot was hatched that night in the basement cells at Qala-i-Jangi. If the foreign Taliban members were released the next morning, they would leave without incident. If not, they would revolt—the Northern Alliance still hadn't searched their prisoners well, and a few had been able to sneak their weapons into the cells. When the time came, the armed detainees would lead the fight.

The planning continued for hours among a small group of the Taliban fighters. Others listened but stayed quiet. They might not join the uprising, but they certainly knew it was coming.

The next morning, two members of the CIA's paramilitary Special Activities Division walked through an open-air courtyard at Qala-i-Jangi, searching for al-Qaeda members among the detainees. About 150 prisoners were lined up in rows, on their knees with their hands tied behind their backs.

The grenade attacks from the night before had unnerved the Northern Alliance fighters. Rather than questioning the prisoners, one guard suggested that they should shoot them, one by one, until somebody identified the al-Qaeda members. The Americans said no. They would use interrogation.

One agent, Johnny Michael Spann, approached a thin, bearded man dressed in a sweater that was usually issued to British soldiers. This prisoner was of particular interest—someone had told Spann that he spoke English.

"Hey you," Spann said. "Right here with your head down. Look at me. I know you speak English. Look at me. Where did you get the British military sweater?"

The prisoner did not look up and did not speak, so Spann walked away. Soon after, Northern Alliance soldiers moved the man to a blanket, pushing him down. Spann returned and squatted down.

"Where are you from?" Spann asked. "You believe in what you're doing here that much, you're willing to be killed here? How were you recruited to come here? Who brought you here?"

The man said nothing. Spann snapped his fingers in front of the prisoner's face. "Hey! Who brought you here? Wake up! Who brought you here to Afghanistan? How did you get here?"

A pause. "What, are you puzzled?" Spann asked. He knelt down on the blanket, trying to photograph the man with a digital camera.

"Put your head up," Spann said. "Push your hair back. Push your hair back so I can see your face."

Silence again. A Northern Alliance soldier grabbed the man's hair and pulled. Spann snapped the picture.

"You got to talk to me," Spann said. "All I want to do is talk to you and find out what your story is. I know you speak English."

The second agent, Dave Tyson, walked toward Spann and called out to him. Spann remarked that the prisoner wouldn't talk.

"Okay, all right," Tyson said. "We explained what the deal is to him."

"I was explaining to the guy we just want to talk to him, find out what his story is."

"The problem is," Tyson said, "he's got to decide if he wants to live or die and die here. We're just going to leave him, and he's going to fucking sit in prison the rest of his fucking short life."

It was the prisoner's decision, Tyson said. "We can only help the guys who want to talk to us."

Spann faced the detainee. "Do you know the people here you're working with are terrorists and killed other Muslims?" he asked. "There were several hundred Muslims killed in the bombing in New York City. Is that what the Koran teaches? I don't think so. Are you going to talk to us?"

The man said nothing.

The agents gave up; they had offered the prisoner his chance. A Northern Alliance guard approached and took the man—John Walker Lindh, soon to be known as the "American Taliban"—back to the line.

• • •

The uprising began about two hours later with explosions and gunfire. Taliban prisoners jumped Spann and tackled him, kicking and tearing at him.

Tyson scrambled toward his comrade and shot four of the men with a nine-millimeter pistol and then seized Spann's AK-47. When a group of fighters charged him, Tyson opened fire, backpedaling as he shot.

The Taliban fighters dashed to the cells and freed their comrades. From there, they stormed an armory inside the fort, grabbing rifles, grenades, ammunition, and rockets. They rushed back out, prepared for battle.

Amid all the shooting and explosions, Spann lay on the ground, shot twice in the head. He was the first American to die in combat since the war in Afghanistan began.

Ben Bonk was at home when his phone rang early that morning. "One of our people is missing," the caller said. "Something's happened."

Bonk knew that nothing more could be said over the unsecure line. He hurried to his car and drove the short distance to CIA headquarters.

Information coming out of Qala-i-Jangi was sketchy. American Special Operations Forces had descended on the fortress and were fighting for control. Tyson was trapped but alive. No one knew what had happened to Spann.

A group of senior agency officials gathered together in the office of Hank Crumpton, who was heading the CIA effort in Afghanistan. Tenet came down; Cofer Black and Crumpton briefed him on the developments.

Black thought of Spann's wife, Shannon, also a CIA employee. She was on maternity leave and away from her home in California, taking a mini vacation with her family.

"We're going to have to tell Shannon before she finds out herself," Black said.

"You can't leave Washington," Tenet replied. "Not in the middle of this."

The task fell to Bonk. He gathered some of Shannon's friends and a member of her husband's unit to join him on the trip to the West Coast. They flew by government jet to John Wayne Airport in Orange County, where other colleagues had already rented cars for them. By the time they reached Spann's house, Shannon was there. She and her family had returned home after she received a call letting her know that a group from headquarters was on the way.

Bonk rang the bell. Shannon opened the door, a newborn baby in her hands.

"Shannon, can we come in? We need to talk."

"Sure."

She handed the baby to a member of her family and led everyone to the living room. Bonk relayed the information that the agency had learned about the shoot-out at Qala-i-Jangi.

"We don't know where Michael is at this moment," he said. "But given what's happened, I think the chances are remote that this is going to work out well."

Shannon asked some questions but held together. "This is what he wanted to do, and he knew it was important," she said softly. "We'll get through this."

They spoke until there was nothing left to say. All of them would be staying at a nearby hotel, Bonk said, and would keep Shannon updated.

Days passed until word came that Michael Spann had been killed. Bonk returned to the Spann home to break the news.

The dusty journey of al-Qaeda's caravan to the mountains of Tora Bora had been, as usual, rough going. As the flat expanse of Jalalabad gave way to the first glint of rocky mountains, the cars clattered over large stones, generating teeth-rattling jolts.

After three hours of tortuous travel, the peaks of Tora Bora loomed above. Cars veered up a steep narrow path, one with no pretensions of being a road. They skirted the cliffs, coming perilously close to tumbling down the mountain. Another hour, and driving became impossible—the fighters had to hike the rest of the way through a barren vista. Thousands of feet up, there were huts that bin Laden had once used as a home; this time, he and his followers would hide out in the mountain's honeycomb of caves. At the end of the climb, groups of al-Qaeda members were assigned to stay in particular caves. But they soon noticed that their leader was nowhere to be found. Bin Laden had simply vanished.

On the eleventh day of Ramadan, November 26, bin Laden reappeared and joined some of his fighters in their cave at Tora Bora. He sat with them while holding a warm glass of green tea, then launched into his standard refrain about the call to jihad.

"Hold your positions and be ready for martyrdom," bin Laden told them.

He stood. "I'll be visiting you again, very soon."

Followed by his guards, he walked out of the cave and disappeared into the pine forests, leaving his fighters behind to fend for themselves.

•　•　•

On the morning of November 27, Tommy Franks was speaking with Victor Renuart Jr., director of operations with Central Command. With Afghani fighters in hot pursuit of al-Qaeda and bin Laden, the two generals were working on plans to provide air support in the battle that was moving into Tora Bora.

Rumsfeld telephoned for Franks.

"General Franks, the president wants us to look at options for Iraq," he said. "What is the status of your planning?"

Out-of-date, Franks said. The Afghan conflict itself presented some issues for the Iraq strategy, called OPLAN1003. Force levels in the region were different, and much of what had been learned in the past few weeks about the use of Special Forces units needed to be incorporated.

"Okay," Rumsfeld said. "Please dust it off and get back to me next week."

The following day, the anxiety was palpable in the hearing room of the Senate Judiciary Committee.

The anthrax letter mailed to Senator Leahy, the committee chairman, had been discovered twelve days earlier. Traces of the bacteria were found in three more locations at the Hart Senate Office building. And new cases of anthrax infections—including some that were fatal—had been reported. But the business of Congress continued on this day with the first Senate hearings about the military commissions order.

Among those sitting at the witness table was Neal Katyal, the law professor who expounded to his students what he considered the constitutional horrors of the order. His wife, Joanna Rosen, had begged him not to go to the hearing, out of fear that he might contract anthrax. When he told her that this was something he had to do, she made one request of him: Don't breathe too deeply.

Katyal listened in silence as other experts testified in support of the plan. Michael Chertoff, the head of the criminal division of the Justice Department, presented the administration's case. Finally, it was Katyal's turn. From his opening sentence, he attacked the order, calling it an unconstitutional assumption of power by the president.

"Our Constitution's structure," he said, "mandates that fundamental choices such as these be made, not by one person, but by the branches of government working together. Ignoring this tradition charts a dangerous course for the future."

While there had been rare times in history that the government had to temporarily dispense with civil trials, such an action was never before taken by a single person.

"A tremendous danger exists if the power is left in one individual to put aside our constitutional traditions when our nation's at crisis," he said. "The safeguard against the potential for this abuse has always been Congress's involvement in a deep constitutional sense. The default should be faith in our traditions and faith in our procedures."

Bush's decision to bypass Congress set a dangerous precedent, Katyal said. Any future president could unilaterally declare that specific types of crimes—such as drug trafficking or gun offenses—should be outside the legal system and shifted, instead, into the commissions. The examples might seem unbelievable, Katyal said, but they were smaller steps than the ones already being taken.

"I believe the administration is trying to do its best, but that's part of the point," he said. "Our constitutional design can't leave these choices to one man, however well intentioned or wise he might be."

Katyal paused. "We don't live in a monarchy."

With those final words, Neal Katyal took his first tentative steps in what would prove to be his multiyear court challenge to the Bush order. His client would be Salim Hamdan, the bin Laden driver who had been seized at a road-block in Afghanistan just four days earlier.

Over several days near Kunduz, combatants loyal to General Dostum continued taking custody of men who surrendered, including confessed Taliban members and Muslims who claimed to be innocents trapped by the bombing. Dostum maintained his policy of sending the Afghanis back home while detaining the foreigners captured by his troops.

On November 28, another group of Muslims riding in a truck outside of Kunduz gave themselves up to Dostum's militia. At gunpoint, the men were removed from the vehicle and forced to their knees while Dostum's fighters searched them for weapons and identification. Three of the men—Shafiq Rasul, Ruhal Ahmed, Asif Iqbal—were British citizens from Tipton, England, who would later insist that they had come to Afghanistan the previous month to provide humanitarian aid. The only reason they were in the region, they would say, was that they had traveled to Pakistan in September for a wedding.

But they mentioned none of this when they were seized on the road outside of Kunduz. As Britons, they were foreigners, no different under Dostum's edict from Pakistanis or Egyptians or any other outsiders. The Northern Alliance fighters tied the hands of the hundreds of new prisoners behind their backs then drove them for more than a day to Mazar-e Sharif, where they were sealed into large containers ordinarily used to transport cargo. From there, they were moved to Dostum's prison at Sheberghan and locked into large cells.

Many of the detainees died during the journey, from the heat and cramped conditions in the containers. But the British men survived and would be turned over to the American military for interrogation.

Before long, they would be dubbed the "Tipton Three," and their names would be known worldwide.

The Battle of Tora Bora began on November 30. The Jawbreaker team had conducted an arduous expedition to a mountaintop and discovered hundreds of al-Qaeda fighters. An air force combat controller in the group called in airstrikes; a laser that the team had brought with them was used to "paint" the targets, giving the bombers something to lock onto. Explosions rocked the mountainous region.

The rebellion at Qala-i-Jangi was put down six days after it blazed through the fortress. When guns and bombs failed to quell the uprising, the Northern Alliance turned to more vicious alternatives. They poured liquid fuel into the basement where the prisoners were making their last stand. When that didn't force them out, the soldiers diverted a stream, sending down a flood of freezing water. The fort filled with the screams of drowning men until finally the remaining Taliban announced their surrender.

More than eighty prisoners crawled out of the subterranean vault—dirty, hungry, and suffering from hypothermia. A few guards handed out fruit to the starving survivors. One gave an apple to a thin, disheveled man who was holding himself up on a stick.

"Thank you," John Walker Lindh said in English.

The flatbed trucks pulled into the rubble-strewn fortress courtyard, evidence of the American bombs that struck Qala-i-Jangi over the past few days. Forcefully, the Northern Alliance soldiers wrangled the survivors on board.

Rumors circulated that one prisoner could speak English and perhaps was an American. Colin Soloway, a freelance reporter from *Newsweek*, heard the story from his translator and decided to find out for himself. He stepped up on a truck bumper, then looked around at the dirty, injured Taliban members inside. A guard pointed to a man sprawled on the flatbed. Soloway thought this fighter looked like a hippie.

"Are you an American?" Soloway asked.

"Yeah," Lindh replied.

A fifteen-minute conversation ensued. Lindh spoke in measured, carefully chosen words. He had come to Afghanistan, he said, to help create a true Islamic state.

But Lindh was with a Taliban fighting force. Was he al-Qaeda? "Did you support the September 11 attacks?" Soloway asked.

"That requires a pretty long and complicated answer. I haven't eaten for two or three days, and my mind is not really in shape to give you a coherent answer."

Soloway pressed the question. Did he support the terrorist attack on the United States?

Lindh relented. "Yes," he said. "I supported it."

Nearby, Matthew Campbell, a correspondent for the *Sunday Times* of London, was counting the drenched and tattered men as they passed, asking questions that none of them would answer. Then a barefoot prisoner wearing a soaked green tunic stopped in front of Campbell.

"Where are you from?" the reporter asked.

"Where am I from?" the man replied. His English was perfect.

He glanced around the compound and sniffed the air before responding. "I was born in America," he said.

"Where?"

Another pause. "Baton Rouge," he said. "Baton Rouge, Louisiana. You know it, yeah?"

An American? Who was he? How had he come to fight here, so far from his home? Campbell asked.

Before the detainee could answer, a guard pushed him forward. The man glanced back once as he walked away, heading toward the trucks.

Months would pass before United States officials would realize that the man, Yaser Esam Hamdi, was indeed an American, the second to be captured at Qala-i-Jangi. Until then, he would be held by the military alongside the foreign fighters.

Bombs ripped apart a valley in Tora Bora that al-Qaeda had hoped would be a stronghold. With the fighters cleared out, a member of the Jawbreaker team went to inspect the area.

On the ground, he saw a mangled body clutching a Yazoo radio, the kind al-Qaeda favored. He listened to it and realized that it was tuned to the frequency used by the terrorist group. He could hear them calling for food and water, and proclaiming their desire to kill Americans.

Then there was a voice he recognized from more than fifty intercepts and tape recordings. It was bin Laden, urging his men to keep up the battle.

Another fighter spoke. "Zamat, how is the sheikh?"

Someone answered, "The sheikh is fine."

This was the proof. Bin Laden was nearby, no farther than the radio frequency's range.

The reporters at Tora Bora seemed to outnumber the American fighters. The Jawbreaker teams were convinced that more troops were necessary—they were at a watershed moment, just days or maybe hours from a final confrontation with bin Laden. The terrorist leader who had brutally killed so many Americans could soon be dead or imprisoned, if the Pentagon was willing to make a push.

At this point the Pakistanis and the Eastern Alliance were the only hope of catching bin Laden, but neither seemed up to the job. Since it was Ramadan, the Eastern Alliance members who had been fasting all day retreated from the battleground for dinner once the sun set; the Pakistani military had left numerous paths from Tora Bora to their border uncovered, and members of the Jawbreaker units questioned whether those soldiers would stop—or aid—escaping al-Qaeda members.

The Americans could fix those problems. All that was needed, the Jawbreaker leaders agreed, was a battalion of Army Rangers dropped behind al-Qaeda's positions. They would stand the best chance of blocking the terrorists from reaching Pakistan.

The request reached Tommy Franks and Rumsfeld. And they turned it down. Both now wanted to avoid committing many troops and instead rely on the Afghani allies working with Special Forces teams. The United States needed to keep a light footprint in Afghanistan, Rumsfeld argued, or there might be a rise in anti-American sentiment that would fuel an insurgency. Plus, throwing together the troops and the means for keeping them supplied might be too difficult to accomplish in such a short time. Suddenly, when the Pentagon was most needed for the fight, Rumsfeld was no longer willing to become more involved. With the CIA and Special Forces having led the way to victory without much input from the Pentagon—and over Rumsfeld's demands that the armed forces spearhead the fight—the defense secretary and his lead general packed up their marbles and went home.

The escape routes into Pakistan remained open.

Seasoned oak crackled in the fireplace of the Oval Office on the morning of December 10. Ashcroft and Bush were there, separated only by the presidential desk built from planks of the nineteenth-century British frigate HMS *Resolute.*

"Mr. President," Ashcroft said, "I have been discussing this issue with my senior staff and recommend that Zacarias Moussaoui be tried in civilian court by the Department of Justice."

This was the man suspected of being the twentieth hijacker for the 9/11 attacks, Ashcroft said, but who had already been arrested weeks before the strike took place. Bush had stated that military commissions were another option and that, when appropriate, terrorism trials would be conducted in civilian court. That would be the best choice for Moussaoui. He would be the first suspected al-Qaeda member tied to 9/11 who would be brought to justice. A public trial would allow the American people to have a greater understanding of the evil facing the country.

"This case has already been presented to a grand jury," Ashcroft said. "We are ready to indict, as soon as tomorrow."

"If this was handled in a criminal court, civilian criminal court, would national security be endangered?" Bush asked. "Would sources or methods be compromised?"

"No, sir," Ashcroft replied.

Moussaoui had been arrested by the FBI inside the United States. Proper criminal procedures had been followed—Moussaoui had been read his rights, no searches had been conducted without warrants, and only civilian law enforcement had been involved in the case. No intelligence agencies played a direct role in the investigation.

Ashcroft finished his presentation. Bush nodded thoughtfully.

"I agree," he said.

The next afternoon, an al-Qaeda lieutenant radioed General Zaman of the Eastern Alliance to negotiate terms of surrender.

As a Pashtun, Zaman could scarcely refuse. His people's identity and social structure are defined by a unique social code called Pashtunwali. Under its precepts, Zaman was obligated to grant personal protection to anyone who requested it, even an enemy. Had he turned away the al-Qaeda entreaty, Zaman would have been accepting a great shame by abandoning his honor.

A translator ran to a sergeant on Alpha Team 572.

"Stop," the translator said. "No more bombs."

That was a good sign. Air assaults were always halted when Eastern Alliance forces moved forward, to avoid shelling them by mistake. Then, when they seized their new position, the attack resumed.

Time passed—ten minutes, twenty minutes, more. Usually the Eastern Alliance troops reached their destination faster than this. Perplexed, the staff sergeant approached the translator.

"Why are we stopping for so long?" he asked.

The translator waved his hands. "No, no. Don't drop any more."

Bin Laden, still hiding miles from his fighters, knew nothing about the supposed negotiations being conducted with the Eastern Alliance. Instead, they were being orchestrated by Ibn al-Shaykh al-Libi, the commander for the Tora Bora fight and an al-Qaeda loyalist who was considered by the Americans to be one of the terrorist group's most dangerous members. Yet here he was, ignoring his longtime leader and forging a policy of his own.

Over the past few days, al-Libi's opinion of bin Laden had sunk. The vaunted jihadist leader was blithely putting his fighters in harm's way while keeping himself at a healthy distance. Even when the three clusters of al-Qaeda fighters moved back into Tora Bora, bin Laden had seemed more concerned about his own self-preservation than that of his men and had implored al-Libi to lead his group. But al-Libi had refused. Instead, he chose to protect a squadron of untested al-Qaeda combatants by guiding them to the mountains.

Just as damning as bin Laden's faintheartedness, in al-Libi's mind, was his strategic ineptitude. By leading his men into a single location, the al-Qaeda leader had increased the risk of pulling back farther. If the fighters attempted a mass escape, al-Libi knew, they would have to move into the open, blundering their way toward Pakistan, potentially making them easy prey for the American bombers roaming the skies.

More than eighty of the men who had followed bin Laden into the mountains were young, naive, and untrained. He obviously felt no compunction about sending these novices to pointless deaths, but al-Libi did. He had to get them out of there, and their best chance for survival would be to trick the Alliance and the Americans into suspending the bombing campaign for about two days. That reprieve would enable al-Libi to lead the men into Pakistan and safe passage to their embassies there. But bin Laden would not be welcome to tag along. The al-Qaeda leader, al-Libi decided, was on his own.

With the bombing pause, al-Libi prepared for the march to Pakistan. Everything now depended on how long the Americans could be held off by the "surrender" gambit.

The next morning, American and British commandos arrived at a sparsely treed area and saw Zaman with his men. The Pashtun commander was sitting on a boulder, smoking a joint. Something big was going on, Zaman told an American soldier—al-Qaeda was cutting a deal for its surrender. No more fighting was allowed until the details were worked out.

The Special Forces teams were doubtful that this development was anything more than an al-Qaeda stalling tactic, but deferred to their indigenous allies. As the negotiations dragged on, the American fighters grew itchy. Zaman occasionally returned with al-Qaeda's terms, such as a demand that they be allowed to carry weapons at the site of their surrender. Absolutely not, the Americans said. This deal had to be unconditional.

Despite Zaman's unwavering confidence, no al-Qaeda fighters appeared. The bombing resumed.

A ground station of the highly secretive National Reconnaissance Office positioned a satellite over Tora Bora. Images captured from hundreds of miles above the earth were transmitted to the CIA via secure microwave links, from the top of the NSA headquarters at Fort Meade to the agency's headquarters in Langley.

The mountainous section of eastern Afghanistan ran like a scar near the country's border. On the eastern side, the images showed Pakistani military positions. Huge pathways remained unguarded that al-Qaeda could use to escape into the tribal areas of Pakistan.

Hank Crumpton from the CIA was in the Situation Room with Bush and Cheney, displaying the satellite images and explaining how, with so much of the area wide open, bin Laden and al-Qaeda could slip away. The briefing, the agency hoped, would persuade Bush to order the Pentagon to secure Tora Bora, despite the foot-dragging by Rumsfeld and Tommy Franks.

"Do the Pakistanis have enough troops to seal the border?" Bush asked.

"No, sir," Crumpton replied. "No one has enough troops to prevent any possibility of escape in a region like that."

Still, Army Rangers needed to be deployed to Tora Bora if there was to be any reasonable hope of catching bin Laden. Bush and Cheney heard the message.

That same afternoon, Ashcroft stepped up to a podium at the Justice Department conference center flanked by FBI director Mueller. Cameras flashed as he began to speak.

"Today, three months after the assault on our homeland, the United States of America has brought the awesome weight of justice against the terrorists who blithely murdered innocent Americans."

That morning, a federal grand jury had indicted Zacarias Moussaoui, Ashcroft said, on charges that he conspired with bin Laden to murder thousands of people.

"For those who continue to doubt al Qaeda's role in the murders of September 11, our indictment offers thirty pages of chilling allegations of al-Qaeda's campaign of terror," he said. "The indictment today is a chronicle of evil."

Ashcroft congratulated an array of officials for their investigation and hard work on the case. He made no mention of the FBI and immigration agents in Minnesota who had arrested Moussaoui, recognized the danger he presented, and unsuccessfully fought for weeks to persuade official Washington to pursue a case. Instead, it was official Washington taking the bow.

No one had given the Defense Department a heads-up about the criminal charges against Moussaoui. And with the battles in Afghanistan on the front burner, few Pentagon officials even noticed Ashcroft's announcement.

The next morning, Wolfowitz and Haynes were scheduled to testify about military commissions before the Senate Armed Services Committee. They were riding in the backseat of an armored Suburban on the way to Capitol Hill when they first heard about the indictment.

It was a heart-stopping moment. In a matter of minutes, they would be in front of the senators responsible for Defense Department oversight, being asked to justify why a new system of justice was needed for terrorists. The legislators were sure to demand that they explain why, if military commissions were necessary, Moussaoui would be tried in civilian court.

"What do we say?" Haynes asked.

"Hey, look," Wolfowitz said. "We've got to say the truth. We didn't know about it."

They arrived at the Russell Senate Office Building and made their way to Room 325. Senator Edward Kennedy raised the Moussaoui indictment in his opening statement.

"We're talking about a person who is going to be charged with the kinds of crimes that threaten American citizens," he said. "That decision is a clear expression of the administration's about competency in the federal courts and where all the rights and protections will be accorded to the defendant in that."

He glanced over his glasses at the witness table. "We are now considering military tribunals, and we're going to be interested in what protections are going to be there."

Wolfowitz gave his prepared remarks and the senators asked their questions. Kennedy brought up Moussaoui again.

"Mr. Wolfowitz," he said, "if you would be good enough to tell us what were the considerations in making the decisions to proceed in the federal courts as opposed to the military tribunal."

"To the best of my knowledge," Wolfowitz replied, "that was a decision made by the Justice Department."

"You weren't involved in this?"

"I was not personally," Wolfowitz said.

He turned toward Haynes. "I don't believe we were as a department, were we?"

Haynes leaned toward the microphone. "No, we were not involved."

Kennedy looked puzzled. "Do you have a view, Mr. Secretary, on that?"

"No," Wolfowitz replied. "I don't."

The questioning continued for another twenty minutes. Then Senator Joseph Lieberman returned to the Moussaoui case.

"I'm troubled by the precedent that this sets as to what the administration will do regarding those who have violated the laws of war," he said. "If we will not try Zacarias Moussaoui before a military tribunal—a noncitizen alleged to be a co-conspirator that killed four thousand Americans—who will we try in a military tribunal?"

Wolfowitz had little to say in reply. No one had consulted the Pentagon, he repeated. Lieberman expressed relief; at least the Defense Department hadn't been involved in something so incomprehensible.

"I think it takes a large risk to bring him before the district court, with all the rights that he would have there that he doesn't deserve, frankly," Lieberman said.

The hearings ended, but the senators' grumbling about the Justice Department continued even after the observers left. The attorney general had sandbagged the Pentagon and, in turn, shown disrespect to the Armed Services Committee. Aschcroft had been a senator, a member of the club, the legislators muttered. He should have known better.

For more than two weeks, Dr. Ayman Batarfi had waited amid the bombing, death, and starvation in Tora Bora to meet with whoever was in charge.

Trained as an orthopedic surgeon, Batarfi had worked at a clinic in Jalalabad and fled the city when the Northern Alliance attacked. He had hoped to reach safety in Pakistan and headed east toward the mountainous region.

Now he was trapped, with no medical supplies to help the wounded. They couldn't even light a fire for warmth or to cook food; that would give the bombers a target. Batarfi struggled with the arduous existence. His throat and eyes burned from the severe cold, and he feared he would not survive. He yearned to get out of Tora Bora and believed his only hope was to gain the help of the man in charge.

He had asked for someone to arrange a meeting but heard nothing in response. Finally, after fifteen days, an armed guard approached to inform Batarfi that they would take him to meet their leader. They escorted him on a four-hour walk to an area that appeared deserted. Bin Laden emerged from behind some trees and called over Batarfi.

"I would like to leave the mountain," Batarfi said.

Bin Laden's face was expressionless. "I don't even have a place to go," he said. "I can't leave the mountains myself."

The comment struck Batarfi. Bin Laden had dragged his people into this catastrophe, had pulled back to Tora Bora without preparations or supplies. But in his first words, he didn't offer plans for saving his dying fighters, the men he had left in the bombing sites while he cowered far away. Instead, his first thoughts were about himself.

Did bin Laden care about anyone else? Batarfi wondered. Had he placed his men in groups, hours away, to distract the Americans by giving them a bigger target to bomb?

For a man who preached the glories of martyrdom, bin Laden certainly seemed quite resistant to the idea of sacrificing his own life for the cause he supposedly held so dear.

At a CIA guesthouse in Kabul, Gary Berntsen, leader of the Jawbreaker forces in eastern Afghanistan, was yelling at Major General Dell Dailey, commander of the Special Operations Forces in Afghanistan.

The Rangers were needed *now*, Berntsen barked. This was the make-or-break. Bin Laden was going to get away!

The orders from Central Command were clear, Dailey replied. No more American troops would be deployed. The military was worried about alienating the Afghan allies.

"I don't give a *damn* about offending our allies," Berntsen yelled. "I only care about eliminating al-Qaeda and delivering bin Laden's head in a box!"

There would be no more soldiers, Dailey repeated. Tommy Franks's position was firm.

That same day at Tora Bora, the snow was deep, the air was thin, and Osama bin Laden was composing his will.

"Allah bears witness that the love of jihad and death in the cause of Allah has dominated my life," he wrote. He had fought the pagans, and would wake reciting the verses of the Koran that called for the battle.

He finished with messages for his family. He instructed his wives not to remarry. And he apologized to his children for having dedicated his life to jihad.

Two members of the Jawbreaker team were listening to the Yazoo radio that had been taken off a dead al-Qaeda member. A voice came on.

"Forgive me."

Bin Laden. Words of regret poured out of the radio, effusive apologies for getting his men trapped in Tora Bora under the withering assault of American airstrikes. There were sounds of mules and people moving. The radio went dead.

In the gray and freezing dawn near Tora Bora, two guides led al-Libi and his young charges across the Afghani-Pakistan border in Nangarhar Province, where the al-Qaeda leader hoped to reach safety.

But in reality, the guides were delivering them into a trap. The eighty-four fighters arrived on December 14* in an area of Shiite tribes who loathed the Taliban, al-Qaeda, and their Sunni fundamentalist doctrine. A man posing as their host persuaded the fighters to turn over their weapons, then gathered them in a mosque. Immediately, Pakistan forces burst in and arrested them.

The two guides were paid handsomely for their deception. Al-Libi was the most important al-Qaeda leader captured since the war began. Ultimately, his detention and brutal interrogation would contribute to the deaths of thousands of American soldiers in Iraq.

In Maryland, Bruce Ivins sat down at his home computer and typed an e-mail to a friend. He was sending her a poem, he wrote, about having two people inside him.

> *I'm a little dream-self, short and stout*
> *I'm the other half of Bruce—when he lets me out.*
> *When I get all steamed up, I don't pout.*
> *I push Bruce aside, then I'm free to run about!*
>
> *Hickory dickory Doc—Doc Bruce ran up the clock.*
> *But something happened in very strange rhythm.*
> *His other self went and exchanged places with him.*
> *So now, please guess who*
> *Is conversing with you.*
> *Hickory dickory Doc!*
>
> *Bruce and this other guy, sitting by some trees,*
> *Exchanging personalities.*
> *It's like having two in one.*
> *Actually, it's rather fun!*

Two days later, just past 8:30 A.M., Ivins e-mailed one of his bosses. When, he asked, would his team get access to more anthrax spores?

•   •   •

---

*It has been frequently reported that this journey ended on November 11, but that is incorrect. Several al-Qaeda members who took part in the trip, as well as classified government records, reveal that the date is December 14. See Notes and Sources.

On December 16, bin Laden left Tora Bora for the last time. Accompanied by some guards, he slipped, unnoticed and unimpeded, into Pakistan. The Northern Alliance and American Special Forces arrived victorious at the al-Qaeda caves the next day.

On a cold evening in late December, Gonzales took a seat at an oval table, joining a dozen other officials in a large suite across the street from the White House.

The room—called, unimaginatively, the Former Office of the Secretary of the Navy—is one of the most opulent in all of Washington. Ornamental stenciling and allegorical symbols of the Navy Department festooned walls hand-painted in Victorian colors. A floor of mahogany, maple, and cherrywood connected two fireplaces made of Belgian black marble. With its luxurious appearance, the room was often used for ceremonial events, but on this day, it would be the site of a brewing battle among members of the administration.

Hundreds of al-Qaeda and Taliban fighters were being captured in Afghanistan. The president had already decided how they would be tried; top advisors were debating where they should be held. The open question remaining: How should they be treated?

At the center of the debate were the Geneva Conventions, a group of four treaties that set international standards for the humanitarian treatment of enemy soldiers and civilians during wartime. The treaties were adopted over many decades, the natural outcome of the horrors of war. At one time, abuse of enemy soldiers and civilians was something that took place in secret—rumored, but unseen and often unreported. With the growth of international communications and the evolution of increasingly brutal weaponry, images and tales of ever more gruesome abuse came out of the shadows, shocking the public consciousness. Nations decided that all was not fair in war, that rules had to be established to ensure that anyone captured by the enemy was treated humanely.

Then came World War II and with it the onset of some of history's most vicious and abhorrent cruelty during international hostilities. The Holocaust, the Bataan death march, the Malmédy massacre, the Katyn Forest massacre—these crimes demonstrated a willingness on the part of combatants to torture and murder wantonly. In response, the conventions were updated and expanded.

In the years that followed, three parts of the revised conventions grew to particular significance. Article 4 of the Third Geneva Convention spelled out who would qualify for prisoner-of-war status during a conflict. In turn, Common Article 3, which appears in each of the treaties, governed the treatment of prisoners of war.

That did not mean, however, that people who did not qualify as prisoners of war could be abused. The Fourth Geneva Convention dictated requirements for humane treatment of civilians. That left one question seemingly unanswered: Do fighters who are not part of a regular army and who violate the laws of war—placing them outside the requirements for POW status—qualify for protection under the Fourth Convention? While that had been a subject of debate for some time, in 1998 a United Nations war crimes tribunal stated that *everyone* held by an enemy during a military conflict fell under the protections of either the Third Convention or the Fourth Convention.

At bottom, though, for all the apparent complexity, the conventions had long been interpreted broadly to mean, simply, that people captured during wartime, regardless of status, were to be treated humanely and with dignity.

In the United States, a failure to apply the conventions properly was fraught with legal peril for administration officials. In 1996, overwhelming majorities of both houses of Congress approved the War Crimes Act, which made it illegal for any nation—including the United States—to commit a "grave breach" of the Geneva Conventions. The punishment for violating the law could be life imprisonment, unless the breach led to someone's death. If so, the defendant could be executed.

These were the issues on the table at the meeting convened for this day by Gonzales. The primary question: Should al-Qaeda members or the Taliban—or both—be granted prisoner-of-war status, and if not, what rights would they then have?

That required resolving different perceptions and interpretations of the conventions throughout the administration. Gonzales brought together everyone with an interest in the outcome—representatives from the Joint Chiefs of Staff, the Pentagon, the CIA, the State Department, the NSC, and the Justice Department.

While he fell far lower than almost everyone else in the room on the bureaucratic ladder, John Yoo was easily the most important person there. Weeks before, Gonzales had instructed him to prepare a memo that would provide the analysis of both the conventions and the War Crimes Act which Bush could then use to reach a decision. All the other officials there could only make suggestions; it was Yoo who would ultimately put everything on paper.

Gonzales took his seat at the center of the table.

"I've asked you all here to discuss the options under the laws of war," he said. "Because we're definitely capturing people, and we need to know how we're supposed to treat them."

The first to respond was William Taft IV, the general counsel at the State Department. Al-Qaeda, he said, was an easier issue—no one thinks terrorists are prisoners of war. But Taliban fighters were a different matter.

"The plain language of Geneva demands that they be granted POW status," he said. "The Taliban is the government in Afghanistan. The Taliban we're capturing are their armed forces."

Yoo spoke next. He agreed that the status of al-Qaeda under the Geneva Conventions was an easy call—it was a criminal organization, not a nation. The issues involving the Taliban, on the other hand, were more complex. They were not the leaders of Afghanistan. Indeed, he said, the State Department had maintained for years that there was no central Afghani government, just groups of warring factions. The Taliban controlled only 90 percent of the country, and its borders of authority were continually shifting. They were incapable of maintaining government institutions or law and order. Civil society had been destabilized by violence.

"Throughout the time of Taliban's existence, Afghanistan has been incapable of meeting the conditions and responsibilities of a sovereign nation," he said. "It is a failed state, and the United States can't apply a treaty to a country that effectively doesn't exist."

Taft strongly disagreed. The United States couldn't simply analyze its way out of the obligations of the treaty by redefining the enemy.

"This country had consistently applied Geneva in every conflict for the past fifty years," he said. Changing that now would contradict the position of every nation that signed the treaties.

From the other side of the table came another objection, this time from Jane Dalton, the legal counsel to the chairman of the Joint Chiefs of Staff.

"Our position is that everyone, al-Qaeda and the Taliban, should be treated as POWs," she said. "Merely from a policy point of view, we should give them protections because we want our soldiers to have protections."

That was unrealistic, one official argued. Neither the Taliban nor al-Qaeda was going to treat the American military in accordance with the conventions. Any soldier who was caught would be killed, probably by beheading.

The debate continued for more than an hour, and by the end, no one had given an inch; each agency had simply reiterated its original stance. Gonzales thanked everyone for coming. He promised that the discussion would continue.

Leaflets fell from the sky like snowflakes, littering the ground around the border between Pakistan and Afghanistan.

Some showed a drawing of a man with a disheveled beard and wearing a *hijab* head covering. To the right of that, a sketch of a large pile of money. Then the third and final image depicted the same man, this time behind prison bars. The leaflet had been designed by the Psychological Operations unit of the U.S. Army Special Operations Command to communicate a message for illiterate Afghanis and Pakistanis: Anyone who turned in members of the Taliban or al-Qaeda would be paid.

The written versions of the pamphlets were much clearer. "You can receive millions of dollars for helping the anti-Taliban force catch al-Qaeda and Taliban murderers," one read. "This is enough money to take care of your family, your village, your tribe for the rest of your life."

The United States was as good as its word and started shelling out bounties. A member of al-Qaeda brought in as much as $20,000; one of the Taliban, about $5,000. The money was an enormous incentive to turn over somebody—*anybody*—to the American military.

In the desperately poor country crippled by centuries of bitter factionalism, tribes turned on tribes, Pakistanis on Arabs, neighbors on neighbors. Around the country, hundreds of farmers, shepherds, ne'er-do-wells, and nobodies were snatched up by locals, tossed into trucks, and driven to the nearest American military unit. Cash filled outstretched palms, and the new detainees were thrown into cells. Al-Qaeda and Taliban members were part of the mix, but no one in the military or intelligence community knew how to tell the terrorists apart from the innocent.

In Paris, American Airlines flight 63 pulled onto the runway at Charles de Gaulle International Airport just before 11:45 on the morning of December 22. The Miami-bound plane was already an hour behind schedule, but few of the almost 180 passengers on board grumbled about the delay. With the images of 9/11 still fresh, there were more jitters than complaints.

Close to three hours later, as the plane flew over the Atlantic, the man in seat

29H stood up and made his way to the lavatory in the back. In the adjoining seat, 29J, a man with long hair and a scraggly beard glanced over his shoulder, watching until the other traveler passed a video monitor at row 33.

The man, Richard Reid, bent over, removed his ankle-high shoes, and placed them on his lap. The waffle-patterned cushioning cells at the bottom of the hiking shoes were packed with plastic explosives. Fuses laced with black powder ran from an improvised detonator with the unattached end at the inner sole.

Reid took the right shoe in his hand and pulled out the fuse. He opened a book of matches, lit one, and held it to the blackened cord.

A flight attendant, Hermis Moutardier, was walking down the aisle, picking up trays from the meal service. Passengers mentioned that they smelled an odor, and Moutardier detected a whiff of sulfur. She walked past row 29 and saw Reid bent over, a lit match in his hand. "Sir," she said, "you have to extinguish that. Smoking is not allowed."

Reid looked up at Moutardier and promised to stop. He placed the burning side of the match in his mouth, extinguishing the flame.

Unnerved, Moutardier walked away to find a member of the flight crew so that she could report what she had just seen. A few minutes later, she returned and saw Reid bending down in his seat again.

"Excuse me," she said, sounding angry. "What are you doing?"

Then she saw it. Reid had a shoe between his legs, and was holding a burning match to a cord coming out near the tongue. It was a fuse.

Moutardier reached down and grabbed Reid. He pushed away. She tried again, and this time he pushed so hard that she fell back against the armrest across the aisle. For a moment she thought Reid might not be stopped.

I'm going to die.

She jumped up and tore down the aisle toward Cristina Jones, a flight attendant who was working in the galley.

"Get him!" Moutardier shouted. "Go!"

No mention of the shoe or the match. But Jones ran back toward Reid's seat and realized something terrible was happening. Even though she saw only that this passenger had his back to the aisle, she knew he was trying to destroy the plane and kill them all.

"Stop it!" she yelled, grabbing Reid around the upper body.

He bent his head down and bit Jones's hand, and she let out a scream. Other passengers heard the commotion and came running. Jones wanted to get out of the way, but Reid wouldn't open his mouth, as if he were trying to rip the flesh off her hand. As the other passengers finally restrained him, Reid let go. Jones, in shock, reverted to her usual duties; she lifted and fastened the tray table in the seat next to Reid.

Fearful that there might still be a lit match, Moutardier returned carrying bottles of Evian water that she and a few passengers poured all over Reid. Within minutes, Reid was restrained with plastic handcuffs, seat-belt extensions on his feet, plus belts and headphones wrapped around his body. Valium was brought out of an in-flight kit and administered by a doctor on board.

Reid did not lose consciousness. A flight attendant later offered him water; he bared his teeth, saying nothing. He tried to get loose, but failed. Finally, he gave up and started to rock and pray.

On a tree-shaded street in the Philadelphia suburb of Wynnewood, a smattering of academic psychologists gathered with law enforcement and intelligence officers to brainstorm about Islamic extremism.

They were at the home of Dr. Martin E. P. Seligman, a renowned psychologist who in 1967 conducted foundational research involving a theory called "learned helplessness." Experiments by Seligman and a colleague appeared to demonstrate that experiences of pain or other distress beyond subjects' control could drive them into a state of emotional surrender. The research led to fundamental reevaluations of depression and won Seligman international acclaim.

The meeting on this evening focused on what drove some Muslims to fanaticism and what measures could be taken to counter the trend. At a break in the discussion, a man approached Seligman with his hand extended. He introduced himself as Dr. Jim Mitchell, a psychologist who had recently retired from a military survival-training program called Survival, Evasion, Resistance, Escape, or SERE.

In the ensuing conversation, Mitchell heaped praise on the older psychologist for his groundbreaking work. His compliments struck Seligman as a bit effusive, perhaps even bewildering. Still, after all these years, it lifted his spirits to hear a colleague express such admiration for his work.

Years later, Seligman's good feelings about that night were replaced by grief and horror when he discovered that, even as the psychologist was lauding him, Mitchell had been at work preparing to use the findings on learned helplessness to justify an American program of brutal interrogation for suspected terrorists.

• • •

For the most part, the experts on interrogation in military intelligence and at the CIA were old, retired, or dead. With the collapse of the Soviet Union and an interlude of relative peace that had lasted since the Vietnam War's end in 1975, captured enemy combatants had become all but extinct. By the mid-1990s, intelligence and military interrogations were a subject more of academic study than of practical application.

But now the emerging terror wars would be changing all that. The agency and the military needed people skilled in the art of getting the enemy to talk. Al-Qaeda members were almost certainly going to be the largest source of intelligence about the group but only if someone knew how to get them to spill the information.

While both were searching for the same skills, the Pentagon and the CIA each struck out on its own to put together interrogation programs.

The military did have one group that was, in a convoluted way, connected to interrogation. It was called the Joint Personnel Recovery Agency, and it ran the SERE programs designed to train American fighters how to tolerate brutal questioning. The soldiers were subjected to abusive tactics that had been employed by the Chinese Communists decades before to obtain false confessions that could be used for propaganda purposes. The names of the methods were bland—sensory deprivation, sleep disturbance, slapping, waterboarding—but the impact on the well-being of those subjected to such treatment was extensively documented.

None of these methods were used in the Defense Department programs to produce interrogation results. No one at SERE cared whether the abuse worked; the sole concern was whether American military personnel were braced to withstand cruel questioning tactics.

That distinction was quickly lost in the rush to develop new interrogation programs. Officers responsible for the SERE programs began selling themselves to higher-ups as invaluable sources for training soldiers to question terrorists. All they had to do was reverse engineer the SERE program—rather than teaching American fighters to resist abusive interrogations, they would instead be instructed on how to use the Chinese tactics against terrorist detainees.

By December, the supposed benefit of transforming SERE experts into interrogation coaches was bouncing around the echo chamber of the Pentagon. Small, ad hoc programs to train interrogators using SERE tactics had already begun. Defense Department officials reached out to SERE instructors for information about detainee "exploitation," the first rumblings that those tactics could be widely adopted for the questioning of terrorists by the military.

Since the CIA didn't have its own SERE schools, it decided to bring in an outside consultant. The agency hired Jim Mitchell, the recently retired air force SERE psychologist who bubbled excitedly about how the concept of learned helplessness that had been studied by Dr. Martin Seligman could be used in interrogations to break detainees. CIA officials asked Mitchell if he would be willing to analyze some al-Qaeda training manuals and see if he could devise an interrogation program based on what he read.

Mitchell agreed to give it a try and sought out a former SERE colleague, Dr. Bruce Jessen, for his input.

These two psychologists—who had never conducted an interrogation, who never performed research on the subject, who knew nothing about al-Qaeda— were now the point men for the CIA in structuring its interrogation program.

It was called the "Manchester Manual," and both the British and the American governments considered it one of the most important pieces of intelligence ever obtained about al-Qaeda's operations and tactics.

The document had been discovered on a computer of a suspected terror-ist, Anas al-Liby, following a police raid of his home in Manchester, England. Since the late 1980s, al-Liby had been a member of al-Jam'a al-Islamiyyah al-Muqatilah—the Libya Islamic Fighting Group—dedicated to the overthrow of Muammar al-Gaddafi, the Libyan dictator. In the mid-1990s, al-Liby fled Tripoli and gravitated toward al-Qaeda; the American government believed that he had played a role in the East African embassy bombings.

Al-Liby avoided arrest in Manchester, slipping away before the raid. But in his haste to escape, he had left behind his computer, a trove of records, and other evidence, including the manual.

The document—handwritten in Arabic—had been scanned into a digital file; the police found no evidence that it had been e-mailed to anyone, and it was not apparent how al-Liby had obtained it. It was shipped to law enforce-ment and intelligence agencies in both Britain and America, and officials were awed by the find. With this training manual, they felt sure that they now knew the step-by-step instructions provided by al-Qaeda to its members on topics ranging from the use of weapons to espionage to operations.

But what officials in both countries found most intriguing was what the document called the seventeenth lesson, a section on how to resist the various interrogation tactics practiced by police and prosecutors. This was one of the main items that the CIA wanted Jim Mitchell to study in formulating a plan for questioning terrorists.

There was, however, a problem with building an interrogation program based in part around the Manchester Manual: Despite the assurances of British and American officials, it was not an al-Qaeda document at all.*

It was, instead, a booklet written by at least two men a decade before, at a time when al-Qaeda was in tatters and bin Laden was living at home in Saudi Arabia. It espoused different goals, using different means, from al-Qaeda's. While it did contain instructions on how to commit terrorist acts, much of that information was amateurish, particularly in the areas of training and weapons usage.

The manual—which does not mention al-Qaeda or bin Laden, or say anything negative about the United States or any Western country—is instead focused on methods for overthrowing a Middle Eastern government. Its contents deal with the specifics of that government's modus operandi—identifying the agency that arrests suspects, summarizing the training of its officers and prosecutors, and even describing the different rooms where detainees are held. The details match only one country: Egypt.

The "resistance techniques" laid out in the document were almost laughingly naive. The manual described some of the most gruesome forms of torture being practiced in parts of the Middle East, including tearing out fingernails, burning skin with lit cigarettes and fire, beating victims with sticks and electric wire, and shocking their genitals with electrical current. And how were the terrorist trainees to fortify themselves against such torments? The manual advised memorizing prepared answers for questions, disobeying orders, taking heart in the likelihood that the torture would likely end more quickly if none of the questions were answered, and praying to Allah. At no point did it suggest that someone who is arrested should fabricate torture claims, as both American and British officials would later contend.

---

*Even a casual reading of the Manchester Manual makes it clear that this document was written not for al-Qaeda, but for another group entirely. Two members of a Middle Eastern intelligence service confirmed that analysis, with one calling the idea that the manual was intended for al-Qaeda "absurd." See Notes and Sources.

Once Mitchell and his colleague Bruce Jessen finished their review of the al-Qaeda training manuals, they wrote a paper infused with psychological jargon analyzing the terrorist group's thinking and recommending that the Americans adopt the tactics used in SERE—including slaps, sleep deprivation, walling, and waterboarding—to wring information out of captured terrorists.

Mitchell assured CIA officials that the methods would strike fear into the hearts of terrorists comparable to that experienced by pilots of a plane about to smash into a building. The officials liked what they heard—tough, muscular techniques coated in the dispassionate lexicon of science.

But the recommendation by Mitchell and Jessen was counterintuitive—if the "resistance techniques" in the manual were intended to help a terrorist avoid confessing when being burned by fire, why would less abusive tactics, like waterboarding, succeed?

All of those flaws and questions escaped the attention of the two men and the American government as they hastened to develop a program for harsh interrogation of suspected terrorists. None of them realized that this aggressive—and unprecedented—American policy was being formulated by these unqualified psychologists based in part on an obscure, near-meaningless, and wildly misinterpreted document.

Paul Wolfowitz liked Alcatraz. That, he argued, would be a good place to hold and interrogate al-Qaeda and Taliban detainees.

A group of Pentagon officials had gathered in Rumsfeld's office to debate possible choices for detention centers. It was a Sunday afternoon, after Rumsfeld had just returned from church, a time when the group had agreed to once again kick around ideas.

The debate had been set off by Tommy Franks, who told Rumsfeld that he wanted the detainees out of his hair. So, it was left to the defense secretary and his team to decide where to put them.

"I think Alcatraz is a great choice," Wolfowitz said. "In American eyes, it's the symbol of where you put the worst of the worst."

It wouldn't work, Haynes replied. "It's in a metropolitan area," he said. "It would take months to refurbish, and it's not DOD property."

There were also legal questions to consider. There was sure to be litigation, and the Ninth Circuit Court of Appeals, where a case from Alcatraz would be heard, was the most liberal in the country.

Then perhaps, Wolfowitz said, the Aleutian Islands in the Pacific. That would have a good climate, which would help limit illness among detainees.

There were other possibilities. Colin Powell had been beating the bushes for ideas, calling allies to see which might be willing to provide a location for the prison. Douglas Feith, the undersecretary for policy, judged each new suggestion based on five factors—security, safety, logistical support, cost, and applicable law. The best options, the group concluded, would place the detainees out of the reach of American courts.

The list of options rapidly grew. Powell persuaded both Panama and Granada to help. South Korea, Diego Garcia, and Wake Island were other available choices. Then there was the possibility of loading detainees onto ships at sea.

But one alternative kept rising to the top. It was an American base on an island governed by military law. It was relatively close. The climate was warm. And the captured terrorists could not possibly escape.

After the analysis was wrapped up, the officials agreed: Detainees should be sent to Guantanamo Bay.

Bush took his seat at the head of the table in the White House Situation Room, surrounded by the full war council and their staffs. Condoleezza Rice sat directly across from him.

"Mr. President, Don has been through this and recommends that we put the detainees in Guantanamo Bay, Cuba," she said. "And we support that."

Cheney spoke up. "Where do they come from, and how do you get them there?"

A chart was brought out listing those issues, and others. At the bottom of the chart for each topic were small diamonds.

"What's that symbol?" Cheney asked.

"Each diamond is a decision point," Rice said.

There was the question of what to do with captured Americans; Lindh was already in custody, being held on a naval vessel. The consensus was that citizens should be brought back into the United States, tried in civilian court, and—if convicted—sent to prison.

"What if a detainee is dangerous, but we can't try them?" Bush asked.

One of the lawyers took that question. "If they are enemy combatants in a conflict, the rules of war allow us to hold them as long as the conflict continues."

Bush and Cheney asked a few more questions. Then the president decided to accept his advisors' recommendation.

Guantanamo Bay, on the southeastern end of Cuba, was dubbed "Puerto Grande" by Columbus when he landed there in 1494. In the centuries since, the harbor emerged as a trophy sought by numerous combatants eager to take possession of its strategic location and natural beauty.

In the aftermath of the Spanish-American War in 1898, when American naval ships rode out a hurricane in Guantanamo Bay, Washington saw the harbor as a prize of great value. America had seized Cuba from Spain and, in 1903, worked out a deal with its newly installed government allowing the United States to lease Guantanamo Bay in perpetuity under an agreement that granted complete jurisdiction of the area. The military built a naval base there, covering forty-five miles of land and water.

By 2001, the Guantanamo naval station was America's oldest, and the site of constant renovation. By December, the lead construction superintendent at the base had been working there for a year and a half. Late that month, he was overseeing a crew handling a project on the leeward side of the base when his department manager issued new instructions.

"I need you to close down your project," the manager said. "We're going to be starting a project to renovate and build another area."

They were under orders to construct a detention center, the manager said, one that would hold some of the world's most dangerous terrorists. And this would be a rush job—they needed to have something ready by January 31, just over a month away. Neither man could have known the deadline would soon be moved up by a couple of weeks.

There were already about forty cells, remnants from the early 1990s, when the naval station was used to house Cuban and Haitian refugees. There was plenty of space for expansion, but Washington hadn't spent enough time planning for the larger facility; no new supplies were available—no wood, no fencing, no concrete. The detention center for suspected terrorists would have to be built from scraps.

The supervisor ordered his crews to wander the island, gathering materials. They removed old chain-link fences, posts, whatever they could find. With that, they constructed frames for the cells. Showers were built using some of the same materials, with fencing on the sides and the top. There was nowhere to cover up; whenever detainees showered, they would be visible to everyone, including female soldiers. There would be no hot water.

The workers would eventually have to build a real detention facility, but for now, this jerry-rigged version, soon to be dubbed Camp X-Ray, would have to do.

BOOK TWO

THE DISMAL SHADE

7

A group of Afghani musicians played in darkness near a C-130 turboprop at Bagram Airfield. Prime Minister Tony Blair and his wife, Cherie, stepped off the aircraft and walked briskly down a red carpet toward a fit, bearded man wearing a long cape and karakul hat. Blair smiled as he shook hands with the man, Hamid Karzai, the newly installed chairman of the Afghan Transitional Administration.

Karzai was a Pashtun leader who had been forced into exile after emerging as a fierce opponent of the Taliban. The American air campaign in October gave Karzai a chance to return to his homeland and take up arms against Taliban rule. Days after the bombing began, he and three colleagues rode motorcycles to the Pakistani border and crossed into Afghanistan. They traveled to Kandahar, where Karzai spent a few weeks taking the pulse of residents, trying to judge if they had tired of the Taliban's stranglehold on their lives. Quietly, the Afghanis poured out their feelings of bitterness and fear of the regime; the population, Karzai decided, was ready for political change.

To take charge of that mission, Karzai needed supplies, and lots of them. Using his ever-present iridium satellite phone, he contacted American embassies in Rome and Islamabad dozens of times, seeking materials and weaponry so that he and his growing militia could join the campaign against the Taliban. Aid flooded in, and the Americans quickly recognized him as a charismatic and knowledgeable leader who was able to rally people to his side. When the Taliban collapsed, prominent Afghanis gathered in Bonn to form the Transitional Administration. With American support, they named Karzai as chairman of the governing committee.

When Blair arrived in Bagram on January 7, 2002, he was the first Western head of state to visit Afghanistan's new leader. Out of deference to the danger of this gathering, the arrival ceremony was brief; a group of soldiers from British Special Forces quickly whisked the official party to a line of armored, four-wheel-drive vehicles.

As the caravan made its way slowly over endless tank traps, Karzai spoke confidently about the future of Afghanistan—perhaps a bit too confidently, Blair thought. Finally, the group reached a Russian barracks where Blair was scheduled to sit down with eight other ministers.

They gathered in a large meeting area inside the building. A collection of tables and chairs had been positioned around the room. A drab spread of sweets had been laid out and would remain uneaten.

Karzai opened the discussions but seemed to have little control over his government's bickering factions. Even as he attempted to express graceful thanks to Blair, other ministers interrupted, openly aggressive and belligerent.

One of the first to speak was a rotund man who bore a striking resemblance to Orson Welles. For several minutes, he thundered about the challenges facing Afghanistan with its crippling poverty and war-weary citizenry.

"We need help," he said in a derisive tone, suggesting that he doubted Britain would deliver.

"We understand the difficulties faced by your country," Blair said. "And I want to assure you that Britain will stay with you for the long term."

Even with all of its problems, Karzai said, his country's future was brighter. "Afghanistan is well rid of the terrible leadership that came before," he said. "The Taliban almost destroyed this country, but its people are now prepared to do what is necessary to rebuild."

The hopeful words did nothing to quiet the tone of distrust and anger in the room; Karzai felt embarrassed about how his compatriots were treating the prime minister. Later, as the meeting drew to a close, he spoke again, trying to rekindle an air of optimism and gratitude.

He faced Blair. "We are all so glad that such a distinguished person as yourself has come to see us, taken the risk," Karzai said with a smile. "You have demonstrated such goodwill. When the Afghan people hear that you visited us, they will be proud and thrilled."

The gathering broke up with a few remaining grumbles. On one side of the room, a Special Forces member leaned toward Alastair Campbell, a senior Blair aide.

"Welcome to bandit country," the soldier whispered.

• • •

The classified threat matrix was delivered by hand and electronically to senior administration officials and to national security outposts around the world. And almost daily, at least one item on this list of potential dangers terrified official Washington.

Since the days after 9/11, the White House had demanded that all information about potential threats be transmitted around the government through the matrix; then intelligence or law enforcement officials were assigned to investigate each item. The data came with almost no filtering; it was, instead, raw intelligence, the kind not usually provided to policy makers. Such information was too easy to misinterpret—the unschooled in the art of spy craft would likely give great weight to insignificant or unreliable reports.

Now every bit of material—from the CIA, the FBI, the Defense Intelligence Agency, the Department of Defense Human Intelligence Operations—was dumped into the matrix. Intelligence was no longer served by the glass, but shot from the fire hose.

Over time, those reviewing the daily list of potential threats found that the experience could be overwhelming—and then numbing. And far too many listed items were absurd on their face.

An official from a CIA office in the Middle East reported that al-Qaeda was preparing to launch a kamikaze-style air assault on an American naval base at a South Pacific island; the navy never had a base on that island, nor had any ship from the Pacific fleet ever docked there. Still, the threat—to a base that didn't exist—was added to the matrix. Another cable came in from a military investigations unit that bin Laden had been spotted shopping at a post exchange on an American base in East Asia. One investigator joked to a friend that perhaps the United States could locate the al-Qaeda leader by tracing the Visa card he used at the PX. The news about bin Laden's shopping trip appeared in the matrix.

Then there was a phenomenon called "circular reporting." After 9/11, hundreds of millions of dollars were pumped into intelligence and law enforcement agencies, which in turn used portions of the money to hire analysts. Within a few months, there were hundreds of new people available all around government to examine and interpret the same bits of detail. A report flowed in from a CIA analyst and was disproved. Days later, the same information—tweaked differently by another analyst—reappeared in the matrix. If investigators could not confirm that the supposed threat was a repeat, they had no choice but to chase down the worthless allegations again.

In one instance, an alcoholic was stopped by local law enforcement in Cleveland; he blurted out that there was a plot to destroy an American Airlines flight leaving from Chicago O'Hare International Airport. The man's statement bubbled up the line and landed in the matrix. The threat was investigated and dismissed as drunken ravings. Days later, another agency reported a plot to attack an American Airlines plane in Chicago, and a new investigation led back to the same alcoholic. The story reappeared on the threat list at least two more times.

But the matrix could not be ignored, because alongside the junk were terrifying nuggets of credible intelligence. There was detailed and corroborated intelligence about terrorist plans to murder hundreds of schoolchildren, to rapidly execute scores of citizens in ways designed to leave Americans feeling unsafe even in their homes, to use truck bombs and other explosives to destroy buildings or infrastructure, and others.

Information from foreign intelligence services was equally frightening. One European agency reported that radiation meters had detected potentially lethal material coming across a border; subsequent information suggested that it had been smuggled from one country to the next by a terrorist group. But the suspects—along with their unknown shipment—had disappeared into the second country. Multiple reports came in from overseas that al-Qaeda was engaged in an aggressive effort in Malaysia to develop anthrax weapons, raising strong concerns in Washington given the recent terrorist attacks using the bacteria.

These domestic and international reports weighed heavily on Bush—it was a daily dose of horror, depictions of the depraved cruelty that the human mind could conceive. No matter how unlikely some of the scenarios might be, they seemed less improbable than the idea of crashing hijacked planes into buildings would have been before 9/11.

Bush and Cheney told their staffs that they would not stand by agonizing about these heinous plots to murder untold thousands. The administration was going to be aggressive, forward-leaning, pushing as far to the line as possible. Their job was to ensure the safety and security of the American people, and they would do whatever it took to meet that duty.

A group of American diplomats and generals strutted into the Sarajevo office of Alija Behmen, the prime minister of Bosnia-Herzegovina.

A secretary greeted the visitors—Christopher Hoh, the deputy United States ambassador, and three others from the embassy; General John Sylvester, the American commander for the NATO-led Stabilization Force, known as SFOR, which was tasked to serve as a peacekeeper in the war-ravaged country; and General David Petraeus, assistant chief of staff with SFOR. Seconds later, Behmen emerged from his office, an expression of cautious cordiality on his face.

"Please, come in," he said, inviting the group to a meeting room.

The prime minister felt apprehensive as everyone found their seats. He had heard that the Americans were about to pressure him to do something bordering on illegality—maybe even crossing that border. Three months earlier, they had demanded that Behmen order the arrests of six Algerians; they were, the Americans said, cooking up a plot to bomb the United States embassy in Sarajevo. While the Americans gave no information supporting the allegation, they repeatedly assured Behmen that it existed.

Over the past three months, Federation authorities had gathered all of the evidence they could find. They searched the men's homes and offices, downloaded and analyzed data on their computer, took the machines apart and examined the pieces, checked phone records, interviewed witnesses, and sought information from agencies such as INTERPOL, the FBI, and NATO security forces. They turned up—nothing. Federation officials begged the Bush administration to give them access to the proof that the United States found so convincing, to no avail. The men must stay locked up, the Americans insisted, but neither the police nor the courts could be told why.

There *was* a piece of paper found in one search that listed a phone number and a name similar to that of a senior al-Qaeda operative. But there were problems with the document, and members of the Federation police whispered among themselves that it might have been manufactured by the Americans to ensure these men were taken off the street.

Any defendant in the country could be held without charge for only ninety days, and that time was almost up for the Algerians. With the men's release looming, the embassy called Behmen and asked for this urgent meeting.

Hoh opened the gathering, discussing the status of the case and the Americans' knowledge about the likely outcome.

"I'm here to inform you," Hoh said, "that senior United States officials—including the president, the vice president, and the secretary of defense—have been briefed about the status of the investigation of these six men and the likelihood that they are about to be released because of a lack of evidence."

Bush and *Cheney* and *Rumsfeld were directly involved in this?* Behmen's anxiety was turning into outright fear.

"Mr. Prime Minister," General Sylvester said, "I have a direct order from the top level of my command to use SFOR troops to rearrest these men, if necessary."

Behmen sat back in his chair, lifting up his overturned hands. *The Americans might use their troops against Federation law enforcement?*

"What am I supposed to do?" Behmen asked. "I can't order for these men to be held in prison when we have no evidence."

Behmen needed to think this through, Sylvester said. "In my view, the direct involvement of SFOR in this case would be a serious mistake. This problem needs to be resolved by the authorities of Bosnia-Herzegovina, without that direct involvement."

If the Algerians could not be held, then the Federation needed to immediately turn them over to the SFOR after their release. If not, the American military would be forced to act. Sylvester would not ignore an order from the president.

This wasn't much of a choice. If Bosnia refused to turn over the Algerians, Behmen knew, the United States would make good on its threat. The Americans would launch a military operation in central Sarajevo and use every means at their disposal to take custody of these suspects. Innocent people might be killed in the upheaval. All for six men.

The Federation could sidestep the law or take a stand on principle. Either way, the Americans would seize the Algerians. There could be violence and danger, or safety and security.

The Americans gave Behmen and his ministers less than a week to decide.

The ferry churned slowly toward the dock on the windward side of Guantanamo Bay. On board were about ten interrogators from the Naval Criminal Investigative Service and the Army Criminal Investigation Command, better known as CID. They had traveled to the island under orders from General Donald Ryder of Southern Command to form a joint criminal task force to conduct law enforcement interrogations of suspected terrorists at Guantanamo.

The ferry docked and the agents hurried off. They were met by a colleague, there to show them around the place. Countless numbers of uniform-clad soldiers bustled about, readying the naval station for its new role. The colleague mentioned that military jets were arriving every day with army and marine personnel, assigned to Guantanamo by Southern Command as part of a troop buildup.

Blaine Thomas, an assistant special agent in charge for the NCIS, decided that the group should check in with the detention center's chief of staff. He and Ray Romano, a senior agent from CID, walked up a hill toward the main building. Thomas saw Marines everywhere, a good sign; as a former marine himself, he expected to be readily accepted by the troops.

The two men stepped inside the building and wandered through some hallways. When they reached the office, the chief of staff signaled for them to wait outside while he handled another matter. Minutes passed. Finally, they were called in. Thomas reached out to shake hands.

The chief ignored him. "Who are you, what the fuck are you doing on my island, and why the fuck are you eating my food?"

Okay, Thomas thought. *That's how it's going to be.*

"We're here representing General Ryder, who was tasked by Secretary Rumsfeld to set up this task force," Thomas said. "I'm a special agent with NCIS, and I'm a former marine."

The chief shrugged. "Yeah? So what?"

His priority was detention, the chief said. Everything else—intelligence, criminal investigations—was secondary to him.

"If you get a chance to do interviews, that's fine," he said. "If you don't, don't come complaining to me."

Romano cleared his throat and decided to try the personal touch. He held out a hat, emblazoned with the CID letters. "I thought you might like to have this," he said.

The chief glanced down at the offering with a look of contempt.

"I don't wear hats," he snapped.

With that, Thomas and Romano left the office, already certain that this would be a very unpleasant assignment.

The office at Bagram Air Base in Afghanistan was bitter cold despite the brazier of burning coal. Two American law enforcement officials sat in silence across from Ibn al-Shaykh al-Libi, the al-Qaeda military commander who the Americans officials believed was the highest-ranking member of the terrorist group in their custody.

Al-Libi had been captured near Tora Bora after two guides lured him and some young al-Qaeda fighters into a trap, turning them over to Shiite tribes in Pakistan for money. The Shiites gave al-Libi to the Pakistani military, which then surrendered him to American troops on December 19.

Army interrogators gladly yielded the task of questioning al-Libi to law enforcement. The job fell to Russell Fincher, a special agent from the FBI's anti-terrorism unit at the New York Field Office, and Marty Mahon, a New York City detective who had been part of the Joint Terrorism Task Force for years. They knew how to conduct an effective interrogation and were moving slowly through the paces.

Some time had passed since the two had walked into the room. They had read al-Libi his rights but had said nothing else. Al-Libi was being given some time to relax, to understand he was safe—but was also being thrown off balance by Americans who were not saying or doing anything.

"Hello," Fincher said finally. He offered al-Libi some coffee.

He pointed southwest. "Mecca is in that direction," he said. All devout Muslims, no matter where they are in the world, pray while facing the Kaaba, a building in Mecca that is the most sacred site in Islam. Fincher had just helped al-Libi meet his Islamic duties.

Fincher explained that he was a devout Christian and joined with al-Libi in prayer sessions, followed by discussions about God, Muhammad, and Jesus. No questions, no yelling, just the slow process of developing a relationship with their witness.

Al-Libi seemed taken aback. This was not what he had been taught to expect. There was no torture, no pain. These men were friendly, even likable. He had no fidelity to bin Laden; he never felt particularly close with the al-Qaeda leader and had begun to consider him selfish.

So he talked. He wasn't a member of al-Qaeda, he said, having never formally pledged his allegiance to bin Laden. But he mixed with the group quite easily and knew many of its senior members. He was acquainted with Richard Reid, the man now called the shoe bomber, who had attempted to blow up an American Airlines flight bound from Paris to Miami. Reid had trained with al-Qaeda and stayed in the group's two-floor guesthouse in the Shar-e Naw area of Kabul, near the Pul-e Khishti Bridge. He didn't speak much, and stayed aloof from others. Al-Libi also provided information about Zacarias Moussaoui, the al-Qaeda member arrested in Minneapolis shortly before 9/11.

While he denied any connection between al-Qaeda and Iraq, he did reveal a critical secret—al-Qaeda was in the final stages of a plan to blow up the American embassy in Aden. This was actionable intelligence, information that could save American lives.

The raw information from al-Libi was typed up quickly into FBI 302s—notes of interview—and transmitted to the Pentagon, the CIA, and the senior leadership of the FBI. The interrogators in Bagram had every reason to believe that the sessions with al-Libi would be seen as an unmitigated success.

The message shot out from the CIA station chief in Kabul: The FBI was screwing up. Al-Libi was holding back.

That opinion reached the White House the same day. Clearly, the station chief was right. Al-Libi had to know more than he was telling. He was a senior member of al-Qaeda, and claimed not to know anything about the group's connections to Iraq? Absurd!

The order went out. This gentle approach wasn't working. The CIA needed to take over. It was time to get rough.

Fincher and Mahon were conducting another day of questioning with al-Libi when a Toyota Tundra pulled up to the building. Without warning, a CIA officer in his mid-fifties climbed out of the truck, then burst into the interrogation room with military troops.

"You're going to Egypt!" the CIA man barked, pointing at al-Libi.

As Fincher and Mahon stood by helplessly, the soldiers grabbed al-Libi and strapped him to a stretcher. They bound his feet and hands, sealed his mouth with duct tape, and pulled a hood over his head. Troops lifted al-Libi onto the stretcher, took him out to the Toyota, and put him inside a box in the back. Then the truck drove away.

On January 11, pilots from the 445th Airlift Wing banked a C-141 cargo carrier over the mystically lucid sapphire waters of the Caribbean Sea. Ahead, the sheltered inlet of Guantanamo Bay appeared, its surrounding lowlands rising steadily through foothills toward blue and purple mountains in the distance.

The Lockheed Starlifter passed over the rocky shoreline and touched down on a small, unwelcoming airstrip encircled by scorched grass and scrub. After a twenty-seven-hour flight from Kandahar, the first twenty suspected terrorists had arrived at the detention camp.

Four Humvees—three with fifty-caliber machine guns and the fourth with a grenade launcher—ringed the plane. A navy Huey helicopter circled overhead. Forty marines with rifles, helmets, and face shields crowded around the airstrip in an intimidating show of force.

Just before 3:00 P.M., the rear doorway of the aircraft opened, and a manacled figure appeared. He was dressed in a fluorescent-orange jumpsuit and cap, a turquoise surgical mask over his mouth, blacked-out goggles, and sound-blocking earmuffs. On the tarmac, he was frisked by military police.

After being searched, the detainees were loaded onto a white bus with windows that had all been blacked out. Once the twenty prisoners were secured, the bus drove down to the bay and onto a ferry, beginning the twenty-minute journey from the leeward to the windward side.

A group of marines waited in silence outside of Camp X-Ray. Hours before, they had heard that the first detainees had arrived at the airfield and, since then, had received intermittent updates on their location. The last notification had just been radioed in—the terrorists would arrive in sixty seconds.

A bus appeared, escorted by two military Humvees. As the line of vehicles came to a stop, the marines could hear their comrades inside the bus yelling at the detainees.

"You're the property of the U.S. now!" one soldier shouted.

The marines outside lined up in groups of two in front of the bus exit. The door opened and the first man appeared, wearing leg irons and a belly chain. He was thrown to the waiting soldiers, who grabbed him by his arm and his shirt. As they dragged the man away, someone called out that the detainee had only one leg; seconds later, his prosthetic limb was tossed off the bus.

Detainees were placed on their knees in a line until all twenty had been brought out. The pairs of marines then hauled them toward a holding area. Each man was taken to a chair and examined by a medic. Afterward, they were fingerprinted and assigned an internment serial number, or ISN. Their goggles, masks, and earmuffs were removed for a moment while they were photographed, then put back on.

From there, they were taken to their cages in Alpha Block. The detainee designated as ISN 374—a man in his late fifties or even his late sixties, one of the soldiers guessed—was terrified. As he was taken toward his cell, the man shook and stopped lifting his feet. The guards carrying him started to yell.

"Walk faster!" one shouted.

The man was taken inside his cage and placed on his knees. One of the soldiers bent down and unshackled the leg irons as his partner held the man around his upper body. The soldier then came around in front to remove the handcuffs. The detainee began swaying back and forth. Both guards, along with an interpreter, yelled at him to stop.

The soldier unlocked the handcuffs. The detainee pulled away, pushing into the marine holding him.

The marine grabbed the man by his biceps and his shirt collar and slammed him face-first onto the cement floor. Then he fell on top of the detainee, holding him down by his neck so that the man couldn't move. The guard's partner left the cage as the officer in charge hustled over. He shoved the cage door closed, then spoke into a radio.

"Code red! Code red!"

Seconds later, the gate flew open again and other marines ran in. They grabbed their colleague, who was still pinning the detainee to the ground, and pulled him out of the cage. Then they jumped on top of the man and hog-tied him with cuffs and chains.

He was left in that position, facedown, for a few hours.

The next morning, the left side of detainee 374's face was bruised and scraped. The marine who had been bumped by the man the day before came by to check on him. He had done his assigned job by physically controlling this man, but still his conscience was eating at him.

Why had the man resisted? What was he trying to accomplish? The marine couldn't let the questions go, and a few days later, he heard from another detainee on the block what had happened.

The man had arrived at Guantanamo without having heard or seen anything for more than a day. He had no idea where he was or what his captors' plan for him was. His home country was a violent place, and he had seen people he knew executed right in front of him. But before they were killed, they were forced onto their knees.

When his shackles were removed, the man, terrified that he was seconds from death, pulled away in a feeble attempt to protect himself. So the guards, unaware of what was happening, shoved him to the floor and piled on top.

A row of nineteenth-century double-gallery houses lines the 900 block of Euterpe Street in the Lower Garden District of New Orleans, a tangible record of the city's golden age. Named for the muse of music of Greek mythology, the street has attracted an eclectic collection of residents—artists, lawyers, businesspeople—eager to be immersed in the trappings of a long-gone era.

Among the residents in early 2002 were Clive Stafford Smith and his wife,

Emily Bolton. Stafford Smith, born in Cambridge, England, had decided to become a lawyer so that he could provide representation to criminal defendants facing execution. He worked on hundreds of death penalty cases for the Southern Prisoners' Defense Committee in Atlanta, earning a reputation as an attorney willing to confront what he saw as the racism in the legal system that drove the American push toward executions.

A series of death penalty cases had drawn him and Emily to New Orleans, and their love of the aesthetic persuaded them to buy a tumbledown house on Euterpe Street. Each day, he worked at the offices of Reprieve US, the American offshoot of a British legal charity he had founded. Each night, he returned from his office to the house, its lights cutting through the street's darkness. There, he would spend part of the evening unwinding while reading a newspaper.

On a night in January, Stafford Smith was poring over the paper when an article caught his eye. The United States was shipping terrorist suspects to a detention center in Guantanamo Bay. The men had no lawyers, no access to courts, and no means for contesting their incarceration.

This is a catastrophe. Stafford Smith had an overwhelming sense of horror; this was unlike anything he had ever encountered in the free world. These people were being held beyond the reach of civilized society, in a place where they would have no legal rights. America was fighting a war to defend itself and its principles and the first thing it does is abandon the rule of law? This was *exactly* the kind of injustice he was fighting in the death penalty cases, he thought.

Stafford Smith was spitting mad and took the paper to his wife. "I cannot believe what these people are doing!"

"You need to calm down," Bolton replied.

The next morning, Stafford Smith was still seething. He put a leash on their golden retriever, Melpomene—the muse of tragedy—and started on his mile walk to the Reprieve offices in the central business district. Inside, he saw an Australian colleague, Richard Bourke. Stafford Smith removed the dog's leash and caught up with his coworker in the kitchen, where he was making some coffee. Bourke already knew about the situation at Guantanamo.

"Can you believe it?" Stafford Smith asked.

"That fucking cunt is outrageous!" Bourke replied, referring to President Bush.

Both men continued raging in anger for a few minutes.

"All right," Stafford Smith said finally. "So what are we going to do about it? And how?"

• • •

Later that same week, the lawyers from Reprieve US went for drinks at Circle Bar, a nightclub constructed inside a New Orleans mansion near the Interstate 10 overpass. The place is funky, in an Addams Family sort of way—furtive and conspiratorial, with chipped plaster and red-glowing candles battling feebly against the Gothic darkness. When there was serious business to discuss at Reprieve, this avant-garde hangout was the off-site conference room.

That evening, the topic was Guantanamo.

"This is the injustice of our age," Stafford Smith said. "It's that simple. We can't just turn away."

But there were practical considerations that they needed to consider before taking on the Bush administration's latest outrage, one of the lawyers replied. Reprieve was already being assailed for its work on behalf of prisoners facing execution—what would happen if they started representing Osama bin Laden's buddies? The 9/11 attacks were still tearing at the American psyche, and now Stafford Smith wanted to jump into the fray on behalf of these terrorists? It would undermine their work for death row inmates. It could well lead to the end of Reprieve.

There was another problem. Bourke's immigration status was more provisional than Stafford Smith's; an Australian who could be sent back home by the government shouldn't be going after the administration in court. Stafford Smith accepted all of the arguments; there were many good reasons for his group to stay out of it.

"All right, here's what we're going to do," he said. "I'm going to get involved, but the office isn't going to get directly involved."

There would be no office funds used, the Reprieve name would not be mentioned and would not appear on any court filings. It would just be Stafford Smith.

Copies of a draft legal opinion were laid out on the conference table in the Situation Room. John Yoo sat near the center, looking satisfied as lawyers from other government departments and agencies studied the document. It had taken several weeks, but he and his colleague Robert Delahunty had finally produced this preliminary version of the memo about the application of the Geneva Conventions to the Afghan War.

The passionate debate hadn't diminished, so Gonzales had once again called a meeting trying to reconcile the conflicting opinions. If nothing else, Yoo could incorporate elements of the different outlooks into the next draft.

Will Taft, the State Department legal advisor who had emerged as Yoo's primary opponent on the topic, was the first to speak.

"Geneva has defined our wars," he said. "It is not possible to have a war unless Geneva applies. We—"

"Well," Yoo interrupted, "does that mean we can't have a war with a country that never signed the Geneva Conventions?"

Taft gave Yoo a quizzical look. "What do you mean?"

"We had the Korean War. North Korea hadn't signed the Geneva Convention, but we had the war. So how could you be right?"

Taft listened, lost in thought. The argument seemed so misplaced—this wasn't some technical question about who put what ink on what document. This was about the policies of the United States, about its unwavering application of the conventions to all hostilities involving its troops.

Everyone began speaking at once. What, someone asked, was the Pentagon's position? Douglas Feith, the undersecretary of defense for policy, took that.

"It's a matter of policy that we want our troops to have the protection of the Geneva Conventions, but we don't want to give these terrorists Geneva protections," he said.

Eyes turned to General Peter Pace, the vice chairman of the Joint Chiefs and the only member of the military at the meeting. He laced his fingers together as he set his hands on the conference table.

"Look, you're the law side," Pace said in a rich baritone voice. "What's important for us is that we train our troops to obey Geneva."

The commitment of America's troops to the conventions did not come with an off switch. The terms and meaning of the treaties were beaten into the heads of new soldiers; it was a foundational part of military training.

"We tell them that if they follow Geneva, then they will be honorably treated when they're captured. That's—"

"General," Yoo said, interrupting, "I just read this report that says that any American soldier who falls into al-Qaeda's hands will get killed right away. They're not interested in taking prisoners. That's one of the reasons they're terrorists. No matter what position you take, they're not going to follow any rules."

Pace didn't back down. "It's important for the United States to be seen as standing for the Geneva Conventions and complying with them in our situation," he said.

Taft and Yoo fell into a discussion about Common Article Three, part of all four of the Geneva Conventions, which dictated that detainees in military hostilities had to be treated humanely, meaning that they couldn't be subjected to pain, humiliation, or degradation. Others listened as the two lawyers dissected individual words, trying to classify the current war. But no matter how many times they examined the text, Yoo said, the law was clear; Geneva didn't apply. Still, he was not there to dictate policy; his job, Yoo said, was to let the decision makers know their legal options.

"You could certainly make the argument that we're not legally bound by Common Article Three but just say that we're going to follow it on our own decision, for foreign policy purposes," Yoo said.

Taft nodded. "I like that idea," he said.

"Wait," Feith said. "Why don't we just publicly say we're going to follow Common Article Three, but then not do it?"

There was an awkward silence.

Hundreds of people, many carrying long-barreled weapons, surrounded the compact five-story building that housed the central prison for Sarajevo. It was January 17. Word had spread among the city's Muslim community that the six Algerians being held in the jail on suspicion of terrorism were about to be released, then handed over to the Americans. A reporter from a local radio station was broadcasting live coverage of the protest and encouraging locals to come protect the men. More people arrived each minute, many of them armed.

The civilians were not alone. SFOR troops were stationed around the prison, encircling the Sarajevo residents. Officials with the Coordinating Team—the Federation's antiterrorism unit—watched the scene with foreboding. The military troops would undoubtedly comply with Bush's order. This could quickly escalate into a bloodbath.

Not far away, Federation ministers gathered for a tense meeting. As the officials considered what to do, they received regular, disturbing updates about the situation from the Coordinating Team.

Every choice was fraught with peril. Memories of the lawlessness and violence from the Kosovo War were still fresh in the minds of the people. If the ministers elected to surrender the Algerians, they would be acting contrary to the orders of the court, ignoring laws that were holding the fragile country together. But if they refused the American demands and the troops moved in, the ensuing violence could race out of control. The Americans might even deem the Federation a country protecting terrorists. Under Bush's "with us or against us" formula, Bosnia-Herzegovina, a nation dependent on the Americans for its existence, could fall into the "against us" category.

The ministers had to choose. There was no time left.

A motion was offered to turn over the Algerians to SFOR, regardless of the court's findings. All those in favor? Hands shot up.

The vote was unanimous.

At about that same moment, a judge from the Federation Supreme Court handed down his decision in the case—there was no evidence that the six Algerians had engaged in or supported any terrorist activities. The charges were dismissed. They were free to go.

The six men were readying themselves to walk out of the prison gate when, without warning, the Bosnian police pulled black hoods over their heads and shackled them. Outside, the SFOR troops took defensive positions. Before anyone in the crowd realized what was happening, the Algerians—their faces hidden—were handed over to the Americans. Rapidly, the soldiers whisked them into an awaiting truck, which immediately drove away.

The time that followed was a blur. Once firmly under the control of SFOR, the men were stripped naked, given medical exams at gunpoint, then hustled onto a military plane. They were chained down. Black goggles, earmuffs, and surgical masks replaced the hoods.

Soon, the aircraft was flying over the Mediterranean Sea; no one had yet told the men why they had been taken or where they were going. After traveling one thousand miles, the plane landed at Incirlik Air Base in Turkey. The men were moved into a hangar and forcibly dressed in jumpsuits. Afterward they were loaded onto a C-141 cargo plane and chained again.

The turboprop flew for thirty hours. The men could feel the plane bump as it touched the ground—but where?

While they were still unable to see or hear, the chains were removed; the shackles remained. Two people lifted each man and took him toward the door of the plane. The first was carried off and hit by a sudden and unexpected blast of heat.

He and his compatriots, soon to be known as the Algerian Six, had arrived at Guantanamo Bay.

• • •

The last of the men who would eventually take the Bush Administration to court over its detention policies were now in hands of the United States.

Hamdi, the American citizen seized in Afghanistan. The Tipton Three. Salim Hamdan, Bin Laden's driver. And the Algerian Six just handed over by Bosnia. They were nobodies, men who had lived anonymous lives, specks on the ever-lengthening scroll of suspects in custody.

But before the decade was out, they would make history, as the centerpiece of Supreme Court decisions that would change the face of American law.

That same day, Gonzales was on the telephone with Bush. He called because Yoo and Delahunty had just issued their formal opinion on the applicability of the Geneva Conventions to the Afghan War. Gonzales was detailing the findings so that Bush could make the decision.

None of the conclusions were a surprise. Yoo and Delahunty had already submitted their less comprehensive memo to the Pentagon nine days ago, but this was the first time Bush heard their judgment.

Common Article Three—dealing with the treatment of prisoners of war—did not apply in the fight against al-Qaeda. There were also strong reasons, Gonzales explained, that the Taliban could not claim its protections. According to the legal analysis, the Taliban were not a constituted government and Afghanistan was not a sovereign country. It was, instead, a failed state with multiple tribal groups battling for control.

The Taliban also did not meet three of the four requirements to be deemed POWs if captured—they did not wear uniforms, did not have a command structure where a military leader was responsible for the actions of subordinates, and did not obey the laws of war. For those reasons, the United States was not bound to grant either al-Qaeda or Taliban members the protections offered POWs.*

The briefing persuaded Bush. That day, he decided that Common Article Three did not apply to the conflict with either the Taliban or al-Qaeda.

Rumsfeld got the word out to the military the next morning, a Saturday, in a memo to General Pace.

---

*The analysis did not examine whether al-Qaeda or Taliban members qualified for Common Article Three protections under the Fourth Geneva Convention, which would have been the required alternative under the ruling of a U.N. tribunal. See Notes and Sources.

"The United States has determined that al Qaeda and Taliban individuals under the control of the Defense Department are not entitled to prisoner of war status for purposes of the Geneva Conventions of 1949."

However, he wrote, commanders were to make sure that the detainees were treated humanely and "to the extent appropriate and consistent with military necessity" in a manner in line with the conventions.

The directive, Rumsfeld wrote, was to be sent immediately to all combatant commanders, who in turn were ordered to provide it to their subordinate commanders, including the head of Task Force 160, the military unit responsible for the care of detainees at Guantanamo. The memo was transmitted that afternoon to officers in the field by secure telex. By morning, those officers began notifying the troops. The standards of the Geneva Conventions that soldiers had been taught almost from the first moment they joined the military were no longer fully in effect.

Within hours, it became clear that the debate about the Geneva Conventions hadn't quite ended. When Powell heard Bush's decision, he reached out to the president, urging him to reconsider. There were options that had not been presented to Bush, he said, and downsides of the decision that had gone unexplored.

None of Bush's close advisors could ever remember the president changing his mind once he made a decision. But given Powell's impassioned plea, the president agreed to reopen the discussion.

"Where's bin Laden?" the CIA officer barked.

Al-Libi said he didn't know, an answer he knew carried severe risks. From the moment when he had been snatched away from Bagram Air Base, his captors had threatened that they were going to take him to Cairo for questioning, a terrifying prospect. The Egyptians were widely known as brutal interrogators who resorted to horrific torture if they didn't like a prisoner's answers.

Now he was being questioned by the Americans while on board the USS *Bataan,* and it was clear that they didn't believe him. What chance would he have of persuading the Egyptians?

The CIA officers told al-Libi to remove his socks and gloves, then put him onto the floor. The room was freezing, but that was nothing compared with what might happen to him in Egypt. After about fifteen minutes, the interrogators brought him back up and put him into a chair.

By then, al-Libi had decided—he would tell the Americans what they wanted to hear. Maybe if he lied, they might change their minds about sending him to Cairo.

Yes, he told them, he was a member of al-Qaeda, and proceeded to recite names he had already told the FBI. The American interrogators eventually came back to the issue of Iraq. What were the connections? How was al-Qaeda tied to Saddam Hussein?

There might be training of al-Qaeda fighters in Iraq, al-Libi said. An extremist named Abu Abdullah had told him that a senior al-Qaeda leader had sent him to Iraq three times since 1997 so he could be trained in the use of poisons and mustard gas.

As al-Libi fabricated his stories, the treatment from his interrogators improved. But it still wasn't enough. He was flown to Egypt a few days later.

No one in the government could reasonably argue that he didn't know what would happen to al-Libi in Cairo. CIA computers were bursting with voluminous files about the brutal techniques of torture employed by the Egyptians.

The agency knew from a source in the country's security service that twelve suspects had been tortured to death by authorities since 2000. The CIA files revealed that subjects of interrogation were taken to the offices of the State Security Investigations Services, where they were handcuffed, blindfolded, and abused to extract information and confessions. Suspects were electrocuted, doused in cold water, beaten with metal rods, raped, suspended in the air for hours by ropes that pulled their tied hands behind their backs—the list of inventive cruelty was endless.

Now the Egyptians would be employing their brutal skills on al-Libi, searching for more secrets about al-Qaeda, including its connections to Iraq that the Americans considered undeniable.

A team of administration lawyers boarded a Gulfstream jet at Andrews Air Force Base two days later for their first trip to the Guantanamo Bay detention camp.

On the way down, Gonzales approached John Yoo and Will Taft, legal advisor to the State Department. The stalemate about the Geneva Conventions decision had to be resolved. Given that they had some time on their hands, he wanted them to hammer out their differences.

"Figure out a compromise," Gonzales said.

The two lawyers sat beside each other, with Taft on the aisle and Yoo at the window. One of them brought out a pen and paper and started taking notes as they spoke.

Yoo restated his argument, with Taft at first only asking questions. When Yoo finished, Taft shook his head.

"I don't agree with your 'failed state' analysis," he said. "And you're hanging a lot on that one definition."

Maybe, Yoo said, they were handling this wrong. Even if Afghanistan was not a failed state, there were other reasons to deny the Taliban POW status—they didn't follow the laws of war, for example. There was evidence that they had become so thoroughly intertwined with al-Qaeda that they were not so much a government as an extension of the terrorist organization. That alone was reason to justify treating them as unlawful combatants.

"The president can go two possible routes," Yoo said. "We could include both options."

Yoo promised to send the next draft of his memo over to the State Department and try to incorporate Taft's position.

"Gentlemen, welcome to Guantanamo Bay."

Brigadier General Michael Lehnert smiled as he greeted the group of lawyers who had just joined him in a meeting room at the naval station. Everyone found a seat, the lights were dimmed, and Lehnert began a PowerPoint presentation about the detention center.

An image was projected on the screen. "Guantanamo Bay," it read. "The least worst place."

Everyone laughed. Rumsfeld said those words at a recent press conference, when a reporter asked what made Guantanamo the best location to hold the detainees.

"Any day, we're going to have T-shirts made up with that on it," Lehnert joked. The soldiers were clearly proud of Rumsfeld's nickname for the base.

From there, Lehnert laid out the plans for the detention center. The Power-Point displayed an image of Camp X-Ray.

"We don't have a new facility, but here's what we're doing with the existing facility," he said.

The next image. Drawings of a new camp.

"Here's what we're going to build, what it's going to look like," Lehnert said.

Then, the basic statistics. How many detainees could X-Ray hold, how many were already there, how long until the new camps were built. From there, it was on to the tour. An aide to Lehnert escorted them to old empty cages made from chain-link fencing.

"We used these to hold the Haitians back in the 1990s," the aide said. "We don't have enough space otherwise."

"How do you know they're still secure?" one of the lawyers asked. "It's been ten years since they were used."

"Simple. We locked a couple of our guys in there and told them that if they could get out, they could have all the beer they wanted. They were shaking it and banging it, and they couldn't get out. So, yeah, I think they're secure."

The group walked around the holding area, most of the lawyers averting their eyes from detainees who were sitting cross-legged inside their cells.

"We're trying to emphasize safety," the aide said. "No one's allowed to be alone with a detainee. They're constantly under observation from the watch-tower. There are guard dogs. Last thing we want is for one of these guys to try and hurt somebody."

None of the marines on base questioned whether these were dangerous men. "The first guy who got here, when he landed, started shouting that he wanted to kill Americans," the aide said. "We're not going to let that happen. There are always people watching to make sure that the detainees don't surprise anybody."

The tour ended, the lawyers ate lunch, and then they returned to the jet. As they took their seats, one of them chuckled.

"Just a few weeks ago, those people were fighting in Afghanistan," he said. "And now look. They're all sitting back here."

Everyone agreed—this was a moment to be happy. The administration was taking down the enemy.

The plane took off. As it was winging its way over the Caribbean, Addington approached Gonzales. Under the commissions order, Bush was supposed to designate each person who was to be tried before a military tribunal. But no one at Guantanamo was going to be heading into the American courts.

"I think you should seek a blanket designation of all of the detainees being sent to Guantanamo as eligible for trial under the president's order," Addington said.

Gonzales agreed.

The intelligence was sketchy. A detainee had told American interrogators about a man known as Sufaat—they hadn't yet divined his full name—who was rumored to be running al-Qaeda's biological weapons program. The previous summer, members of the group had helped Sufaat move laboratory equipment from Karachi to Kandahar, and while no one was told why al-Qaeda needed the sophisticated material, there was gossip that it was being used to grow the bacteria that cause anthrax. When the anthrax attacks began in the United States, at least one of the men involved in transporting the equipment believed that al-Qaeda was striking America with Sufaat's microbes.

The CIA ran the name through its bulging list of al-Qaeda members and associates. There were more than a few "Sufaats," so there was no telling who, if any of them, was the right man.

The raw intelligence was included in the threat matrix report, delivered through the national security system. There were strong reasons to suspect, administration officials concluded, that al-Qaeda was behind the anthrax mailings.

Then, another scrap of information: Sufaat had fled Afghanistan for Pakistan to set up a new anthrax lab. The Americans believed they had even learned the location where the experiments were being conducted. FBI agents involved in the investigation of the anthrax attacks headed to Pakistan and searched for the laboratory.

They were close to the truth. Sufaat was the researcher responsible for al-Qaeda's anthrax program, he had fled from Afghanistan to Pakistan, and he had resumed his work there. But the information divined by the Americans about where he was hiding was wrong.

The FBI agents returned to the United States, convinced that the lab was in some part of Pakistan. They just didn't know where.

Canadian authorities fanned out across Ottawa on the morning of January 22, conducting searches and interviews in their continuing investigation of Maher Arar and Abdullah Almalki.

At that point neither man was in the country. Almalki had traveled to Malaysia with his wife, children, and parents to visit his wife's family. Arar was in Tunisia to attend to his father-in-law, who was ill. His wife, Monia Mazigh, was pregnant and couldn't make the trip.

At 7:30 A.M., two Mounties arrived at Arar's apartment in Nepean, a city adjacent to Ottawa. Corporal Randy Buffam knocked on the door and Mazigh answered. Buffam and his colleague identified themselves.

"Could I speak to Maher Arar?" Buffam asked.

"He is not home."

There was a moment's pause. "Where is he?"

"Abroad."

"What do you mean by abroad?"

"Overseas."

"How long has he been gone?"

"He's been away for three weeks."

Mazigh grew increasingly uncomfortable. She had no idea why these men were at her door or what they wanted with her husband.

"How long until he returns?"

"Maybe three days."

"Whereabouts is he overseas?"

"Tunisia."

This wasn't going anywhere. Buffam left his business card and asked Mazigh to have her husband call.

In a different part of town, the Mounties were questioning Almalki's brother. They wanted to know about the radios that Almalki's company, Dawn Services, was selling to a Pakistan corporation. Similar radios had been found in Afghanistan—not necessarily the same radios, just the same make and model. Still, they believed Almalki might have been the one who was shipping the technology to al-Qaeda. The brother knew nothing, and the Mounties left.

As the years passed, the Mounties would conduct innumerable interviews trying to connect Almalki's radios to the ones found in Afghanistan. But they would never check serial numbers against those in Almalki's shipping documents. They wouldn't even contact Microelectronics, the Pakistani company that Almalki had told them was his customer. Officials with Microelectronics later said they would have gladly confirmed their purchases from Almalki if someone had just asked.

Arar telephoned Canadian officials from Tunisia later that day and left a voice mail. Why, he demanded, were the Mounties going to his apartment so early in the morning without warning? They had disturbed his pregnant wife.

Buffam called back and for several days they traded calls until Arar returned to Ottawa. The officer reached him there and asked him to come in for an interview.

"For what reason?" Arar asked. "How did you get my name?"

He couldn't discuss an ongoing investigation over the phone, Buffam said.

"We'd like to meet you in person to simply clarify some issues which have surfaced as a result of our inquiries."

Arar said that he had just returned from Tunisia and could not meet Buffam until the next day.

The call unnerved Arar. He decided that, if he was going to be questioned by the police, he wanted a lawyer there. He telephoned Michael Edelson, who agreed to meet with Arar. The lawyer immediately called Buffam and left him a voice mail. He said that he was representing Arar, and if the police wanted to speak to his client, they needed to go through him. Moreover, Edelson said that if he arranged for officers to speak with Arar, his client's statements couldn't be used against him in any future legal proceeding. The interview would be used to provide whatever clarification was needed. Nothing more.

Buffam consulted another officer with the Mounties. They agreed—the meeting with Arar should be canceled if they couldn't use his comments in a prosecution. It was a waste of time to question him just to gather information.

The final debate about the Geneva Conventions issue was scheduled to be held at a meeting of the National Security Council. In preparation, officials were pulling together memos in support of their positions.

The day after returning from Guantanamo, Yoo had sent Gonzales a new thirty-seven-page opinion; it contained modest changes, but the document still amounted to a robust argument that the conventions were irrelevant in the war against the Taliban and al-Qaeda.

Memos from other administration officials—including Powell—hadn't arrived yet, but Gonzales decided to put together a document summarizing the various arguments so that Bush wouldn't be caught off guard at the meeting. On January 25, he turned the job of preparing the summary memo over to his deputy, Flanigan, who in turn sought Addington's help.

Flanigan was already at his computer working on a first draft when Addington arrived, placed a chair behind him, and started reading. At first, Addington made some suggestions while Flanigan did most of the writing. When he finished, Flanigan sent an electronic copy of the memo to Addington for an edit.

The draft strongly supported Bush's original position. It presented a truncated—and inaccurate—representation of Powell's arguments along with a lengthy series of bullet points about why Bush had been right.

The legal opinion of the Justice Department, the memo said, was definitive: Bush had the constitutional power to deem the conventions inapplicable, and such a decision was allowable under the treaties. From a policy perspective, this was a new kind of war, one never conceived by the original negotiators of the conventions, and Bush could not allow himself to be locked into an inflexible system that didn't apply to the current situation.

Addington reviewed that portion of the memo. Too many people seemed to be unaware of the scope of Geneva's requirements. He wanted some way to emphasize how off the mark the conventions were in this new world.

He started typing.

"This new paradigm renders obsolete Geneva's strict limitations on the questioning of enemy prisoners," he wrote, "and renders quaint some of its provisions requiring the captured enemy to be afforded such things as commissary privileges, scrip [i.e., advances in monthly pay], athletic uniforms and scientific instruments."

That was good, he thought. Anyone wondering why the conventions didn't fit with this war would now have to contemplate the al-Qaeda football team marching to the grill for some bin Laden burgers.

By 3:30 that afternoon, Flanigan and Addington were running up against a deadline. Gonzales had promised to have a draft of the memo sent to other officials, particularly Powell, and the time had come to ship out what had been written so far.

Flanigan printed Addington's edited version and handed it off to Gonzales, who wrote in a few revisions by hand. Flanigan typed in the changes, printed the draft again, then sent it to be faxed from the Situation Room.

He took a moment to catch his breath, then gave Addington's edit a careful read. While going over the second page, he winced.

"... and renders quaint some of its provisions ..."

A little too snide, Flanigan thought. He liked the idea Addington was trying to convey, but hated the words. He edited out the line.

Powell was annoyed. Gonzales's draft memo was wrong, or at least misleading.

The memo said that Powell wanted Bush to rule that the Geneva Conventions applied to both al-Qaeda and the Taliban, but gave no further explanation what that meant. Then it suggested Powell was willing to settle on an agreement whereby al-Qaeda and Taliban fighters could be determined not to qualify as POWs under the conventions, but only on a case-by-case basis.

Completely false. Powell never said any such thing. But that was why he needed to see the draft. Gonzales wanted Powell's comments, and now he could try to get the memo to be accurate.

His comments filled up a one-page, single-spaced memo. At the top, he re-wrote the summary of his position.

> *The Secretary of State believes that al Qaeda terrorists as a group are not entitled to POW status and that Taliban fighters could be determined not to be POW's either as a group or on a case-by-case basis.*

Somehow, his argument had just slid by others in the administration. Powell was not demanding that *anyone* to be granted POW status. He just wanted Bush to publicly proclaim that the Geneva accords applied to the Afghan War. That's all. Under Geneva, the administration would be in its right to declare that neither group qualified as POWs. There was no need to take the extreme step of announcing that the United States was going to ignore the conventions, Powell thought, when the same result could be reached by following them.

From there, Powell tore at the underpinning of the memo's logic. The "failed state" argument that had been advanced by Yoo and Delahunty was problematic—it contradicted the policies of the United States and the international community, which consistently held Afghanistan to its treaty obligations and identified it as a party to the Geneva Conventions. If Afghanistan was no longer a sovereign nation, then there could be no consequences for its failure to abide by *any* treaties. Again, a serious and unnecessary outcome, growing from a flawed legal interpretation.

Powell attached his summary comments to his own letter for Gonzales. In it, he presented his real argument. There were two choices—the president could choose to determine that Geneva did not apply to the Afghan War and deny POW status to the Taliban and al-Qaeda. Or the president could determine that Geneva *did* apply to the Afghan War and deny POW status to the Taliban and al-Qaeda.

Both options, he wrote, provided the same flexibility on how detainees were treated, including with respect to interrogation, detention, and trials. Both allowed the administration to withhold the benefits and privileges of POW status. Neither option entailed significant risk that American officials would be prosecuted under domestic law on the grounds that they had committed a grave breach of the conventions.

By applying Geneva to the Afghan War, the president would be continuing to espouse the country's unwavering support for the conventions. It would preserve America's credibility and moral authority, provide the strongest legal foundation for the administration's actions, and maintain the POW status for American soldiers.

His argument, Powell thought, was hard to refute.

The next morning, Gonzales checked his BlackBerry and saw that the *Washington Times* had an exclusive story on its front page.

POWELL WANTS DETAINEES TO BE DECLARED POWS, the headline read. MEMO SHOWS DIFFERENCES WITH WHITE HOUSE.

A memo. It was Gonzales's draft memo, the one he was preparing for Bush. The one that incorrectly portrayed Powell as pushing for al-Qaeda and Taliban detainees to be deemed POWs. Now that error had been publicized as fact.

Worse, this was legal advice to the president from the White House counsel. This wasn't just some policy memo; it was protected by attorney-client privilege. And someone had handed it over to the press.

Gonzales was furious. The draft had been circulated to the State Department and the Pentagon. It had gone out the previous afternoon specifically seeking everyone's comments, so that it could be revised. A new version already existed, and there was at least one more rewrite to go. What was the purpose of leaking a work in progress, particularly when it was wrong?

He placed some calls to determine who had had access to the draft memo. The answer stunned him—once a document went into regular circulation, the number of officials able to get their hands on it was very large.

This was a harsh lesson for Gonzales. Washington played a type of hardball that was new for him. He couldn't drop his guard or assume that everyone was on the same team. He would have to be more careful.

The final version of the memo went directly to the president. No one on the staff other than Gonzales, Flanigan, and Addington was allowed to even hold a copy.

That same day in Damascus, guards entered the cell of Ahmad El-Maati and once again pulled a hood over his head.

His interrogation in Syria was complete—he had confessed to the bogus plot to bomb the Canadian Parliament, he had implicated Abdullah Almalki and Maher Arar as al-Qaeda members, he had admitted that the map found in his truck so many months before was part of a terrorist plan. All lies, but the torture stopped.

Now he was rushed to an airport and put on a plane. He prayed that he was being taken back to Canada but soon realized his torment was not over. The jet landed in Cairo, where he was handed off to the Egyptians. Once again, he was imprisoned and brought into a room for interrogation. When asked about his confessions in Syria, El-Maati tried to persuade his new captors that he had been lying. In response, they beat him.

At one point El-Maati could hear the screams of a woman nearby, obviously being subjected to torture. One of his interrogators leaned toward him, smiling.

"That's your sister in the next room," he said. "We're about to rape her."

In Building 1425 at Fort Detrick, an FBI agent sat across from Bruce Ivins, conducting his second interview with the anthrax researcher. The bacteria contained in the Daschle letter had been identified as a virulent form called the Ames strain, and investigators had turned to a handful of labs and researchers around the country that held samples of the microbe. Ivins was one of those scientists.

Ivins lectured the agent about the history of the Ames strain, explaining that the researchers in Fort Meade had first obtained it around 1981. He provided some information about a number of labs with the bacteria.

Then he offered suggestions of others the FBI should interview. There were plenty of people who had raised his suspicions, he said, some of whom had even talked about how to weaponize anthrax. He gave a list of names. The FBI, he said, should take a close look at those people. One of them might be the anthrax killer

The House sergeant at arms stood just inside the doors of the House chamber, facing the rostrum.

"Mr. Speaker!" he called out. "The president of the United States!"

Hundreds of politicians and government officials stood and applauded as Bush made his way down the center aisle in the chamber of the House of Representatives. He stopped frequently, shaking hands and pointing through the crowds in an informal greeting to certain members of Congress.

It was just after nine o'clock on January 29, the night of Bush's first State of the Union address. Not everyone in the administration was in attendance; a large group of officials, including a cabinet officer, was outside of Washington in a secure location. They were the shadow government for the evening, the people who would step in as the new administration if terrorists somehow managed to kill everyone attending the president's speech.

Bush took his place at the clerk's desk, then turned around and handed manila envelopes containing copies of his speech to Cheney and Tom Daschle, the House Speaker.

After more applause, Bush began his address. Despite all of the troubles facing the country, he said, the state of the union had never been stronger.

"The American flag flies again over our embassy in Kabul," he said. "Terrorists who once occupied Afghanistan now occupy cells at Guantanamo Bay. And terrorist leaders who urged followers to sacrifice their lives are running for their own."

He provided a litany of the American's actions and successes in taking on terrorists. While the most visible military action was in Afghanistan, he said, the United States was acting elsewhere. American troops were in the Philippines, providing counterterrorist training to that country's military. The navy was patrolling off the coast of Africa to prevent the establishment of terrorist camps in Somalia.

And specific threats had been quelled. "Our soldiers, working with the Bosnian government, seized terrorists who were plotting to bomb our embassy," he said.

Three days later, on the morning of February 1, members of the war council arrived at the Situation Room for another meeting about the Geneva issue—this time with the president.

Everyone stood when Bush walked into the room. He said a few pleasantries, then took a seat. He already had a good sense of what was coming; Gonzales had just briefed him again on everyone's opinion.

After Condoleezza Rice opened the meeting, Powell calmly stated his case. He laid out the two choices he had described in his memo, underscoring that Bush could accomplish everything he wanted without abandoning the conventions.

"We have an image to uphold around the world," Powell said. "If we don't do this, it will make it much more difficult for us to try and encourage other countries to treat people humanely."

Every day, Powell said, they were working on persuading more nations to work with the United States in the war on terror. Deciding not to apply Geneva could make that job much more difficult.

General Pace spoke next, giving his now-familiar refrain about the military's commitment to the accords. The discussion went around the table, and then Cheney spoke.

"This is a matter of law," he said. The Taliban and al-Qaeda were not lawful combatants; they didn't follow the rules of war.

"We all agree that they'll be treated humanely," Cheney said, "But we don't want to tie our hands. We need to preserve flexibility. And under the law, we can do that."

After about forty-five minutes, Bush gave a nod and thanked everyone for their input. The discussion was over.

About an hour later, Ashcroft called a meeting in his office for a group of about half a dozen department lawyers. Powell, he told them, had written a memo for Bush about Geneva before the NSC meeting. Now he wanted to write something, too.

"We need a letter to the president laying out our position," he said. This was a legal question, and the Justice Department had provided its legal advice. Ashcroft wasn't going to allow Powell to make an end run and take control of the issue.

The lawyers broke out legal pads and took turns crafting paragraphs for the letter. They finished in about twenty minutes, and the material was sent to a secretary to be typed up. The draft was presented to Ashcroft. He scowled as he read it.

"I don't like this," he said. "This isn't how I want to say it."

This wasn't about foreign policy, Ashcroft said. That wasn't his area of responsibility. But Powell wasn't supposed to be delving into the law either.

The lawyers took another shot, but Ashcroft rejected it again. He took a deep breath in frustration. "Okay!" he said. "Everybody out! I'm going to write this myself."

As his staff lawyers left the room, Ashcroft began composing the letter in longhand. He agreed with Powell that there were two basic theories establishing that neither al-Qaeda nor the Taliban was entitled to POW status.

But, it was risky to declare the conventions as relevant to this war. There was a higher chance of litigation against administration officials—or even criminal prosecution. Plus, there was no need to fear that some other country might someday declare that American forces didn't qualify for Geneva protections. His department's analysis was based on the concept that Afghanistan was a failed state; other countries would not be able to reasonably make that same argument about the United States. The legal opinion could never be turned back against the country that produced it.

• • •

That same day at the University of Washington in Seattle, a microbiologist sat at her computer composing an e-mail to the FBI about the anthrax killer.

Shortly after the attacks, the American Society for Microbiology sent an e-mail to its forty thousand members, asking them to alert the authorities of any suspicions they might have. Only this one researcher replied. She had a queasy feeling about a scientist who had been obsessed with her years before after he learned that she was a member of the Kappa Kappa Gamma sorority. His name was Bruce Ivins.

All those years ago, he had stalked her, and she was sure he was also the person who had spray-painted the letters *KKG* on the sidewalk outside her house. She had not heard from him in eighteen years; then—just three days after the first anthrax letter was mailed—he had e-mailed her and followed up with a phone call. In their conversation, Ivins chatted about her children, revealing details of their lives that he should not have known. Then he discussed the important role he played in anthrax research, and how—given the 9/11 attacks—he was on edge, concerned that terrorists might use biological weapons against Americans. It was all too bizarre, and the more she thought about him, the more convinced she became that the FBI should question this strange man.

She began her e-mail by identifying herself and explaining that she was responding to the microbiology society's request to help the authorities with the anthrax case.

"I would like to speak to someone about a former colleague who presently works with anthrax at Ft. Detrick," she wrote. "I believe that this individual is somewhat mentally unstable and has the profile of someone who COULD be capable of such an act."

She would not give her home phone number or address, she wrote, because Ivins scared her. He was adept at computer snooping, and she was afraid for the safety of her children and herself. He had e-mailed her recently to let her know he was working with anthrax, she wrote, a detail that seemed inconsequential at the time but that now struck her as ominous.

"Please," she typed, "take this seriously."

FBI agents soon contacted the microbiologist and quizzed her about her concerns. She repeated everything she had written and again implored the Bureau to take a strong look at Ivins.

But the agents disregarded the tip. After all, Ivins had joined the federal inquiry into the anthrax attacks. The FBI was relying on him for his expertise in the field. He was offering up the names of numerous suspects. His help was invaluable.

Why would they waste time investigating a man who was providing such crucial help in tracking down a murderer?

Bush reached his final decision about the Geneva Conventions issue on February 7. Colin Powell won.

In a written order, Bush stated that he accepted the Justice Department's legal opinion that the provisions of Geneva were irrelevant to the global conflict with al-Qaeda, meaning that none of its members qualified for prisoner-of-war status. He also maintained that, while he had the authority to suspend the conventions, he would not do so in the Afghan War.

"I determine that the provisions of Geneva apply to our present conflict with the Taliban," the order said.

As a result, the status of the Taliban had to be examined under the terms of the accords. Based on that review, Bush declared that the Taliban were unlawful combatants, so they, too, did not qualify for POW status.

The analysis was incomplete. Bush made no finding as to whether the Taliban would be covered as civilians, given that a human rights tribunal had ruled that everyone fell under the terms of either Geneva Convention 3, which dealt with armed forces, or Geneva 4, which applied to civilians.

Still, Bush declared, the detainees would be treated humanely. "As a matter of policy, the United States Armed Forces shall continue to treat detainees humanely and, to the extent appropriate and consistent with military necessity, in a manner consistent with the principles of Geneva," the order said.

The FBI issued subpoenas worldwide for more than one thousand specimens of anthrax. Perhaps, investigators hoped, a test that was in development would soon be available to detect a biological fingerprint in the bacteria, allowing them to compare the submissions with the microbes found in the letters. If they found a match, they might be able to trace the spores from the attack back to their source and snare the culprit who sent them.

One of the researchers who received a subpoena was Bruce Ivins. In February, he put together eight samples, including two from a batch he had developed called RMR-1029—the source of the anthrax used in the attacks. The FBI had included instructions to the researchers for preparing the anthrax, and Ivins followed them precisely with six of the submissions. But he disregarded them for the two from RMR-1029, making them useless for any analysis.

If it was an attempt at a cover-up, it worked perfectly—at least for now.

After the CIA flew al-Libi to Egypt, he was delivered to the Mukhabarat al-Aama, the country's general intelligence and security service. The agents transported him to the Mukhabarat headquarters in the Abdeen district of Cairo and immediately took him to be interrogated.

Al-Libi was brought into a room and pushed into a chair. An Egyptian official stood over him and, as he had to so many other prisoners, made a promise.

"You are going to confess," he said. "Thousands of people have been in that chair before you. All of them have confessed."

There was no reason to hold back, the man said. Al-Libi could do this the hard way or the easy way. It was his choice.

So, Al-Libi talked. He made up stories about upcoming al-Qaeda attacks. He lied about where senior members of the organization were hiding—no one would have accepted that he didn't know.

Eventually, the interrogators moved on.

The new topic: al-Qaeda's connections to Iraq. They wanted details, and al-Libi tossed out some fictional information. They beat him—they knew he was lying, one interrogator said. Tell the truth!

He stumbled to reply, but the words didn't come fast enough. An interrogator hit him several times. Then he was picked up and shoved into a box, so small that just a minute inside was agony. More than fifteen hours passed until they finally took him out. The interrogator again instructed him to tell the truth.

Al-Libi gave an answer. The interrogator struck him in the chest with his forearm, then pushed al-Libi to the floor. He was punched and kicked for a quarter of an hour. Beaten and bruised, al-Libi was allowed to sit down in the chair. An interrogator approached him, demanding again that he tell the truth.

Small lies hadn't worked. A big one would.

Three al-Qaeda members had traveled to Iraq to be trained in the use of nuclear weapons, he said. He named real people, although the story was completely false. His interrogators were pleased and allowed him to eat.

Days later, the interrogators pressed again, this time for information about al-Qaeda's work with Iraq in developing biological weapons. Al-Libi didn't know how to lie—he wasn't sure what *biological* meant. He struggled but failed to put together a story. The torture resumed.

• • •

The information was relayed to Washington through the CIA within a matter of days.

It was shared among very few officials, but it engendered a great deal of relief. A senior al-Qaeda member not only had revealed the connections between the terrorist organization and Saddam, but in the process had confirmed that Iraq was continuing work on a nuclear program.

Now they had proof—Saddam presented a danger to America and the world. The United States would have to do whatever it could to stop him. The work on plans for a war in Iraq needed to be stepped up.

8

The court clerk studied the twenty-two-page legal document with a practiced eye, looking for imperfections. He flipped back to the first page and reread the caption. No doubt, this case would be unusual.

The plaintiffs included three Guantanamo detainees, each with a relative representing him in the case, and relatives of other captives held at Guantanamo. The defendants were four government officials, including the president. And the document, headed "Petition for Writ of Habeas Corpus," demanded that administration officials prove they had the evidence and the legal authority to keep the men in custody.

The three lawyers who had just filed the document watched as the clerk picked up the date stamp and pounded the papers into the court docket.

They had to pay a filing fee, the clerk said flatly.

One of the attorneys—Stafford Smith, the lawyer with Reprieve in New Orleans—demurred.

"We'd like to file it in forma pauperis," he said, a designation of their clients' indigence. That might save them pocket change today but would spare them much larger future expenses, such as for deposition transcripts.

Did they have a sworn affidavit from the clients confirming that they couldn't afford court costs? the clerk asked. No, and they couldn't get one. Their Guantanamo clients didn't even know they had lawyers. The administration, which had repeatedly refused the detainees contact with anybody, including their families, certainly wasn't going to act as a courier of legal documents.

Without the affidavits, there was nothing the clerk could do. One of the lawyers paid the fee.

It was February 19, 2002. *Rasul et al. v. Bush,* the first major case challenging the administration's detention policies, had been set in motion.

In John Marshall Park, next to the courthouse, a small crowd of journalists gathered for a press conference. They watched as Stafford Smith and the two other lawyers—Bill Goodman from the Center for Constitutional Rights and Joseph Margulies, a civil rights lawyer who taught at Cornell University Law School—emerged from the courthouse and approached a cluster of microphones.

Goodman introduced himself, then got to the point. "We have, today, filed a lawsuit which tests the power of the federal government and the President of the United States to hold whomever he chooses simply because he does not like them," he said, "Or simply because he wants to hold them indefinitely without having any legal authority to do so."

Next was Margulies. "From one perspective, we believe this case is really very easy," he said. "The President of the United States and the executive branch simply cannot hold a person for the rest of his life without legal process, without judicial review, without being charged, without counsel, particularly when one possible outcome is the death penalty."

Was the United States, Margulies asked, really going to jettison the rule of law and scuttle the Constitution to appease the fury of a nation traumatized by the 9/11 attacks?

"And that's what this case is about," Stafford Smith added. "To ensure that hatred doesn't overcome human rights."

Stafford Smith returned home that same night, shaken by the media's reaction to his declaration of noble intent.

The reporters at the press conference had turned almost combative, hammering him and the other two lawyers with questions that suggested their initiative was a waste of time and, worse still, an offense to the American people. What merit did the habeas petition have, one journalist asked, given that Bush had already decided on the use of military commissions? What had their clients been doing in Afghanistan? Why did any of this matter, given that the men had been caught in the act of trying to kill American soldiers? But the low point came in a subsequent television interview, when a reporter asked Stafford Smith several times if he was a traitor.

This was a sign of how badly 9/11 had battered the American psyche, he thought. The journalists were making assumptions—for example, that the men had been fighting Americans in Afghanistan—that no one, not even the lawyers, knew to be true or false. Yet he had been all but accused of betraying the United States for seeking to hold the government accountable to a fundamental precept of common law and the Constitution: the state must prove that prisoners were being lawfully detained.

Stafford Smith arrived home late that night. The light on his answering machine was blinking. He pushed the play button.

A voice snarled. "You fucking faggot liberal, you're fucking ruining this country, you fucking pro-terrorism piece-of-shit faggot."

Stafford Smith stared at the machine. *Quite articulate*, he thought.

Message after message spewed the same hatred and contempt. So much fear, so much anger about the dictates of the American Constitution, he thought. The whole experience left Stafford Smith wondering.

How did they get my phone number?

Somebody needed to take charge of the interrogations at Guantanamo. Paul Wolfowitz thought he knew the perfect candidate.

Major General Michael Dunlavey was an army reservist and trial lawyer working with the NSA. He had thirty-five years' experience in counterintelligence and had recently served as the army's assistant deputy chief of staff for intelligence. Over his career, he told associates, he had conducted three thousand interrogations.

Dunlavey was ordered to meet with the defense secretary in a week. On February 21, he arrived at Suite 3E880 on the E-ring of the Pentagon and was escorted into Rumsfeld's office. He noticed a twisted piece of aluminum on a nearby coffee table; it was debris from American Airlines flight 77 that Rumsfeld had picked up outside of the Pentagon on September 11.

Rumsfeld gestured toward a chair at a round table, and Dunlavey plopped down into it. A satellite photograph beneath a glass covering on the table depicted Asia at night, with Japan and South Korea speckled white from the burning lights of their bustling societies and North Korea sunk in complete darkness. Rumsfeld called the line between black and white the "knife edge" of civilization, where tens of thousands of American soldiers stood guard, separating the flames of freedom from the dark gloom of tyranny. The metaphor captured Rumsfeld's vision of the American military's calling not only in Asia but in the ongoing conflict as well.

Wolfowitz and several other Pentagon officials joined the meeting. Rumsfeld spoke bluntly.

"We need you to set up the interrogation operations for the war on terror," he told Dunlavey.

Five days earlier, he said, Southern Command had been ordered to establish Joint Task Force 170 as the coordinator of all American interrogation efforts. Dunlavey, Rumsfeld said, would be the commander of the unit, working in Guantanamo Bay.

"We've picked up a lot of bad guys," he said. "These people are very well schooled on resistance to interrogation. We want to identify the senior Taliban and al-Qaeda operatives and find out about what they were planning, what operations they had going."

This mission, Rumsfeld said, was about getting the information America needed to prevent another 9/11. "I want the intelligence," he said, "and I want it now."

Several members of Guantanamo's Initial Reaction Force were lolling about in a large wooden shed at the back of the detention center. As a small-scale riot squad, the soldiers were under orders to steamroller any detainee who posed a threat to the military or to other prisoners. But when the camp was quiet, there was nothing for them to do but wait.

A call came in on the radio. The team was needed immediately at Bravo Block. The soldiers snatched up their equipment and scrambled over; the officer in charge was waiting alongside a member of the military police. The MP pointed at one of the detainees.

"This guy over here called me a bitch a couple of times," she said angrily. "Whip his ass!"

The response team decided to storm the detainee's cage and hog-tie him. The squad assembled at the door. Inside, the man was screaming.

"Shut up and lie down!" one of the soldiers yelled.

The detainee stared at the team, unmoving.

One of the officers unlocked the cage door. Immediately the detainee turned around, dropped to his knees, and put his hands behind his head. The lead soldier tossed aside the protective plastic shield he was holding, ran a couple of steps, and hopped into the air. His knee slammed into the detainee's back, smashing his face onto the cement floor. With the first soldier still on top of the man, the other team members ran in and piled on, slugging and kicking him.

Someone yelled out for the MP. She walked inside the cage, approached the man, then punched him twice in the head. Once the detainee was handcuffed, the soldiers stood. The man didn't move; blood seeped onto the concrete. One of the soldiers pushed him to get up. No response.

A stretcher was brought into the cage and the detainee was carried to a military ambulance. Response team members climbed inside the vehicle for the ride to the main medical facility at Guantanamo. No one spoke during the drive.

Later that night, the soldiers returned and sat down with a few friends. The group recounted the confrontation inside the cage. The detainee was in bad shape. One of the team members said that the man had gone into cardiac arrest in the ambulance.

The conversation was laced with anxiety. All of the soldiers knew that video cameras kept watch on the detainees. Could the attack this evening have been recorded? One of the soldiers reassured them that all would be fine.

"The videotape has been destroyed," he said. "So we have nothing to worry about."

In the hamlet of Chapri on the western border of Pakistan, an ancient stone arch marks the border between the country's settled areas and its tribal wild lands. On one side, modernity and democracy had taken root. On the other, lawlessness and the rule of the gun held sway.

In late February, two militiamen with the Khattak, a Pashtun tribe, stopped a battered Mitsubishi Pajero jeep. Inside were four men and three women wearing burkas. One of the militiamen asked where they were going. No response, apparently because the man he was questioning didn't understand the Pashtu language. He was a Yemeni, fleeing Afghanistan.

"Get out," the militiaman said, signaling with his hands.

The seven emerged from the jeep, and the soldiers noticed that the women were unnaturally tall; one was wearing men's sandals. Pointing their guns, the militiamen shouted at the group, demanding that they drop to the ground. A quick inspection revealed that the women were not women at all, but three African men in disguise—two from Sudan and one from the island nation of Mauritius off Africa's southeast coast.

This was quite a find. Pakistani officials were sure to want to question these suspicious people. Inquiries were made, money changed hands, and the seven were turned over to agents from the intelligence service. The driver and the other three men—all Pakistanis—answered whatever was asked of them once their palms, too, were greased. The driver revealed that the foreigners had been headed to his hometown of Faisalabad.

The questioning of the three Africans got nowhere and they remained mute. Perhaps, the intelligence agents decided, FBI officials working in a nearby town would have more success. They drove the suspects there and handed them over.

Again, out came the money, and again, tongues were loosened. They were part of al-Qaeda, the men said, and were heading to Faisalabad to join confederates hiding out in safe houses. One of them, the Africans said, was a man named Abu Zubaydah.

The agents were stunned. Abu Zubaydah was considered by the intelligence community as one of bin Laden's most trusted—and dangerous—lieutenants. If they moved quickly, the Americans might be able to snag him.

The news about Zubaydah was flashed to Washington, then back to the senior CIA officer in Pakistan, Bob Grenier. He summoned his subordinates and told them that there was now strong intelligence that Zubaydah was in Pakistan, most likely in Faisalabad.

"We've got to catch him," he said. "And we want him alive."

But first, they had to find the safe house where Zubaydah was holed up.

Christopher Meyer, the British ambassador to the United States, was fuming.

Since the 9/11 attacks, no government leader had been a more steadfast ally than Tony Blair. Britain was second only to the Americans in the number of troops it had committed to the multination coalition fighting in Afghanistan. The Pentagon already knew that the Royal Marines were days from deploying one of their elite fighting units, 45 Commando, which specialized in mountain and cold-weather warfare.

Then, the inexplicable. On March 5, as British and American forces fought side by side, the White House announced new tariffs on steel imports, including British specialty steel.

It defied political reason. Bush was a *conservative,* and conservatives were supposed to abhor tariffs as an assault on free trade. It was also diplomatic lunacy. The British *needed* a healthy steel industry; war demanded weaponry, and that required steel. How could the White House embrace Britain as its closest partner in Afghanistan—and even now begin wooing the Blair government to join in its efforts to oust Saddam Hussein in Iraq—while simultaneously treating it so disdainfully as an economic adversary?

Meyer contacted Karl Rove, a senior advisor to Bush. The two men had been friends since they first met years before in Austin, Texas, but today that relationship took a backseat. The ambassador made no attempt to hide his anger.

"What in Christ's name do you think you're doing?" Meyer snapped.

The United States had no choice, Rove calmly replied. "The steel industry is in terrible trouble. And it's in states that are important to the president's reelection effort."

Reelection? Was Rove kidding? The White House was willing to strain relations with the British to win a political chit for an election more than two years away?

"It's just politics," Rove went on. "But what we'll try to do is pass this tariff thing and we'll try to mitigate the consequences for you afterward."

Meyer ended the conversation more exasperated than ever. Not only was the Bush administration sandbagging Britain, it was doing so under the pretense that it was all about economic necessity, when in fact the decision was being driven by petty politics. And, it didn't seem that the administration cared if the tariffs accomplished anything. The implicit pledge to make up for any losses his country might incur—probably by ordering more steel from Britain—made the policy pointless. It was a zero-sum game, an economic nonevent, but one that allowed Bush to crow about his concern for the nation's Rust Belt.

These tariffs were a public slap in the face to America's most loyal friend, delivered with a private wink that it was really just a charade. This decision, Meyer fumed, was reprehensible.

The next week on March 11, Cheney arrived at Number 10 Downing Street in London for a meeting with Tony Blair. He was on an international tour, trying to gauge the support in foreign capitals for military action against Iraq. Britain was the first stop; from there, the vice president would travel to Turkey, Saudi Arabia, Jordan, Kuwait, and eight other Middle Eastern countries.

Cheney's best bet for winning over the Arabs, Blair said, was to present the administration's plans on Iraq as part of an overall Middle East peace strategy. Treating Iraq as just one piece in a giant puzzle the administration was seeking to solve, and not as the puzzle itself, was the key to the success of his mission.

"We're very conscious of the importance of a peace plan," Cheney responded matter-of-factly.

His manner was quiet, his tone calm, but for all his air of gravitas, the words he spoke seemed almost flippant, as if Blair's advice were bothersome. Neither the prime minister nor his aides believed that Cheney or Bush *got it,* could see the Middle East forest beyond the Iraq tree.

Nevertheless, Blair pushed ahead. "If you are going to deal with something like Iraq," he said, "you have to think ahead about what might happen and include things you might not expect. The best-laid plans disappear in the fog of war."

Not a problem, Cheney said. The administration would plan for all contingencies. However, it would not compromise its mission of regime change in Iraq simply to gain the support of other nations. America could go it alone.

"A coalition would be nice," Cheney said. "But it's not essential."

Later, Blair's team retired to the prime minister's residence for dinner. Cheney's final words had hit hard, their message inescapable. The vice president wasn't dismissing just the Arab nations in his calculus of power. He was also saying that the British didn't matter much to the outcome of the coming conflict.

On the morning of March 13, the sun peeked through a double-size guard tower looming over the detention center inside Kandahar Airport, now the main base for American and allied military operations in the Afghan provincial capital.

A truck accompanied by a military escort drove out of the compound, turning onto a road toward the city. Inside the first vehicle, four investigators—two FBI agents, a member of the Army Criminal Investigation Division, and an interrogator with the army 202nd Military Intelligence Battalion—rode with a slightly built Yemeni man. He was Salim Hamdan, the bin Laden driver taken into custody at the eastern border of Afghanistan several months before.

Soon after his capture, Hamdan had been transported to Kandahar, where military interrogators and FBI agents questioned him repeatedly. He offered little resistance; after two days of attempting to deceive his interrogators, he tried to answer whatever he was asked, although sometimes he struggled to understand the poorly translated queries. He had pointed out al-Qaeda safe houses and other facilities on maps of Afghanistan. He had identified a picture of Richard Reid, the shoe bomber, and linked him to al-Qaeda. And he recounted statements bin Laden had made and actions he had taken before 9/11 that showed the al-Qaeda leader knew a major attack was coming.

Today, Hamdan was accompanying investigators into Kandahar for the second time. A few weeks earlier, he had taken them to two former bin Laden residences and a safe house; American bombing had destroyed the largest of the three structures. This time, the Americans wanted Hamdan to guide them through Tarnak Farms, the main al-Qaeda training camp, near the airport.

First, Hamdan showed the investigators another guesthouse and a cemetery. It was there, he said, that he had buried the body of Abu Hafs, also known as Mohammed Atef, the al-Qaeda military commander. Then it was on to Tarnak Farms, reduced by the American air campaign to a landscape of destruction. Hamdan pointed to the ruins of one building.

"This was a mosque," he said. Shortly before the 9/11 attacks, bin Laden and Ayman Zawahiri, now the terrorist leader's second in command, had gathered about two hundred people inside the mosque. There, they announced the merging of al-Qaeda with Zawahiri's terrorist group, Egyptian Islamic Jihad, Hamdan said.

The two FBI special agents—Robert Fuller from New York and William Vincent from Los Angeles—inspected the wreckage of the mosque, strewn alongside a bomb crater fifty feet wide and fifteen feet deep.

Something caught their attention: two booklets, their pages fluttering in the wind. Before picking up the documents, the agents photographed them with a Sony FD Mavica digital camera to show where they had been found and how they looked.

One was an address book, handwritten in Arabic, with thirty entries of names and organizations that included home, business, and fax numbers. Within thirty-six hours, the NSA would begin monitoring all of them.

The other document was even more intriguing—a checkbook issued by a Saudi bank. It contained detailed information about all deposits and withdrawals. The balances ranged from 20,000 to 185,000 Saudi riyals, or about $5,000 to $50,000. Five men's names were listed on the account.

The bank name had just weeks before come to the attention of American intelligence, which had traced flows of cash from extremist groups and suspect charities through accounts there. Already, members of the administration were debating how hard they should push the Saudi government to crack down on the institution. And soon, thanks to one of bin Laden's trusted assistants, CIA officials would be able to provide fresh evidence to spark the Saudis' interest.

That night in Washington, Condoleezza Rice sat down for dinner with David Manning, the chief foreign policy advisor to Tony Blair. The calls for action against Iraq had been growing louder, some European leaders were slamming Bush for considering such an idea, and the meeting with Cheney that month had sown confusion about the administration's view of Britain's role. In a few weeks, Blair would be visiting Bush at his ranch in Crawford to discuss Iraq, and had sent Manning to impress upon the administration his concerns and suggestions about how to manage world opinion on the issue.

Blair fervently believed that Saddam posed a serious threat to the West and had been publicly sounding the alarm for years, beginning with a 1999 speech he delivered in Chicago. But his stance, and his allegiance to Bush, had already aroused hostility in Parliament and in the British press, which had taken to deriding him as the president's "poodle." The Americans had to understand the political minefield that Blair was attempting to negotiate.

"The president is deeply appreciative of your government's support," Rice said. "And he's strongly aware of the criticism the prime minister is getting."

Manning expressed his thanks. "The prime minister will not budge in his support for regime change," he said. "But he does have to manage a press, a Parliament, and a public opinion that is very different from anything in the States."

Bush could help Blair keep the upper hand in the debate, Manning said, by giving Britain a role in the formulation of policy, both diplomatic and military, aimed at driving Saddam from power. Blair would, in fact, insist on a carefully calibrated collaboration between the two countries.

"Failure is not an option," Manning said.

Bush was still wrestling with numerous questions, Rice said. How could he persuade the international community that military action against Iraq was necessary? What value should be put on Iraq's opposition in exile? And, perhaps most important, after war succeeded, what then?

Other factors needed to be considered, Manning said. "We realize that the administration could go it alone if it wanted," he said, tipping his hat to Cheney's breezy assertion of American autonomy. "But if it wants company, it will have to take into account the concerns of its potential coalition partners."

Saddam's 1998 decision to throw U.N. weapons inspectors out of Iraq was not enough to justify a military action *now*, almost four years later, he said. The Americans would have to work with the U.N. in an attempt to get the weapons inspectors back into the country. If Saddam refused to grant them unfettered access to suspect sites, his obstructionism would be a persuasive argument, even to a hesitant Europe, for a military solution.

The time had come to raise the issue that had been brushed aside by Cheney; the most important element of any strategy, Manning said, was tackling the Israeli-Palestinian conflict.

"Unless we do," he said, "we could find ourselves bombing Iraq and losing the Gulf."

The next day, Manning sent a private memo to Blair.

"My talks with Condi convinced me that Bush wants to hear your views on Iraq before taking any action," he wrote. "He also wants your support. He is still smarting from the comments by other European leaders about his Iraq policy."

Bush's diplomatic near-isolation gave Blair tremendous leverage for influencing American policy, Manning wrote, not only on getting U.N. weapons inspectors back into Iraq but also on planning for any military action. Clearly, Manning suggested, the United States could also use outside guidance to help trim back its expectations.

"I think there is a real risk that the Administration underestimates the difficulties," he wrote. "They may agree that failure isn't an option, but this does not mean that they will avoid it."

Bedlam reigned at Guantanamo Bay.

The intelligence interrogators were untrained. Translators barely had the fluency to order a cup of coffee in Saudi Arabia, much less to bridge language barriers with the detainees. No one seemed to grasp Arab culture or religion. The interrogation hut—built by members of Construction Battalion 423, known as the Seabees—allowed anyone, even prisoners, to see who was inside.

Major General Dunlavey was appalled. He had just arrived at Guantanamo to assume control of Joint Task Force 170, the coordinator of detainee interrogations, and it didn't take him long on his first walking tour of the detention center to grasp the magnitude of the disorder.

Even security was lax—to him, the facility looked like nothing more than a dangling fence. He learned that there had been a small riot. One detainee had sharpened a spoon into a knife, while others had gotten their hands on pieces of metal, like welding rods, and fashioned weapons out of them. Defense Department photographers wandered around unimpeded, snapping pictures for publication without showing the slightest concern about the potential of disclosing valuable information to al-Qaeda.

Then there were the detainees themselves. Only 5 percent of them had been picked up by the United States. It soon became obvious that far too many of them weren't terrorist masterminds, but dirt farmers turned over by Afghanis and Pakistanis seeking a bounty. One was hard of hearing and appeared to be over a hundred years old; guards nicknamed him "al-Qaeda Claus." Three others appeared to be in their seventies and eighties.

Dunlavey decided that spending time interrogating—or even guarding—these old-timers was a waste of resources. He pushed the Defense Department to send the men home. The Pentagon refused for ten months, then quietly released them. No information had ever been discovered suggesting that the old men had any connection to terrorism.

At a conference table in Jim Haynes's office at the Pentagon, David Addington was fidgeting with a black binder. He was there for a briefing from Haynes about the Pentagon's progress in setting up military commissions and—as expected—the news was infuriating.

The binder alone provoked Addington's rage; he wouldn't even bother to open it, and refused to pay much attention to Haynes's explications of its contents. The thickness of the file told him all he needed to know—the Pentagon had produced a nightmare of bureaucratic red tape. This policy had been rammed through the decision-making process in a matter of days so that the tribunals would be ready to go immediately. All for nothing.

The document that Haynes was presenting described, in excruciating detail, the procedures the tribunals would have to follow and the responsibilities each participant would have to shoulder. It covered every base, from defining the rules of evidence to setting the qualifications of the presiding judge to prohibiting the filming of the proceedings.

Addington stewed. Franklin Roosevelt had managed to pull together his military commissions in a matter of days. Why was the Pentagon dragging out the process for what seemed to be an eternity?

Part of the problem, Addington knew, was that Rumsfeld uncharacteristically had abandoned his usual decisiveness. Instead, he appointed "the wise men"—people like former attorney general Griffin Bell, who knew both the law and the ways of Washington. Predictably, creating this group led to more consultations, debate, and delay.

As he listened to the briefing, Flanigan pondered all the energy being expended on these rules. Haynes was a good friend, so Flanigan was trying to find a nice way of asking the question on his mind: *What the hell are you doing?*

Addington beat him to the punch. "Well," he said sharply, pushing the binder away, "this looks like just a repeat of the Prosper Commission."

That task force, chaired by Pierre Prosper, had dawdled for weeks delving into the minutiae about how to try terrorists, Addington said. That was why he, Flanigan, and Gonzales had stepped into the breach to get an order out.

"All you're doing is replaying those issues," he said. "And by the way, when are you going to be ready to stand up one of those tribunals you're talking about?"

Not to worry, Haynes said. "It won't take very long to do. We'll get them up and running quickly."

"But you have the president's order," Addington said. "Why not just use a simple, streamlined process for constituting a tribunal and get moving?"

"You know we can't do that," Haynes said. "The secretary wants it done this way."

Addington shook his head. "Does the secretary read the president's military order as an order? Or does he read it as a license to create a new judicial system?"

This wasn't about keeping things simple for the sake of simplicity. The military had plenty of detainees at Guantanamo, Addington said. He had no sympathy for them, but they at least should be given a chance to go to trial.

Gonzales held up a hand. Addington, he thought, was being too brusque. This was not a way to handle the situation.

"It looks like you're doing a very good job," he said to Haynes, smiling. "Looks like you're talking to the right people. Keep us informed."

The meeting came to an end and the lawyers went their separate ways, confident that the Pentagon would abandon its sluggish approach and get the military commissions running soon. They could not have imagined that years would pass before the first trial would be held.

A group of boys laughed and shouted as they played soccer on a street alongside a sprawling beige villa in Faisalabad. A misplaced kick sent the ball flying into the gated yard of the house, called Shabaz Cottage. A man sprang to the door.

"Get out!" he yelled at the boys in Arabic.

A passing policeman heard the ruckus and took a look. Not only did the man in the house speak a foreign language; he was too pale-skinned to be Pakistani. A little more surveillance, a few quiet questions around the neighborhood, and the policeman learned that a large contingent of Arabs lived there, kept the shutters closed at all times, and never left the property. Something suspicious was going on, the policeman decided. He reported the information to his superiors, who relayed it to Pakistani security forces. They passed it on to the Americans.

• • •

The NSA was conducting electronic surveillance of Shabaz Cottage, the surrounding neighborhood, and thirteen other houses identified through intelligence gathering as terrorist havens. The report from the Pakistani policeman confirmed many of their suspicions. At least two of the locations—Shabaz and another called Issa—were determined to be safe houses operated by Lashkar-e-Tayyiba, one of the largest Islamist organizations in South Asia. Some of the initial intelligence indicated that the two were part of a network of houses and operatives enlisted by Zubaydah after the fall of Kandahar to help al-Qaeda fighters escape from Afghanistan.

Analysts listened in on satellite calls from those residences to Saudi Arabia, Yemen, and other countries. Evidence piled up; authorities grew confident that Zubaydah was hiding at Shabaz Cottage.

At the Civil Lines Police Station in Faisalabad, Pakistan, officers were readying themselves for a raid. The assignment seemed routine—the industrial and agricultural city was a magnet for illegal immigrants, and police often arrested crowds of them in late-night sweeps.

Just past midnight on March 28, the police chief, Tsadiqui Hussain, was busying himself in his colonial-era office when a throng of men clad in bulletproof vests paid him a visit. They included officials with Pakistani intelligence, the CIA, and the FBI; they told Hussain that they needed his help.

The raid tonight would not be a typical roundup, one of the Pakistani agents told Hussain. It involved much bigger prey than usual, a Middle Eastern terrorist that the United States wanted locked up. One of the Americans brought out a stack of photocopies and passed them around. Each page contained a picture of an Arab man and many showed how the man might look if disguised—clean-shaven, with a goatee, with long hair, with short hair.

The man, the officials told Hussain, was Abu Zubaydah, a key player in al-Qaeda. If he was captured, American officials were confident they would gain unparalleled insight into the terror group's inner workings, and possibly obtain the evidence they needed to track down bin Laden himself.

This would be, the officials cautioned, a very dangerous undertaking. The terrorists would be well armed with guns and explosives, and they had already demonstrated a willingness to kill. But the police couldn't just go in shooting—finding out what the terrorists knew was the goal.

"You need to capture the subjects alive at all costs," one of the Pakistanis told Hussain.

The chief called in reinforcements. More than one hundred officers were assigned to raid Shabaz Cottage, while others were stationed at checkpoints on roads in Faisalabad or dispatched to cover alternate means of escape.

The police arrived at the mansion at 3:00 A.M. and scaled the front gate. After snipping the electric wire at the top, they dropped down into the yard and made their way to a garage. Three guards were sleeping there, and the assault team subdued them. The police called out for the men inside to surrender. When there was no response, they bashed open the door and pushed their way inside.

Zubaydah was there. He and three other Arabs snapped up cash and fake passports in the house and ran upstairs to the roof, with the police just steps behind. Trapped, Zubaydah and the other men took a running leap off the house, soaring over barbed-wire fencing and landing on the roof of the villa next door. But the Pakistanis had anticipated that escape route—four officers were waiting for the Arabs and grabbed them. Zubaydah exploded in anger.

"You're not Muslims!" he shouted.

"Of course we are," one of the officers replied.

"Well, you're American Muslims!" Zubaydah said.

Suddenly one of his comrades lunged at a police officer, grabbing his AK-47. A firefight broke out, and Zubaydah was hit in the stomach, the leg, and the groin. The man who grabbed the gun, Abu al-Haznat, was shot dead. Another terrorist and three police officers were injured.

John Kiriakou, a CIA agent, rushed to the scene and grabbed the senior Pakistani security officer. "Where is Abu Zubaydah?" he shouted.

The officer pointed to a bloodied body sprawled on the ground. "This is Abu Zubaydah," he said.

This had to be a mistake, Kiriakou thought. He had studied Zubaydah's appearance, and this guy didn't look like him at all. He was fatter, maybe by forty pounds. His hair was wild. His face was different. Kiriakou sought out a colleague for advice.

"Get me a picture of his iris," the colleague said. Optical identification through biometric scanning would do the job.

Kiriakou leaned down to Zubaydah. "Open your eyes!" he ordered. It was no use—the man's eyes were rolled back in his head.

"Okay," the colleague said. "Then get me a close-up of his ear."

Ear identification? That was something new to Kiriakou. The Dutch had been the first to try it and had solved a series of gas-station robberies by examining the image of an ear captured on video. The CIA adopted the technique soon after.

Kiriakou snapped a picture and, using his cell phone, sent it to his colleague. A moment passed. "It's him."

Kiriakou looked down at Zubaydah. His wounds were severe; he was almost certainly going to die. They had to get him medical attention right away.

The senior Pakistani security officer disagreed. Zubaydah had killed one of his men. "We will fuck with him," he said. "Then he's going to die."

No, Kiriakou snapped back. "I'm going to get fucked if he dies before we get him to the hospital," he said. "Those are my orders. This is nonnegotiable."

Zubaydah was handed off and dumped in the back of a Toyota mini truck that raced away from the scene.

Shabaz Cottage and the other safe houses proved to be gold mines of intelligence. Searches turned up computers, three dozen memory disks, cell phones and notebooks filled with phone numbers, electronic notes, an al-Qaeda artillery manual, and ten thousand pages of other material. On a table was a partially built bomb, along with evidence that indicated it was to be used in an attack on a school. A roster on the wall listed the names of those in the house assigned kitchen duty; the most fascinating entry read "Saturday, Osama."

Whatever resentments lingered between the United States and Pakistan over bin Laden's escape from Tora Bora melted away. The joint raid by police and security agents was celebrated as proof that Islamabad was becoming a full partner in the war on terror.

Pakistan soon enjoyed the fruits of that cooperation when the administration paid a bounty of millions of dollars for its help in capturing Zubaydah.

The hospital room was stifling and infested with mosquitoes. Zubaydah lay in the bed motionless, with wires and plastic tubing connected to his body. A few feet away, John Kiriakou was sitting in a fold-up metal chair; he had been ordered to watch Zubaydah until he woke up. Hours passed as the agent swatted at the buzzing insects while sweating through a crimson T-shirt emblazoned with the image of SpongeBob SquarePants.

At last, Zubaydah stirred. Kiriakou walked to the head of the bed. His captive opened his eyes and fear spread across his face. His heart rate jumped, setting off an alarm. A doctor and nurse ran into the room and administered Demerol, a narcotic. Zubaydah drifted back to sleep.

Time passed. Zubaydah woke again for a few seconds, delirious and asking for wine. After another few hours, he came around a third time, fully conscious. He motioned to Kiriakou. The agent walked over and moved his oxygen mask.

"Please, brother," Zubaydah said, weeping softly. "Kill me."

"Kill you?"

"Yes, please, brother, kill me. Take the pillow, put it over my face, and kill me."

"No, my friend, no one is going to kill you. You're very important to us. We worked hard to find you. And we have a lot of questions we want to ask you."

Zubaydah sobbed. "Please," he moaned, "please kill me."

The Chilterns lie northwest of London, a vista of sweeping grasslands, honeysuckle-draped cottages, and the crack of cricket bats on plush village greens. Church bells ring out across the leafy stillness, adding an almost mystical aura to the scene's unearthly beauty.

Unobtrusively tucked into the chalk hills is Chequers, the sixteenth-century mansion that serves as the official country residence of Britain's prime minister. The estate overflows with treasures from European history, including letters written by Oliver Cromwell, Napoléon, and the poet Robert Browning, as well as a ring worn by Queen Elizabeth I.

While Chequers is traditionally used as a weekend getaway, Blair and his staff traveled there on Tuesday, April 2, for an in-depth and hard-edged debate about Iraq. The meeting with Bush at the Crawford ranch was three days away, and this would be Blair's best opportunity to hammer out a strategy for bending the president's will a bit closer to his own.

The British officials gathered at ten that morning on the first floor in the Long Gallery, and Blair described his predicament.

"I believe that Bush is in the same position I am," he said. "It would be great to get rid of Saddam, but can it be done without terrible unforeseen consequences?"

British intelligence presented an assessment of the situation in Iraq. The state of its military forces was adequate, the opposition to Saddam was feeble, and

Saddam himself—well, he was a maniac. Those elements made a combustible and unpredictable mix. The consequences of an American-led invasion were anybody's guess.

Admiral Sir Michael Boyce, the chief of defense staff, launched into a diatribe about the West's near helplessness to influence the course of events in Iraq. Worse, he said, was the Bush team—members of the administration were secretive, even hiding information about the plans for Iraq from their own colleagues. It was hard to tell if *anyone* in Washington grasped the wider strategic picture.

"Only Rumsfeld and a few others know what's being planned," Boyce said to Blair, mispronouncing the name as Rums*field*. "You may speak to Bush or Rice, but do they really know what's going on?"

Blair waved off Boyce's doubts. "In the end, Bush will make the decisions," he said.

Another problem—Blair had been pushing for a new U.N. Security Council resolution against Iraq before launching a military campaign, but the Americans didn't think it necessary. Bush and his aides believed that earlier U.N. declarations about Iraq provided a sufficient legal basis for war.

Lieutenant-General Sir Anthony Pigott, who had coordinated Britain's efforts in Afghanistan, was invited to give his views. It was possible, he said, to launch a full-scale invasion that culminated with an assault on Baghdad.

"It would be bloody," he said, "And it would take a long time."

Even then, he said, victory could not be proclaimed with the defeat of the Iraqi army and the overthrow of Saddam. The preparations for war *had* to include a realistic plan about how the allies would manage Iraq once the fighting ended. "The Americans believe they can replicate Afghanistan, but this is very, very different," he said.

Boyle piped up again. A British soldier based in Tampa and working with U.S. Central Command, he said, had told his superiors in London that he could not get a read on General Tommy Franks. The Americans seemed to be planning for something later, maybe around New Year. By all appearances, Franks was considering using solely airpower and Special Forces to topple the Baathist regime. If so, the game plan was woefully inadequate.

"If they want us to be involved in providing forces," Boyle said, "then we have to be involved in all the planning."

The military men finished their presentation, and Blair stroked his chin.

True, he said, the Americans' planning and strategy was flawed. But that left him caught in a conundrum.

"Do I support totally in public and deliver our strategy?" he asked. "Or do I put distance between us and lose influence?"

The primary issue, Pigott said, was defining the goal of any military assault. Was the central aim to target Iraq's weapons-of-mass-destruction capabilities, or was it to oust Saddam and usher in a new regime?

"It's regime change, in part because of WMD," Blair said. "But more broadly because of Saddam's threat to the region and the world."

Just saying "weapons of mass destruction" would not persuade the public that this was a war worth fighting, Blair said. "People will say that we've known about WMD for a long time."

So many uncertainties, so many problems. Only one thing was guaranteed, Blair said. "This will not be a popular war. And in the States, fighting an unpopular war and losing is not an option."

The U-Tapao Royal Thai Navy Airfield is located ninety miles southeast of Bangkok on the coast of the Gulf of Thailand. During the Vietnam War, the United States used it as a forward operating base for B-52 Stratofortress bombers and KC-135 Stratotankers, refueling aircraft of the Strategic Air Command. In the recent bombing runs over Afghanistan, U-Tapao served as an indispensable refueling station, although the Thai government kept that secret to avoid inflaming the country's Muslim population.

Now, in April 2002, the United States turned to U-Tapao once more. A small, disused warehouse at the airfield was hastily secured as the site of a temporary secret prison where the CIA could hold and interrogate senior al-Qaeda operatives far from the public eye.

Their first guest was Abu Zubaydah. After receiving his medical treatment in Pakistan, he had been whisked by the CIA to U-Tapao for interrogation. Ali Soufan and Steve Gaudin—two FBI agents who had worked on the investigation of the 1998 embassy bombings—were dispatched by Washington to assist in the questioning.

Their supervisor, Charles Frahm, gave them specific instructions. The CIA was in charge of Zubaydah, and its operatives would call the shots. Zubaydah was not to be read his Miranda rights. If the CIA did anything that discomforted the two agents, they were to leave the facility and call headquarters.

Speed was of the essence. Interrogation subjects are at their most vulnerable from the chaos and trauma they feel just after being caught—the so-called shock of capture. The agents needed to get to Thailand fast so they could take advantage of this period of overwhelming confusion for Zubaydah.

Soufan and Gaudin arrived before the CIA interrogators. They went to Zubaydah and spoke with him in Arabic and English; Zubaydah was fluent in both languages. At first, Zubaydah insisted he was not the person that the agents thought. His name was Daoud, he said, not Zubaydah.

Soufan smiled. "How about I call you Hani?"

It was the nickname Zubaydah's mother had given him as a child; Soufan had found that tidbit by digging through FBI files. Zubaydah couldn't hide his surprise. These men had come prepared.

"Okay," he said.

With that, the agents and the terrorist began to talk.

Soon after, Zubaydah went into septic shock from his gunshot wounds. His condition was grave, and the CIA was not equipped to treat him. Worried that Zubaydah might die—taking his secrets with him—the agents rushed him to a nearby hospital.

Soufan and Gaudin stayed with Zubaydah, dabbing his lips with ice, cleaning him up after he soiled himself, changing his bandages, and pushing for better medical care. When he was conscious, they prayed with him.

"Ask God for strength," Soufan told Zubaydah.

The agents weren't acting solely out of compassion; rather, this was another tactic, known as "dislocation of expectations." It is designed to disarm a suspect who is braced for harsh treatment. Most captured terrorists expected to be manhandled and tortured—they were caught off guard by acts of kindness from someone versed in their language and culture. Psychologically unsteady and deprived of a frame of reference, they often responded by cooperating.

As Zubaydah's health improved, the agents questioned him again. They had come to Thailand with a handheld computer containing pictures of suspected al-Qaeda operatives, in hopes that Zubaydah would identify them. Gaudin asked Soufan to show Zubaydah a photograph of Abdullah Ahmed Abdullah, a suspect in the 1998 embassy bombings. The wrong picture popped up.

Zubaydah stared at the photo. "How do you know Mukhtar?" he asked.

"We know all about Mukhtar," Soufan replied without skipping a beat.

He was lying. The FBI had been struggling to identify a person called

"Mukhtar" who had been mentioned in bin Laden recordings. The CIA had been pursuing leads about the man for a year, but it wasn't the top priority. The name seemed like just another drop in an ocean of data.

But by pretending he knew of Mukhtar, Soufan retained dominance in the interrogation. Had he expressed excitement about the name, Zubaydah would have realized he had information that the agent coveted and could have seized the position of power merely by clamming up. In this game of mental poker, Soufan had no choice but to make a high-stakes bluff.

Soufan moved on to other pictures, then casually returned to the photograph of Mukhtar.

Zubaydah looked up. "How did you know he was the mastermind of 9/11?"

Neither agent answered. Instead, they plowed ahead on other topics, silently containing their elation.

After the night's questioning, they forwarded the information to Washington. CIA analysts pored over their records about Mukhtar. They located an August 28 cable that gave the man's real name.

Mukhtar was Khalid Sheikh Mohammed.

How, the CIA officials debated, would they force Zubaydah to *really* talk?

Sure, the FBI had made some headway, but the information was mostly flotsam. Admitting who he was? Identifying Mukhtar? Not enough.

Once again—as they had with al-Libi before whisking him off to Egypt for more abusive interrogation—agency officials believed that their captive knew far more than he was letting on. A source had revealed that Zubaydah had assembled plans to strike Israel, or Saudi Arabia, or perhaps India. His name had been linked to a plot involving an attack on a school—and possibly not just one. Evidence confirming that intelligence had turned up in Zubaydah's safe house. There, authorities had found a map of a British school in Lahore near a table loaded with bomb components. Then there was "chatter" being intercepted by the NSA—it was spiking again, just as it had been before 9/11.

Something bad was about to happen; people were about to die. There was no time, agency officials argued, for the FBI's treasured "relationship building." If Zubaydah wouldn't speak, then the CIA had to pry the information out of him.

At a series of meetings at agency headquarters in Langley, top counterterrorism experts floated ideas for tactics. Perhaps they should place Zubaydah in a cell filled with corpses. Surround him with naked women. Administer electric shocks to his teeth.

None of the agency officials knew much about interrogating captured terrorists, and all but one man in the room expressed doubts about which road to take. That lone exception was Jim Mitchell, the former SERE psychologist who had analyzed the Manchester Manual for the CIA. Despite his own lack of expertise in the methodology of interrogations or the psychology of Arab terrorists, Mitchell's calm self-assurance captivated the others in the room.

"The thing that will make him talk," Mitchell told them, "is fear."

As the CIA officers listened to Mitchell expound on the benefits of aggressive tactics in interrogation, a classified report that would have shown him up as a fool lay buried deep within the bowels of their own headquarters.

Decades before, agency psychologists and interrogation specialists had conducted extensive research on successful interview techniques, publishing the findings in a 1958 classified report. The study reached two unequivocal conclusions: Interrogators who cultivated relationships with captives got results, while those who threatened and bullied got nowhere.

"Maltreating the subject is, from a strictly practical point of view, as shortsighted as whipping a horse to his knees before a thirty mile ride," the report said. "It is true that most anyone will talk when subjected to enough physical pressures, but the information obtained in this way is likely to be of little intelligence value."

Even the theory at the heart of the argument in favor of rough treatment—that it would eventually push the interview subject into confessing to the lies he had previously spun during less aggressive questioning—was wrong, the study found. Instead, subjects had to be gently guided into a tacit, yet unspoken, acknowledgment of their deceit, sparing them the indignity of having to admit it.

"Showing some subjects up as liars is the very worst thing to do, because their determination not to lose face will only make them stick harder to the lie," the report said. "For these, it is necessary to provide loopholes by asking questions which let them correct their stories without any direct admission of lying."

The approach, the study said, was somewhat different from that used by law enforcement, because the focus of an agency interrogator should be on what persuaded a subject to talk, rather than on whether the information could be used as evidence in a court. But the technique used by the FBI of establishing a relationship was the best for CIA interrogations, too.

"An interrogation yields the highest intelligence dividend when the interrogee finally becomes an ally," the report said.

That was what the best minds of the CIA urged. But their report was languishing in a forgotten corner of the agency's headquarters. Elsewhere in the building, a psychologist who didn't know what he was talking about was clamoring for the approach that the experts had long ago concluded was worse than worthless. And the officials listening to his breezy assurances were eager to get going on Mitchell's advice.

The London bureau for Al Jazeera overlooks the Albert Embankment on the south side of the Thames, directly across the river from the headquarters of MI5, Britain's domestic intelligence service.

On an early April morning, Yosri Fouda, a reporter with the Arab television network, had just arrived at the office when his cell phone rang. The line crackled.

"*Salaam-u-alaikum,* Brother Yosri," a man said. "I am someone who means well."

The caller hadn't given his name, and Fouda didn't recognize his voice. But the man sounded friendly and was apparently devout—the first words he had spoken were an Islamic greeting.

"I hope you are thinking of preparing something special for the first anniversary," the man said. "Because if you are, we can provide you with some exclusive stuff."

The first anniversary. It was still a long way off, but was this man talking about 9/11?

The caller asked Fouda for a secure fax number and, as soon as the reporter gave him one, hung up.

A three-page fax arrived a few days later. It was an outline for a three-part documentary about the 9/11 attacks, complete with instructions on where to do the filming, whom to contact, and what to say. Fouda could scarcely believe the arrogance of this anonymous author in assuming that he could dictate the content and structure of a report by a global news organization.

Uncertain how to proceed, Fouda took the fax home with him that night so he could reread it. After he arrived, his cell phone rang again. The mysterious man was calling back.

"Would you like to come to Islamabad?" he asked. "We will make sure that you are, God willing, fine and that you get what you want."

A religious man, apparently with detailed knowledge about 9/11, wanted him in Pakistan so he could be given information. Fouda wasn't sure where this was going, but he smelled a scoop.

"Absolutely," he replied. "As soon as I can get a visa, you will find me, God willing, at your end."

He had arrived on the first flight of detainees brought to Guantanamo and had been assigned Internment Serial Number 9, abbreviated in the center's documents as ISN 009. The official list of captives' names identified him as Himdy Yasser, but no such person existed at Guantanamo. Instead, he was Yaser Hamdi, a name mangled during sloppy processing.

The Americans had picked him up with dozens of other men, including John Walker Lindh, at Qala-i-Jangi following the uprising in the compound. Like Lindh, he stood apart from the others. He was American. But unlike Lindh—who had been brought to the United States and indicted on felony charges—Hamdi was locked up at Guantanamo.

When he told his interrogators he had been born in Louisiana, they didn't believe him, though his English was flawless. And because he had lived in Saudi Arabia since he was a toddler, even he didn't realize that his birth in Baton Rouge made him an American citizen. In early April, someone checked his story and found his birth certificate. Hamdi had been telling the truth.

The news rocketed to Jim Haynes at the Pentagon. He could scarcely believe it—*another* American had been fighting alongside the Taliban. What was this?

Haynes alerted Rumsfeld, who seemed flummoxed about what to do.

"I recommend that we bring this guy into the United States," Haynes said. "We've already been through this with John Walker Lindh. We need to be consistent."

The situation also posed a potential legal threat to Guantanamo, he said. A court was far more likely to extend its reach to the detention center in Cuba if an American citizen was there. Moving Hamdi out would solve the problem.

Rumsfeld agreed. Officials at Guantanamo received the order and hurried Hamdi from his cell. Taking Hamdi back to the United States required some care. If he was going to be handed over to the Justice Department, he shouldn't travel by military transport, Washington officials decided. Instead, he was loaded onto a jet that belonged to the FBI.

Haynes's deputy, Whit Cobb, called John Yoo to alert him to the news.

"You won't believe this," Cobb said. "Looks like we found an American citizen among the people at Guantanamo."

"You've got to be kidding!" You replied. "How'd that happen?"

"It appears he was born in the U.S., then left as an infant for Saudi Arabia. So he's a citizen."

Not good news. "This guy *has* to be brought back to the United States," Yoo said. "We can't have him at Guantanamo Bay."

While Hamdi was in transit, administration lawyers rushed to an emergency meeting in Gonzales's office. Not all of them bought Haynes's argument that this detainee should be allowed on American soil, citizen or not. Maybe, some thought, the plane should be diverted before it had a chance to land.

"I don't think this is a good idea," Addington said.

"The decision's already been made by the secretary of defense," Haynes replied.

Flanigan broke in. "It could cause some real problems," he said. "It's going to completely shut off the military commission process."

Instead, Addington said, bringing Hamdi to the United States would put a possible habeas corpus case on a fast track. Then some judge somewhere could order the administration to produce Hamdi and potentially reveal evidence that the administration had against him.

Haynes strongly disagreed. "He is a U.S. citizen," he said. "We *have* to bring him back to the United States."

Anger flashed across Addington's face. "This should have been more carefully vetted," he said. "This is a decision that's going to have far-reaching consequences."

They needed to limit the potential damage, Addington said. If Hamdi was going to be brought to the country, then the administration had to make sure he wasn't taken to a region covered by a federal circuit that might be unfriendly to the government. The best choice, the lawyers agreed, was the Fourth Circuit. The appeals court there was conservative and most likely to lean toward the administration's argument.

The instructions went out. The plane carrying Hamdi was ordered to fly to Norfolk, Virginia, inside the Fourth Circuit.

• • •

The afternoon of April 5 was brisk but sunny when the FBI plane from Guanta-namo landed at Chambers Field in the Norfolk Naval Station. At 2:15, a green minivan with tinted windows pulled beside it. Soldiers walked Hamdi, chained and blinded by black goggles, off the plane and into the van. It drove down Hampton Boulevard toward the base's brig. It would be his home for much of the next three years.

That same evening at Bush's ranch in Crawford, Tony Blair sat down at a dining table, his back to three off-white bookcases stuffed with historical works and autobiographies.

It was the first day of the two leaders' summit to discuss the Middle East. Until a week ago, Iraq had been the front-burner topic. Then world events in-terceded. The Israeli Defense Forces had launched a military operation in the West Bank, the largest since the Six-Day War in 1967. The action, called Op-eration Defensive Shield, followed a series of attacks against Israel carried out by Palestinian armed groups, part of the uprising known as the Second Intifada. The fighting had intensified three days earlier, with an Israeli siege at Jenin, a Palestinian refugee camp, followed by a ferocious counterattack.

As they dined, Bush and Blair discussed the rapidly deteriorating situation. Any hopes for advancing the Middle East peace process were now dashed. And this was not an isolated issue, Blair said. He repeated the message he had deliv-ered to Cheney weeks before—the conflict between the Israelis and the Pales-tinians had to be part of the strategy for Iraq.

"These are not divisible problems," he said. "It is one problem with differ-ent facets, and this Israel-Palestine conflict is an important one of them. Reso-lution of that would have an enormously beneficial impact with the Muslim world."

"I understand your position, Tony," Bush replied. "But I don't believe we can wait for one problem to be solved before we address the other."

Blair expanded on his argument. The linkage was fundamental, and address-ing it was vital to any success. But, to his frustration, Blair could tell that Bush didn't buy it. The prime minister asked where the administration now stood in its strategy for Iraq.

"We don't have a war plan set," Bush said. "But I have set up a small cell at CENTCOM to do some planning and think through the various options. When they've done that, I'll examine their suggestions."

Blair again urged caution. If there were openings for resolving questions about Iraq's weapons of mass destruction without going to war, they had to be pursued. A new initiative with the United Nations, he said, could be presented to Saddam as his last chance.

Bush didn't have much faith in the U.N. approach. But, he said, he was no warmonger either. "If Saddam allows the U.N. inspectors in to do their work, unfettered," he said, "that would mean adjusting our approach."

The reverse, of course, also held, Blair said. If the peaceful, international route didn't work, then a coalition had to be ready to act decisively to remove Saddam. But in preparation, they needed to pursue a public relations campaign that could address the growing international hostility against a military action. Bush agreed.

Blair went to bed that night feeling relieved. Bush, it seemed, *did* want to build a coalition of nations to work with the Americans on Iraq; he communicated none of Cheney's disdain for such an approach. In fact, Blair mused, Bush seemed to tacitly distance himself from the hawks in his administration.

The next morning, the sky over Crawford was black with thunderstorms, a welcome sight for the local farmers and ranchers who had been struggling through a dry spell.

At 9:30, just after breakfast, Bush, Blair, and their top aides gathered in the president's office, a one-story building about half a mile from the main house. Bush, Andy Card, and Condoleezza Rice sat one side of the room; Blair, David Manning, and the prime minister's chief of staff, Jonathan Powell, were across from them.

Bush and Blair gave an account of their discussion from the previous day. They were still in the stage of reviewing options, the men said. No final positions had been taken; nothing had been set in stone.

After that short briefing, Iraq was cast aside, and the group turned to the Middle East conflict. A conference call connected the group to Powell and Stephen Hadley, Rice's deputy. General Anthony Zinni, who had been appointed by Bush as a special envoy to Israel and the Palestinian Authority, joined the call from Tel Aviv and described a meeting he had just had with the Israeli prime minister, Ariel Sharon. While Sharon insisted that Operation Defensive Shield would not end until the Palestinian terrorists had been routed, Zinni explained, he had agreed to allow the general into the West Bank so that he could meet with Yasser Arafat, the Palestinian Authority chairman.

For the rest of the morning, the British and American officials hashed over ideas for managing the Israeli-Palestinian standoff. Years later, critics would cite this meeting as the time when Bush and Blair agreed to invade Iraq. Not only was there no such deal; Iraq was not even the main topic of conversation.

At about that same time, Frank Dunham Jr. was sitting at the breakfast table in a house on a dead-end street in Virginia Beach, reading a front-page article in the local newspaper.

U.S-BORN TALIBAN HELD IN NORFOLK, the headline read. The piece reported that Yaser Hamdi had been seized in Afghanistan during a prison uprising, sent to Guantanamo, and then, when military officials determined he had been born in Baton Rouge, transferred to the United States.

What struck Dunham was that officials were not recognizing any of Hamdi's basic rights as an American. He had no lawyer, and, at least according to the article, the Bush administration was holding him without pursuing criminal charges, as it had against John Walker Lindh.

That's just wrong, he thought.

Dunham knew that, as the head of the public defender's office for the Eastern District of Virginia, he would be getting involved in the case as soon as he returned to work on Monday. He had already taken up the defense of an accused terrorist, Zacarias Moussaoui. But in its treatment of Hamdi, the government seemed to be taking its stance toward captured jihadists in a troubling new direction. Moussaoui, a foreign national accused of involvement in the 9/11 plot, had been criminally charged and granted the constitutional rights afforded any defendant in an American court. Not this time.

Given that Hamdi was a citizen with no apparent links to the hijackings, Dunham would have expected him to be afforded at *least* the same rights as Moussaoui. And Lindh? The same people had arrested him on the same day in the same place under the same circumstances; he was in federal court, too. The unfairness of Hamdi's fate seemed inescapable, and certainly looked bad— while the American son of a wealthy California family and the Frenchman were sent to civilian court, the American of Saudi descent who lived in the Middle East was locked up in a brig, uncharged.

Dunham had no compunction about stirring up this hornet's nest. Even though he already represented an accused terrorist, no one could paint him as some wild-eyed radical. He was a conservative Republican who had served in the navy, a former federal prosecutor who had gone into private practice as a defense lawyer in white-collar and military cases. Then he abandoned that lucrative career to be the federal public defender in the district, at half the pay. With meager resources, he had managed to assemble a group of lawyers for the office in little more than a year.

He had learned to make do with the basics. So that morning, he reached for a pad and pencil and began drafting a letter, seeking to represent Yaser Hamdi.

At eleven o'clock that morning, Bush and Blair held a press conference inside the gymnasium at Crawford High School; any hope for meeting with reporters outdoors had been dashed by the torrential rain.

Both men gave opening statements summarizing the topics they had covered in their two days of talks—terrorism, the Middle East, weapons of mass destruction. They made no mention of Iraq.

Bush invited questions. The first two journalists asked about the Israeli incursions into the West Bank. Then Bush called on Adam Entous, a reporter from Reuters.

Had the problems in the Middle East threatened Bush's effort to build a coalition for military action against Iraq? Entous asked. And had Bush convinced Blair that a military solution was necessary?

They had indeed talked about Iraq, Bush said. Both he and Blair agreed that Saddam Hussein was obligated under the years-old U.N. resolutions to prove he had no weapons of mass destruction.

"I explained to the prime minister that the policy of my government is the removal of Saddam and that all options are on the table," Bush said.

He turned to Blair. Any sensible person, the prime minister said, would recognize that the region, the world, and the Iraqi people would be better off with Saddam out of power.

"This is a matter for considering all the options," he said. "But a situation where he continues to be in breach of all the United Nations resolutions, refusing to allow us to assess, as the international community have demanded, whether and how he is developing these weapons of mass destruction—doing nothing in those circumstances is not an option, so we consider all the options available."

The men sounded as if they were in agreement. They were open to trying anything that might rein in Saddam Hussein. And if diplomacy failed, then war could well be the only alternative.

• • •

After returning to the ranch, a few of the British and American officials were chatting outside a bungalow. As they spoke, Bush's dog, Barney, trotted over.

Bush motioned toward the dog. "This is my Leo," he said.

Leo? The prime minister's son?

Alastair Campbell, a senior Blair aide, blurted out the thought that was on everyone's mind

"Hold on," he said. "Leo's not a dog."

Bush smiled. "Yes, I know," he said. "But Barney's the substitute for the little boy I never had."

It was a charming moment, one that reinforced Campbell's growing impression that Bush had evolved into a more confident leader. At press conferences, Campbell had sometimes winced at the president's slouching posture and inartful delivery that seemed to reflect a lack of confidence. But today was different. Bush appeared energetic and self-assured. Everything in his demeanor, including his willingness to engage in lighthearted banter, proclaimed that the president had found not only his voice, but his purpose.

That night before dinner, Campbell mentioned to Bush how serene he had seemed during the press conference. True, Bush said. Since the last time he had met with Blair, he said, he had changed his attitude about himself and his job.

"In the early days, I really got knocked when they put down the way I mangle words, and it really made me hesitant," he said.

But now, Bush said, he had given up caring what the reporters thought about his verbal gaffes, and that made all the difference.

"The truth is, I have a limited vocabulary," he said. "I'm not great with words, and I have to think about what I say very carefully."

The two spoke for some time—about reporters, about Iraq—when Bush noticed that Campbell was one of the few in the room who wasn't nursing a beer.

"Why aren't you drinking?" Bush asked.

A shrug. "I'm a recovering drunk," Campbell said.

Bush nodded. "Yeah. Me, too."

"How much did you drink?"

"Well, two or three beers a day," Bush said. "A bit of wine. Some bourbon. But I gave it up in August 1986."

The two men compared their histories with alcohol. Bush's drinking didn't come close to matching Campbell's daily binges.

"Having a breakdown and not drinking has been the best thing that ever happened to me," Campbell said. "It was like seeing the light."

Bush glanced at him quizzically. "But you still don't believe in God?" he asked.

This was the second time that day the question had come up. In the morning, Campbell had fallen into a conversation with a woman in Bush's e-mail prayer group who had asked if he had faith in God. She seemed to pity Campbell when he told her no. And he gave Bush the same answer.

At dinner, Bush and Campbell engaged in a spirited conversation about running. After the meal, Blair grabbed a guitar and started strumming and singing along with Daddy Rabbit, a band hired for the occassion. The evening ended with a few after-dinner toasts.

"All right, everyone can leave," Bush announced, sounding jovial. "I want to go to bed."

Pleasant though the evening had been, the British officials puzzled over one striking aspect of it—Bush seemed more at ease with them than he did with his own staff. The president's aides showed great deference to him, Campbell said to Blair, but none of them kidded around with him. They didn't seem to recognize that Bush had a touch of Austin Powers, the fictional—and goofy—secret agent from a series of movies.

"That's why he seems to enjoy the banter with us," Blair said. "He doesn't seem to have anyone there who just has a laugh."

On April 15, Bruce Ivins carried a plastic test tube into his office at the army's infectious disease research center in Fort Detrick. Standing beside his bookcase, he brought out a stick that looked like a Q-tip with a wooden handle. It was a sterile swab, often used to test for bacterial contamination in his anthrax lab.

Ivins swiped the swab across part of the bookcase, inserted it into the test tube, broke off the wooden handle, and pushed a cap onto the container. He wandered around the "cold side" of the lab—the portion where no tests of the bacteria are conducted—and swabbed other spots the same way.

The previous day, two researchers had spilled a negligible quantity of anthrax bacteria inside the hot suite. A quick decontamination was performed, the area was tested, and everything came back negative—no bacteria. But Ivins wasn't satisfied. He went to his supervisor and demanded more samplings, this time on the cold side. His insistence puzzled the supervisor; there was no evidence—

indeed, no reason to believe—that there had been any contamination outside of the hot suite. She told Ivins he could not swab those areas without permission.

Flouting her instructions, he was now walking around the cold side taking samples in several areas including his office, the men's changing room, and a lab technician's desk. A number of the tests came back positive for anthrax.

But Ivins alerted no one. Instead, the next day, he did additional tests. Contamination turned up in even more spots, including multiple areas of his office, on an electrical box, and in the changing room. This time, he reported his findings to his supervisor, who was furious at his insubordination but duty-bound to order a comprehensive survey of Building 1425.

Out of twenty-two offices, only Ivins's was contaminated. The women's changing room was negative. The bacteria were found in three areas, all of them directly linked to Ivins. The test results were eventually turned over to the FBI agents conducting the anthrax investigation.

The details were striking. In total, 1,197 samples were obtained. Of those taken by Ivins, 27 percent yielded positive results, compared with 0.18 percent for those swabbed by others. In other words, Ivins's swabs detected bacteria at a rate 15,000 percent higher than those conducted by colleagues. It was as if he knew exactly where to test.

Frank Dunham's first letter about Hamdi arrived by fax to the Norfolk Naval Base brig on April 17. It was addressed to William Paulette, the commanding officer of the military prison, and asked him to find out if Hamdi wanted to be represented by a lawyer. Dunham requested an immediate reply.

But Paulette was not authorized to contact anyone outside of the military about Hamdi. Instead, he forwarded the letter to the Combat Logistics Force, which shuffled it farther up the line to the Joint Forces Command. Paulette was ordered to ignore Dunham.

9

Yosri Fouda checked into a modest hotel in Islamabad on April 17. A few weeks had passed since a mysterious man had invited the Al Jazeera reporter to Pakistan with hints that he could help create a news package marking the first anniversary of 9/11. But Fouda had made the journey on faith—he had no means of contacting the source and had no idea if the man would call again.

A shower, a meal, a book, a little television. Fouda did whatever he could to pass the time. After twelve hours with no word from his contact, he became bored, impatient, and increasingly doubtful that anything was going to come from this trip.

The hotel phone rang. It had to be his contact. No one else knew he was there. Fouda picked up the receiver.

"Thank God you have arrived safe," a man said. "Take the night flight to Karachi."

A dial tone. The man had hung up.

On the two-hour flight the next day, Fouda's nerves were frayed. His contact seemed tied to al-Qaeda. When he arrived, would there be a gang of fundamentalists lying in wait to kidnap him?

His plane landed at Quaid-e-Azam Airport. Fouda left the terminal, flagged down a cab, and told the driver to take him to the Karachi Marriott Hotel on Abdullah Haroon Road. As the taxi maneuvered through traffic, the anonymous source—whom Fouda had taken to calling Abu Bakr, the name of the prophet Muhammad's father-in-law—called the cell phone again. Fouda told him that he was on his way to the Marriott.

"Ask the driver to take you to the Regent Plaza instead," the man said.

Fouda gave the new destination and the driver changed course toward one of the city's major boulevards, Shara-e-Faisal. The hotel resembled a white, multi-tiered wedding cake amid schools, shopping centers, and government buildings. Fouda checked in to Room 322 and stepped into a hot shower, only to hear a knock at the door. He dashed out to welcome . . . whoever it was.

The man came inside and greeted Fouda. About twenty minutes later, as they shared a meal, Fouda's visitor mentioned almost casually that bin Laden was still alive and was a devoted viewer of Al Jazeera.

"How does he watch us now?" Fouda asked.

"Do not worry, Brother Yosri. Sheikh Osama, God protect him, is alive and well. Whatever he misses he gets on tape."

The conversation turned to Al Jazeera programming and the fax that the man had sent to Fouda weeks before with a detailed proposal for a 9/11 anniversary news package. They were drinking tea when the al-Qaeda envoy ended the conversation.

"Do not worry, Brother Yosri," he said. "You will, God willing, know everything tomorrow."

Following new instructions, Fouda slipped out the back door of the hotel, hailed a taxi, and made his way to another location. There, he stood by a staircase for several minutes until another stranger arrived.

"I have just given my mother-in-law a lift home," the man said. "We can go now."

Fouda was ushered into a car and driven to another part of town. His host parked, left the car, and walked to a phone booth. When he returned, another changeup—Fouda was to take a rickshaw to the next location. There, he was picked up by another automobile, then driven out of Karachi to a road where a third car waited.

A different man appeared. He blindfolded Fouda for the next leg of his circuitous journey.

They arrived at the final stop. With his eyes still covered, Fouda was led into a building and up four flights of stairs. He heard a doorbell. Once he was inside the room, someone removed his blindfold.

"It is okay now," a voice said. "You can open your eyes."

Fouda blinked. A bearded man was standing two feet away from him. It was Khalid Sheikh Mohammed, the mastermind of the 9/11 attacks.

Sheikh Mohammed led Fouda to another room. A second man was there waiting, and the reporter recognized him as Ramzi bin al-Shibh, a 9/11 conspirator who was a close friend of Atta, the ringleader of the hijackers. He, like Sheikh Mohammed, was one of the United States' most wanted terrorists.

"Recognized us yet?" Sheikh Mohammed said.

The men sat down.

"They say you are terrorists," Fouda blurted out.

Bin al-Shibh smiled, but said nothing.

"They are right," Sheikh Mohammed replied. "We are terrorists."

Hours passed. The men prayed, drank tea, chatted, but there was none of the bare-knuckled back-and-forth that resembled an interview with a journalist. This was just a time for the three men to grow comfortable with each other. The only useful information that Fouda garnered so far was the realization that bin al-Shibh had written the fax he had received in London. Finally, at almost ten o'clock at night, Fouda ventured into his first real question.

He looked Sheikh Mohammed in the eye. "Did you do it?" he asked.

"No filming today," Sheikh Mohammed replied without a hint that he had heard the question. "And you do not have to worry about a camera or a cameraman for tomorrow. We will provide everything."

Bin al-Shibh broke in. "You will be going straight from here to your flight whenever we are done."

Fouda resigned himself to learning nothing of value that day. But then Sheikh Mohammed stared him in the face, his shoulders erect and his chin up.

"I am the head of the al-Qaeda military committee," he announced. "And yes, we did it."

The hearing for Zacarias Moussaoui on the morning of April 22 was supposed to be a routine judicial housecleaning. His lawyers, led by Frank Dunham, had filed motions with the Federal District Court in Alexandria seeking to improve the conditions of their client's imprisonment while he awaited trial. There was no excitement among reporters packing the gallery; it wasn't likely they would get a story out of such a dry proceeding.

At ten o'clock, Judge Leonie Brinkema mounted the bench and the clerk called the case. Moussaoui, clad in a green prison jumpsuit, was led in by the marshals through a side door.

"Will counsel please state their appearance for the record," the clerk said.

The prosecution spoke first. "Good morning, your honor. Rob Spencer, Ken Karas, and Dave Novak for the United States."

Dunham stood. "Good morning, your honor. Frank Dunham, the federal public defender, Jerry Zerkin, and Ed MacMahon—"

Moussaoui raised his arm, one finger to the sky. "Ma'am," he called. "No, I am sorry to note, they are not my lawyers."

A jolt raced through the courtroom. Apparently, this wouldn't be a routine day after all.

"Mr. Moussaoui," Brinkema said, "Go up to the lectern, please."

Moussaoui stood and walked forward. "Thank you."

Brinkema cautioned him that the prosecutors could use anything he said in court against him. Moussaoui said that he understood.

"Just speak up loudly, Mr. Moussaoui," Brinkema said. "Go ahead."

There was a pause. All eyes were fixed on Moussaoui, and he seemed to be enjoying the attention.

"In the name of Allah," he began, "I, Zacarias Moussaoui, today the twenty-second of April 2002, after being prevented for a long time to mount an effective defense by overly restrictive and oppressive condition of confinement, take the control of my defense."

He was firing his lawyers, Moussaoui said, and would represent himself at trial. They worked for the government and were part of a conspiracy against him.

"Greed, fame, and vanity is their motivation," Moussaoui said in a calm but forceful voice. "Their game is deception. Their slogan is no scruple."

He began reciting portions of the Koran, then listed countries that he said should be under the control of Muslims.

"I pray to Allah, the powerful, for the return of the Islamic Emirates of Afghanistan and the destruction of the United States of America," he said. "America, I'm ready to fight in your Don King fight, even both hands tied behind the back in court."

He was just getting started. In a rambling fifty-minute monologue, he inveighed again against his lawyers, quoted more passages from the Koran, and explained his reasons for wanting to represent himself with the help of a Muslim lawyer.

"All right," Brinkema said when Moussaoui finished. "Let me first advise you that you have the absolute right under our law to be your own attorney. You already know that. But you do not have the right to pick and choose the lawyer you want appointed to you."

Before they went any further, she said, she wanted to hear from his attorneys.

Moussaoui shook his head. "I do not want you to refer to them as my attorney," he said. "They are not my attorney."

"I understand."

Moreover, Moussaoui said, he did not want them to reveal anything about his legal strategy.

"These men will not," Brinkema said. "They're experienced attorneys."

"Yeah, yeah, I believe that they're experienced." Moussaoui smirked. "They're experienced in deception."

Brinkema ruled that Moussaoui could represent himself, pending a psychiatric evaluation. But, she said, in the event that he proved unable to handle the job, Dunham and the other lawyers would remain in court as standby counsel.

Outside the courtroom, reporters surrounded Dunham. Moussaoui's position was understandable, he said. "If somebody thrusts a lawyer on you that you didn't pick, it's hard for you to trust them, especially in a case like this."

In the White House, disbelief, once again, was engulfed by more disbelief. The Moussaoui case was supposed to follow a simple script: indictment, trial, conviction, sentence—the only question had been whether the prosecutors would succeed in persuading the court to impose a death sentence.

But now this man was out there, babbling away in front of the national press corps, speaking in Arabic, quoting the Koran. Was he sending coded messages? Why didn't the judge put a stop to this dangerous charade?

The Moussaoui case, administration lawyers fretted, was turning into a circus. And the first day of the trial hadn't even been held.

Shortly before 4:00 P.M. on May 3, Saudi Arabian Airlines flight SV667 banked northwest, beginning its final approach into Damascus International Airport. On board the plane, Abdullah Almalki glanced out of a window at the lush greenery below of the Ghouta, a belt of farmland on the outskirts of Damascus that Syrians revered as near paradise. The area had special meaning to Almalki;

his family owned land there, and he affectionately remembered playing with his brothers as a child amid its fruit trees and orchards.

He had not seen Syria since he moved to Canada as a teenager fifteen years before and was returning now after hearing some bad news. A few days earlier, he had received word that his grandmother had fallen ill and that several members of the family, including Almalki's parents, had flown to Damascus to be at her bedside. He had promised to join them as soon as he could.

As he watched his homeland rush by beneath the plane, Almalki could not have known that a noose was tightening. Canadian officials had been investigating him on suspicion of terrorist activities. Records from their inquiry had been sent to the CIA, which in turn passed them to Syrian intelligence. Since then, the Syrians had tortured Ahmad El-Maati until he confessed to having met Almalki and Maher Arar at an al-Qaeda training camp in Afghanistan. The allegation was false, but given in desperation. El-Maati had buckled to stop the torture.

Now, in the airport below, Syrian intelligence officials waited. Shortly before, the Americans had informed them that Almalki was on his way to Damascus. They were ready to pounce on him as soon as he arrived.

Crowds of well-dressed travelers packed every square foot of the terminal at the Damascus International Airport. The crush of people was so large that some of them had to hold their luggage on their heads.

As Almalki made his way off the plane and waded inside, he saw a well-dressed woman holding a sign with his name on it. He approached her and introduced himself.

"Okay," the woman said. "I'm here to take you to your mother."

She escorted Almalki through the run-down terminal, leading him to the VIP lounge. His mother was there, along with a cousin he had never met before. After hugs and introductions, Almalki took a sip of his mother's lemonade while waiting for someone to bring him a glass of his own.

Immigration officials arrived at the lounge doorway. By policy, none of them were allowed into the room; instead they stood at the entry, and asked the staff to summon Almalki over so that they could speak with him.

Almalki thought nothing of the request and headed to the door. They had some questions for him, one of the officials said, adding that they needed to make sure he was allowed in the VIP room.

The questions were standard fare for Syria. *What's your name? What's your date of birth? What's your father's full name? What's your grandfather's name?* Probably, Almalki figured, they just wanted to make sure he was who he claimed to be.

The questioning ended. "Please come with us," one of the officials said.

Almalki told his mother he would be right back. Some immigration issue needed to be cleared up, that was all. His cousin said he would accompany him. The two men walked out of the lounge, with Almalki leaving his bag and laptop behind. No need to bring them along, he thought, since he would be back in a few minutes.

He never returned.

The immigration officials escorted the two to a security office at the airport. Almalki felt certain that he knew what this was about. All Syrian men are ob-ligated to serve time in the military, and Almalki never had. But that wouldn't be a problem; after his family had departed for Canada, his father had faithfully filed the necessary documents to keep Almalki's deferral valid.

The group arrived in an office, where a security official was sitting behind a desk. "I need your Syrian identification card," he said.

"I don't have one," Almalki replied. "Does this have anything to do with my military service? I've been in Canada for fifteen years and have been filing for a deferral every five years."

"No," the official replied. "This has nothing to do with military service."

Almalki's cousin grew angry. "What is going on?" he demanded.

One of the officials told him to leave. He hesitated, then walked out of the room.

The man behind the desk told Almalki that his name had come up on a com-puter search as someone who was wanted, although the security officials didn't know why. One of them brought out a book and started flipping the pages. He found Almalki's name.

"Oh, sir, this is recent," he said. "It's a report received from the embassy on April twenty-second."

Embassy? What embassy? Maybe it had something to do with the Pakistanis, since his biggest customer was headquartered there.

Before Almalki could ask more questions, the official stood up from his desk and led him into another room. There, two other men bombarded him with questions about his family and the reasons for his long absence from Syria.

One of the officials looked at the other. "He is wanted for Branch 235," he said.

"Branch 235?" Almalki asked. "What's that?"

"Far' Falastin." The Palestine Branch.

Almalki didn't know what that was, but one of the officials assured him that the visit there wouldn't take long. They brought him outside, where a minibus was waiting. As he rode through Damascus, Almalki chatted with his escorts, who seemed friendly enough.

After thirty minutes, the driver pulled up to a gate at a large compound. Almalki stepped off the bus and was shepherded through. He looked around the compound and saw men carrying machine guns. No one explained what was happening as they led Almalki into an old, two-story building. Inside, he saw a blindfolded man. He started to worry; this was a bad place to be.

All of this was a mistake, he thought, and he could straighten it out if he could just speak to someone. He had yet to realize that he was in a prison. Far' Falastin was the most notorious torture site in all of Syria.

Almalki was blindfolded and moved to another room, where he was left alone for a short time. Suddenly he heard the noise of people coming through the door. A man approached him.

"You are in Syria, not in Canada," the man said. "You have to speak. You don't get a lawyer."

Almalki listened, his fear rising.

"Which treatment would you like?" the man asked. "The friendly one or the other one?"

Not a difficult question. "I choose what you would choose," Almalki said.

"Bring him a chair!" the man barked at someone else in the room.

The chair arrived and was placed next to Almalki.

"Sit," the man said. "Give me ten, fifteen minutes. I'll clear up any misunderstandings."

Almalki heard paper rustling. His inquisitor apparently had some report in his hands.

"Why are the Americans, the Canadians, the British, the whole world so interested in you?" the man asked.

Almalki opened his mouth but was cut off by the next question.

"Do you know Ibrahym Adam?"

The Canadians. This was the exact question he had been asked months before by a Canadian intelligence agent, the one who had lied to him about being unable to find Adam. And now the Syrians were asking about him. Somehow, Canada's information had been delivered to the Syrian government. But why?

"I know Ibrahym," Almalki responded. "I was asked about him in Canada. I think that the investigator was interested in him because he is a Muslim and a pilot."

"Who is Ahmad El-Maati?"

El-Maati. The man with the map. But Almalki didn't recognize the name. He knew him as Ahmad Badr; like many Egyptians, El-Maati used his father's name, Badr, as a sign of respect. Almalki had no reason to be aware of that. He had barely ever spoken to El-Maati.

"I don't know who that is," Almalki said.

A third question, another name. Again, Almalki had never heard it before.

There was a moment of silence, as if a storm was about to arrive. "You must prefer the nonfriendly treatment!" the man yelled.

He slapped Almalki hard in the face.

Almalki's thoughts raced. In barely an hour, his world had turned upside down. His university degrees, his business contacts—none of that mattered here. He had entered into a nightmare.

"You know Ahmad El-Maati!" the man barked.

"I don't know anyone by that name!"

"You know him!"

Desperate, Almalki asked for someone to describe this person. He was big and an Egyptian, the man responded. A few more details, and Almalki realized who it was.

"Yes, now I know who you mean," he said, his voice quivering. "But I know him by the name Ahmad Badr, not Ahmad El-Maati."

Another moment passed. His interrogator spoke, his voice calm.

"Take off your shoes, your socks, and your jacket," he said. "Then lie down on the floor on your stomach."

Almalki screamed as two or three men whipped the bottom of his feet with electric cables. He had never experienced pain remotely like this. It was as if his feet were on fire.

Others in the room gathered around and kicked him—in the head, in the shoulders, everywhere. He instinctively rolled onto his back.

"Lie on your stomach!" someone yelled.

He turned over. One man stood on Almalki's head, and another on his back, ensuring that he would remain facedown. The whippings and kicking resumed.

"How do you know Ahmed Khadr?" someone shouted. Years before, he had worked with Khadr in Afghanistan for a few months but had left out of his dislike for the man.

Before Almalki could answer, the questions kept coming.

"Have you dealt with bin Laden and al-Qaeda?"

"Did you sell equipment to al-Qaeda and the Taliban?"

"What kind of computers did you sell to them?"

"I don't sell computers!" Almalki shouted.

For a moment the beatings stopped and his tormentors poured cold water on his legs and told him to stand. It was a Syrian torture technique, designed to keep the circulation going so that, no matter how long they whipped him, the pain wouldn't subside.

The torture resumed.

"What is your role with al-Qaeda?"

"Admit that you are bin Laden's right-hand man!"

"That makes no sense!" Almalki screamed. "Everyone knows that Zawahiri is bin Laden's right-hand man!"

"Fine," one of the torturers responded. "Then you are his left-hand man."

Almalki couldn't bear up under the pain. Telling the truth wouldn't stop these men. Neither would logic. There was only one option remaining. He would lie.

"Yes!" he screamed. "I know bin Laden!"

"From where?"

"From years ago, when I worked with United Nations development projects in Pakistan and Afghanistan."

The beating stopped, and the Syrians spoke among themselves. Then they left the room.

Minutes later, they returned. "You're lying!" one of them screamed. "Bin Laden was in Sudan when you were in Pakistan and Afghanistan!"

Almalki felt as if he was going crazy. Even lies didn't work with his tormentors.

"I never met bin Laden!" he cried. "I only said that to stop the torture!"

The beatings resumed. They promised that they would shock him with electricity, tear off his nails, stuff him into a tire, whatever it took to force out the truth.

After more than an hour, Almalki couldn't speak anymore. He passed out and was dragged from the room. The torture was over for the day.

The men took him downstairs and threw him into a small, filthy cell. It was number three, two cells down from where Ahmad El-Maati had been held months before.

The cells around him were occupied by men who had been interrogated by the CIA and other Western intelligence agencies before being delivered to Syria. Two—one a teenager—had been with Abu Zubaydah the night of the raid in Pakistan. Another had been arrested in Pakistan and delivered to Syria on a CIA plane. The Americans had interrogated a third, a computer designer, before they transferred him to Damascus. And all of them had been tortured into confessing their membership in al-Qaeda.

The Syrians abused Almalki in increasingly cruel and painful ways. On one day, an interrogator merely asked him questions about twenty different Muslims living in Canada. Some Almalki knew, some he didn't.

The interrogator mentioned a man from Ottawa.

At first, Almalki didn't understand; his questioner's pronunciation was all but unintelligible. But when he repeated himself, Almalki recognized the name. It was someone he had dined with at Mango's Café a few months previously, followed by a trip to Future Shop to purchase printer ink.

Yes, Almalki said. He knew that man.

He knew Maher Arar.

Abu Zubaydah, the recently captured al-Qaeda operative, was still struggling to recover from his wounds. His infection had spread to one eye; soon, a doctor would have to remove it surgically. Zubaydah would be left wearing a patch.

The two FBI agents, Soufan and Gaudin, exploited Zubaydah's ordeal to their advantage. They maneuvered between an almost intimate attentiveness for his damaged condition to a show of seeming omniscience as they recounted information about al-Qaeda and Zubaydah himself.

Over several days, Zubaydah spun out his worldview, infused with an ardor for socialism and hostility to the corporations spawned by capitalism. At one point he lost steam and glanced at Soufan.

"Could you get me a Coca-Cola?" he asked.

He was requesting a soft drink manufactured by one of the world's largest corporations. Soufan flashed a smile. Zubaydah suddenly recognized the humor of his request. They broke out laughing.

For the FBI agents, each new scrap of information they pulled from Zubaydah was proof that their approach was working. To the uninformed, Zubaydah would seem to have no reason to say *anything*. No one was hurting him or even threatening him. He could clam up or spin lies with no prospect of unpleasant consequences. Yet he was talking and telling the truth. That didn't surprise the agents—not only were these interrogation techniques found in study after study to be the most effective, but they had perfected them in the course of interviewing more al-Qaeda members than anyone else in government. They were the professionals.

Then the amateurs arrived.

A team of CIA officers, psychologists, and support staff arrived in Thailand on an agency plane. Zubaydah was still in the hospital recovering from his injuries, which would delay the implementation of the new arrivals' aggressive interrogation plan.

Soufan and Gaudin met with senior members of the group at a nearby hotel and briefed them on their progress. Soufan took an instant dislike to one member of the CIA team—Jim Mitchell, the retired SERE instructor who was now a consultant to the CIA on interrogation issues. Mitchell was never one to listen and learn; instead, he spoke frequently in a tone of absolute arrogance that Soufan found grating.

There wasn't much he could do about it, though. At the beginning, their boss had told Soufan and Gaudin that the CIA was in charge. The two agents had no choice but to relinquish responsibility for the interrogation.

The cell had no bunk and no blankets. Zubaydah, still weak from his wounds, had been stripped naked. The air-conditioning had been turned up; he shivered and at times turned a bluish hue. He was alone; no one spoke to him.

The cell door opened and a CIA officer stepped inside. He stood motionless for a few seconds, staring at Zubaydah.

"Tell me what I want to know," the interrogator said. He turned and left the cell without saying another word.

Rather than opening up, Zubaydah shut down. The harsh tactics were backfiring. For days, the FBI agents had been sending cables to Washington chock-full of revelations. Now nothing.

So the CIA stepped up its offensive. Mitchell, in consultation with the Counterterrorist Center at the CIA, added sleep deprivation, bombarding Zubaydah's cell with loud hard rock and funk music, including songs by the Red Hot Chili Peppers. As planned, the noise kept Zubaydah awake for twenty-four to forty-eight hours at a time. Yet he remained silent.

Hoping to break the logjam, Mitchell spoke directly to Zubaydah. But unlike the CIA officers, he never showed his face, instead hiding behind a mask. Still, Zubaydah refused to speak. After days of failure, the CIA team invited the FBI agents back in hopes that they could overcome Zubaydah's resistance.

Soufan was horrified at what he saw. Why was Zubaydah naked and freezing? The agent turned the heat back up and covered Zubaydah with a towel. Out of Zubaydah's earshot, Mitchell fumed, saying that Soufan was undermining his efforts.

"Have you ever interrogated anyone?" Soufan snapped.

"No, but it doesn't matter," Mitchell shot back. "Science is science. This is a behavioral issue."

That's absurd, Soufan replied. The FBI techniques had been proved effective over and over again.

Mitchell rolled his eyes. "Look, I'm a psychologist," he said dismissively. "I know how the human mind works."

Amazing. Somehow, this contractor had convinced himself that, even with no real knowledge or experience, he was more qualified to conduct interrogations than anyone else there. He almost seemed to be saying that the professionals were working at a disadvantage by having actual knowledge. No matter—the CIA team had invited Soufan and Gaudin back in, and they were going to conduct their interviews the way that worked.

The agents sat with Zubaydah and spoke kindly to him. It took time to regain his trust, but finally, the relationship was restored and Zubaydah started talking again. He told the agents that he had heard about an Islamist with a Latino name who had plans to use a "dirty bomb" that would spread radiation over a small area inside the United States. Sheikh Mohammed had instructed the man to get a new passport in Jordan, then head to America for the attack.

The agents contacted the American embassy in Amman and asked officials to search their records for a Hispanic man who had recently applied for a passport.

The name José Padilla turned up. The embassy sent the photo on file back to Thailand, and Soufan showed it to Zubaydah.

"Is this the guy?" Soufan asked.

Zubaydah nodded. Padilla was the terrorist.

This breakthrough did nothing to persuade the CIA to change course. With Zubaydah no longer resistant to talking, Mitchell proclaimed, he could now be induced to spill more information under aggressive questioning.

The CIA took over. And again, Zubaydah went silent. Increasingly frustrated, the intelligence agents issued a murder threat.

"If one child dies in America and I find out you knew something about it," one of the CIA officers shouted at Zubaydah, "I will personally cut your mother's throat!"

The Yoo memo had specifically forbidden interrogators from telling a detainee that either he or another person would be killed. But a later review by CIA lawyers declared that the threat that Zubaydah's mother would be killed was lawful. Grammatically, the sentence began with the subordinate conjunction *if*. That meant it was conditional. And that, the lawyers declared, was fine.

The sequence never varied. The FBI used relationship building and Zubaydah talked. The CIA stepped back in with its harsh methods, and he stopped. Then the agency officers brought back the FBI and the cycle repeated itself.

None of this meant that rough questioning techniques didn't work, Mitchell told the agency officers. They just needed to be more aggressive.

Days later, John Rizzo, the acting general counsel at the CIA, telephoned Bellinger, the NSC legal advisor.

The agency had captured Abu Zubaydah, Rizzo explained, and was interrogating him overseas. They had already been using some severe tactics in questioning him, but nothing had worked. A psychological consultant was urging the interrogators to step up the intensity of the interrogations by using some rougher techniques, including waterboarding. But the CIA officers feared that if they followed the recommendations of the consultant, Jim Mitchell, they might face criminal charges.

The agency, Rizzo said, wanted the Justice Department to issue a formal decision that it would decline to prosecute any CIA interrogators for violating antitorture statutes in their questioning of Zubaydah.

Bellinger promised to set up a meeting with the Justice Department. The CIA could make its case directly to officials there.

That Saturday, John Yoo was shopping when he received a call on his cell phone from the Justice Department Command Center. The official on the line told him that a meeting had been scheduled for 11:00 A.M. that day in Bellinger's office. The man offered no details before clicking off the line.

Yoo drove to the Eisenhower Executive Office Building across from the White House and headed upstairs. Bellinger was already there, along with a few men Yoo did not recognize.

"We have a problem," Bellinger said. He nodded toward the other men in the room. "They'll tell you about it."

They were from the CIA. One of the men introduced himself only by a first name, which may or may not have been his real one. He was an average-looking guy, dressed in a blue button-down shirt without a tie.

They needed Yoo's input, the official said. The agency had captured Abu Zubaydah, the operational planner for al-Qaeda, and CIA officers had been questioning him.

"He's resistant to interrogation," he said.

Resistant? "What do you mean?" Yoo asked.

"For everything we do, he already has a countermove ready," the official said. "It's like playing a grand master in chess. He's the most difficult person I've ever encountered."

Zubaydah would talk sometimes, the official said, but never gave away anything worthwhile. And everyone at the agency knew this man had a treasure trove of knowledge about al-Qaeda. He was someone who could unquestionably help the United States deter terrorist attacks.

"If we can break him," the official said, "it will be the greatest achievement in my career at the CIA."

"Isn't there some kind of truth serum?" Yoo asked.

"No, we don't have one. We've never had one. People seem to think the Russians had one, but we don't know if that's for real."

Okay. No truth serum. That's just the movies.

"We may want to use more aggressive interrogation methods," the official said. "And we need to know what's legal and what's not legal."

Yoo looked at Bellinger. "Who's allowed to know about this? Who can we consult with? I mean, obviously, I can't give you an opinion off the top of my head. I'm pretty sure this is a complicated issue."

Secrecy was paramount, Bellinger cautioned. Yoo could inform Ashcroft and whatever colleagues in his office were needed to conduct the legal analysis. But no one else.

"Can we consult with the State Department?" Yoo asked. The top experts on the laws of war worked there.

Bellinger shook his head. "Access to this program is extremely restricted," he said. "The State Department shouldn't be informed."

Condoleezza Rice walked briskly into the White House Situation Room and took a seat at the head of the conference table. Other officials straggled in over the next few minutes.

"All right, let's get started," Rice said after everyone found a seat.

She nodded toward Tenet. "George believes that we need to do some things in the interrogations of terrorists to help gather information," she said. She turned the floor over to him.

"We are facing a very dedicated adversary, and they have been trained on how to resist our interrogation techniques," he said. "Now we have intelligence about specific possible threats that are potentially coming, and some of the people we've captured have knowledge of these threats."

The types of people being targeted for murder by al-Qaeda were across the board, from schoolchildren to shoppers—all innocent, all in danger.

"The interrogations we've been conducting up to this point have not been sufficient to get the al-Qaeda members in our custody to give up the information they have about these threats," Tenet continued. "And so, some of our experts in interrogation have put together a series of new techniques that they think might be more effective."

Rizzo, the CIA lawyer, explained that he had already appealed to the Justice Department for a formal statement declining to prosecute agency officers who conducted harsh questioning. But no such assurance had been provided.

The interrogators were already taking risks with some of the less controversial techniques—forced nudity, slaps, exposure to cold, sleep deprivation—without legal clearance. But their most important capture, Abu Zubaydah, was still resisting. He had obviously gone through the training contained in the Manchester Manual, the CIA officials concluded. The officers needed greater leeway to wring information out of him.

There were a series of techniques that had been recommended by the agency's psychological consultant, Tenet said. He passed around a document that contained a list of them—confining an interrogation subject in small boxes, taking advantage of his fears, forcing him to stand in uncomfortable positions for hours, extending the length of time he was deprived of sleep. The most aggressive, Tenet said, was a technique called waterboarding.

"Do we really need to do this?" Gonzales asked.

"Under the right circumstances to get the right information, yes," Tenet said.

As the discussion continued, Gonzales decided to let Bush know that the CIA had come in with an important request. But he had already concluded that the president shouldn't be told much else.

Gonzales reached the Oval Office and stood in the doorway. Bush was working at his desk.

"Mr. President," Gonzales said.

"Fredo!" Bush replied, using his nickname for the White House counsel.

Gonzales stepped into the room and sat down in a chair next to the president's desk. He explained that Bush's top aides were meeting downstairs in the Situation Room.

"Tenet is saying that the CIA needs to adopt some new interrogation techniques for al-Qaeda terrorists," he explained. "There are some threats the agency knows about, and he thinks this is the best way to get the information."

"Well, what are we talking about?" Bush asked.

"Mr. President, I think for your own protection you don't need to know the details of what's going on here," Gonzales replied.

Bush paused, then gave a nod of understanding.

"All right," he said. "Just make sure that these things are lawful."

Downstairs, the conversation had turned to the legality of the CIA's requests. The Office of Legal Counsel, Ashcroft said, was already working on that analysis.

"All right, John," Rice said. "But I'd like you to review their work personally."

Yoo reached a preliminary finding that certain of the CIA's proposed tactics, such as confinement, were lawful. The analysis of others, like waterboarding, was going to take more time.

• • •

Two dark wooden boxes were placed in a room at the secret prison where Zubaydah was confined. One looked something like a coffin; the other was much smaller.

Soufan saw the larger box and was horrified. His mind raced with questions and fears. Was the CIA planning to bury Zubaydah alive? He immediately confronted the agency interrogators.

"We're the United States of America, and we don't do that kind of thing!" he shouted. "Has anybody given you the legal authority to do what you're doing?"

One of the officers brought out a document. "This has been approved at the highest levels in Washington," he said, waving the paper in Soufan's face. "These approvals are coming from Gonzales."

The White House counsel.

Soufan didn't care *who* had approved this; he wanted no part of it. He stormed off to a secure phone. His bosses at the FBI, he decided, needed to know what was happening.

"I swear to God," Soufan shouted, "I'm going to arrest these guys!"

On the other end of the line, Pasquale D'Amuro, the bureau's assistant director for counterterrorism, spoke in measured tones, trying to calm Soufan. He understood his concerns, D'Amuro said. This wasn't the way that the FBI would do the job. But the CIA was in charge.

Soufan, he said, should just come home. Gaudin would join him a few weeks later.

When the time came to use the boxes, the interrogators started with the larger one, placing Zubaydah inside and putting a cover on top.

His movements were severely restricted. The heat was oppressive and Zubaydah found it difficult to breathe. Sweat, pressure, and friction combined to make it impossible for him to squirm into a comfortable position. He was left inside for up to eight hours at a time.

The smaller box was worse. It was shorter than Zubaydah, forcing him to crouch down as long as two hours. Once again, he could not move.

Over time, the CIA's Office of Medical Services would deem that the cramped confinement technique should no longer be used. The problem: It was too much of a relief for the detainee, since being sealed inside the box offered hours-long breaks from interrogation. This experimental, untested technique simply didn't work.

On the afternoon of May 8, two FBI agents from New York were hiding in a utility closet near U.S. Customs at Chicago's O'Hare International Airport, preparing to confront a suspected terrorist.

Outside the door, a passenger who had just arrived from Zurich was speaking with Andy Ferreri, a customs agent. Ferreri asked the man for his passport and declaration form. He read the name on the documents.

José Padilla. The American who had just been identified by Abu Zubaydah as an al-Qaeda terrorist planning to detonate a dirty bomb.

Ferreri searched Padilla's belongings and found a wad of cash—$10,526. But Padilla had declared only $8,000.

"Sir, I'm going to have to confiscate this currency," Ferreri said. He escorted Padilla about twenty yards to a conference room and asked him to sit down.

Ferreri left the room and walked to the utility closet. He went inside and told the two FBI agents—Russell Fincher and Craig Donnachie—about the cash Padilla had been carrying.

The investigators had flown in that day from New York, where they worked with the counterterrorism squad. Almost a dozen other Chicago-based FBI and customs agents had been assigned to help in the confrontation with Padilla, mostly by making sure he didn't escape or hurt anyone.

After briefing the two agents, Ferreri took them to the conference room where Padilla was waiting. About eight other FBI and customs agents stood guard at the door.

Fincher and Donnachie went inside accompanied by two colleagues, R. J. Holley and Todd Schmitt. A long table surrounded by almost two dozen chairs dominated the room. Padilla had settled near one end.

Fincher sat down at Padilla's left, while Donnachie took the chair to his right. Holley and Schmitt sat at the far end of the table; they would be only observers. Just before 3:15, the agents brought out their credentials.

"Mr. Padilla, my name is Russell Fincher, and I'm an FBI agent. This is Craig Donnachie, and he's also an FBI agent, as are our colleagues at the other end of the table."

He stared directly into Padilla's eyes. "We need to ask you some questions," he said.

"All right."

"We've been made aware of the ten thousand dollars that you were carrying into the country. Would you be willing to talk to me about where it came from and what you were planning to do with it?"

Padilla shrugged. "Sure."

A good FBI interrogation rarely starts with hard questions that might frighten a suspect into silence. Instead, agents lob a few softballs to lull the interview subject into a false sense of security.

That's where Fincher began, asking Padilla for basic information—his date of birth, Social Security number, and address in the United States.

"I can't provide you with a U.S. address," Padilla replied. "I've lived outside the country since 1998."

"Well, where do you live now?" Fincher asked.

"In Egypt. In Cairo and Tanta."

"All right. And what are your addresses in those cities?"

Padilla thought for a moment. "I don't remember," he said.

The first lie, the agents thought.

"Well, then just give me a description of those residences," Fincher said.

"I'm sorry. I can't really say."

"You can't describe the places where you live?"

"No," Padilla said. "I'm not good with that kind of thing."

The second.

"Well, what's your phone number in either location?"

"I don't know."

Third.

"You don't know your own phone number? How to reach your family?"

"I don't remember."

"Do you have a cell phone?"

"Yes. I just bought a new one. But I can't remember the number. It's a new one, so I can't remember."

Fourth.

This line of questioning wasn't going anywhere.

"Why have you come to Chicago?"

"I'm on a trip to visit my mother and my son."

His mother's name, he said, was Estela Ortega Lebron. He handed Fincher a slip of paper with her name, address, and phone number on it. The note also instructed him to ask for Estela Lebron.

"The thing is," Fincher said, "you haven't arranged to travel from Chicago to Florida. Why not?"

"I'm in Chicago to visit my son," he said. He gave the boy's name and said that he was about twelve or thirteen years old.

"And where does your son live?"

"I don't know."

Lie number five, maybe six.

"I'm planning to call my mother to find out how to contact him," Padilla said.

The boy lived with his mother, he added, somewhere in the northwest section of Chicago. He himself had never really been close with the mother, Marisol Rivera. He got her pregnant when her boyfriend was in prison. When his son was born, Padilla said, he took the last name of the boyfriend.

Fincher returned to Padilla's background, and the memory lapses vanished. He could name the streets where he had lived, the three schools he had attended before dropping out in the seventh grade, and other details. He had drifted aimlessly, Padilla said, and had joined the Latin Disciples gang. When he was thirteen years old, he murdered someone and was arrested; he served five years in St. Charles Juvenile Detention Center. Afterward, he lived with his mother in Florida and took a busboy job at a Hilton Hotel but again succumbed to the lure of gang life. He was arrested in 1991 on a weapons charge and was sent to prison for about a year.

It was there, Padilla said, that his life was transformed. First, he met a fellow inmate who was a member of the Nation of Islam, the African-American religious movement founded in Detroit. Padilla didn't agree with everything the man said, but it set him to thinking about Islam. Then he got into a fight with another inmate and was thrown into solitary confinement.

"And it was during that time I had a dream that seemed really important," Padilla said. "In just a brief moment in the dream, I saw myself floating and wearing a black hood and a robe."

"Why was that important to you?" Fincher asked.

"It was a vision. It's what inspired me to focus intently on studying Islam."

After his release, Padilla said, he began his religious training in Florida, then in 1998 moved to Egypt. He attended a university there and studied under several tutors.

"What were the tutors' names?" Fincher asked.

"I don't remember."

Lost count.

"How did you find them?"

"I really couldn't say."

Fincher pressed for more details about the university, to no avail.

In either 1999 or 2000, Padilla said, he had made a pilgrimage to Mecca during the holy month of Ramadan. There, he met two men, one who asked him to move to Saudi Arabia, and the other who pressed him to come to Pakistan. He decided to travel to Pakistan, where there were schools that could help him speed up his study of Islam.

"What were the names of the two men you met?"

"I don't remember."

A few minutes later, at 4:25 P.M., Fincher said that they should take a break so that Padilla could have dinner and visit the restroom.

At 5:35, the interview resumed.

"Let's talk about the money you were carrying when you arrived here."

"Oh, I'm happy to tell you about that."

Fincher brought out Padilla's customs form that he had filled out on the plane. "You claimed here that you were carrying about eight thousand dollars. But you really had more than ten."

"I was tired when I filled that out," Padilla said. "I didn't count it correctly."

"Were you aware that U.S. law requires you to declare amounts of ten thousand dollars or more when you enter the country?"

"No, I didn't know that."

Fincher sat back in his chair. "Come on. This is absurd. You're coming into the United States, carrying this huge sum of money, to visit a relative in a distant city. But you don't have any travel arrangements? That doesn't make any sense."

"That's why I came, to visit my mother and son," he insisted. In fact, he said, he wanted to call his mother.

"Why do you want to call her?"

Padilla shook his head. "Never mind. Let's just finish."

Back to the money. Where did it come from?

"A man in Egypt gave me some of it in an envelope," Padilla said. "I also received money in Pakistan."

Some of it was just income, money he was paid for teaching English in Egypt and Pakistan. "Muslims in both countries also gave me some of it as a donation, so I could visit my mother and son in the United States," he said. "I also want to take my son to Puerto Rico once I meet with him in the U.S."

A few more questions about the money, the same evasive replies. Time to see if he would disclose the types of people who were his associates.

"Is there anyone in Egypt or Pakistan that you particularly admired or trusted or befriended? And are there any events you want to elaborate on?"

"There are many people and events," Padilla responded. "But I really can't recall any of them. I'm just too tired from traveling."

Fincher kept pushing, and Padilla kept pleading exhaustion. "I might be able to tell you more if I was more rested," he said.

That would be fine, one of the agents said. They could resume the interview in the morning.

"Listen, I've been here a long time and I've answered all your questions," Padilla responded. "I want to call my mother. And I'm worried about my money. But I'm done. I don't want to talk to you tomorrow."

"A few more questions," Fincher said. "Tell me the countries you've traveled to."

"I've only been to Switzerland, Egypt, Pakistan, and Saudi Arabia."

"Ever been to Afghanistan?"

"No," Padilla said. "Never."

"Now, you recently got a new American passport while you were in Pakistan," Fincher said. "What happened to your old one?"

"I lost it in a marketplace in Karachi. I reported it lost to the U.S. consulate there and got a replacement."

"Did you sell your old passport to anyone?"

"No."

"Did you tell the consulate the truth about how you lost it?"

"Of course."

"Okay," Fincher said, "what's the name of the market where you lost the passport?"

"I don't know the name."

"Well, what area in Karachi is the market in?"

"I don't know that name either."

At 6:10, Fincher called another break.

• • •

They resumed ten minutes later. Padilla seemed testy.

"I want to get my money back," he said. "I don't know what's happening to it. And I want to talk to my mother."

Again, the agents suggested they stop for the night and resume the questioning in the morning.

"I don't want to spend the night in a hotel, and I don't want to speak with you tomorrow."

Still, Padilla again continued answering questions for another few minutes. Perhaps, one of the agents suggested, their standoff could be resolved if Padilla agreed to take a polygraph.

"No, I'm not going to do that," Padilla said. "You don't need it. I'm being cooperative. And there's no scientific basis for those tests."

He had answered all of their questions, Padilla said. He wanted to leave. He wanted to call his mother and visit his son.

Fincher took a breath. The soft-spoken and polite approach wasn't working. It was time to try confrontation.

He suddenly turned his chair toward Padilla and leaned in.

"Let me tell you what I think," he said, his voice raised. "I think you *have* been to Afghanistan. I think you had military training there and met with high-ranking al-Qaeda officials. I think they sent you back to Pakistan, where you met up with other associates. And I think you left Pakistan en route for somewhere to commit an act of terrorism."

For a full minute, Fincher laid out in rapid fire the details he had been holding back. Padilla had been delayed in his travels. He was accompanied by another foreign national who was using a false passport. He and the other man had been detained in Karachi. He had traveled from Zurich to Egypt and back before flying to Chicago. And he had come to the United States to conduct surveillance for a terrorist attack.

Padilla's face was expressionless. He jumped out of his seat. "This interview is over," he said. "It's time for me to go."

Wait, Fincher said, standing. "I'd like you to volunteer to work with me and help me understand the things I've presented to you," he said. "If you don't want to volunteer, I'm going to serve you with a grand jury subpoena and compel your testimony in New York City."

Fincher brought out the subpoena and showed it to Padilla. A second passed. Padilla looked puzzled.

"What's a grand jury subpoena?" he asked. "What would happen if you served me with it?"

The agents would take him to New York, Fincher said, and he would be brought before the grand jury. He would have to answer questions. If he lied, he could be charged with perjury.

"But if you volunteer to go, we'll put you up in a hotel tonight and then take you to New York tomorrow."

"Would I be represented by a lawyer?"

"If you want one," Fincher replied, "We could arrange it."

Padilla paused. A haughty look spread over his face.

"I'm not going to volunteer to go to New York," he said, sounding cocky. "If you want me to go, you have to arrest me."

Damn. Fincher wanted a witness, not a defendant.

"I do have a material witness arrest warrant in your name," he said. "But I would much rather you volunteer the information than serve you with the warrant."

Again, Padilla looked confused. "A material witness warrant?"

That meant the government believed Padilla knew information that was relevant to a criminal investigation, Fincher said. A federal judge had reviewed the FBI's evidence and agreed that Padilla could be detained to testify before the grand jury. He had signed the warrant just before Padilla's plane landed.

Fincher reflected for a moment. Padilla had repeatedly invoked his mother during the interview, at one point fretting about what she might think if she heard the FBI was questioning him. That was an angle to use.

"I'm concerned that if I serve this, it's going to go on your arrest record," he said. "I know you've had a clean record for ten years. I'm worried that if I have to arrest you, your mother is going to think you're in some kind of trouble again."

Padilla stayed silent.

"José, I don't need and I don't want to arrest you."

"I'm not going to volunteer," Padilla responded. "You want me in New York, you have to arrest me."

Fincher sighed. "All right."

He brought out a pair of handcuffs.

"José Padilla, I'm arresting you pursuant to a material witness order."

Fincher read him his Miranda rights.

• • •

Three weeks had passed since Frank Dunham sent his letter to Norfolk Naval Station asking if Hamdi wanted a lawyer, and he had received no reply. Stung by the brush-off, Dunham decided to turn to the courts.

On Friday, May 10, a lawyer from his office walked down Granby Street in Norfolk to the Federal District Courthouse, passing several construction sites along the way. He pulled open the glass-and-chrome doors of the four-story building and made his way to the clerk's office. There, he filled out the necessary paperwork and filed a habeas corpus petition, demanding that the government produce Hamdi and prove that he was being lawfully detained.

It was, Dunham knew, a long shot. He was filing as a "next friend"—a term of law meaning that he was acting on behalf of someone who was unable to look after his own legal interests. But the courts required a next friend to have had a prior, meaningful relationship with the person being represented, and Dunham had never met, spoken to, or even seen Yaser Hamdi. He would never be able to establish that he met the requirements.

Dunham had tried to get around that problem by recruiting a substitute next friend with credentials to act the part. He had tracked down Yaser Hamdi's father, Esam Hamdi, in Saudi Arabia. But Esam expressed no interest in being named as the next friend. Dunham had no choice but to seek the role himself.

With the petition filed, the clock was ticking. A judge could well throw out the case if Dunham didn't find a legitimate next friend. He put out another feeler to Esam Hamdi.

The following Monday, a copy of the habeas petition arrived at the Pentagon's Office of the General Counsel. One of the lawyers there reviewed the filing, then briefed his boss, Jim Haynes, about it. Haynes was delighted.

He had been a participant in the administration's months of debates about what to do with United States citizens who joined the Taliban or al-Qaeda in fighting American troops. To Haynes, the right answer seemed obvious. All citizens fell under the protections of the Constitution; the government was proscribed from throwing aside those rights when detaining or trying an American on any charges that could result in the loss of freedom. Deciding, by fiat, that those constitutional demands didn't apply to terrorists seemed unsupportable. Haynes admired Dunham for his willingness to lock horns with the government over an issue of such fundamental import.

Haynes decided to let Dunham know what he thought. He dashed off a note to the public defender saying how much he respected him for the work he was doing.

At Guantanamo, General Dunlavey, the new commander of Task Force 170, was speaking by video teleconference with officers at Southern Command.

Dunlavey had settled in to his new job at the detention center, and had quickly developed a distaste for both law enforcement and the International Committee of the Red Cross. Both groups, Dunlavey grumbled, were interfering with interrogations of detainees by the military's intelligence teams.

The Criminal Investigation Task Force at the detention facility was criticizing the rough treatment used in the intelligence interrogations, and the Red Cross officials were complaining that they were not gaining access to all of the captives. But that couldn't be helped. As part of the effort to instill "learned helplessness" in the detainees, they were supposed to be kept isolated from everyone except their interrogators. If they were allowed to meet with the Red Cross—or even be exposed to the gentler "relationship" technique of law enforcement—then the intelligence program would collapse, he argued.

During the video teleconference, Dunlavey complained to the SOUTH-COM officers about the Red Cross. The group wasn't helping the military, he said, and was repeating the detainees' stories of torture—which were all lies. The Pentagon already knew from the Manchester Manual that al-Qaeda members were trained to falsely claim to have been subjected to brutality by interrogators. Why weren't these people aware of that?

"Yeah, the Red Cross is trouble," he said. "They *are* al-Qaeda."

On a high floor at the Metropolitan Correctional Center in Manhattan, a team of federal marshals unlocked the door to the cell holding José Padilla. They instructed him where to stand, then slapped on handcuffs, leg irons, and shackles.

It was May 15. Padilla had been transported to the prison the previous night and was scheduled to appear that morning before Chief Judge Michael Mukasey in the federal courthouse next door. Mukasey was well versed in terrorism cases, having sat on some high-profile prosecutions including the trial of Omar Abdel-Rahman, known as the "blind sheikh."

He was also familiar with the Padilla case. He had been the judge who signed the material witness warrant, based on an affidavit by Special Agent Joseph Ennis that attested to the government's evidence on Padilla.

The marshals led Padilla through a side door in Courtroom 21A. He shuffled toward a table where Donna Newman, a defense lawyer, was waiting. After a short hearing, Mukasey appointed Newman as Padilla's attorney.

For the next few weeks, the lawyer and her new client conferred about what course to follow. Prosecutors provided them with a copy of the Ennis affidavit; none of the information it contained was particularly strong. Newman wrote a motion challenging the government's right to hold Padilla.

It wouldn't take long to get a ruling on her motion, Newman figured. Mukasey had scheduled a conference for June 11, where she expected him to issue a decision.

The conference would never take place.

10

Blaine Thomas sprawled out on his bed at Guantanamo Bay and clicked on the television to watch cable news. The room was nothing much to look at, just four blank walls inside dilapidated housing that had been vacant for years. A decrepit air conditioner wheezed ineffectually against the oppressive heat, and Thomas was drenched in sweat.

He didn't much care; he treasured these rare moments of solitude so he could rest and think. As the assistant special agent in charge with the Criminal Investigation Task Force assigned to the detention center, he spent his days juggling one demanding task after another—watching over his interrogators, working with analysts to tease out connections among detainees, and transmitting classified findings over a secure network called SIPRNet to his superiors at Fort Belvoir.

That was the work that gave him professional satisfaction. It was the other part—the turf warfare—that he found wearying. He wasted untold hours battling the intelligence interrogators and their lead cheerleader, General Dunlavey, the officer in charge. Dunlavey and his team openly scorned their civilian counterparts, snickering and rolling their eyes whenever they heard about trying to "build relationships" with detainees during interrogations—it was too gentle, too . . . lame. There was no shouting, no poking, no slapping or any of the other tough methods that the soldiers in the intelligence unit had been told were the most effective.

Thomas and his colleagues could only shrug; the only intelligence that they detected in Dunlavey's team was in its name. They were mostly kids who seemed to have acquired their tough-guy tactics from the movies. Their sessions with the detainees always started with the same shouted questions—*Where's bin*

Laden? When's the last time you saw him? Since most of the prisoners had *never* seen bin Laden, these pointless inquisitions gave away their interrogators as ignorant and easily fooled.

The hostility between the two camps left Thomas exhausted at the end of the day, longing for the sanctuary of his stifling room, where he could kick back with the television or a book. But there would be no rest for him tonight.

Shortly after eleven o'clock, there was a knock at the door. It was the supervisor for the FBI agents stationed at Guantanamo.

"I've got a message for you," he said. "There's a problem."

Thomas had heard about the trouble long ago. Around February, the Pentagon had learned that terrorists had set up a bomb-making operation at three safe houses established by the former lieutenant governor of an Afghani province. The size and type of the explosives were particularly lethal, and plans were in the works to use them against American troops. That information had been conveyed to the intelligence unit at Guantanamo with orders to do whatever it took to wring the location of the safe houses out of the detainees.

The interrogators sprang into action like a bunch of Keystone Kops, dragging random detainees in for questioning and screaming at them to reveal what they knew about the bomb plot. It was like shooting in the dark at an unseen target in the desperate hope of hitting the bull's-eye.

If this was old news to Thomas, the urgency of the threat was not. Time was running out. The military had learned that the bombs would be used in about ten days and had alerted the criminal task force at Guantanamo in hopes its interrogators could ferret out what the intelligence unit could not.

Ten days. Not much time. Just grabbing detainees to interrogate wouldn't work; Thomas knew that he had to start off by figuring out which ones might actually know something about the safe houses.

Thomas turned it over in his mind. He was equipped for the task, having actually read the files on every detainee. And while he normally had a poor memory, details of each prisoner stuck in his head.

The name of the province rang a bell. One of the detainees had been identified as the governor in that very region. Since the intelligence suggested that one of that man's former deputies was running the safe houses, he was an obvious candidate for questioning.

He hurried to another part of the barracks to find his operations chief. "I need you to get me two of our best interrogators, right now," he said.

• • •

The detainee was brought into an interrogation room by military police. Two members of the military's criminal investigative team and two FBI agents were waiting for him, alongside two interpreters. Thomas and the bureau supervisor were in the next room.

The police put the detainee in a chair, then chained him to an eyebolt drilled into the floor. "All right," one interrogator said, "here's why you're down here."

He told the prisoner what the Americans had discovered about the bombing threat. They knew he was an important man in the province, the interrogator said, important enough to know about the location of the safe houses.

"We need you to be cooperative," the interrogator said.

Seconds ticked by. The detainee's expression was impassive. Finally, he spoke, his tone respectful. "I know what you're talking about," he said. "I know where these safe houses are."

"Then tell us."

The detainee shook his head. "There's nothing I can do for you. Not unless you do something for me."

The man had not seen his wife and daughter for months, and in all that time they had been caught in a war zone. Every day, he ached with the fear that they had been killed. He had to know what had happened to them.

"Find out if my wife and daughter are alive. Then I will tell you what you want to know."

One of the interrogators walked to the next room, where Thomas waited. He related the detainee's condition for talking.

Thomas rubbed his face. "Oh, shit! How are we going to find that out?"

The detainee provided a phone number in Afghanistan—not his own, but a neighbor's. That man would be able to find the detainee's wife.

"If I can dial this phone number and speak to my wife," he said, "then I will give this information to you."

The interrogators were getting close, but allowing a detainee to make a phone call was a command decision. Thomas walked into the room. One of the investigators introduced him as the boss.

"Okay," Thomas said. "We're going to make this happen."

But he had his own conditions. Two translators would sit next to the detainee, listening to every word. If the conversation veered onto any other topic, or if a woman wasn't put on the phone, an agent would immediately disconnect the call. The detainee accepted the terms.

Thomas brought a telephone into the room, dialed the number, and handed it to the detainee. Within a few minutes, the man's wife was on the line. She was fine, she told him, and their daughter was safe. Tears filled the man's eyes, and the call quickly came to an end.

The detainee spent a moment pulling himself together. He looked up at the interrogators. "I keep my word," he said.

Then he spelled out, in minute detail, where the Americans could find the safe houses.

Within a day, military officials stationed in Afghanistan confirmed that high-powered bombs were being built at the identified locations. Missiles destroyed the houses an hour later.

There were plenty of high fives among Thomas and his team when they heard the news. Their work had saved the lives of American troops in Afghanistan.

It had also proved a point. The intelligence interrogators had failed to find an iota of information about the safe houses. Roughing up detainees, yelling at them, depriving them of sleep—none of that had accomplished anything. But when the criminal investigators took over, thought the situation through, and then treated a detainee like a human being, they got what they were looking for in just a few hours.

Maybe General Dunlavey and his crew would finally figure it out, Thomas said. What better proof was there that the tactics of criminal investigators worked, and the ones being used by the intelligence teams did not?

A few days later, the deputy commander of the joint task force at Guantanamo dropped in to speak with Thomas. He seemed almost shamefaced.

"Hey," he said, taking a seat. "General Dunlavey has ordered me to do a 15-6."

"A 15-6?" Thomas asked, sitting bolt upright in his chair.

An investigation under Army Regulation 15-6. He would have to interview witnesses, gather evidence, and then submit a report with his findings.

"Dunlavey's saying you broke protocol by letting a detainee make a phone call."

"What we did saved lives, and you're going to investigate us for it?" Thomas snapped.

"I know, it's unbelievable. But I've been given an order. I have to follow it."

Thomas sank back down. "You guys don't even understand what a real investigation is! You do a real investigation when someone does something wrong! And nothing was done wrong here."

He left it at that. After all, he couldn't blame the deputy commander, who was only following orders. It was Dunlavey who had some explaining to do. Thomas tracked him down.

"What the hell's going on?" he demanded.

Dunlavey was unruffled.

"I can't talk to you," he said. "Not until I get the report back on the 15-6."

Thomas stormed off, having no doubt why this was happening. Dunlavey was mad that the criminal investigators showed up his interrogators.

In Guantanamo's house of mirrors, Thomas realized, success didn't breed admiration. It triggered retribution.

The word in Norfolk legal circles about Magistrate Judge Tommy E. Miller was mixed. Lawyers considered him to be extremely knowledgeable of the law and a stickler for the rules of procedure. Still, some prosecutors questioned his even-handedness, scenting an antigovernment bent. So, when the habeas petition for Hamdi was assigned to Miller, there were groans at the United States Attorney's Office and cheers among the public defenders led by Frank Dunham.

Their responses proved prophetic—by May 21, Miller had given the government a judicial shellacking. Over the prosecutor's objections, he accepted Dunham as a next friend of Hamdi, appointed him as counsel, and ordered the government to allow him to meet with his new client. And there were to be no mysteries about Hamdi—if the government wasn't going to charge him with a crime, Miller declared, it would have to come up with a persuasive argument for his continued detention.

What exactly did "severe pain" mean, anyway?

That was the question bouncing around the Office of Legal Counsel, as John Yoo and other lawyers there worked on their assessment of the CIA's proposal for harsh interrogations.

The phrase was a set piece in all of the domestic and international prohibitions against torture. If an action is taken with the intent to inflict severe pain, unless it is part of a lawful punishment imposed for crimes, then it constitutes torture, the rules read.

But that description, the administration lawyers concluded, was murky. They set out to clarify it.

Jennifer Koester, a junior lawyer in the office just a year out of Yale Law School, had been assigned to determine the meaning of the words. She began by looking up the word *severe* in two dictionaries. She studied the legislative or ratification history of relevant rules—the antitorture prohibitions under Title 18 of the Federal Criminal Code and the U.N. Convention Against Torture—as well as a handful of cases heard before both domestic and overseas courts.

When she finished that review, Koester prepared a first draft of her analysis, arriving at a conclusion that was even vaguer than the words *severe pain*. It was the result, she wrote, of "extreme conduct" that went beyond cruel, inhuman, or degrading treatment.

The draft went to John Yoo, and he wasn't satisfied. There had to be a stronger basis in the law, he believed, for coaxing out a more precise meaning.

On May 23, he wrote a comment about the draft. "Is severe used in this way in other parts of the US Code?"

Koester and other lawyers got back to work, looking for any law that used the words *severe* or *severe pain*.

The legal fight over Yaser Hamdi resumed on May 24.

Judge Miller, government lawyers decided, had exceeded his authority. He was a magistrate, essentially an assistant to the district court judge. He was supposed to be handling pretrial issues, but his orders amounted to granting the habeas motion.

The government filed its objections with Federal District Judge Robert Doumar, who had authority to toss out Miller's orders.

The filing marshaled a number of precedents to contest the orders, asserting that Miller improperly applied the next friend rules and did not have the power to appoint an attorney to Hamdi. That was bad enough, the document said, but by ruling on issues that should not have been taken up until later, Miller had robbed the government of the chance to present its arguments for keeping Hamdi isolated.

For example, the military needed to interrogate Hamdi for any knowledge he might possess about al-Qaeda and its plans. Plus, evidence showed that al-Qaeda operatives could use a meeting with *anyone* for strategic—and dangerous—advantage.

"It is well known," the filing said, "than an al Qaeda training manual uncovered by the United States provides instructions for passing concealed messages to their colleagues from behind bars after they have been captured—even through unwitting intermediaries."

After the document was filed, a local reporter called Dunham to ask him about the claim that Hamdi might use him to communicate with other al-Qaeda members.

"It's so ridiculous, I just won't give it the time of day," Dunham replied.

The lawyer could not have known, but the government's claim was also wrong. The filing was referring to the Manchester Manual, which was found not by the United States, but by Britain. And despite the claim that it was "well known" that the document described how to pass secret messages from prison, it did nothing of the sort.

"That sounds idiotic, doesn't it?"

Federal Judge Robert Doumar scowled as he spoke the words to Gregory Garre, the assistant to the solicitor general. It was May 28, and Doumar had taken up the Hamdi case days before, putting on hold all of Magistrate Judge Miller's orders. But now, in his first hearing on the case, the white-haired jurist was erupting in anger at the government in ways that made Miller's show of annoyance seem tame by comparison.

Garre had just argued that Hamdi had no right to a lawyer, since he had not been charged with anything. But, as a captured enemy combatant, he could be held indefinitely. Doumar rolled his eyes.

"We're not dealing with a novel doctrine here," Garre said. The military historically had the right to capture enemy combatants under the rules and customs of war, and could hold them until the end of the conflict.

"That is mind-boggling!" Doumar responded. "When are these hostilities going to end? Can he be held forever? Can he be held for life?"

Frank Dunham, the federal public defender, argued that if he was not allowed to speak to Hamdi, there would be no way to challenge the government's designation that he was an enemy combatant.

"Allow me to see him so I can develop his side of the story," he said. "He could well say that 'I was standing around tending my camel when I got rounded up.' "

Doumar agreed. "Not letting Hamdi see a lawyer just seems to run counter to the very basic right to counsel that is part of the constitution," he said.

He issued his ruling, upholding Magistrate Miller's order. The government had three days to allow Dunham to meet with Hamdi, in private. And its lawyers had to provide a written explanation for why Hamdi was being detained.

The three days, Doumar said, should be enough to give the government the chance to challenge his ruling in a higher court.

"How much time would you need to drive to Richmond or Washington to file an appeal?" he asked.

Then he smiled. "And if you can find a judge to overturn my decision," he said, "more power to you."

John Yoo shook his head as he lingered over the words from Doumar's ruling.

This is outrageous. This country was at *war*. Hamdi had been seized on the battlefield. And the administration was supposed to treat him like a common criminal defendant? Maybe summon a few soldiers from Afghanistan to Norfolk so they could describe the circumstances of Hamdi's capture, just to ease Doumar's concerns?

This judge's ruling wasn't just some distraction on the sidelines of the war on terror, Yoo fumed. It struck at the very heart of the conflict. If left unchallenged, it would set a precedent that could wreak untold damage.

He contacted Ted Olson, the solicitor general. "Ted, you know, I'm really worried about this case. It could go to the Supreme Court, and I think it's going to raise some fundamental questions of whether we're at war."

It was a bad idea, Yoo said, to leave a matter of this importance in the hands of some local federal prosecutors. They needed to put together a special team of administration lawyers reporting to Olson, which would handle Hamdi and the other habeas cases.

A good idea, Olson said. "We need to make sure we put the best people on this," he said.

Dozens of administration lawyers gathered around a conference table in an ornate, ceremonial room on the fifth floor of the Justice Department. Like Yoo, they had been staggered by Judge Doumar's ruling; most in the group had assumed that he would brush aside the Miller orders, or maybe limit them. But certainly not *uphold* them.

The legal team that had been assembled to handle the habeas cases was just getting its footing, but now there was no time left for preparations and debate. Ted Olson had called this meeting to set the strategy for the next few weeks on how to manage the Hamdi problem.

"All right, you know what Judge Doumar's decision has been on Hamdi, and we're going to have to figure out what our response is going to be," he told his colleagues. "I want to hear everybody's views."

The first suggestion was simple: Do nothing. A number of lawyers said that the administration should not appeal Doumar's ruling, to avoid alienating him. Whatever a higher court ruled, the case would be kicked back to Doumar. He was renowned for his anger and had the habit of tongue-lashing lawyers who challenged him. In Norfolk, the joke was that Judge Judy, the brutal television jurist, quaked when she saw Doumar coming.

"We should just give Doumar the answers he wants," one of the assistant United States attorneys from the district said. "Work with him in the four corners of the decision."

That was the best idea and didn't seem to have much downside, another lawyer said. Even if Doumar demanded to hear from the soldiers who had picked up Hamdi, so what? Bring them back, take them to court, have them answer some questions. Simple.

Lawyers from the State Department and the Pentagon agreed. "It's not like this is a trial," a lawyer from State said. "He's basically saying this raises constitutional concerns and he wants a briefing on the constitutional issues. We can—"

Yoo interrupted. "This judge has to be slapped down," he said. "He's gone way beyond his authority."

The administration had no choice, Yoo said, but to appeal. "It's important that this judge not be allowed to interfere with decisions that are going to have implications with military and intelligence operations," he said. "This guy's acted way outside what he's allowed to do, he cited no precedent for it, and he shouldn't be allowed to get away with it."

Doumar was casting himself, in an act of misplaced grandiosity, as some sort of judicial monarch, Yoo said. "I don't think this one guy, this one judge, this outlier should, because of the luck of the draw, be allowed to dictate how American detention policies can work!" he snapped.

The vehemence of his outburst took his associates aback. Yoo was usually coolheaded, but this time he was unable to contain his fury at the idea of knuckling under to this single judge.

The debate dribbled on for a bit longer, but no one in the room came close to matching the intensity of Yoo's passion.

On Saturday, June 8, Gonzales was in Austin preparing to deliver a speech when he received a call from Jim Haynes at the Pentagon.

"I need to speak to you on a secure line," Haynes said.

"Okay. Call me back at two."

He instructed Haynes to dial the office of Johnny Sutton, the United States attorney for the Western District of Texas. Gonzales made his way a few blocks to a building on the corner of Ninth and Congress. Ordinarily, Sutton's tenth-floor suite was locked on the weekend, but someone had been told to open it for the White House counsel. Gonzales walked into Sutton's personal office, where the black, bulky secure phone was hooked up. The call came through right on time.

"Everyone has reached an agreement on Padilla," Haynes said. The military was going to take him into custody.

The debate about what to do with Padilla had been raging for weeks, with officials racing to reach a decision before Judge Mukasey's next hearing, scheduled to be held in three days. Mukasey could well order Padilla's release from prison unless the government charged him with a crime; a material witness warrant might not be enough to hold an American citizen for months.

But indicting him was inconceivable. Too much of the evidence against him had come from Abu Zubaydah and another suspect, Binyam Mohamed, who had been beaten by Pakistani intelligence officers when they questioned him. National security was at issue. The administration couldn't just trot out two high-level enemies of the United States who had been secreted away in prisons overseas.

Not only that, but trying suspected terrorists in civilian court had proved to be messy affairs. Moussaoui had already transformed his criminal trial into a circus, firing his lawyers, launching into lengthy diatribes against the West, and trumpeting his wish for the destruction of America. The trial of John Walker Lindh hadn't gone much better—his lawyers were mounting an aggressive defense, releasing government photographs that showed their client bound, naked, and blindfolded; demanding access to detainees at Guantanamo; and seeking to subpoena members of the military and the FBI. Criminal prosecutions, some administration lawyers argued, were too unpredictable for cases that blended the usual types of evidence with classified intelligence.

Still, the process for making the decision was complicated. The CIA compiled a written assessment of the available intelligence about Padilla, including the statements from Zubaydah. That information was then turned over to the Pentagon, which added data collected by the Defense Intelligence Agency. An assessment of whether Padilla qualified as an enemy combatant was signed by Rumsfeld and forwarded to Ashcroft. There, the final analysis was prepared, attesting that Rumsfeld's determination complied with the law, that the military could legally take Padilla into custody, and that Ashcroft recommended the decision as a matter of policy. The full package of information was then sent back to Haynes at the Pentagon.

Gonzales thanked Haynes for the update. He would take the recommendation to Bush once he got back to Washington.

The next morning, Sunday, Gonzales dropped by Addington's office to read through the Padilla recommendation. The vice president's counsel and Flanigan had been shepherding the documents through the approval process and both men had kept copies.

Addington was waiting. Gonzales greeted him, picked up the paperwork, and sat down on a couch to review it. He recommended a few changes and the two men tinkered with the wording. It was ready for the president.

Gonzales made a call and was connected to Bush. "Mr. President, I've got the paperwork on Padilla."

Fine, Bush replied. He told Gonzales to bring it by that evening.

Bush was sitting at his desk in the White House residence, reading through a single-page declaration. It said Padilla was an enemy combatant, was closely associated with al-Qaeda, and posed a continuing threat to the United States. Everything seemed in order.

Bush dated the document and signed it.

At about the same time, federal prosecutors in New York visited Judge Mukasey at his home with a motion to toss out the material witness order. If it remained in effect, the transfer of Padilla from the custody of the Justice Department to the Pentagon would be impeded. Mukasey approved the request.

That night, military officials arrived at the Metropolitan Correctional Center and took custody of Padilla. He was shackled, blindfolded, then flown to the Naval Weapons Station Charleston in South Carolina. Members of the navy's masters-at-arms branch brought Padilla off the plane, taking him to Building 3107, the Consolidated Naval Brig. He was locked in a cell away from the rest of the population.

The next day, Padilla's lawyer, Donna Newman, was preparing for a hearing before Mukasey that was scheduled to be held in twenty-four hours. No one had told her that the warrant against her client had been vacated, or that he had been turned over to the military. She was notified of his fate just before the rest of the world learned about it.

A press release had been written about Padilla and an information packet prepared. White House officials prided themselves on their skill at controlling "the message" of any event, making sure an announcement was carefully readied. This one was going to take particular skill. A United States citizen arrested on American soil, dirty bombs, enemy combatants—these were complex issues that had to be framed well. They couldn't overstate the threat, yet at the same time they had to justify the military's custody of Padilla as necessary for national security.

Both Rumsfeld and Ashcroft were overseas, so the responsibility for handling the press conference had been turned over to their deputies—Wolfowitz and Larry Thompson—as well as Mueller from the FBI. There had been some debate about where to conduct the briefing, but the White House wanted it held at the Justice Department pressroom.

The planning was still under way when a document arrived at the White House from Moscow. It was a statement about Padilla that had been composed by aides to Ashcroft, who was traveling in Russia. Until that moment, no one at the White House even suspected that the attorney general was preparing to hold his own—unvetted and unapproved—press conference in Russia.

Ashcroft was rehearsing his statement while one aide applied hair spray and another brushed off his shoulders.

"We have captured a known terrorist," Ashcroft said.

He stopped and loudly cleared his throat. "Let's try that again," he said. "We have captured . . ."

• • •

About fifteen minutes later, Ashcroft peered grimly into a Russian camera, his face bathed in an eerie red glow. The image was spooky, something like the opening scene of a horror-movie marathon.

"I am pleased to announce today a significant step forward in the war on terrorism," Ashcroft began. "We have captured a known terrorist who was exploring a plan to build and explode a radiological dispersion device, or dirty bomb, in the United States."

So far, so good. Despite Ashcroft's appearance—and the apparent urgency conveyed by his delivering his statement from Moscow—the words he had spoken so far were finely tuned, the essence of diplomatic understatement. Padilla was "exploring a plan"—just the right way to phrase it. There was no talk of an imminent threat.

The attorney general described Padilla's background, explaining that he had also gone by the name Abdullah al-Mujahir, and gave details about his arrest in Chicago. Then Ashcroft fouled it up.

"We have disrupted an unfolding terrorist plot to attack the United States by exploding a radioactive dirty bomb," he said. "Now, a radioactive dirty bomb involves exploding a conventional bomb that not only kills victims in the immediate vicinity, but also spreads radioactive material that is highly toxic to humans and can cause mass death and injury."

In the White House, Addington watched Ashcroft's performance in utter astonishment. *Disrupted an unfolding terrorist plot?* Padilla had barely entered the planning stages. *Mass death?* Mass overstatement! People were going to think that the country just dodged a nuclear attack or something.

Not good.

Ashcroft's face filled the television screens on the floor of the New York Stock Exchange and in trading rooms across Wall Street. His words flashed across Bloomberg and Reuters news terminals.

The stock market had been having a good day, a rarity since the collapse months before of Enron, the energy conglomerate. In fact, the Dow had gained just over one hundred points.

But, as Ashcroft spoke, the market swooned. The advances for the day were all but wiped out in minutes.

• • •

It's never easy to walk a cat backward. But somehow, the White House had to undo Ashcroft's alarmist talk without suggesting that the administration didn't know what it was doing.

The duty fell to Wolfowitz, Thompson, and Mueller. The original press conference went forward; reporters were notified that there would be a briefing at 11:15 that morning. After a twenty-minute delay, the three men appeared. Thompson spoke first.

"By now, all of you have heard the attorney general's statement regarding the arrest of Abdullah al-Mujahir and his transfer to military control," he said. "Secretary Wolfowitz has a few brief remarks."

Wolfowitz took over, choosing his words carefully in an effort to project a sense of calm. Padilla had been *discussing* plans; he had only been conducting reconnaissance. His soothing tone didn't satisfy the crowd of journalists; they wanted facts.

"How far did they get?" one reporter asked. "Have they assembled any part of the weapon?"

Thompson glanced at Mueller. "I'll defer to the director on that question."

Mueller said a few words thanking the CIA for their work. "Now, with regard to the specific question, as it states, I think, in the attorney general's statement, there were discussions about this possible plan, and it was in the discussion phase," he said. "It had not gone, as far as we know, much past the discussion phase."

Another reporter asked whether the attack was planned to take place in Washington. Mueller turned that question over to Wolfowitz.

"As Director Mueller said, this was still in the initial planning stages," Wolfowitz said. "It certainly wasn't at the point of having a specific target."

While Padilla seemed to have some knowledge of the Washington area, that wasn't particularly important. "I want to emphasize again, there was not an actual plan," Wolfowitz said. "We stopped this man in the initial planning stages."

The press conference lasted just over six minutes. The stock market edged higher.

Yosri Fouda had kept his secret for months. The Al Jazeera reporter who had interviewed Khalid Sheikh Mohammed and Ramzi bin al-Shibh in Pakistan had been waiting to tell his bosses about the coup until the al-Qaeda terrorists sent him the tapes from the meeting. But now he was ready to let them in on the news about the remarkable interviews.

Among those Fouda informed was Sheikh Hamad bin Thamer al-Thani, the chairman of Al Jazeera. Soon, al-Thani notified his cousin the emir of Qatar, Sheikh Hamad bin Khalifa al-Thani. The emir, in turn, shared the information with George Tenet. The CIA obtained copies of the Al Jazeera interview. Now CIA agents had recordings that could be used to match the two terrorists' voices to those from calls intercepted by the NSA.

Ted Olson wasn't on time for the latest meeting about the appeal in the Hamdi case, so his deputy, Paul Clement, sat at the head of the table. "Let's get started," he said. "I hope everybody has had a chance to review the filing."

A hearing before the Fourth Circuit Court of Appeals was scheduled to be held in a matter of days; Olson had come down in favor of Yoo's argument for putting Judge Doumar in his place.

The number of lawyers in this meeting was much smaller than in the early strategy session. This time, the goal was to make sure that the Justice Department, the Pentagon, and the counsels for Bush and Cheney were all agreed on the arguments that Clement should make.

The centerpiece of the case would rest on the authority of the president and the military in a time of war. The habeas petition was a challenge to the president's powers under the Constitution. Courts could not intervene with a military or presidential decision that declared an individual to be an unlawful enemy combatant; the judiciary was not qualified to make that kind of judgment and had no authority to question such a determination. Should the courts want to review the rights of an unlawful enemy combatant, they could. But that was different from challenging the designation.

On the specific issue of a habeas petition, there was strong precedent to argue that such filings from military captives should not be considered. There was *Ex Parte Quirin,* the German saboteurs case that the administration had used as the basis for establishing military commissions—one of the defendants was an American citizen, and his habeas petition had been tossed out. In 1950, in a case called *Johnson v. Eisentrager,* the Supreme Court ruled specifically that the judiciary should not consider a habeas petition filed by a foreign enemy. Another case, *In re Territo,* was directly on point—an Italian soldier who was born in the United States had been captured on the field of battle. The Ninth Circuit Court of Appeals ruled that Territo's citizenship was irrelevant and that he had no right to file a habeas petition. The only weakness in that case was that, while it was the only precedent that dealt specifically with the issues raised in the Hamdi case, it was a circuit opinion. The Supreme Court did not hear an appeal.

There was something missing, Addington thought. "We should also mention that, even under the Third Geneva Convention, POWs don't have a right to a lawyer and can't challenge their detention," he said. "Certainly, unlawful enemy combatants don't get more rights than POWs."

Good point. Clement wrote it down.

Olson arrived and listened to the discussion in silence. He sat back in his chair.

"I'm pretty pessimistic about the Supreme Court on the access-to-a-lawyer issue," he said. "We may not get four votes for that, let alone five."

Addington looked at Olson with an expression of disbelief. He had enormous respect for the solicitor general—so did Cheney—but he couldn't imagine Olson was right. The precedents were all on the administration's side! The court would have to reverse standing law stretching back decades!

"I'm surprised," Addington said. "Do you really think so?"

Absolutely, Olson said. Four of the justices—John Paul Stevens, David Souter, Ruth Bader Ginsburg, and Stephen Breyer—were probably lost causes. Anthony Kennedy was a strong believer in the right to counsel, so he was going to be a problem. Even Sandra Day O'Connor was a question mark; she might have issues with the procedure that went into designating someone as an enemy combatant.

"They would have to reverse the precedents," Addington said.

Olson nodded. That very well might happen. It was the same argument that Yoo had made months before—the Supreme Court was as much a political body as a judicial one. The mind-set of each justice had to be considered in predicting outcomes. And, under that analysis, the administration's chances didn't look good.

The argument before the Fourth Circuit Court of Appeals, Olson said, would be handled by Clement. An appearance by the deputy solicitor general would underscore how important the administration considered these issues. Some of the other lawyers were surprised, since they had expected Olson himself to appear in court.

As the meeting broke up, Olson approached Flanigan, drew him aside, and handed him a DVD.

"This is something I'm giving to friends," he said. "It's a tribute that Larry King has done for Barbara."

Flanigan was touched. Olson's wife, Barbara, had been killed on 9/11, when her plane crashed into the Pentagon.

King, the television personality, had assembled the video to honor his murdered friend. Perhaps, Flanigan thought, Olson's grief might have something to do with his decision not to argue before the court on behalf of the administration. A lawyer was supposed to approach a case without emotion, and in this instance, no one could expect Olson to suspend his personal feelings.

Just a mile down Pennsylvania Avenue, in the offices of the law firm Shearman & Sterling, Tom Wilner was preparing for a different legal assault on the administration's detainee policy.

Months before, Wilner had filed a suit on behalf of twelve Kuwaiti men held at Guantanamo, captioned *al-Odah et al. v. United States*. The case was joined with *Rasul v. Bush*, the habeas petition brought by Clive Stafford Smith, Joseph Margulies, and the Center for Constitutional Rights. *Rasul* had been going nowhere for months, but now the combined petitions were about to be heard in Federal District Court for the District of Columbia.

The bar that the lawyers faced was high. Unlike Hamdi, none of the plaintiffs were American citizens or were even detained in the United States. Instead, they were alien nationals seized overseas and held at Guantanamo. A court was far less likely to grant constitutional rights to foreign enemy combatants than to a citizen, and less likely still if they were being held at Guantanamo naval base in Cuba. Unlike in Norfolk, where Hamdi was imprisoned, the United States had no sovereign control over Guantanamo, the administration argued. That meant American courts had no jurisdiction over activities there.

To deal with those complexities, Wilner threw the equivalent of a baseball pitcher's changeup to knock his adversaries off balance. He didn't file a habeas petition—in fact, he didn't challenge his clients' confinement at all. Instead, his motion sought only to compel the administration to grant the Kuwaitis basic rights—access to the courts, the right to a lawyer—so that they could raise claims about the *conditions* of their confinement. The distinction was subtle, but Wilner hoped, by focusing solely on procedure, it could serve as the first step toward a full-throated challenge to the government's policy.

For the strategy to succeed, though, Wilner and his team needed to dig up a precedent showing that constitutional rights apply to foreigners held in overseas locations controlled by the United States. It seemed a long shot, but such a prior ruling would strike at the heart of the government's claim that Guantanamo lay outside the reach of American law.

Associates at the law firm scoured legal databases, and several times a week dumped piles of cases on Wilner's desk that contained any discernible relevance to a range of issues raised by the lawsuit. Then, one day, a lawyer on the team dropped off a Xeroxed copy of the decision in a little-known 1977 case called *Ralpho v. Bell,* heard in the court of appeals for the District of Columbia. The district where Wilner's case was being heard!

The case had nothing to do with war or detention or enemy combatants. Instead, it involved a man from Micronesia who was contesting the procedures followed by United States officials in deciding how much he was paid out of a compensation fund administered by the government. There had been no hearing prior to the determination that Ralpho was owed little, and he had no idea how the conclusion had been reached. The American response was simple—while the United States had political control of Micronesia through a trust agreement, it had no sovereignty over the territory. No sovereignty, no constitutional rights, no need for due process.

With each sentence he read, Wilner's excitement grew. Then came the clincher:

> *It is settled that there cannot exist under the American flag any governmental authority untrammeled by the requirements of due process of law.*

It didn't matter, the court ruled, that the United States had no sovereign authority over Micronesia. Ralpho had the right to due process—hearings, lawyers, everything.

"Shit!" Wilner exploded in delight. "This is our case!"

He rushed to show the decision to his colleagues. As far as he was concerned, their position had just become ironclad.

Two military officers stood at the doorway of an interrogation booth in the recently constructed Camp Delta at Guantanamo Bay. Camp X-Ray, the makeshift quarters thrown together before the first detainees arrived, had been shuttered, and now the rooms for questioning detainees were more private and had a more professional appearance.

One of the officers was Britt Mallow, the commander of the Criminal Investigation Task Force that was charged with conducting interviews for use in prosecutions against detainees. The other was a senior official with the Defense Intelligence Agency, who was purported to be one of the military's most experienced interrogators. The two were chatting about nothing in particular, and the conversation drifted onto the topic of interrogation tactics.

"You know, all these guys are the same," the intelligence officer said. "All you've got to do is find what button to push and they'll tell you anything you want to know."

Mallow stared at his colleague. *How fucking stupid is that?*

"I don't get where you're coming from," Mallow said. "You've got to take into account the backgrounds of these people for an interrogation. Are you saying that a guy from India is going to have the same cultural background as a guy from North Africa as a guy from Eastern Europe and a guy from South Texas?"

Most of the detainees were rural laborers, not trained soldiers or cunning spies. The majority were terribly unsophisticated. An individual approach had to be used for all of them—a cookie-cutter plan might work with some and shut down others. Questioning them was a delicate dance.

The intelligence officer sneered. "I've been around," he said. "I know how to do this."

Mallow's heart sank. The ranks of the intelligence interrogators were filled with kids in their late teens, with all of the arrogance and ignorance of youth. Many didn't bother to read the files of the captives they berated. They were green, Mallow had told himself. They would grow into their jobs.

But this intelligence officer had been around the block on interrogations. And he had no idea what he was talking about.

There was no one to teach these kids how to do the job. This was a problem with no easy fix.

The lawyers gathered at the White House counsel's suite were ready to do battle. With just days to go before the next hearing in the Hamdi case, the debate over how best to win legal support for administration policies had yet to be resolved. Judge Doumar was beside the point—his ruling would certainly be appealed, no matter what his decision. But Ted Olson continued to worry about the Supreme Court; however valid the White House considered its legal analysis to be, Olson was doubtful the court would agree.

At the meeting in Gonzales's office, Bradford Berenson was arguing that Olson had good reason for his misgivings. Berenson had worked as a clerk for Justice Anthony Kennedy, who was frequently the swing voter between the Supreme Court's conservative and liberal jurists; Brett Kavanaugh, another White House lawyer who had worked for Justice Kennedy, agreed.

"You have to understand," Berenson told the group, "Justice Kennedy will never accept that the president has absolute discretion to lock up an American citizen and deny him access to a lawyer. His feelings about the right to counsel are very, very strong."

Addington broke in. "It's ridiculous to surrender the president's authority based on a supposition about what Kennedy *might* do. No one knows that."

"David, you've got two people in this room who have both worked very closely with Justice Kennedy," Berenson said. "We are the best source of information you've got about how he thinks. And both of us are telling you the same thing. He will never go along with this."

"That's naive," Addington said.

"And that is *know-nothingness*!" Berenson shouted, slapping the coffee table. His hand caught the edge of an empty candy dish; it flipped into the air, landing with a clatter.

The shouting continued, when a secretary appeared at the door of the office. "Everything okay in here?" she asked.

"Yes, it's fine," Gonzales replied with a smile. "Don't worry."

The secretary left and closed the door. For a moment, no one spoke.

Addington broke the stillness. His voice was calm. He had shifted from anger to teaching mode. He glanced around at each of his colleagues.

"Is there anybody in this room who believes that what we are about to do here is actually unlawful or unconstitutional?" he asked.

No one replied.

"And is this the policy that is the most protective of the citizens of the United States?"

Again, silence.

Addington sat back as he raised his arms and shrugged. "So what more is there to discuss?" he asked.

The debate ended, and the decision was left to Gonzales. He sided with Addington. The administration would push the most aggressive legal position possible.

On the afternoon of June 24, a group of reporters was waiting in the White House Rose Garden when Bush stepped behind a podium to deliver a speech that had been billed as a major policy address.

He opened his remarks at 3:47. "For too long, the citizens of the Middle East have lived in the midst of death and fear," he said. "The hatred of a few holds the hopes of many hostage."

It was intolerable: Israelis were captive to terror, Palestinians were living in squalor and humiliation. Without change, there was little reason to hope for a resolution of the Middle East conflict. But there was a way out of the impasse.

His vision, Bush said, was for the creation of two states living side by side in peace. To accomplish that, changes had to be made.

The Palestinians had to elect new leaders, people who were not compromised by their involvement in terrorism. They needed to construct new political and economic institutions, implement new security measures with their neighbors, adopt a new constitution granting authority to the Palestinian parliament, and embrace a working democracy.

"Today, Palestinian authorities are encouraging, not opposing, terrorism," he said. "I've said in the past that nations are either with us or against us in the war on terror. To be counted on the side of peace, nations must act."

Bush spoke of the obligations of the Palestinians for almost eight minutes. He stated that the United States would support the creation of a Palestinian state only once all of those conditions were met. Then for just over a minute, he said that, once steps were made to improve security in the region, the Israelis had to withdraw their forces to positions held the previous year, stop settlement activity in the occupied territories, and release frozen Palestinian assets.

"The choice here is stark and simple," Bush said. "The Bible says, 'I have set before you life and death . . . therefore choose life.' The time has arrived for everyone in this conflict to choose peace and hope and life."

The Bush speech landed with a decided thud in the Blair government. British officials were at a loss to understand why the president had bothered making it. It could only stir up more enmity.

They found the concluding words particularly astonishing. In addressing a conflict between Jews and Muslims, the president quoted from *the fifth book of the Hebrew Bible*? Who thought *that* was a good idea?

The problem wasn't with the speech's premises; on those, Bush was right. Palestinian terrorism *was* undermining the peace process. Palestinian leaders *were* advocating violence. The Palestinian legislature *was* toothless, and needed real power that could come only from a new constitution. And Israel could not change its policies until the country's security was ensured.

No, the largest problem was with the speech's timing in the midst of heightened hostilities. The Palestinians saw the Israelis as the aggressors and viewed terrorism as the only choice they had to stand up to a regional superpower. They considered demands by the United States to be suspect from the start. Dismissing all of those realities would do nothing to calm the churning waters.

Perhaps, some of the British officials suggested, the speech was Bush's attempt to satisfy Blair's insistence that his Iraq policy must be folded into the pursuit of a broader Middle East peace initiative. If so, it failed miserably.

There were no federal judges in the Richmond courtroom when the June 25 hearing began on the Hamdi appeal. Instead, the three-judge panel was listening in from their chambers by teleconference, with one in Charlottesville, Virginia, and the other two in Greenville, South Carolina.

Clement presented his argument first, describing the historic power of the military and the president to detain an enemy during a time of war.

Judge J. Harvis Wilkinson III interrupted from Charlottesville. "How will you decide when the end of hostilities has happened, and the detainees can be released?"

True, Clement said, that posed a challenge. "But it's crystal clear that there are hostilities now," he said.

Wilkinson pressed his point. "This is a different kind of war," he said. "There is not going to be a VE Day. There is not going to be a VJ Day. What does it mean for this detainee? Is it open-ended?"

The real issue, Clement said, is whether the executive branch had the right to hold a detainee during wartime. The fact that the end of a war couldn't be predicted didn't deprive the president and the military of that authority.

If, instead, the courts intervened and required evidence justifying the designation of an individual as an enemy combatant, the consequences would be enormous.

"Are we really going to call as a witness a U.S. military official who right now is on the front waging a war, and call him back to Norfolk so he can be a fact witness?" Clement asked. "Deference, a proper respect for the military's judgment about who is an enemy combatant, a judgment the military has been making for two centuries, avoids that parade of horribles."

Meddling with military judgments by bringing these cases into court, Clement said, would impede the ability of the armed forces to obtain critical intelligence and protect American lives.

"In an extraordinary case like this," he said, "access to counsel would really interfere with the ongoing interrogation."

Next, Hamdi's side. Geremy Kamens, who worked with Dunham in the public defender's office, stepped to the podium. "Your honor," he said, "I believe the Constitution prevents the indefinite detention of an American citizen."

Wilkinson broke in again. "What is the violation of constitutional law when the United States is detaining someone who has taken up arms against America and is captured on the field of battle?" he asked. "This has been done in every war that I know. I don't know of any court decisions that said this is unconstitutional."

Without the appointment of an attorney, Kamens replied, there was no check on whether the military's designation was correct. They had provided no evidence that Hamdi was, in fact, an enemy combatant.

"The appointment of counsel means an end of intelligence-gathering efforts, doesn't it?" Wilkinson asked.

"I'm not sure it would."

"Sure it would!" Wilkinson snapped.

Once counsel was appointed, Wilkinson said, he couldn't conceive of how the entire panoply of constitutional rights could be withheld from a detainee.

Then, trouble. Wilkinson suddenly lashed out at Judge Doumar, dashing any hopes of keeping the jurist from being antagonized by the appeal. "How in the world could the district court have proceeded to decide all these questions and potentially preempt them by appointing counsel without even giving the government a chance to be heard?" he railed. "That seems to have flunked the fairness test. I don't understand it."

The local paper in Norfolk picked up the words. By the next day, Doumar would be reading Wilkinson's condemnation. Most likely, the lawyers figured, this was going to make their lives more difficult.

The next morning, Hamdi stirred as he heard footsteps approaching his cell at the Norfolk Naval Station. It was an officer he knew, coming by on his early rounds. He liked the man; he clearly cared about Hamdi's well-being.

Still, Hamdi wasn't feeling well. He was depressed and frustrated. He had tried to find ways to pass the time—asking for a deck of cards and a Game Boy—but his requests either went unanswered or were rejected. So he sat alone, hour after hour, with nothing to do and no one to engage in conversation. The morning rounds were the most exciting part of his day.

The officer arrived at Hamdi's cell. "Good morning," he said. "How are you today?"

"Not so good," Hamdi replied. "I just . . . how much longer am I going to be kept here? And why haven't I been given a chance to meet with a lawyer?"

"I understand this is very hard for you," the officer replied. "I can assure you that your situation is under review, but it's outside our control at this facility."

Hamdi shook his head and tears welled in his eyes.

"Have faith," the officer said. "In time, these matters will work themselves out."

"All rise."

The lawyers in the Washington, D.C., courtroom stood as federal judge Colleen Kollar-Kotelly took her seat behind the bench. It was 2:00 P.M. that same day, and Clement was ready to fight two more detainee cases.

These, he thought, were the easier ones—*Rasul,* brought by Clive Stafford Smith, Joe Margulies, and the Center for Constitutional Rights; and *Odah,* filed by Tom Wilner from Shearman & Sterling. None of the detainees were American citizens, all of them had been picked up by the military in Pakistan and Afghanistan. No one, he thought, could reasonably expect to win an argument that the United States was remiss in holding them incommunicado.

After the lawyers introduced themselves, Kollar-Kotelly glanced at some papers on her desk. There were two suits here, she said, one a habeas petition and the other—something else, premised on statutes and constitutional rights. She asked Clement to speak first. He ticked off the same arguments he gave in Richmond: The president had the authority, the military designation of an enemy combatant couldn't be challenged, threats to national security had to be considered. At times, his words were identical to those he had delivered the day before.

"The notion that they have no access to courts does not mean they are without rights," Clement said. "The scope of those rights is for the political and military branches to determine."

Kollar-Kotelly launched into questions that echoed those asked by the judges in the Hamdi case. How were these men designated enemy combatants? When would hostilities be considered over? Would they ever be charged?

"Is it an open-ended detention that doesn't have finality to it?" Kollar-Kotelly asked.

"There will be an end point to the detention, but it's the government's contention that that decision is for the executive branch to make," Clement replied.

Margulies came next, arguing that his clients were being held improperly, that the United States was acting as judge and jailer, and that the court had the power to grant the habeas petition.

Then, it was Wilner's turn, and from the outset, the judge questioned whether his case differed from the others filed on behalf of detainees.

"We are not at this time seeking their release," he said.

The primary reason, he said, was that he had no basis claiming they *should* be freed, because the lawyers knew none of the facts that led to their detention. "We are seeking basic rights while they are in confinement," Wilner said.

The judge was perplexed. Wilner wanted due process rights for his clients, she said, which were not significantly different from what Margulies was seeking. "I don't understand why this is really not a writ of habeas corpus, although you have obviously framed it differently," she said.

"Your honor," he replied, "the total fact is we don't know what we are entitled to, because we've had no access to them. We don't know what's happening. So, as a very first step at this point, we want basic rights for them."

Kollar-Kotelly still struggled with the argument. "So," she said, "you're claiming that they are lawfully in custody?"

"We are not challenging the government's right to take people into custody," Wilner replied. "We are challenging the conditions of their custody, being held without certain rights."

The judge flipped to a page in Wilner's motion and took a moment studying a particular sentence.

"You say that the government's position would, quote, enable federal officials to capture foreign nationals anywhere in the world, forcibly transport them to and hold them incommunicado in exclusive enclaves," she said, "denying them not only the most basic procedural rights of due process, but substantive rights as well, including guarantees against torture."

She looked up at Wilner. "Isn't this somewhat of an extreme proposition?"

At that moment, just over a mile away, lawyers at the Office of Legal Counsel were reviewing the latest memo defining torture.

They had successfully located the words *severe pain* in other statutes. But those laws had nothing to with punishment or the intentional infliction of harm; rather, they regulated government health care programs.

Still, just as in the antitorture laws, the phrase *severe pain* was not defined and instead was used as a descriptor for something else—in this case, an emergency medical condition. The language of the law identified such urgent threats as:

. . . a condition manifesting itself by acute symptoms of sufficient severity (including severe pain) such that the absence of immediate medical attention could reasonably be expected to result in placing the individual's health [or the health of an unborn child] in serious jeopardy, serious impairment to bodily functions, or serious dysfunction of bodily organs.

Even without a definition of severe pain, the language of the health care law made clear that the phrase referred to a *symptom*. Severe pain did not *cause* jeopardy to health, impairments of bodily functions, or dysfunction of bodily organs. Quite the opposite—those conditions could cause severe pain.

There was another issue: The wording of the health care statutes was as vague as that found in the antitorture laws. How could an interrogator determine whether a harsh technique caused "a jeopardy to health" or any of the other outcomes those laws listed?

To solve that puzzle, the lawyers resorted to creative linguistic license—they changed the words. *Jeopardy to health* became *death. Dysfunction of bodily organs* became *organ failure. Serious impairment to bodily functions* became the more unwieldy *permanent damage resulting in a loss of significant bodily functions.*

With that, the lawyers concluded, severe pain rising to the level of torture had been clarified.

The next phrase to parse: *specific intent.*

The antitorture statute didn't just say that inflicting severe pain was illegal. Rather, its wording required that an individual had to have the "specific intent" to cause pain. That wording had always been applied in a simple way—essentially, if an action taken by an official accidentally caused severe pain, it was not illegal. If a prisoner tripped and landed on his face while being moved from one place to another, it didn't qualify as torture under the law.

The attorneys at the Office of Legal Counsel concluded that they needed to provide a more detailed analysis of the term, at least in regard to its application to aggressive interrogation techniques.

Such questioning, they decided, did not fall under the specific intent to cause severe pain. When they used the harsh techniques, the interrogators did not have the objective of hurting detainees; rather, they were applying the tactics for the purpose of compelling answers to questions. They believed that the aggressive methods would not harm detainees—whether that belief was reasonable, the lawyers concluded, was irrelevant. And the fact that individuals with medical training would be observing the interrogations—and could stop them at any time—also suggested a lack of specific intent.

The antitorture prohibitions, the lawyers decided, did not apply to harsh questioning of suspected terrorists—in this case, Abu Zubaydah. No specific intent to cause severe pain, no legal violation.

The officer who checked on Hamdi at the naval brig every morning was at his computer, typing an e-mail to a superior. He related his encounters with Hamdi and expressed concern about the detainee's deepening depression.

"After eight months in detention facilities (Kandahar, Camp X-Ray, Norfolk Brig) with no potential end in site and no encouraging news and isolated from his countrymen, I can understand how he feels," the officer wrote.

Things weren't helped by the fact that every time Hamdi asked a question, the officer had to reply with words that always amounted to "I don't know."

This was a delicate assignment. "I will continue to do what I can to help this individual maintain his sanity," the officer typed, "but in my opinion we're working with borrowed time."

Officials from the Pentagon and Britain's Ministry of Defense began three days of meetings on June 27 to discuss plans for a military strike against Iraq. And the Blair government reacted with near horror.

A report summarizing the discussions was sent to David Manning, Blair's foreign policy advisor, and Jack Straw, the foreign secretary. Straw was bowled over by what he read. The Americans seemed to be planning a war based on wishful thinking that bordered on fantasy. There was nothing to suggest they understood the magnitude and complexity of military action against Iraq, and they seemed to have reverted to the mind-set that, if other nations didn't see it their way, they would just go it alone.

On July 8, Straw prepared a three-page memo to Blair deriding the American plans as fatally flawed by logical inconsistencies and pie-in-the-sky assumptions.

The Bush administration had "no strategic concept for the military plan and, in particular, no thought apparently given to 'day after' scenarios," Straw wrote.

It blithely took for granted the dubious conjecture that its military could swoop in, then rapidly identify and destroy Iraq's weapons of mass destruction. The Bush team simply asserted that Kuwait would happily host a large-scale military action by the United States for up to two years, that other Gulf states would jump in with support, and that Iran and Syria would sit quietly on the sidelines as Western armies invaded their next-door neighbor.

"The support even of key allies such as Kuwait cannot be counted on in the absence of some serious groundwork by the US," Straw wrote.

It also seemed that Blair's discussions with Bush at the Crawford summit had been for naught. All of the prime minister's conditions for British involvement in a war—first seeking new diplomatic action through the U.N., incorporating the Middle East peace process into any plan of attack, and pursuing an aggressive campaign to temper the global public hostility toward a military action—went unmentioned in the strategic discussion with the Americans.

"The fact that the US plan apparently ignores these conditions causes me particular concern," Straw wrote. "Are they determined to go ahead regardless? Does the omission signal a weakening of US commitment to work for progress in these areas before deciding to launch a military action? None of them is getting any easier."

The speech by Bush about the Israeli-Palestinian conflict had certainly done nothing to improve the situation, Straw added.

"The key point," Straw wrote, "is how to get through to the Americans that the success of any military operation in Iraq—and protection of our fundamental interests in the region—depends on devising in advance a coherent strategy."

Bush could not simply prepare to celebrate military victory. There also had to be a strong assessment of the economic and political repercussions of the war itself.

"They must also understand," Straw concluded, "that we are serious about our conditions for UK involvement."

Under CIA questioning, Abu Zubaydah was dribbling out bits of information. In Afghanistan, he told his interrogators on July 10, he had run two terrorist training camps, called Khaldan and Derunta. Al-Qaeda controlled neither, although Zubaydah had agreed that bin Laden could invite the trainees from those camps to join his group.

Scanty though the information was, it opened up a window on one of bin Laden's methods for recruiting terrorists.

The ruling on the Hamdi appeal was handed down two days later, on July 12. And the results were a mixed bag.

The three-judge panel was unanimous in its decision to throw out Doumar's order. Hamdi did not have the right to a lawyer and could be held without charge. But it wasn't a total victory for the government. The judges expressed deep skepticism about Clement's position that the decisions of the administration and the military on detainees could not be contested in court.

If they accepted the administration's argument, and threw out the Hamdi habeas petition, the ruling said, the judges "would be summarily embracing a sweeping proposition—namely that, with no meaningful judicial review, any American citizen alleged to be an enemy combatant could be detained indefinitely without charges or counsel on the government's say-so."

The case would continue, with a judicial inquiry into Hamdi's status as an enemy combatant. The lawyers were heading back to Judge Doumar's court.

11

Security guards in dark SWAT uniforms patrolled an FBI compound hidden away in the rolling hills near Clarksburg, West Virginia. Inside the nine-mile perimeter, a small forest surrounded the world's most technologically advanced storehouse for biometric crime data, the bureau's Criminal Justice Information Services Division.

Since the 9/11 attacks, examiners at the sprawling headquarters had been searching through terabytes of records from the unit's Integrated Automated Fingerprint Identification System, hoping to identify terrorists. Each scanned image of loops and swirls required about ten minutes to investigate, as high-powered computers combed through more than ninety million sets of fingerprints collected from civil and criminal agencies throughout government.

In July, one of the analysts punched a few keys on her computer, calling up a thumbprint that had been electronically recorded at Guantanamo on a portable Cross Match ID 1000 system. The mainframe started processing, and in minutes, a match appeared on the analyst's screen. It was part of a complete set of fingerprints from a Form FD-249 that an immigration agent at Orlando International Airport had taken on August 4, 2001. The information was immediately forwarded to FBI headquarters in Washington.

The passport used by the man in Orlando identified him as Mohammed al-Qahtani, and immigration records showed that he was refused entry and sent back to London shortly before 9/11. The investigating agents cross-checked the information with FBI data that laid out the hijackers' movements in the years and days leading up to the attacks in New York and Washington. The results left them dumbfounded.

While Qahtani was being detained at immigration, Mohammed Atta, the lead hijacker, was at the Orlando Airport making calls from a public phone. He used his AT&T card five times that afternoon and evening, from 4:30 to 8:30, to contact a mobile phone with a Dubai number. A check of security tapes showed that Atta was waiting at the airport in a rental car, leaving at 9:04, long after Qahtani was supposed to have arrived.

There had always been a mystery about the 9/11 attacks. Every plane had four hijackers, except for the one that crashed in Pennsylvania; only three boarded that flight. FBI agents were certain that there was a twentieth hijacker who had somehow been thwarted. The assumption, until now, had been that Moussaoui was the man, even though the evidence was scant.

Now the FBI had strong proof that Qahtani might be the missing hijacker. And he was locked up, available for questioning.

Another attack was coming, a big one. This time, al-Qaeda terrorists were planning to destroy a nuclear reactor, most likely Unit 1 at Three Mile Island in Pennsylvania, but maybe Indian Point in New York. Or at least, that was what new intelligence was indicating.

The first hint of a threat came from a Middle Eastern intelligence service, one with a checkered track record for accuracy. But a mosaic of other information, including a spike in chatter among known terrorists, was raising fears in the Bush administration that al-Qaeda might be on the verge of an onslaught even more deadly than the 9/11 strike. An attack on a nuclear facility wouldn't be easy—thick concrete containment shields protect the reactor core, and breaching them would require a massive explosion. But, if targeted accurately, a plane that crashed into a power plant could trigger the release of a lethal amount of radioactive iodine, a component of the reactors' fuel rods.

The intelligence indicated that the blow might be launched over the July 4 weekend, but once that date came and went, the rumbles of an impending disaster didn't quiet down. Instead, new data suggested that an attack might come on the first anniversary of 9/11. Administration officials—from the White House, the CIA, the Pentagon, and the Justice Department—debated whether to warn the public of the danger.

They decided to wait but agreed that the questioning of detainees in Guantanamo, Afghanistan, and the secret prisons had to be stepped up. If any of those men had an inkling about such a monstrous plot, then the interrogators needed to wrench it out of them.

• • •

Dressed in a green prison jumpsuit, John Walker Lindh sat at the defendant's table in an Alexandria courtroom, listening as federal judge T. S. Ellis III recited the precautions that would be taken to protect the identities of witnesses at his criminal trial.

The judge asked if the lawyers were satisfied with his plans to use black curtains to block the public's view of some of the people who would be testifying.

James Brosnahan, one of Lindh's lawyers, stood. "We have no objection to it, your honor, in view of what's occurred."

"All right," Ellis responded without missing a beat. "Well, I suppose, then, you had better tell me what occurred."

The defense and prosecution had agreed to resolve the case at about one o'clock that morning, Brosnahan said. Under the terms of the deal, Lindh would plead guilty to two felonies—supplying services to the Taliban and carrying an explosive device while committing that felony. In exchange, the government agreed to recommend a twenty-year sentence.

"All right," Judge Ellis said. "Mr. Lindh, you may come to the podium, sir."

Lindh stood and walked to the center of the room, facing the bench. Ellis went through the usual procedural niceties, asking Lindh if he knew the consequences of changing his plea, if he was in a state of mind to make such a decision, if he understood that the agreed-upon sentence wasn't binding on the judge. Lindh simply said, "Yes" in response to each question.

"Now, Mr. Lindh," the judge said. "Tell me, sir, in your own words what you did."

Lindh replied with a mutter, and Ellis told him to speak up.

"I'm sorry, sir," Lindh responded. "I provided my services as a soldier to the Taliban last year, from about August to November. In the course of doing so, I carried a rifle and two grenades. And I did so knowingly and willingly, knowing that it was illegal."

After Lindh made his statement, the prosecutors spent several more minutes rattling off details of his actions.

Ellis looked at the podium. "Mr. Lindh, how do you now plead?"

"I plead guilty, sir," he said.

When the session ended, two marshals escorted Lindh from the courtroom through a side door. He made no eye contact with his father, mother, sister, and older brother, who were seated in the second row.

Outside, he was placed into a vehicle in a convoy of four SUVs. They drove away for the short trip back to prison, where Walker could remain for the next two decades.

The information culled from interrogations at Guantanamo was disappointing at best. Each time General Dunlavey flew to Washington to brief Rumsfeld, he complained that the tactics used by the intelligence group lacked teeth. A more dynamic mix of techniques needed to be applied.

Rumsfeld delegated the task of coming up with options to Jim Haynes. The trouble was that Haynes had no idea what unit in the Pentagon knew about questioning enemies—it certainly wasn't anyone in his office. He consulted Richard Shiffrin, the deputy general counsel for intelligence.

"Dick," he said. "Where's the expertise in the Defense Department on interrogation?"

"I'm not sure," Shiffrin replied. "We've been out of that business for a long time, at least since Vietnam."

But perhaps, Shiffrin suggested, the Joint Personnel Recovery Agency—the group responsible for coordinating the military's capability to recover missing or captured soldiers—could help. That unit oversaw the SERE program, which taught military personnel how to resist aggressive interrogation.

"There's got to be some scholarly professional literature on the subject," he said. "And perhaps they have some."

Shiffrin telephoned Fort Belvoir, the JPRA headquarters, and was connected to the agency's chief of staff, Lieutenant Colonel Daniel Baumgartner.

"I wanted to see if I could get some information on the use of physical pressures in SERE training," Shiffrin said.

At first, Baumgartner was caught off guard. "Are you asking for the information to use physical pressures in interrogations?" he asked.

"Yes. One of the things we want is whatever information you have to see whether we can reverse engineer the techniques."

Now Baumgartner understood. The Pentagon was looking into whether it could apply the methods used to teach resistance to American soldiers and essentially turn the process around—a training plan to teach defensive strategies would instead be converted into an offensive line of attack.

"I want to be helpful," Baumgartner replied. "But the SERE techniques are designed to show Americans the worst possible treatment they may face. Any use of those techniques on detainees would require administration approval."

Understood, Shiffrin replied. But he still needed to review whatever written information the JPRA might have about the procedures used in SERE.

"Well, we have a library of information," Baumgartner replied. "But it's at Fairchild Air Force Base. It's going to take some time to get it."

An entire library, at Fairchild. Outside Seattle. This, Shiffrin knew, was going to be difficult.

Tony Blair's top military and national security advisors delivered their conclusions on July 23—the Americans had made up their minds. They were going to invade Iraq.

In private conversations, Bush administration officials had essentially written off the U.N.'s effort to rein in Saddam Hussein as ineffectual. Stephen Hadley, deputy national security advisor for Bush, had pointedly told one British official that there was no need to wait for another resolution to be pushed through by Kofi Annan, the U.N. secretary general; how many times, Hadley asked, were they supposed to stand by while the Iraqis stiffed Annan? Condoleezza Rice was a bit more restrained in her comments, one official told Blair, but not by much.

"Will the Iraqis welcome an invasion or not?" Blair asked.

Jack Straw, the foreign affairs minister, answered. "The regime will appear popular until it tips," he said. "But when it tips, it will tip quickly."

The group discussed the Americans' preparations for mounting an invasion, and the international challenges they faced. Kuwait, Diego Garcia, Cyprus, Turkey—all were key players in the evolving military plan. But the invocation of Saddam's probable possession of weapons of mass destruction in winning the cooperation of those countries could backfire.

"Of the four countries posing a potential threat from WMD—Iran, Korea, Libya, and Iraq—Iraq would be fourth," Straw said. "Saddam doesn't have nukes, although he does have some offensive WMD capabilities."

That raised the key question: What made the Americans so dead set on invading Iraq? Was this about weapons of mass destruction, or instead about the overthrow of Saddam? Was this folly?

"It's worse than you think," Blair said. "I actually believe in doing this."

Still, he added, he was acutely aware of how difficult it would be to sell an invasion to the Parliamentary Labor Party and the British public.

"What if we just don't go in with the Americans on this?" Straw asked.

Not a chance. "That would be the biggest shift in foreign policy in fifty years," Blair said. "I'm not sure it's very wise."

On the other hand, they should not let the Americans lead Britain around by the nose. "On the tactical level, showing maximum closeness publicly is the way to maximize influence privately," Blair said.

Geoff Hoon, the secretary of state for defense, wasn't sure that the Blair government could do much to sway the Bush administration toward seeking a new U.N. resolution before taking military action. "The Americans' clear view is that they already have legal justification," he said.

"Well, first, I need to be convinced of the workability of a military plan," Blair said. "And, second, of an equally workable political strategy."

There could be an impasse, Straw cautioned. "We could probably get the votes for a U.N. ultimatum," he said. "But the Americans may not want to go down that route."

Perhaps not, Blair said. "But I see regime change as the route to dealing with WMD."

The legal tug-of-war between Judge Doumar and the government over the Hamdi case intensified with each passing day.

Since the court of appeals tossed out his ruling that Hamdi be allowed to consult a lawyer, Doumar had pressed for the government to justify, with evidence, why Hamdi was being detained without charge. He ordered that the administration provide him with copies of Hamdi's statements, the names and addresses of his interrogators, and the name of the person who decided that he was an unlawful enemy combatant.

The government lawyers shot back, essentially telling Doumar to take a hike. They argued that he had no right to any of that information because it involved national security matters linked to the conduct of the war. They would not comply. At a hearing, an enraged Doumar slammed the government for ignoring his order, suggesting that the refusal could lead to a contempt citation.

Just as the tussle seemed to be moving toward all-out legal warfare, the government blinked. It filed papers that included, without explanation, a link to a Web page where it had posted the Manchester Manual and attached a two-page declaration about Hamdi from Michael Mobbs, special advisor to Douglas Feith, the undersecretary of defense for policy.

In the document, Mobbs said that, based on a review of relevant records, he was familiar with the circumstances surrounding Hamdi's capture and detention. Hamdi had received weapons training from the Taliban, Mobbs wrote, and he had surrendered to Northern Alliance forces following an intense battle. He had relinquished his rifle, was taken to a Northern Alliance prison, and had been present during an uprising there. Military screeners determined that Hamdi fitted the criteria for an enemy combatant. He was then handed over to American forces.

Doumar reviewed the filing. And he wasn't happy with what he read.

At Fort Belvoir, Colonel Baumgartner was gathering information about the psychological effects of the SERE program. He knew next to nothing about the topic, but Shiffrin from the Pentagon had asked him to write a memo describing how the harsh interrogations—especially waterboarding—affected the mental health of soldiers.

For research, Baumgartner brought together some subordinates—a group he called "the exploitation answer stuckee team"—and they were forwarding any useful material they found. Baumgartner also did his own digging and telephoned Dr. Jerald Ogrisseg, chief psychologist at the air force's SERE school.

"I wanted to get your thoughts on waterboarding the enemy," Baumgartner said.

Ogrisseg was taken aback. "Wouldn't that be illegal?"

That wasn't a judgment for Baumgartner to make. "People from above are asking about using waterboarding in real-world interrogations," he replied.

The whole idea seemed misguided, Ogrisseg thought. No one at SERE was an expert in interrogations.

"Well, aside from being illegal," he said, "this is a completely different arena than we at the survival school know anything about."

Even so, Ogrisseg agreed to review the data. He found that, in SERE, the long-term psychological effects from aggressive interrogations were minimal.

There were sound reasons for that. The air force worked hard to prevent temporary damage to a trainee's mental state from spiraling into something harmful. During training, the air force performed three extensive debriefings, giving participants the opportunity to describe their experiences; this mitigated the risk that a dramatic experience would transform into a traumatic one. Also, air force personnel who took SERE training knew that they would be waterboarded for a short period of time, were aware of what to expect, and had the chance to stop the process at any point if panic set in.

None of those controls would be incorporated into a real interrogation.

Whatever happened at the SERE schools was irrelevant in assessing the psychological impact of waterboarding an enemy.

Baumgartner wrote his memo in the most diplomatic tone he could muster. A lieutenant colonel couldn't exactly send a message to the Pentagon saying, "Are you people crazy?"

The JPRA, he wrote, indeed had at its disposal experts on the use of harsh interrogations, called exploitation techniques. His unit had already briefed intelligence agencies on those methods and would be happy to do the same for the military. He was sending some documents, he wrote, that contained academic analyses of interrogation tactics, based on what had been effective against captured American soldiers in the past.

Then he tiptoed toward a warning. "The ability to exploit, however, is a very specialized skill set built on training and experience," he wrote. This was not for amateurs.

The memo sparked some questions from the general counsel's office, so Baumgartner set to work on a follow-up the next day, July 26. He tossed subtlety aside—this memo included an unsigned attachment that was the bureaucratic equivalent of flashing lights and sirens.

"Upwards of 90 percent of interrogations have been successful through the exclusive use of the direct approach, where a degree of rapport is established with the prisoner," the document read.

Translation: The law enforcement approach works. As for aggressive tactics?

"Once any means of duress has been purposely applied to the prisoner, the formerly cooperative relationship can not be reestablished. In addition, the prisoner's resolve to resist cooperating with the interrogator will likely be increased as a result of harsh or brutal treatment."

Skilled interrogators relied on subtle, nonverbal behaviors to assess a prisoner's psychological state, gaining insights that could be used to foster cooperation and to judge the veracity of the subject's statements.

"The prisoner's physical response to the pain inflicted by an interrogator would obliterate such nuance and deprive the interrogator of these key tools."

The paradox was that the harsh techniques that reduced the ability to gauge a prisoner's truthfulness simultaneously increased the probability of lying.

"If an interrogator produces information that resulted from the application of physical and psychological duress, the reliability and accuracy of this information is in doubt," the attachment said. "In other words, a subject in extreme pain may provide an answer, any answer, or many answers in order to get the pain to stop."

Baumgartner assembled the packet of information and sent it to the Pentagon. The CIA received no such warning that conducting brutal interrogation was foolish.

In a secret prison, a CIA operations officer had both of his hands wrapped around a detainee's neck. He manipulated his fingers, then pressed down on the carotid arteries to cut off the blood flow to the man's brain.

The detainee nodded off, close to passing out. The officer released his grip and shook him.

"Come on," he shouted. "Wake up."

Then he did it again. And again.

Years later, when questioned about the event, the officer would inform investigators that he had never been trained in interrogation techniques before he began questioning al-Qaeda suspects.

At Guantanamo, the interviews of Mohammed al-Qahtani weren't going well. In the week since the discovery of evidence suggesting he was the twentieth hijacker, FBI agents and military personnel had interrogated him every day, without much luck. He was combative and evasive. He projected unbridled arrogance.

He had never traveled to the United States, Qahtani insisted, and if anyone was saying that he had, well, they were lying. The interrogators then revealed that they had records showing he had tried to enter the country the year before in Orlando. Qahtani changed his story—that was just a business trip, he said. He had come to America to sell used cars. Despite the obvious contradiction, Qahtani would not budge from his cover story. The interrogators decided to try isolating Qahtani to see if a lack of social support from other detainees might make him more compliant. They moved him to the maximum-security facility at Camp Delta on July 27, but Qahtani's resistance didn't change.

Frustrated, the case agent decided that he needed the help of Ali Soufan, the crack FBI agent whose questioning of Abu Zubaydah had identified Sheikh Mohammed and José Padilla.

Four lawyers from the Office of Legal Counsel were seated around a coffee table on a couch and two overstuffed chairs. They had gathered in the office of Jay

Bybee, the assistant attorney general in charge of the unit, for one last debate about CIA interrogation tactics.

The resolution of the "severe pain" issue had dealt with only half of the restrictions in the antitorture laws. The infliction of "severe mental pain or suffering" that caused prolonged psychological harm was also illegal, and now the lawyers were wrestling with whether any of the proposed CIA practices violated that prohibition. The meanings were fairly explicit in the statutes—issuing threats of death, or inflicting pain that caused psychological problems, or using mind-altering drugs were all forbidden. So each proposed method had to be checked against those restrictions.

Even before the meeting was called, the lawyers had tossed out one of the CIA's suggestions without much debate—interrogators could not bury detainees alive. While the coffins would have hidden oxygen tanks and cameras to watch for trouble, the people inside wouldn't know about those safeguards or of their interrogators' intent to pull them out if necessary. Clearly, the lawyers agreed, the tactic constituted a threat of death, so it was illegal. Also, warning detainees that they might be turned over to other countries for torture— something the CIA had already done—was against the law.

All but one of the other tactics passed muster. Slapping, stress positions, confinement, sleep deprivation—none of those, the lawyers decided, caused prolonged mental harm. A technique called "walling"—in which a thick collar would be placed around a detainee's neck and used to slam him into a wall— was also acceptable, so long as the wall was false and flexible. But one method remained that John Yoo feared *could* cross the line.

"I'm concerned that the waterboarding measure might violate the statute," he told the others. "I don't have a problem with the other ones. I don't think they come close. But that one, it's either on the line or it's a little over the line."

The problem, Yoo said, was twofold. Since waterboarding creates the sensation of drowning, couldn't that be considered as a threat of death? Also, he and Jennifer Koester had reviewed records from the military's SERE training, in which soldiers and seaman were subjected to waterboarding. While there were no instances of long-term physical damage, some percentage of the subjects felt so traumatized by waterboarding that they requested psychological counseling.

"If soldiers are experiencing psychological issues from a controlled exposure to waterboarding, then we really have to consider what it would mean when it's used in a real interrogation," Yoo said.

It might be still possible for the CIA to use waterboarding, Yoo said, but only if the issue was kicked up to the president. Under his commander-in-chief powers, Bush had the authority to order actions he deemed to be of military necessity. If he instructed the agency to conduct waterboarding, Yoo said, then it might make a technical violation of the antitorture statute allowable.

Bybee and another lawyer, Pat Philbin, disagreed.

"I don't think we need to address the constitutional issue, because I think under our statutory analysis, it's okay to do," Philbin said.

Yoo sat back on the couch. "Look, if it's something we're doubtful about, we should go ahead and discuss the constitutional side of it, because there could be disagreement," he said. "There may be people who think it's a violation of the statute. And in that case, we haven't provided a complete answer about the legal issue."

The two lawyers stuck to their guns. "We're headed in a circle here," Bybee said. "Let's mull it over."

The next day, Bybee contacted Yoo.

"I thought about it, let's go ahead and do it," he said. "Write up the constitutional issue."

In a few days, the language was inserted into the next draft of the memo analyzing the CIA interrogation procedures. The president had the constitutional power in a time of war, it read, to order the performance of actions that otherwise might be deemed a violation of the relevant part of the antitorture statute—Section 2340A.

"We conclude," the memo said, "that the Department of Justice could not enforce Section 2340A against federal officials acting pursuant to the President's constitutional authority to wage a military campaign."

Not only were prosecutors prohibited from charging the interrogators with a crime, but no laws—none—could be used to restrict Bush's directive.

"Any effort by Congress to regulate the interrogation of battlefield combatants would violate the Constitution's sole vesting of the commander-in-chief authority in the President," the memo said. "Just as statutes that order the President to conduct warfare in a certain manner for specific goals would be unconstitutional, so too are laws that seek to prevent the President from gaining the intelligence he believes necessary to prevent attacks upon the United States."

Now the lawyers were satisfied with the verdict on waterboarding. The technique, the memo said, was legal. But even if it wasn't, the president could order waterboarding, and nothing in the law could stop him.

• • •

In his large corner office at Shearman & Sterling, Tom Wilner was behind his desk, angrily gripping a small sheaf of papers. It was past 2:00 P.M. on July 31, and federal judge Colleen Kollar-Kotelly had just handed down her ruling in the *Rasul* and *al-Odah* cases, brought by Wilner and other defense lawyers on behalf of several Guantanamo detainees. The decision was a slam dunk for the government.

She could not consider the merits of either case, Kollar-Kotelly wrote, because she had no authority over foreigners held at Guantanamo. "As the Court finds that no court would have jurisdiction to hear these actions, the Court shall dismiss both suits with prejudice."

With prejudice. While the lawyers could appeal her decision, Kollar-Kotelly was barring them from ever refiling a petition.

As Wilner flipped each page, his rage grew. Not only was Kollar-Kotelly wrong, he thought; she was misrepresenting the case law to maneuver her way to what seemed like a predetermined outcome.

Guantanamo was not a United States territory, just a place that America leased—even though it had full control and authority there, and refused to comply with Cuban demands to nullify the treaty. Wilner felt sure that the *Ralpho* case, which established that the United States was required to grant rights to residents in Micronesia after World War II, established that an area where America was in control but had no sovereignty was governed by the Constitution. But, no—Kollar-Kotelly flipped *Ralpho* on its head: The ruling in that case had compared the status of Micronesia with that of American territories like Guam. Therefore, she concluded, Micronesia was, for legal analysis, a territory of the United States and Guantanamo was not. Wilner read that portion of the decision several times, dumbstruck; it made no sense.

Kollar-Kotelly had, in essence, established Guantanamo as a lawless land. American courts had no role, no controlling sovereign had ever signed a treaty on its behalf, and no one held there was protected by the Constitution or the Geneva Conventions. Detainees could be imprisoned without trial, without charge, forever—and no one could stop it. Could Bush order detainees shot without trial? Under Kollar-Kotelly's decision, why not? Was there much difference between taking people's liberty without charge and executing them without trial?

Kollar-Kotelly's decision wasn't just preposterous, Wilner thought; it was obnoxious. She dismissed out of hand Wilner's attempt to give his clients legal redress for the conditions of their confinement. In hostile language, the judge essentially called Wilner a liar, saying his filing was a habeas corpus petition written deceptively to make it appear like something else. And, she wrote, since it was really a habeas petition, the precedents demanded that she toss it out.

Wilner swiveled in his chair toward his computer. He wanted to send an e-mail to Kuwait for one detainee's father, Khalid al-Odah, to update him on the developments.

"We believe it is a very unsophisticated and uncourageous opinion," he wrote. "We really thought we had outdone the government, but it seems not to have mattered to this judge. Hopefully, the judges on the court of appeals will have more courage."

An e-mailed response from al-Odah arrived in Wilner's in-box at about four o'clock the next morning. "We were prepared for such a ruling," he wrote. "We should have the same spirit when we started and we should continue with the same spirit to the end."

Jim Haynes was developing a lot of impatience for the work of Doug Feith, the undersecretary of defense for policy. Everyone in the administration knew that harmless Arabs had been inadvertently snatched up in Afghanistan and Pakistan, then delivered to Guantanamo. Dunlavey was complaining that some of those elderly and sick detainees—the ones who had been given nicknames like "half-dead Bob" and "al-Qaeda Claus"—ought to be released, and it was Feith's job to get it done. But nothing was happening.

Not by design, though. Haynes believed that Feith was too disorganized to successfully manage a birthday party, much less the policies for a detention center. His dithering wouldn't matter much if he was put in charge of the Pentagon dining room, but it mattered a great deal when he was assigned the task of establishing policies to free innocent nobodies locked up at the naval base.

Finally, Haynes had enough of waiting and went to see Feith.

"This system at Gitmo isn't working," Haynes said. "We have *got* to get a review process that's better than what we're doing. If we've got any mistakes, we ought to find them."

Feith nodded. "Okay, yeah. Fine."

Months passed, with Haynes riding Feith for a proposal. They finally hammered one out and sent it to Wolfowitz, the deputy defense secretary and a celebrated procrastinator in his own right. But this time he signed off on the document quickly and transmitted it to Rumsfeld for final approval.

The new process was in place for dispatching the luckless men from Guantanamo who had been inadvertently caught up in the hunt for terrorists. Many had languished in their cells for more than eleven months.

Abu Zubaydah stood flat against a concrete wall with a thick roll of cloth draped around his neck. The CIA officer in front of him grabbed the cloth and forcibly jerked him forward. The interrogator immediately shoved Zubaydah back, slamming his shoulder blades into the hard wall. He moaned in pain.

This was the first time that the CIA used "walling" on any detainee, and the interrogator was, inadvertently, doing it wrong. The Justice Department's Office of Legal Counsel had approved exploiting the technique only if the subject was thrown against a false and flexible wall. That detail had escaped the attention of the CIA officers at the secret prison where Zubaydah was being held. The tactic they were using was not authorized; it would not be the last time interrogators went beyond the legal restrictions provided by the Office of Legal Counsel. The semantic fine points that the lawyers had invoked to separate potentially illegal acts from lawful ones had been lost in a big-league game of telephone—from the Justice Department to the CIA general counsel to the agency's Directorate of Operations, and finally to the interrogators on the ground.

The manhandling had been going on for just under an hour. At the start of the session, the CIA officer had told Zubaydah that he would do whatever it took to squeeze important information out of him. He had begun by slapping Zubaydah in the face or the abdomen whenever he seemed to be putting up resistance.

After the walling, Zubaydah was placed inside a confinement box for several hours. While he was there, one of the CIA officers realized they were supposed to have used a false wall; they fetched some plywood and leaned it against the concrete. When Zubaydah was removed from the box, he was walled again into the sheet of wood.

When the first session ended, the interrogators chained Zubaydah into a standing position with his arms above his head so that he couldn't sleep. He was naked, except for a diaper. In part to ensure that he had no solid food in his stomach, he was placed on a liquid diet—the doctors on-site feared he might throw up when he was waterboarded later and inhale chunks of his own vomit.

Before the interrogation resumed, a doctor and psychologist checked Zubaydah. Then, questioning, slapping, walling. This time, though, a new tactic was introduced—cold water was poured on him repeatedly for several minutes. Afterward, it was back to the chains, the diaper, and the liquid diet.

With each session, the aggressiveness increased. But still, the CIA officers believed he was not telling the full truth. He was saying nothing about the possible attack on a nuclear reactor, and administration officials believed that was imminent. Zubaydah, they felt sure, knew of information that could stop a 9/11 sequel, but he wouldn't talk. So the interrogators checked with Langley and got the green light to waterboard him.

Zubaydah was brought into a room and strapped down on a gurney, which was leaned back about fifteen degrees. After Zubaydah exhaled, leaving his lungs collapsed, one of the interrogators held a black cloth against his mouth while another poured water from a plastic bottle onto his face. The liquid flowed into his mouth and nose; the cloth acted like a one-way valve, allowing water to run in but preventing Zubaydah from coughing it out. The fluid filled his head, sinuses, and throat. Even though, because of the incline of the gurney, no liquid could enter his lungs, Zubaydah sucked in the water as he struggled to breathe, experiencing an uncontrollable sense of impending death. He was a drowning man who could not drown.

After less than thirty seconds, the interrogator stopped pouring the water, the cloth was removed from Zubaydah's face, and the gurney was elevated to a vertical position. Liquid flowed out of his head as the straps dug into his injuries. As expected, he vomited.

A moment passed. Then the gurney was leaned back again, the cloth placed over Zubaydah's mouth, and water poured on his face. Terrified, Zubaydah urinated on himself.

He would be waterboarded eighty-three times during August.

Colin Powell could feel it. The administration was rushing toward a unilateral military showdown in Iraq. Several advisors were urging the president to disregard the talk about international coalitions; decisive action was called for, they argued—every minute of delay increased the threat Saddam posed to American security. Fretting over world opinion was a dangerous waste of time.

On the evening of August 5, Powell seized his chance to make the case for diplomacy. He met with Bush and Rice at the White House residence, prepared to spell out in the starkest terms the potentially ruinous, yet rarely stated, consequences of an invasion of Iraq.

It could well destabilize Saudi Arabia, Egypt, and Jordan—all allies in the war on terror. Bush would become the Western autocrat of a proud Muslim nation until some sort of indigenous government could be cobbled together.

Then there were the British. If Bush refused to pursue a diplomatic solution, he would be virtually thumbing his nose at the Blair government. The prime minister *needed* cover from the U.N. Jack Straw, the foreign affairs minister, had hammered home that point repeatedly to Powell. Ignoring the political minefield Blair was stepping through would not only imperil his political future, it would raise unnecessary tensions between Britain and America. Blair had, in many ways, become an indispensable ally. He could not be taken for granted.

Bush looked at Powell. "What should I do?" he asked. "What else can I do?"

"You can still make a pitch for a coalition or U.N. action to do what needs to be done," Powell said.

But, he said, the president had to be aware of one possibility: The U.N. might resolve the problem by disarming Iraq and leave Saddam in power.

At Guantanamo, Ali Soufan was sitting in front of Qahtani, conducting another interview. The FBI agent was handling the interrogation in his usual style—trying to establish a relationship, discussing Islam, speaking about Arab culture—all in a calm but firm tone.

In session after session, Soufan stressed that, at some point, Qahtani would talk and that opening up now was the best choice. "You will find yourself in a difficult situation if you don't speak with me," Soufan said.

Qahtani refused to buckle. Soufan recommended that he be moved to an even more remote location at Guantanamo where his isolation would be complete. It was not a tactic commonly resorted to by law enforcement, but this was an uncommon case.

On August 8, after the bureau and the military approved of the plan, Qahtani was transported by ambulance from his cell in Camp Delta to the navy brig. There, his life took a desolate turn. Under Soufan's instructions, the guards stopped speaking to him and would not allow him to look at them. When they entered his cell, they would cover their faces or order him to turn away. Seclusion, Soufan believed, would chip away at his captive's resolve.

And indeed, Qahtani found the brig to be the most miserable place he had been detained. The windows were covered at all times. He never knew if it was night or day. He didn't know when to pray. He didn't know how to face Mecca.

Though Qahtani's confinement had become more onerous, Soufan stayed respectful. He was never aggressive. He would pray with him and offer him tea. Other than his admonition that Qahtani would crack sooner or later, Soufan never said anything that could even vaguely be interpreted as a threat.

It worked. Qahtani began to open up.

He revealed that he had a relative living in Chicago. The man, named Ali Saleh Kahlah al-Marri, had already been detained on a material witness warrant, but the statements from Qahtani convinced law enforcement that his relative was an al-Qaeda sleeper agent.

Qahtani also disclosed that he had attended the Farouq training camps in Afghanistan, where he had been taught about tactics and weapons. He had sworn his allegiance to bin Laden in early 2001 and vowed that he would do whatever the al-Qaeda leader asked of him. Then he admitted that he had planned to join the other hijackers in the 9/11 strikes. He knew little about the operation, he said, and even less about other al-Qaeda plans.

His denials struck Soufan and other FBI agents as credible—Qahtani had been recruited to serve as a "muscle" hijacker, responsible only for subduing the passengers. Bin Laden and al-Qaeda's standard practice was to keep information about an attack compartmentalized, even from the participants; each was told only enough to do his job. Someone in Qahtani's role would not have been informed of much.

Soufan's coups from his interrogations with Qahtani were another success for the FBI. Yet once again, intelligence officials bushed aside the accomplishment, certain that the al-Qaeda terrorist was tricking law enforcement. The military told the FBI to get out of the way—Qahtani knew more and just wasn't telling. If they were going to learn anything, the military officers said, then they were going to have to get rough.

A group of FBI agents, postal inspectors, and state police approached a blue mailbox near the corner of Bank and Nassau Streets, across from Princeton University.

Numerous cases of anthrax infection had months before turned up among New Jersey postal workers connected to a sorting center in Hamilton. Since that time, investigators had gathered more than six hundred samples from mailboxes and other locations where letters might have been held, sending them to the state health department in Trenton for testing. The Princeton mailbox had just come back positive for anthrax spores. Now the investigators knew where the anthrax killer had mailed the deadly letters.

While agents and police went door-to-door along Nassau Street questioning shop owners, workers removed the mailbox. It was taken to an airport and airlifted to a laboratory for further testing.

• • •

Judge Doumar summoned lawyers in the Hamdi case to a hearing on August 13. After court was called to order, he brought out the two-page declaration from Michael Mobbs that the government had filed weeks before as the explanation for Hamdi's continued detention.

Doumar held up the document. "I'm going to be focusing exclusively in this hearing on the Mobbs declaration," he said. "If I rely on this, then I must pick it apart."

He glared down at Gregory Garre, the assistant solicitor general appearing on behalf of the government. "If you gave me the information," Doumar said, "then all of this could have been avoided."

The questions tumbled out. Who is this Mobbs person? What qualifies him to be a "special advisor"?

"He's an undersecretary of defense," Garre replied, "and he's substantially involved in detainee issues."

But Mobbs seemed to have no personal information about Hamdi. All the declaration said was that he had read documents and was familiar with circumstances in the case.

"My secretary's familiar with the Hamdi case," Doumar said. "Should she decide? She's *my* special advisor."

Mobbs also gave no indication about how long Hamdi would be detained, Doumar said. "How long does it take to question a man?" he asked. "A year? Two years? A lifetime?"

Garre was unruffled. "We couldn't answer that question now any better than we could eleven months after Pearl Harbor," he said.

The back-and-forth continued, with Doumar frequently complaining that Garre wasn't giving him straight answers.

"Can the military do anything they want with him, without a tribunal?" the judge asked.

"The present detention is lawful," Garre replied.

"What restraints are there?" Doumar shot back.

"The detainee has asked to speak to diplomats from Saudi Arabia."

"Can I beg you to answer my question," Doumar snapped. "If the military sat him down in boiling oil, would that be lawful?"

"I don't think anyone's suggested that," Garre replied.

• • •

Three days later, Doumar issued his ruling, and given his comments at the hearing, the decision was not a surprise: The Mobbs declaration, he said, was inadequate to justify the continued detention of Hamdi.

"There is nothing to indicate why he is treated differently than all the other captured Taliban," Doumar wrote. "There is no reason given for Hamdi to be in military confinement, incommunicado for over four months and being held some eight to ten months without any charges of any kind."

It was obvious that prosecutors were not contemplating criminal charges, and if Hamdi was going to continue to be held, an effort had to be made to present the court with the reasons for that decision.

"We must protect the freedoms of even those who hate us and that we may find objectionable," he wrote. "The warlords of Afghanistan may have been in the business of pillage and plunder. We cannot descend to their standards without debasing ourselves."

The ruling was uncompromising. There was no doubt that the administration was headed back to the Fourth Circuit Court of Appeals.

The meeting at the Justice Department had been eye-opening for Pasquale D'Amuro, the FBI's assistant director for counterterrorism. Weeks before, he had heard the dismay in Soufan's voice as he recounted the abusive methods being used by the CIA against Abu Zubaydah. D'Amuro had brought up the matter with Mueller, the bureau director, and the two had agreed that agents should not participate in any CIA questioning sessions that distressed them.

Still, D'Amuro thought the FBI could play a helpful role in the interrogation of high-value detainees like Zubaydah. He made an appointment with Michael Chertoff, head of the criminal division, to discuss it.

They met in Chertoff's office and were joined by Alice Fisher, his deputy. D'Amuro laid out his case, saying that FBI participation in the interrogations would be of enormous value, particularly since its agents were so familiar with the most prominent detainees from earlier investigations.

That wasn't going to work, Chertoff declared. The CIA's interrogation tactics had gone far beyond anything FBI agents did, and the Office of Legal Counsel at the Justice Department had sanctioned it.

"The CIA got a legal opinion from OLC that they could legally use waterboarding, throw people into walls, confine them in boxes," Chertoff said.

As he ran down the list, D'Amuro listened in shock. These methods weren't just immoral—they were *stupid*. The FBI's rapport-building techniques had been successful time and again. Harsh tactics didn't work, and even if they did, the detainees came from a part of the world that employed brutal torture. The CIA was using a less effective option, he thought, and one that was less horrific than the detainees would have expected.

Chertoff assured D'Amuro that this was not some rogue operation. The idea had been approved all the way up the line at the Justice Department—John Ashcroft himself had been involved from the start and had given his stamp of approval to the OLC findings.

After the meeting, D'Amuro returned to FBI headquarters on Pennsylvania Avenue and tracked down Mueller to report what he had heard. Bureau agents, he said, could not be part of these abusive interrogations.

"We don't do that," D'Amuro said.

What was happening was not going to stay secret. Eventually, D'Amuro said, Congress was sure to investigate.

"Someday," he said, "people are going to be sitting in front of green felt tables having to testify about all of this."

The National Security Council meeting had just broken up and officials were heading out the door. The group had been discussing possible al-Qaeda connections to Saddam Hussein, but the evidence was thin gruel. A couple of detainees had given statements about such links, but Tenet kept brushing them off as imaginary. Still, some officials thought he was wrong.

Hadley, the deputy national security advisor, accompanied Wolfowitz out the door. The two were still discussing the intelligence on al-Qaeda and Iraq as they reached the staircase.

"Paul," Hadley said, "it's just not there."

Wolfowitz tightened his lips. "We'll find it," he said with certainty in his voice. "It's got to be there."

Over at the Pentagon, Ben Bonk was incredulous. "This isn't true," he told a group of Defense Department officials. Iraq was not behind al-Qaeda.

Bonk, the former deputy chief at the CIA's Counterterrorist Center, had been moved out of the unit months before and assigned instead to deal with Iraq. And it seemed every day he was fighting the same battle, trying to persuade officials outside the CIA—particularly at the Pentagon—that Saddam was not al-Qaeda's secret puppeteer.

In fact, the evidence more strongly supported the opposite conclusion. Bin

Laden had raged against Saddam since the early 1990s. The Iraqi dictator ran a secular ship, and bin Laden was committed to the creation of an Islamic caliphate. Sure, they both hated America, but so did the North Koreans, and no one was suggesting that Kim Jong Il was chummy with bin Laden.

But there were those—like Wolfowitz and Feith and Cheney—who didn't want to hear all that. To Bonk, it seemed they believed that the failure to find evidence of a malign partnership didn't mean there wasn't any. It was the kind of logic that could be used to argue that Saddam was conspiring with Harry Potter—after all, there might be proof out there somewhere that could verify the notion, even if it hadn't been found.

To Bonk's mind, the true believers at the Pentagon were grasping at straws, like a supposed meeting in Prague between Mohammed Atta and a senior Iraqi official. That information had come from Czech intelligence; the CIA had dug into it and concluded it wasn't true.

That revelation didn't faze the Pentagon, where officials criticized the intelligence agency for failing to see the whole picture. So it was on this day that Feith and some of his Defense Department colleagues visited the CIA to make their case to Tenet and his top aides. As Bonk and his team listened, their reaction was the same—their visitors were serving warmed-over tidbits that proved nothing.

Something definitive had to be assembled, Bonk decided, a report that laid out all of the government's intelligence about Iraq and al-Qaeda, establishing once and for all who was right. He told Tenet that he and his group would get to work on a comprehensive paper right away. It would take them a few weeks to finish, he said.

After almost a month of harsh treatment, Zubaydah said he was willing to answer any questions.

"Brothers who are captured and interrogated are permitted by Allah to provide information when they believe they have reached the limit of their ability to withhold it in the face of psychological and physical hardships," he explained to his CIA captors.

And so, Zubaydah talked. He filled in gaps in the agency's knowledge about al-Qaeda's organizational structure, its key members, and its method of operation. He discussed the role played by the group's Shura Council, which he described as al-Qaeda's governing body, ranking just below bin Laden in seniority.

He discussed Abd al-Rahim al-Nashiri, a planner of the *Cole* attack who was known inside the organization as an egomaniac. The CIA officers asked if he knew of any links between al-Qaeda and Saddam Hussein—a question that had been relayed from Washington. No, he replied. He didn't.

What about other al-Qaeda members? Who could most likely pass for a Westerner, maybe lead an attack on the United States or Europe?

"Ja'far al-Tayyar," Zubaydah replied. *Ja'far the Pilot*—an al-Qaeda nom de guerre. But Zubaydah didn't know his real name.

Who was he?

"From what I heard, he was the other Mohammed Atta," Zubaydah said. "He was told to deliver an American Hiroshima."

Not much of this was new—Zubaydah had already provided a lot of the same information to FBI agents. They had heard of Ja'far and had opened a file on him, unknowingly under one of his aliases. They had also already learned some of the al-Qaeda operational information. While Zubaydah's disclosures to the CIA were somewhat more detailed, the agency had been interrogating him for almost two months; using the relationship approach, the FBI had obtained important admissions from Zubaydah in a matter of days. Years later, a report by the CIA inspector general would say that Zubaydah might well have given up the same information without any harsh interrogation.

But the words used by Zubaydah about Ja'far—*the other Mohammed Atta, an American Hiroshima*—grabbed renewed attention in Washington. Throughout the administration, the press was on to answer three questions: Who was Ja'far the Pilot? Where was he? And was he planning to strike America?

Months of agonizing investigation would pass before officials learned that Ja'far was a naturalized American citizen, a longtime resident of Fort Lauderdale, a former student at Broward Community College, and one of al-Qaeda's most dangerous terrorists. But by the time the FBI raided his family home, Ja'far the Pilot was in the wind.

At a Tuscan restaurant just off Piazza Risorgimento in Milan, Robert Lady, the local CIA station chief, was enjoying dinner with a law enforcement official from the Carabinieri, Italy's national gendarmerie. Lady had befriended the officer, Luciano Pironi, earlier that year and the two often met for a beer or a quick meal. On this day, their wives were both on holiday, so the two men had decided to have a leisurely get-together at one of the better eateries in the area.

But the two weren't just sharing pleasantries—business was being conducted. About ten months had passed since Bush had persuaded Prime Minister Berlusconi to allow American intelligence operatives to snatch up a suspected terrorist in Italy and spirit him out of the country. Now, in August, planning for the operation was finally under way. There was a man named Abu Omar who was living in Milan, Lady said, an Egyptian cleric who was both influential and extremely dangerous.

"I received a tip that he's planning to hijack a school bus from the American School, over by the opera house," Lady said.

The bus would be carrying children anywhere from the ages of five to eighteen. They would be Americans, Brits, and an array of other nationalities. The plan was diabolical—a suicide bomber would board the bus and detonate his explosives, or the children would be forced off the vehicle into a fusillade of machine-gun bullets. Either way, this was a plot that had to be stopped.

Pironi had told Lady long before that he wanted to move from the Carabinieri to Italy's primary intelligence group, Servizio per le Informazioni e la Sicurezza Militare. This planned snatch was going to be a big operation, the CIA officer said. Maybe Pironi could play a role in it. That, Lady said, would certainly give him a leg up in switching jobs.

The idea sounded great. Make sure to give him updates on how he could help, Pironi said.

The usual medley of cars and bicycles clogged a retail district in Serang, Indonesia, on the afternoon of August 22. Despite the crowds, business was slow at the Toko Elita Indah jewelry store.

It wasn't the merchandise that kept customers away—sometimes, it was the owners. They were Chinese Christians, a group that made up less than 1 percent of an overwhelmingly Muslim population that reviled outsiders as contaminants to their ethnic and religious purity. Such intolerance put the businesses and safety of all Chinese Christians at risk, particularly from extremists who believed that killing such infidels, much less robbing them, was sanctioned by the Koran. One local Muslim leader had proclaimed as much, telling his followers that if Islamists could take the lives of nonbelievers, surely they could take their property.

The Islamist threat appeared that day. Three armed extremists wearing ski masks stormed the jewelry store, waving their pistols at the family members who were working behind the counter.

"Gold!" one of the robbers shouted.

The men grabbed whatever they could. Terrified, Vini Khian, the owner's eighteen-year-old daughter, screamed; one of the assailants shot her in the abdomen. Seconds later, the bandits ran out of the store carrying five and a half pounds of gold and $500 in cash.

The owner phoned an ambulance and then the Serang police. The girl was rushed to the hospital and survived. The two officers who arrived at the store shrugged off the heist as a standard-fare snatch-and-grab. The thieves knew what they were doing; gold and cash were impossible to trace. For months, the crime lay in limbo.

It was only later, amid piles of rubble and hundreds of dead bodies, that the authorities would realize that this seemingly inconsequential robbery had been orchestrated to help finance what would be the largest terrorist attack since 9/11.

Four hundred miles away, three men sat in a darkened car outside of a Surakarta gas station near the Klewer Market in Central Java.

At the wheel was Amrozi bin Nurhasyim, a member of the Southeast Asian offshoot of al-Qaeda called Jemaah Islamiyah. Beside him sat Imam Samudra, an operations planner for the terrorist group. Two other terrorists—one an expert in bomb making, the other in electronics—hunched in the backseat. The four had joined up that night to celebrate the success of the jewelry store robbery by their brothers-in-arms in Serang, who had grabbed enough loot to pay a good part of the cost for their ambitious bombing plot.

"Today we have begun a big project," Samudra boasted. "Today we have declared war on America."

Eight months before, the leadership of Jemaah Islamiyah had met in Thailand with Riduan Isamuddin—an al-Qaeda heavy hitter better known as Hambali—to toss around ideas for the next terrorist strike. A plan to bomb embassies and other targets in Singapore had been thwarted by that country's Internal Security Department, and Hambali had pushed the Southeast Asian terrorists to focus instead on "soft targets"—bars, cafés, or nightclubs frequented by Westerners. Using a series of code words, he suggested five countries where an operation could be launched, including "Terminal"—the name for Indonesia. Whatever nation was chosen, Hambali emphasized, the primary goal was to kill a lot of "white meat," his code for Americans.

Hambali was now pushing for the attack to take place on the first anniversary of 9/11, but Samudra refused. They weren't prepared. They still needed to purchase bomb-making equipment and choose the attack site.

"We will have to wait before establishing a target and a plan," Samudra told the others in the car. "We need time to seek the target, the means, and, most importantly, the funds."

The money from the jewelry store robbery was the first step, and Hambali was supposed to provide another $30,000. Despite the delay, Samudra was confident that he and his compatriots would soon inflict renewed fear on America and its allies.

Zubaydah begged his CIA interrogators to stop as they strapped him down onto the gurney and rotated it fifteen degrees downward. The black cloth was held over his mouth and an officer poured water on his face. Zubaydah's head filled with liquid.

Nearby, a group of agency officials from Washington watched as Zubaydah tried fruitlessly to struggle. He urinated on himself again, no longer able to control his bladder anytime he was terrified.

The interrogators didn't want to do this. They had reported to CIA headquarters that Zubaydah had been broken and was now fully cooperative. Senior officials didn't believe it—he seemed to know bits and pieces, organizational structures of al-Qaeda, a few names, but no details of planned attacks. His name had turned up in so many interceptions of al-Qaeda conversations that they were still convinced Zubaydah was the third-highest-ranking member of the terrorist group, below only bin Laden and Zawahiri.

The information coming out of the interrogations was far different. He was no al-Qaeda mastermind—in fact, there was something *off* about him, almost as if he was mentally ill. He had said repeatedly that he was *not* an al-Qaeda fighter or even a member. He was, instead, a facilitator whose duties were to act as a logistics chief, no more than a terrorist travel agent. His name appeared in so many intercepted conversations—and was linked to so many different attacks—because the al-Qaeda members involved in the terrorist operations were contacting him to help arrange their trips, he maintained.

If true, none of this made Zubaydah a useless catch—far from it. He was a cog inside the al-Qaeda wheel, and his revelations expanded the American government's knowledge of the terrorist group's activities. But his information was often sketchy, and he provided few detailed insights about impending attacks.

To reassure themselves that he was holding nothing back, the CIA officials wanted to observe Zubaydah's behavior during a harsh interrogation. Afterward, their bosses agreed—Zubaydah was cooperating. He had been waterboarded again for nothing.

The black, double-folded cable slashed at Abdullah Almalki's feet, his Syrian interrogators cracking it like a whip. It was August 24, and Almalki—the Canadian citizen who had been seized during a trip to Damascus to visit his sick grandmother—was approaching his fourth month in captivity.

Throughout that time, he had been tortured relentlessly. They had beaten him with the cable for seven hours straight, counting off a thousand lashes. They had stuffed him into a tire while pounding him, hung him off the ground by his arms, slapped him, kicked him. He occasionally was able to peek from under his blindfold and saw that his tormentors were formulating their questions from documents they were studying.

Eventually, he came to believe that the Canadian government was aiding the Syrians. At one point he was asked questions about his business that could have come only from paperwork seized in his office during a search by Canadian law enforcement. Another time, he was asked questions about material found in his parents' house; police officials took that, too. The Canadians would later deny having shared any of the information with the Syrians. They had, however, provided it to the Americans.

The belief that his country had abandoned him—and, indeed, was participating in his torture—nearly overwhelmed Almalki with grief. Most galling of all was the sheer pointlessness of his ordeal. If he lied, he was tortured. If he told the truth, he was tortured. If he said nothing, he was tortured. There was no way to make the brutality stop.

The blackest moment, though, came when he realized that children were in this horrible place. Almalki was in an interrogation room when he saw a boy, about eight years old, taking his younger sister to the bathroom. He learned that up to twenty mothers and ten children were being held. The mothers were tortured; he could hear them when they were returned to their crying children, broken, bloodied, and moaning in pain.

• • •

In a seventh-floor office at CIA headquarters, Cofer Black sat at his desk, angrily writing on a yellow legal pad. He was sick of politicians yammering about how the agency's counterterrorism unit had fallen down on the job before 9/11. This testimony he was preparing would be his first chance to publicly slam the critics that he saw as reckless and uninformed.

Black had stepped down as head of the Counterterrorist Center in May and since then had been working out of an office in the suite of the CIA's general counsel, John Rizzo. He filled his days reviewing documents and putting thoughts to paper as he readied himself to appear before Congress's Joint Select Committee on Intelligence, which was investigating the 9/11 attacks.

Members of the committee had offered him the chance to speak at the hearing from behind a screen to protect him against potential retribution from terrorists. He refused—he wasn't going to hide. His people who had been on the front lines for years in the war against the jihadists—those men and women who had dedicated so much of their lives to protecting the country—were being smeared as responsible for the deaths of three thousand of their fellow citizens. Black wanted to stand in public, telling the truth about the selfless commitment of these anonymous heroes who had struggled valiantly with too little money, too little support, and too much work. The White House knew it; Congress knew it; the entire national security apparatus knew it. The CIA's inspector general had even issued a report, just weeks before 9/11, saying what a good job the unit was doing, particularly given its meager resources.

But even *with* all of those hurdles, his people had detected the rumblings of the coming attack. He had personally briefed Rice about the warning signs of an imminent terrorist strike. Then the White House did . . . nothing. And now senior members of the administration were—just as Black had always expected—blaming the CIA for not warning them enough, or not pinpointing the time and place of the attacks.

It took 9/11 to sweep aside all of the impediments. The counterterrorism unit received all the money and people it needed. After months of administration hemming and hawing over using the armed Predator, the bird was cleared for takeoff. Restrictions against sharing intelligence with the FBI were tossed out. There was no longer hand-wringing from the White House about conducting proactive operations against terrorists.

Black was never one to use mealymouthed words to get a point across. So he needed some hard-edged phrase to convey to Congress how restrained his CIA unit had been before 9/11, and how everything had changed afterward.

Some sort of graphic analogy. Something like "unchained the junkyard dog." But not quite. America wasn't a junkyard and the counterterrorism personnel weren't dogs. It was the wrong metaphor.

He gave it more thought, and the perfect phrase popped into his mind. He scribbled it down on his legal pad.

"After 9/11," he wrote, "the gloves came off."

On the evening of August 27 in Karachi, an al-Qaeda operative removed the lid on a Nera WorldPhone and connected to an Intelsat communications satellite stationed over the Indian Ocean. The terrorist—one of the planners of the 9/11 attack—entered a phone number into the desktop system and reached an associate who was also tied to the terrorist group.

The first man spoke in code, his words beamed into orbit. Before the flow of digital data could be relayed back down to earth, it was intercepted by another satellite operated on behalf of the NSA by the American government's National Reconnaissance Office.

Technical experts picked through the conversation and began to suspect that the unidentified caller was involved in transporting al-Qaeda members out of Pakistan, where many of them had fled after the war in Afghanistan began. The analysts ran voice comparisons with other recordings and hit the mother lode. They matched the voice with one on the yet-to-be-broadcast Al Jazeera interview with bin al-Shibh and Sheikh Mohammed, a recording that had been turned over to the CIA by the emir of Qatar.

The man on the phone was bin al-Shibh. American intelligence now knew the city where one of the planners of 9/11 was hiding. The Pakistanis had proved themselves trustworthy in the capture of Abu Zubaydah and perhaps could help with this search. The CIA passed the information to the Directorate for Inter-Services Intelligence, asking for help. The hunt would last fifteen days.

Cheney was angry. The Iraq debate had been playing out around the world—in newspaper articles, think-tank reports, speeches by geopolitical Einsteins—but the administration had barely made a peep to explain its position. It was imperative, the vice president told Bush, to let the public know where they stood, and why. And he would like to make the case himself. Bush agreed, but didn't ask Cheney for details of what he planned to say.

• • •

The stage at the Nashville convention for the Veterans of Foreign Wars was splashed in red and blue from the curtains to the lighting to the dais. After an effusive introduction, Cheney stood and approached the podium, taking a place in front of a giant, red oval emblazoned with the group's logo.

"As members of the VFW," he began, "you are united by common experiences and shared commitments."

For the next few minutes, Cheney wandered down familiar paths—praising the integrity of veterans, their history of leadership on great issues of the day, their closeness with the administration. Predictably, he spoke, too, about homeland security, 9/11, the war in Afghanistan, and the pursuit of bin Laden.

Then, a shift. "Containment is not possible when dictators obtain weapons of mass destruction and are prepared to share them with terrorists who intend to inflict catastrophic casualties on the United States," he said. "The case of Saddam Hussein, a sworn enemy of our country, requires a candid appraisal of the facts."

Since the rout of Iraqi forces in the Gulf War, Saddam had agreed to abide by U.N. resolutions calling for him to cease the development of nuclear, chemical, and biological weapons. But he broke his promises.

"We now know that Saddam has resumed his efforts to acquire nuclear weapons," Cheney said. "Among other sources, we have gotten this from first-hand testimony of defectors."

Attempts by the international community to keep Saddam in check had failed, Cheney said, because he devised an elaborate program to hide his arms-building efforts.

"One must keep in mind the history of the U.N. inspection teams in Iraq," he said. "Even as they were conducting the most intrusive system of arms control in history, the inspectors missed a great deal."

That track record provided strong reason to question any suggestion that bringing the weapons inspectors back would end the threat posed by Iraq. "On the contrary," Cheney said, "there is a great danger that it would provide false comfort that Saddam was somehow 'back in his box.' "

And while the world relaxed to the soothing assurances from U.N. inspectors, Saddam would just keep plotting.

"There is no doubt that Saddam Hussein now has weapons of mass destruction," Cheney said. "There is no doubt he is amassing them to use against our friends, against our allies, and against us."

Americans could not wish away this mortal threat, he said. Their elected leaders instead had to consider all available options. Those who believed that opposing Saddam would damage the broader war on terror were wrong. Instead, Cheney said, regime change in Iraq would inspire freedom-loving people to topple dictatorships in other lands. Extremists would have to rethink their strategy of jihad. The people in Iraq would celebrate the overthrow of their tyrants, just as Afghanis in Kabul had welcomed their American liberators.

"With our help," Cheney said, "a liberated Iraq can be a great nation once again."

After a few closing remarks, Cheney stepped away from the podium. The crowd erupted in applause.

At the White House, horror.

Cheney had issued what amounted to the moral equivalent of a declaration of war. He had gone far beyond any policy yet decided by Bush. He had stuck a finger in the eye of the U.N., dismissing weapons inspection as not only foolhardy, but dangerous. And his backhanded slap at the international community had been delivered at a time when Blair was phoning several times a week, urging Bush to give the U.N. one last try. To the president's consternation, Cheney had just put America's partnership with Britain into jeopardy, at a time when Blair's support for the administration's policy was crucial.

And no one in the White House had known ahead of time that Cheney was going to publicly utter such inflammatory pronouncements.

Reassurances to the British were delivered in a phone call from Rice to David Manning, one of the Blair's chief foreign policy advisors.

Just ignore Cheney's comments, Rice said. Nothing had changed, and the president was eager to hear what the prime minister had to say about seeking a U.N. resolution in a speech he was scheduled to deliver on September 12. There had been no final decisions, regardless of how Cheney made it sound.

The damage control continued through the week. Powell gave an interview with the BBC, attesting to America's respect and faith in U.N. weapons inspectors. The message to Number 10 Downing Street was clear: Blair would gain political cover. Cheney would not be allowed to engage in diplomatic freelancing again.

At the British embassy in Washington, Ambassador Christopher Meyer was preparing for a meeting between Bush and Blair that was scheduled for the next morning at Camp David. It was the evening of September 6, and once again

Blair was traveling to America to press Bush about seeking a new U.N. resolution on Iraq before launching a military invasion.

The Cheney speech—or, as one of Blair's advisors called it, "the train wreck"—had provided the prime minister with a taste of the political heat he would face if the United States stiff-armed the U.N. Already suspicious of the American designs on Iraq, the British press and public greeted Cheney's comments with a mixture of hostility and disdain. With his staff, Blair was steadfast, almost belligerent, in insisting that taking on Iraq was the right thing to do. But after the Cheney debacle, he returned to his role of coaxing the Bush administration into an internationalist frame of mind.

Meyer had high hopes for the Camp David meeting. While the militarists like Cheney and Rumsfeld were reckless in their go-it-alone arrogance, Bush was much more of a statesman. The president might be hawkish, but he was not a fool; his instincts were balanced with a strong dose of realpolitik. The world should thank God that it was Bush—and not Cheney—sitting in the Oval Office, Meyer thought.

The phone rang in his study. On the line was one of the most talented foreign policy experts from the Clinton administration, someone whom Meyer had long ago grown to trust.

"Just to let you know," the caller said, "Dick Cheney is going to be present throughout the prime minister's discussions with the president."

A *Clinton* official was conveying confidential information from the *Bush* administration?

"How the hell do you know?" Meyer asked.

"Don't ask, don't tell," came the reply. "But Blair had better watch out."

The next morning at Camp David, a line of soldiers stood at attention as Tony Blair and his entourage of advisors passed. Bush greeted them warmly, then escorted the group into the main building.

A few of the aides for both men took seats while Bush brought Blair and Manning to his study. The two had assumed that only Rice would be joining the meeting—they hadn't heard yet from Meyer about the warning that Cheney would be attending.

Then the vice president appeared. The assemblage suggested that this meeting was about far more than persuading Bush—Blair's job was to pull him away from the voices in his own administration clamoring for war. The prime minister, in essence, had to beat Cheney.

• • •

Over the next two hours, Blair was unshakable.

He marshaled all of the usual arguments about the need to seek a U.N. resolution on Iraq—military action would shatter global alliances, Middle Eastern allies would be forced by the demands of their own people to turn against the West, the peace process would be crippled, the motivations for the attack would be distrusted.

There were questions that still hadn't been answered to the public's satisfaction: Why Saddam? Why now? What was the commitment of America and Britain to the Middle East? A new U.N. resolution would help provide answers. It would demonstrate that the recognition of the danger posed by Saddam was multinational, and not just something being pushed by the United States. Iraq's refusal to comply with a renewed U.N. effort toward disarmament would prove that it was time to force Saddam's hand. And, with both the United States and Britain strongly advancing the notion that this was part of a broader Middle East policy, they could not only win more allies and support throughout the region but also advance the peace process.

Occasionally, Cheney came in with a counterpoint, and Blair parried the vice president's objection—and at times slammed it down, diplomatically. At one point Cheney argued that bringing in the U.N. for more inspections could well upend the effort for regime change.

"The British government's aim is for disarmament," Blair countered. "It is not for regime change. If the result of disarming Saddam was regime change, that would be positive, but it is not our primary goal."

"Well," Cheney countered, "we want regime change in order to disarm Saddam Hussein, not the other way around."

That approach, while understandable, would be disastrous, Blair said. The Americans and the British couldn't tell the world that they didn't care whether Saddam was armed, they just wanted him out. Justifying that position would be next to impossible. They would be back struggling with the question: Why Saddam? There were other armed enemies, so why attack one that could be neutralized without war?

"Now, you may have objections to a U.N. resolution, but actually, I believe we might need two," Blair said. "One to set the conditions and one to take action if those conditions weren't meet."

He looked at Bush. "Our message should be either the regime must change in response to U.N. pressure and to U.N. resolutions," Blair said, "or it would be changed by military action."

Bush suppressed a smile. Blair's performance was impressive. Cheney could be an intimidating figure, but Blair wasn't taking any guff. He was knocking the vice president back, without batting an eye.

Boy, Blair has cojones, Bush thought.

He could see the virtues of Blair's position, Bush said. There could be victory without war.

"If, by chance, Saddam accepted and implemented the terms of a new resolution," he said, "we would have succeeded in changing the very nature of the regime."

His smile broke through. "We would have cratered the guy," he said.

The aides waiting in the other room were summoned to the president's study. Bush asked the British officials for a briefing about the staff's discussions.

Alastair Campbell, a senior Blair aide, spoke directly to Bush. The administration, Campbell said, had to consider the importance of sending out a clear message of its benevolent intent.

"I feel like you really have to *get* the anti-Americanism in Europe and the Middle East," he said. "A lot of it is jealousy and some of it resentment that they felt obliged to feel sympathy and solidarity post-9/11."

But there were other important factors feeding into anti-Americanism that could not be shunted aside. Some of the disdain for the United States, Campbell said, came from a fear of its power. That was why the British officials were worried about the language that members of the Bush administration were using in their public statements.

A look of anger flashed across Cheney's face. "You mean we shouldn't talk about democracy?" he snapped.

Campbell faced the vice president. "Not if what people take out of it is not a message about democracy, but a message about Americanization," he said.

Bush nodded. Whatever Cheney's thoughts, Bush, it seemed, got it. There was a break in the discussion and Blair headed to the restroom.

"Hey, big guy!" Bush called out to Campbell.

Campbell walked over. A few of Bush's aides were beside him.

He looked at Campbell, an amused look on his face. "I'll say this," Bush said, "and I don't want it on the record, and with apologies to the mixed audience, but your guy's got balls."

. . .

The meeting resumed, and Bush took control.

"I've decided to go down to the U.N. and put down a new Security Council resolution," he said. "But I can't stand by. At that point we've got to say to Saddam, 'Okay, what will you do?' "

Blair and his aides breathed a sigh of relief. They had won the day. When Bush gave his speech on Iraq to the U.N. in four days, he would be declaring his preference for diplomacy before military action. Cheney had been checked.

Dinner than night was anticlimactic. The vice president ate his meal in near silence, and Blair, suffering from severe stomach cramps, barely ate at all.

Bush held forth, filling the group in on a dispute unfolding at the Augusta National Golf Club about whether women could be admitted as members. It was a silly battle, Bush said. The club was going to have to let women in at some point, so why not just accept the inevitable?

A member of the British contingent commented that, while the rest of the world wanted the Iraq issue to be resolved a step at a time, Americans would probably question why Bush was seeking a diplomatic solution at the U.N., rather than just sending in the troops. Cheney smiled across the table. Without saying a word, everyone understood—that was his question.

As dinner wrapped up, Blair excused himself and headed to his cabin. Bush accompanied Campbell out the door. "I suppose you can tell the story of how Tony flew in and pulled the crazed unilateralist back from the brink," he joked.

After 9:30 the next morning, Rumsfeld was in his Pentagon office reviewing an intelligence report. He had asked a few weeks earlier for an assessment by the Directorate of Intelligence Joint Staff of what the United States did and did not know about an Iraqi program for weapons of mass destruction. Although the analysis had been completed four days earlier, this was the first time Rumsfeld had laid eyes on it.

The findings were disconcerting. The opening page cautioned that all of the assessments of Iraq's arsenal were based heavily on analytic assumptions. There was very little hard evidence.

"Our knowledge of the Iraqi nuclear weapons program is based largely— perhaps 90%—on analysis of imprecise intelligence," the report said.

As for biological weapons, the intelligence officers could not confirm the identity of any Iraqi facilities that produced, tested, or stored them. And while they believed that Iraq had seven mobile production plants for such weapons, they could not locate them.

In every category, the information was sketchy. The analysts didn't know if Iraq had the processes in place to produce chemical devices, and they couldn't confirm the identity of any Iraqi sites used to produce the final agents needed for a weapon. While Saddam had short-range ballistic missiles, they doubted that he could produce longer-range weapons. Information about staging and storage sites for ballistic missiles was "significantly lacking," the report said.

Rumsfeld decided that General Myers, the chairman of the Joint Chiefs, needed to see this report immediately. Just after 9:45, he addressed an e-mail to Myers, attaching a copy of the report.

"Please take a look at this material as to what we don't know about WMD," he typed. "It's big."

BOOK THREE

THE THREAT

12

Three Yemeni men emerged from a five-story building in a Karachi housing project and walked across the street toward an outdoor food stall.

A detachment of paramilitaries rushed out from behind cars and doorways, pointing AK-47s and handguns at the men. Without a word, the squad of Pakistani soldiers tackled the Yemenis, yanking back their arms and pushing their faces into the concrete.

It was shortly after seven o'clock on the morning of September 11, 2002. Since the previous afternoon, a group of Army Rangers, police officers, and operatives from the ISI—Pakistan's premier intelligence agency—had been conducting surveillance of the building. Just fifteen days before, American intelligence had informed the ISI that it had intercepted a call from Ramzi bin al-Shibh, a top al-Qaeda terrorist and 9/11 plotter. The CIA determined that the call came from Karachi but couldn't narrow down the location. The ISI took over the hunt, but without more information, the chances that its agents would locate bin al-Shibh were slim.

Then, a breakthrough. Police and ISI agents had raided an apartment in the suburb of Bahadurabad, where they believed a group of Arab terrorists was hiding out. The suspects had already fled, but the gatekeeper at the complex knew where they had gone and led authorities to Building 63C in a project called Commercial Area Phase 2.

Now, thirty-six hours later, the appearance of the three Yemenis on the street was the first confirmation that the ISI had found a terrorist safe house. After cuffing the men's hands, the soldiers pulled them off the ground, dragging them away from 63C.

Fighting his captors, one of the men turned his head, looking up to the building's fifth floor. "Brothers!" he screamed. "Arm yourselves!"

The paramilitaries subdued the man, but it was too late. They had lost the element of surprise. They had to launch the raid immediately.

Rangers and ISI officers fanned out, surrounding the building. Without warning, machine-gun fire sprayed from the fifth-floor windows. As some soldiers and officers took cover, another team blitzed the building, rushing up its single stairwell. Just as the officers passed the third floor, they saw two Arabs and grabbed them. The men shouted to their compatriots, who threw grenades down the stairs. Withering gunfire chopped at the ground as police struggled to pull two injured officers out of harm's way.

A pitched battle had begun, and despite their superior numbers, the authorities were heavily outgunned; rifles and pistols were no match for automatic weapons. The Pakistanis needed heavily armed reinforcements.

More than two thousand Rangers and local police flooded the area. The authorities cordoned off a square kilometer around the building, evacuating residents and shopkeepers from what had become a war zone.

As the hours passed, the air was thick with the smell of cordite. Bullet holes pockmarked the building. Some of the men inside the apartment climbed up to the roof, shielding themselves under a low cement barrier as they fired at the authorities. The police tried to root them out with tear gas; the canisters bounced off the walls and landed on the officers below.

Rangers in full body armor rushed toward the building under the cover from smoke grenades, then took up positions beneath an overhang on the ground floor. Before they moved again, there was a lull in the gunfire.

"You cannot get away!" someone yelled.

"Allahu Akbar!" came the response. God is great.

Inside the apartment, one of the militants had been badly wounded and was bleeding profusely. He made his way to the kitchen wall and smeared a message in his own blood: *There is no God but Allah, Mohammed is his messenger.*

About noon, five Rangers stormed the building, praying as they ran. They bolted up the stairs and into the apartment, where they found survivors crouching in a windowless kitchen, armed only with a rifle.

"Surrender!" a soldier called out.

"Bastard! Bastard!"

One of the extremists leaped to his feet and darted out; he was shot dead.

The man with the rifle took aim at a Ranger and pulled the trigger. A click, then nothing—the gun had jammed. He and a surviving companion grabbed whatever they could—forks, bottles, pans—and hurled them at the soldiers. Then the men held knives to their own throats, threatening to kill themselves rather than be taken into custody. The Rangers fired tear gas and the two men stumbled out of the kitchen, gasping, their hands raised.

Suddenly one of them lunged for a Ranger's gun, and the paramilitaries jumped on them. Both men struggled as the soldiers physically pinned them down.

"You're going to hell!" one screamed. "You're going to hell!"

It was all over by one o'clock. Shell casings and chunks of concrete littered the street; the building's roof was smeared with blood. Seven of the terrorists survived; two were dead.

The men were blindfolded with rags and led outside. Bin al-Shibh, one of the survivors, thrust his hand in the air just before he was thrown into a waiting vehicle.

Searching the apartment, the police found more than twenty remote radio detonators, documents belonging to members of the bin Laden family, laptop computers, mobile phones, and records of terrorist plots, including an attack planned for that very day—killing Pervez Musharraf, Pakistan's president, by shooting rockets at him as he attended a defense exhibition in Karachi.

Later that day, a sheaf of papers arrived at Number 10 Downing Street from the White House. It was a draft of the Iraq speech that Bush was preparing to deliver the following morning at the U.N. General Assembly Hall. And Blair was alarmed as he read it.

There was no call for a new U.N. resolution. The draft read as though it had been written by Cheney and Rumsfeld—bursting with bluster and saber rattling, and not much else. This *had* to be a mistake. The president had made a commitment to Blair that he was going to seek diplomatic action through the U.N. And Bush had never gone back on his word before.

With less than twenty-four hours to go, Blair decided to inject himself into the administration's debate once again. If White House policy makers and speechwriters couldn't figure out what to say, then Blair would do it.

He handwrote a short passage for insertion into the speech and gave it to

David Manning, his foreign policy advisor. Manning transmitted it to Condoleezza Rice and then telephoned her. She told him that the words would be included, but later British officials heard disturbing rumblings that called her assurances into question. Cheney had launched a last-ditch offensive urging Bush to ignore the calls for a new U.N. resolution, and Colin Powell had joined the fray, challenging the vice president's advice as dangerously misguided.

By day's end, the battle within the administration seemed to have been resolved. Manning was told that there was no doubt: Bush would be calling for the resolution.

At 10:35 the next morning, Bush ascended the green marble podium in the vast U.N. General Assembly Hall and walked to the large wooden lectern. He looked out on the applauding crowd of delegates seated in the auditorium. On each side of the podium, semitransparent mirrors reflected the teleprompter screen below. The words from the speech scrolled forward.

"Mr. Secretary General, Mr. President, distinguished delegates and ladies and gentlemen," Bush began, "We meet one year and one day after a terrorist attack brought grief to my country and brought grief to many citizens of our world."

He paid homage to the mission of the U.N. and its commitment to human dignity and collective security. He called for peace in the Middle East, reaffirming his support for an independent Palestine.

"Above all," he said, "our principles and our security are challenged today by outlaw groups and regimes that accept no law of morality and have no limit to their violent ambitions."

Terrorists were lurking within many nations, he said. The threat that rogue regimes could provide them with weapons to kill on a massive scale was a dreadful reality.

"In one place—in one regime—we find all of these dangers in their most lethal and aggressive forms," he said.

In London, Tony Blair watched the speech on television. So far, everything was going as planned. Bush was describing the history of the efforts by U.N. weapons inspectors and Saddam's flouting of the body's resolutions.

"We know that Saddam Hussein pursued weapons of mass murder even when inspectors were in his country," Bush said. "Are we to assume that he stopped when they left?"

That's good, Blair thought. The public reaction to this would almost certainly be favorable.

The words continued to scroll by on the teleprompter mirrors. Bush was reaching the critical point, where he would declare his commitment to a renewed U.N. diplomatic effort to disarm Iraq.

"My nation will work with the U.N. Security Council to meet our common challenge," Bush said. "If Iraq's regime defies us again, the world must move deliberately, decisively to hold Iraq to account."

He glanced at the teleprompter, looking for the phrase calling for a new resolution.

It wasn't there.

The purposes of the United States should not be doubted . . .

That was the next sentence on the teleprompter—an attestation to the country's might and willpower. There was nothing about diplomacy. The words that had been the subject of such great debate had simply disappeared.

Bush took a breath. And then he winged it.

"We will work with the U.N. Security Council for the necessary resolutions . . ." he began.

Resolutions? That's odd.

Christopher Meyer, the British ambassador, was flummoxed by Bush's use of the plural. Blair had been pushing for two resolutions, of course, but Bush had always demurred. Now, after all the fighting over whether to accept even one, the president announced he would go for two? Without warning?

It was almost as if Bush had reached his decision at the last second. Meyer had no way of knowing that he had just witnessed the president of the United States announce what seemed to be a major international initiative by mistake, owing to a technical flub.

Slips of the tongue don't establish national security policy, and so the calls went out quickly to inform allies that the president had misspoken. He wanted one resolution, not two.

Rice delivered the message to the Blair government in a phone call to David

Manning. There had been a slipup, she explained, and Bush had gone further in his statements than he had intended.

"We gave the president the wrong text," she said. "He was ad-libbing."

Early on September 15, a bespectacled, balding man arrived at the thirty-nine-story Secretariat Building at U.N. headquarters in Manhattan. He was Hans Blix, head of the international body's commission in charge of disarming Iraq and monitoring the country's compliance.

The group—the United Nations Monitoring, Verification and Inspection Commission, known universally as UNMOVIC—had been unable to check Iraq's activities since its formation in 1999; Saddam had thrown out a group of weapons inspectors the previous year.

Blix—a Swedish diplomat with a long pedigree promoting the peaceful use of nuclear energy—had come out of retirement in 2000 to become the new head of UNMOVIC at the request of the U.N. secretary general, Kofi Annan. If weapons inspectors went back into Iraq, it would be Blix who led them. Now, just days after the Bush speech, Annan had summoned Blix to his office for an urgent Sunday meeting. The news was breathtaking—Saddam had blinked.

"The Iraqis are going to declare that they accept the return of inspectors," Annan said. "They want early discussions in Baghdad or Vienna about practical arrangements."

"Great," Blix replied. "But I want the talks to be in Vienna."

If Blix and other members of UNMOVIC rushed to Baghdad, the world might see it as a sign that Saddam had capitulated. But the Iraqis might then turn around and reject the conditions for moving forward—it could be made to look as though the U.N. team had fumbled in the negotiations.

"We should go to Baghdad and offer Iraq the benefit of inspection only when they accept the practical arrangements we need," Blix said.

The effort would be worthwhile, Blix said, only if Saddam allowed full and free access to suspected weapons sites and accepted other terms that would ensure the credibility of UNMOVIC's work. Annan agreed.

The letter from Iraq's foreign minister, Naji Sabri, was delivered to Annan the next afternoon. In it, Sabri declared that Iraq had decided to allow the weapons inspectors back, with no conditions.

This, the letter said, was the first step toward assuring the world that Iraq no longer possessed weapons of mass destruction.

• • •

The first inklings of a planned terrorist attack in Indonesia were picked up in mid-September by MI5, Britain's Security Service. Based on electronic intercepts and reports from informants, the intelligence agency determined that the plot included a weekend bombing of nightclubs frequented by American, British, and other Western tourists. Most likely, the strike would take place in Bali.

Word of the threat was passed on to Britain's diplomatic service, the Foreign and Commonwealth Office, which was responsible for issuing travel advisories. But MI5 didn't inform Britain's government outposts or other interests in Indonesia of the growing danger.

The Gulfstream jet taxied toward the hangar at Guantanamo Bay. A delegation of administration lawyers in business suits stepped out and was greeted by General Dunlavey.

It was September 26. The group—including Addington, Haynes, Rizzo, and several other attorneys—was making a quick stop at the detention center to review its operations. They were taken by ferry to the windward side of the base and then boarded a bus to Camp Delta. After a short briefing, they were escorted through a building that held two dozen detainees clad in orange jumpsuits. Some of the men studied the lawyers with vacant expressions. Others glared, their eyes flashing in anger. Afterward, the group observed the questioning of a detainee; the interrogators used the relationship-building tactics of law enforcement.

But the most important topic of discussion was al-Qahtani. The lawyers knew that the interrogation of the man thought to be the twentieth hijacker had begun and were eager to learn details of its progress.

"What do we know about this guy?" Addington asked. "Have we gotten anything out of him?"

Not much. Since the military questioning had begun, Qahtani had been unshakable in his resistance; one of the interviewers was a former member of the Jordanian military, but even his knowledge of both Arabic and aggressive techniques wasn't helping. The interrogations might proceed more quickly, Dunlavey said, if there weren't so many constraints on what his teams were permitted to do.

"We'd like to be able to take the Koran away from some detainees, and hold it as an incentive," Dunlavey said. The request had been sent up the line to SOUTHCOM, he said, but no one had signed off on it.

SOUTHCOM approval might not be necessary, Haynes said. "You should have the authority in place to make those calls, per the president's order," he said.

After three hours, the tour ended and the entourage flew to the naval brig in Charleston, where Padilla was being held. From there, it was on to Norfolk to see Hamdi.

The group was brought to a room with a black-and-white, closed-circuit television that showed Hamdi's cell. Jack Goldsmith, who had just taken the job as special counsel to Haynes at the Pentagon, felt uncomfortable as he watched the detainee. Something just seemed wrong.

This twenty-two-year-old American citizen, a foot soldier with the Taliban, was all alone, held in a tiny cell at a dingy prison. He had no access to a lawyer—indeed, almost no contact with any other human being.

Goldsmith had no doubt that Hamdi was being held legally. But, as he looked at this stupefied, pathetic man, Goldsmith was struck by the realization that law wasn't the point. The administration's legalistic frame of mind gave short shrift to prudence. Officials had spent plenty of time determining that the rules allowed them to stuff Hamdi into a cell and leave him in isolation. They never stopped to question whether it was a smart thing to do.

That same morning, Congressman Porter Goss picked up a gavel and pounded it once. It was the fifth day of public hearings—sponsored by the intelligence subcommittees of both the House and the Senate—into the events leading up to 9/11. Until now, no official had stepped forward to explain what the government knew before the attacks and whether they could have been stopped.

At the witness table sat two balding middle-aged men, both looking more like college professors than warriors. They were Cofer Black from the CIA and Dale Watson, a former top official with the FBI's counterterrorism unit.

"Mr. Black, welcome," Goss said, glancing up from his prepared statement. "The floor is yours, sir."

Black folded his hands on the witness table.

"Mr. Chairman," he said, "I'd like to express my appreciation to you and to the committee for offering me a screen to protect my identity and to enhance my security. Good security is always a very good idea. And if this were normal circumstances, I would accept your offer."

But, he said, the work of the committee was too important for him to be a voice behind a screen. "When I speak, I think the American people need to look into my face, and I want to look the American people in the eye."

After expressing his deep horror over the murder of three thousand people, Black described the realities of his former unit's work. The CIA *had* provided the administration with warnings of an impending attack, he said, but could not specify the time and place. And that intelligence was obtained despite enormous challenges imposed by Washington.

"You need to appreciate fully three factors," he said. "There were choices made for us. These choices were made for the Central Intelligence Agency and they were made for the Counterterrorism Center. These involved numbers of people, money, and operational flexibility."

As cloak-and-dagger as the word *counterterrorism* might sound, his former unit spent a lot of time in mundane—and often unsuccessful—battles against Washington bureaucracy. His people were shortchanged on every side, Black said. The center struggled with constant shortages of cash, forcing a shutdown of some efforts to combat terrorists. The staff was small, given its responsibilities. There were 25 percent fewer covert officers in 1999 than nine years before.

Despite their success in navigating through those challenges, they were impeded when it came time for action. Politicians fearful that someone—even bin Laden—would be killed had derailed plenty of operational plans. There had been proposals to aid Afghanis in an attack on the al-Qaeda leader, to assassinate him, to use an armed Predator, to grab him when he was in Sudan—all of them thwarted. By the late 1990s, they were told that they had the authority to capture bin Laden, but no one would approve actually doing it. What were they supposed to do if they couldn't kill him or snatch him? Curse at him?

Now, with three thousand people slaughtered, the politicians *got* it. There was no more hand-wringing about whether to strike or what weapons to use. The policy was simple: Destroy al-Qaeda and bin Laden.

Black wanted to discuss everything that had since been green-lighted, but most of it remained classified. He could only hint at the magnitude of the problems caused by skittishness among policy makers—and their recent conversion to born-again belligerence in the war on terror.

"This is a very highly classified area, but I have to say that all you need to know is that there was a before 9/11 and there was an after 9/11," he said. "After 9/11 the gloves come off. Nearly three thousand al-Qaeda and their supporters have been arrested or detained. In Afghanistan, the al-Qaeda who refused to surrender have been killed. The hunt is on."

Good. Black had made his point. Sharp, succinct, clear, and without revealing any classified information. Perhaps now, he thought, the public would understand how counterterrorism had been mismanaged—out of neglect and cowardice—and the horrific impact of those mistakes.

It was not to be. Instead, Black learned the danger of speaking in metaphor. Reporters and politicians eventually seized on the "gloves came off" comment as proof that there was a policy to inflict brutal treatment on detainees. He could only shake his head—he wasn't even *working* with the counterterrorism unit when the decisions were made about waterboarding and other harsh tactics. Did these people really believe he would appear on television, casually disclosing classified programs? Particularly those created after he left the unit? Critics were infusing his clichés with meanings that weren't there.

It all went to reinforce Black's long-held opinions: He despised politicians—and hated reporters even more.

Staff Sergeant Patrick Callaghan of the Mounties' AO Canada unit received a call that afternoon from the FBI's legal attaché's office in Ottawa.

Maher Arar, a target of ongoing inquiries in both the United States and Canada, was due to arrive in New York on a flight from Zurich, the attaché said. Arar had gained the attention of Canadian officials when he was seen having lunch at an Ottawa restaurant called Mango's Café with Abdullah Almalki, who had already been under investigation. The two men had been seen walking in the rain together—or at least, that's how the filed reports described what had been in reality a light misting—and that raised suspicions among the Mounties that nefarious intrigue might be hatching.

In recent months, more information had turned up that reinforced those suspicions. Ahmad El-Maati, who had been stopped a year before at the Canadian border carrying a map of federal facilities in Ottawa, had been arrested by the Syrians and confessed to having been trained at al-Qaeda camps with Almalki and Arar. Then Almalki was also seized in Damascus, and he admitted knowing Arar. Those confessions—forwarded from a country notorious for unrelenting torture during interrogations—struck the Canadians as a powerful indictment of Arar's intentions.

Now, with Arar's expected arrival in New York, the investigators would have their chance to confront him. The FBI official told Callaghan that the United States intended to deny Arar entry. If the Canadians had any questions to ask him, the official said, they should send them down in writing. The fax arrived at two o'clock.

At that same time, American Airlines flight 65 from Zurich reached its gate at John F. Kennedy International Airport. Arar stood to gather his belongings and squeezed into the line of passengers jammed in the aisle. He had a few hours to kill on this layover before his connecting flight to Canada.

At immigration, the agent entered Arar's information into the computer, then asked him to stand aside. Minutes later, officials escorted him to another part of the airport.

"Why am I being pulled aside?" he asked.

"Just regular procedure," an agent responded.

Arar was fingerprinted and photographed. Airport police searched his bag and his wallet. When Arar asked for an explanation, no one replied. He requested to be allowed to place a phone call and was refused.

After two hours, officials from the Joint Terrorism Task Force—including investigators with the INS, the FBI, and the New York Police Department's intelligence unit—showed up to question Arar.

"I'd like to contact a lawyer," Arar said.

"No," an FBI agent replied. "You're not an American citizen. You have no right to a lawyer."

The cross-examination lasted hours. The Americans asked Arar about his work, his income, and his travels in the United States. They pressed him for information about a trip he had taken recently to Japan. They fished for details about aspects of his life that were so private Arar assumed they had learned about them from the Canadian government.

The agent then asked if he knew Ahmad El-Maati, the man who, under torture in Syria, had identified Arar as an al-Qaeda member.

"Yes, I know him," Arar responded. "But not well. I met him a couple of years ago at a garage in Montreal where I was getting my car fixed."

And what about Abdullah Almalki?

"Yes, I know him," Arar said. "But I know his brother better."

The encounter grew increasingly heated. The agents bombarded Arar with rapid-fire questions and raged at him if he hesitated before replying. They in-

sulted him and accused him of having a selective memory. Arar couldn't understand why they had become so abusive, or why they seemed to think he was
lying.

Still, the interview didn't produce enough new evidence, even with the information already in investigative files, to justify arresting Arar. All the United
States could do was ship him out of the country. An INS inspector led him
to an office, asked a few questions, and typed the answers into a Form I-275,
a formal request for Arar to submit that would withdraw his application for
admission into the United States. The agent printed the form and told Arar to
sign it. The Syrian-born engineer had no idea what the document was but was
too exhausted and too hungry to put up a fight. He scribbled his name on the
signature line. Arar had unwittingly agreed to be sent back to Zurich on a flight
the next afternoon. Until then, he would have to be detained.

At 1:00 A.M., federal marshals arrived. Arar was chained and shackled, then
taken outside to a waiting van. They drove him to another building, a small jail
at the airport, and locked him in a cell.

No one had yet told him what was going on.

That evening in Washington, the INS commissioner, James Ziglar, called his
chief of staff and other lawyers to a meeting in his office. He wanted to discuss
what to do with Maher Arar.

Just a few hours had passed since Arar arrived at Kennedy, setting off a flood
of phone calls between officials in New York and Washington. Word had circulated within the administration that this Canadian was a high-level al-Qaeda
member, active in a terrorist cell plotting a new attack against the United States.
The evidence was sketchy, little more than raw intelligence, but it was enough
to put the White House on edge.

For Ziglar, the Arar issue had popped up at an unusual time. He was winding
down a particularly troubled tenure as INS commissioner, vilified for his agency's slipshod screening of foreign visitors to the United States—a reputation
that was sealed when it sent visa approval papers to two of the 9/11 hijackers
exactly six months after the attack. Ziglar, who had come to the job with no
background in immigration law, would be leaving at the end of November. The
decision of what to do with this suspected al-Qaeda member named Arar would
be one of his last.

"All right," he said, "so who is Maher Arar?"

One of the lawyers explained that Arar was a citizen of both Canada and

Syria, and had been the subject of investigations by authorities in Washington and Ottawa. When Arar flew in that day from Zurich, his name popped up during a routine screening through the Advance Passenger Information System, identifying him as a foreigner who was barred from the United States.

Given the criticism over the past year that the INS had been lax in confronting possible terrorists at the border, there was no question that Arar would be refused entry. The agency consulted officials from the Department of Homeland Security and all agreed that Arar had to be removed. Maybe to Canada or Switzerland. Or maybe, one official suggested, to Syria.

Monia Mazigh, Arar's wife, saw her husband standing in front of her, scowling. She asked him why he seemed angry, but he would not answer. She tried to approach him. He vanished.

She awoke. It had been a dream. She had stayed up as long as she could the night before, worried that something had happened to Arar. He hadn't arrived home, he hadn't called, and no one knew where he was. She had slept only two or three hours, but when she did doze off, the nightmares about the disappearance of her husband returned.

The tense circumstances were suffocating her. Arar's business was struggling, and they had been forced to give up their rented house in Canada. She was now with her children in her native Tunisia, where the family had traveled for a much-needed holiday. However, this week, Arar had returned to Canada to handle some developments with his work.

And now he had dropped out of sight.

Climbing out of bed, Mazigh stepped into the living room and glanced at the phone. Maybe the line was disconnected—maybe that was why she hadn't heard from Arar. She lifted the receiver and listened to the hum of the dial tone.

"What do you think about Osama bin Laden?"

Arar stared at the FBI agent who had asked the question. *What in the world is he talking about?* Arar responded with angry words about the al-Qaeda leader.

One day had passed since Arar's arrival in New York. His interrogation had resumed that morning at eight when two FBI agents took him out of his cell to another room. They wanted one more chance to interview him before he was sent back to Zurich.

Again, the questions came fast, not only about bin Laden, but also about the Palestinians and Iraq. They asked for information about the mosques he attended, his bank accounts, and his e-mail addresses. They inspected his Palm-Pilot. But they still refused to tell him why he was being held.

The agents broke for lunch, although no one brought food for Arar. Instead, he was returned to his cell in shackles. He was famished—his last meal had been on the plane. When he asked to be fed, he was ignored.

By five o'clock, the agents and investigators with the Joint Terrorism Task Force had finished with Arar. The interviews and searches turned up nothing. The information in the government computers was vague and unpersuasive. This was a waste of their time.

The message was passed to immigration officials: The counterterrorism agents had no interest in Arar as an investigative subject. As far as they were concerned, they were free to remove him from the country.

An order came down that same afternoon from J. Scott Blackman, the INS eastern regional director.

Following instructions from Washington, Blackman declared that Arar was not to be sent to Zurich that day, as had been planned, and his original "withdrawal of application" was canceled. Instead, he said, Arar should be told that he could withdraw his application only if he agreed to be sent to Syria.

Two INS agents met with Arar to present him with the new conditions. "We want you to voluntarily go back to Syria," one of the men said.

Back to Syria? He hadn't lived there for eighteen years, since he was a teenager.

"No way," Arar replied. "Send me to Canada, where I was going."

The agent looked angry. "You are a special interest, okay?" he snapped.

Arar didn't understand. A special interest to *whom*? A boss? Another country? It didn't matter—he would not willingly go to Syria.

"Send me back to Switzerland or Tunisia," he said.

That wasn't an option. "If you don't agree to return to Syria," one agent said, "you will be charged as a terrorist."

The agents left the room. At about eight that night, Arar was chained up again, placed in a van, and driven to the Metropolitan Detention Center in Brooklyn. He was strip-searched and dressed in an orange jumpsuit. Maher Arar, Canadian entrepreneur, was now inmate number 61339053.

• • •

Still no word from her husband. After more fitful sleep, Monia Mazigh decided to stop waiting and take some action.

She telephoned the Canadian embassy in Tunis and reached a woman named Thérèse Laatar. After answering a few initial questions about where she lived in Canada and where she was staying in Tunisia, Mazigh told her story.

"My husband, a Canadian citizen, has not contacted me since leaving Tunisia two days ago," she said. "He was scheduled to arrive in Montreal, but didn't."

There was a long silence. Mazigh assumed that Laatar either was taking notes or didn't understand the situation. When she spoke, her tone was almost dismissive. She would contact the Consular Section in Ottawa, she promised.

"I'll call you back on Monday," Laatar said. Three days later.

Not good enough. Mazigh placed another call, this time to the office of Michael Edelson, the lawyer Arar had consulted when Mounties had sought to interview him months before. She explained the situation again. Edelson promised to call the Crown Prosecutor's Office to find out if they knew what had happened to her husband.

Mazigh hung up. Nothing she had tried was working.

In Damascus on the evening of September 30, Abdullah Almalki was brought upstairs from his cell at Far' Falastin prison. His tormentors were waiting.

The head of interrogation, George Salloum, handled the questioning. "I want you to list everyone you know by the name of Maher," he said.

Almalki tossed out a few names, then mentioned Maher Arar. Salloum's eyes lit up.

"That is the one!" he said.

They needed to hear what Almalki knew about Arar, Salloum said. Almalki was handed some paper and a pencil, and ordered to write it all down.

Salloum glared at him, the wisp of a smile on his face.

"Arar is detained now somewhere, and we are going to question him," he said. "If his story is different than your story, I will torture you myself."

Joseph Witsch was troubled.

An instructor in the military's SERE program, Witsch had been part of a team dispatched to Fort Bragg to conduct training sessions on aggressive tactics for questioning detainees—a task they weren't qualified to carry out and that, in any case, was worse than pointless.

SERE training was about learning to resist harsh tactics, not about effective interrogation. Sure, harsh tactics might force detainees to talk—but they couldn't make them tell the truth. Using these methods in Guantanamo was going to produce information that was unreliable and misleading, Witsch thought. He wrote a report to Chris Wirts, senior civilian in the Joint Personnel Recovery Agency, urging caution.

On October 1, he sent a more strongly worded follow-up memo to Wirts. The handling of the detainees, he wrote, "is a screwed up mess and everyone is scrambling to unscrew the mess."

The only way they could make a contribution, Witsch wrote, would be to consult with high-level officials in the government, and not spend time with lower-level personnel who would then have to teach their own bosses how to properly use the information about SERE.

The bottom line—everyone involved in SERE needed to get away from training Guantanamo interrogators. Eventually, the whole effort was going to blow up.

"We don't have an established track record in this type of activity and we would present an easy target for someone to point at as the problem," Witsch wrote. "The stakes are much higher for this than what you and I have done in any activity before."

Prison guards at the Metropolitan Correction Center in Brooklyn accompanied Maher Arar to a telephone that same afternoon. He had been held for five days and had not been allowed to contact anyone; he was certain that his family was in near hysterics. He needed to calm them—and get their help.

A guard unchained Arar.

"You have two minutes," the guard said.

Two minutes. Not enough time to reach his wife in Tunis. Or a lawyer. Or anyone in the Canadian government. The best choice was his mother-in-law in Canada.

The call connected and she answered. Arar quickly told her that he was being held in a Brooklyn prison and gave her a short summary of what had happened.

"I'm not being treated well," he said. "And I'm scared, because they're talking about sending me to Syria. I need a lawyer. Somebody needs to help me."

The guard interrupted. "Time's up."

• • •

Arar's mother-in-law immediately telephoned her daughter in Tunis. "Maher just called," she said. "He's being held in the United States."

The words echoed with malevolent force through Mazigh's head. "What did he say?" she asked.

"He wants a lawyer. He's afraid he'll be sent back to Syria. That's all he told me."

"Didn't he tell you why he's in prison, what he's charged with?" Mazigh asked.

A sigh. "No. No, he hung up right after that."

The next morning in London, an official with Britain's diplomatic service finished editing a travel advisory warning of a heightened danger in Indonesia. The information had been received days before from M15, but the e-mail hadn't been ready to send until now.

Much of the advisory was filled with routine language that had appeared in official warnings for months. No key points were highlighted; the text was paragraph after paragraph of mind-numbing bureaucratese. The new information was slipped in almost haphazardly, worded in the same cumbersome language.

In the run up to the fasting month which starts around 5 November, activists are more likely to show their disapproval of many of the bars and nightclubs which are popular with Indonesians and foreigners, especially on Friday nights. British citizens should avoid these establishments.

Terrorists had become *activists*. *Attack* had become the more delicate *show their disapproval*. *Ramadan* had become *the fasting month*. And neither *Islamic* nor *Muslim*—words that would have leaped out at any reader who waded through the familiar verbiage—appeared at all. Someone had couched the alert in terms so benign that they seemed almost designed *not* to sound an alarm.

The next afternoon at 1:40, military and intelligence officials met at Guantanamo to again discuss how to break detainees during interrogations. They began with a review of tactics used on soldiers in the SERE program.

"Harsh techniques used on our service members have worked and will work on some detainees," said Lieutenant Colonel Jerald Phifer, the director of intelligence at Guantanamo. "What about those?"

"Force is risky," replied Major John Leso, an army psychologist.

Just being in this room, having this conversation, filled Leso with anguish. Young, slender, and earnest, he had been delighted when he was deployed to Guantanamo, assuming that he would be providing counseling to soldiers. But after he arrived, Leso was ordered to teach interrogators psychological tactics that might force detainees to talk. The assignment threw him—Leso knew nothing about interrogations. Since then, he had witnessed harsh questioning—involving sexual humiliation, stress positions, and the use of dogs—and the experience had left him distressed. Now he was sitting at a table, listening as plans were hatched for even more abusive methods. His dedication to helping people had been twisted into an ugly quest to hurt them.

Leso stayed mostly silent as the group reveled over the success of aggressive interrogation in breaking the resistance of al-Qahtani, the suspected twentieth hijacker. Their self-congratulations were misplaced—al-Qahtani had said nothing that he hadn't already told the FBI before the military took over the questioning. None of the intelligence interrogators had so much as glanced at the FBI agents' notes of their interviews with al-Qahtani and so never knew that he was simply repeating himself. And there was no one at the meeting to stress that point—the criminal interrogators had not been invited to attend.

The camp needed to be shaken up, one of the participants said, by creating an environment of controlled chaos. But they would have to be careful—the International Committee of the Red Cross was occasionally checking to see if detainees were being treated in accordance with international standards.

Dave Becker from the Defense Intelligence Agency said that there were already plenty of reports being issued by the ICRC about the use of sleep deprivation against detainees held at Bagram Air Base.

"True," said Lieutenant Colonel Diane Beaver, the top legal advisor to the military's interrogation unit at Guantanamo. "But officially, it's not happening. It is not being reported."

Beaver then repeated that ICRC inspections at Guantanamo were a serious concern. "They will be in and out, scrutinizing our operations, unless they are displeased and decide to protest and leave," she said. "That would draw a lot of negative attention."

A CIA lawyer, John Fredman, mentioned that the Office of Legal Counsel at the Justice Department had offered a lot of guidance on the issue of rough tactics. As for the ICRC, the Department of Defense had already found ways to work around any problems.

"In the past when the ICRC made a big deal about certain detainees, DOD just moved them away," he said. "Then when the ICRC asked about their whereabouts, the DOD's response has been that the detainees merit no status under the Geneva Conventions."

There were other laws protecting detainees, of course, but based on the Justice Department analysis, those weren't matters of much concern.

"Under the Torture Convention, torture has been prohibited by international law, but the language of the statutes is written vaguely," Fredman said. "Severe mental and physical pain is prohibited. But the mental part is explained as poorly as the physical part."

Fredman then recited the definitions for "severe pain" that had been cobbled together by the Office of Legal Counsel based on interpretations of health care laws. For an action to count as physical torture, he said, it had to cause permanent damage to major organs or body parts. Mental torture had to meet similarly high standards—the tactics were illegal only if they led to permanent and profound damage to the senses and the personality.

"It basically is a matter of perception," he said. "If the detainee dies, you're doing it wrong."

That same day in Damascus, Abdullah Almalki was lying in his prison cell, aching and exhausted. He had been interrogated about Arar for two days, but hadn't given Salloum the answers he wanted. So, they hurt him.

Almalki wasn't sure how much more of this he could take. The beatings, whippings, and other forms of torture had left him in constant pain. Even on those days when he wasn't tortured, he endured horrors. When he tried to sleep, large rats came into his cell and crawled over his legs. Cats urinated on him from a grating in the ceiling. Lice covered his body. He had lost fifty pounds, and his ribs stuck out of his chest. The skin on the top of his mouth was almost gone from his screaming.

Despite everything that had been inflicted on him, Almalki hadn't been crippled or emotionally incapacitated. His tormentors had been careful not to kill him or leave him in catatonic despair; they wanted him talking, not dead or incapable of speech. And so, they followed only the most time-tested torture techniques, making sure to avoid inflicting long-term damage to Almalki's major organs and body parts or causing permanent and profound harm to his senses and personality. If they knew about the classified standards being used by the Americans to define torture, the Syrians could reasonably argue that they were in compliance.

• • •

Almalki was brought upstairs a few hours later for more interrogation about Arar. Salloum again handled the questioning. For him to be involved day after day signaled that, whatever was going on with Arar, the Syrians considered it important.

"I want to know if Arar has been to Pakistan or Afghanistan," Salloum said.

Almalki feebly shook his head. "No, not that I know of."

Salloum kept rephrasing the question, but Almalki's answer never changed.

"I want you to say that Arar is with al-Qaeda!" Salloum snapped.

"I don't know anyone with al-Qaeda."

"You're lying!"

"I don't know anyone with al-Qaeda," Almalki repeated, sounding weak.

Salloum turned to one of the other interrogators.

"Send a report about these questions to headquarters, so they can be faxed by noon," he said.

Faxed where? Almalki thought. Someone in Damascus? Canada? The United States? Who was involved in this?

Salloum turned back to Almalki.

"Arar will be here soon," he said. "And if I find out you've lied, I'm going to put you in a barrel of human excrement, and cut your food rations, and torture you until you're paralyzed."

Almalki's chest clutched in fear. "I've told you everything I know!" he cried. "If you want more, give me a blank paper and I'll sign it. You can fill it in yourself."

Salloum stared at Almalki in silence. He turned to leave the room, glancing at another interrogator on his way out the door.

"Torture him," Salloum said. "And be ruthless."

Maher Arar couldn't stop sobbing.

He was in a cell-like room at the Brooklyn prison, sitting at a table across from Maureen Girvan, the Canadian consul in New York. It was October 3, Arar's eighth day in detention and his first chance to speak with a government official from his home country.

He described to Girvan what had happened to him since his arrival in New York. He told her of being chained and unfed, of his captors' refusal to allow him to contact a lawyer. The Americans wouldn't even let him have a toothbrush. At one point, he said, he was taken to a doctor and given a shot, but no one would tell him what it was.

They had, however, finally given him papers with the allegations against him—that he was inadmissible to the United States because he was a member of al-Qaeda. He showed Girvan the documents.

"This is insane!" he cried. "I'm innocent!"

He was not an enemy of America. He had always admired the United States, he said, and had never experienced trouble in the country before.

"I'm very scared," he said. "They're talking about sending me to Syria."

The meeting ended. Girvan returned to her office and prepared a case note for her superiors in Ottawa. It consisted of eleven words.

"Mr. Arar is alleged to be a member of al Qaeda."

Girvan spoke with Arar's wife about an hour later, describing her visit to the prison. "He was disoriented, he cried a lot and wanted to know how you all were," she said.

The description of her husband's anguish tore at Mazigh. "Have the Americans given a reason for his arrest?" she asked.

"He showed me a sheet of paper saying that they were denying him entry to the United States because he belongs to the terrorist group, al-Qaeda."

Al-Qaeda!

"But he's innocent!" Mazigh cried. "Maher doesn't belong to al-Qaeda or any terrorist group."

There was a long silence.

The Americans had made their decision, Girvan finally said. Arar needed to get a lawyer as fast as possible.

Later that day, the CIA sent a fax to Corporal Rick Flewelling, an officer with the Mounties who monitored AO Canada. The intelligence agency was seeking any information the Canadians might have that could be used by the Americans to charge Arar with a crime and keep him locked up. Flewelling assigned some officers to see if they could pull something together.

The call wasn't memorable, just a two-minute chat that sealed Maher Arar's fate.

Richard Armitage, the deputy secretary of state, was in his office when a secretary told him Larry Thompson, Ashcroft's deputy, was on the line.

"We've got a man named Maher Arar detained up in New York," Thompson said. "He's a member of al-Qaeda, and he has dual citizenship, Canadian and Syrian. We want to send him to Syria, but wanted to check whether State had any foreign policy objections."

"He's not an American citizen?" Armitage asked.

"No, just Syrian and Canadian."

This didn't strike Armitage as a hard issue. Syria had been secretly aiding the Bush administration in the fight against al-Qaeda. Relations between the two countries were improving. There was no reason to think that Syria would object to taking one of its own citizens, even if he had ties to terrorism.

"Okay," he said. "There's no problem. We don't have any objections."

Green light.

"Resist!" the detainee yelled in Arabic. "Resist with all your might!"

The military police inside an interrogation booth at Camp Delta in Guantanamo screamed at the detainee to shut up. But the man just ignored them, and continued calling out to his fellow prisoners. Finally, the chief of the detention center's Interrogation Control Element came out of his office to find out who was causing the ruckus. He arrived at the booth and looked inside. The detainee was still screaming, but the interrogator, the translator, and some guards were frozen in place, unsure of what to do.

"Keep that detainee quiet!" the chief shouted.

A moment passed. "I have some duct tape," one of the MPs said.

After consulting with a superior, the chief told the soldiers to go ahead and tape the detainee's mouth shut.

Down the hall, two supervisory special agents from the FBI's Behavioral Analysis Unit were watching agents question another detainee. The head of military interrogations walked into the observation room and signaled to them.

"Hey, come here," the officer said. "I want to show you something funny."

The agents followed him to another observation area, which was packed with military personnel watching events unfolding in an interrogation room.

A detainee was inside, handcuffed and chained to the floor. Two bands of duct tape wrapped his head, covering his eyes and his mouth. The man had a beard and a full head of hair; when the duct tape was eventually ripped off, it would tear hair from his flesh. Four Americans were in the room—two interrogators and two guards. One interrogator was yelling at the detainee. The scene both perplexed and disturbed the FBI agents. How, they wondered, could the man answer questions with his mouth taped shut?

"Was he spitting on someone?" an agent asked.

"No," the officer replied. "He just wouldn't stop chanting the Koran."

"How do you plan to take the tape off without hurting him?"

The officer just laughed, saying nothing.

The agents left the room and contacted the FBI's Office of Special Counsel to report that they might have just witnessed a crime.

Ben Bonk was sitting in his office at the CIA, his heart sinking as he read a new National Intelligence Estimate about Iraq.

What happened? For weeks, Bonk had spent most of his time hunkering down with his staff to produce a lengthy analysis shooting down the administration's contention that Iraq was working with al-Qaeda. But now it felt as if there had been a switch-up—al-Qaeda was almost irrelevant in the Iraq debate; it was all "weapons of mass destruction." Bonk hadn't even considered the issue worth discussing. There was analysis dating back years that demonstrated Saddam had no such arsenal. Yet even though it was his group that handled Iraq, it hadn't been asked for input on the National Intelligence Estimate.

Was Bush even getting all of the intelligence? And was the Pentagon burying its own findings? The Defense Intelligence Agency had *just* issued an analysis that had made its way up the line to Rumsfeld. Bonk had reviewed it—the report showed that no one knew a damned thing. Every piece of information they knew about Iraq's weapons was, at best, hazy.

The Pentagon report acknowledged that 90 percent of the intelligence on Iraq's nuclear capabilities was imprecise; that the existence of biological facilities could not be proved and the supposed "mobile weapons labs" could not be found; that the presence of sites to produce chemical agents for weapons could not be confirmed; and that there was no proof that Iraq had *any* facilities to produce chemical devices. This was the best that the saber rattlers at the Pentagon could do?

Then came this CIA report, roaring with certitudes that put the Pentagon's timid findings to shame. The agency's analysts stated they had "high confidence" that Iraq was continuing and even expanding its chemical, biological, nuclear, and missile programs; that it possessed chemical and biological missiles; and that it could make a nuclear weapon in a matter of months once it obtained weapons-grade fissionable material.

Weighing the two reports against each other was dizzying. The CIA had no doubt that the weapons were there, while the Pentagon was unsure whether the capacity to make them even existed. It was as if the intelligence analysts were saying that they were confident that Saddam's wife was ready to give birth, but remained uncertain if she was pregnant.

Bonk finished reading, then walked down the hall to confront one of the agency's senior people who had been involved in preparing the intelligence estimate.

"How did we get to this point?" Bonk asked. "What are we saying here? This isn't even what we said four months ago."

His colleague fumbled for an answer, but all he could do was mutter some vague generalities. Bonk walked away in near despair. Maybe he could have stopped this if he had seen it coming. It just seemed so obvious to him that Saddam's arsenal was an illusion. He never anticipated that anyone would conclude this imaginary threat was real.

After twenty-four hours of hunting, Canadian police had come up dry in their search for information to give the CIA. There wasn't a lot of evidence that could be used to keep Arar locked up.

At 6:10 P.M. on Saturday, October 5, an FBI official called the home of Corporal Rick Flewelling, the RCMP official who was coordinating the search. He told the American that his force hadn't found anything that could definitively tie Arar to al-Qaeda.

"Well," the FBI official replied, "Washington's afraid that we don't have enough evidence to charge Arar with anything."

If neither country could conjure up an irrefutable link to the terrorist group, couldn't the Canadians come up with *something* to indict him with so that Arar could be locked up or barred from returning home? the FBI agent asked. The bosses in Washington wouldn't be happy if the guy was allowed to wander around Canada at will.

There wasn't much he could do, Flewelling said. They couldn't imprison Arar without evidence.

"And since he's a Canadian citizen, he would have to be readmitted to Canada," Flewelling said.

The call ended without a resolution of their conundrum and with both men befuddled by the difficulty of nailing down Arar's terrorist leanings. Neither considered the obvious explanation—the evidence didn't exist because Arar was an innocent man.

About an hour later, Arar was taken from his cell to a visiting area at the prison. A woman who appeared to be Moroccan was waiting for him on the other side of a wall of glass. He picked up a handset so they could speak.

"My name is Amal Oummih, and I'm an immigration lawyer," she said. "I've been speaking with your family, but I haven't been formally retained yet."

Arar started crying again. "They want to send me to Syria!"

"You need to calm down. You will be allowed to choose where you want to go, and there will be a hearing where you can argue your case. You don't need to be worried about this."

Arar didn't believe her. The Americans had made no secret of the fact that they wanted to ship him to Syria.

"Please," he begged. "Please do everything you can."

The meeting lasted about an hour and a half. Before she left, Oummih again told Arar not to worry. This would all be straightened out.

As Arar was meeting with Oummih, INS headquarters contacted asylum officers in New York with instructions to interview Arar the following day. It was standard procedure for a foreigner like Arar who was being forcibly removed to a country where he thought he would be tortured. Arar couldn't just declare that he was scared; he had to provide specific evidence to support his fear.

But Arar would be hard-pressed to produce any grounds by himself. He had been locked up for days. Only his lawyer could gather the proof.

Twenty-four hours later, after 4:30 on a Sunday, an e-mail arrived at the INS Command Center in Washington. A lawyer for the service instructed officials at the center to contact Arar's lawyers immediately. They needed to be informed that an asylum hearing would be held for their client in four hours.

A call was placed to Oummih's office about five; unsurprisingly, she was not there late on a Sunday afternoon. The INS official left a voice-mail message. A second call reached a Canadian lawyer who had worked with Arar, but he pointed out there was no way he could get to New York in four hours. If the hearing were rearranged for the next day, the lawyer said, he could attend.

The INS official refused. The hearing would go forward as scheduled.

• • •

Guards unlocked Arar's cell just before nine o'clock that night. "Your lawyer is here to see you," a guard told him.

The timing seemed odd—Oummih was visiting on Sunday night?—but Arar was relieved to hear the news. He was escorted to a room where a group of asylum officers waited. Arar didn't recognize them. Oummih was not there.

"Where is my lawyer?" Arar asked.

One of the asylum officers responded. "We called, but he refused to come."

What? Were they lying? Oummih was a woman; why did they say "he"? He didn't imagine they were talking about a lawyer from another country.

The asylum officials instructed Arar to sit down, and the questioning began.

"Why are you opposed to being sent to Syria?"

"I'll be tortured there," Arar replied. "I don't want to go to Syria. Send me to Canada or Switzerland or Tunisia. Don't send me to Syria."

"Why do you think you'll be tortured?"

Arar thought for a moment. "I haven't performed my mandatory military service. They'll arrest me."

"But why would they torture you for that?"

A pause. "Please, don't send me to Syria," Arar pleaded.

"So, is the question about military service the only reason you're frightened?"

"Please, don't send me to Syria. Send me to my family. Please don't do this."

The asylum officer leaned forward, his elbows on the table. "Mr. Arar, if you don't want to go to Syria, you have to explain why you believe you'll be persecuted there."

Arar rubbed his hands over his face, then stared at the asylum officer.

"I'll be persecuted because I'm a Sunni Muslim."

"All right. Why do you think that?"

Arar teared up. "I don't know. But they'll persecute me for that."

No one was persuaded by his claim; he was acting out of desperation. Sunni Muslims were the largest religious group in Syria.

"I'm not a member of a terrorist organization!" Arar blurted out.

"We're not here to discuss that, Mr. Arar. The purpose of this is to find out if you have a reasonable basis for believing you would be tortured in Syria. Is there anything else that makes you afraid?"

Arar didn't answer. He didn't know what to say.

"Mr. Arar, you need to tell us if there is any other reason you have for being afraid that you will be persecuted."

Arar covered his eyes with one hand. "I don't know," he mumbled.

"It's important that you explain your reasons, Mr. Arar. We need to understand why you believe this."

Silence. Arar stared at the ground, looking broken. He couldn't think of anything to say.

Throughout the meeting, the asylum officers repeatedly left the room to brief senior officials at INS headquarters in Washington about the questions and Arar's answers. They were fed suggestions for follow-ups.

After five and a half hours, the interview ended. Arar was handed a typed statement summarizing the discussion and was told to sign it. He refused.

The asylum officers reached their decision. There was no reason that Maher Arar could not be sent to Syria. He had no reasonable basis to believe that he would be tortured.

If Arar had been given sixty seconds to do an Internet search, he could have called up all the evidence he needed to prove his fears were justified. It was posted on United States government Web sites, in the Syria section of the State Department's annual report on human rights practices worldwide. Syria tortured prisoners, the report said. Those suspected of ties to terrorism—like Arar—were frequently subjected to the most abusive treatment.

The methods of torture, the report said, included administering electrical shocks; pulling out fingernails; forcing objects into the rectum; beatings, sometimes while the victim was suspended from a ceiling; hyperextending the spine; and using a chair that bends backward to fracture the detainee's spine.

In his prison cell, though, Arar had no access to the report. And the INS pretended that it didn't exist.

A sixteen-year-old boy was escorted into an interrogation room at Bagram Air Base, where an FBI agent was waiting to question him. The teenager was Omar Khadr, a Canadian citizen born in Pakistan. He had been captured in July by American forces in Afghanistan and accused of killing a soldier with a grenade, and since then he had been questioned about the Taliban and al-Qaeda.

It was October 7. The agent, Robert Fuller, had come with a photograph to show Khadr, in hopes the boy could confirm that the man in the picture was tied to al-Qaeda. Fuller showed Khadr the photo.

"Do you recognize this man?" the agent asked.

Khadr stared at the picture. "I'm not sure."

"Okay," Fuller said. "Let me give you a couple of minutes to think about it."

After a short break, Fuller showed Khadr the photograph again. This time, the teenager admitted that, in September or October 2001, he had seen the man at a Kabul safe house run by Abu Musab al-Suri, an al-Qaeda operative.

Done. That was the proof that Washington had been so diligently seeking. Khadr had identified Maher Arar as having ties to al-Qaeda.

The information was transmitted to Washington. Justice Department officials met in their command center to discuss the breakthrough. There was no question now; Arar, they decided, could not be sent to Canada. Since he could not be arrested there, he might sneak back across the border and launch some attack.

The best place to ship Arar, they decided, was Syria.

Khadr had lied. He had never seen Arar in Afghanistan. Later, he would say that he had told Fuller only what he thought the agent wanted to hear.

Once again, the sloppiness of the investigation went undetected. No one checked the records that could prove that Khadr's statements were at odds with reality. And those documents were already in the hands of the FBI and the Mounties.

Arar could not have been in Kabul during either September or October 2001. Through their investigation, FBI agents had already shown—incontrovertibly—that Arar was in California during September. As for October, the evidence of Khadr's lies was even stronger. For it was on October 12 that Arar had met with Almalki at Mango's Café. Several surveillance teams had watched as they lunched. Afterward, Arar's movements were monitored. He was, the Canadian investigation established, in Ottawa.

And now the American investigation had established that, at about the same time, he was also in Kabul.

At 4:00 A.M. the next day, Arar's twelfth day in limbo, a group of men arrived at his cell and woke him up.

"You're leaving," one of the guards said.

Arar struggled to stand. "Where am I being sent?" he asked.

"Let's get going, come on."

After a strip search, he was handcuffed, shackled, and taken to an office. A woman stood in front of him, holding a sheaf of papers. She read the first page, saying this was the decision of Blackman, the eastern regional director.

"I have concluded on the basis of classified information that Arar is unequivocally inadmissible to the United States," the woman read, quoting Blackman, "in that he is a member of an organization that has been designated by the Secretary of State as a Foreign Terrorist Organization, to wit: al Qaeda."

Arar shook his head. "No," he pleaded. "No . . ."

He would be removed to Syria, the woman read. The INS commissioner had determined that shipping him to Damascus was consistent with the international Convention Against Torture, she said. There was no reason to believe that Arar would be persecuted there.

Arar grew hysterical. "Please, please don't do this to me," he begged. "Please . . . I'll be tortured. They'll torture me. Don't do this."

Everyone in the room ignored him. Instead, they ordered him to change out of his orange prison suit into a brown one. Then he was hustled out to a government car and driven to Teterboro Airport in New Jersey.

Waiting there was a Gulfstream III. Arar was removed from the car and brought up the steps into the plane. It took off at 5:40 A.M.

Arar never saw the evidence against him that was cited in the removal order from Blackman. The classified information was nothing more than the statements from El-Maati and Almalki that had been extracted by torture, and Omar Khadr's false identification of Arar.

Other pages included the unclassified reasons the government concluded he was with al-Qaeda. Arar was friendly with both Almalki and El-Maati, the document said. Another reason for suspicion, it said, was that Almalki exported radios overseas, and one of his customers was the Pakistani military—both an incorrect and a bizarre assertion. His customer was another company that in turn sold equipment to the Pakistanis. And the Pakistanis were being celebrated as an ally in the fight against al-Qaeda. How could selling radios that ended up in the hands of a military ally be suggestive of wrongdoing?

Arar had held three business meetings with Almalki, the document said. Blackman cited one lunch that took place at a restaurant as particularly suspicious, since Arar had been seen walking in the rain with Almalki.

The false weather report, with its illogical connection to terrorism, helped drive the decision to ship Arar to Syria.

• • •

The Gulfstream III landed in Amman, Jordan, at about two on the morning of October 9. While the Syrians were willing to hold Arar, they would not take him directly. Their cooperation with the United States—ostensibly an enemy— had to remain a secret.

Arar was handed over to Jordanian officials. They blindfolded him, chained him with new shackles, and loaded him into a van.

"Put your head down," one of the Jordanians said.

Arar complied. Then the men started beating him on his face and head.

Through a grating above his cell, Abdullah Almalki detected the sounds of a new arrival. The guards searched the man's bags, asking him to identify various items.

"That's Swiss chocolate," Almalki heard the man say. He recognized the voice. Maher Arar had arrived at Far' Falastin.

Almalki listened as Arar asked the same questions he had posed on his first day in this hell. Where was the bed? Where was the pillow? Still so naive.

It wouldn't be long, Almalki knew, before he would hear Arar's screams.

13

The first snow of the Russian winter dusted the tree-shrouded hunting lodge at the Zavidovo nature preserve. As a motorcade approached, Vladimir Putin and his wife, Ludmilla, stepped outside onto a porch to greet their visitors.

The caravan stopped. Tony and Cherie Blair emerged from a limousine and walked toward the Putins. As flashbulbs popped, there were handshakes and airy kisses. The Russian president gestured toward a flag hoisted above the building.

"I made it a point to meet you under the Russian flag," he said in practiced English.

The Putins escorted the Blairs inside for a tour of the house, then settled in an elegant drawing room beside an unlit, ornate fireplace. A group of reporters appeared at the doorway. One of them asked the prime minister what he thought of Zavidovo.

Breathtaking, he said, and a wonderful place to meet. "I'm looking forward to my talks with President Putin," Blair said.

The prime minister had traveled to Russia on this day, October 11, hoping to persuade Putin to support a new U.N. resolution on Iraq. Both Blair and Bush had been lobbying members of the Security Council all week; in a phone call two days earlier, Bush had urged Jacques Chirac, the French president, to support a single declaration threatening Saddam with severe consequences if he failed to comply. But Chirac was wary; he told Bush that he preferred a two-tiered approach, with weapons inspectors returning to Iraq and leaving the question of military force until later. It was the same position that Blair had advanced to the president privately, without success.

Bush had ceded responsibility for winning over the Russian president to

Blair, with good reason—the prime minister had cultivated a strong rapport with Putin, while relations between Russia and America remained frosty at best. If Blair could convince Putin that the U.N. resolution was just as important to the British government as it was to the Bush administration, he thought, it would go a long way toward winning him over.

To sway Putin to their cause, both London and Washington had assembled their evidence of Saddam's malfeasance, delivering separate unclassified intelligence reports in the days leading up to the Zavidovo summit. What Blair didn't know as the two men prepared to square off was the futility of the mission— Putin had already privately brushed off the "Dossier" from Britain and the "National Intelligence Estimate" from the United States as rehashes of old information that he had previously scorned as inadequate.

The wives headed out of the sitting room, leaving Blair on a couch with Putin across from him in an armchair. Two interpreters stood by while the Russian president continued flaunting his growing proficiency in English with small talk; his fluency wasn't up to the subtleties of diplomatic discourse.

In short order, Putin laid out his main message—he wasn't happy. Almost alone among the Russian leadership, he was dedicated to pursuing a pro-Western policy, he said, but the Bush administration seemed to have no appreciation for his willingness to go out on a limb.

"This is very important for the West," he said, "but I feel I am getting very little in return for this from the United States."

Blair nodded. "I think Bush gets it, but I'm not sure of some of the others," he said.

As the hours passed, Putin repeatedly returned to the same theme. His show of petulance filled Blair with frustration—from the first time he met Bush, Blair had urged the president to display a show of trust to Putin. Now, as he listened to Putin's carping, he realized his message had gone unheeded. The administration had misplayed its hand by failing to show proper deference to Putin, frittering away its influence over an important player in the war on terror.

"I understand," Blair said. "I'll talk to Bush about it."

Not enough. The United States was strong-arming the international community, Putin said, with no recognition of the challenges facing its allies.

"If there is something the Americans are worried about, they expect the whole world to share their concerns and drop everything," he said. "But if it is something that the rest of the world is interested in, like the Middle East peace process, they don't get the urgency."

His exasperation didn't end there. The hypocrisy of the Bush administration in wooing him to join *its* campaign against extremists, while at the same time impeding *his* crackdown on terrorists at Russia's gate, was a wonder to behold, he said.

"Suppose we act against Georgia, which is a base for terrorism against Russia," he said. "What would you say if we took Georgia out? Yet the Americans think they can do whatever they like to whomever they like."

This wasn't going well. The Americans' cavalier treatment of the proud and thin-skinned Russian leader had offended him deeply—and now they wanted him to jump on their bandwagon. Sure, it was Blair who was making the case for the Iraq policy, but Putin knew that the White House had formulated it.

"I understand," Blair repeated. "I appreciate your importance and the importance of Russia in these endeavors, and I know President Bush does as well. I'm sorry if this hasn't been communicated well. Both the British and American governments recognize that Russia must be part of any Iraq policy. We want your thoughts. Again, I will contact President Bush to discuss this, but I know his respect for you and for Russia is the same as mine."

Putin nodded, his expression inscrutable.

Blair discussed the steps under way to formulate a U.N. resolution, adding that, of course, Russian input was indispensable. But time was running out. The dossier sent to Putin only days before made clear the situation's urgency, he said.

Impassively, Putin sat back in his chair. "I saw nothing there to support the claims that Saddam Hussein possesses weapons of mass destruction," he said coolly. "The information from the CIA was not any better."

Blair went white. He *should* have been told this was coming. His staff had failed miserably on this one.

"We believe there is important data there," Blair said. "At the very least, it raises significant concerns about Saddam's designs. It is essential that we make sure about his weapons. That's why we need the inspectors to go back into Iraq."

"I agree," Putin said. "But I do not see the need for a fresh resolution. The U.N. has already made its demands on Iraq. We just have to make sure that the will of the U.N. is respected."

Before Blair could respond, Putin signaled the possibility of compromise. "That does not mean I am ruling out supporting a new resolution in the future," he said.

Still, why was Iraq all-important? Putin asked. Islamic extremists were the real danger. The flood of that intelligence had not let up; there were threats in Indonesia, Britain, Spain, the United States, and of course, in Russia. Terrorists linked to al-Qaeda were everywhere. Why was Bush squandering time and resources going after Saddam Hussein?

"Do you really think that Iraq is more dangerous than this fundamentalism?" Putin asked.

Blair shook his head. "Course not."

That same day in Denpasar, Indonesia, three Muslim extremists scooped a granulated explosive into twelve plastic filing cabinets. After months of planning, the men and their coconspirators—all members of the Southeast Asian terror group Jemaah Islamiyah—were working on the final stages of what would prove to be the deadliest terrorist attack since 9/11.

The targets were two Bali nightspots frequented by American and Australian tourists—Paddy's Irish Pub and the Sari Club. They had been selected as part of a strategy formulated earlier that year with a senior al-Qaeda operative known as Hambali—rather than striking at well-protected buildings like embassies, they would attack "soft targets" like bars and discos. The first step in the plan took place in August, when two of the extremists robbed a Serang jewelry store. The stolen loot, combined with $30,000 provided by al-Qaeda, was used for safe houses, vehicles, and chemicals for bombs.

After several days of stirring together the chemicals—potassium chlorate, aluminum powder, and sulfur—the lethal mixture was ready for the filing cabinets. Once the containers were full, the conspirators roped them together with 490 feet of explosive cord and inserted 94 RDX electric detonators. A drawer of TNT was added to serve as a kicker for the explosion.

The next afternoon, Ali Imron, a Jemaah Islamiyah terrorist, pulled his green Suzuki Vitara to the front of the Hotel Harum. Waiting for him outside were two young men barely out of their teens, known by the aliases Iqbal and Jimi. They climbed in and Imron drove away, heading to the Denpasar safe house on Pulau Menjangan Street. There, over the next few hours, his passengers would be taught how to blow themselves up.

The sons of rice farmers, Iqbal and Jimi were achingly poor and uneducated men who had grown up in tiny wooden huts with no electricity and no running water. They had few possessions and little hope for a better future. But they found solace in Islam and, like many young men in their town of Malimping, had been swept up by the calls to jihad. Imam Samudra, one of the Jemaah Islamiyah plotters, promised that they could trade their earthly misery for the joys of paradise if they martyred themselves by murdering unbelievers. The two young men excitedly told Samudra that they had both dreamed of having visited Afghanistan and embraced bin Laden, who asked them if they wanted to die as martyrs. Their tale left Samudra with no doubt. These devotees of the faith were meant to be the suicide bombers for the Bali attack.

The plan required two vehicles, and both were parked at the Menjangan safe house—a white 1983 Mitsubishi L300 van and a Yamaha FZ1R motorcycle. All but the van's front seat had been stripped out, making room for the filing cabinets jammed with explosives. To ensure that the van could not be linked to them, the terrorists had ground down the vehicle identification numbers—commonly known as VIN numbers—stamped onto the chassis and the engine.

The motorcycle had been purchased the day before to transport a much smaller bomb that would be detonated on a street beside the American consulate. That explosive wasn't expected to kill anyone; instead, it was meant as a message to the United States that its policies were responsible for the carnage at the nightclubs.

Imron brought Iqbal and Jimi inside to explain the plans for that night. They would drive the van to Kuta, the nightlife capital of Bali, then park outside of the Suri Club. Jimi would remain in the vehicle, and Iqbal—wearing a six-pocketed vest filled with TNT—would walk into Paddy's and blow himself up. Survivors were sure to run for the exits while the revelers across the street at Suri would be lured outside by the commotion. Then Jimi would detonate the van; the large bomb would tear apart partiers on the street and—hopefully—destroy both nightclubs, murdering everyone inside.

Jimi and Iqbal were thrilled. To be martyred in such an attack was an honor, one that they prayed would be a call to arms for all Muslims.

The motorcycle headlight illuminated small trees that lined a curb on Hayam Wuruk Street in Denpasar. Ali Imron rode with one hand on the handlebars and the other clutching a plastic bag containing TNT, a Nokia 5110 mobile phone, and human excrement.

As Imron approached the American consulate, he flipped a "kill" switch he had installed the previous day on the Yamaha motorcycle. The engine sputtered and died, just as he had planned. He leaned toward the curb, pretending to fiddle with a stubborn motor, and tossed the plastic bag onto the adjacent foot-path. It looked like any other unremarkable piece of roadside trash.

Pulling himself back up, he hit the switch again and revved the engine. He drove off, back to the safe house where the Mitsubishi van was ready to deliver its deadly cargo.

That night, Blaine Pecaut lay down and slid on a pair of headphones. The young American had just finished washing up in his room at the Cempaka Hotel Kuta and was taking a moment to relax after a full day of surfing. Ear-lier, he had eaten dinner with two friends and three British surfers they had just met—Marc Gajardo, Hannabeth Luke, and Melanie Cohen. Over their meal, the Britons suggested that they all go partying at the Sari Club nearby. While his two friends said they were too tired, Pecaut agreed to join the others.

But exhaustion caught up with him. He fell asleep and didn't wake up when his new acquaintances knocked on the door. Getting no answer, the group left without him and walked the five minutes to the nightclub.

The usual bumper-to-bumper traffic filled the one open lane on Legian Street in Kuta's buzzing central strip. A swirl of bright lights and pounding music punc-tuated the laughter of young tourists as they barhopped past vendors hawking knockoffs of high-end clothes.

At about eleven, the bomb-laden Mitsubishi van was driving down Raya Kuta Street and reached the Legian intersection. Ali Imron turned right onto the clogged street. The van moved slowly, weighed down by the one-ton bomb. Coming to a stop, Imron left the driver's seat and Jimi took the wheel. Behind them in the cargo area, Iqbal was slipping on the vest loaded with TNT.

Imron got out and glanced around, looking for a fellow conspirator named Joni Hendrawan, also known as Idris, who was supposed to have ridden the Yamaha motorcycle there. He spotted Idris at the side of the road, ran over, and jumped on the back of the bike. Then, as the two men roared off, Idris fumbled for his cell phone. He was preparing to call the Nokia 5110 mobile phone that was wired to the bomb lying on a curb near the American consulate.

Jimi stepped on the gas, nudging the van inch by inch down Legian Street. A taxi followed closely behind, ferrying a Japanese couple, Kosuke and Yuka Su-zuki. It was their honeymoon.

• • •

The rhythms of Eminem's "Without Me" pumped through speakers inside the Suri Club as lights flashed in sync with the music. The place was packed with more than three hundred people drinking, dancing, and shouting over the ruckus. At the bar, several members of the Kingsley Amateur Football Club from Perth were in high spirits on their first night of a vacation to celebrate a successful season.

One of the team members, Corey Paltridge, jumped onto the dance floor and launched into an air-guitar impression of Angus Young, the leader of the Australian rock group AC/DC. His friends laughed as other revelers backed away, giving the twenty-year-old room for his performance.

A few feet away, a teammate named Bradley McIlroy was sitting with three Swedish girls. One of them, who said her name was Joanne, seemed particularly interested in him, and McIlroy slid his arm around her.

Two friends from Melbourne, Shelley Campbell and Belinda Allen, had been in the Sari Club for only a few minutes before they heard that two professional soccer players from Australia—Michael Martyn and Jason McCartney—were across the street at Paddy's. Shelley knew Jason, and suggested to Belinda that they head over to say hi. The two women started to make their way out when Belinda stopped.

"I need to go to the toilet," she said.

Belinda moved through the crowds toward the ladies' room, and Shelley followed. They both went inside. Eminem's hip-hop song faded to an end and was replaced by the pop-disco rhythm of Cher's "Believe." Marc Gajardo, the thirty-year-old British surfer who had walked from the Cempaka Hotel with his girlfriend and another woman, made a face of mock disgust.

He leaned in to speak to his girlfriend, Hannabeth Luke. "I'm sorry," he said, "I really can't dance to this."

Marc headed for the door, grabbing a chance for some fresh air. Outside, a white Mitsubishi van pulled in front of him. The door opened and a man wearing a heavy vest stepped out, then crossed the street toward Paddy's.

Inside, Natalie Gould was standing at the bar, just a few feet away from her longtime friend Nicole McLean. The two had been in Bali for only four and a half hours, and Paddy's was their first stop of the evening.

Near the center of the room, the two members of Australia's professional football league, Michael Martyn and Jason McCartney, were nursing a couple of beers. They had been at the bar for fifteen minutes.

An Indonesian man wearing a vest made his way through the crowds, passing Michael and Jason. He thrust his hand into his pocket and flicked the switch.

A burst of current flowed through electrical wires in a nanosecond, simultaneously reaching multiple detonators. The impulse vaporized thin wire filaments inside the blasting caps, setting off an explosive charge. Each solid molecule of TNT was converted into fifteen molecules of hot gas and powdered carbon. The blast expanded at a velocity of more than twenty-nine thousand feet per second, creating a percussive wave that could tear apart everything in a sixty-foot radius.

The force of the explosion lifted Michael and Jason off the floor, then slammed both men into the ground. Natalie was knocked unconscious. Something—she would never know what—hit Nicole in the arm and sent her flying.

The lights went out amid pandemonium. Jason struggled to open his eyes, but couldn't. "I can't see!" he yelled. "I'm blind!"

He wasn't. His eyelashes had been welded together by the heat.

Nicole couldn't move one of her arms. She reached down to pick it up. It had been severed and was attached by only a flap of skin.

Nearby, Michael got to his feet and gaped at the bloodbath surrounding him.

A few people left the Sari Club to find out what had happened. Their view was blocked by the white van parked directly in front of the door in the drop-off area.

Inside the ladies' room, Shelley Campbell felt a vibration. The floor and walls shook. A woman beside her glanced around.

"What the fuck was that?" she yelled.

"Must have been an earthquake," Shelley replied.

Out in the bar, Bradley McIlroy still had his arm around Joanne when he heard what sounded like firecrackers. He looked through a window and saw the white van.

Fifteen seconds had passed.

Sitting at the wheel of the Mitsubishi, Jimi had his hand on the electric switch. He flipped it, sending current to dozens of detonators.

• • •

The oxygen in the air caught fire amid the tremendous release of gas, heat, and light. A massive wave of pressure blew a rolling wall of flames in every direction.

The taxi behind the van was thrown skyward, flipping several times before it landed on its wheels three car lengths back. The driver and his passengers, the Japanese newlyweds, were killed.

Inside Paddy's, the fireball hit Michael Martyn in the face. He and his friend Jason McIntyre burst into flame. Burning people and body parts were thrown everywhere. Pieces of the wall and ceiling collapsed.

The blast propelled Marc Gajardo backward and the front wall of the Sari Club fell on him. The building's roof collapsed in a rush of flame and pressure.

Bradley McIlroy was blown away from Joanne, but he got up quickly as fire and screams filled the room. He was about twelve feet from Joanne and took a step toward her.

He stopped in his tracks. She had been cut in half, just above the waist.

Back in the ladies' room, the blast hit Shelley Campbell and flattened the wall beside her. As she screamed, another woman, Deborah Carey, burst out of a stall and grabbed Shelley, pulling her away from the rapidly moving flames.

Then Shelley saw Belinda's feet. The stall door had blown in on top of her, and her legs were sticking out from under it.

"Belinda!" Shelley screamed, shaking her friend's leg.

She didn't move or respond. Shelley tried to lift the door, but it wouldn't budge. She glanced around and saw some men climbing a wall to escape.

"Help!" she screamed to them. "My friend is trapped!"

The men ran toward her, but were blocked by the fire.

"You have to get out!" one of them yelled.

He grabbed Shelley and Deborah Carey and pushed them into a line that had formed of people trying to get over the wall. Neither woman could climb it. Two men appeared at the top of the wall, grabbed their arms, and pulled. Another man pushed them from behind.

Jake Ryan, one of the soccer players in the club, was knocked flat onto his back. People started running over him in a desperate effort to escape. He sat up, pushing off two corpses, then saw the fire.

Shit! It's time to get out of here!

He glanced around. His teenage brother, Mitch, was somewhere in the building, but Jake couldn't see him. He heard an Australian voice calling from a wall. "Up here, mate!"

"My brother's in here!" Jake shouted. "I can't leave him!"

"Look around!" the Australian yelled back.

He turned. All he saw were people on fire. He couldn't walk forward into the blistering heat. So instead, he climbed the wall and scrambled across a roof to safety. He was bleeding profusely; one of his heels had been cut off and he had a gaping shrapnel wound in his stomach. But he wasn't going to give up on saving his brother. He hobbled to the front of the club, where he saw Steven Febey, a fellow soccer player. The two rushed inside the burning building, looking for people to help. Mitch was nowhere to be found; Jake wouldn't discover until the next day that his brother had survived.

Jake and Steve stumbled through the wreckage when they heard a woman screaming for help. Her legs had been cut off and her body was in flames. Both men struggled to reach her, but the fire was too intense. They saw her burn to death.

On the motorcycle roaring blocks away from the Sari Club, Idris and Ali Imron heard the tremendous explosion. Seconds passed, then Idris hit the send button on his phone.

The call connected to the cell phone in the bomb near the American consulate. The component that allowed the phone to vibrate rotated as usual, completing a circuit. Electricity shot through an attached wire to a detonator.

The small amount of TNT exploded, ripping a chunk out of the curb. Message delivered—the bombing at the nightclubs was about America.

Blaine Pecaut was still asleep in his hotel room when the ceiling partially collapsed on him. The mirror on his closet shattered, everything on his nightstand fell to the floor, and the lights went out. He couldn't see his hand in front of his face.

Down in the hotel courtyard, he heard screaming and yelling. One of his friends called out, "Bomb! Bomb! Where's Blaine?"

"I think he's at the Sari," came the response.

Pecaut groped in the darkness. The floor was covered with glass, but he managed to find his sandals. He sprinted out of the room to the courtyard. The scene was mayhem, with people running and screaming. He tracked down his two friends to let them know he was all right, then ran to Legian Street, hoping to find the three British surfers he had befriended, including Marc Gajardo.

He turned the corner and stared into the horror. Corpses everywhere. People walking in a daze, missing arms and legs, skin blackened from burns. Pecaut saw a man on the ground, still alive but severely wounded, with fire inching toward him. He bent down and wrapped his arms around the stranger, trying to drag him away from danger. Before they could move, Pecaut felt something wet and slippery. He pulled back his arm and saw it was dripping with blood, but not his own—the man had a three-foot gash running down his back. Pecaut hadn't put his arms under the stranger; he had slid them inside his body.

He looked at the injured man's face and saw only a blank stare. Pecaut was sure that he was watching the expression of someone who knew his death was moments away.

In the aftermath of the Bali attack, world leaders faced the same question: With Islamic terrorists still slaughtering innocents, why focus on Iraq? Saddam wasn't indiscriminately killing civilians; bin Laden was.

The criticism began in Australia, which lost dozens of its citizens in the bombings. Speaking from Canberra, Senator Bob Brown challenged the decision of Prime Minister John Howard to stand with America in pursuing Iraq.

"This event underscores the need for Australia to have a policy of regional defense and engagement rather than global stratagems at the behest of Washington," Brown said. "Australia should not join the invasion of Iraq. We should concentrate our resources in the neighborhood."

Another senator, Andrew Bartlett, joined in urging a policy shift. "We expect in the coming months the debate on Australian security will focus more on Southeast Asia and our nation's responsibilities in our region," Bartlett said.

But Howard would have none of it. In a hastily arranged press conference that afternoon, he declared that the peril from al-Qaeda and other Islamic terrorists could not be separated from the dangers posed by Iraq.

"It's unrealistic of anybody to believe that if you just deal with terrorism in one part of the world, then it's solved in other parts of the worlds," he said. "Terrorism is a worldwide threat. It needs to be responded to on a worldwide basis."

In the United States, Bush addressed the question three times that day—once in a press conference on the South Lawn and twice in speeches in Michigan. His message: The Bali attack only made the case against Saddam Hussein stronger. If this was what terrorists could do on their own, he said, imagine what would happen if the Iraqi dictator armed al-Qaeda with weapons of mass destruction.

"This is a man that we know has had connections to al-Qaeda," Bush said at a fund-raising dinner in Dearborn. "This is a man who, in my judgment, would like to use al-Qaeda as a forward army."

Tony Blair confronted the issue two days later, during the "Prime Minister's Questions" session with Parliament. Before any of the members could ask, Blair attempted to shoot down the controversy in an opening statement.

"We have had a fresh reminder, if we needed one, that the war against terrorism is not over," he said. "Some say that we should fight terrorism alone, and that issues to do with weapons of mass destruction are a distraction. I reject that entirely. Both, though different in means, are the same in nature."

He glanced up from his prepared statement. "Both are threats from people or states who do not care about human life, who have no compunction about killing the innocent," he said. "Both represent the extreme replacing the rational, the fanatic driving out moderation."

Then, the questions from members. "Does the prime minister agree that, in the wake of the tragedy, the international community must take stock of the campaign against terrorism?" asked Charles Kennedy. "Does he share the anxiety expressed by European Union commissioner Chris Patten, who said that he hopes that the efforts against Iraq do not distract us from the needs for further efforts in Afghanistan and Pakistan and against al-Qaeda itself?"

Blair gripped the lectern. Both Iraq and Islamic terrorism were threats that had to be addressed, he said. "We should show the same firmness with respect to both."

Another member, Alice Mahon, sharpened the tone. "In light of the latest outrage," she said, "should we not be targeting all our resources and energies on fighting terrorism, rather than starting another war in the Middle East? Surely the prime minister will agree that to start such a war would fan the flames of fundamentalism across the whole area and make matters much worse."

Blair stuck to his guns. "This is not an either/or. We really need to tackle both of these issue, as both are threats to the stability and order of the world."

The critics were not appeased.

. . .

Almost daily, Washington grilled the officers running Guantanamo about their floundering efforts at interrogating Mohammed al-Qahtani. How, the officials demanded, could a terrorist who had been one of the conspirators in the 9/11 attacks not know volumes of information about al-Qaeda?

Immediately after their October 2 meeting with the CIA about counterresistance methods, military interrogators at Guantanamo began employing SERE techniques against al-Qahtani—depriving him of sleep, blaring loud music, and flashing bright lights into his cell, confronting him with military dogs to scare him. But nothing had worked.

So, on October 11, Guantanamo officials sought permission to get tougher with al-Qahtani. The director of intelligence, Lieutenant Colonel Jerald Phifer, prepared the requests.

He broke them into three groups, from least to most aggressive. The first category would allow interrogators to yell at the detainee and deceive him, specifically by misrepresenting themselves as being from a foreign country with a reputation for torturing prisoners. Category II stepped things up a bit— interrogators could force detainees into stress positions, like standing, for up to four hours; show them documents and reports; isolate them for up to thirty days; deprive them of light, sound, or anything else that would give them comfort, including religious materials; question them for twenty hours at a time; remove their clothing; forcibly shave off their facial hair; and exploit their phobias by exposing them to whatever they found frightening.

The techniques in Category III were the most drastic—convincing detainees that either they or their families were about to be killed; exposing them to cold weather; waterboarding; and using noninjurious physical contact, such as grabbing or poking them.

Phifer's memo went to Diane Beaver, the chief legal advisor at Guantanamo, and she prepared an analysis concluding that the suggested tactics were lawful.

Beaver noted that, by Bush's order, the Guantanamo detainees were not protected by the Geneva Conventions. What that meant, she wrote, was that only domestic laws against torture were relevant. "An international law analysis is not required for the current proposal because the Geneva Conventions do not apply to these detainees."

On the other hand, she wrote, military interrogators *were* bound by the federal antitorture statute, the Eighth Amendment's prohibitions against cruel and unusual punishment, and the Uniform Code of Military Justice. The Constitu-

tion presented no problem. If an interrogation technique was used for a legitimate government purpose, then it wasn't cruel or unusual.

Nor would any of the practices lumped into the three categories violate the
antitorture statute, she wrote. So long as they were employed without the specific intent of causing physical or mental pain or suffering, they would pass legal
muster. In al-Qahtani's case, for example, the intent was to gain information,
not to inflict pain. But it would be illegal if motivated by sadism.

To reach that conclusion required a mix of verbal gymnastics and Orwellian
logic, where the word *forbidden* became the word *permitted.* The antitorture
statute specifically stated that threats of imminent death violated the law. But,
Beaver wrote, that didn't mean such threats violated the law. The words of the
statute could be ignored if the administration, by virtue of its duty to protect
American citizens, declared it so. Black was black, unless the government decided that it should be white.

The Beaver analysis and the Phifer memo were sent to General Dunlavey,
the commander of the intelligence unit at Guantanamo. He signed off on the
proposal, and forwarded it to the SOUTHCOM commander.

In a cover memo, Dunlavey, who was just days from being replaced at Guantanamo, wrote that the proposed methods would make it easier for interrogators to extract information from detainees.

And, based on Beaver's analysis, he wrote, "I have concluded that these techniques do not violate U.S. or international laws."

A video teleconference over a secure satellite link was set up that week between
Guantanamo and Washington. By then, the working relationship of FBI and
military intelligence had frayed beyond repair, with each side arguing that the
other had no clue how to question al-Qahtani.

This call was the chance for both sides to make their case. Almost everyone directly involved with interrogation issues was either on the line or in the
room—officials from the Pentagon, the CIA, and the Justice Department; law
enforcement agents; and Major General Geoffrey Miller, who had just been
named to replace Dunlavey.

The military interrogators were preening—after many hours of questioning,
they bragged, al-Qahtani had blurted out the name "Mohammed Atta." A real
breakthrough, they asserted, and indisputable proof that harsh tactics worked.

Ridiculous, an FBI psychologist replied. Al-Qahtani had yelled out a name
that had been on the front pages of every newspaper in the world and only be-

cause he wanted the interrogators to let him eat and go to the bathroom. That was hardly "intelligence."

Lieutenant Colonel Phifer described the new tactics that he wanted approved, saying they would build on the military's already impressive achievements.

"The aggressive approach we've used up until now has already produced some useful intelligence," Phifer said. He began to tick off information he claimed had been extracted from al-Qahtani.

The FBI unit chief broke in. "Look, everything you've gotten thus far is what the FBI gave you on al-Qahtani," he spat.

Nods around the room.

"That is *not* true," Phifer shot back.

"It is," the psychologist said.

"Look, the techniques you guys are using don't work," the unit chief said. "They're completely ineffective. You're not getting good intelligence."

Voices were raised and accusations flew. There was no bridging the gap between diametrically opposed and inflexible positions. The meeting broke up and the teleconference ended.

The news from Bob Lady was a nasty surprise.

For the first time, the CIA station chief in Milan was informing his counterpart with SISMI, the Italian intelligence agency, about the American plan to kidnap one of the city's residents. Months before, he had tipped off a friend who was an officer with the Carabinieri, but this time, while speaking to an equal, he held back nothing—the entire idea, Lady said, was stupid.

The SISMI officer, Stefano D'Ambrosio, could only listen in disbelief as Lady described the madness of the undertaking. Snatching the suspected terrorist, Abu Omar, from an allied Western country—one that was more than willing to share intelligence about the man—was irrational. Italy wasn't Pakistan; there was no reason to take such an extraordinary step.

Worse, Lady said, he now knew that Italy's premier law enforcement and state security service—DIGOS—was conducting surveillance of Abu Omar. The group had tapped his phones, which had already led to other suspects. Investigating the Egyptian cleric was invaluable in obtaining new intelligence about Italy's Islamic extremists. Leaving him alone while law enforcement watched was certainly a better choice than making him disappear.

"I'm telling you this because I wanted to see if you were already aware of the plan to collect him," Lady said.

The operation, Lady said, had been worked out by Jeff Castelli, head of the CIA in Rome. "And he's following a range of precise directives from agency headquarters in Langley," he said.

A CIA squad belonging to a unit called the Special Operations Group was already in Milan, preparing for the abduction. "These guys are the heavies, the ones who conduct special intelligence operations," Lady said. "All of them have military and operational experience. They're not just confined to investigative work."

There were several steps to the plan, Lady said. Once Abu Omar was grabbed in Milan, he would be driven to an air base near Ghedi, in the province of Brescia. Then he would be moved onto a plane from Ramstein Air Base in Germany and flown to another location. Lady did not mention that Abu Omar was being taken to Egypt.

"SISMI personnel are at work near Ghedi right now to find a suitable place to hold him until we can get him on the plane," Lady said. The ones involved weren't renegades; all of this was being done with the knowledge and approval of the director of SISMI, General Nicolò Pollari.

After finishing his description of the plan, Lady shook his head. "None of this makes sense," he said again. "This man is being subjected to an excellent and thorough investigation by DIGOS. Why in the world is it necessary to damage our fruitful collaboration with them?"

Plus, no one at the CIA was recognizing obvious problems. He had been forced to betray the confidence of DIGOS by keeping it in the dark about the scheme, Lady said, and that could well put everyone in danger.

"This man and all the other suspects are being tailed," Lady said. "But no one is considering how DIGOS is going to react when they see someone abducted off the street in front of them. There might even be shooting."

Feeling bowled over, D'Ambrosio sat back in his chair. "I agree with your criticisms," he said. "But what you might not know is that the air-base commander at Ghedi, Colonel Bellini, would never have consented to using his base for this. When he finds out, he will be furious."

Lady spread his arms out in despair. "What can I do?"

"Why has such an action been planned?"

"It's a project intended to remove a subject from circulation who's held to be extremely dangerous."

"But this is just one man," D'Ambrosio replied. "Once he's been taken away, he'll probably just be replaced by somebody else who we'll have trouble fingering. And then we won't be able to place this new fellow under observation. Plus, if DIGOS continued their work, they could develop more evidence sufficient for Abu Omar's arrest and sentence in a court."

"I agree," Lady said. "But this is a plan that is now decidedly close to the hearts of Castelli, as well as Sabrina de Sousa."

D'Ambrosio recognized the name. De Sousa worked at the Rome embassy; Castelli had sent her to Milan, Lady said, to keep tabs on him and push him in the right direction. Lady bad-mouthed de Sousa, and then began to belittle Castelli.

"What do you expect someone who's a Buddhist, burns incense in his office, and listens to the music of Bob Marley to know about terrorism?"

Both men chuckled.

"Well, despite being the section head for SISMI in Milan, I know nothing of this plan," D'Ambrosio said.

"I suppose I shouldn't be surprised," Lady replied. "None of the activities here involve your staff. It's SISMI people coming directly from Rome."

A moment passed, then Lady's eyes flashed with a new zest. "I cannot believe that Pollari is in on this!" he snapped.

If the detainee dies you're doing it wrong.

Mark Fallon, head of the Criminal Investigative Task Force at Guantanamo, was stunned by what he was reading. The words leaped out at him from the minutes of the October 2 debate between the military and the CIA on subjecting al-Qahtani to harsher interrogations. Fallon wasn't supposed to have seen the document, but one of his colleagues, Blaine Thomas, had snagged a bootleg copy and e-mailed it to him.

With every sentence he read, his revulsion deepened. Waterboarding, plans to hide abusive techniques from the Red Cross, the need to have medical personnel at the ready during interrogations—it was all abhorrent. Yet the people involved chattered on about this cruelty in such a relaxed, banal way, as if they were discussing plans for a weekend barbecue. Members of Fallon's team hadn't been invited to the meeting, and no wonder. A criminal investigator would never have sat through it without raising hell—and might even have deemed the discussion to be an illegal conspiracy.

On October 28, Fallon forwarded the e-mail to other members of his team and included his own analysis.

"This looks like the kind of stuff that Congressional hearings are made of," he typed. The ideas being tossed about "would, in my opinion, shock the con-science of any legal body looking at using the result of the interrogations."

But this was not just about how a court or tribunal might judge the military's interrogation plans. "Someone," Fallon wrote, "needs to be considering how history will look back at this."

That day, Paul Clement stood in the well of a Richmond courtroom, preparing to argue the latest government appeal in the Hamdi case. The deputy solicitor general had been readying himself for this moment through moot court ses-sions at the Justice Department, with colleagues playing the role of the three-judge panel on the Fourth Circuit Court of Appeals. The exercise honed his argument that the government was not under any obligation to provide more information about its reasons for detaining Hamdi, as had been demanded by Judge Doumar of the lower court.

Reporters and onlookers packed the courtroom, including several govern-ment officials who had quietly slipped into the gallery. David Addington and Tim Flanigan had arrived about an hour early, but had been careful not to identify themselves to anyone at the courthouse; the last thing they needed was to be swarmed by journalists.

Both sides trotted out the same arguments they had presented to Doumar. Clement maintained that the declaration of Michael Mobbs, a Pentagon of-ficial, that had been filed by the administration in July spelled out everything Doumar needed to know about Hamdi's detention. The courts should have no further role; this was solely a matter for the president.

"I think it's important to give discretion to the executive branch to handle detainees as it sees fit," Clement said. "It is possible for the United States to handle an individual seized in the United States as an enemy combatant."

Not good enough, argued Frank Dunham Jr., Hamdi's lawyer. The Mobbs declaration was nothing more than a series of government assertions, all with the implied message "Trust us." The administration was refusing to allow Hamdi to even *see* the declaration—vague as it was—to say whether any of it was true.

"Nobody knows what his version of the facts might be," Dunham said.

The passage of time had also undermined the government's claim about the need to question Hamdi, he said. Of course any decision made on the battle-field was entitled to deference, and the government's interest in gathering intel-ligence from a captive was understandable. But—given the months that had passed—how much could Hamdi know that he hadn't already revealed?

Chief Judge Wilkinson seized on that thread of inquiry. Was Hamdi even worth holding? After all, the Mobbs declaration said that Hamdi had been in Afghanistan only a few months before he was caught.

"Is Mr. Hamdi still of use to you in your intelligence-gathering operations?" Wilkinson asked. "Is Hamdi still of importance?"

Absolutely, Clement replied. Anytime another suspected terrorist was captured, Hamdi could be prodded to reveal whatever secrets he might know or insights he might have about the man. Intelligence was a mosaic, where bits and pieces of information came together to form an understanding of reality.

But wait, Dunham retorted. The very expectation that Hamdi should be held because he might cough up new evidence placed the government under the obligation to explain *why* it considered him so valuable. "We still don't know if he's an enemy combatant, that's the sixty-four-dollar question," he said. "The precedent that the administration is setting has a long-term potential for incursions on our liberties."

Wilkinson all but threw up his hands at the quandary being thrust upon him and his colleagues. It was the job of the court to strike the right balance between protecting the safety of American citizens and upholding the country's values. But demanding that the administration bring more evidence to court could well insert judges into the war.

"I'm worried about wading in over my head with these production orders," he said. "Doesn't that move the battlefield right into the courtroom?"

"Our freedoms don't come cheap," Dunham replied. "They can't be swept away."

The arguments continued for two hours. At the end, Wilkinson nodded to the lawyers on both sides. "The American people have been beautifully served by the quality of the advocacy," he said.

Then, following a tradition of the Fourth Circuit, Wilkinson led his two colleagues down from the bench to shake hands with the battery of attorneys.

A White House van pulled up to one of Washington's premier hotels at 8:30 on the morning of October 30. The driver scampered out and opened the doors for two dignitaries, Hans Blix and Mohamed ElBaradei, the men designated to oversee the new searches in Iraq for weapons of mass destruction.

The groundwork for inspections had been under way for more than a month. The new U.N. resolution demanding that Iraq disarm would be approved in a few days. Blix had been crisscrossing the world in preparation—negotiating with the Iraqis, meeting with Russian officials, consulting members of the Bush administration. Then, two nights before, Colin Powell had telephoned Blix to say that the time had come for him to speak with the president.

The van drove Blix and ElBaradei—director general of the International Atomic Energy Agency—and their aides to the portico outside the West Wing of the executive mansion. The aides were left to cool their heels while Blix and ElBaradei were escorted to Cheney's office.

The vice president greeted his guests and invited them to take a seat. Cheney had no real questions. Instead, he did most of the talking.

Blix was somewhat uneasy. He was still troubled by Cheney's speech in August in which he dismissed weapons inspectors as essentially useless and gave his confident assertion that Iraq undoubtedly possessed weapons of mass destruction. There was a strong chance that Iraqis might be hiding illegal weapons—particularly anthrax, Blix thought. But Cheney seemed to be willfully overlooking evidence—such as the results of earlier inspections—that contradicted his narrative, placing his faith instead in the stories spun by Iraqi defectors about secret weaponry concealed throughout the country. Inspections would have to combat assertions.

It all came down to the safety of American citizens, Cheney said. "I always take the security interests of the United States as the starting point," he said. "Nothing else overrides that. And if inspections don't get results, they're not going to go on forever."

He looked Blix in the eye. "The United States is ready to discredit inspections in favor of disarmament," he said.

Blix got the message. If his team found the weapons that Cheney was certain had been secreted away, they had done a good job. If they didn't, they were a naive collection of bumblers, and Saddam would have to be defanged by military might.

Heads I win, tails you lose.

Minutes later in the Oval Office, Bush shifted about in his chair as he spoke with Blix and ElBaradei. He was a sharp contrast to his dour and unflappable vice president, Blix thought—charming, with an air of almost boyish enthusiasm. And his message was almost the antithesis of Cheney's.

"The United States genuinely wants peace," he said. "Contrary to what you may have heard, I'm not some wild, gung ho Texan bent on dragging the U.S. into war."

He was willing to stand by while the U.N. Security Council debated a new resolution, but not for long. The League of Nations delayed and debated about disarmament without ever making real progress—a failure that set the stage for World War II. The United States was not about to commit the same colossal blunder.

"But America has full confidence in you and Mr. ElBaradei," Bush said. "We are going to throw our full support behind you."

"Thank you, Mr. President," Blix replied. "We appreciate that. I consider the support of the United States to be essential for our success."

The two diplomats headed off for meetings with the president's national security team. The conversation with Bush had been devoid of any real substance—probably on purpose, Blix surmised. He had just been subjected to a good-cop, bad-cop routine, with Bush's cheery tone meant to convey American hopes for his success and Cheney's forbidding demeanor intended to afford him a glimpse of the consequences of failure.

That same day, Stefano D'Ambrosio, the head of the Milan office for SISMI, was walking down a street in Bologna alongside Marco Mancini, the second in command for Italy's military intelligence agency.

A few days had passed since D'Ambrosio had heard from Bob Lady—the CIA station chief in Milan—about the American plan to abduct one of the city's residents, Abu Omar. Despite Lady's insistence that the director of SISMI was part of the operation, D'Ambrosio felt obligated to warn his bosses of the CIA officer's qualms about the scheme and to express his own dismay as well.

Mancini listened in silence, his face stony, as D'Ambrosio spelled out his and Lady's concerns.

"I seriously urge you to advise the director of these issues," D'Ambrosio said. "But please don't let him know that I was made directly aware of this plan by Bob Lady." Lady, he said, might suffer serious consequences for having filled in D'Ambrosio without permission.

"Also, I want to be clear," D'Ambrosio added. "It is not possible for SISMI and CIA operatives to come into my territory without my knowing about it."

Mancini turned to D'Ambrosio, glaring at him. "But was it really Lady himself who told you?" he asked.

"Yes, it was."

A grunt. "I find that very disturbing."

"Well," D'Ambrosio replied, "might it be opportune to make a written note of this?"

"That's not necessary," Mancini replied. He would personally alert Gustavo Pignero, SISMI's director of counterespionage.

The meeting ended. And while D'Ambrosio didn't know it yet, he had just critically damaged his career.

Bruce Ivins was sitting at a table, scrawling messages to himself. The anthrax researcher was increasingly troubled. He had made mistakes. His decision to decontaminate his work area against his boss's instructions had led the FBI to question him; he confessed not only to testing and cleaning there in April 2002, but also a few months before, in December.

At this point the FBI still considered him a valued member of the investigative team and dismissed his actions as just the behavior of a quirky guy. But having to explain himself to the bureau unnerved Ivins. He was embarrassed and anxious. He tried to appear blasé about it—he laughed to colleagues that maybe the government thought he might be the killer, as if such an accusation was the most absurd idea conceivable.

But when he was alone, symptoms of his stress bubbled over. He had long been fond of composing bizarre poems, and now he dashed them off more frequently, with stranger twists than ever. He wrote about a colleague's circumcision, another's obesity, manically jumping from topic to topic. Recently, he had gone a step further, scrawling notes to himself that vaguely threatened his perceived enemies.

His hand swooped maniacally as he wrote his latest tirade on a steno pad in wild block letters interspersed with flowing cursive strokes. The words were laced with rage at unspecified adversaries.

I DON'T CONGRATULATE
OPPONENTS, I
HUMILIATE THEM

I DRAW FIRST BLOOD . . . AND
LAST

I'M NOT YOUR OPPONENT—
I'M YOUR ENEMY.

Ivins finished his scribbling. He ripped the page off the pad and stuffed it into a drawer.

A forensic investigator with the Indonesian police slowly scanned the light beam from a Mini-CrimeScope 400 down the mangled remnant of a car chassis. The five-foot length of metal discovered at the Bali bombing site had been examined repeatedly for clues, without success. Now, with the case underway for weeks, investigators were falling into near desperation. The trail was going cold, and they still didn't have a single suspect.

The investigation had seen successes in the early days. The morning after the bombing, a team from the Australian Federal Police offered to assist the Indonesians with the inquiry. That same day, officers discovered the Yamaha motorcycle used by the terrorists dumped at a nearby mosque. They tracked down the shop where the bike had been purchased, and witnesses there provided enough information for police sketches. Still, authorities had no names and no hints of where else to look.

The investigators thought they had obtained critical evidence when the twisted piece of chassis was discovered on the roof of a nearby bank. If they could track down the owner of the car, they knew, they stood a fair chance of closing in on the perpetrators.

But their hopes collapsed as they examined the chunk of metal. The terrorists had filed down the two vehicle identification numbers—the VIN numbers—rendering them illegible. If they were smart enough to take that precaution, police officials feared, the chance that they left behind other clues was slim.

The man leading the investigation for the Indonesians, General I Made Mangku Pastika, fell into a deep depression about the lack of progress. He ordered his men to reexamine the evidence and then, without telling anyone, he left the office. A devout Hindu, he decided to visit his temple and pray for a breakthrough.

The investigators gave the chassis another look. It was the same exercise in futility—it was nothing, just a scrap of steel with unreadable numbers. But one forensic investigator hadn't given up. As he illuminated each spot, he studied it meticulously, looking for something—anything—that might help.

Wait.

He saw a tiny piece of metal, just one and a half inches long. On previous inspections, it had appeared to be part of the chassis, but this time the investigator could see that it was welded on. It somehow looked different from the rest of the frame, with a slight variation in color.

The investigator reached for a tool and pried off the sliver of metal. He fixed the light on the spot that had been covered. And his heart leaped.

"Come here!" he yelled out to his colleagues. "I have something!"

Pastika was in the middle of his devotions at the temple when his cell phone rang. One of his deputies was on the line.

"General, where are you?" the deputy asked. "Are you not in the office?"

"No," Pastika replied. "I'm praying for the success of the investigation."

The deputy laughed. "Your prayers have been answered," he said. "We just found a number on the chassis."

The discovery of another VIN number was so far-fetched that more than a few of the investigators suspected there might have been some divine intervention.

The terrorists had unwittingly purchased the wrong kind of van in the wrong country. They had known that Indonesian cars and trucks had two VIN numbers, one stamped on the chassis and the other on the engine. But, under Indonesian law, commercial vehicles like the van were required to have a *third* number, also stamped on the chassis. The perpetrators had successfully filed down the usual two, but had no inkling that the third even existed.

Perhaps a mundane misstep, but it was another factor that led some officers to see the hand of providence. The bombers hadn't just missed seeing the number—by virtue of an improbable act, it had become almost impossible for them to have discovered it. A former owner of the van had welded a support strut onto the chassis, and by sheer chance, it had covered the VIN number. That not only hid it from the bombers, but also shielded it from the explosion. The van had been torn to pieces in the blast, but the third VIN number emerged unscathed.

The police ran the number through a computer database and found the names of the vehicle's previous seven owners. The most recent, Amrozi bin Nurhasyim, had a record. He was a member of Jemaah Islamiyah, the Asian terrorist organization affiliated with al-Qaeda, and the brother of Ali Imron. And now the authorities knew his address.

The next morning, November 5, teams of Indonesian police raided Amrozi's home in East Java. The forty-year-old mechanic was sleeping in the rear of the house. When the officers kicked in his door, he made no attempt to flee. Instead, he started to laugh.

"You guys are very clever," he said with a smile. "How did you find me?"

The authorities swept through the house, quickly locating vital pieces of evidence. They found Amrozi's cell phone, which had numbers for other conspirators; bags of bomb-making chemicals and the receipts from where they were purchased; training manuals on ambush techniques; and copies of speeches by Osama bin Laden.

Officers handcuffed Amrozi and ushered him outside. He beamed as he was led through the gaggle of investigators, shoved into the back of an armored van, and driven to the police station.

Amrozi readily confessed. He not only took responsibility for his role in the attack, but also identified other plotters. He was proud of what they had done and seemed to delight in talking about it.

In his confession, he told the police that he hadn't been near Kuta on the night of the bombing. Instead, he learned that it had been successful the next morning at seven, when he heard a news report on Radio Elshinta.

"I was very happy," he told the police. "How can I describe it? It was like when I was still a bachelor trying for a girl and you finally get to meet her. It was that sort of excitement. But this was even better."

Eventually, the police put on a public show of Amrozi's bizarre grandstanding. Questioned behind glass, he merrily recounted the bombing as dozens of reporters and photographers listened in. He described the allure of Jemaah Islamiyah and bin Laden as well as his own dedication to jihad.

He pointed at the journalists. "These are the sort of people I wanted to kill," he said.

The debate about revving up the interrogation of al-Qahtani to harsh new levels was going nowhere. Dunlavey's request to establish three ascending categories of aggressive techniques had been sent up the line; discussions had been held, but after a month, no decisions had been made.

By November, Dunlavey was gone, replaced by General Miller. His superior, General Tom Hill, the SOUTHCOM commander, had taken responsibility for consulting Rumsfeld about the proposals.* Finally, on November 12, Hill

*Testimony of Pentagon officials in at least two internal investigations, as well as one report, suggests that Rumsfeld may have provided verbal approval to Hill. However, the evidence is not conclusive either way. See Notes and Sources.

gave a verbal approval for the use of Category I and Category II techniques. That meant interrogators could yell at or deceive detainees, force them to assume stress positions, question them for twenty hours at a time, take away their clothes, forcibly shave them, and turn their phobias against them. But there would be no waterboarding of Guantanamo detainees, no death threats, no exposure to frigid cold.

That day, military intelligence officials at Guantanamo wrote an interrogation strategy for al-Qahtani, and it went far beyond anything approved by Hill. Entitled the Special Interrogation Plan, it involved four phases, not just three. Before questioning began, al-Qahtani would have both his beard and hair forcibly shaved. During the first stage of the interrogation, he would be subjected to pressures such as stress positions but would be forbidden to talk. If he tried to speak, the interrogators would tape his mouth shut. Military dogs would be brought into the room to frighten him. Then, when al-Qahtani was allowed to speak, the proposal said, he would be eager to "tell all."

The second phase would not be controversial—a government translator would pose as a fellow detainee and try to pry out his secrets. Phase three would employ the techniques requested by Dunlavey in the October 11 memo.

Then, phase four: torture. American soldiers would not *personally* inflict pain on al-Qahtani. Instead, he would be shipped out of Guantanamo, temporarily or permanently, to either Egypt or Jordan, where beatings, burnings, and other abuses were routinely deployed. The strategy "would allow those countries to employ interrogation techniques that will enable them to obtain the requisite information," the plan said.

General Miller was all for it. The director of intelligence at Guantanamo, Lieutenant Colonel Phifer, sent him an e-mail within hours, informing Miller that interrogators would begin using the techniques in two days.

There were times when Britt Mallow wanted to jab a pencil in someone's eye.

Mallow, the commander of the Criminal Investigative Task Force at Guantanamo, had been battling the Pentagon and the intelligence unit for months. At the detention center, he had witnessed some of the asinine interrogations conducted by young, poorly trained soldiers. No one had yet seemed to notice that screaming, "Where is bin Laden?" at detainees had zero effect.

Then those same interrogators who had resorted to contrivances started using tactics that looked as though they had been lifted from *24,* the counterterrorism television show. Flashing lights, loud music, stress positions—the approach was ridiculous. Worse than ridiculous. Counterproductive.

Mallow had tried to persuade Dunlavey that the methods used by the criminal investigators were the most fruitful. But the general had just waved him away, captivated by the false glories of an intelligence unit that brandished information obtained by criminal investigators as its own.

Dunlavey's false claims of success climbed up the line of command to the Pentagon, giving credence to the belief that screaming and jumping were strong components of a national defense. Mallow's disparagement of that approach had earned him some screams of his own—from get-tough-on-terrorists Defense Department bureaucrats.

That's when he hit the slow burn—or not so slow. These *suits* who had never questioned anyone outside of a job interview, who had never seen combat, who had never confronted the enemy, had the arrogance to tell the military officers trained for the job to butt out.

Then, in mid-November, Mallow saw Dunlavey's October request to allow measures that were even more severe to loosen al-Qahtani's tongue. The reason for the appeal: because the already rough treatment being meted out wasn't working.

No kidding.

It was the proverbial slippery slope. Rather than acknowledging defeat, the intelligence officers wanted to double down on a failed approach. Harsh interrogations would work, they were arguing, if only they were harsher.

This madness had to be stopped, Mallow decided. On November 14, he sent an e-mail to Miller saying that he strongly opposed the tactics described in the Dunlavey proposal.

"I feel they will be largely ineffective, and that they will have serious negative material and legal effects on our investigations," he wrote. "I am also extremely concerned that the use of many of these techniques will open any military members up for criminal charges."

Mallow had no way of knowing that an even more disturbing solution was in the making—the just-written Special Interrogation Plan that was scheduled to be used on al-Qahtani within the next twenty-four hours.

The skies were overcast in Ottawa that same day as Colin Powell led an eleven-member diplomatic contingent to the headquarters of the Foreign Affairs Ministry. It was Powell's first formal visit with senior Canadian officials, and the main topic of discussion was expected to be Iraq.

Six days earlier, the U.N. Security Council had unanimously approved Resolution 1441, declaring Iraq in breach of its cease-fire agreement from the Gulf War and offering Saddam a final opportunity to give up his weapons. Powell had traveled to Ottawa in part to ask, without suggesting specifics, what Canadian officials would be willing to contribute to a coalition military force in the event an invasion of Iraq proved necessary.

A working lunch had been scheduled, but first Powell met with Bill Graham, the foreign minister. Powell opened with the usual diplomatic fare about the important friendship of the two countries, then acknowledged recent frictions that had marred it—an American program that required all Canadians of Arab descent to be fingerprinted and photographed before being admitted to the country, the arrest and detention of a Canadian hunter who had wandered across the border carrying a rifle, the deportation of Maher Arar to Syria.

"But we should never lose sight of the great overall relationship," he said, citing the high volume of trade and tourism between the two countries.

"Well, thank you, Mr. Powell," Graham said. "And let me welcome you and extend my government's deepest appreciation for your visit today."

After dispensing with the niceties, the two men ranged over the international scene, discussing Iraq, North Korea, border restrictions, and security issues.

The last topic gave Graham the opening he needed to return to the topic of Maher Arar. The press had been lambasting Ottawa about the Arar case, he said, with commentators demanding to know why America had deported a Canadian to Syria. Graham wanted to know the answer himself.

"Mr. Powell," Graham said. "We believe very strongly in security. But security will only come if our own citizens believe that it is being handled in a way where the right balance is being struck."

Graham leaned on his elbows. "We don't believe the balance was maintained here."

"I understand your concern," Powell said, "But we had evidence about Mr. Arar's contacts and we were justified in doing what we did. He was a national security threat to the United States of America, which we were entitled to ascertain in our own sovereign right."

As close as Washington's relationship was with Ottawa, Powell said, the Canadians were not in the position to tell the Bush administration which individuals were or were not security threats.

"Well, look," Graham said, "we are protesting that you did this."

The United States had the absolute right to deport Arar the way it did, Powell responded. "And by the way," he added, "your guys knew what we were doing all along. They gave a go-ahead."

What the hell? Graham had heard nothing of the kind. On the contrary, he had been told that no one in the government even knew that Arar had been shipped to Syria until days after it had happened.

"Okay," Graham said, "if somebody by a wink or a nod or something explicit said something, tell us who it is and we can go to that person and find out what happened."

Powell nodded solemnly. "I'll see what we can do."

Two experienced FBI interrogators read the new plan for al-Qahtani with alarm. Where did the military come up with these ideas?

The agents poked around and were incredulous when they discovered that the "force him not to speak and then he'll tell all" theory came from a single army translator. Other than the crackpot notion of a linguist with zero understanding of interrogation, the military had no data, no study—nothing—to back it up.

The scariest part of the initiative, though, was the provision in phase four that would allow for detainees to be shipped to Middle Eastern countries where they were sure to be tortured. Never mind that it was wrongheaded—torture just plain didn't work—it crossed the line from foolish to illegal.

If the agents were disturbed by the contents of the plan, they were even more taken aback by the attitude of the people who would be following the proposed rules. They attended a meeting to discuss the policy with their military counterparts, who laughed and joked as they showed an undisguised glee about its cruelty.

The circuslike atmosphere of the meeting put the FBI agents on edge. Was it the baseless expectation that they might be able to pry information out of al-Qahtani that aroused the military interrogators' enthusiasm? Or was it the anticipation of revenge, the opportunity to hurt a man who had been part of the plot that murdered thousands of their fellow citizens?

The two agents sent a memo to Washington. If this plan was not overhauled, and if a decision was made to implement the tactics that it authorized, their people in Guantanamo would have nothing to do with it.

In private discussions, members of the full Criminal Investigative Task Force were even blunter. If military intelligence officials tried to carry out phase four, then the agents would have to arrest them.

The explosion of anger from law enforcement prompted General Miller to postpone the execution of the Special Interrogation Plan and instead order a review. In his recent e-mail, Britt Mallow had suggested that the intelligence unit and criminal investigators work together in developing a common strategy based on the traditional relationship-building approach. Miller gave the go-ahead for the two sides to hammer out an agreement.

The result was a hybrid that combined ideas from both groups. The law enforcement approach would be pursued for about a week. If that didn't work, the military's plan would be put into effect, minus some of its harsher provisions.

One of the criminal investigators told his colleagues that the compromise was the best they could hope for—the "lesser of two evils." Others disagreed, saying that if they accepted it, the military would assume the agents were giving their blessing to the remaining abusive techniques.

In the end, nobody was happy. The military interrogators grumbled that they wanted to reject any proposal that excluded SERE techniques and the option of sending al-Qahtani to the Middle East for torture. Inflicting severe pain, one officer said to an agent, worked with terrorists.

"Haven't you seen *24*?" he asked.

On November 21 in the Czech Republic, Bill Graham was wandering through the Prague Conference Center on the lookout for Colin Powell. It was a challenging hunt—the center was packed with crowds of dignitaries attending the first NATO summit since the Bali massacre and only the second since 9/11.

From the time of the last meeting between Graham and his American counterpart, the Canadian foreign minister had angrily instructed his aides to find out who had approved of Maher Arar's deportation to Syria. But everyone contacted—from Graham's own department, the Mounties, Canadian intelligence—insisted that they had known nothing of the Americans' plans.

Finally, Graham located Powell and pulled him aside.

"Look, I want to speak to you for a couple of minutes about the troubling issues around Mr. Arar," Graham said. "My information still is that nobody in Canada had any participation in the decision that he be taken to Syria. Would you please continue looking into this?"

"Bill," Powell replied, "my answer is exactly the same. You are not getting the straight goods from your guys. I am telling you my information is that there were people involved in this decision in Canada."

Graham nodded. But again, he asked Powell to identify them. The case was becoming a cause célèbre in Canada, and he needed to tamp down the furor. Powell again promised to do his best to get a name.

The two shook hands and Powell disappeared into the sea of faces. Graham boiled; someone in his government was lying. When he returned to Ottawa, he was going to pound some tables—his aides were going to find this person!

Or were they? Graham couldn't shake a nagging doubt. What if the Canadian officials were telling the truth? What if Powell was wrong, and the United States had sent Arar to the Middle East without telling anyone? What if this citizen had been snatched away from his home and sent to a Syrian prison based on bad intelligence?

No trial, no chance to defend himself, Graham thought. *What chance did Arar have for justice in this Kafkaesque situation?*

At a private room in another part of the Prague Center, Bush met with Blair and a few of his top subordinates.

He smiled as he glad-handed all around. "How ya doing?" he said with each handshake. A few of the aides noticed that Bush was wearing a showy pair of cowboy boots—an unusual yet somehow endearing choice for a NATO meeting.

Bush and the prime minister then launched into a discussion about Iraq. Just sitting back to see how Saddam reacted to the new resolution wouldn't cut it, the president said.

"We need real pressure to build on him, through troop movements, international condemnation," he said. "We need really tough and unpredictable inspections, to throw Saddam off balance."

They also had to be ready to move, if necessary. "Once we've made the call agreeing that Saddam is in breach, we have to do something militarily, and quickly," Bush said. That meant a quick, sustainable bombing raid, he added, followed by boots on the ground.

The first inspection by Hans Blix's team was set to begin in six days, but Bush made it clear that he wasn't impressed with the Swedish diplomat.

"He's wringing his hands and talking war and peace," he said. "But that's our judgment."

Blair wasn't so downbeat. "I feel there's a twenty percent chance that Saddam will cooperate," he said.

Bush shrugged. "I don't know what cooperation means."

Well, if Saddam failed to meet the terms of the resolution and there was a military action, his government would fall pretty quickly, Blair said. Bush agreed, adding that the CIA and MI5 should be put to work to help that along, even before an invasion.

Back to inspections. "Saddam's making Blix and the U.N. look like fools," Bush said.

The British officials walked away from the meeting with a feeling that Bush had drawn his line in the sand. How much proof would it take to convince him that inspections were working if he was condemning Blix before the diplomat and his team had even arrived in Baghdad?

Two days later at Guantanamo, the military initiated the new interrogation strategy for al-Qahtani. General Miller and other officers had formally adopted the modified hybrid plan—starting with relationship building but reverting to an aggressive approach if gentleness failed.

At 2:25 in the morning, a hooded al-Qahtani was escorted into an interrogation booth at Camp X-Ray. After a guard sat him down, his chains were bolted to the floor and his hood was removed. There were two interrogators, one translator, and an army psychologist in the room.

The sergeants handling the questioning began the rapport-building process—at least as best as they understood it. Al-Qahtani refused to look at one of them, a woman, saying eye contact with the opposite sex was against his religion. She asked Qahtani if he wanted water, but he didn't answer.

The other sergeant stepped in. Not answering, he said, disrespected his colleague, he said.

"No," al-Qahtani said. "I don't want any water."

His first response.

1:45 P.M. Into the eleventh straight hour of interrogation.

A television was moved in front of al-Qahtani and one of the soldiers loaded a DVD in the attached player. The screen filled with images of the World Trade Center on 9/11. Planes smashing in the buildings in balls of fire. People jumping to their deaths. The towers collapsing.

Al-Qahtani stared at the video, exhibiting no emotion. Photos of the hijackers appeared, and he reacted for the first time by averting his eyes.

• • •

2:15 P.M.

One of the guards calmly engaged al-Qahtani in a conversation about family and dreams.

Al-Qahtani grew upset. "Why are you causing me pain talking about family and things I can not have?" he asked.

He started to cry.

7:20 P.M. The eighteenth straight hour.

The third shift of interrogators arrived.

You will be judged by Allah, one of them told al-Qahtani. The leaders of al-Qaeda had twisted the words of the Koran.

"How did this come about?" the sergeant asked. "Why are you the only one holding on and everyone else is speaking?"

No response.

"Don't worry about a military judge," he continued. "Worry about Allah. The Koran doesn't say kill the innocent. Make things right. Repent."

Al-Qahtani cried again. He said that if the guards took him back to Delta Camp, where other detainees were held, he would answer their questions.

"You have to earn your way back to Delta," an interrogator responded.

12:00 A.M. Into the twenty-second straight hour.

Al-Qahtani had not said a word for more than four hours. He was unchained and taken back to bed.

The military's first day of "rapport-building" interrogation had ended.

November 24, 4:00 A.M.

After allowing al-Qahtani four hours of sleep, one of the sergeants woke him. The detainee was struggling to stay conscious, so the sergeant walked him around for five minutes. He was then chained to the floor.

"I want to perform sunrise prayer," al-Qahtani said.

"The sun hasn't come up yet," the second sergeant said. "I'll allow prayer later."

When did Ramadan begin? al-Qahtani asked.

"We'll talk about that later."

Besides, al-Qahtani had announced the previous day—after eating—that he was on a hunger strike. So why would Ramadan make a difference? He was already fasting.

"I don't know how to answer the question," al-Qahtani responded.

6:45 P.M. Into the fourteenth straight hour of interrogation.

Al-Qahtani had spoken only a few times since the morning. Nothing much, and usually just asking to pray or go to the bathroom. A doctor arrived to check him, to make sure that he was physically able to continue.

"I want to sign a form or a release saying I do not want any medication," he said.

"No such form exists," the doctor responded.

One of the interrogators looked at al-Qahtani. "Mo," he said, using a nickname they had given him. "We are not going to let you die."

12:00 A.M. Twenty straight hours of interrogation.

Al-Qahtani had remained mostly silent. His feet were swollen, and the soldiers put on a pressure wrap to combat the problem. Then he was put to bed.

November 25, 6:00 A.M. Beginning the third straight hour of interrogation.

The sergeants played the 9/11 DVD for al-Qahtani again. One of them came up behind him and leaned in close.

"What is God telling you right now?" he whispered. "Your nineteen friends died in a fireball and you weren't with them. Was that God's choice? Is it God's will that you stay alive to tell us about his message?"

Without warning, al-Qahtani threw his head back, smacking the sergeant in the eye. Two guards jumped on him, pinning him to the ground. The sergeant crouched down, and al-Qahtani spat at him.

The sergeant smiled. "Go ahead and spit on me," he said. "It won't change anything. You're still here, I'm still talking to you. And you won't leave until you've given God's message."

The two guards pulled up al-Qahtani and put him back in the chair.

9:15 A.M.

Al-Qahtani asked to go to the bathroom. The interrogators told him no. He could use a bottle instead. He refused.

• • •

9:40 A.M.

Three and a half bags of liquid had been infused into al-Qahtani by IV. He moaned and spoke to one of the guards.

"I'm willing to talk if I can urinate," he said.

A female sergeant came into the interrogation booth from another room.

"Who do you work for?" she asked.

"Al-Qaeda."

"Who was your leader?"

"Osama bin Laden."

"Why did you go to Orlando?"

"I wasn't told the mission."

"Who was meeting you?"

"I don't know."

"Who was with you on the plane?"

"I was by myself."

The second sergeant grunted. "You're wasting my time."

10:00 A.M. Into the seventh straight hour.

"I need to go to the bathroom," al-Qahtani said.

The male interrogator responded. "You can go in the bottle."

"I want to go to the bathroom. It's more comfortable."

The interrogator shook his head. "You've ruined all trust," he said. "You can either go in the bottle or in your pants."

Al-Qahtani didn't respond. Then he wet himself.

1:20 P.M.

A new shift of interrogators entered the room. The lead questioner engaged al-Qahtani in some small talk, trying to establish a bond. He asked him about al-Qahtani's statement that he was with al-Qaeda.

"I was mad," al-Qahtani said. "And under too much pressure."

He asked for some food, saying that he would end his hunger strike if the IVs were removed from his body. The lead interrogator continued speaking with al-Qahtani in a calm, almost friendly voice. The Saudi suddenly began crying in deep, racking sobs.

"When I came to Orlando, I was turned away due to a visa problem," he said. "I was coming on my own. I am not part of al-Qaeda. I do not know Osama bin Laden."

He went silent for a moment. "I don't know what God wants."

The lead interrogator described how al-Qaeda members swore allegiance to bin Laden. Al-Qahtani sat in silence. The interrogator finished his comments.

"I know nothing about Osama bin Laden," al-Qahtani responded.

2:20 P.M. Into the eleventh straight hour.

Al-Qahtani was eating a military meal ration, his third of the day, and drinking a full bottle of water. The interrogators continued to question him. But as he downed the food, al-Qahtani became increasingly evasive.

"After I ate, I feel better and will not talk."

The intelligence officers continued their questioning, while al-Qahtani stayed silent. Then, suddenly, he started yelling.

"You are working for the devil!" he shouted. "You can take me back to my brothers. I will not eat anymore, I will not drink anymore, and I am not going to talk anymore."

He wept.

That same Monday, Stefano D'Ambrosio, the head of SISMI's Milan office, was waiting in a hallway at Fort Braschi, the headquarters on the outskirts of Rome for the Italian military intelligence service.

He was there to meet with Gustavo Pignero, SISMI's director of counterespionage, after having been summoned on Saturday by an urgent phone call to his house. Now, as he stood outside of Pignero's office, he couldn't help but wonder why he was there.

One of Pignero's aides approached and took D'Ambrosio aside.

"What did you do to Mancini?" the aide asked. "He's absolutely furious with you."

Mancini? D'Ambrosio's only recent contact with SISMI's second in command was a few weeks back, when he had raised his concerns about the American plan to kidnap a resident of Milan. But why would that discussion cause a problem? All he had done was warn Mancini about the plot and explain that the CIA's Milan station chief, Robert Lady, was deeply opposed to the idea.

There had to be some other issue, D'Ambrosio thought. "I don't know what's going on," he said.

Seconds later, D'Ambrosio was invited into Pignero's office. The head of the counterterrorism division was alone, sitting at his desk.

There were no pleasantries. "You are being transferred immediately to central headquarters in Rome," Pignero said. "So, of course, you're leaving Milan."

That was it. No explanation, no rationale, just *You're gone. Good-bye.*

"I've worked efficiently during my time in Milan," D'Ambrosio said. "Did I do something wrong for you to come to such a decision?"

"No, not at all. You've done good work. But it's like I'm a football coach, and I have a player on the field who was worth eight out of ten. But on the benches there was another player who could be worth ten out of ten. So he is the one who has to be brought in to play."

D'Ambrosio thought for a moment, and couldn't imagine who the "ten out of ten" player might be.

"When do I have to move?"

"Immediately," Pignero replied.

The meeting ended. And while D'Ambrosio would never be told the truth, he suspected that his bosses had pushed him out of the way because of his objections to the kidnapping plan. Nor would he know that the CIA had lobbied for that decision.

Two days later, Rumsfeld was meeting with his senior staff when he threw his hands up in frustration.

Nothing had been done about Dunlavey's request to allow Guantanamo interrogators to use more aggressive tactics against al-Qahtani. General Hill, the SOUTHCOM commander, had relayed the proposal to the Pentagon, but had never received a response. The interrogators down in Guantanamo were still waiting for guidance from the top, Rumsfeld said.

"You guys couldn't find your fanny with both hands!" he snapped. "Hill is telling me he wants an answer. I need a recommendation!"

The group promised to get back to Rumsfeld quickly. Then an interrogation plan could be put together for al-Qahtani.

None of them knew that new tactics were already being used against al-Qahtani. Major General Miller was the highest-ranking official who approved the hybrid plan. The Pentagon had never heard of it.

The senior Pentagon aides left Rumsfeld's suite through the dining room and headed to the office of Paul Wolfowitz, the deputy secretary.

They all took seats at a conference table, with Wolfowitz at the head, then brought out copies of the Hill memo and the attached Dunlavey request.

"All right," Wolfowitz said, "What do we think?"

The men started reading down the list of recommended tactics. Category I seemed easy—yelling at a detainee, deceiving him, suggesting that the interrogators were from countries with reputations for torturing prisoners. Scaring them, tricking them—those were all techniques used in police interrogations. No problem there.

On to Category II: standing for four hours; using falsified documents; isolation; deprivation of light, sound, and comfort items; twenty-hour interrogations; leaving prisoners naked during questioning; forced shaving of facial hair; exploiting detainees' phobias.

Most of these didn't involve even touching the detainees, with the possible exception of the forced shaving. There was no real pain associated with any of the other actions, just fear and discomfort. This was a closer call than Category I, but again, the tactics struck the men as allowable.

Category III, the most aggressive of all. The officials took a moment to read the requested methods: convincing detainees that either they or their families were about to be killed; exposing them to cold; waterboarding; and using physical contact, such as grabbing or poking.

"These are icky," said Feith, the deputy secretary for policy.

Haynes spoke. He knew that the Office of Legal Counsel at the Justice Department had declared techniques like these to be lawful. But that, he argued, didn't mean they should be used by the military.

"The DOJ is very permissive in what's allowed," he said. "But I think it's a real mistake to go this far."

Heads nodded. Most of these ideas were over the line.

Still, one seemed less troublesome—grabbing and poking. Not inflicting pain, more like asserting authority. Didn't police do this, too? The group agreed; such mild physical contact was allowable.

Someone had to write up the recommendation. Haynes volunteered. It wasn't really the kind of job he should have been doing; he was supposed to comment on the legality of policy initiatives, not write the proposals himself. But Feith and Wolfowitz worked slowly, and he figured it would take them forever to put together a memo; others in the room had even weaker credentials for the job.

Haynes headed to his office and typed up the one-page document. He finished at 1:00 P.M.

• • •

The next day was Thanksgiving and Rumsfeld stayed home, where he reviewed the Haynes memo along with the attachments, including the letter from Hill and the request from Dunlavey.

Rumsfeld didn't return to the office until the following Monday, December 2. He brought out the memo at the senior staff meeting that morning and read it over one more time.

"What's the big deal about standing for four hours?" he asked.

Before anyone answered, he signed his name, approving the recommendation. At the bottom of the page, he scribbled a message reflecting his question, almost as an addendum.

"However, I stand for 8–10 hours a day," he wrote. "Why is standing limited to 4 hours?"

14

The late afternoon meeting in the Pentagon suite of the navy general counsel broke up amid a flurry of files and papers gathered from the conference table. The office was luxurious, with elegant drapes and bookshelves that reached from the floor to the high ceilings. Symbols of naval history dotted the office—a large model of a notable World War II ship, sextants, compasses, and artwork portraying great moments from past conflicts. Only the green-tinted light that colored the room—coaxed in from windows specially coated to prevent electronic eavesdropping—offset the plush atmosphere.

As his lieutenants headed out, the general counsel, Alberto Mora, rose from the head seat at the conference table and made his way toward his desk. Once the others were gone, David Brant, head of the Naval Criminal Investigative Service, approached him.

"You have a minute?" Brant asked.

"What's up?"

"I just need to talk to you about something."

There were some troubling reports coming in from NCIS investigators stationed at Guantanamo, Brant said, choosing his words with care.

"My people are saying that detainees are being abused down there," he said. "They haven't participated in it, and they haven't witnessed it, but it's apparently been inflicted by members of JTF-170," the intelligence task force.

Has to be some sort of rogue operation, Mora thought.

Brant hesitated, but only for a flicker of a second. "Now, the rumor is that this has been approved at the highest levels," he said. "We think it's repugnant. We think it's unlawful and contrary to American values."

Even if ordered to take part in these interrogations, Brant said, his people would refuse. In fact, some of them wanted out of Guantanamo completely, to escape being associated with a place that stank of barbarity.

"Do you want to know more?" Brant asked.

Mora realized that Brant was giving him a way out. He appreciated the consideration—he could say no and hide behind a wall of ignorance if these rumors blew up into scandal. He doubted that would happen. Whatever misdeeds might be uncovered would surely be the work of a few misguided mavericks. But even if he was wrong, even if there was something more ominous going on, Mora wouldn't be walking away from this.

"I have to know more," he said. "If this is true, it's very serious."

They agreed to get together the next day with other military officials who should know about any suspicious goings-on.

The meeting was held the following afternoon in Mora's office. He invited four other Pentagon officials to hear Brant out, including Dr. Michael Gelles, the chief psychologist for NCIS.

Brant repeated what he had told Mora. He explained that, even though the navy investigators had not witnessed abusive interrogations, there was ample reason to believe their suspicions were true.

Gelles agreed. "Guantanamo isn't a big place, it's like a small village," he said. "The different commands go to the same restaurants, work out of the same jails. They engage in the same recreational activities."

As a result, Gelles said, the criminal investigators mingled constantly with their counterparts in the intelligence unit who pulled no punches about what they were doing in the interrogation rooms.

"The guards and interrogators with JTF-170 are under immense pressure to produce results," he said. "And they've begun using some abusive techniques with the detainees."

A document was passed around that read like a transcript of a recent interrogation. It described treatment, like forcing detainees to wear women's underwear, making them hold their bodies in painful positions, and subjecting them to coercive psychological techniques.

Mora read each page with rising disgust, but not outrage. Yes, the tactics described were aggressive and crude, but in his view they didn't rise to the level of inhumane treatment—much less torture.

Then Gelles dashed that thought. "This isn't the full scope of what's going on," he said. "What we're hearing is there are harsh interrogations taking place where there is physical abuse."

And, he said, there was no dissuading the military interrogators from venturing down this destructive path. "They believe that these techniques aren't just useful, but necessary to get the information they want."

Regardless, Gelles said, the interrogators were transgressing the boundaries they had been taught to respect and committing acts that would constitute crimes if used against an American citizen.

Whoever approved these techniques had no familiarity with the voluminous literature on interrogation, and that meant they had no understanding of the dangers they had unleashed, Gelles said.

Unlike seasoned law enforcement agents—who by trial and by training had mastered the art of interrogation—these loose cannons were young and inexperienced, with no grasp of how free-for-all tactics could corrupt them.

"Once the initial barrier against the use of force has been breached, it can set in motion a concept known as 'force drift,' " Gelles said. "It's an observed phenomenon among interrogators who rely on force."

Permission to mistreat prisoners conveys the unmistakable message that cruelty works, leading raw interrogators to the seemingly logical conclusion that if mild abuse doesn't get results, inflicting a higher amount of pain might.

"So the level of force used against an uncooperative witness tends to escalate such that, if left unchecked, it could reach levels that include torture," he said. "I'm very concerned that the conditions at Guantanamo are such that it's ripe for this phenomenon to emerge."

There was an uncomfortable urgency in Gelles's words that struck Mora hard. The doctor had an unrivaled reputation for his expertise in the practical application of psychology to law enforcement and national defense—he had helped the military question spies and had worked closely with the CIA. He was exactly the kind of specialist who should have been consulted on how to put together an effective interrogation program. But based on what he was saying, it appeared that the military had decided to wing it without soliciting the advice of its own experts. If Gelles was this worried, then Mora was, too.

Brant leaned forward, looking uneasy. "These guys don't know what they're doing," he said. "But like I said, this is not some rogue operation. And this isn't just something that's been sanctioned by the local command. It's reportedly been authorized at a high level in Washington."

"Do we know who authorized it?" Mora asked.

"No," Brant replied. "We don't have any more information on that."

They would soon enough, though. "A lot of people are talking about it at Guantanamo," he said, "And it's bound to get out."

Mora glanced around the table, taking in the dismay that knotted the faces of his colleagues as they waited to hear his verdict.

"This could be unlawful and certainly contrary to our national values, even if this is limited to one individual," he said. "That in itself would be a scandal and would create legal exposure to everybody associated with this."

Mora praised Brant, Gelles, and their associates at NCIS for taking the initiative to divulge the irregularities they had uncovered and he promised to take swift action. The meeting ended in an almost mournful silence.

Rear Admiral Michael Lohr stayed behind. Alone with Mora, he shook his head and grimaced. "I can't believe I'm hearing this," he said.

2:00 A.M. Eight hours later. Second straight hour of interrogation.

The sergeants questioning al-Qahtani had hung a photograph of a scantily clad model around his neck to demean and offend him. They knew that, like most fundamentalist Muslims, he considered viewing women dressed in provocative clothing to be an affront to God.

Al-Qahtani was unbolted from the floor and led by the guards to the bathroom. As he walked out, he ripped off the photo. The guards grabbed him and pushed him to the floor.

"What do you think you're doing?" one of the guards asked.

"What do you think you are going to do to me?" al-Qahtani replied.

3:00 A.M.

The interrogators brought out a binder filled with pictures of women in bikinis. One of them started holding up the images to al-Qahtani.

"Tell me, are the women the same or different?" he asked.

Averting his eyes, al-Qahtani began to struggle. One of the interrogators sprinkled water on his head.

"Are they the same or different?" the interrogator asked again.

Al-Qahtani looked at the photos. "They are different," he said.

7:40 A.M.

The United States had captured a lot of al-Qaeda members and seized their computers, one of the interrogators said.

"Do you think we're going to find your address on the confiscated computers?" he asked.

"You might find it. It's possible."

An admission. A big one.

"Why is it possible that we would find your address on an al-Qaeda computer?"

Al-Qahtani's eyes narrowed. "You must have misunderstood me," he said. "My address won't be found on any of the al-Qaeda computers."

Later that day at the Pentagon, Mora telephoned his counterpart in the army, Steven Morello. Maybe, he thought, the other general counsels might be able to work with him to find out what was going on. He and Morello had a friendly professional relationship, so he seemed the best person to contact first.

"Steve, I hear some rumors that there are some interrogation abuses going on at Guantanamo," Mora said.

"Yeah, I know something about that," Morello replied. "Come on down."

Mora's jaw dropped. Morello *already knew.* The gossip from Cuba was apparently making the rounds fast at the Pentagon. He hurried to Morello's office two floors below.

Morello and his deputy, Tom Taylor, were waiting for him in a small conference room. The three took seats at a small round table, and Morello pushed a document over to Mora.

"We tried to stop this," he said.

It was the memo from Jim Haynes that had been signed by Rumsfeld two weeks before, along with the attachments that described the methods that Guantanamo interrogators wanted to use.

Mora scanned it quickly and, at first, saw nothing disturbing. *Sensory deprivation techniques*—well, sure, put the guy in a dark room for ten minutes. He had the same reaction to every proposal: nothing wrong with doing this, nothing wrong with doing that.

Then a thought struck him. *Where are the limits?*

How long could a man be forced to stand in a darkened, soundless room? Ten minutes? Ten hours? Ten days? The memo gave no hint of the answer. That crucial decision—which could transform a clever tactic into brutal cruelty—had apparently been left to the interrogators. And the memo provided no guidance. Mora's gaze shifted to the bottom of the Haynes memo and fastened on Rumsfeld's scrawl.

However, I stand for 8–10 hours a day. Why is standing limited to 4 hours?

It had to be a joke, Mora thought—but a stupid one to make. In a courtroom, those blithe words could be interpreted in a very ugly way. Rumsfeld should never have written them, but once he did, Haynes should never have circulated the memo.

Mora sighed. *Poor Jim Haynes,* he thought.

He knew that the Pentagon general counsel had been at the office around the clock almost every day for more than a year. His workload was just impossible. Haynes had told him that he had once fallen asleep at the wheel while driving home and jerked back awake in the nick of time.

Jim just missed it, Mora thought. His mind numbed by overwork, he had no doubt skimmed over the notation without registering its significance. And besides—what was Haynes doing writing this memo, anyway? Did somebody who wanted to keep his name off this dump it on him? Sure, it had legal ramifications, but the document was primarily a policy statement. It should have been written by Feith or Wolfowitz, not foisted on the general counsel.

Mora thumbed through a few more pages. A whole bevy of lawyers at various rankings had approved the techniques. Of course Haynes was going to defer to their collective judgment. It wasn't his job to conduct legal research.

Haynes's people had failed him, Mora thought, hadn't looked out for him the way they should have. They themselves probably didn't grasp the implications of what they were rubber-stamping, or recognize how this could blow up in everybody's face, all the way to Rumsfeld, if the public ever got wind of it.

Mora decided that he needed to read the document through again more thoroughly. There was no reason to force Morello to sit there and watch him do it. He asked to borrow the memo; sure, came the reply.

"Thanks for sharing this with me," Mora said as he headed for the door.

This is absurd!

Mora was at his desk, reading a legal analysis about detainee treatment that had been sent from Guantanamo months before. *This* mess—written by the chief legal advisor at the detention center, Diane Beaver—was what the Pentagon had relied upon in approving harsh interrogation tactics? Everything in it—its logic, its interpretations, its conclusions—was not only wrong, it was laughably wrong. In a mere six and a half pages, Beaver had single-handedly managed to annul hundreds of years of jurisprudence.

International law didn't apply. Mora could only shake his head at the colossal misjudgment. The president makes a declaration and suddenly the United States is not bound by the rules that govern every nation? What if the Russians tried that ploy, or the Chinese? How could Beaver not realize that this wild idea would drain the meaning out of every international human rights agreement ever written?

The rest of the memo only amplified the folly of her reasoning. Cruel, inhuman, and degrading treatment could be inflicted on Guantanamo detainees with near impunity because, at that location, no law prohibited it. No court would have jurisdiction to rule on an abuse allegation, so no interrogator could be subject to criminal prosecution. The military had created a toxic stew at Guantanamo: poorly trained interrogators, told to mistreat prisoners, with no limitations and no exposure to the law. This was a disaster. The potential damage to America's security, prestige, and moral bearing was incalculable.

This travesty of justice rested on a precarious tower of policy misjudgments and legal error. He had to knock it down, Mora decided. Rumsfeld's decision had to be rescinded—and quickly.

December 20, 11:15 A.M. Into the eleventh straight hour.

"Bark!" an interrogator yelled.

Al-Qahtani struggled, closing his eyes tightly.

"Dogs are held in higher esteem than you. At least they know right from wrong, and know that they have to protect innocent people from bad people. So do some dog tricks. Then we can elevate you to the social status of a dog."

No reply. Al-Qahtani grew more agitated.

"Bark!" the interrogator repeated.

Then "stay." Then "come."

"You're going to learn your dog tricks," the interrogator said.

1:00 P.M.

"Bark!"

"Stop this! I should be treated like a man!"

"You have to be trained," the interrogator replied. "You have to learn who to defend and who to attack."

An assortment of pictures was brought out. One of the interrogators showed the first set to al-Qahtani. They were photographs of victims from 9/11.

"Bark happy for these people."

Al-Qahtani said nothing.

"Bark happy for these people!"

A pause. Then al-Qahtani barked.

The interrogator brought out a second set of photographs. They were images of the 9/11 hijackers.

"Growl at these people!"

Al-Qahtani growled.

The dog tricks ended, and it was on to the next indignity. One of the interrogators wrapped a towel around al-Qahtani's head.

"Time for your dance lessons," an interrogator said.

The two sergeants began to instruct al-Qahtani on how to dance. He reared back and tried to kick one of the guards. No one reacted, and the dance lessons resumed.

Later that day, Mora was waiting outside Haynes's office when his boss appeared in the doorway.

"Alberto, how are you?" he said. "Come on in."

Mora had told Haynes only that they needed to discuss some issues involving Guantanamo, and he knew he would get a respectful hearing. That was Haynes's way with subordinates. Though he rarely spoke or even reacted in one-on-one meetings, he always listened closely to their concerns and never cut them off until they had said their piece. Mora felt certain that his distress would be resolved before he left Haynes's office.

The two men took seats at a small conference table. Haynes leaned forward, a finger on his temple.

"What's this about?" he asked.

Mora told him of the reports from NCIS agents about abuse at Guantanamo. He mentioned that he had obtained a copy of the Rumsfeld memo and attached documents.

"I'm surprised that the secretary was allowed to sign it," he said. "I know this wasn't the intent, but in my view, some of these authorized techniques could rise to the level of torture."

"They don't," Haynes replied.

"Jim, think this through a little more carefully," Mora said.

Consider how vague the language is, he said. What, for example, did "deprivation of light and auditory stimuli" mean?

"Could a detainee be locked in a completely dark cell? And for how long? A month? Longer?"

Then there was the approval for using the detainees' fears against them. "What precisely did that permit?" Mora asked. "Could a detainee be held in a coffin? Could phobias be applied until madness set in?"

Nor could the rightness or wrongness of an interrogation tactic be measured in isolation from the others, Mora said. Ordeal could be piled on ordeal, strung together in a sensory overload that would cross the line into torture.

"There are no limitations spelled out," he said. "There is no boundary for prohibited treatment. And that boundary has to be at the point where cruel and unusual punishment or treatment begins."

Haynes said nothing, but his eyes were fixed on Mora as he drank in every word. He was in his "downloading information" mode, Mora thought.

"And you shouldn't rely on the Beaver legal brief," he continued. "It's an incompetent piece of legal analysis."

Its chief flaw was to set torture as the start and end point of the analysis. But that was not the boundary for permissible behavior; the treatment of a detainee did not have to rise to the level of torture to be illegal. Beaver's memo was an astonishing repudiation of historic laws and jurisprudence that prohibited cruel, inhumane, and degrading treatment—actions that fell short of torture.

Take a step back and look at the conclusions, Mora said—international law didn't apply, because the president says it doesn't; domestic law doesn't apply, because the detainees were being held at Guantanamo; and even if the laws were deemed worthy of consideration, only the most horrendous violations would be reviewed.

Then there was the approval signed by Rumsfeld, and the potential for political fallout from the secretary's flippant remark about how many hours each day he spent on his feet.

"I'm confident that the secretary was meaning to be jocular," Mora said. "But the defense attorneys for the detainees are sure to view it differently. If the memo isn't withdrawn quickly, it's going to be discovered and used at the military commissions. And, since his signature is on it, the secretary is certain to be called as a witness."

Any competent defense lawyer would portray Rumsfeld's note as a signal to interrogators that they shouldn't worry about the limits spelled out in the authorization and instead should feel free to do whatever was necessary to obtain the information they needed.

The stakes were enormous, Mora said. "These memos and the practices they authorized threaten the entire military commission process."

That was all Mora had to say. Haynes nodded.

"Thank you for bringing this to me, Alberto," he said. "I'll pay attention to what you said and think about it."

Mora left the office in a flush of relief. Haynes had listened to everything he had said. Problem solved, and just in time. He and his family were about to jet off to Florida for the holidays. Now Mora could enjoy his vacation.

December 21, 10:23 P.M. Into the tenth hour of interrogation.

An army sergeant shoved al-Qahtani into a sitting position on the floor and stood over him.

"You don't deserve to be seated in a chair like a civilized human being," one of the interrogators said. "You're beneath me. You should be at my feet."

Al-Qahtani looked down.

"You're a weak-minded coward," the interrogator said. "You kill innocent women and children who are created by God."

Nothing.

The interrogator launched into a monologue about Saudi Arabia, al-Qahtani's homeland. The Saudi government had been making big changes, she said. It was cracking down on the terrorists, locking them up. As she spoke, she moved closer to al-Qahtani.

"Get away from me!" he snapped.

He pressed his hands and feet against the floor to thrust his body backward, but the guards lunged at him and flattened him on his back. The interrogator straddled him without putting any weight on him. As she continued speaking, al-Qahtani tried to knock her off by bending his legs; the guards grabbed his shins and held him down.

He turned his head and started praying loudly. The interrogator ignored him.

Al-Qaeda was on the run, she said. Qaed Salim Sinan al-Harethi, one of bin Laden's top associates and a suspect in the *Cole* bombing, had recently been killed by the CIA.

"He was in a car in Yemen," she said. "He probably thought he was safe, didn't think we could find him. We hit him with a missile. Blew him up where he sat. Al-Qaeda can't hide from us. It's done."

The linguist leaned in toward al-Qahtani as she translated the interrogator's words.

"Get out of my face!" he spat.

She didn't move and continued interpreting.

December 23, 12:30 A.M. Thirty minutes.

The lead interrogator walked into a booth where al-Qahtani was being held. A recording of white noise was playing and pictures of swimsuit models dangled from his neck. He looked distraught.

"How are you doing, Mo?" the interrogator asked.

"I have problems."

"What are the problems?"

Al-Qahtani glared. "They are between me and God."

"Tell me your problems. They can't be solved unless you say what they are."

Al-Qahtani wept.

The pictures of the swimsuit models he was forced to wear, the incessant questioning he was forced to endure, the stiff metal chair he was forced to sit on, all the other indignities he was forced to endure—those were his problems.

"I cannot handle this treatment much longer," he said.

"Is there anything else that's a problem for you? Are you in pain?"

No, al-Qahtani said.

For several minutes, the interrogator explained to al-Qahtani why he was being treated so roughly. The soldiers knew that he found all of these things unpleasant. That was the point. They wanted al-Qahtani to understand that they were in charge, that his situation was futile, that no matter how hard he resisted, they would never relent.

"You chose this lifestyle," the interrogator said.

Al-Qahtani said nothing.

After a moment, the interrogator removed the pictures of the scantily clad women from around al-Qahtani's neck.

"The test of your ability to answer questions is going to begin now."

Al-Qahtani fell into a sullen silence. Then he looked up at the interrogator.

"I will answer your questions after you pour water over my head, and tell me you will do that to me day after day," he said.

Al-Qahtani seemed to be looking for a way out. Perhaps he thought he could rationalize cooperation with the enemy if he himself set the rules for his mistreatment. But the interrogators couldn't allow him to take control, even by agreeing to his request to mistreat him.

"Think about your decision to answer questions," the interrogator said. "I'll only ask questions if you fully cooperate."

January 1, 11:00 P.M. Fourth hour.

Al-Qahtani was struggling to stay awake. An interrogator was discussing the Koran and the obligations it imposes on Muslims to observe justice for orphans. Al-Qaeda had left many children orphaned, the interrogator said. They deserved justice. Al-Qahtani could bring them justice by telling the truth.

"What made nineteen Saudi Arabian men want to kill themselves?" the interrogator asked.

"I'm not sure. Maybe they were tricked."

"How could one man, bin Laden, convince nineteen young men to kill themselves?"

Al-Qahtani's head rocked and his eyes closed. He was drifting in and out of sleep.

The interrogator loudly repeated the question. Al-Qahtani opened his eyes.

"They were tricked," he said. "He distorted the picture in front of them."

"Does that make you mad?"

"Yes."

"Are you mad that your friends were tricked?"

"Yes."

The interrogator felt pleased. Al-Qahtani did not realize he had just been lumped in with the hijackers.

"Did your friends know about the plan?"

"No." Al-Qahtani's head lolled.

"Did you know about the plan?"

"No."

"Did Mohammed Atta know about the plan?"

"I don't know."

"Does it make you mad that he killed your friends?"

"Yes."

"Are you glad you didn't die on the plane?"

"Yes."

"Are your parents glad you didn't die?"

"Yes."

"Did you call your parents after you didn't get on the plane?"

"No."

"You knew getting on the plane was wrong, didn't you?"

"Yes."

"But you still wanted to fight?"

"Yes."

Al-Qahtani's head drooped and his words slurred. He said nothing more.

The weary eyes of John Leso, the army psychologist, filled with tears.

He had been stationed at Guantanamo Bay for six months, and had been deeply shaken by what he had seen. When given the assignment, he thought he would be treating psychologically distressed soldiers but was soon ordered to join the Behavioral Science Consultation Team, with responsibility for serving as a psychological advisor for interrogations. He had sat through a meeting that fall where members of the military and the CIA nonchalantly bandied about theories on how best to conduct abusive questioning—and how to make sure the Red Cross never found out. Now, in January, he was being rotated out and replaced as chief psychologist by an associate, Colonel Larry James. He was ready to leave Guantanamo, but feared that it would never leave him.

When James arrived at Guantanamo, he was shocked by Leso's appearance. Once a bundle of eager energy, he had become a haggard, listless hulk of his old self. James couldn't imagine what had happened but recognized the signature symptoms of trauma.

Leso had escorted James to his quarters and the two men had sat down. James waited for Leso to tell him what had happened.

Then the tears began.

"I was pressured to teach interrogators procedures and tactics that were a challenge to my ethics as a psychologist and my moral fiber as a human being," he said. "Being part of this has been just devastating to me."

Leso had witnessed bodies twisted in pain, sexual humiliation, the snarling of attack dogs used to frighten defenseless detainees. He had spent two days observing the interrogation of al-Qahtani, a near bystander with no authority to put a halt to even the most abusive treatment. The senior officers had not uttered a murmur of protest—in fact, they got their marching orders from higher-ups back home. He had tried to persuade the interrogators to ease up, and while they sometimes relented for a while, they always went back to playing rough. They were convinced that abusive tactics worked, even though detainees clammed up when they were used.

For the better part of the evening, Leso spilled his stories, and James played the role of caring sage to suffering patient. By the end of the discussion, Leso's frayed nerves seemed to have steadied. He proposed a quick trip to the mess hall before the place closed. The two headed outside to the SUV.

As they bounced along, Leso stole a glance at his visitor. The hurt in his eyes, James thought, was startling.

"Colonel . . ." Leso began, and then stopped.

He paused, then started again.

"Colonel, you need to be real careful down here," he said. "You can step in a minefield every hour of the day at this place."

Buried explosives, at Guantanamo? Then, in a flash, James realized that Leso wasn't talking about munitions. He was warning him to step carefully, because at any moment he might confront a direct attack on his values—not only as a psychologist, but also as a human being.

Alberto Mora walked into the kitchen in his mother's Key Biscayne home and picked up the phone. It was David Brant, the head of NCIS.

"I'm sorry to be calling you during your vacation," Brant said. "The abuse is still going on in Guantanamo."

Mora took a deep breath and glanced out the window at his mother's swimming pool, collecting his thoughts.

Nothing had changed? Maybe he had been wrong. Maybe this policy of abuse wasn't some fumbling mistake.

"I'll have to deal with this when I get back," Mora said. He returned that same week.

At his fifth-floor office in the heart of historic Old Town Alexandria, Frank Dunham Jr. was reading the ruling just handed down in the Hamdi case. More than two months had passed since Dunham, the federal public defender, had argued before the Fourth Circuit Court of Appeals that the administration had to provide evidence that its detention of Hamdi was legal. But the three-judge panel disagreed.

Since Hamdi was picked up on a battlefield in Afghanistan, the administration had the legal right to designate him as an enemy combatant, the ruling said. An American could go to court to compel the government to justify his detention, but that required officials only to provide the basic facts and legal authority for the determination. Of course, the panel's decision did not grant the government unlimited power—their ruling, the judges said, applied only when the detainee had been seized in a theater of war.

By the time Dunham reached the final page of the ruling, he knew the case was far from closed. It was heading to the Supreme Court.

"Jim," Mora said, "I was really surprised when I got back to hear that the detainee abuse is still going on."

It was the afternoon of January 9. Mora was in Haynes's office again, this time ready to make a stink. Since his return to the Pentagon six days earlier, Mora had been consulting navy officials and reviewing a legal analysis about the issue written by the navy's legal arm, the Judge Advocate General Corps. The brief was detailed and lawyerly, and its conclusion was straightforward—what was going on in Guantanamo was beyond the legal pale.

Mora handed Haynes a copy of the navy's new legal opinion. Haynes gave it a glance; more advice on the pile of conflicting information.

"I understand your position, Alberto," Haynes said. "But there are people here who believe these techniques are necessary to get information out of a few Guantanamo detainees."

These were some of most dangerous enemies faced by the United States, the worst of the worst. They had been entwined in the 9/11 plot and were privy to al-Qaeda's designs to kill more innocents. This wasn't a simple, black-and-white issue, and the administration was doing its best to walk the fine line between respecting their rights and protecting American lives.

"I understand," Mora replied. "I recognize that the ethical issues here are very difficult."

He raised the classic "ticking bomb" scenario. What if a captured terrorist knew of an imminent nuclear attack on an American city? What limits should be placed on interrogating him? Mora said he didn't know.

"If I were the interrogator, I would probably apply the torture myself," Mora said. "And I would do so with the full knowledge that I could face potentially severe personal consequences."

But none of that had any bearing on Guantanamo, Mora said. There was no ticking bomb. There was no justification for abandoning America's cherished laws and values.

"Does the threat of one common criminal against the life of one citizen justify torture or mistreatment?" Mora asked. "If not, how many lives have to be in jeopardy? Where's the threshold? I just don't think that that's something we should be deciding in the Pentagon."

As Mora pressed his case, Haynes gave him his full attention, but his face was inscrutable. Mora's frustration got to him.

"Jim, these policies could threaten the secretary's tenure and could even damage the presidency," he said. "Protect your client."

In a closed session that day, Hans Blix and Mohamed ElBaradei briefed the U.N. Security Council on the weapons inspectors' progress in Iraq.

The inspections had been under way since late November, and the team had searched a long-suspect presidential palace. In early December, Iraq had issued what it called a complete accounting of its weapons programs. The Americans had dismissed the disclosure as a sham. Iraq, they claimed, was hiding information about nerve gas, anthrax, fuels for ballistic missiles, mobile labs for biological weapons, and its efforts to obtain uranium from Niger—a false allegation that later would be proved to have been based on forged documents.

The U.N. inspectors spent several weeks reviewing Iraq's twelve-thousand-page assessment, and also weren't happy with what they found.

Blix opened the briefing with a rundown of the inspectors' recent findings. "If we had found any 'smoking gun,' we would have reported it to the Council," he said. "Similarly, if we had met with a denial of access or other impediment to our inspections, we would have reported it to the Council. We have not submitted any such reports."

The Iraqi declaration, however, was far from adequate. "It is rich in volume but poor in new information about weapons issues and practically devoid of new evidence on such issues," he said. Almost all of the supporting documents were nothing more than rehashes of what had been provided to the U.N. during the inspections of the 1990s.

"Iraq must present credible evidence," he said. "It cannot just maintain that it must be deemed to be without proscribed weapons so long as there is no evidence to the contrary."

Years later, looking back on the declaration, Blix acknowledged that Iraq had been in a difficult bind.

"It was very hard for them to declare any weapons," he said, "when they didn't have any."

• • •

The next day, Larry Di Rita, a Pentagon spokesman, burst into Haynes's office with urgent news.

"There was an enema administered to al-Qahtani in his interrogation," Di Rita said.

"What?"

"They gave al-Qahtani an enema."

Haynes sat back in his chair. *Not good.* Using enemas for interrogation, that would be *way* over the line. He doubted it was true; there were plenty of rumors flying around. Then again, maybe it did happen, maybe there was something to this concept of force drift after all. Whatever the case, jitters were spreading through the Pentagon. They needed to step back and take a closer look at the interrogation policies.

As soon as Di Rita left, Haynes walked down to Rumsfeld's office.

"Boss, I just received a report that al-Qahtani was given an enema as part of his interrogation," Haynes said. "We have to stop this and take another look."

"Why? Just tell them not to do that."

He's blowing this off. "No," Haynes said. "Even if this is just indicative of a rumor, that alone isn't good. There is too much friction in the system."

He told Rumsfeld about Mora's misgivings. If the general counsel of a military branch was alarmed, they couldn't ignore this growing storm without feeding even more damning rumors.

Haynes left Rumsfeld's office uncertain whether the defense secretary was taking the matter seriously. No matter—it was imperative to call an emergency meeting of everyone involved in this controversy. Then he would get back to Rumsfeld and force the issue before it spun out of control.

Mora didn't know whether he should shout "Hallelujah," but by that afternoon, he was convinced that Haynes was taking his concerns seriously. Without explanation, he had set up meetings for Mora with the top lawyers at the Pentagon, offering him the chance to lobby them to reconsider the interrogation policy.

By day's end, Mora had met with the chief legal officers for each branch of the military, the Joint Chiefs of Staff, and the Judge Advocate General Corps. He reviewed the contents and implications of the Rumsfeld authorization with each one and repeated the arguments he had given to Haynes about why it should be rewritten.

Late in the day, Haynes called.

"Alberto, I wanted you to know that the Secretary has been briefed about your concerns," he said. "We're reviewing the matter, and I think changes in the interrogation policy are in the offing. That might happen as early as next week."

Mora smiled. "Thanks, Jim. That's great to hear."

The next day, Saturday, Haynes went back to Rumsfeld.

"Boss, we need a breather on this policy," Haynes said. "I strongly recommend that you rescind everything you approved so we can take a look at everything and make sure all of this is being done right."

Rumsfeld gave a vague and noncommittal reply. His mind was elsewhere—on preparations for an invasion of Iraq. This clamor about Guantanamo was an unwanted distraction. Haynes left the office with no clue of what his boss might do to resolve the problem.

Colonel Larry James, the new Guantanamo psychologist, was making the rounds at about 1:00 A.M. in the buildings that housed the interrogation booths. From an observation room, he heard yelling, screaming, and the sounds of furniture being thrown around. He peeked into the booth from behind a one-way mirror to see what the ruckus was all about.

Inside, James saw one interrogator and three guards wrestling with a detainee. The man was wearing only pink panties, a wig, and lipstick, and now the soldiers were struggling to dress him in a pink nightgown. James felt an urge to rush into the booth and call a halt to the frightening episode but hesitated. Maybe something was happening that he didn't understand. He opened his thermos and poured a cup of coffee, watching as he waited for the events to play themselves out.

They didn't. After several minutes, the fighting hadn't let up.

I need to stop this right now.

James knocked on the door and walked in. He tried hard not to register any shock or disgust on his face at the bizarre scene unfolding in front of him. He called out to the interrogator.

"Hey," he said calmly, "you want some coffee?"

The interrogator got off the detainee, breathing hard. "I sure do, Colonel," he said. "I'll take you up on that."

James looked over at the three guards. "Let the detainee up and put him in a chair," he said. "Give him a break."

He poured the interrogator a cup of coffee and the two of them stepped out of the booth.

The next step. James the army psychologist was about to assume the role of James the army interrogator—although he would be questioning the frustrated soldier, trying to nudge him away from the fruitless path of confrontation. And he would go about it by using relationship-building techniques.

Over the next few minutes, James spoke calmly to the soldier about everything other than the interrogation. Fishing, hunting, the relative quality of a .45-caliber pistol compared to a nine-millimeter.

Slowly, James maneuvered the conversation around to the session he had just witnessed. The interrogator was still simmering over an insult the detainee had screamed at him two days earlier after spitting at him.

" 'I'm gonna butt-fuck your wife' is how I think the interpreter said it, sir," the interrogator said, the anger boiling up.

Still, he had doubts about how he was handling the situation. "Would you be willing to review the case with me tomorrow, sir?" he asked.

"Sure," James replied.

The detainee was a very bad guy. His file revealed that he was a hard-core terrorist and had been aggressively resistant to questioning. But manhandling and humiliating him were guaranteed to fail, James knew.

When he held the promised review with the interrogator, James asked him how it was going.

"Sir, the problem is that the fucker won't talk to me," he replied.

Okay, James said. He asked what the detainee was being fed. The same meals that soldiers in the field get, the interrogator said. Nothing hot, nothing particularly tasty, but good enough.

"Here's what I recommend," James said. Go to the base McDonald's and pick up a fish sandwich. Then buy the *Sports Illustrated* swimsuit issue at the PX, he said; Muslim or no, the man hadn't seen a woman in a year.

The soldier looked aghast. "You don't want me to give that stuff to him, do you, sir?" he asked. "'Cause that just ain't right, sir."

Not yet, James said. Instead, go into the interrogation booth and eat the sandwich. Have some pistachios and tea as well. Read the magazine. Don't ask the man a single question, don't yell at him. Do the same thing for three days.

"Well, hell, I don't mind eating and looking at girls, sir, but that's not my job," the interrogator said. "I'm supposed to be getting intel from this guy."

Just give it a try, James said. "At the end of the week, bring an extra fish sandwich. Let's see what happens."

It worked. When the soldier arrived with the extra meal, he casually handed it to the detainee. He let him have the magazine. Slowly, the prisoner warmed to his former tormentor. He started talking, revealing useful intelligence.

A meal from McDonald's had pulled off what a year of abuse had failed to achieve.

At the White House, Bush was meeting with his national security team for an in-depth review of the administration's counterterrorism efforts.

One of the biggest challenges they faced, Tenet said, was al-Qaeda's continued success in attracting new foot soldiers. Rice and Wolfowitz agreed, fretting that American efforts had failed to stem the influx of jihadist recruits.

Bush waved a hand dismissively. "Victory will take care of that problem."

Some of the people in the room were flabbergasted. In a single sentence, they thought, Bush had revealed volumes about his strategic thinking. There was no question that he was referring to the impending invasion of Iraq. Somehow, Bush had come to believe that ousting Saddam would—what? frighten? impress?—extremists so much that they would abandon jihad.

It was, one aide believed, an extraordinarily dangerous assumption.

"Should the interrogations of al-Qahtani continue?" Rumsfeld asked.

It was Sunday, January 12, and Rumsfeld had just telephoned General Tom Hill, the SOUTHCOM commander. Jim Haynes had reported that interrogators had forced an enema on al-Qahtani, Rumsfeld said. Now he was pushing for Rumsfeld to withdraw his authorization for the aggressive interrogation techniques. But if the military was done questioning al-Qahtani, the whole point was moot.

Hill replied that he didn't know where things stood with al-Qahtani. "I'll discuss the question with General Miller," he said.

He contacted Miller at Guantanamo that same day and explained the secretary's concerns. He called back Rumsfeld in less than an hour. No enema had

been given to al-Qahtani in an interrogation, he said, and the detainee had yet
to provide much information.

"I recommend that we continue the interrogation," Hill said.

Rumsfeld agreed.

His decision didn't last long. A few hours later, Rumsfeld called Hill again.
Stop everything but Category I techniques, he said. He needed time to think
about this.

That afternoon, the secure red line phone in Haynes's office rang. General Hill
was calling, and he was furious.

"Jim, I heard from the secretary, and what you're telling him is bullshit!" Hill
fumed. "We gave al-Qahtani an enema a month and a half ago because the doc
said he needed one. We don't do that stuff in interrogations!"

Already, Hill said, they were suffering the consequences. Rumsfeld ordered
him to suspend everything except Category I. They could yell at al-Qahtani and
deceive him. Great, like that was going to work all by itself.

"Tom, I'm glad you're not doing anything wrong," Haynes replied. "But it's
my judgment that we should take a breather and take another look at this because there are too many rumors."

Hill grumbled a response and hung up.

The partial—and temporary—suspension of the harshest forms of interrogation wasn't enough, Haynes decided. It was a halfhearted half measure.
The entire authorization needed to be rescinded and a new one written from
scratch.

Haynes typed a memo for Rumsfeld that would withdraw his interrogation
order. Now all he had to do was persuade the secretary to sign it.

On the morning of January 15, Alberto Mora handed his assistant a draft memo
and asked her to drop it off with Haynes's secretary. His high hopes from the
previous Friday had been dashed. Haynes had arranged for those meetings with
the lawyers and then . . . nothing. No new information, no suggestion from
Haynes that the policy was under review.

That morning, he realized he had never put his objections in writing. So he
wrote the memo detailing his concerns about the interrogation policy and his
belief that it authorized, at a minimum, cruel treatment and, at worst, torture.

He addressed the draft to Haynes and Jane Dalton, chief legal advisor to the Joint Chiefs.

After the memo was left at Haynes's office, Mora called him to explain why he had felt compelled to write it.

"Jim," he said, "I've been increasingly uncomfortable, given the amount of time that's passed, that I haven't put my view on the interrogation issues in writing."

He hadn't signed the memo yet, Mora said, so it didn't need to be treated yet as an official document. "But," he said, "I'll be signing it out late this afternoon unless I hear definitively that the use of the interrogation techniques has been or is being suspended."

Haynes asked Mora to stop by that afternoon. He didn't mention that he had already sent Rumsfeld the proposed withdrawal order, but he still had to discuss it with the secretary before he could be confident it would be signed.

By the time Mora showed up in his office, Haynes hoped, the whole issue would already be resolved.

About that same time in London, Tony Blair was attending a meeting at the Ministry of Defence for a briefing on Iraq. An array of senior officers, including Admiral Michael Boyce, the chief of the defense staff, and the heads of each armed forces branch, was there in full uniform. The room was packed, with staffers crammed against the walls on three sides.

Boyce spoke first. The Americans, he said, were set to launch an invasion of Iraq. "We anticipate that President Bush will make a decision on February 15 and they would go within twelve days or so to a massive air, sea, and land operation," he said.

He glanced up from some notes. "It is going to be called 'Shock and Awe' and the scale will reflect that," he said. "There will be hundreds of plane sorties from day one, aimed at wiping out Saddam's infrastructure and playing for a 'house of cards' effect."

Britain would deploy large numbers of planes and ships, along with up to forty-two thousand troops. The Americans would send in as many as three hundred thousand soldiers. Iraq's oil fields would be seized immediately, which, he said, might inflame the conspiracy theories about the war's true purpose.

That probably wouldn't be a problem, said naval commander Alan West.

"There will be so much going on in the first day or so that the international media won't know where to go," he said.

Either way, the fields had to be secured quickly in order to prevent the ecological disaster that would ensue if Saddam blew them up in hopes of sowing global economic chaos.

"What if Saddam retreats to fortress Baghdad?" Blair asked.

The expectation, Boyce said, was that the scale of the attack would break Saddam's grip on Iraq, and without the terror he inspired in his people, he would have nowhere to hide. His own countrymen would turn him in.

"Give me your judgment on the plan," Blair said. "Will it work?"

"Yes," Boyce replied. "It will."

"But I'm concerned about the number of bombs planned to be dropped on Baghdad and the risk of collateral damage and civilian casualties," Blair said.

The technology was different than in the Persian Gulf War, an advisor from British intelligence said. The accuracy of the precision-guided munitions— smart bombs—had improved dramatically since then. Still, this was sure to be a bloody war, and the scale of the bombing campaign would unquestionably result in civilian deaths.

Blair mulled that over. "We need to get the proper humanitarian support in place," he said.

Plans should be formulated immediately for dealing with Iraq in the aftermath of the invasion, he said. Millions of people would suddenly be without a government, probably without water or electricity. America and Britain had the moral duty to tackle those problems and couldn't wait until after Saddam fell to prepare a plan.

Then, the biggest question. "What is the chance of Saddam using his WMD?" Blair asked.

He might want to try, Boyce said, but probably couldn't succeed. "The intelligence leaves no ambiguity over Saddam's willingness to use WMD if he judged the time was right," he said. But, since the Iraqi dictator was currently concealing his weapons from the U.N. inspectors, he might not have enough time to get them ready for action.

"That's the reason Tommy Franks has gone with the doctrine of overwhelming force," Boyce said. "The Americans believe that Saddam is operating on an assumption that the operation would be done by air strikes first, and then move in on land. The plan is to catch him off guard."

Anxiety was etched on the prime minister's face. "What could the worst outcome of action be?" he asked.

Of course, the use of weapons of mass destruction, Boyce replied, and the burning of the Iraqi oil fields—just because they doubted Saddam could do either one didn't mean they were right. Then, the day after, when Saddam was gone, chaos might ensue.

"Any rapid regime collapse followed by a power vacuum could result in internecine fighting between the Shia and Sunni populations," Boyce said, "and adventuring by adjacent countries and ethnic groups that could irretrievably fracture the country."

Blair thanked the officers and left the room with a coterie of assistants. As the group marched solemnly down a dimly lit hallway, the only noise was the clicking of heels on the floor.

Outside, they climbed into waiting cars. Blair said nothing. The die was cast; the Americans were going on the attack. The shooting and dying could begin in just a few weeks. And they weren't prepared for the aftermath.

A few hours later, Mora arrived for his meeting with Haynes. The deputy general counsel, Daniel Dell'Orto, joined them.

Haynes slid Mora's draft memo across the table to him. "I don't know what you're trying to accomplish with this," he said. "Surely you must know how I feel about these issues and the impact of what you've done."

"No, Jim, I don't. I have no idea if you agree with me totally, or disagree, or come out somewhere in the middle. You never said anything."

Haynes laughed. "Yeah, I know."

A moment passed. "Well, I can tell you that the secretary is considering suspending his authorization later today," Haynes said.

Considering? What did that mean? Maybe even Haynes didn't know, Mora thought. He hesitated before speaking.

"Well, I'm delighted to hear that," Mora finally said, choosing his words carefully. "Then I won't be signing out my memo."

Haynes nodded. "Let me get back to you later," he said.

He called Mora within a few hours.

"Good news," he said. "Rumsfeld suspended the techniques."

Mora smiled. "That's great, Jim."

• • •

In Paris, a swarm of police motorcycles escorted a black SUV down the rue du Faubourg Saint-Honoré toward the Élysée Palace, the official residence of President Jacques Chirac.

The entourage reached the front gate encased by a massive archway and headed inside. Hans Blix and Mohamed ElBaradei stepped out of the SUV and were greeted at the entrance by an aide who accompanied them inside for a meeting with Chirac.

It was January 17. Blix and ElBaradei had come to Paris to brief the French head of state on their progress in Iraq. The news was not good. Inspectors had just located a crate of warheads for the delivery of chemical weapons. They contained no illegal agents, but that was beside the point. The Iraqis were still required to have reported them to the U.N. Then the inspectors turned up a stash of documents at the home of a nuclear scientist describing how to use lasers for uranium enrichment missile guidance. The Iraqis insisted this was just an instance of a single scientist squirreling away his own papers, but the weapons inspectors didn't buy that.

Chirac listened impassively as Blix laid out the facts. "The situation has been very tense," he said. "There hasn't been any real effort by the Iraqis to solve any of the outstanding disarmament issues."

Still, the inspectors were stymied. They hadn't uncovered any indisputable evidence that Iraq was secreting away weapons of mass destruction. Mobile labs for creating toxins and anthrax, underground facilities, dual-use equipment ready for rapid transformation into weapons—nothing like that had turned up yet. His team would have to keep looking for them.

"It is also possible," he said, "that few weapons of mass destruction actually exist."

Chirac was unimpressed. "I do not believe that Iraq poses any real threat, at least not one that would call for a military intervention," he said. "Our intelligence service does not have any serious evidence that these weapons exist."

There was no doubt that, in the early 1990s, Iraq had possessed such armaments. "It is my view that the original weapons inspections revealed what we needed to know," Chirac said. "They succeeded. Iraq has already been disarmed."

So why go to war? Why would the Americans—or anyone, for that matter—

consider a military action when the evidence of a threat was little more than wisps of rumors?

"War is the worst solution," Chirac said. "It will fuel Muslim hatred of the West. It will create terrorists. France is not ready to be drawn into such a war."

As the conversation wound down, the French president questioned whether Saddam understood the dangers he faced. "He is locked up in an intellectual bunker," Chirac said. "None of the people around him dare tell him the truth. If there is war, he will be eliminated."

Saddam's only choice, Chirac said, was to back down, to offer conciliatory and positive statements. Perhaps, though, the Iraqi dictator would prove incapable of acting in his own best interest.

Jim Haynes walked into his conference room for the weekly meeting with senior lawyers at the Pentagon, including the general counsels for each military branch and their aides. As usual, there was no written agenda, just an opportunity for the attorneys to update him on their projects and raise any concerns. Once those presentations were finished, Haynes made an announcement.

"The secretary has ordered me to set up a working group for the different services to put together a study examining the issues associated with detainee interrogation," he said. "He said that he wants this done very quickly, so we have very tight deadlines for this."

Mary Walker, the air-force general counsel, would be in charge, Haynes said, and would divide the responsibilities among her colleagues.

Haynes glanced around the room. "Any questions?"

None. "Okay, let's get back to work," he said.

The members of the working group probably weren't up to the job on their own, Haynes mused. The legal quagmires they faced—interrogation techniques, constitutional law, antitorture statutes, international treaties, the rules of sovereignty—were far from their areas of proficiency. They would need outside expertise.

He knew just the unit—and just the man—to handle the job: the Office of Legal Counsel at the Department of Justice, specifically John Yoo.

Haynes phoned Yoo. "John, we've put together a working group that's going to examine the interrogation issues top to bottom," he said. "Our folks want to know what they can do, and we just haven't provided enough guidance. Could you put together an analysis that defines the corners of the box of what's legal?"

Sure, Yoo replied. The two men discussed the points that needed to be addressed, then Yoo promised to get back quickly with a draft.

Yoo hung up, questions racing through his mind. He had kept his cards hidden—neither Haynes nor anyone else at the Pentagon knew that the CIA had already been granted the authority to conduct extremely aggressive interrogations. Yoo had written a memo dated August 1, 2002, laying out the scope and limits of the law for agency interrogators. He wondered if he could simply give Haynes a copy of that, or at least call him back to tell him what his conclusions would be.

Whatever decision he made, Yoo thought, a bigger issue was at play here. Granting the military the same interrogation authority enjoyed by the CIA was a mistake, one that could easily come back to bite the administration.

That afternoon, Yoo dropped onto the couch in the White House counsel's office, where he had come seeking the advice of Gonzales and Addington on how to handle the request from the Pentagon.

"Some of the legal issues are different, because the interrogations are on Guantanamo," Yoo said. "But other than that, this is the same question we answered for the CIA."

If the White House gave the go-ahead, Yoo said, he could provide Haynes with the original CIA memo. But exposing the agency's activities to a broader audience might be a problem.

"My proposal is that we just write the opinion for Jim as if it were a fresh opinion and not tell him where it comes from," Yoo said. "They'll just think we did it for the first time with them."

Gonzales nodded. "I think that's the best approach," he said.

"And that way," Addington said, "Jim's going to think you're the fastest-working lawyer in the world."

They all laughed.

"There is one thing we need to talk about," Yoo said. "I don't think it's a good idea for DOD to be doing this. I wish we could just tell them not to."

The Department of Defense was not the Central Intelligence Agency, Yoo said. Inexperienced soldiers were much more likely to botch the job of conducting aggressive interrogations than trained CIA professionals.

"Putting aside the legality," he said, "the military's just so big, and they just use so much of a 'one size fits all' philosophy. I don't think they'll have the same level of quality control that the agency does."

"You're right," Addington said. "The military's like that. They run by the blunt force of numbers and the CIA's more surgical."

The meeting ended and Yoo stood. "I just wish we could tell Jim not to do it," he said again.

15

Light from a chandelier of gilt bronze and crystal spilled across the hand-carved Louis XV desk where Jacques Chirac was working. His office, the Salon Doré, was an opulent holdover from nineteenth-century France, its golden walls adorned with Gobelin tapestries that surrounded the most valuable antiques in all of the Élysée Palace. But on this day, the familiar grandeur barely registered with the French president as he waited for yet another phone call from Bush: the topic, again, would be Iraq. Just weeks after the first U.N. resolution demanding that Saddam comply with his disarmament obligations, the Bush administration was pushing the Security Council to take the next step, authorizing a U.N.-backed invasion. Chirac remained unconvinced that military action was necessary: he still considered the evidence that Iraq possessed weapons of mass destruction to be flimsy at best. Rushing into battle based on hunches and theories struck him as the height of folly.

Bush had been particularly unpersuasive in making the case, Chirac thought. Months before, the American president had leaned on him to support an authorization for military action as part of the *first* U.N. resolution. Chirac refused, arguing that it was too soon to be discussing the use of force, since the weapons inspectors had yet to have begun their work. Even now, the U.N. team had barely been on the ground long enough to have located their hotel in Iraq, much less find hidden armaments. Yet here was Bush, tub-thumping about war again. Chirac would have none of it; authorizing an attack at this stage would make the original resolution seem like a cynical cover for a premeditated attack.

The call came through and the two men traded diplomatic pleasantries.

"Jacques," Bush said, "Saddam is digging in. He is lying to the world and he is lying to Blix. We can't let him think that the U.N. is a paper tiger that won't enforce its own resolutions."

"I understand your concerns, George, but the inspectors need more time. War should be the last option, and it will be our admission of failure. I am not convinced that the situation is urgent, or even that the weapons are there. Before we take an irreversible step, we need to be certain of our beliefs."

Delay would serve only to embolden Saddam, Bush replied. "He has to hear a unified message from us, a declaration that the world is allied against him," he said. "We know he will not comply unless he feels the pressure."

Bush wasn't listening to him, Chirac thought. Instead, he was jumping all over the rhetorical map in search of the magic words that would win him over. Saddam was lying; the U.N. had to prove itself; the allies had to work together. Perhaps, but all beside the point if illegal armaments weren't found. What if, in fact, Saddam was telling the truth? With the U.N. staring him down and inspectors roaming the country, Saddam couldn't do anything with his arsenal, even if it existed. War would change that. If foreign forces cornered the Iraqi leader, and if he really did have such weapons at his disposal, they wouldn't remain hidden anymore. Instead, they would be trained on American soldiers and anyone allied with them.

Before Chirac could elaborate on that point, Bush veered in another direction.

"Jacques," he said, "you and I share a common faith. You're Roman Catholic, I'm Methodist, but we are both Christians committed to the teachings of the Bible. We share one common Lord."

Chirac said nothing. He didn't know where Bush was going with this.

"Gog and Magog are at work in the Middle East," Bush said. "Biblical prophecies are being fulfilled."

Gog and Magog? What was that?

"This confrontation," Bush said, "is willed by God, who wants to use this conflict to erase His people's enemies before a new age begins."

Chirac was bewildered. The American president, he thought, sounded dangerously fanatical.

After the call ended, Chirac called together his senior staff members and relayed the conversation.

"He said, 'Gog and Magog.' Do any of you know what he is talking about?"

Blank faces and head shakes.

"Find out," Chirac said.

• • •

Near Lake Geneva in Switzerland, Thomas Römer, a theology professor at the University of Lausanne, was in his office when the phone rang. On the line was the head of the Biblical Service at the Protestant Federation of France with an odd request: Jacques Chirac wanted to know the meaning of "Gog and Magog."

"He recently spoke with the president of the United States, and he brought up Gog and Magog in relation to the recent events in the Middle East," she said. "Could you write a page about it, explaining the meaning?"

The original appeal for help had come from Chirac's aides at the Élysée Palace, she said. They had first sought out the Protestants for an answer, since Bush belonged to the evangelical Christian movement. But the question was beyond the federation's expertise—its scholars focused on the New Testament, while the concept of Gog and Magog had its origins in the Old Testament. So they turned to Römer, a world-renowned expert on the Hebrew scriptures.

"I'd be happy to help," Römer said. He understood Bush's reference; it would be easy to put into plain words for Chirac.

At his computer, Römer typed the explanation. The phrase *Gog and Magog* shows up in two books of the Old Testament, Genesis and Ezekiel. The available translations of the text were quite cryptic and theologians had long debated their meaning. In Genesis, they appear to refer to two creatures, but Ezekiel used them in the description of a future war. Groups such as the evangelicals seized on the passages as a prophecy of an apocalyptic conflict between good and evil in the time of the Messiah.

That interpretation was reinforced by the use of the term in the New Testament's Book of Revelation. Although that mention of Gog and Magog does not refer to the same people or events, it does pertain to a war fought at the end of the millennium, with Satan attempting to deceive the nations of the world and engage in a battle against Christ and His saints. According to that rendition, the righteous would emerge victorious, and Satan would be flung into a lake of fire.

That Bush was invoking this biblical concept as a justification for his foreign policy didn't surprise Römer—for some reason, American presidents seemed to have a weakness for Gog and Magog. Ronald Reagan, for example, had proclaimed this biblical confrontation between good and evil would pit the United States against the Soviet Union, which had abandoned God at the time of the Russian Revolution.

Now, with America's old enemy defunct, Bush had apparently decided that

Moscow had nothing to do with the battle of Gog and Magog. Instead, the forces of evil had emerged in Baghdad.

The response from Römer confirmed the worst of Chirac's fears—biblical writings were influencing Bush's decisions about war in the Middle East. A certainty of God's will would surely blind any political leader to the evidence of man—weapons inspections would never persuade the administration if Bush believed a clash with Iraq was being guided by God. And that sealed it—Chirac would oppose all military action. France was not going to fight a war based on an American president's interpretation of the Bible.

At the Versailles Palace on January 22, the white wine was a German Riesling; the red, a French Bordeaux—carefully chosen symbols for an extraordinary party. It was the fortieth anniversary of the friendship treaty between the two countries, and both governments—including all 603 members of the German parliament and their 577 French counterparts—had gathered at the magnificent château of French kings for the unprecedented celebration.

Chirac and German chancellor Gerhard Schröder arrived together through the Marengo Room, hung with canvases that portrayed the victories of Napoléon. To a drumroll, they entered the assembly hall, an extravagant auditorium decked out in red velvet and gold leaf.

Chirac spoke first, calling for the two countries to deepen their ties at every level, from government cooperation to cultural exchanges. Then he raised the issue of Iraq.

"War is not inevitable," he said as the assembled delegates burst into vigorous applause. "For us, war is always the proof of failure and the worst of solutions, so everything must be done to avoid it."

There was only one framework for a legitimate solution to the challenge of Iraq, he said, and that was the United Nations. Germany and France, Chirac added, were joining together in favor of a peaceful solution. Any attempt by the United States to secure a resolution in support of an invasion, he hinted, would be vetoed by both nations.

In his comments, Schröder skipped the hints. "Don't expect Germany to approve a resolution legitimizing war," he said. "Don't expect it."

The slap from Europe infuriated Bush. So he slapped right back.

"Surely our friends have learned lessons from the past," he told a group of reporters gathered in the Roosevelt Room at the White House. "Surely we have learned how this man deceives and delays. He's giving people the runaround."

Regardless of whether the French and Germans blocked a second U.N. resolution, Bush suggested, America and its supporters would act. "Time is running out," he said. "I believe in the name of peace, he must disarm. And we will lead a coalition of willing nations to disarm him. Make no mistake about that. He will be disarmed."

During an afternoon press briefing at the Pentagon, Rumsfeld decided to follow his boss's lead in taking a poke at the French and Germans—but this time, with a much sharper stick.

It came in response to a query posed by Charles Groenhuijsen, a journalist with Dutch public television. "Sir, a question about the mood among European allies," Groenhuijsen began. "It seems that a lot of Europeans rather give the benefit of the doubt to Saddam Hussein than President George Bush. These are U.S. allies. What do you make of that?"

Rumsfeld engaged in some lighthearted banter with Groenhuijsen before answering.

"What do I think about it?" he said. "Well, there isn't anyone alive who wouldn't prefer unanimity. I mean, you just always would like everyone to stand up and say, 'Way to go! That's the right thing to do, United States.' "

But rarely did all countries reach common accord on *anything*, he said. On the other hand, the transatlantic partnership had been different. Almost always, Europe joined hands with America if the facts justified taking action.

"Now, you're thinking of Europe as Germany and France," he continued. "I don't. I think that's old Europe. If you look at the entire NATO Europe today, the center of gravity is shifting to the east."

There were plenty of new countries that had been invited to join NATO, he said. But still, he acknowledged, Groenhuijsen was right.

"Germany has been a problem, and France has been a problem," he said. "But you look at vast numbers of other countries in Europe, they're not with France and Germany on this, they're with the United States."

Rumsfeld's broadside was greeted in France and Germany with a mixture of bemusement and irritation. Inept diplomacy aside, Washington appeared to be signaling that any ally—no matter how strong its historical friendship with the United States—could be elbowed aside if it disagreed with the administration's policy. It was childish, as if the White House believed its "with us or against us" mind-set forbade any country from reaching an independent conclusion about Iraq.

Still, some politicians relished being cast as the elder statesmen lecturing their impetuous cousin in the New World. "When one is an old continent, a continent with an old historic, cultural, and economic tradition, one can sometimes inherit a certain wisdom, and wisdom can be a good advisor," said Jean-François Copé, the French government's official spokesman.

The German foreign minister, Joschka Fischer, was delicate in his response. "We should try to treat each other sensibly," he said. "Our position is not a problem, it is a constructive contribution."

Others showed less restraint. Asked by a reporter for her view, Roselyne Bachelot, the French environment minister, responded, "If you knew what I felt like telling Mr. Rumsfeld . . ."

She stopped herself, saying that the word she had in mind was too offensive.

Yoo's draft memo for the Pentagon on interrogations was delivered that same week to Mary Walker, the air-force general counsel. As head of the working group reviewing interrogation policy for Guantanamo, Walker declared that she alone would be allowed to keep a copy of the legal analysis. To ensure the highest level of security, she said, her counterparts at the other military branches would be allowed only to read the document in her office.

Her fellow lawyers grumbled among themselves about her pronouncement. They were supposed to be working together to form policy. The Yoo opinion—and who was this guy John Yoo, anyway?—was going to be the template for everything they did. Forcing them to rely on notes scribbled during a reading session in Walker's office would crimp their ability to do their job. And the lawyers couldn't help but wonder—since Jim Haynes had appointed Walker, did that mean he didn't trust the rest of them either?

Still, Alberto Mora was looking forward to reviewing the memo. The Office of Legal Counsel, he knew, was the most respected group of lawyers in government, composed largely of academics renowned for the brilliance and subtlety of their reasoning. Years before, as general counsel of the United States Information Agency, he had read plenty of OLC memos and unfailingly found them to be models of legal draftsmanship. He was eager to see how attorneys with that level of expertise and knowledge would configure the legal limits for detainee interrogation.

Mora scheduled an appointment to study the Yoo memo in Walker's office. When he arrived, Walker removed the document from a safe where she kept classified material. Mora sat at a table and started taking notes as he read.

He gave a start. Something was missing. He stopped writing and leafed through the memo, his consternation growing as he flipped each page.

He found references to torture—reference after reference after reference. A law said this about torture, a treaty said that. And that was it.

What's the boundary where harsh treatment becomes degrading? When did degrading treatment become cruelty? The answers weren't there! The memo frequently mentioned "the Torture Convention" but even *that* nickname ignored the international agreement's wider scope. Its actual name was "the Convention against Torture and Other Cruel, Inhuman or Degrading Treatment or Punishment." The terms *cruelty* and *degrading treatment* were right in the title, but didn't make it into the analysis.

Mora turned back to the first page and read through the memo again, this time more closely. It wasn't possible, he thought, that such a core element of the issue had simply been ignored. But it had been.

This memo doesn't get it, he thought. *It can't reach the right conclusions if it's not asking the right questions.*

Then Mora reached the portion that dealt with the president's authority in wartime, and what he read struck him as grotesque and dangerous. Yoo's assertion that the executive's power was virtually unbounded during war amounted to a declaration that the presidency was a supreme branch of government, beyond the law, beyond the authority of Congress, beyond the review of the courts.

My God. They're arguing that the president can do whatever he wants.

Walker left her office before Mora finished. He planned to call her as soon as possible so he could let her know that this memo was garbage.

A chief petty officer at the Pentagon took an elevator down to the main level and found John Yoo waiting. The first meeting of the Detainee Interrogation Working Group was being held on this day, January 23, and Yoo had been invited to give a presentation.

The working group was already reviewing thirty-six aggressive techniques, including sleep deprivation, stress positions, use of phobias, and waterboarding. Before anything was approved, though, the military lawyers wanted to get a better understanding of Yoo's reasoning and to challenge him on some of his conclusions.

Yoo arrived upstairs to find more than a dozen people waiting in a conference room. Walker introduced him.

"John's here to discuss his draft memo and then answer whatever questions you have about it," Walker said. "So, John, go ahead."

Yoo explained each element of his analysis—the definition of torture, the requirement that an interrogator must intend to cause pain, and the sweeping powers a president was permitted to exercise during wartime.

"Under the conventional doctrine, the president can order that the U.S. violate international law," he said. "That doesn't mean it's legal under international law. It still could be a violation if a country gets harmed or asks for a remedy or whatever compensation it's seeking. But we do have the right to violate international law."

Across the table, an army officer with the Judge Advocate General's Corps shook his head. "No, that's not true," he said. "International law binds us."

Yoo leaned forward. *This is going to be like being a law professor again.*

"The Constitution creates certain powers and gives them to the president," he said. "Where does it mention international law binding the constitutional powers of the executive branch?"

"That's what we always teach to every soldier in basic training, that they are bound by international law."

"But there's a landmark case, *Paquete Habana v. U.S.,* that says a president can order actions inconsistent with international law."

"Well, we have to be bound by international law," the army officer responded.

"Why?" Yoo asked.

"If we violate international law, the other side is going to violate it, too, in treating our soldiers when they're captured."

"Look, if you think al-Qaeda is going to follow any rules of war, that's nice, but we have no factual evidence that's true."

The other issue to consider, Yoo said, was that their objections were about policy, and that wasn't relevant in a discussion about constitutionality.

Another JAG officer spoke. "This is going to be very bad for the image of the military in other countries."

Yoo nodded. "That's a very good point, and it could certainly be valid," he said. "But again, that doesn't tell us anything about how to interpret the law."

The meeting lasted for an hour and a half. The military lawyers raised objection after objection, but Yoo remained unflappable, batting down their arguments as being in the realm of policy, not the law. Then, after Walker thanked Yoo for his input, he headed out.

The meeting was a disaster, Yoo thought. *I knew we shouldn't be doing this with the Pentagon.* The use of harsh treatment by soldiers wasn't going to work. The military was too big, and the resistance to adopting such a policy was going to be too strong.

But he fervently believed that it wasn't his place to make such an argument to the Defense Department. He was just a lawyer, not a decision maker.

The next day, Tony Blair sent a confidential note to Bush. The two men were set for another tête-à-tête on Iraq, and the prime minister wanted to do as much spadework as possible. He felt confident, he told his advisors, that he could persuade the president to postpone any invasion until after the Security Council approved a second resolution.

Blair opened his missive with flattery. Bush's strength, the prime minister wrote, had forced Saddam to allow weapons inspectors into Iraq. But much more needed to take place before gearing up for war.

Public support for military action was essential, Blair wrote, and time was needed to build it. The British people opposed an aggressive Iraq policy; he couldn't even say that a majority of his own cabinet was in support.

They needed to keep their effort on a multinational track, Blair wrote, but it wasn't going to be easy.

Haynes was doing his best to juggle the wildly divergent opinions coming in about interrogations. Yoo, and, in turn, Walker, were insistent that the military had the authority to conduct aggressive questioning. But Mora was banging the drum that the legal analysis leading to that conclusion was incompetent. Cruelty and degrading treatment had to be defined and contained, he insisted.

He telephoned Alberto Gonzales.

"Al," Haynes said, "there's a lot of friction over here about interrogation policy."

"Well, you've got to work it out."

Thanks so much for your help.

"A lot of the push-back on this is coming from Alberto Mora," Haynes said. "He is strongly disagreeing with John Yoo on this."

There are always going to be disagreements about legal interpretations, Gonzales replied, even when they come out of the Department of Justice.

"But at the end of the day, somebody's got to make the final call on the legality," he said. "And it's not Alberto Mora. It's the DOJ."

At a BBC television studio in London, the sounds of a brassy orchestral piece faded and a camera crane swung over David Frost. The British talk-show host was seated on an overstuffed armchair, with Tony Blair perched on a couch beside him. It was January 24, and Blair had decided to appear on a Sunday-morning program—*BBC Breakfast with Frost*—to again make his case on Iraq to the British people.

Frost looked into the camera lens. "And now the news is that the prime minister's here. Good morning, Prime Minister."

"Good morning, David," Blair responded with a smile.

Straight to Iraq. Hans Blix would be presenting a new report to the U.N. the next day, Frost said. If the weapons inspectors hadn't been able to complete their work yet, would they be allowed to keep searching?

"They've got to be given the time to do the job," Blair said. "But it's important to define what the job is, because this is where I think a lot of the confusion comes in."

The inspectors were charged with certifying whether Saddam was cooperating, and that meant more than just granting access to sites, Blair said. Saddam had to say where the weapons material was hidden, show it to the inspectors, and then destroy it.

"So, we would give him extra time—Hans Blix?"

"We've gone down the U.N. route precisely because the inspectors have got to be the means of trying to resolve this peacefully. If the inspectors are able to do their job, fine. But if they're not able to do their job, then we have to disarm Saddam by force."

His talking point out of the way, Blair returned to Frost's question. Blix's team should be allowed whatever time it needed, he said, but Saddam had to cooperate by revealing everything.

"What we know is that he has this material," Blair said. "We know there is something like three hundred and fifty tons of chemical warfare agent. We know that there is something like thirty thousand special munitions for the delivery of chemical and biological weapons."

What's more, Saddam was engaged in a deadly game of hide-and-seek, moving his illegal weaponry to different parts of the country in an elaborate scheme of concealment.

With the U.N. weapons inspectors playing such a critical role in the decision for military action, Frost asked, would the British government need, require, or prefer a second resolution on Iraq?

"Of course we want a second resolution," Blair replied. Without one, he said, Britain would take military action only under two conditions.

"That is the circumstance where the U.N. inspectors say he's not cooperating and he's in breach of the resolution that was passed in November," Blair said, followed by a U.N. failure to act "because someone, say, unreasonably exercises their veto and blocks the resolution."

As he spoke, the prime minister was engaged in a complex balancing act—or, more accurately, was deceiving the world. For just ten days earlier, Blair had received an analysis from his attorney general declaring that the very policy he was now advancing was, in fact, illegal.

In the confidential memo, the attorney general, Peter Goldsmith, wrote that Britain was very limited in what actions it could legally take regarding Iraq. Unless the U.N. adopted a second resolution to authorize a military campaign, Britain could deploy troops only for self-defense or as a humanitarian intervention—and neither condition applied here. He was, Goldsmith wrote, "ruling out the use of force without a further decision of the Council."

Some members of the Blair government had suggested the U.N. could be ignored if one of the permanent members of the Council "unreasonably" vetoed a second resolution. But, Goldsmith wrote, the international organization's charter did not support that supposition.

"In these circumstances, I do not believe there is room for arguing that a condition of reasonableness can be implied as a precondition for the lawful exercise of a veto," Goldsmith wrote.

The attorney general's analysis was a bitter secret, one Blair was unwilling to share even with Bush. How could he tell the president that, despite their months of planning, Britain might not join the United States in a war against Iraq?

The next day in Manhattan, the Security Council chamber was packed with delegates, reporters, and other observers. The anticipation was almost palpable as the crowd awaited the latest report from the Iraqi weapons inspectors.

Representatives from the fifteen state members of the Council found their seats at the horseshoe-shaped mahogany table. Blix and ElBaradei from the International Atomic Energy Agency were at the side of the room, waiting to be invited to make their presentations.

Blix spoke first. "Iraq has not come to a genuine acceptance—not even today—of the disarmament which has been demanded of it and which it needs to carry out to win the confidence of the world and to live in peace," he said.

Iraq had cooperated on the process of the undertaking, Blix said, granting access to all sites the inspectors wanted to see. Even so, problems remained—the Iraqis refused to guarantee the safety of a U-2 plane that the inspectors wanted to use for aerial imagery and surveillance, for example. And there had been instances where inspectors were harassed.

Substance was another matter, Blix said. Iraq was not providing active assistance but simply allowing the inspectors to look around. "It is not enough to open doors," he said. "Inspection is not a game of 'catch as catch can.'"

There was evidence that the Iraqis possessed a weaponized version of a toxic nerve agent known as VX. Also, records indicated that Iraq had produced more anthrax than it had disclosed, and officials provided no convincing proof that the biological agent had been destroyed. There was more: Baghdad maintained that its missiles could fly no farther than the 150-kilometer limit imposed by its disarmament agreements, but the inspectors were skeptical.

"Our Iraqi counterparts are fond of saying that there are no proscribed items and if no evidence is presented to the contrary, they should have the benefit of the doubt, be presumed innocent," Blix said. "Presumptions do not solve the problem."

Then, ElBaradei. His take on Iraq's nuclear capabilities was far more upbeat.

"We have to date found no evidence that Iraq has revived its nuclear weapons program since the elimination of that program in the 1990s," he said.

The lack of substantiation, of course, wasn't enough to give Iraq a clean bill of health. But, with the verification system that had just been put in place, a final verdict would be possible.

"We should be able within the next few months to provide credible assurance that Iraq has no nuclear weapons programs," ElBaradei said. "These few months would be a valuable investment in peace because they could help us to avoid a war."

Time. All they needed was more time.

• • •

"The start date for the military campaign is penciled in for March 10," Bush said. "That's when we're planning to get going with the bombing."

It was five days later, January 31. Bush and Blair were meeting in the Oval Office for another review of the strategy for Iraq. Joining Bush in the American contingent were Andy Card, Condoleezza Rice, and Dan Fried, one of her senior assistants. Blair was aided by Jonathan Powell, his chief of staff; David Manning, his foreign policy advisor; and Matthew Rycroft, his private secretary.

Blair was, once again, urging Bush to join him in pushing for a second U.N. resolution. He was trying not to sound desperate, but couldn't bring himself to reveal the terrible truth that if America chose to attack without U.N. support, the British might have to stay on the sidelines.

Bush wasn't buying that the U.N. was important. "We're going to put everything we can into getting a new resolution," he said. "We'll twist some arms and even threaten if we have to. But, I've got to say, if we fail, we're going to take military action anyway."

The air campaign would probably last four days, Bush said, demolishing as many as 1,500 targets. "We're going to be very careful to avoid hitting innocent civilians," he said. "But I don't think there's going to be much danger for them for too long. The bombing is going to ensure a quick collapse of Saddam's regime. It's going to destroy his 'command and control' very quickly. The army's going to fold."

The military timetable was tight, Bush said, so they could give the Security Council only a short time for a second resolution.

Blair nodded. "It's essential for us both to lobby for the second resolution," he said. "It would give us an insurance policy against the unexpected."

And they had to recognize that there were plenty of unknowns. "If anything went wrong with the military campaign," Blair said, "or if Saddam increased the stakes by burning oil wells, or killing children, or fomenting internal divisions within Iraq, a second resolution would give us international cover, especially with the Arabs."

It was important, though, for the wording of the resolution to be tough. "I think we should make it clear that it amounts to Saddam's last opportunity to comply," he said. "We have been very patient. Now we should be saying that the crisis must be resolved in weeks, not months."

"I agree," Bush responded. "I'm not itching to go to war, but we can't let Saddam keep playing with us."

The "last chance" approach might give them the ability to force the Iraqi dictator out without firing a shot, Bush said. "Probably after passing the second resolution, assuming we get it, we should warn Saddam that he has a week to leave," he said. "We should notify the media, too. Then we'd have a clear field if he refused to go."

Of course, the recent reports from the weapons inspectors weren't helping persuade holdouts on the Security Council, Blair said. They suggested that Iraq was engaged in some cat-and-mouse games but didn't explicitly accuse Saddam of violating the terms of the November resolution. Bush agreed—getting the resolution through would be easier if Blix actually found prohibited weapons, or, failing that, at least took a harder line against Saddam's mischief.

They had been considering a few options to deal with that, Bush said. If Blix couldn't handle the job, maybe they should just provoke Saddam into a confrontation.

"Blix mentioned at the U.N. that Saddam wouldn't guarantee the safety for a U-2 reconnaissance flight," Bush said. "So we were thinking of flying one over Iraq with fighter cover, but paint it with U.N. colors. Then, if Saddam fired on them, he would be in breach."

That would undoubtedly persuade every member of the Security Council to support a second resolution—or might even justify immediate military action against the Iraqi dictator.

"We've also been thinking about bringing out a defector, and having him give a public presentation about Saddam's WMD," Bush said.

Then there was one last option under consideration: assassinating Saddam Hussein. The lawyers at the Office of Legal Counsel had reviewed that alternative and concluded that Bush had the authority at a time of war to give an order for Saddam—or any other enemy he designated—to be killed.

At that same time, other Blair aides were in the office of Dan Bartlett, a close advisor to the president. The topic of discussion: the political nightmare enveloping the prime minister.

Some 70 percent of British citizens opposed joining the United States in a military operation, said Alastair Campbell, a senior Blair aide. Without a second U.N. resolution, the prime minister's government could be forced to sit out the war if it could not win wider public support.

"We've really got our balls in a vise here," Campbell said.

Not a problem in the United States, Bartlett said. "We believe that both politically and legally we can go without a second resolution."

Minutes later, the group joined their bosses in the Oval Office to offer advice on the message they should convey at a press conference that was about to begin.

"I'm up for the idea of saying that I'm open for a second resolution," Bush said.

"That's a good way to frame it," Rice said.

Ari Fleischer, the White House press secretary, broke in. "I strongly disagree," he said. "If we say that, it will be seen as a shift in U.S. policy. A better way to say it is that we're hopeful that the U.N. will approve the second resolution, but we are prepared to move forward either way."

"Wait a minute," Campbell said. "After everything Tony has said in press interviews, that's going to end up with a 'split' story." The president and the prime minister would be portrayed as being in disagreement.

Blair and Bush listened impassively as their aides debated how to portray the meeting to the press. After several minutes, no agreement had been reached, and Bush grew tired of the discussion. He stood.

"Let's just do it," he said.

Shortly after 4:10, Bush and Blair strode together down Cross Hall toward the East Room, where the press corps waited. Both men dispensed with opening statements. Bush called on Ron Fournier from the Associated Press.

"Thank you, sir," Fournier said. "First, quickly to the prime minister, did you ask President Bush to secure a second U.N. resolution and give the weapons inspectors more time?"

Blair began his answer by saying that the U.N.'s November Resolution 1441 had been Saddam's final chance to disarm and that Blix had subsequently established that the Iraqi leader was failing to meet his obligations.

"What is important is that the international community come together and make it absolutely clear that this is unacceptable," he said. "So this is a test for the international community."

Standing nearby, some of Blair's aides winced. He had bobbed and weaved, and hadn't answered the question—did he ask Bush to get a second resolution and give the weapons inspectors more time? But Blair couldn't give a straight response; he didn't know what Bush was going to say and it was imperative that they show unanimity in their plans. Above all else, they had to avoid creating the impression that Bush was waving off pleas from Blair.

Second question, from Andrew Marr of the BBC. About seeking a new resolution, what was the status of that, and was it worth the effort?

Uneasiness flashed across Bush's face. His body language exuded discomfort.

"This needs to be resolved quickly," he said. "Should the United Nations decide to pass a second resolution, it would be welcomed if it is yet another signal that we're intent upon disarming Saddam Hussein. But 1441 gives us the authority to move without any second resolution."

The answer virtually threw Tony Blair under a bus. *Welcomed.* Not "needed" or "encouraged" or even "hopeful to have." If a second resolution showed up, well, that would be fine. But Bush didn't much care—the United States could legally invade Iraq under the first resolution. He still didn't know that Britain's attorney general disagreed.

As the short press conference ended, Campbell glanced at Sally Morgan, Blair's director of political and government relations. She grimaced. Holding the press conference without proper preparation had been a mistake.

Major Nick Lovelace from the military's Joint Staff Directorate for Intelligence sent an e-mail that week asking for more information on SERE techniques.

His request went to Joseph Witsch, who had formerly conducted training at the Army's SERE school. Witsch had known for months that the harsh methods employed in SERE training had been used at Guantanamo, which in his mind was a prelude to fiasco. He had warned his superiors against the idea, saying that the tactics might be usesful for toughening up American soldiers, but there was no evidence that they would work in a real interrogation. His objections had been ignored.

Now the e-mail from Lovelace suggested that the Pentagon was pushing for an escalation of SERE tactics at Guantanamo. A working group on interrogation had just contacted him for additional details on how SERE worked, Lovelace said. Witsch replied that he had already provided that information to the Defense Intelligence Agency. Not enough, Lovelace said—the Pentagon needed more detail.

Frustrated, Witsch wrote his own email to Lieutenant Colonel Dan Baumgartner, the chief of staff for the Joint Personnel Recovery Agency, which oversaw the SERE schools. He reiterated his objections to using SERE tactics at Guantanamo, this time more forcefully than before.

Word would get out about what they were doing, he warned, and it would get out quickly. The backlash would be immediate. Their group would be blamed and investigated when Guantanamo interrogators went too far. None of them had any idea how the information they were providing to the intelligence units was being used.

One problem, he wrote, was more important than the rest. "The physical and psychological pressures we apply in training violate national and international laws. We are only allowed to do these things based on permission from DOD management and intense oversight by numerous organizations within DOD. I hope someone is explaining this to all these folks asking for our techniques and methodology!"

Witsch said that he understood interrogators might consider the tactics "cool," and he was not suggesting that the SERE experts remove themselves completely from the effort. But it was reckless to simply toss information about the techniques to anyone who asked.

"We must get a handle on all these people seeking information on our stuff," he wrote. "This is getting out of control!!!"

Haynes arrived late to the February 4 meeting of the interrogation working group. "Sorry, everybody," he said as he rushed into the room. "Let's get going."

A draft "final report" on harsh tactics was passed around the room. Inside was a chart listing the various methods, each marked with a stoplight color. Green meant there was no reason to worry about legal ramifications. Those marked with yellow were lawful, but had problems that could not be eliminated. Red was saved for those that might be illegal or present other significant challenges.

The report concluded that thirty-six techniques could be used to different degrees without moralistic fanfare. An additional ten options, the report said, ought to be reserved for exceptional cases. These included isolation, prolonged interrogation, slapping, and other abusive techniques. Only waterboarding was marked as "red," but the report recommended its use anyway.

Jane Dalton, the legal advisor to the Joint Chiefs of Staff, studied the chart with growing alarm. One column graded the techniques for their adherence to customary international law. In that category, all of them were marked as green; methods that any foreign body would deem illegal were now declared to be fine, because Yoo's analysis decreed that international law had no sway in American jurisprudence. The premise, Dalton thought, was wrongheaded and an embarrassment to national honor. It would have to be removed.

In Conference Room A at the Cabinet Office Building in Whitehall, no one knew yet what was going on, but MI5 was working hard to find out.

Operatives with the British security service had picked up a swirl of intelligence that al-Qaeda terrorists were planning a massive attack at London Heathrow Airport. The information was good, but sketchy; the terrorists intended either to shoot down civilian aircraft with surface-to-air missiles, or to hijack planes and crash them into the terminals.

The February 10 meeting at Whitehall of the group—known as COBRA—had been called to weigh options for disrupting the attack. London police were already sweeping through the city, arresting suspects and anyone else linked to Islamic extremist groups. That program, the COBRA members decided, would continue. From there, they agreed to bring in the military, dispatching troops and tanks to Heathrow to serve as both a deterrent and an offensive force if the terrorists turned up. A third option, closing the airport, was raised. Blair rejected that; the British people would not accept such a drastic move unless the government turned up very specific information about a possible strike.

Blair emerged from the conference room filled with pride at the diligence of Britain's intelligence service in uncovering the plot in time to thwart it. He could not have known that the Americans would eventually claim credit for detecting the threat to Heathrow by waterboarding a terrorist suspect—one month after the COBRA meeting.

On the afternoon of February 10, Alberto Mora was walking down the hallway on the third floor of the Pentagon's E-ring. Jim Haynes had asked him to drop by so they could discuss Mora's thoughts about the draft report finished six days before by the working group.

Mora was not going to have any good words about it. The report was as bad as—no, worse than—he expected. Again, it made no mention of limits on questioning techniques to ensure that interrogators didn't violate laws forbidding cruel or degrading treatment. Either the lawyers running the working group didn't know the law, or else they didn't care about it.

The process that led to the writing of the report was deeply flawed, Mora thought. Members of the group were allowed to voice their concerns about the proposed tactics. Then, without warning, their opinions were ignored. The Yoo memo dictated every answer—if his analysis said a proposal was lawful, then it was recommended. And there wasn't much that Yoo considered unlawful.

Mora had met with Yoo directly but emerged from that discussion even more convinced that the Justice Department lawyer was dangerous. He had never witnessed such unsullied arrogance. If Yoo thought something met the standards of law, well, then it did, period. Any disagreements were legal sideshows, he declared, pointless excursions into policy making. Mora decided to push Yoo's opinion to its logical extreme and asked him if the president could lawfully order a detainee to be tortured. Yes, Yoo replied, he could.

The only hope for stopping this madness, Mora thought, was Haynes, so he was delighted when the Pentagon general counsel invited him for a chat.

Both Haynes and his principal deputy, Daniel Dell'Orto, were waiting for Mora in a conference room. "Thanks for coming, Alberto," Haynes said. "So, I'm eager to hear your thoughts."

"They're very negative, Jim," he said. "The working group was a flawed process and it did not lead to a paper that's a quality product."

He criticized Mary Walker, the group's head, for ignoring dissident opinions. There were no clear standards set on how far any technique could go, and no restrictions explored on cruelty and degrading treatment.

"This shouldn't be issued," Mora said. "What you should do is thank Walker for her service, then stick the report in a drawer and never let it see the light of day again."

Haynes listened, saying nothing as usual. Mora didn't take that as a bad sign. He knew that there weren't going to be any debates at this point.

"So, those are my thoughts, Jim," Mora said.

Haynes paused a moment, then stood. He shook Mora's hand. "Thanks for coming by, Alberto," he said.

On First Avenue in Manhattan, Hans Blix arrived at the building that housed the American delegation to the U.N. and was taken to the office of the ambassador, John Negroponte. It was February 11, three days before Blix was scheduled to deliver his next report to the Security Council, and he had come to the American mission to provide Condoleezza Rice with a preview of what he planned to say.

Three officials were waiting for him in Negroponte's office—the ambassador, Rice, and John Wolf, the assistant secretary of state for nonproliferation.

Blix began with a discussion of surveillance flights. At the time of his last report, the Iraqis were refusing to guarantee the safety of any U-2 that entered the country's airspace, unless Blix accepted certain requirements. He had refused. Now that impasse was moot.

"It's my understanding that they have accepted U-2 surveillance without restrictions," he said, "and we'd like to start the flights as soon as possible."

Overall, he said, there appeared to be more willingness among the Iraqis to cooperate actively. It was always possible that Baghdad's seeming compliance was a delaying tactic, but he had no proof either way. The Iraqis turned over a lot of documents, none of them amounting to anything significant.

And the Security Council wasn't providing much help. "I must say, I haven't been terribly impressed with the intelligence provided by member states so far," he said.

"That's the nature of intelligence," Rice replied. "It goes stale very quickly. We're not withholding any intelligence, but that information is no substitute for what Iraq needed to do voluntarily."

Blix had to remember, she said, that American intelligence wasn't on trial; Saddam Hussein was.

Neither Blix nor Rice knew the magnitude of the American intelligence community's failure to assist the U.N. inspection effort. The agencies had identified 105 sites that were the most probable hiding places for weapons of mass destruction. Despite public proclamations by Tenet and other top intelligence officials that all of this information had been shared with Blix, it had not; twenty-nine of those locations—about 30 percent—had been withheld.

Still, Rice insisted, Saddam was compelled to disclose his weapons, whether the U.N. team could find them or not. "The aim of Resolution 1441 was to force Iraq to make a strategic decision to disarm," she said, "but he's still playing a process game. He can't be allowed to get away with that."

Saddam was undermining the credibility of the Security Council, she said, and yet the international body was showing a weakening resolve to enforce its own resolutions. The United States was not going to stand by and endlessly tolerate wavering.

"This issue is quickly coming to an end," she said.

Shortly before noon on February 17, a young police officer on a motor scooter parked at Piazza Maciachini in Milan. He began to lock his bike when a dark Volkswagen zipped up behind him. The driver opened his window.

"I'm Bob's friend," he called out in perfect Italian. "Get in!"

The officer, Luciano Pironi from the Carabinieri, felt a rush of excitement. This nameless, fortysomething man worked with Bob Lady, the CIA officer who had told Pironi in August about the agency's plan to kidnap a resident of Milan. Lady had agreed to give Pironi a role in the operation, and now, after weeks of practice, the day for the abduction had finally arrived.

Pironi climbed into the passenger seat, and the car took off. The two men barely spoke. After a few minutes, they reached a side street called Via Bonomi and came to a stop just before the intersection with Via Guerzoni.

For several minutes, the two men remained still and silent. The driver's mobile phone rang. On the line was Lady, letting him know that their subject, Abu Omar, was on the move.

"Yes, all right," the driver replied.

He started the car and drove to the intersection of Via Guerzoni and Via Davanzati. Then, they watched.

The heavyset, bearded man was walking briskly down Via Ciaia, coming from Piazza Dergano. He arrived at Via Guerzoni. Ahead of him, a Volkswagen sat in the intersection.

There he was. Pironi and the driver saw Abu Omar.

"You're going to have to stop him near the white van parked over there, on Via Guerzoni," the driver said, pointing at the vehicle.

"All right."

A telephone rang. It was the Samsung cell phone that Lady had given to Pironi for the operation.

"Don't answer that," the driver said.

Pironi nodded and removed the battery from the phone.

The driver turned the key and headed down Via Guerzoni toward Abu Omar. He came to a stop and Pironi got out, standing in the middle of the road as the target approached.

"Sir!" Pironi called out in Italian, flashing his badge. "Let me see your papers."

Abu Omar looked perplexed. "I don't speak Italian," he said in English.

Pironi switched languages. "All right," he said. "Let me see your passport."

He told Abu Omar to follow him and they edged toward the back of the white van. His suspect produced a residency card and his passport. Pironi studied them as he waited for someone to leap out of the van.

Seconds ticked by, and nothing happened. Pironi felt nervous; he could stare at these documents only so long before raising suspicions. He took out his phone, hoping Abu Omar didn't notice that it had no power. He pretended to make a call to run a check on the papers.

The van's front right-hand side door opened, and a man leaned out, facing Pironi. "What are you doing?" the man yelled.

Both Pironi and Abu Omar jumped back, startled by the shouting. Two sets of arms reached out from the van and grabbed Abu Omar, whisking him inside and throwing him to the floor. The door clattered shut, the engine roared, and the van made a rapid U-turn before racing away.

Pironi remained standing in the street, openmouthed and still holding Abu Omar's papers.

The presentation by Blix to the Security Council that same day had a little bit for everyone, with a glass half-full, glass half-empty theme. That proved to be the problem.

There was no specific evidence of any weapons violations, and the Iraqis were beginning to show real signs of cooperation, Blix said. On the other hand, the inspectors had located some prohibited missiles and engines, and Baghdad had failed to account for a range of other material.

Still, there should not be a rush to judgment. The Americans had been marshaling data that they contended established the existence of illegal Iraqi arms programs, but Blix found their case weak.

"Inspectors, for their part, must base their reports only on evidence, which they can, themselves, examine and present publicly," he said. "Without evidence, confidence cannot arise."

ElBaradei of the International Atomic Energy Agency delivered the second report on possible nuclear programs, and his findings were more conclusive than Blix's. His agency had neutralized Iraq's past nuclear program by 1998, he said, leaving no unresolved disarmament issues.

"Hence, our focus since the resumption of our inspections in Iraq, two and a half months ago, has been verifying whether Iraq revived its nuclear program in the intervening years," he said. "We have to date found no evidence of ongoing prohibited nuclear or nuclear-related activities in Iraq."

ElBaradei stepped away from the Security Council table, leaving behind the delegates of fifteen nations who were more at odds than ever.

• • •

A Gulfstream jet carrying Abu Omar arrived the next morning in Egypt, less than twenty-four hours after the CIA had abducted him in Milan. He was brought out of the plane and turned over to Egyptian security officers. They tossed him into a car and drove to the Tora prison compound in Cairo. There, he was locked in an isolation cell.

For the next seven months, Abu Omar would be interrogated and tortured. He was beaten and burned. Electrodes were attached to his genitals to give him shocks. His tormentors demanded that he tell them about his terrorist activities; he protested that there was nothing for him to tell.

The Egyptians wrote reports on everything Abu Omar said. They turned over the documents to American intelligence, sharing the near-worthless answers they had managed to extract through torture.

The pressure was growing on Tony Blair. The Security Council seemed hopelessly split, and if that dissension wasn't resolved, Bush would launch the Iraqi invasion in a few weeks without a second resolution.

But the prime minister was still facing the ugly reality that, given the analysis of his attorney general, Britain could not lawfully join a military action without specific U.N. authorization. If Blair didn't find a middle ground, his country's historic relationship with America could be irretrievably damaged.

A possible answer might be with Hans Blix. Perhaps, Blair thought, he could persuade Blix to advance a proposal that would be less aggressive than an authorization for an invasion, but stronger than nothing. Blair arranged to speak with Blix by phone.

On February 20, Blix called Number 10 Downing Street on a secure telephone line at the New York office of Jeremy Greenstock, the British ambassador to the United Nations.

Blair's voice was calm. "The Americans were quite disappointed in your report," he said. "It undermined their faith in the U.N. process."

Well, Blix thought, *it undermined their faith that the U.N. process would lead to the authorization of the military route.*

"The Americans are attracted by a second Security Council resolution, up to a point," Blair said. "But they don't feel like they need one. There's a risk of the U.N. being marginalized."

There was an alternative, the prime minister said. He could offer the Americans a type of ultimatum that would include a requirement to meet certain benchmarks—dates when Saddam would have to achieve individual disarmament requirements—and impose a duty to cooperate actively. Then, if Iraq failed to comply with any of those step-by-step deadlines, it would be declared in breach of the original resolution.

Blix liked the idea. "Full cooperation could be defined, or, as you suggest, listed in categories," he said.

But the Bush administration seemed unbendable. "There should be room for compromise in the American position," Blix said. "They are going ahead too fast."

So they were agreed. Blair said he would pursue the benchmark idea with Bush and gain time for Blix. With luck, Blair thought, this process would resolve the legal barrier he faced about using military force against Iraq.

16

A thunderstorm rolled across Rawalpindi, Pakistan, after sunset on February 28, rattling the windows of a pink two-story house in the middle-class neighborhood of Westridge. Inside, a group of Islamic men knelt on prayer rugs, whispering the nighttime *Isha'a* devotionals. They ended their reaffirmation of faith in the ritual position, with their feet folded under their bodies.

One of the men grunted as he hefted his bulky frame off the ground. He raised a hand and stroked his double chin, a postprayer habit he had developed when a thick beard covered it. Now there were just a mustache and a shadow of stubble, a change in appearance intended to disguise his true identity as Khalid Sheikh Mohammed, mastermind of the 9/11 attacks.

Sheikh Mohammed had been on the run for nearly eighteen months, most of the time shuttling to cities throughout Pakistan. Unlike bin Laden, he was not the kind to hide in an Afghani cave; he much preferred the creature comforts available in safe houses, despite the higher risk of capture.

But his success in evading capture had made Sheikh Mohammed complacent, even sloppy. He met with strangers—friends of friends of associates. He used unencrypted cell phones. Documents and audio recordings were strewn around the house where he was staying. Financial records, telephone numbers, and other electronic data had been saved on unsecured computers.

His recklessness would be his undoing—the authorities were closing in. The noose started to tighten three weeks before, when intelligence operatives intercepted a series of coded instructions issued over the Internet by bin Laden's spokesman, Abul Baraa Qarshi. The messages included details about a planned attack against bridges and gas stations in the United States and repeatedly mentioned "Mukhtar"—Sheikh Mohammed's code name.

From that cybertraffic, investigators gleaned information that indirectly led them to a house in Wahdat Colony, a ramshackle area of Quetta where an Egyptian aide to al-Qaeda was holed up. American agents began to monitor the aide's calls; several were placed to 18A Nisar Road in Rawalpindi. Electronic surveillance of the house began immediately, allowing for eavesdropping on calls placed and received by Sheikh Mohammed.

About that time, an informant contacted the Americans; he knew of the comings and goings at the house on Nisar Road. He offered to help capture Sheikh Mohammed, in anticipation of receiving the $25 million bounty on the terrorist.

It all came down to this night. The informant had joined in the prayers at the house, then engaged in chitchat with the people there. They included Ahmed Abdul Qadoos, a Pakistani Islamist; Mustafa al-Hawsawi, an al-Qaeda financial expert; and Sheikh Mohammed. Eventually, the informant excused himself, went into the bathroom, and took out a cell phone that the Americans had given him. He typed a text message.

"I am with KSM," it said.

Hours passed with the capture team quietly watching the house, waiting for the predawn darkness. Not only timing but tactics compelled the delay—they wanted the element of surprise, with their targets unaware and undressed.

At about 3:00 A.M., more than twenty commandos brandishing rifles slipped silently across the remote shadows on the lawn, smashed down the front door, and stormed inside. In a bedroom, they found Sheikh Mohammed, groggy in half sleep. Before he could grab a weapon, they pulled him from the bed, slipped a hood over his head, and dragged him outside to a waiting vehicle.

A search of the house yielded a trove of high-value information. A computer hard drive included instructions that Sheikh Mohammed had sent to an al-Qaeda associate, directing him to case targets in America; spreadsheets of payments sent to the families of al-Qaeda members; transcripts of chat sessions with a 9/11 terrorist; and three letters from Osama bin Laden. But the prize was an al-Qaeda address book—a computer file listing phone numbers, e-mail addresses, and other contact information of fellow terrorists.

It was the largest haul of intelligence about al-Qaeda ever—enough to fill a small cargo plane, the investigators joked. And all because of a supposed mastermind's foolishness.

For three days, Sheikh Mohammed refused to answer any questions posed to him by Pakistani intelligence agents. He sat in a near trance, reeling off verses of the Koran. One of the Muslim agents in the room was surprised by what he heard—Sheikh Mohammed made repeated mistakes in his recitations. For someone eager to murder innocents in the name of Islam, he hadn't bothered to develop much familiarity with the religion.

Finally, on March 4, the orchestrator of the 9/11 attacks began to speak, but only to condemn his Muslim captors as apostates.

"Playing an American surrogate won't help you or your country," he snarled. "There are dozens of people who will give their lives but won't let Americans live in peace anywhere in the world."

For several minutes, the Pakistanis listened to Sheikh Mohammed's railings. Finally, one of the agents asked a simple question. "Is bin Laden still alive?"

Sheikh Mohammed laughed. "Of course he is," he said. In fact, he had met with the al-Qaeda leader just a few months earlier in Afghanistan. Both bin Laden and his fighters were ready to act if America invaded Iraq.

"Let the Iraq war begin!" he said. "The U.S. forces will be targeted inside their bases in the Gulf. I don't have any specific information, but my sixth sense is telling me that you will get the news from Saudi Arabia, Qatar, and Kuwait."

A CIA officer in the room saw the chink in Sheikh Mohammed's armor. *Arrogance.* He opened his mouth not to insult or deceive his interrogators, but to suggest that he was someone at the center of the jihad against the West. A real warrior would never reveal anything just to boast about his insider knowledge. Sheikh Mohammed was an amateur, a braggart. He wasn't a soldier, just a psychopathic murderer. No doubt, he would break under interrogation.

Later that day, the Pakistanis hooded Sheikh Mohammed again and drove him to the nearby Chaklala air force base in Rawalpindi, where he was turned over to the Americans. The CIA spirited him away to an interrogation center at Bagram Air Base in Afghanistan.

The next day in Paris, the foreign ministers of France, Germany, and Russia emerged from a meeting and released a statement, calling on Iraq to be more cooperative in disarmament and praising the work of the weapons inspectors. Banal stuff, but they saved the bombshell for the end.

"We will not let a proposed resolution pass that would authorize the use of force," it said.

The declaration hit the Blair government hard. That day, the prime minister had telephoned Bush again, arguing that world opinion was hostile to an invasion and that countries reluctant to support a second resolution needed to be given a reason—maybe even a cover—to end their opposition. He suggested that he could travel to Chile, which was struggling to find a middle ground in the dispute over the second resolution.

But Bush seemed almost indifferent to the diplomatic squabble. He still didn't know that Britain would be unable to join in a military operation against Iraq without further action by the Security Council.

Jack Straw, the foreign secretary, dropped in for a chat with Blair. It was not too late for Britain to switch course and disentangle itself from America's military adventure, he said, aligning itself instead with the coalition of nations committed to a diplomatic solution. Marching alongside the military hawks in the United States was simply too grave a choice.

"If you go next Wednesday with Bush, and without a second resolution," Straw warned, "the only regime change that will be taking place will be in this room."

A report issued in the name of the Detainee Interrogation Working Group was circulated around the Pentagon the following day. While it was meant to be the group's final statement on permissible techniques, it suffered from a significant problem—most of the group's members opposed its analysis.

The findings were based almost exclusively on the Yoo memo, a fact that enraged a majority of the military lawyers. Whatever words the Defense Department put on paper, the detractors argued, few of these findings would be accepted by international tribunals or, in some cases, even American prosecutors. Members of the military could well be subject to arrest, they maintained. Adopting these standards would invite enemies—not just al-Qaeda, but any enemy in the future—to torture American soldiers. Detainee statements might be prohibited from being admitted in criminal prosecutions, including those before military commissions, since they could be deemed as having been obtained illegally. Topping it off, there was *no* evidence that these methods worked.

Just before the report's release inside the Pentagon, Major General Thomas Romig, the army judge advocate general, sent a memo to Jim Haynes, expressing his reservations. The Justice Department memo, he wrote, sanctioned techniques "that may appear to violate international law, domestic law, or both."

Haynes forwarded Romig's complaint to Yoo. Nothing was changed.

Members of the British government were planning for the resignation of Tony Blair.

The likelihood of pushing a second resolution through the U.N. had all but evaporated. Bush and Blair had both appealed to Vladimir Putin to reconsider his decision but instead the Russian president had hardened his position, declaring that his government would veto not only the resolution as currently written, but any other proposed authorization of military force as well.

On the other hand, there was still some cause for hope, in the view of British officials—Bush had postponed the attack date twice, from the original March 10, to March 12, and then to March 17, giving the Security Council an extra week to act.

Now Blair was juggling two challenges to his leadership—impending votes in the U.N., and also in the House of Commons. The prime minister was seeking parliamentary approval for British troops to fight alongside the Americans in Iraq, if an invasion took place.

Bush had won approval from Congress for his own war resolution in a lopsided vote held in October. But the politics of Britain were much more complex. Blair's own Labour Party was teetering on open revolt, and if the British Parliament rejected his proposal on the heels of a veto at the Security Council, the prime minister would have no choice but to step down. Already, the cabinet secretary was exploring how to establish a caretaker government.

Blair gathered with a few of his aides for a gloomy meeting laced with black humor and speculations about his potential political demise.

Still, he remained unshaken in his decision. "I still feel like we're doing the right thing," he said.

A Gulfstream V executive jet landed at the remote Szczytno-Szymany Airport in northeast Poland at 4:00 P.M. on March 7. Military officers and border guards secured the perimeter; the civilian employees at the facility had been ordered inside the terminal building. On the edge of the runway, a few vans were waiting, their engines running.

The plane taxied to a halt. The vans raced out to the far end of the runway, stopping near the jet. A team of CIA agents scrambled out of the vehicles and boarded the aircraft. Soon, they brought out Khalid Sheikh Mohammed, shackled and hooded, and placed him inside one of the vans. The vehicles turned on their brights and drove past the terminal through the security gate, onto a tarmac road lined with pine trees.

About fifteen minutes later, the vans reached an unpaved road, little more than a path, next to a lake. They came to a stop at the Stare Kiejkuty intelligence training base maintained by the Polish government. A group of hulking men in black outfits dragged Sheikh Mohammed out of the vehicle and took him to the basement of the building. There, they put him in a cell, chained his arms above his head, and slashed off his clothes. They left him naked.

Sheikh Mohammed had arrived at the CIA's premier secret prison.

That same day, Blix and ElBaradei delivered their latest—and what would be their last—formal report on the weapons inspections in Iraq.

For days, members of the Bush administration had been pushing Blix—sometimes to the point of rudeness—to declare that he had found two types of equipment that violated the requirements imposed by the U.N. on Iraq. But the inspectors believed, at least for now, that the items they had located were insignificant. One, a drone aircraft, was powered by a motorcycle engine and constructed mostly from balsa wood. The second was a cluster bomb, which administration officials maintained was designed to strew smaller bomblets containing biological or chemical material across a large area; the device had been found by the inspectors in an old factory store and appeared to be nothing more than rusting scrap metal. It contained no traces of any life-threatening agents. Neither of these was sufficient—or there simply was not enough information about them—to declare Iraq in breach of its agreements, Blix concluded.

Before the presentation, Blix and ElBaradei took an elevator to the thirty-eighth floor at the U.N. building, then walked to the office of Kofi Annan, the secretary-general. The three men headed down together to the Security Council chamber. Everyone took a seat at the table and Blix was invited to speak first.

The inspectors had followed down the leads provided by Western intelligence services, yet made no damning discoveries. There was no evidence to support claims that Iraq was operating mobile weapons labs. Allegations that Saddam maintained underground armament facilities could not be substantiated; sites identified by the West had been inspected and ground-penetrating radar had been employed, to no avail. The Iraqis were demolishing what little material had turned up, including some rockets, engines, and the like.

"We are not watching the breaking of toothpicks," Blix said. "Lethal weapons are being destroyed."

There was greater cooperation, Blix said, although Iraq's seriousness of purpose still had to be assessed. The inspectors needed more time, if only to verify whether full disarmament was taking place. "It will not take years, nor weeks, but months," he said.

ElBaradei spoke next and ticked off the searches that been conducted for each item supposedly maintained by Iraq. "After three months of intrusive inspections," he said, "we have to date found no evidence or plausible indication of the revival of a nuclear weapon program in Iraq."

The presentations changed no minds among the Security Council members.

Anonymous attacks against Blix and ElBaradei appeared in news articles worldwide. The *New York Times* reported that Washington officials were angered that Blix had failed to mention cluster bombs that had been found by the inspectors. A Reuters dispatch said that the White House was annoyed at his failure to disclose the existence of the drone in his presentation. The State Department issued a "fact sheet" falsely claiming that inspectors had concluded that the drone was definitely a violation by Iraq.

These were the smoking guns, officials maintained, that had been hidden by Blix in his desperation to avoid war. Rarely was it mentioned that both items had been included in a document provided by Blix to the Security Council.

The effort to publicly undermine ElBaradei's credibility was spearheaded by the vice president. The supposed nuclear expert, Cheney argued in an appearance on *Meet the Press*, didn't know what he was talking about.

"I think Mr. ElBaradei frankly is wrong," the vice president said. "If you look at the track record of the International Atomic Energy Agency and this kind of issue, especially where Iraq's concerned, they have consistently underestimated or missed what it was Saddam Hussein was doing."

Peter Goldsmith, Blair's attorney general, changed his mind. Britain could lawfully invade Iraq with the Americans after all.

The dramatic turnaround had been weeks in the making. Just six days earlier, Goldsmith had sent a note to Blair, amending his earlier ruling with waffling, on-the-one-hand, on-the-other-hand language. The small step struck Blair and his other advisors as a sign that Goldsmith might, if pushed, reverse his original decision. The prime minister went all out: Give a final judgment, he told Goldsmith. And make it explicit, yes or no.

On March 13, Goldsmith met with Jack Straw, the foreign secretary, with the news that he was reversing himself. "I've decided to come down on one side," the attorney general said: "1441 is sufficient."

Resolution 1441 was the declaration approved by the Security Council in November setting out the new requirements for Iraq's disarmament. One resolution—not two—would carry the day.

Goldsmith's new analysis depended on comparing the November resolution with Resolution 687 from 1991, which imposed a cease-fire in the Persian Gulf War if Iraq disarmed. In Resolution 1441, Iraq was declared in breach of Resolution 687—in other words, Goldsmith maintained, Saddam had failed to comply with the terms of the cease-fire. An invasion now would not be an independent event. Instead, it was a resumption of hostilities in the Gulf War.

"In public, I need to explain my case as strongly and unambiguously as possible," Goldsmith said. "And I might need to tell the cabinet when it meets on March 17 that the legal issues were finely balanced."

Straw disagreed. It would be better to distribute a draft letter from Straw to the relevant committee in Parliament and make it Goldsmith's official explanation. Delving into a detailed conversation with the cabinet members would be a mistake.

"You need to be aware, there's a problem with the cabinet," Straw said. "They leak everything."

The following day, an annual awards ceremony took place at the Pentagon. It was a formal affair, held to honor civilian employees who had made exceptional contributions to the mission of the Defense Department.

Three men selected to receive the Decoration for Exceptional Civilian Service wore boutonnieres designating them as the winners. Some of the army's top brass milled around them, offering congratulations for everything they had done in their technical work with anthrax at the research institute based at Fort Detrick.

The ceremony began, and a presenter lauded the recipients' role in helping the United States respond to the threats posed by the deadly bacteria.

Each of the scientists was handed the award. Bruce Ivins, the mentally unstable researcher who would soon be the prime suspect in the anthrax killings, beamed as he accepted his medal.

Sheikh Mohammed's cell had no windows, denying him any perceptions of night and day. Bland and uninviting meals were served at ever-changing intervals and the hum of white noise was pumped incessantly through a speaker. Interrogations were conducted irregularly. Eventually, he lost all sense of time— a classic technique designed to throw him off balance.

This was not what he had expected. When the terrorist mastermind was turned over to the Americans, he proclaimed with cocky self-assurance that he would not speak until he was taken to New York and assigned a lawyer. But there would be no lawyer, no court, no rights. He was now, an interrogator told him, the property of the United States government.

The smirk stayed on Sheikh Mohammed's face; he would not reveal anything, he said. Americans were weak and lacked resilience. They wouldn't do what was necessary to stop jihadists from achieving their goals.

An interrogator pressed him for information about future attacks. Sheikh Mohammed just smiled.

"Soon, you will know," he said.

The arrogance would not last. In the earliest days, Sheikh Mohammed was subjected to what the interrogation plan called "conditioning techniques." He was shackled to the ceiling standing up, with his hands handcuffed in front of him; he was left in that position to prevent him from sleeping and was kept awake for more than ninety-six hours. He was nude at all times, except when he was forced by his chains to stand up; then he was dressed in a diaper so that he didn't have to be released when he needed to go to the bathroom. His diet was manipulated, with a near-tasteless liquid substituted for his usual meals.

None of those tactics were used to force him to deliver answers. Instead, by demonstrating that he had no control over his basic needs, they were intended to induce a high state of anxiety in hopes that he would begin to value his own welfare more than the secrets he held.

The questioning followed the traditional good-cop, bad-cop routine, although the chasm between good and bad was enormous. The gentler portion was handled by Deuce Martinez, a CIA officer who had worked much of his career as a narcotics analyst. Martinez spoke no Arabic and had no background with interrogations, but quickly demonstrated a skill with Sheikh Mohammed that astonished CIA colleagues.

The two men discussed religion as Martinez fed dates to his subject. The CIA officer listened with seeming compassion when Sheikh Mohammed expressed anguish over the likelihood that he would never see his children again. The terrorist composed poems for Martinez's wife as a sign of respect; they were sent instead to CIA psychologists for analysis.

Sheikh Mohammed grew relaxed and almost friendly in Martinez's presence. He spent time explaining the similarities between Martinez's Christianity and his own Islamic beliefs.

"Can't we get along?" Sheikh Mohammed eventually asked.

"Isn't it a little late for that?" Martinez replied.

A different team replaced Martinez when the time came for rougher treatment. The interrogators began with what they called "corrective techniques"—slapping Sheikh Mohammed in the face and the abdomen, holding his head motionless, and grabbing him when his attention wandered. They escalated to the interrogation plan's "coercive techniques," repeatedly throwing him against a false wall; dousing him with water of about fifty degrees; and forcing him into stress positions and cramped confinement. Finally, they pushed the trauma button—waterboarding. During his first month in the Polish secret prison, Sheikh Mohammed was waterboarded 183 times.

Before March ended, Sheikh Mohammed began to talk. Much of his information struck interrogators as little more than attempts at deception. But before long, he was divulging details that were confirmed to be true.

He described the traits and profiles for Western sympathizers that al-Qaeda had begun to seek out as recruits after 9/11, and gave details of how the terror group selected and conducted surveillance of its targets. He exposed active terror plots in America. He said he had been scheming with a man named Sayf al-Rahman Paracha to smuggle explosives into the United States for an attack in New York; as a result, Paracha was named an enemy combatant and his son was arrested. He described how a truck driver in Ohio named Iyman Faris was conspiring to blow up the Brooklyn Bridge; that led to Faris's arrest and his agreement to act as a double agent for the FBI by sending deceptive e-mail and text messages from a safe house in Virginia to his terrorist commanders.

Sheikh Mohammed also told his interrogators about a plan to attack Heathrow Airport, but that news was outdated; the British had already caught wind of the threat and averted it by making mass arrests.

The biggest payoff from questioning Sheikh Mohammed was not a single revelation, but the sheer volume of information that the CIA could use to trick other detainees into spilling their secrets. Sheikh Mohammed, at times, didn't even realize what he had done. In one instance, he said that he had met three men running al-Qaeda's project to produce anthrax, identifying one as Yazid Sufaat, who was already in custody. The interrogators thought Sheikh Mohammed revealed the information because he believed—falsely—that Sufaat had told his captors about his work. The CIA then confronted Sufaat, who was so shaken by the discovery of his role that he identified the other two terrorists working on the biological weapons program. They were promptly arrested.

Over the course of a few months, the leverage against other detainees provided by Sheikh Mohammed's information played a big part in the agency's efforts to cripple al-Qaeda's associated militant network in Southeast Asia, Jemaah Islamiyah. After 9/11, Sheikh Mohammed began to count increasingly on the Asian terrorists for his plots, recruiting Jemaah Islamiyah in an unsuccessful plot to crash a hijacked plane into Library Tower in Los Angeles, as well as to strike targets throughout Asia and Europe. In the course of planning the attacks, Sheikh Mohammed revealed, he had asked an ally named Majid Khan to deliver $50,000 to Jemaah Islamiyah members.

Unknown to Sheikh Mohammed, Khan had been detained weeks before in Pakistan. CIA interrogators confronted him about the money, and Khan cracked, admitting that he had turned it over to a man he knew only as Zubair. Khan provided a description and phone number for the man, and authorities picked up Zubair a few weeks later.

Then, during his debriefings, Zubair revealed that he worked directly for Riduan Isamuddin, better known as Hambali. Dubbed by the CIA as "Osama bin Laden of Southeast Asia," Hambali was one of the most sought-after terrorists in the world; the Bali nightclub bombers had already identified him as a primary director of the attack. And Zubair knew where the terrorist leader was hiding. Hambali was captured by the CIA and Thai authorities at an apartment in Ayutthaya, Thailand; at the time, he was in the final stages of planning attacks on a series of hotels in Bangkok.

Hambali was Jemaah Islamiyah's military commander and chief liaison with al-Qaeda. While his capture dealt a severe blow to the Southeast Asian terror group, the CIA wanted to hammer it harder. So the agency went back to Sheikh Mohammed and told him to identify Hambali's likely successor. He named Hambali's brother, 'Abd al-Hadi.

In short order, the brother was in custody and he, too, was interrogated. He identified a cell of Jemaah Islamiyah terrorists who had been sent by Hambali to Karachi so that they could serve as martyrs in future al-Qaeda operations. When confronted with that information, Hambali confessed—the cell members were being groomed for attacks in the United States involving hijacked airplanes. The instructions to set up the cell, Hambali said, had been transmitted to him by a senior al-Qaeda terrorist—Khalid Sheikh Mohammed. With the new information, authorities took down the terror cell.

The process had gone full circle—starting with Sheikh Mohammed and ending with the destruction of a terror cell he had helped create. Asia's worst terrorist group was, at least for a while, left in shambles.

Bush peered out a window on *Air Force One* as the coastline of Portugal's Azores Islands came into view. It was March 16, a Sunday, and the president had just flown more than two thousand miles to the idyllic archipelago in the North Atlantic for an emergency summit with the prime ministers of Britain, Spain, and Portugal.

Hopes that the Security Council would pass a second resolution authorizing the use of military force against Iraq had all but evaporated. Some last-minute diplomatic efforts were brewing—representatives from Chile were still attempting to broker a compromise resolution, but their effort was faltering. There were also rumblings out of the Middle East that other Arab states were negotiating Saddam's departure from Iraq, but that apparently was all they were—rumblings.

So instead, Bush called for this meeting in the Azores with three countries that had already committed their support for an Iraqi invasion. He was tired of debate, and done with it. This discussion would not be so much about whether to close the door on more U.N. wrangling, but rather how hard to slam it shut.

The president's plane landed at Lajes Field, a military base shared by the air forces of Portugal and America. Other large jets were just off the runway, including a British Airways 777 airliner that had been chartered to carry Tony Blair and a handful of his advisors to the meeting. *Air Force One* came to a stop and Bush came down the stairs. He stepped into a limousine that was part of an enormous motorcade—so large it seemed designed more to convey an air of urgency than to shuttle around politicians.

The convoy swung by a building on the Portuguese side of Lajes where the prime ministers were waiting. Blair was invited to join Bush in his limousine, while José Maria Aznar of Spain and José Manuel Barroso of Portugal climbed into other cars. Then the motorcade sped off to the American portion of the base. There, the group was led to its meeting room.

As the leader of the host country, Barroso welcomed his guests and launched into a long, cumbersome speech about the road that lay ahead.

"We have to make a last effort for peace," he implored. "We need to try one last time to reach a political solution."

There were formulaic nods and mutterings of agreement, amid an unspoken understanding that diplomacy had almost certainly failed. They had to present the U.N. with an ultimatum, Bush said—accept the resolution as written within twenty-four hours, or get out of the way.

"This is our last effort," he said. "Everyone has to be able to say that we did everything we could to avoid war. But this is the final moment, the moment of truth."

There would be no more hand-wringing, Bush said. Saddam still had the means—indeed, the incentive—to deliver weapons of mass destruction to al-Qaeda terrorists. The civilized world could not simply stand by, waiting for calamity to strike.

"I am just not going to be the president on whose watch this happens," Bush said. "I love my country and these people threaten it by their hatred for us."

But, he promised, he would pursue more than just a military action against Iraq—this was just a stage in his grander ambition to advance the Middle East peace process, and once Iraq was liberated from its tyrant, he would pursue that cause with vigor.

Blair quickly struck a cautionary note. "The vote in Parliament is on Tuesday," he said. "And if the vote fails, I'll have to resign as prime minister."

That eventuality, Bush knew, would be a huge blow to the Iraq mission. If Blair was forced from office, Britain would pull out of the coalition and America would lose its most important ally. The entire military strategy would have to be rethought.

The men and their aides crafted a statement declaring their commitment to disarming Saddam and aiding the Iraqi people. Once they were finished, everyone prepared to leave the room. Alastair Campbell, a Blair aide who over the years had struck up a friendly relationship with Bush, approached the president. He was going to be participating in a charity run, Campbell explained.

"If I do a sub-four-hour marathon, will you sponsor me?" he asked.

Bush smiled. "If you win the vote in Parliament, I'll kiss your ass."

"I'd rather have the sponsorship," Campbell replied.

Minutes later, Bush spoke to the assembled reporters, making no effort to mask his anger or sugarcoat his message.

"Tomorrow is a moment of truth for the world," he said. "Many nations have voiced a commitment to peace and security. And now they must demonstrate that commitment in the only effective way, by supporting the immediate and unconditional surrender of Saddam Hussein."

Blair agreed. "More discussion is just more delay, with Saddam remaining armed with weapons of mass destruction," he said. "We are in the final stages because, after twelve years of failing to disarm him, now is the time when we have to decide."

The reporters didn't quite know what to make of what they had just heard. *Tomorrow, final stages, time to decide.* Had Bush and Blair just thrown down the gauntlet and given the U.N. twenty-four hours to act?

Ron Fournier from the Associated Press asked the question. "When you say tomorrow is the moment of truth, does that mean that tomorrow is the last day that the resolution can be voted up or down and, at the end of the day tomorrow, one way or another, the diplomatic window has closed?"

Bush didn't hesitate. "That's exactly what I'm saying."

When the press conference ended, the four world leaders stood together, shaking hands as they bade their good-byes. Bush patted Blair on the shoulder, then walked off toward *Air Force One,* accompanied by Condoleezza Rice.

"I hope that's not the last time we see him," she said to Bush. In days, they knew, Blair could be a private citizen again.

The president and his entourage climbed onto the plane. They gathered at a wooden table in the aircraft's conference room and began hammering out what they called "the ultimatum speech," which Bush would deliver in an Oval Office address the following night. The message was simple: Hussein had to leave Iraq in forty-eight hours from the time Bush gave his address—by Wednesday at 8:00 P.M. Washington time—or face the fury of American might.

They completed the draft and settled in for a movie. Bush munched on pop-
corn as the lights dimmed. The film *Conspiracy Theory* began. Bush didn't like it.

Two days later, Tony Blair was reviewing documents in shirtsleeves, his suit
jacket beside him on the table. He was in a private room in the House of Commons, directly behind the Speaker's chair, preparing to beseech Parliament to
authorize the use of military force against Iraq.

The room was a hive of activity, with aides giving him last-minute information and suggesting pungent turns of phrase for his speech. Amid the tumult,
one of them studied Blair. The intense machinations of the past year had ex-
acted a toll on the prime minister. He had lost weight and his face had paled.
But his energy had not waned—he was reaching the tail end of what would be
an eighteen-hour day, and his staffers were still struggling to keep up with him
as he rushed from place to place.

The time approached 12:30 P.M. Blair slipped on his jacket and stepped into
the House chamber.

Blair stood at a wooden podium in front of his seat in the House of Commons,
the spot where prime ministers historically addressed the members.

"This is a tough choice indeed," he said, "but it is also a stark one: To stand
British troops down now and turn back or to hold firm to the course that we
have set. I believe passionately that we must hold firm to that course."

Already, some of the House members saw a difference in Blair, changes in
style that underscored the gravity of the moment. There were no sneers or head
shakes directed at those he considered fools as there had been so often in the
past. There was no cadence of the pulpit. Instead, the words were simple, raw,
and respectful. But above all, they were bleak.

"The outcome of this debate will determine more than the fate of the Iraqi
regime," Blair proclaimed. "It will determine the pattern of international politics for the next generation."

He reviewed the twelve-year history of the U.N.'s efforts to disarm Iraq,
reciting the dashed hopes, the endless delays, the fruitless talks. Now Security
Council members were singing that same old song. The choice was no longer
about whether action against Saddam would be postponed, Blair said. It was
about whether there would be any action at all.

"The tragedy is that the world has to learn the lesson all over again that weakness in the face of a threat from a tyrant is the surest way not to peace but, unfortunately, to conflict," Blair said.

These were not simple issues, the prime minister said, and reasonable people could disagree in good faith on how to proceed. There had, of course, been efforts to link Saddam with bin Laden, though no firm proof of a meaningful relationship had yet been found.

"At the moment," he said, "I accept fully that the association between the two is loose. But it is hardening."

Blair's voice stayed steady, but his hands began to tremble. His wife, Cherie, watched from the gallery, her face frozen.

"To retreat now, I believe, would put at hazard all that we hold dearest," he said, "to tell our allies that, at the very moment of action, at the very moment when they need our determination, Britain faltered."

He looked around the packed room. "I will not be a party to such a course," he said.

With that, Blair pushed aside his prepared remarks.

"This is the time not just for this government—or indeed for this Prime Minister—but for this House to give a lead," he said, "to show, at the moment of decision, that we have the courage to do the right thing."

Blair stopped speaking, and the members erupted in applause and cheers.

The debate lasted late into the night. At 10:00 P.M., a majority beat back an amendment offered by 139 members of Blair's own party, declaring that the case for war had not been proved. Learning of his victory, Blair breathed deep and sighed. The revolt against his war policy had been quelled. Britain would be joining the Americans in the fight to defang Saddam Hussein.

On the afternoon of March 19, in the private dining room just off the Oval Office, members of the war cabinet were showing Bush maps of Baghdad and pointing out a proposed strategic target.

The combined CIA and army Special Forces unit—called the Northern Iraq Liaison Unit—had turned up intelligence the previous day. As relayed by an important source, information from Iraq's communications headquarters indicated that Saddam, his sons, and other top members of his government would be hiding out at Dora Farms, an estate owned by the dictator's wife. Aerial reconnaissance suggested that the location's security had been tightened. Rather than fleeing Iraq and seeking asylum abroad before Bush's forty-eight-hour deadline expired that night, Saddam apparently planned to hole up at the small complex on the outskirts of Baghdad.

Bush clasped his chin. "How good are your sources on this?" he asked Tenet.

"Very good," Tenet replied. "But we can't guarantee that it isn't wrong, or that it isn't a trick."

Saddam was capable of doing anything to stay in power. He might have moved an orphanage to the site, luring the United States into unknowingly raining bombs on children and earning the censure of the world. Or maybe Dora Farms was just a stopping point on his way out of the country. But, Tenet said, the intelligence that placed Saddam there was as good as it got.

The president furrowed his brow. Launching an air war now would be a drastic departure from the carefully choreographed invasion plan; there were supposed to be two days of covert operations before bombing began. Plus, he couldn't underestimate Saddam's ruthlessness, he thought. Launching this strike could annihilate the Iraqi dictator and his lieutenants, or it could kill innocents put in danger by that sociopath. Bush wanted more information before making a decision.

Either way, General Tommy Franks, head of U.S. Central Command, had to be briefed on the situation. General Dick Myers, chairman of the Joint Chiefs of Staff, walked out of the room to call him.

At that moment, just west of Doha, Qatar, Tommy Franks was asleep in his bedroom at the Al Udeid Air Base, the forward headquarters of CENTCOM. As he dozed, a movie—a 1949 John Wayne western called *She Wore a Yellow Ribbon*—was playing, unwatched and unheard, on his television.

By his bed, the secure phone rang. It was Myers.

"Tom," the general said, "I'm in the White House with the president, Secretary Rumsfeld, and George Tenet. Are you aware of the emerging target at Dora Farms?"

Franks knew about it. He had heard from the CIA the previous day of the intelligence suggesting Saddam and some of his senior lieutenants might be planning to hide out on March 19 at the compound. He told Myers that his group had been laying the groundwork for an aerial attack on the grounds.

"Can you strike it tonight?" Myers asked.

Franks pulled on his boots. This would be a last-minute change in the strategy. There would be none of the long-planned "shock and awe" from the initial moments of attack, more like puzzlement and laughter. Still, Franks understood that there was a chance to end this war by taking out Saddam in one shot. The American military would have pulled off a feat to astonish the world.

Timing was tight.

The intelligence indicated that there was an underground concrete shelter at Dora. The only aircraft in the area that could carry a bunker-busting bomb, hit a precise target in the middle of a populated area, and, with luck, return safely was an F-117 Stealth Fighter. Sending a bomber now, without having first crippled Baghdad's air defenses, would never be authorized in normal circumstances. F-117s could barely be detected by radar, and at night, they were almost impossible to observe from the ground. But in daylight, they could be seen and shot down. For this mission, the Stealths would have to drop the bombs, then flee the Baghdad skies before the first glow of dawn. To pull that off, Bush had give the go-ahead for the attack by no later than 7:15 P.M. Washington time, just three hours away—and forty-five minutes before the deadline Bush had given Saddam for leaving Iraq.

Tenet had more news. Saddam had been spotted arriving at Dora in a taxi.

Bush paused as he considered the new development. It was 7:11, four minutes before the deadline Franks had set for a decision. The president looked around the room at his advisors.

"Do you favor a strike?" he asked. Each of them—Myers, Rumsfeld, Tenet, Cheney, Rice, and Powell—said yes.

"Let's go," Bush said.

7:12 P.M. The moment that Bush issued his last major policy decision in the terror wars, launched on a clear day in Washington some eighteen months before.

Three minutes later, Tony Blair was in his private residence on the third floor of Number 10 Downing Street, watching soccer highlights on the ITV television network. He was disheartened to see that his favorite team, Newcastle United, had been knocked out of the Champions League tournament with a 0–2 loss to Barcelona.

The telephone rang. David Manning, the special advisor on foreign affairs, was on the line. "I just received a call from the White House," he said. "The president has just authorized a decapitation strike against Saddam and the Iraqi high command."

A last-minute change. The war wasn't supposed to start this way. Blair mentioned that he wanted to speak to Bush, to hear more about what was happening.

There wasn't much else to learn, Manning said. "And the president's gone off for dinner."

Blair thanked Manning and hung up.

George and Laura Bush were sitting in the living room of the White House residence when a call came through from Andy Card, the chief of staff. It was 8:05 P.M. The deadline Bush had issued two days before had passed.

"Mr. President," Card said, "our intelligence officials say they have no information that Saddam has left Iraq."

Now there was no longer any reason for Bush to call off the F-117s that were hurtling toward Baghdad. They would reach their target, he knew, in just over an hour and a half.

At 5:34 Baghdad time, the Stealth bombers dropped laser-guided GBU-28 bunker busters on Dora Farms. Explosions thundered over the sleeping city. Apparently, the Iraqi military had not been expecting a morning attack; a full minute passed until air-raid sirens sounded, followed by another lengthy delay before antiaircraft fire began.

A crowd of senior administration officials dashed into and out of the Oval Office dining room, making calls in search of news from Baghdad. Bush came down from the residence and joined his advisors just after ten o'clock. Steve Hadley, the deputy national security advisor, approached him.

"Mr. President," he said. "It appears that the bombing mission went according to plan. The planes are still in stealth mode and are heading back to base."

Bush nodded. "Let's pray for the pilots," he said.

Everyone in the room bowed their heads in silence. When the moment passed, Bush walked into the Oval Office and sat at his desk, the same one used twelve years before by his father, President George H. W. Bush, when he announced the commencement of bombing against Iraq in the opening salvo of the Persian Gulf War.

Now, once again, a camera and sound equipment rested on wooden planks that had been laid across the floor. A member of the television crew approached Bush, brushed his hair, applied some makeup, and straightened his lapel. When she finished, the president glanced at an aide and pumped his fist.

"Feel good," he said.

Seconds before 10:15, the countdown began. His image appeared on televisions worldwide.

"My fellow citizens," he began. "At this hour American and coalition forces are in the early stages of military operations to disarm Iraq, to free its people and to defend the world from grave danger."

He spoke for four minutes, then sat completely still with his eyes focused on the camera.

"And, we're out," the director said. "Thank you, Mr. President."

Bush stood and approached the men and women who had helped guide him through the tumultuous months since 9/11, shaking their hands and accepting their congratulations. Then he strolled away, leaving his aides behind as he headed upstairs for bed.

EPILOGUE

Beneath a flawless late-summer sky, two bagpipers and a drummer played "Amazing Grace" in the concrete canyon where the World Trade Center once stood. Alongside them, police officers and firefighters unfurled the tattered American flag that had previously fluttered over the rubble of the towers, as a tribute to the terrorists' victims and a display of the nation's resolve.

The crowds that gathered for the second anniversary memorial service were smaller than the previous year, and fewer official ceremonies were taking place around the country. Still, thousands had come to Ground Zero this day, wearing ribbons of remembrance and holding photographs aloft of loved ones who had perished on 9/11. At 8:46, exactly two years after American Airlines flight 77 smashed into the North Tower, a single bell chimed and the crowd went silent.

A boy named Peter Negron, dressed in a dark suit that hung loosely over his thin frame, stepped up to a wooden podium near the flag. He was no longer the eleven-year-old mischief maker he had been on the day his father was murdered. He was a teenager with an ache that wouldn't go away and eyes that wept whenever he recalled his father's last words to him: "I love you, champ."

Peter leaned in to the microphone. "I wanted to read you this poem," he said, "because it says what I am feeling."

In a reedy, tremulous voice, Peter recited an elegy called "Stars," describing his affection for the lights in the sky because they never told him to cheer up or asked him the reasons for his sadness, yet somehow calmed him in their silent vigil.

He reached the final lines. "I felt them watching over me, each one—and let me cry and cry till I was done."

Peter was followed by two hundred other children who had lost loved ones in the attack and who now stood, two at a time, to speak the names of the dead. It was a poignant and potent scene. These were the youngest victims, the sons, daughters, nieces, nephews, and grandchildren of the three thousand who lost their lives that day.

And gradually, with the passage of time, they were being forgotten by an emotionally exhausted nation. Patriotic fervor was giving way to doubt. Sorrow had been subsumed by anger and protests—about Iraq, Guantanamo, detainee treatment, military commissions. Soon, the domestic political conflict would spread to other controversies, with the disclosures of the NSA's new powers to monitor electronic communication, the CIA's secret prisons, and the legal analyses proclaiming the president's almost unfettered powers at a time of war. The revelations spilled out, one after another, ripping the national fabric as nothing had done since Vietnam.

Bush was already losing credibility. The invasion of Iraq was emerging as a strategic debacle—there were no weapons of mass destruction, no connections to 9/11, no adequate preparations for the aftermath of victory. Looting, blackouts, and mayhem were turning the Iraqi people against the United States. Bush and some of the strongest advocates for the war revised the rationale, nudging aside the claims about nuclear and biochemical arsenals and about Saddam's connivance with al-Qaeda, proclaiming instead that the mission was largely to free Iraqis from the rule of a tyrant. But a growing number of Americans were unconvinced—that same day, even as crowds were softly weeping at Ground Zero, a new Gallup poll was released showing that Bush's approval among Americans had tumbled to its lowest level since the 9/11 attacks. By the time Bush left office, he was the most unpopular departing president in history, with Gallup showing a final approval rating of 22 percent.

In Britain, as the casualties mounted in Iraq, Tony Blair faced a similar collapse in support. Widespread public anger at the prime minister intensified on the 9/11 second anniversary, when a just-issued parliamentary report revealed that British intelligence had warned him military action against Iraq would *increase* the risk of terrorists' obtaining weapons of mass destruction.

By 2005, Blair had become a drag on his Labour Party, which lost almost one hundred seats in Parliament. Pressure mounted within the party for him to resign, and in 2007, he stepped down as prime minister. But that didn't end the Iraq controversy for Blair—in 2009, Prime Minister Gordon Brown announced the formation of an independent committee to investigate decisions and intelligence that led Britain to join the invasion. Blair was summoned to testify multiple times.

The abruptness of the American public's pivot away from wrath at al-Qaeda to preoccupation with Iraq was breathtaking, and was reflected in Bush's own statements. In the last half of 2003, he mentioned Osama bin Laden only three times—in each instance, in response to questions at a press conference specifically about the terrorist leader. He uttered Saddam Hussein's name in almost 150 instances in the same period. The words *al-Qaeda* passed his lips nine times, once to state that Saddam Hussein had been tied to the terrorist group. He talked about Afghanistan nineteen times; Iraq, ninety-six.

Disputes about the reliability of the information used to justify the invasion of Iraq continue to this day. George Tenet publicly accused Dick Cheney and other hawks in the administration of pushing the country into war without ever seriously evaluating whether Saddam Hussein posed an imminent threat to the United States. Tenet resigned from the CIA in 2004 and is now a managing director with the financial firm Allen & Company.

Cheney became a lightning rod for public criticism; by the time he left office, Gallup reported that 59 percent of Americans disapproved of his performance as vice president. According to associates, when he first returned to private life, Cheney was angry with Bush for rejecting much of his advice in the second term. However, the two men have since put their differences aside.

Colin Powell, who stepped down as secretary of state in 2005, felt betrayed and abused by how the Bush administration had used him in the buildup to the Iraq war. During the attempt to secure a U.N. resolution authorizing military action, Powell had delivered a detailed presentation to other member nations about the intelligence that proved Iraq's misdeeds. The speech was, Powell later said, the lowest point in his career, because so much of the information he had been provided by members of the administration proved to be false. One of the primary sources of information in the speech—Rafid Ahmed Alwan al-Janabi, or "Curveball," as his U.S. and German handlers called him—admitted in 2011 that he had fabricated evidence of Iraq's supposed biological weapons program. In February of that year, Powell called on the CIA and the Pentagon to explain why they had failed to alert him to Curveball's unreliability before his address at the U.N. Beyond that dispute, Powell has maintained a low profile since his resignation and is now an honorary board member of Wings of Hope, a charitable group that combats poverty.

Condoleezza Rice succeeded Powell as secretary of state and remained with the Bush administration until its final day, then returned to Stanford University to resume her position as a political science professor. John Ashcroft left the Justice Department in 2005 and set up a Washington consulting firm, the Ashcroft Group.

At the Pentagon, Iraq also played a role in the departure of Donald Rumsfeld. He resigned in November 2006 after Republicans suffered bruising losses in midterm elections, in large part because of public furor over Iraq. In 2007, he formed the Rumsfeld Foundation, a charitable group. Paul Wolfowitz served as president of the World Bank but resigned in 2007 amid accusations that he violated ethical rules in arranging a generous pay and promotion package for Shaha Ali Riza, his companion. He is now a visiting scholar at the American Enterprise Institute.

Throughout the post-9/11 political tumult, the most contentious controversy was about the treatment of detainees, with administration critics contending it amounted to torture that produced no information of value, while supporters countered that it was legal, necessary, and effective. At the center of that dispute were an assortment of administration lawyers—Yoo, Gonzales, Addington, Flanigan, and Haynes.

Yoo left the Justice Department in 2003 after he was passed over to run the Office of Legal Counsel. He recommended Jack Goldsmith, a professor on leave from the University of Chicago Law School, for the position. He then returned to the faculty of Berkeley Law School at the University of California. Six weeks into the job, Goldsmith read Yoo's memos on detainee treatment and was troubled by what he saw as narrow definitions of torture, shoddy legal analysis about presidential powers, and flawed conclusions. He withdrew the opinions in 2004, rendering them irrelevant to the administration's policy considerations.

Partially in response to that decision, the Office of Professional Responsibility at the Justice Department launched an investigation of the Office of Legal Counsel and the analyses it had conducted on terrorism issues. Yoo's decisions were a primary focus of the inquiry.

The investigative report concluded that Yoo "knowingly provided incomplete and one-sided advice in his analysis" on the president's power at a time of war. It also criticized his determination that an interrogator was not engaged in torture if his mistreatment of a detainee was for the purpose of obtaining information, rather than simply to inflict pain; the report concluded that this was insufficient and failed to convey the ambiguity of the laws in this area.

The accusation against Yoo that he intentionally crafted his constitutional interpretation to fit the needs of the administration is suspect. First, his writings *before* he joined the Office of Legal Counsel, most of which appeared in law reviews, advanced the same argument on presidential powers that he included in the memos. Moreover, some lawyers who worked with him in the Justice Department say that Yoo was—and remains—a passionate advocate for his analysis, and that they have no doubt he believes his legal reasoning is sound.

Still, those lawyers also believe Yoo inadvertently set up the administration for trouble because of an arrogant certainty that drove his writing. He waved away differing opinions, these lawyers said, and failed to reconsider his interpretation when the implications of its findings became nonsensical.

Based on his analysis, the president at a time of war could lawfully set up concentration camps for Muslims, murder the children of terrorist suspects to force the suspects to talk, and whatever else he chooses to do so long as he believes it is necessary for national security. Yoo acknowledged as much during his questioning by lawyers with the Office of Professional Responsibility for their report; when asked if the president could lawfully order the massacre of a village of civilians during wartime, Yoo's response was "Sure."

The lawyers who relied on the Yoo memos paid a price for that decision. Both Haynes and Flanigan lost coveted positions in government. Haynes had been nominated for a federal judgeship; Flanigan was selected by Bush to serve as deputy attorney general. Both nominations set off debates on Capitol Hill, largely because of their connections—sometimes amounting to little more than attending a briefing—to policies related to detainees and other terrorism issues. Flanigan returned as a partner to the law firm of McGuireWoods, where his practice focuses on international transactions and government investigations. Haynes was hired as the chief corporate counsel at Chevron.

With controversies swirling around them, both Gonzales and Addington struggled to find work after they left government service. Addington finally landed a job in 2010 as the vice president of domestic and economic policy studies at the Heritage Foundation; in 2009, Gonzales began teaching political science as a visiting professor at Texas Tech University.

However the decisions on the interrogation tactics are viewed, they have to be considered in context. While Goldsmith was deemed by some as a hero for withdrawing the original interrogation memos, he bristled at the hostility shown to Yoo and other lawyers by the press and the public. None of this was a "struggle between the forces of good and evil," he wrote. No one wanted to shred the Constitution. Administration lawyers began formulating analyses when the Twin Towers and the Pentagon were still burning and the number of dead was still unknown. Everyone—at the White House, in Congress, at the CIA, at the Pentagon, in business and among the general public—believed correctly that al-Qaeda was plotting more attacks. Lawyers were caught up in an almost unbearable dilemma of being forced to make rulings, on the fly, that might deflect an unimaginably destructive second blow by al-Qaeda, but perhaps at the cost of sacrificing, if only for a time, certain of America's founding principles. Those who believe such decisions would be easy, Goldsmith argued, are fooling themselves.

The huge volume of documents and other records that have been made public in the years after the decisions were reached do not expose reckless personalities who cavalierly issued life-and-death decisions, but rather, officials who were struggling to find a proper balance between national security and legal rights. Or, as Goldsmith said, "How aggressively to check the terrorist threat and whether and how far to push the law in doing so are rarely obvious, especially during blizzards of frightening threat reports, when one is blinded by ignorance and desperately worried about not doing enough."

Even as the horrors of 9/11 receded in the undertow of memory, that desperate worry continued to transfix the Bush administration, which—whatever the final judgment of history about its tactics, successes, and failures may be—never wavered from its central focus of averting the next deadly terrorist assault that its members feared was on the horizon. The information contained in the daily threat matrix had not gone away. And there were constant reminders of the price that was paid on 9/11 for Washington's failure to exercise greater vigilance amid the growing warnings of terrorist threats.

While Bush did not attend the memorial at Ground Zero on the second anniversary of the attacks, White House officials said that he was deeply affected by the hundreds of grieving children, both for their losses and for their bravery in standing before the crowds of mourners to recite the names of the dead. Many of them added heartrending personal messages: "You're the ultimate father and I love you in my heart"; "I love you, Daddy, and I miss you a lot"; "My mother and my hero. We love you."

The final speaker was Michele Stabile, who saved her father's name, Michael Stabile, as the last she uttered. "I miss you, Daddy," she said before stepping away from the microphone.

Then the sound of Taps filled the air.

• • •

The following month, on the afternoon of October 6, 2003, an Air France flight landed at Dorval International Airport in Montreal. On board, Maher Arar, sickly and pale, stood up and made his way to the exit. After two years in a Syrian prison, he was back home.

Arar had just been released without advance notice, for no apparent reason. In truth, he had become a pawn in a game of international diplomacy. Syria had tried to curry favor with the United States—by providing intelligence on al-Qaeda and agreeing to imprison accused terrorists turned over by the Americans—in hopes it would help improve its relations with Washington.

But that optimism proved wrong. The administration did not temper its criticisms of Syria—Bush even characterized it in 2002 as part of an "axis of evil," linking it to both Saddam's Iraq and North Korea. As the administration continued its condemnations, a judgment was made at the highest reaches of the Syrian government to limit its cooperation. While Arar was a Canadian, he had been delivered by the Americans, through Jordan. Syria had no interest in holding him and no reward if it did. And so, he was released.

Arar stepped off the plane just after 12:30 and was taken to the airport's secure arrivals area. Waiting for him was his wife, Monia Mazigh, who had spent the last two years pleading with the Canadian government, the press, lawyers, anyone she thought could help rescue her husband.

She saw that he was very thin, his black sweater drooping over his body. He looked terrified. Mazigh approached him.

"You are safe now," she whispered in his ear.

He was taken to an airport lounge and was stunned to see a swarm of reporters waiting for him. He decided to make a short statement.

"I'm very glad to get back home," he said softly. "I'm so excited to see my family again."

The delicacy of his statement prompted Mazigh to add some words of her own. "This has been a terrible tragedy for our family," she said. "This is just the beginning of justice."

It was indeed. The Canadian public pressured the government to explain how and why Arar had been sent to Syria by the United States. Much of the anger was directed at the Canadian intelligence agency and the Mounties, based on suspicions that the two groups had worked in concert with the Americans in the Arar case. The Canadian government formed an independent investigative commission. After two years of hearings and document reviews, the group concluded that no evidence had ever existed to suggest that Arar constituted a threat—he was not a member of al-Qaeda, never was, and had no connections at all to Islamic extremists. In 2007, Canada paid him a settlement of $10 million and issued a formal expression of regret.

"On behalf of the Government of Canada, I wish to apologize to you, Monia Mazigh and your family for any role Canadian officials may have played in the terrible ordeal that all of you experienced in 2002 and 2003," Stephen Harper, the Canadian prime minister, wrote in the letter to Arar. "I sincerely hope that these words and actions will assist you and your family in your efforts to begin a new and hopeful chapter in your lives."

The United States, which had played a far more significant role in Arar's deportation, has refused to apologize or acknowledge any error. Arar sued, but the Bush administration successfully convinced the courts that its officials could not be held liable for his injuries on the grounds that the case involved classified national security issues.

While Washington has never acknowledged the full truth, at least one of the reasons behind Arar's deportation was a lie. Shortly after Arar had been sent to Syria, William Graham, Canada's minister of foreign affairs, repeatedly asked Colin Powell for details about how the United States came to deport a Canadian citizen to the Middle East. Each time, Powell assured him that Canadian officials had provided the intelligence leading to Arar's removal and had authorized it. Graham launched his own inquiry to identify the culprits in his government, without success. Then, on December 1, 2003, just two months after Arar's return, he learned why his search failed. Powell called him and revealed that others in the administration had misled him about the evidence on Arar; none of the information had been provided by Canada, and no one in Ottawa had authorized the departation.

The sham evidence against Arar came primarily from two sources—Ahmad El-Maati, the man with the map; and Abdullah Almalki, whom Canadian intelligence had seen have lunch with Arar. Under torture, El-Maati stated that both Arar and Almalki were part of al-Qaeda; subsequently, Almalki acknowledged to his abusers that he knew Arar, proof, supposedly, of an al-Qaeda connection.

The Syrians also released Almalki and El-Maati. El-Maati, who was both a Canadian and an Egyptian citizen, was sent to Cairo in 2002 after being detained in Syria for three months. There, he was tortured again. He was released in January 2004 and flew back home. For years, he remained unable to work and lived in an apartment with his mother.

In July 2004, a Syrian court cleared Almalki of any connection to terrorism; he also returned to Canada. Years after the ordeal ended, Almalki still experienced severe pain from the torture, once collapsing on his driveway screaming while passing a basketball to one of his children.

Canada appointed another independent commission to investigate the cases of El-Maati and Almalki. Following that inquiry, in 2009, the House of Commons voted to offer an official apology and an undisclosed settlement to both men.

The Canadian government never did so.

Almost five years after the CIA snatched him off a Milan street, Abu Omar was released from an Egyptian prison when a Cairo court found the allegation against him to be unfounded. He did not return to Italy, where he still faced arrest on terrorism charges.

Five days after the cleric was freed, Armando Spataro, deputy chief prosecutor in Milan, secured the indictment of twenty-six Americans who were directly involved in the kidnapping. In 2010, after being tried in absentia, twenty-three of them were convicted on the charges by an Italian judge. Robert Lady—the CIA station chief in Milan who had vigorously opposed the idea of abducting an Italian resident—was sentenced to eight years in prison.

He and the officials convicted in the case are now considered fugitives by the Italian government.

The legal fights challenging the president's policies on the detention and treatment of suspected terrorists played out over several years. And in the end, with each ruling by the Supreme Court, the administration lost.

The names of the men whose cases changed American policy became known worldwide—Shafiq Rasul, one of the members of the Tipton Three and the first to file a habeas petition; Yaser Esam Hamdi, the American citizen captured in Afghanistan and then held in a navy brig in Norfolk; Salim Hamdan, bin Laden's former driver; and Lakhdar Boumediene, one of the Algerian Six who had been reluctantly turned over by officials in Bosnia-Herzegovina after they were threatened by the United States.

The High Court slowly chipped away at policies that had seemed impervious to attack. The *Rasul* ruling held that American courts had the authority to determine whether foreign nationals detained at Guantanamo were lawfully imprisoned. Under *Hamdi,* the court decided that American citizens had the right to challenge their designation as enemy combatants before an impartial judge. The *Hamdan* case was the most earth-shattering, declaring that only Congress, and not the president, had the authority to set up military commissions, and found the panels established by Bush ran afoul of both the laws of military justice and the Geneva Conventions.

Congress responded in 2006 with the passage of the Military Commissions Act, which gave the government the authority to try suspected terrorists before the tribunals. The law also included relaxed rules of evidence, allowing the admission of hearsay and information obtained through coercion interrogations, without the defendants' having any chance to confront their accusers.

The law stood for two years, until the court issued its opinion in the *Boumediene* case, holding that constitutional rights extended to detainees held in Guantanamo. With that foundation to the ruling, the court continued that the prisoners had habeas rights and that the Military Commissions Act was an unconstitutional suspension of those rights.

Almost all of the men whose names are now linked to those decisions were either released without charges or given a minimal sentence. Rasul and the other members of the Tipton Three—Asif Iqbal and Ruhal Ahmed—were sent back to England in March 2004 after being detained for seventeen months. They were freed the next day. That was not the end of the story. In 2007, both Ahmed and Rasul agreed to appear on a British television show where they would be given a lie-detector test. Ahmed failed, and admitted that he had visited an Islamist training camp and had been trained to use an AK-47. Rasul refused to go through with the test.

Also in 2004, Hamdi—who had been captured in Afghanistan with Taliban fighters—was sent back to Saudi Arabia, on condition that he renounce his American citizenship. After being held for two and a half years, he also was never charged.

Salim Hamdan was the first Guantanamo detainee to be tried by military commission. In the case, which was heard in 2008, Hamdan was charged with conspiracy and providing support for terrorists. After eight hours of deliberation, the military officers on the jury found Hamdan guilty only on the second count. The prosecution urged the judge to sentence Hamdan to a term of thirty years to life; the defense sought forty-five months. In a rebuke to the administration's portrayal of Hamdan as a dangerous terrorist, the judge sentenced him to sixty-six months but credited him with the sixty-one months he had already been held. Hamdan was released after five months. He now lives in Yemen with his family.

The story of the Algerian Six proved to be the most disturbing. They had been arrested in Bosnia under accusations that they were plotting to bomb the American embassy in Sarajevo; that allegation was dropped when their case was finally heard before a review board at Guantanamo. Instead, the administration argued that they should continue to be held on the basis of bizarre allegations: that one of the men taught karate to orphans; that another, during his compulsory military service in Algeria, had worked as a cook; that a third wore a ring similar to those favored by a group connected to Hamas. Only a single claim rose to the level of an actual charge—that one of the men had joined al-Qaeda and Taliban fighters in the battle at Tora Bora. The claim was false—at the time of the Tora Bora conflict, he was in a Sarajevo prison at the insistence of Bush administration officials.

The men were held for almost seven years and saw the inside of a civilian court only because of the ruling in *Boumediene.* In their filings, the men contended that there was no basis for their detention, and federal judge Richard J. Leon agreed. He tossed out all charges against five of the men, but ruled that the secret intelligence information against the sixth justified his detention.

In dismissing the case against the five, Leon said, "To allow enemy combatancy to rest on so thin a reed would be inconsistent with this court's obligation. The court must and will grant their petitions and order their release." Their seven-year detention, Leon declared, had been illegal.

By the summer of 2008, the world was closing in on Dr. Bruce Ivins.

The investigation into the anthrax killings of 2001 had overtaken his life. No longer was he the FBI's golden boy, the scientific brains behind the inquiry. Instead, he had become the government's lead—and only—suspect.

A technological breakthrough was the first step in Ivins's transformation from hero to villain. The new test allowed researchers to detect minor mutations that served as a biological fingerprint for anthrax; samples of the bacteria could all be linked to the original source. Using that technique, the government determined that the anthrax used in the attack had been derived from RMR-1029, a batch developed by and in the possession of Ivins.

While some scientists argued that the test was far from conclusive, other evidence developed by the FBI was even more compelling. Investigators reviewed

Ivins's unapproved efforts in April 2002 to decontaminate his work area and determined that the spots he had chosen to clean invariably were tainted with anthrax, an anomaly that went far beyond statistical chance—Ivins, the agents concluded, knew where to look.

The government also learned of his bizarre obsession with the Kappa Kappa Gamma sorority, and discovered that a Kappa location was just 175 feet from the mailbox in Princeton where the anthrax letters were mailed—again, an improbable coincidence. Moreover, the bureau determined that in the days leading up to the anthrax mailings, Ivins had uncharacteristically worked nights in the lab, a change in routine that would have given him time to prepare the deadly weapon. They caught him in lie after lie.

Then there was the code. A review of the first mailings revealed an exceedingly complex message hidden within sentences, specifically, in the letters that had been written in boldface—*TTT, AAT,* and *TAT*. Each was an accepted scientific code for the three acids involved in the makeup of DNA, playing a role in the production of phenylalanine, asparagine, and tyrosine; the single-letter designation for each was *F, N,* and *Y*. The first letter of each acid—*PAT*—spelled out the name of one of the women who had been a target of his obsessions. The letter designation—*FNY*—was a slang term for "fuck New York," a city that was also one of Ivins's fixations and that he hated with a deep-seated passion.

Detecting ciphers hidden in DNA was not an invention by Ivins; the book *Gödel, Escher, Bach: An Eternal Golden Braid* dealt in part with hidden messages, including DNA codes. Ivins was fascinated by the book, which had been given to him long before by the microbiologist from Kappa Kappa Gamma whom he had stalked for years. When he realized that he was a suspect, Ivins went out late at night and threw the book into the garbage. The FBI was watching, and agents immediately snapped up the trash as evidence.

Ivins had been exposed by his own deceit and lies. He was forced to testify before a federal grand jury at least twice. Agents had searched his house, his office, and his cars—anyplace where he might have hidden something. Indeed, nothing in the anthrax researcher's life was private anymore. Everyone he knew—including people he hadn't spoken with in years—was questioned. Other raids of his garbage turned up more than a dozen pornographic magazines and fourteen pairs of semen-stained panties. If that wasn't embarrassing enough, the bureau demanded that he submit to a DNA test to determine if the semen was his.

But the investigation was about to reach a new stage. The government was preparing to indict Ivins for committing murder through the use of a weapon of mass destruction. His lawyer notified him that he would soon be arrested.

What little remained of Ivins's sanity cracked. He had often told his therapists of his desire to kill himself or others, and his homicidal thoughts were escalating. By July, his obsessions focused on Kathryn Price, a law school lecturer who participated in a television reality show called *The Mole*. Under the rules in that program, a group of ten contestants compete in various tests; however, one of them is the mole, secretly responsible for sabotaging the efforts of other participants. On the final day of the program, Price was revealed as the mole, and Ivins flew into a rage about what he perceived as her betrayal.

On July 6, Ivins opened a new Yahoo e-mail account under the name "Stanford Hawker," a name apparently derived from his fixation on the schools attended by the woman who was now in his crosshairs. Price held degrees from both Stanford Law School and the University of Kansas, where the sports teams were known as the Jayhawks. For the password, he typed a sentence as one word: *killkathrynprice*.

When Price admitted to being the mole, one of the contestants should have killed her, Ivins said in diatribes posted on YouTube. "He should have taken the hatchet and brought it down hard and sharply across her neck, severing her carotid artery and jugular vein," he said. "Then when she hits the ground, he completes the task on the other side of the neck, severing her trachea as well."

Now that the show was over, Ivins wrote, he could only hope that somebody else would give her the punishment she deserved. "The least someone could do would be to take a sharp ballpoint pen or letter opener and put her eyes out."

Three days later, Ivins's fury was boiling over, this time at his colleagues and the FBI. That evening, he attended his regular group therapy session, which was being run by two counselors, including one named Jean Duley. Members of the group were engaged in role-playing, exploring bonds between fathers and sons. As the evening unfolded, Ivins—whose own father had frequently told him that he had been unwanted—grew increasingly agitated.

Duley noticed. "Bruce, is there something you want to discuss?"

Ivins clenched his teeth, shifting his gaze rapidly back and forth across the floor. "There's nothing," he said. "I'm fine."

"Come on, Bruce, this is a safe place. We're here for you. What's troubling you?"

His head jerked up. "All these damn people! The FBI, the government, the whole system! They have been doing everything they can to destroy me! They shouldn't take me on! I'm the wrong guy to take on. I'm not going to let them do this!"

"Bruce," Duley said, "try to focus."

"I'm not going to face the death penalty!" he snapped. "I'll kill myself first!"

Duley leaned in. She needed to explore this suicide threat, to find out whether Ivins was serious.

"Bruce," she said, "do you have a plan for how you would kill yourself?"

Ivins face locked in a bizarre smile. "Yeah, I've got a plan," he said. "I've got a list. I've got a bulletproof vest and I'm going to get a Glock handgun from my son. I can't go get it. The FBI is watching me. But my son can get it. I have a list. My coworkers, the FBI agents, everyone who's gone after me, everyone who's betrayed me. They're all on it. I'm going to get them all."

No one spoke.

Ivins's words rushed out as he jumped from topic to topic. "I've been walking around the ghetto areas of Frederick at night, looking for someone to try and hurt me. I'd just call out 'Come on, nigger boy!' Then I'd stab them in the eye with this sharp pen."

He removed a pen from his pocket and showed the other members of the group. "This is what I would use," he said. "Slam it right in the eye."

Back to the plot for a killing spree. "It could be done," he said. "I've got a bulletproof vest, I can get a gun. It's a good plan. I've really thought it out well. Cleaning it all up could be done. It would all work."

One of the other group members spoke. "If you're innocent, then why are you doing what you plan to do?"

Ivins smiled, but said nothing.

"I'm not going to do anything in the next twenty-four hours, because I'm not ready," he said.

The other members of the group listened to his ravings with fear. Finally, someone told Ivins he was making everyone uncomfortable, and the conversation moved on. After the meeting, Ivins spoke to one of the attendees.

"You'll see me in the papers," he said.

To Duley, Ivins's statements did not sound like fictitious ramblings, so the next morning, she contacted the Frederick Police Department. The authorities obtained an order allowing them to involuntarily commit Ivins to a hospital. He was arrested that day at Fort Detrick and driven to Sheppard Pratt Health System in Baltimore, where he was admitted to the psychiatric unit.

• • •

The FBI was notified of Ivins's statements at his group therapy session and raided his house again. They discovered hundreds of rounds of ammunition, smokeless handgun power for semiautomatic and automatic weapons, a bulletproof vest, and a shield that could be used for body armor. The plans he described for mass murder, the agents concluded, had been real.

Ivins was released from Sheppard Pratt on July 24. A family member protested, urging the hospital to keep him in long-term care, but the doctors ignored the objection. He was given an August 11 appointment for a psychiatric follow-up, eighteen days later.

After his release, Ivins headed to a Giant Eagle store to purchase some groceries, his prescriptions, and Tylenol PM. Just under an hour later he returned, and bought a second seventy-count bottle of the painkiller.

After a quick stop at the C. Burr Artz Library in Frederick, where he used a computer to check on the progress of the anthrax investigation, Ivins headed home. Broken and lethargic, he went straight upstairs to the second-floor bedroom. As he slept, his wife, Diane, left a letter for him on an end table, describing her pain and confusion about his actions over the previous few weeks. He had been cruel to her. And, inexplicably, he had been ignoring his lawyer's advice to stay away from the lab at night and to stop contacting two women he had harassed in the past.

There were also signs of danger. "You tell me you aren't going to get any more guns," she wrote, "then you fill out an online application for a gun license."

Ivins woke later and saw the letter. After reading it, he flipped the page over and grabbed a pen. "I have a terrible headache," he wrote. "I'm going to take some Tylenol and sleep in tomorrow."

He added, "Please let me sleep. Please." Then he scratched out those words.

Ivins stayed in bed for the next two days. Diane let her husband rest, looking in on him every so often to see if he was all right. Outside, FBI agents were keeping the house under surveillance to make sure that Ivins did not have the chance to leave and start on his promised rampage.

On the night of July 26, Diane checked on her husband at nine; he was fine. She headed to a first-floor bedroom where she had been sleeping and read a book before drifting off again.

But at some point that day, Ivins swallowed dozens of Tylenol tablets, washing them down with wine. As any doctor knew, such an overdose would destroy his liver and kill him. Late that night, he made his way into the bathroom and collapsed on the floor.

Diane awoke at 1:00 A.M. and headed upstairs to check on her husband. She found him, still alive and lying in a pool of his own urine. He was cold to the touch and unresponsive. Diane called 911, and Ivins was rushed to Frederick Memorial Hospital. The FBI surveillance unit followed the ambulance.

Six hours later, a nurse called Ivins's name loudly and he awakened almost imperceptibly.

"Bruce," the nurse said, "did you intentionally try to commit suicide?"

Groggily, Ivins nodded. Then he attempted to pull out the tubes in his body; he was placed in restraints. The next day, with Ivins fully unresponsive, he was moved to the intensive care unit. The massive overdose had led to kidney failure and was destroying his liver.

There was little that could be done to save him, and Diane insisted that he would not want to be resuscitated if his heart failed. By the next morning, the doctors concluded that Ivins would not awaken again. They consulted Diane, who decided to stop all aggressive life support. Three hours went by, and at 10:47, with his family at his bedside, his heart stopped beating.

Bruce Ivins, the man deemed by the FBI to be the anthrax killer, was dead.

An elderly, bearded man knelt down beside a palm tree and moved one of the stones encircling the trunk. This was his garden, such as it was, an incongruous patch of pastoral harmony surrounded by the thick walls of a military prison. The vast power he once wielded was gone. A life of gardening, writing, praying, and answering questions was all that remained for Saddam Hussein.

The hunt for Saddam after the invasion of Iraq in March 2003 had taken many months. He had stayed hidden in Baghdad until the week of April 10, when he concluded that the city would soon fall to the coalition. At that point he gathered his senior deputies for a final meeting, telling them that they would now begin to "struggle in secret." He left the city and gradually sent away his bodyguards to avoid attracting attention. Eight months later, he was staying in a mud hut with a lean-to in Ad-Dawr, near his hometown of Tikrit. The military received information that Saddam was hiding out in the area and launched a search mission called Operation Red Dawn. As the First Brigade Combat Team of the army's Fourth Infantry Division swooped in, Saddam went to the backyard, where a small, underground hiding place had been built years before. He climbed through a "spider hole" that had been dug into the ground, big enough to hide one person. His housemates covered it with a Styrofoam plug, some dirt, and a few ratty carpets. Saddam lay down in the coffinlike space and stayed quiet as the military searched above him. Soon, the soldiers discovered the hole and Saddam climbed out, his hands raised in surrender.

Now he was High Value Detainee Number 1 at Camp Cropper, the military facility at the Baghdad International Airport. His interrogations had begun on February 7, 2004, with the interviewer, FBI supervisory special agent George Piro, using the tried-and-true relationship-building techniques. Each day of questioning began early in the morning and lasted for hours, with Saddam offered breaks to eat, pray, and putter around in the garden.

The first few weeks had focused on Saddam's history in Iraq. But by March, as it became clear that Iraq possessed no weapons of mass destruction, Piro's supervisors told him to find out why. How could intelligence agencies worldwide have been so wrong?

On May 13, Saddam returned from a break to his nine-by-twelve tiled cell and took a seat on a metal chair across from Piro. The FBI agent and the former dictator of Iraq engaged in a casual conversation, and the discussion soon turned to Iraq's weapons of mass destruction.

"The U.N. weapons inspections achieved their objectives," Saddam said simply. "Iraq does not have any WMD and has not for some time."

"A lot of people think that you were reluctant to cooperate with the inspections process."

Saddam tossed up his hands. "We cooperated for seven years! We granted the inspectors access to the entire country, including the presidential palaces."

Piro challenged Saddam, saying that there were instances where illegal components had been hidden.

"There were individuals in the government who were initially reluctant to cooperate with the inspectors," Saddam replied. "It was difficult for them to be told one day to open all of their files and turn over all of their work and government secrets to outsiders. It took time and occurred in steps."

By 1998, he said, all of the weaponry was gone. There had been claims that he had secreted away the weapons in presidential palaces. His own palaces! It was an absurd idea. The entire Iraqi leadership would have been put at risk if such armaments were kept there. Before they were destroyed, the weapons had been stored in remote locations in the desert, he said.

"The coalition has gathered information indicating that Iraq was either maintaining or redeveloping its WMD capability," Piro said.

"They may think so," Saddam replied, "but it's not true."

"Would others in your country do this without your knowledge?"

Saddam shook his head. "No," he said. "I had meetings with all of my ministers and asked them specifically if Iraq had WMD that I was unaware of. All of them said no."

He had made it clear to them long before, Saddam said, that he wanted the country to shed all of the chemical and biological weapons and disband any nuclear projects. They knew this, and followed his instructions.

"Iraq," Saddam Hussein declared, "did not have WMD."

Cows and chickens scampered about in fear as a team of twelve Navy SEALs ran through an animal pen in Abbottabad, Pakistan. Behind the men, their MH-60 Black Hawk helicopter rested at an angle on a wall where it had just crashed.

It was early morning on May 1, 2011. After America's decadelong hunt for Osama bin Laden, the elite military force was closing in on the terrorist leader's recently discovered home. Bush had been out of office since 2009, and the raid this night had been green-lighted by his successor, Barack Obama. Shortly after assuming the presidency, Obama had ordered his director of the CIA, Leon Panetta, to set in motion plans for capturing bin Laden. A number of new and expanded initiatives were adopted but still the location of the terrorist leader remained a mystery. Then, in August 2010, the intelligence agency believed it had located a bin Laden courier, a man who had been identified through interrogation at Guantanamo. Operatives with the CIA and the National Reconnaissance Office tracked the courier, who eventually led them to the Abbottabad compound. Months of intelligence gathering and preparation for an assault followed, culminating in that night's operation.

The SEAL team sprinted toward the steel gate of the animal pen. A three-man demolition team stuck C-4 explosives to the metal, squeezing it like hardened ice cream onto the hinges. They set off the detonators, and the C-4 blasted open the gate.

From there, more gates and more explosions as the SEALs hustled toward the house where they believed bin Laden was staying. Almost immediately after the American fighters reached the patio, a stocky man appeared brandishing an AK-47. He was shot and killed, along with his unarmed wife, who had been standing beside him.

Some of the SEALs charged the three-story house. They began clearing the first floor, room by room, but the job was more complicated than they could have anticipated. The house was something of a maze, with false doors and blocked entryways that slowed the search.

The SEALs believed that if bin Laden was in the house, he would be on one of the higher floors, probably the third. But another gate blocked entry to the staircase. The demolition team took over again and blasted through. Three SEALs climbed the darkened stairs. On the way, they saw one of bin Laden's sons, Khalid, rushing toward them, an AK-47 in his hands. Khalid fired the weapon, and the SEALs shot back, killing him.

Another gate blocked the stairs again; more C-4 took care of that. A bearded man peered over the third-floor railing. It appeared to be bin Laden himself. One of the SEALs raised his gun and fired, but the terrorist leader fell back and ran into his bedroom.

The SEALs reached the third floor and rushed down a hallway, where one of them pushed open the bedroom door. Inside, he saw two women standing with bin Laden. The younger of the two—bin Laden's fifth wife, Amal—screamed at the SEALs. She approached them, and the first SEAL in the room, fearful that she might have a bomb strapped to her body, shot her in the calf with his M4 rifle. Then he wrapped his arms around her, pushing her and the other woman to the side.

Near the bed, the al-Qaeda chief stood alone, dressed in a traditional Arab outfit of loose, drawstring pants, a tunic, and a prayer cap. The second SEAL team member moved into the room, raised his M4, and trained the infrared laser at bin Laden. He pulled the trigger, and a 5.56-millimeter bullet slammed into the terrorist leader's chest. As bin Laden fell, the SEAL fired another shot that hit him in the face, blowing off part of his head.

The shooter pushed a button on his radio. "For God and country, Geronimo, Geronimo, Geronimo," he said. "Geronimo EIKIA."

The words were code announcing the astounding news—bin Laden was dead.

Hours later, in the Arabian Sea, the flat-bottom rounded nose of a V-22 Osprey came into view of the sailors standing on the deck of the USS *Carl Vinson*. The engine nacelles mounted on the end of each wingtip rotated from horizontal to vertical, and the Osprey descended toward the Nimitz-class supercarrier. The group of waiting sailors ran over to the aircraft when it landed.

A detail of military police climbed out of the Osprey, then worked with the sailors to remove their cargo from the plane's belly. It was the body of Osama bin Laden, delivered to the *Vinson* for its final disposal.

Members of the Obama administration had given careful thought about how to handle bin Laden's corpse. The primary goal was to avoid further inflaming Islamic passions, potentially increasing the dangers faced by Americans from extremists. Photographs were ruled out—releasing a picture of bin Laden, with his head partly gone, would have been not only a strategic blunder, it also would be downright ghoulish. As for bin Laden's burial, the Americans had to be careful to honor Islamic customs while simultaneously ensuring that they did not create a shrine where jihadists could gather.

Bin Laden was removed from the Osprey and placed in a spot out of sight of other sailors on the *Vinson*. The body was washed and wrapped in a burial shroud. Weights were attached to ensure that it would never rise in the water. Then the military police and sailors placed the corpse on an open-air elevator and took it down to the lowest level of the ship, where it was laid out on a prepared flat board. After some religious words were spoken and translated into Arabic, three of the sailors tipped up the board. The body slid down and fell about twenty-five feet, hitting the water with a splash.

Osama bin Laden, the most infamous mass murderer of the twenty-first century, sank silently to the bottom of the sea.

ACKNOWLEDGMENTS

Every so often, a person of immense talent and skill comes along, and I was lucky enough to have one working with me on this book. I first met Jordan Wolf eight years ago when he was a high school student whom I had hired to sort documents for my last book. I was startled by his quick mind and incomparable work ethic and soon promoted him to be one of my researchers. From there, he went to Yale University for his undergraduate degree and Tufts for his master's in philosophy, and now is headed for UCLA School of Law to pursue his J.D. and Ph.D. in law and philosophy. But, while he was in school, Jordan agreed to help me again with *500 Days*. This time around, he did everything—interviewing sources, digging up documents, writing depictions of events, and serving as my all-around partner in thinking through this book. Remember his name—I have no doubt he will go on to great things.

As he has for my last two books, Brent Bowers read over the manuscript and provided unparalleled editing and all-around guidance. His magic has dusted every page. Diane Obara served as my invaluable transcriber, proving herself, as always, to be irreplaceable.

The folks at the Wylie Agency once again were invaluable. On top of everything else he has done for me, Andrew Wylie was the idea man: he was the one who suggested that I write a national security book, a new direction for me, and took a stand as my fiercest advocate. Jeff Posternak was my hand-holder and all-around powerhouse who helped fight off the demons when they needed to be slayed.

The documents that Jordan and I collected for this book proved to be quite overwhelming, filling up two offices, a spare bedroom, and ultimately, rooms in someone else's house. Margie and Terry Tippen became the document wran-glers, organizing thousands of pages of records with such precision that I was actually able to find the information I needed from the mountain of paper. Tim Perkins offered me badly needed office space, as well as his insights about the manuscript. And I would be remiss not to recognize the contributions of Errington Thompson.

One of the biggest thrills for me with this book is that I was once again able to work with one of the finest editors in the business, Stacy Creamer. She showed me almost every day the delight of working with a top-notch pub-lisher. Megan Reid was my endlessly cheerful guide through Touchstone who was willing to jump into the mix whenever I needed help; at times, she also served as my desperately needed taskmaster, pushing me back on track when-ever I began to wander. Lisa Healy, the production editor, and George Turian-ski, the production manager, treated me with patience as I missed deadline after deadline—sorry, guys. Martin P. Karlow, the copy editor, and W. Anne Jones, the proofreader, saved me from myself more than a few times. And Ruth Lee-Mui, the designer, gave a crisp appearance to the whole book.

Finally, as always, my family played the most important role, giving me back my smile when I felt frustrated and encouraging me to keep going when I felt stuck. My wife, Theresa, was there for me every step of the way as both my edi-tor and my best friend. My three boys—Adam, Ryan, and Sam—brought me delight every day and were endlessly patient and supportive when things got rough. Adam also took a direct role in the work by assuming the unenviable job of printing out thousands of pages of e-mails and other records that I had ob-tained in digital format. The four of you have made my life an endless delight. I cannot find the words to express how much I love you all.

On the other hand, perhaps those are the words.

NOTES AND SOURCES

This book is based on more than six hundred hours of interviews, many of which were tape-recorded, with more than one hundred people involved in these events, as well as thousands of pages of documents.

The documents include notes of interviews and interrogations from the United States and other countries, secret government Teletypes and e-mails, medical records, scheduling books, travel documents, personal memos, diaries, recordings and transcripts, formal written statements provided to government investigators and in court trials, sworn testimony from criminal and civil trials and hearings, and an array of other records.

Most of the interviews were conducted on condition of anonymity. However, none of the participants in these interviews will be named. That is because I have found that, in a book, identifying those who spoke on the record makes it far easier to discern the names of others who asked me not to disclose their cooperation. A message, also, to those who sat for lengthy interviews with me but whose information did not make the book—I apologize. The direction of these large projects is often hard to predict in the early going, and the result has been that multiple story lines I pursued in my reporting hit the cutting room floor.

At times, recollections and documents conflicted. In most of those instances, I relied on the documents. However, if those records were unsworn statements, I gave them the same weight as the interviews and set out to resolve the conflict. If I could not reach a resolution, I did not use the information.

Some of the dialogue comes directly from recordings or direct transcripts of the conversation. The majority of those recorded discussions, however, were not in English. There were also a good number of documents and transcripts of wiretaps in foreign languages. As a result, I hired translators to interpret Arabic, Italian, French, German, Spanish, Bosnian (much in the Shtokavian dialect), Balinese, and Polish. I located several of those translators through Link Translations in New York; others I hired were independent, or I located them in the relevant country.

Most of the dialogue was reconstructed with the help of participants or witnesses to the conversations or documents that describe the discussion. In a few, rare instances, secondary sources were informed of events or conversations with a participant. If the secondary sources agreed on what they were told, or they were corroborated by documents, the dialogue was used. However, the dialogue reconstructed by this method never amounted to more than three sentences in a single scene and was never incriminating.

Of course, I am not claiming that the dialogue in these pages is a perfect transcript of incidents that occurred years ago. It does, however, represent the best recollection of these events and conversations by participants. In my books, I have invariably found that these renditions more accurately reflect reality than mere paraphrase would. Indeed, I have had sources summarize a conversation for me, after which I forced them to go back and try to reconstruct the dialogue. In a number of instances, when pushed to dig into their memories—or when aided by documents I placed before them—these sources frequently came to realize that their general recollection was incomplete or even incorrect compared to the dialogue they reconstructed.

In some cases, I was unable to determine the precise date when an event occurred. In those cases I have presented the relevant scene at the point in the narrative that is most consistent with the information contained in the relevant documents and interviews. In those instances, I give no indication of the event's date. For ease of reading, there were also times when a particular event was moved a few days out of order, to allow for a theme in one chapter to be completed. These movements never had any impact on the story, and the scenes had no relationship to any surrounding information.

Descriptions of individual settings come from direct observation, interviews, and documents. Most details of weather conditions come from records of the National Climactic Data Center or Weather Underground at www.wunderground.com.

Every history builds off the work of others, and I was fortunate to be standing on the shoulders of giants. Lawrence Wright, in his astonishing work *The Looming Tower: Al-Qaeda and the Road to 9/11,* Knopf, 2006, provides an invaluable depiction of the formation of al-Qaeda and the events leading to 9/11, as does Steve Coll in his seminal work *Ghost Wars: The Secret History of the CIA, Afghanistan, and Bin Laden, from the Soviet Invasion to September 10, 2001,* Penguin, 2004. Bob Woodward detailed the weeks leading up to the invasion of Afghanistan in *Bush at War,* Simon & Schuster, 2002, and then turned his expert eye toward Iraq in *Plan of Attack,* Simon & Schuster, 2004. Jane Mayer provided an invaluable analysis and depiction of the events and implications of the war on terror in her book *The Dark Side: The Inside Story of How the War on Terror Turned into a War on American Ideals,* Doubleday, 2008.

Prologue

1: The date of the briefing and a confirmation of the Bush attendees from "CIA Briefs Bush on National Security; Aides Rice, Wolfowitz Participate in Session at Texas Ranch," *Washington Post,* September 3, 2000.

2: Bush's appearance at the briefing from photographs of the event.

2: Background on the sarin gas attacks in Tokyo from T. R. Reid, "Tokyo Police Link Sect to Nerve Gas," *Washington Post,* March 22, 1995.

2–3: The briefing for Bush remains classified. However, a senior CIA official directed me to open-source materials about the threat of CBRN and terrorists that contain the same information. They include Richard A. Falkenrath et al., *America's Achilles' Heel: Nuclear, Biological, and Chemical Terrorism and Covert Attack,* MIT Press, 1998; and George Tenet's testimony of February 2, 2000, before the Senate Select Committee on Intelligence, "Global Realities of Our National Security." Other documents I obtained provided statistical and historical references that I was assured were reflected in the Bonk presentation. They include Canadian Security Intelligence Service (CSIS), "Chemical, Biological, Radiological and Nuclear (CBRN) Terrorism," December 18, 1999; Falkenrath et al., *America's Achilles' Heel*; National Defense University, Center for Counterproliferation Research, "Chemical, Biological, Radiological and Nuclear Terrorism: The Threat According to the Current Unclassified Literature," May 31, 2002; and Central Intelligence Agency, "Terrorist CBRN: Materials and Effects, CTC-2003-40058, May 2003. Historic statistical information referenced in the

Bonk briefing is also reported in Kate Ivanova and Todd Sandler, "CBRN Attack Perpetrators: An Empirical Study," *Foreign Policy Analysis,* 2007 (3).

3: Some details of al-Qaeda's pursuit of chemical and biological weapons from a note from Zawahiri to Mohammed Ataf, the al-Qaeda military leader, dated April 15, 1999; September 10, 2008, memo of Admiral D. M. Thomas Jr., Joint Task Force Guantanamo, to the Commander for United States Southern Command in Miami, "Recommendations for Continued Detention Under DOD Control (CD) for Guantanamo Detainee, ISN US9GZ-010016DP (S) (*Detainee Assessment, Abu al-Libi*)." Also see Rolf Mowatt-Larssen, "Al Qaeda Weapons of Mass Destruction Threat: Hype or Reality?" Belfer Center for Science and International Affairs, Harvard Kennedy School, January 2010.

3–7: Some details of Atyani's trip to Afghanistan and experiences with bin Laden from a video of his June 24, 2001, report on MBC-TV.

4: Details of bin Laden's philosophies and histories from a secret twenty-seven-page dossier written by a foreign intelligence service. Under an agreement with an intelligence officer, neither the name on the dossier nor the name of the foreign service can be disclosed. Also see Osama bin Laden, "Declaration of War Against the Americans Occupying the Land of the Two Holy Places," August 23, 1996. Other information from Intelligence Report, "Terrorism: Osama Bin Laden's Historical Links to Abdallah Azzam," April 18, 1997; and FBI Electronic Communication from Counterterrorism, Usama Bin Laden Unit, "Title: Usama Bin Laden IT-UBL/Al-Qaeda OO:NY," April 13, 2001 (*FBI-EC, April 13, 2001*). The fundamentalists' belief in the Zionist-communist conspiracy and its impact on Muslims, from Salah al-Din al-Munajjid, *Amidat al Nakba,* Beirut, 1967. Also see Fouad Ajami, *The Arab Predicament: Arab Political Thought and Practice Since 1967,* Cambridge University Press, 1992. The nature and significance of *jahiliyya* and other details of fundamentalist writers from Sayyid Qutb, *Milestones,* reprinted by Kazi Publications, 2007; Albert J. Bergesen, *The Sayyid Qutb Reader,* Routledge, 2008; and Ajami, *The Arab Predicament.*

4–5: Some military, logistical, and operational details about al-Qaeda from FBI 302 (notes of interview) from the interview of Nasser Ahmed Nasser al-Qaeda-Bahri, aka Abu Jandal al-Qaeda-Gharbi, conducted from September 17 through October 2, 2001, in Sana'a, Yemen. Additional documentary information from the sworn testimony of Jamal al-Qaeda-Fadl, *United States v. bin Laden,* S(7) 98 Cr. 1023, February 6, 2001. Also see FBI 302s of interviews of Salem Ahmed Hamdan, May 26, 2002; June 26 through July 9, 2002; August 6, 2002; August 19, 2002; August 24, 2002; November 13, 2002. More details from "Government's Evidentiary Proffer Supporting the Admissibility of Co-Conspirator Statements," *United States v. Enaa Arnaout,* no. 02-CR-892, filed January 6, 2003. Also see the combined FBI report of interviews with Mohamed Rashed al-Qaeda-Owhali, dated September 9, 1998; Report from the Government of Prime Minister Tony Blair for the United Kingdom, "Responsibility for the Terrorist Atrocities in the United States, 11 September 2001," October 4, 2001; and Decision Support Systems Inc., "Hunting the Sleepers," December 31, 2001.

5: Details of the East African bombings are included in a combined report by FBI agents and a CID agent with the Army Criminal Investigation Command. The report details information from the interviews of Mohamed Rashad Daoud al-Owhali (aka Khalid Salim Saleh bin Saudi Arabia), which took place in Nairobi, Kenya, from August 22 to August 25, 1998. Also see the indictment in *United States v. Bin Laden,* S(10) 98 Cr. 1023.

6: Details of the training video from a copy of the recording. Bin Laden's praise of jihadists from a video filmed at his son's wedding in 2000.

7: Details of the millennium plot from "Complaint for Violation Title 18, Sections 842(a)(3)(A) and 1001," *United States v. Ahmed Ressam,* filed in Federal District Court of the Western District of Seattle, magistrate's docket case no. 99-547M (December 1999). Some details of the preparations for the millennium from FBI Office of the Inspector General, "A Review of the FBI's Handling of Intelligence Information Related to the September 11 Attacks," November 2004; and a September 20, 1999, cable from Tenet to the CIA field. Also see FBI Electronic Communication from Counterterrorism Division, NS#H/SIOC/CAT A/B, "Title: Ahmed Ressam; Usama Bin Laden; Sbih Benyamin; Lucia Garofalo," December 29, 1999.

7–8: Some details of CIA's success in stopping the attack on the Albanian embassy from the testimony of Cofer Black before the Senate and House Intelligence Committees on September 26, 2002. Information related to the planned attack in Turkey from Report of the U.S. Select Committee on Intelligence and U.S. House Permanent Select Committee on Intelligence, "Joint Inquiry into Intelligence Community Activities Before and After the Terrorist Attacks of September 11, 2001," S. Rept. no. 107-351, H. Rept. no. 107-792, December 2002 (*Congressional 9/11 Report*).

8: Some details of the spike in chatter from FBI's Daily UBL/Radical Fundamentalist Threat Update, "Newly Reported Threats and Incidents," June 22, 2001, and FBI-EC, April 13, 2001. Also see National Commission on Terrorist Attacks upon the United States, *The 9/11 Commission Report,* W. W. Norton, 2004 (*the 9/11 Commission Report*); Condoleezza Rice press conference of May 16, 2002; and James Bamford, *The Shadow Factory: The Ultra-Secret NSA from 9/11 to the Eavesdropping on America,* Doubleday, 2008. Also see details of the FBI's knowledge from a memo from Dale Watson, head of the Bureau's counterterrorism unit, to Louis Freeh, the director. The memo, headed "BIN LADEN/IBN KHATTAB THREAT REPORTING," was written in April 2001. Also see FBI Electronic Communication from Usama bin Laden Unit/SIOC to all field offices, "Usama bin Laden," April 13, 2001. The increase in NSA detections of chatter from the Congressional 9/11 Report. Also see a transcript from "News Conference with FBI Special Agent Robert Wright," May 30, 2002.

9–10: Some details of the conversation between Pickard and Watson, as well as some details from the briefing of Ashcroft, from Memorandum for Record from an interview of Dale Watson, conducted June 3, 2004, by the staff of the National Commission on Terrorist Attacks upon the United States (*the 9/11 Commission*); Pickard's letter of June 24, 2004, to Thomas Kean and Lee Hamilton of the 9/11 Commission; Pickard's sworn testimony before the commission on April 13, 2004; agenda briefing records, entitled "Weekly with the Attorney General: Briefing Material," for June 28, 2001, and July 12, 2001; and "Team Six Questions for Attorney General John Ashcroft," an undated document prepared by the staff of the 9/11 Commission. Also see Philip Shenon, *The Commission: The Uncensored History of the 9/11 Investigation,* Twelve, 2008.

There is no dispute that the discussion between Pickard and Watson took place; both Pickard and Watson have agreed in official statements that it occurred immediately after the July 12 briefing. However, there has been disagreement about whether the events Pickard described from his meeting with Ashcroft took place. The evidence leaves little doubt that Pickard's description is true.

Both Pickard and Watson state that their discussion took place within minutes of the Ashcroft briefing. To contend that Pickard's portrayal of the briefing is untrue would, by necessity, mean that immediately after he returned from the briefing, Pickard stepped into Watson's office and lied for no discernible reason at a time when he was about to retire. Such an argument is simply not credible.

Second, Pickard has testified under oath before the 9/11 Commission that these events occurred. He also described them to the staff members of the commission in an earlier interview; the statements were so detailed and Pickard spoke with such conviction that the staff had no doubt he was telling the truth, according to Shenon in *The Commission.*

Third, Pickard has publicly offered to take a lie detector test on this, performed by an independent government agency. Neither Ashcroft nor his supporters have made a similar offer.

Then there is the nature of the denials themselves. Ashcroft's supporters often argue that he refuted Pickard's allegation under oath before the 9/11 Commission. That is a false reading of the record. Indeed, Ashcroft's statement made it seem as if he had denied the allegation before the commission, when in fact he had not. The exchange was:

> *Commissioner James Thompson:* [Pickard says he] briefed you on al Qaeda and Osama bin Laden, and when he sought to do so again, you told him you didn't need to hear from him again. . . .
> *Ashcroft:* . . . I did never speak to him saying that I did not want to hear about terrorism.

The denial is a straw man. No one ever accused Ashcroft of not wanting to hear about terrorism—Pickard's allegation was very specific: Ashcroft did not want to hear about the ongoing chatter that month by al-Qaeda.

Next, there is one uncomfortable fact. The rest of Ashcroft's testimony was loaded with deceptive statements. He falsely claimed that the Clinton administration had no covert action program to kill bin Laden; at the time of his testimony, the commission had obtained a copy of Clinton's 1998 authorization to kill bin Laden. Ashcroft stated that the "wall" separating the CIA and the FBI prevented an investigation of Zacarias Moussaoui, saying that a warrant was rejected because of the division. This is false. Two warrants were prepared. The first was rejected on the grounds that its evidence was "shaky"; the second was prepared as part of an intelligence investigation under FISA, so the wall would have no role at all. Ashcroft claimed the wall prevented the FBI from learning about two hijackers that the CIA had tracked into the United States, when in fact the information could legally have been shared without breaching the wall. Then he attacked Jamie Gorelick, a member of the commission, saying that she was responsible for the wall. As proof, he had declassified a 1995 memo—almost certainly for political purposes—showing that Gorelick had wanted a wall between intelligence and law enforcement in the World Trade Center bombing case of 1993; Gorelick's memo extended no further than that particular case. The wall was instead established sometime later by Attorney General Reno.

The false attack on Gorelick infuriated commission members. Both commission chairmen criticized Ashcroft's comments as "overstated." Slade Gorton, a Republican member of the commission, pointed out that Ashcroft's second in command had reaffirmed the wall procedures in August 2001.

There have been other denials as well, but many of them are equally questionable. For example, Ashcroft's chief of staff, David Ayres, stated in a memo to the commission that he was present at all of the briefings and never heard the exchange described by Pickard. However, Ayres did not have the appropriate clearance to *be* present at a briefing on al-Qaeda chatter. That is why Pickard very clearly states that Ayres left the room before that briefing began. Another written denial came from David Laufman, the chief of staff for Deputy Attorney General Larry Thompson. Laufman states in his letter that he attended the briefing on June 28, and did not hear Ashcroft make the statement attributed to him by Pickard. This is, of course, irrelevant. Pickard testified that the event took place on July 12, not June 28.

This leaves only one piece of evidence on Ashcroft's side—a denial by Deputy Attorney General Thompson. He cosigned the Laufman letter, saying that Ashcroft never refused to hear information about the al-Qaeda threat. Moreover, Thompson has a sparkling reputation as a man of integrity, and I have no reason to doubt his sincerity.

However, this again referenced the irrelevant June 28 briefing. Thompson did, however, have the appropriate clearance to attend a classified briefing on July 12, but he does not mention that meeting.

There is, of course, the possibility of the statement's being forgotten or unheard, but just assuming that would be inappropriate on my part. So, the next level of ascertaining credibility would be, simply, to examine what Ashcroft did in the aftermath of the July 12 briefing.

Unfortunately for Ashcroft, that examination leaves only two possible choices: that he was not particularly concerned about the chatter and its possible meaning, or that he was incompetent. The briefings on the rising threats were frightening. Ashcroft received a similar briefing from the CIA earlier, on July 5, and by that point the agency was pulling no punches in describing the potential magnitude of the problem.

If Ashcroft was, as he portrays himself to have been, concerned about this growing terrorist threat, then his reaction would have been clear: Elevate the significance of terrorist issues and pump up the resources available to counterterrorist efforts. Ashcroft did the opposite.

On August 11, 2001, Ashcroft issued a document called "Strategic Plan: Attorney General Priorities." The document listed thirty-six items, with thirteen of those items highlighted as "AG GOAL." Only one of those items dealt with terrorism, and it was not highlighted.

The budget also did not reflect any concern on Ashcroft's part about a potential terrorist attack. He called for spending increases in sixty-eight programs, none involving terrorism. He proposed $65 million in cuts for state and local counterterrorism grants. He rejected the FBI's entreaty for $58 million in new counterterrorism resources—more agents, analysts, and translators. Pickard appealed that decision, refusing to contest any other cuts in hopes of getting the counterterrorism budget approved. Ashcroft rejected that appeal on September 10, 2001, one day before the attack.

In other words, Ashcroft either knew of the problem but did not care, or did not think the threat levels merited special attention. It is unreasonable to think that Ashcroft would have been callous regarding such a potential threat. The second choice is all that remains.

All of this left me with two outcomes. I have no doubt that the encounter in Watson's office took place, and I have no doubt that Pickard is telling the truth. Some may disagree with my second conclusion, based on the Thompson letter and an assumption that he simply recounted the wrong date; as a result, I have presented this story only through the context of the encounter in Watson's office. I would not have done so, however, if the evidence were not so overwhelming that Pickard's story about his encounter with Ashcroft is true.

10–12: Some details of Qahtani's arrival at the Orlando airport and his questioning from the January 26, 2004, testimony of José E. Meléndez-Pérez (Meléndez-Pérez testimony) to the 9/11 Commission, and "Charge Sheet: Khalid Sheikh Mohammed, Walid Muhammad Salih, Mubarak Bin 'Attash, Ramzi Binalshibh, Ali Abdul Aziz, Ali Mustafa Ahmed, Adam al Hawsawi, Mohamed al Khatani" MC Form 458, submitted to the Convening Authority for the military commissions held at Guantanamo on February 11, 2008 (KSM charge sheet).

12–14: Some details of the investigation of Moussaoui and the subsequent interrogation from an August 18, 2001, electronic communication from Harry Samit to Joe Marang of the ITOS/ Iran Unit, titled "Moussaoui, Zacarias, aka Shaqil, IT—Other"; an August 24, 2001, FBI Electronic Communication from Harry Samit to Michael Maltbie, headed "Moussaoui, Zacarias; IT—Other"; an unsigned application from the same day headed "Mossaoui [sic], Zacaria; IT—Other," seeking a search warrant from the Foreign Intelligence Security Court (FISA); an FBI Electronic Communication of the Field Office to Samit and Maltbie, headed "ZACARIAS MOUSSAOUI, AKA SHAKIL; IT-OTHER; 00:MP; an affidavit by Hussein Ali Hassan al-Attas, dated August 17, 2001, headed "Record of Sworn Statement in an Affidavit Form, Affidavit-Witness"; a September 6, 2001, FBI Electronic Communication from Samit to Maltbie, with most of its heading blacked out as classified; an undated translated copy of al-Attas's will; Samit's testimony of March 9, 2006, in *United States v. Moussaoui;* a single page of notes written by Samit during an August 17 interrogation of Moussaoui; and the 2004 FBI-OIG Report. Also see the hearings before the Senate Select Committee on Intelligence and the House Permanent Select Committee on Intelligence, "Events Surrounding September 11," September 24, 2002.

13: The concern about Moussoaui at the Pan Am Flight Academy from the March 9, 2006, testimony of Clancy Prevost in *United States v. Moussaoui,* criminal case no. 1:01cr455, in Federal District Court for the Eastern District of Virginia. Also see testimony of that same day by Shohaib Kassam.

14: Some details of Jones's call with Maltbie from Samit's March 9, 2006, testimony in *United States v. Moussaoui;* the 2004 FBI-OIG Report; and the September 24, 2002, Joint Intelligence hearings.

15: Some details of Massoud's assassination from *"Onderzoek naar Betrokkenheid Dood Massoud," NRC Handelsblad,* October 19, 2001; *"Verband Rotterdam en 20ste Kaper," de Volkskrant* (Amsterdam), October 20 2001; *"Terroristenlijst," NRC Handelsblad,* December 29, 2001; Michael Elliott, "They Had a Plan," *Time,* August 12, 2002; Emerson Vermaat, "Bin Laden's Terror Networks in Europe," a report released by the Mackenzie Institute, a Canadian research group; Matthew Campbell, "How They Killed the Afghan Lion," *Sunday Times* (London), September 23, 2001; Joseph Fitchett, "Did Bin Laden Kill Afghan Rebel?" *International Herald Tribune,* September 17, 2001; and Thomas Harding, "Blast Survivor Tells of Massoud Assassination," *Telegraph,* October 26, 2001.

16: Some details about the ritual cleansing from an FBI 302 from an interview with a housekeeper at the Days Hotel, taken on September 11, 2001, and numbered 315-280350-302-4160. Record, Boston, Massachusetts, Summary, February 2, 2004.

16–17: Some details of Jawahir's experience with Hamza and Ahmed al-Ghamdi from the FBI 302 of her interview on September 11, 2001, for file no. 265D-NY-280350.

17: Information about the gate for United 175 from "Staff Monograph on the Four Flights and Civil Aviation Security," 9/11 Commission, September 2005.

BOOK ONE

19: The phrase "a war of unknown warriors" is derived from a speech delivered by British prime minister Winston Churchill four days after the Battle of Britain began. His exact words were:

> There are vast numbers, not only in this Island but in every land, who will render faithful service in this war, but whose names will never be known, whose deeds will never be recorded. This is a War of the Unknown Warriors; but let all strive without failing in faith or in duty.

The allusion should be clear. The fight against terrorism is one built on intelligence and secrecy, and the identities of many of those who joined in the battle will never be known.

Chapter 1

21: The timing of the unofficial White House evacuation from the live CNN broadcast on 9/11. The formal evacuation of the executive mansion, called for by White House security, began at 9:45 A.M.

21–22: Some details about Mineta's experiences from his March 23, 2003, testimony before the 9/11 Commission.

22–23: Some details of Cheney's trip down the tunnel to the PEOC were first reported by Dan Balz and Bob Woodward, "America's Chaotic Road to War," *Washington Post,* January 27, 2002.

23: Most details about Moussaoui's learning of the 9/11 attacks from his March 27, 2006, testimony in *United States v. Moussaoui.*

25: Some details of Canoles's experiences from two sets of handwritten notes from a government interview at the FAA on March 25, 2004. Also see Alan Levin, Marilyn Adams, and Blake Morrison, "Amid Terror, a Drastic Decision: Clear the Skies," *USA Today,* August 12, 2002.

25: Timing of events inside the PEOC from the Secret Service log maintained by an agent stationed at the center.

25–26, 27: Some details of the conversations between Mineta and Belger from Mineta's testimony before the 9/11 Commission, and Belger's June 17, 2004, testimony before the group.

26: Details of the speed of flight 77 and the events immediately preceding and after its crash into the Pentagon from American Society of Civil Engineers, *The Pentagon Building Performance Report,* Structural Engineering Institute, January 2003.

26–27: Some details of Sliney's experiences from 9/11 Commission Memorandum for the Record, "Interview with Benedict Sliney," May 21, 2004; "Written Testimony of Benedict Sliney to the National Commission on Terrorist Attacks upon the United States," June 17, 2004. Also see Levin, Adams, and Morrison, *USA Today,* August 12, 2002.

27–28: Some details of Rumsfeld's departure from the Pentagon and his efforts to help responders from a contemporaneous video at the site; Andrew Cockburn, *Rumsfeld: His Rise, Fall, and Catastrophic Legacy,* Scribner, 2007; and Steve Vogel, *The Pentagon: A History,* Random House, 2008.

28, 29: Details of the engineering elements that led to the collapse of the two towers from the Federal Emergency Management Agency, *World Trade Center Building Performance Study,* May 2002.

29: Some details of Bush and Cheney's conversation from the 9/11 Commission Report; Bill Sammon, *Fighting Back: The War on Terrorism—from Inside the Bush White House,* Regnery Publishing, 2002.

29: The location of the limousine's arrival at the Sarasota Airport from a Secret Service log from that day. The proximity of that spot to Jones Aviation from direct observation.

29, 30: The timing of Cheney's arrival in the PEOC from a Secret Service log.

30: The final moments of United 93 were revealed in the 9/11 Report.

31: Some details about the marine barracks attacks in Beirut from Robert McFarlane, "From Beirut to 9/11," *New York Times,* October 22, 2008.

32: The dialogue between Cheney and the military aide was recounted by Norm Mineta in his testimony before the 9/11 Commission. Also see excerpts from handwritten notes of Lewis "Scooter" Libby taken in the PEOC on 9/11. Some details of Bolten's discussion with Cheney also from Libby's notes; notes from an April 5, 2004, interview with Bolten by the 9/11 Commission; and the 9/11 Commission Report.

34–35: The dialogue between Rumsfeld and Cheney from an edited recording played for the author. The conversation was also contained in the 9/11 Commission Report.

38: Some details about Yoo's background from University of California at Berkeley, "Faculty Profile," undated. Background of his writings from Yoo, "Foreign Affairs Federalism and the Separation of Powers," Boalt Working Papers in Public Law, 2001; and Yoo, "Globalism and the Constitution: Treaties, Non-Self-Execution, and the Original Understanding," *Columbia Law Review* 99 (1999).

38–40: Some details of events on Bush's flight from Florida from a press pool report compiled by Judy Keen of *USA Today* and Jay Carney of *Time;* from Lynn Spencer, *Touching History,* Free Press, 2008; and from the Secret Service log maintained at the PEOC.

40: Details of the Dougherty conference room from direct observation. Bush's statement from *Public Papers of the President, George W. Bush 2001,* Vol. 2, United States Government Printing Office, 2003.

40–41: Some details of Blair's experiences on 9/11 from contemporaneous diaries written by Alastair Campbell, the prime minister's director of communication from 1997 through 2003 (*the Campbell Diaries*). Also see Tony Blair, *A Journey: My Political Life,* Knopf, 2010; and the January 29, 2010, testimony of Blair before Iraq Inquiry chaired by Sir John Chilcot (*the Chilcot Inquiry*). The formation of the inquiry was announced by Prime Minister Gordon Brown on June 15, 2009.

42–43: Some details of El-Maati's experience at the border, as well as his background, from the Canadian report, "Internal Inquiry in the Actions of Canadian Officials in Relation to Abdullah Almalki, Ahmed Abou-Elmaati and Muayyed Nureddin," written by an official government commission led by the Honorable Frank Iacobucci (*the Iacobucci Report*); "Report of the Events Related to Maher Arar, Factual Background," Vols. 1 and 2, from the Commission of Inquiry into the Actions of Canadian Officials in Relation to Maher Arar, led by Dennis O'Connor (*the O'Connor Report*); Stephen J. Toope, "Fact Finder's Report" for the Arar Commission (*the Toope Report*); the August 27, 2001, letter written by Ann Armstrong, a manager at Highland Transport; a telex from the U.S. embassy in Ottawa to the secretary of state, "Canadian Media Reporting on Alleged Terrorist Activities," August 4, 2002 (*State Department August 4 telex*); and a copy of the map carried by El-Maati that day.

42–45: The El-Maati story is somewhat complex. The inclusion of El-Maati on lists of suspected security risks in both the United States and Canada was completely reasonable. His presence in Afghanistan for five years, his involvement with the faction of Gulbuddin Hekmatyar, and the intelligence labeling his brother, Amr, as a threat were more than sufficient to raise concerns about him.

However, the evolution of his portrayal by the intelligence agencies—from a person of interest to a primary member of a Canadian terrorist cell—was not reasonable. The Iacobucci Commission concluded that labeling El-Maati as an imminent threat, terrorist, and associate of bin Laden was inaccurate, unreliable, and lacking an investigative basis. The Canadian Parliament's Public Safety Committee voted to issue an apology to El-Maati and the others, and give them compensation. While the Canadian prime minister has not done so, the vote in itself underscores the poor quality of the intelligence labeling El-Maati and the others as terrorist threats.

Several items here must be addressed. There is a great deal of public misunderstanding about Muslims who traveled to Afghanistan to join in the battles there. In essence, there are multiple groups—those who traveled there from the late 1980s to 1990, those who joined bin Laden's Afghan Arabs, those who arrived in 1991 through 1995, and those who traveled there after 1996 to join with the Taliban. The differences are attributable to the chaotic nature of Afghanistan itself—in the early years, the mujahideen and the Arabs were fighting the Soviets, and America backed them; the ones who traveled there in the early 1990s could be there to help the war-ravaged country, join with the government, or wage war alongside the mujahideen who had turned on their own countrymen for power. And, of course, those who arrived after 1996 were, for the most part, dedicated jihadists.

El-Maati was in the second group, traveling to Afghanistan in 1991 and leaving in 1996. In doing so, he was in the company of Muslims worldwide.

"The perception among Muslims was that these people fighting in Afghanistan were victorious over the Soviets by God's aid and a lot of learned people and students started flocking there," said Khaled Abou El Fadl, a professor at UCLA School of Law who was appointed by President George W. Bush to the United States Commission on International Religious Freedom. "Afghanistan in the early 1990s was becoming a mecca for a lot of Muslims who wanted to attain true Islamic knowledge."

In this instance, the bottom line is that there was a reasonable basis for suspicion of El-Maati, but it was not tempered with a sophisticated understanding of the perception of Afghanistan among young Muslim men in the early 1990s.

43–45: Some details of the El-Maati interrogation from the Iacobucci Report. Also see the Arar Report and BC Civil Liberties Report, "Ahmad Abou El Maati: A Chronology."

45–46: Details of the Offutt videoconference from notes of the meeting read to the author.

46: Details of Ashcroft's arrival from Dan Eggen, "Ashcroft Jet Had Scare on Sept. 11," *Washington Post*, September 28, 2001; and John Ashcroft, *Never Again: Securing America and Restoring Justice*, Center Street, 2006.

49: Details of the work on Bush's speech were first reported in Balz and Woodward, op. cit. The author also reviewed notes that were taken during the discussions, and drafts of the address.

50: Bush's words in the Oval Office address from a transcript in *Public Papers of the President*, Vol. 2.

50–51: Some details of the meeting from contemporaneous notes maintained by one of the participants. Also see Bob Woodward, *Bush at War*, Simon & Schuster, 2002.

51–52: Some details of Salim Hamdan's experiences from FBI 302s of interviews with Hamdan, conducted in Guantanamo Bay detention center on June 26 through July 9, 2002; August 6, 2002; August 19, 2002; August 24, 2002; November 13, 2002, from cases numbered 262-NY-277013 and 265A-MM-C99102. Also from CITF, *Report of Investigative Activity*, activity no. 99221031841338, May 17, 2003.

Chapter 2

53–55: Some details of the COBRA meeting from the Campbell Diaries; Blair, *A Journey: My Political Life;* and the January 29, 2010, testimony of Blair before the Chilcot Inquiry. Also see House of Commons Home Affairs Committee, *The Home Office's Response to Terrorist Attacks*, Sixth Report of Session, 2009–2010.

55–56: Most details of the NSC meeting from contemporaneous notes taken by one of the attendees, and confirmed by another participant. Also see Woodward, *Bush at War;* and George Tenet, *At the Center of the Storm*, HarperCollins, 2007. Bush's position is also reflected in an October 1, 2001, State Department Cable to all American embassies and missions, "Subject: September 11: Working Together to Fight the Plague of Global Terrorism and the Case Against Al-Qa'ida." Also see untitled memo of Rumsfeld to Bush, dated September 23, 2001.

58: Some details of Addington's background were first reported by Jane Mayer, "The Hidden Power," *New Yorker*, July 3, 2006.

59–61: Some details of the 1991 Iraq resolution, and its revisions into the 2001 version, from copies of the original 1991 document, a draft of the 2001 version, and the final 2001 resolution.

62: Details of the CIA's review of the performance at the Counterterrorist Center from the CIA Office of the Inspector General, "Inspection Report of the DCI Counterterrorist Center, Directorate of Operations," August 2001.

63–64: The meeting at Salah's house was described by Salim Hamdan in the FBI 302 notes of the August 4, 2002, interview conducted at Guantanamo by Ali Soufan, for file No. 262-NY-277013/265A-MM-C99102. The heading of the document incorrectly gives Hamdan's first name as "Salem."

63: Details of original proposal by Sheikh Mohammed from "Substitution for the Testimony of Khalid Sheikh Mohammed," Defendant's Exhibit 941, *United States v. Moussaoui*. Also see the 9/11 Commission Report; FBI Electronic Communication from New York I-49, "Title: Manila Air; AOT-IT; OO:NY," June 10, 2002; and FBI Electronic Communication from New York I-49, "Title: Manila Air; AOT-IT; OO:NY," July 8, 1999.

64–65: Most details of the September 13 meeting from contemporaneous notes taken by one of the attendees, and confirmed by another participant. Also see Woodward, *Bush at War;* and Tenet, *At the Center of the Storm.*

65: Information about the War Powers Resolution, and its controversy, from Noah Feldman, "Our Presidential Era: Who Can Check the President?" *New York Times,* January 8, 2006.

67: The timing and location of the meeting from the scheduling book of one of the attendees.

68–71: The depiction of the events on the floor of the Senate from a C-SPAN video recording from that day.

69: Dashle's response to the White House request for authority to use force in the United States from Barton Gellman, "Daschle: Congress Denied Bush War Powers in U.S.," *Washington Post,* December 23, 2005.

71–72: Some details of the Bush-Blair conversation, and the subsequent discussion between the prime minister and his aides, from the Campbell diaries. Also see Simon McDonald, "Iraq: Options," a December 3, 2001, paper prepared by the Foreign and Commonwealth Office at Blair's request.

72–73: The description of Camp David from W. Dale Nelson, *The President Is at Camp David,* Syracuse University Press, 2000.

72–75: Some details of the Camp David meeting from the contemporaneous notes of one of the participants. Also see Woodward, *Bush at War;* Tenet, *At the Center of the Storm;* and National Archives, "9/11 Photographic Timeline from George W. Bush Library," undated.

76: Details of the history of and potential damage of smallpox from Stefan Riedel, "Edward Jenner and the History of Smallpox and Vaccination," *Baylor University Medical Center Proceedings,* January 2005; Steve Connor, "How Terrorism Prevented Smallpox Being Wiped Off the Face of the Planet Forever," *Independent,* January 3, 2002; and Richard Preston, *The Demon in the Freezer,* Fawcett, 2002.

77: Some details of Ivins's psychiatric and personal history, including his obsession with Kappa Kappa Gamma, from a confidential analysis prepared by the Expert Behavioral Analysis Panel at the request of Chief Judge Royce C. Lamberth of the Federal District Court for the District of Columbia (*Anthrax Panel Report*). For the report, the panel was permitted to examine all of Ivins's psychiatric records and to interview his former psychiatrists and counselors. Other information from Officer Robert Wayne Pierce, Incident/Investigation Report, July 27, 2008—the formal report assembled by the Frederick, Maryland, Police Department in its investigation of Ivins's suicide that month. Also see the first Arredondo affidavit. His use of Celexa from FBI Electronic Communication from Washington Field Office AMX#3, "Title: Amerithrax; Major Case 184," June 7, 2005.

Chapter 3

78–79: Details of the September 17 meeting from contemporaneous notes kept by one of the participants. Also see Woodward, *Bush at War;* and Tenet, *At the Center of the Storm.*

79: Details of the structure of a Memorandum of Notification from National Security Decision Directive 286, signed by Ronald Reagan on October 15, 1987. Some details of National Security Presidential Directive number nine from a limited summary released by the White House on April 1, 2004. Also see "Sixth Declaration of Marilyn A. Dorn, Information Review Officer, Central Intelligence Agency," January 2007, from the case *American Civil Liberties Union v. Department of Defense,* no. 04 Civ. 4151, filed in Federal District Court for the Southern District of New York.

79: Details of the Bush meeting with reporters, including the location and time, from *Public Papers of the President,* op. cit., and a video recording of the event.

80–81: Details of the military's efforts to secure regional bases from a Pentagon report from the U.S. Army Combined Arms Center at Fort Leavenworth entitled "The United States Army in Operation ENDURING FREEDOM (OEF)," October 2001–September 2005; "A Different Kind of War," June 2009 (*Combined Arms Center Report*); and Center for Army Lessons Learned, "Handbook: Operation Enduring Freedom III," no. 05–06, January 2005 (*OEF Handbook*).

81: Details about the difficulties in the relationship between the Americans and the Russians from James Kitfield, "Putin's Leap of Faith," *National Journal,* October 6, 2001.

82: Details of the *Mayaguez* incident from Major A. J. C. Lavalle, USAF Southeast Asia Monograph Series, Vol. 3, Monographs 4 and 5, *The Vietnamese Air Force, 1951–1975,* Office of Air Force History, United States Air Force, 1976; and John L. Frisbee, "The *Mayaguez* Incident," *Air Force Magazine,* September 1991.

84: Some details about the Nazi saboteur case from Louis Fisher, CRS Report for Congress, *Military Tribunals: The Quirin Precedent,* March 26, 2002; and United States Supreme Court opinion, *Ex Parte Quirin,* 317 U.S. 1, 1942. Also see Lieutenant Colonel Judy Prescott and Major Joanne Eldridge, "Military Commissions, Past and Future," *Military Review,* March–April 2003; and the November 19, 2001, memo from William J. Haynes II to Rumsfeld headed "Info Memo."

84–85: Information about the classified Canadian report of September 18, 2001, from the original document.

85–86: Some details of Almalki's encounters with CSIS from the Iacobucci Report; the O'Connor Report; BC Civil Liberties Association, "Abdullah Almalki: Chronology"; and Kerry Pither, *Dark Days,* Viking Canada, 2008. Also see State Department August 4 telex.

87: Details of Schroen's experiences on the last day before his departure were first reported in Gary Schroen, *First In,* Presidio Press, 2005. Also see Richard A. Best Jr. and Andrew Feickert, Congressional Research Service, *Special Operations Forces (SOF) and CIA Paramilitary Operations: Issues for Congress,* as updated December 6, 2006, Order Code RS22017.

88: Some details of Chamberlain's experience from Casey Chamberlain, "My Anthrax Survivor's Story," September 19, 2006; and Tom Brokaw's testimony of September 10, 2008, before the Commission on the Prevention of Weapons of Mass Destruction Proliferation and Terrorism (*the Brokaw testimony*). Details of the letter from a copy of the original document.

89: Some details of the Feith draft memo from a footnote in the 9/11 Report.

89: Details about the actual contacts between Saddam and al-Qaeda from Report of the Select Committee on Intelligence, "Postwar Findings About Iraq's WMD Programs and Links to Terrorism and How They Compare with Prewar Assessments," September 8, 2006 (*Senate Postwar Report on Iraq*). Details of the administration's military plan for Iran from November 27, 2001, Pentagon memo. The document is unsigned and has no subject line.

90–91: Some details of the Blair-Bush dinner from the Campbell diaries.

91–92: Details of Huden's experience from Eric Lipton and Kirk Johnson, "Tracking Bioterror's Tangled Course," *New York Times,* December 26, 2001.

92: Details of Arteta's performance from an opera review by Joe Banno, "Così: Playing It Safe," *Washington Post,* September 15, 2001.

92: The destruction of the Buddhas from Barry Bearak, "Over World Protests, Taliban Are Destroying Ancient Buddhas," *New York Times,* March 4, 2001; and Bearak, "Afghan Says Destruction of Buddhas Is Complete," *New York Times,* March 12, 2001.

94–95: Bin Laden's meeting with the reporter, and all of the dialogue, from the Foreign Broadcast Information Service with the CIA's Directorate of Science and Technology, "FBIS Report: Compilation of Usama Bin Ladin Statements, 1994–January 2004," January 2004 (*FBIS*

Report); and "Usama bin Laden Says the Al-Qa'idah Group Had Nothing to Do with the 11 September Attacks," *Ummat Karachi,* September 28, 2001.

96–97: Some details about the operations and requirements of FISA from Majors Louis A. Chiarella and Michael A. Newton, "So Judge, How Do I Get a FISA Warrant? The Policy and Procedure for Conducting Electronic Surveillance," *Army Lawyer,* October 1997. Also see *Congressional Record—Senate,* February 26, 2003, p. 4542.

97: Details of the detection on Sana'a phone line and its importance in developing other intelligence from the 9/11 Report; a classified report from an intelligence agency dated December 29, 1999; the prepared statement of Cofer Black for his testimony before the Joint Intelligence Committees of Congress of September 26, 2002.

97–98: Some details of the rules allowing for the NSA to monitor calls coming into the United States from U.S. Department of Justice, "Legal Authorities Supporting the Activities of the National Security Agency Described by the President," January 19, 2006. The existence of this element of the program was first reported by James Risen and Eric Lichtblau, "Bush Lets U.S. Spy on Callers Without Courts," *New York Times,* December 16, 2005.

99: Some elements of the e-mail interception program were first disclosed in an article by Daniel Klaidman, "Now We Know What the Battle Was All About," *Newsweek,* December 13, 2008.

100: The code name for the NSA program was first disclosed by Michael Isikoff, "The Fed Who Blew the Whistle," *Newsweek,* December 13, 2008.

101: Details of the appearance of Stevens's spinal fluid and Dr. Bush's experience were first reported in Preston, *The Demon in the Freezer.*

101–102: Information about the fax from the original document. Some details about Almalki's work from the Iacobucci Report. Also see the O'Connor Report.

103–104: Some details of the personal background revealed by Zubaydah from the CIA document "Psychological Assessment of Zain al-Abedin al-Abideen Muhammad Hassan, a.k.a. Abu Zubaydah," December 30, 2004.

104: Details of Zubaydah's comments on the recruiting video from the original recording. Also see memo of November 11, 2008, written by D. M. Thomas Jr., "Joint Task Force Guantanamo to the Commander for United States Southern Command in Miami, Recommendations for Continued Detention Under DOD Control (CD) for Guantanamo Detainee, ISN US9GZ-010016DP (S)" (*Detainee Assessment, Abu Zubaydah*); and the CIA document "Psychological Assessment of Zain al-Abedin al-Abideen Muhammad Hassan, a.k.a. Abu Zubaydah," dated January 31, 2003.

107: Details of Brokaw's encounter with NBC security from the Brokaw testimony.

107–108: The experience of Zaki and his team was first reported in Preston, *The Demon in the Freezer;* also see John Jernigan et al., "Bioterrorism-Related Inhalational Anthrax: The First 10 Cases Reported in the United States," *Emerging Infectious Diseases Journal,* Centers for Disease Control 7:6 (December 2001); and David Brown, "Stopping a Scourge," *Smithsonian,* September 2003.

108: The work at Fort Detrick with infectious agents is conducted through a division called the U.S. Army Medical Research Institute of Infectious Disease, best known as USAMRIID. The work and appearance of the unit from Memorandum for Commander, "Legal Review—AR 15-6 Investigation into Contamination at USAMRIID," May 15, 2002; undated floor plan of the facility; Memorandum for Record, "Area Surveys for *B. anthracis* Conducted in Bacteriology Division from 15 to 18 April," April 19, 2002; sworn statement of the USAMRIID chief of the bacteriology division, provided on a DA Form 2823, May 5, 2002; sworn statement of the researcher involved in making mutants in anthrax genes, provided on a DA Form 2823, May 6, 2002; sworn statement of Bruce Ivins, provided on a DA Form 2823, May 6, 2002; an FBI case summary memo, "Amerithrax; Major Case 184, case ID 279A-

WF-222936-USAMRIID"; and Colonel Edward M. Eitzen Jr., Memo for Headquarters, Department of the Army, "Subject: Biological Defense Mishap," April 23, 2002. Also see USAMRIID's *Medical Management of Biological Casualties Handbook,* April 2005.

108–109: Ivins's time in the lab from an original work sheet compiled by the FBI and a partial review of laboratory access records for Building 1425. Also see FBI 302, no interviewee, June 18, 2005, for file no. 279A-WF-222936-USAMRIID-1326. The degree to which this differed from his normal practice from Department of Justice, "Amerithrax Investigative Summary," February 19, 2010 (*Amerithrax Report*). Also see "Application and Affidavit, Search Warrant," signed by Marlo Arredondo, February 22, 2008, filed in the Federal District Court for the District of Columbia (*first Arredondo affidavit*); and "Application and Affidavit, Search Warrant," signed by Postal Inspector Thomas Dellafera, October 31, 2007, for case number 07-524-M-01, filed in the Federal District Court for the District of Columbia (*Dellafera affidavit*).

109: Ivins's discovery of the change in the availability of anthrax vaccine, and its impact on his work, from the Amerithrax Report.

109–111: Some of the details of the first anthrax mailing from Department of Justice, "Amerithrax Investigative Summary," February 19, 2010 (*Amerithrax Report*); the Anthrax Panel Report; and the first Arredondo affidavit.

110: Pauley's connection to the sorority from an undated document from Kappa Kappa Gamma entitled "Famous Kappas!"

Chapter 4

113–114: Details of the bombing of Afghanistan from Combined Arms Center Report and OEF Handbook. Also see Peter Baker, "Kabul and Kandahar Hit in Attacks Through Night," *Washington Post,* October 8, 2001; Patrick E. Tyler, "U.S. and Britain Strike Afghanistan, Aiming at Bases and Terrorist Camps," *New York Times,* October 7, 2001; David Rohde, "Thunderous Blasts and Bright Flashes Mark Kabul Strikes," *New York Times,* October 8, 2001.

114: Some details of the events preceding Bush's speech from Laura Bush, *Spoken from the Heart,* Scribner, 2010. Speech transcript, including timing, from *Public Papers of the President, George W. Bush 2001,* Vol. 2, United States Government Printing Office, 2003.

114–115: Bin Laden's comments from the FBIS Report. Descriptions from the video recording.

115: Details of the second anthrax mailing from the Amerithrax Report, the Anthrax Panel Report. Details of the Daschle letter to the Pentagon from the Anthrax Panel Report and the original document.

116: Background of Prince Bandar from Elsa Walsh, "The Prince," *New Yorker,* March 24, 2003.

116: Details of the Pan Am 103 attack and the culpability attributed to Libya from Colin Boyd, "Workshop: Police Investigations of 'Politically Sensitive' or High Profile Crimes: The Lockerbie Trial," International Society for the Reform of Criminal Law, 15th International Conference, August 16–30, 2001.

118–121: Some details of the police search and the detention of Belkacem Bensayah from the declaration of Anela Kobilica filed in *Boumediene et al. v. Bush et al.,* civil action no. 04-cv-1166 in Federal District Court for the District of Columbia; declaration of Nermina Pivic of October 9, 2008; Human Rights Chamber for Bosnia and Herzegovina, "Decision on Admissibility and Merits"; *Mustafa AIT DIR v. Bosnia Herzegovina and the Federation of Bosnia and Herzegovina,* case no. CH/02/8961; Federation Ministry of Interior–Crime Police Department, Receipt of Temporarily Seized Objects, October 8, 2001, no. 12/5-5/-2-01; and the May 6, 2008, testimony of Stephen Oleskey before the House Subcommittee on Foreign Affairs, Subcommittee on International Organizations, Human Rights, and Oversight (*Oleskey testimony*).

118–119: Details of Bosnia's failures to stem terrorism and of its stepped-up efforts after 9/11, from a declaration of Alija Behmen, October 6, 2008; and Evan Kohlmann, *Al-Qaida's Jihad in Europe: The Afghan-Bosnian Network,* Berg Publishers, 2004.

121: Details of the Muhamed Bešić statements and the timing of them from a declaration of Nedim Dervisbegovic, October 17, 2008; and George Jahn, "Police Arrest Terrorist Suspect After Tracing Phone Call to Bin Laden Aide," *Associated Press Worldstream,* October 8, 2001.

121–122, 123–125: Some details of O'Connor's experiences and the testing of her samples from the Brokaw Testimony.

125–126: The description of Mango's Café and the shopping mall from personal observation. Some details of the meeting from the formal surveillance report from that day, as well as depictions from the Iacobucci Report. Information about Arar from the O'Connor Report.

125, 126: The exact nature of the weather on October 12 in Ottawa has been a major element of the RCMP investigation and the resulting suspicions about Arar. There has been testimony as well as documents submitted to investigative commissions about what the surveillance teams saw and reported. But I can find no evidence that anyone ever checked the hourly reports filed by the Ottawa weather station for that date and at that time. Those records are quite revealing. The day bounced between overcast and light rain. At no time was there a rainstorm of any significant size. At five o'clock, when the fateful walk took place, the weather was clearing. The humidity had dropped—from 94 percent to 88 percent—and visibility had increased from seven miles to ten. The overcast sky was breaking up. In other words, not only was it impossible for there to have been a major rainstorm, but the weather station specifically noted that the precipitation was light—and, based on these data, misty. This conforms with Arar's and Almalki's public statements that they did not remember it raining and did not get wet.

There is, however, a more important point to note: The absolute absurdity of the RCMP's purported observations. By the official depiction, both men would have been dripping wet, their clothes soaked through, by the time they arrived at the house of prayer and then at Future Shop. Directly across the street from Mango's Café is a gas station, which sells umbrellas. About a hundred yards farther is a grocery store, which sells umbrellas. And one hundred yards after that is a discount retailer, which sells umbrellas. Moreover, on the walk from Mango's to the prayer house these are multiple other stores that sell umbrellas. It strains credibility to the breaking point to believe that these men would walk in a downpour, arriving drenched at a holy site, when they could have easily purchased an umbrella. Or they could have simply driven in one of their cars. Everything suggests that the RCMP reports are both wrong and illogical.

Assume, for a moment, that the independent data and logic are wrong, and that both men, for some unknown and unnecessary reason, walked in the rain. So what? The implication, of course, is that they were somehow trying to be alone so they could discuss something nefarious. Meeting in public, walking on a busy street—these are not the actions of people trying to maintain a secret. A private meeting, perhaps, but one at a strip mall is hardly suspicious. Then there is the speculation that Arar and Almalki were speaking in a way that appeared to the investigators as if they were trying to keep from being heard. The belief came from the fact that the men "leaned in" when they spoke to each other. The conclusion that there was something being hidden because they were speaking to each other in modest tones—at a time when they were meeting and walking in public—is again an illogical conclusion.

The idea that any of these events led an investigator to conclude that something untoward was occurring—particularly when the evidence from that day proves the official statements to be wrong—is frightening and reflects an utter incompetence on the part of the RCMP, one that ultimately led to the abduction and torture of an innocent man.

126: Details of Brokaw's realization that the powder had been anthrax from the Brokaw testimony.

126–127: Some details of the Castelli-Battelli meeting from a transcript of Battelli's interview with Armando Spataro, deputy chief prosecutor in Milan. Also see Spataro, "The Kidnapping of Nasr Mostafa Hassan alias Abu Omar (Milano, 17.02.2003)," January 23, 2008.

127, 130: Some details of the American rendition program from Note d'Information Commissaire, Royal Canadian Mounted Police, CID/NSIB 2004–14, February 6, 2004.

127–128: Some details about the panic at NBC and the subsequent meeting from the Brokaw testimony.

128: Details of the FBI warning from the original release, headed "Warning of Possible Future Terrorist Attacks," October 10, 2001.

128: Ashcroft's comments from a transcript of a press conference held at the Department of Health and Human Services on October 12, 2001.

128–129: Cheney's comments from Tom Pelton and Scott Shane, "Woman in N.Y. 4th Anthrax Case," *Baltimore Sun,* October 13, 2001.

129–130: Some details of El-Maati's experience seeing the news story from the Iacobucci Report. Also see the O'Connor Report.

131: Some details from the experience in Daschle's office from the Amerithrax Report and a copy of the original letter.

131–132: Some details about Ivins's magazines and relationship with the American Family Association from the Anthrax Panel Report.

132–133: Public details of Bush's meeting with the Italian prime minister from "Remarks Following Discussions with Silvio Berlusconi of Italy and an Exchange with Reporters," October 15, 2001, *Public Papers of the Presidents,* Vol. 2.

133: Some details of Ezzell's experience from Preston, *The Demon in the Freezer.*

134: Some details of the intercepted phone call and related details from Narrative for Petitioners, in *Boumediene v. Bush,* filed in the Federal District Court for the District of Columbia; and Andrew Purvis, "The Suspects: A Bosnian Subplot," *Time,* November 12, 2001.

134: Some details of Ivins's work from the Amerithrax Report; the Anthrax Panel Report; an FBI Electronic Communication from the Washington Field Office Amerithrax-3 Team to Inspection, headed "Amerithrax; Major Case 184," dated May 24, 2005, for case no. 279A-WF-222936-USAMRIID. The report quotes from the original document.

134–135: Some details of the encounter between Behmen and the American officials from a declaration of Alija Behmen, October 6, 2008; the declaration of Wolfgang Petritsch of September 15, 2008; and Ijava Zlatko Lagumdžija (*Lagumdžija declaration*), September 22, 2008.

Chapter 5

137–138: Some details about Blair's frustration with American policy regarding the Northern Alliance from the Campbell diaries.

138–139: The experiences of the Alpha Teams were first reported in the Combined Arms Center Report and OEF Handbook.

140: Details of the Yoo memo to Gonzales and Haynes from original document, John C. Yoo and Robert J. Delahunty, "Authority for Use of Military Force to Combat Terrorist Activities Within the United States," October 23, 2001.

140–141: Some details of the ground assault from the Combined Arms Center Report and OEF Handbook.

142: Some details of the Jack Straw–Dick Cheney meeting from the Campbell diaries.

145–146: Some details of El-Maati's decision to travel to Syria and his experiences at the airport from the Iacobucci Report; the O'Connor Report; and BC Civil Liberties Report, "Ahmad Abou El Maati: A Chronology."

146, 149: Some details of the NSC meeting from partial notes taken by one of the participants and Tenet, *At the Center of the Storm.*

146–147, 149: Some details of the battle from the Combined Arms Center Report; Paul Wolfowitz, speech before the Fletcher Conference, 2001, "National Security for a New Era, Focusing National Power," November 14, 2001; Peter Tomsen, Barnett Rubin, testimony of November 7, 2001, before the House Committee on International Relations in the hearings entitled "The Future of Afghanistan." Also see OEF Handbook.

147: Some details of the flow of intelligence about El-Maati from the Iacobucci Report.

150–151: Some details about the Jalalabad meeting from Philip Smucker, "How Bin Laden Got Away," *Christian Science Monitor,* March 4, 2002.

152–153: Some details of El-Maati's abduction from the Iacobucci Report. Also see the Arar Report and BC Civil Liberties Report, "Ahmad Abou El Maati: A Chronology." Also see State Department August 4 telex.

Chapter 6

156: Details and quotes from the Bush order from the original document.

157–158: Some of the details of Bellinger's reaction to the military commissions order were first reported in Jane Mayer, *The Dark Side,* Doubleday, 2008.

158: Details of the neighborhood surrounding Far' Falastin from direct observation.

158, 161, 162–163: Some details of the El-Maati interrogation from the Iacobucci Report. Also see the Arar Report and BC Civil Liberties Report, "Ahmad Abou El Maati: A Chronology."

158–159: Some details of the convoy's stop in Jalalabad from Smucker, *Christian Science Monitor,* March 4, 2002.

159: Some details of the liberation of Kabul from the Combined Arms Center Report; John Simpson, BBC News, "Eyewitness: The Liberation of Kabul," November 13, 2001. Also see transcript, *NewsHour with Jim Lehrer,* "The Fall of Kabul," November 13, 2001. Also see OEF Handbook.

159–160: Details of the *New York Times* article from the original document.

161–162: Some details of Ivins's testing and cleaning of the lab offices from FBI 302 of the interview of Bruce E. Ivins, April 24–25 2002; an FBI Electronic Communication from the Washington Field Office Amerithrax-3 Team to Inspection headed "Amerithrax; Major Case 184," dated May 24, 2005, for case no. 279A-WF-222936-USAMRIID. Also see the Amerithrax Report.

162: Some details of the creation of the Eastern Alliance, and the antipathy of the militias within it, from the Combined Arms Center Report and Gary Berntsen, *Jawbreaker: The Attack on Bin Laden and Al-Qaeda,* Crown Publishers, 2005. Also see OEF Handbook.

163–165: Some details about the engineering firms and activities at Ground Zero from August Domel Jr., *World Trade Center Disaster: Structural Engineers at Ground Zero,* a report prepared for the National Council of Structural Engineers Association, November 2001.

165–166: Some details about the operations of Sufaat and his interactions with Sheikh Mohammed from Memorandum for Commander, United States Southern Command, "Subject: Combatant Status Review Tribunal Input and Recommendation for Continued Detention Under DoD Control (CD) for Guantanamo Detainee, ISN: US9KU-010024DP(S)," December 8, 2006 (*Detainee Assessment, Khalid Sheikh Mohammed*); Memorandum for Commander, United States Southern Command, "Subject: Recommendation for Continued Detention Under DoD Control (CD) for Guantanamo Detainee, ISN US9YM-000577DP (S)," May 5, 2008 (*Detainee Assessment, Jamal Muhammad Alawi*); and Memorandum for Commander, United States Southern Command, "Subject: Recommendation for Continued Detention Under DoD Control (CD) for Guantanamo Detainee,

ISN: US9MY-010021DP (S)," May 5, 2008 (*Detainee Assessment, Mohd Farik bin Amin*). Also see Rolf Mowatt-Larssen, "Al Qaeda Weapons of Mass Destruction Threat: Hype or Reality?" Belfer Center for Science and International Affairs, January 2010; and the Opening Statement of Robert Spencer, *United States v. Moussaoui,* March 6, 2006.

167–168: Some details of the capture of Salim Hamdan from the December 5, 2007, testimony of Major Henry Smith in Hamdan's trial before a military commission at Guantanamo. Also see the FBI 302 of Hamdan's interrogation of January 30, 2002, by Special Agents Pete Harrington and Craig Donnachie for file no. 265A-NY-2830350-302.

167: Two works that explain a good deal about the Pashtun, the Pakistan-Afghanistan border culture, and the support for fundamentalist Islam there were both published in the journal *International Security* of Spring 2008. They are Thomas H. Johnson and M. Chris Mason, "No Sign Until the Burst of Fire: Understanding the Pakistan-Afghanistan Frontier"; and Seth G. Jones, "The Rise of Afghanistan's Insurgency: State Failure and Jihad."

168–169: Events from the surrender to the first explosion at Qala-i-Jangi were described in "Proffer of Facts in Support of Defendant's Suppression Motion," *United States v. John Philip Walker Lindh,* crim. no. 02-37-A, filed with the Federal District Court for the Eastern District of Virginia. Additional details of the Taliban surrender to Dostum from a video of the event; details of the transport of prisoners from a report to members of the Committee on Foreign Relations, United States Senate, "How We Failed to Get Bin Laden and Why It Matters Today," November 30, 2009 (*the Tora Bora Report*); and details of the arrival and initial attack at Qala-i-Jangi from Alex Perry, "Inside the Battle at Qala-i-Jangi," *Time,* December 1, 2001.

169–170: Interrogation of John Walker Lindh from a video of the event. Also see Criminal Complaint, *United States v. John Philip Walker Lindh,* crim. no. 02-57-M, filed with the Federal District Court for the Eastern District of Virginia. Also see "Findings and Recommendations Regarding 15-6 Investigation of Photographs Taken of Mr. John Walker Lindh by 5th Special Forces Group (airborne)," Report of Proceedings by Investigating Officer/Board of Trustees, February 3, 2003.

171–172: The uprising, Tyson's experiences, and comments from videos and photographs of the event; Corpi d'Élite, "Enduring Freedom Spec Ops: Qala-i-Jangi, 25–28 November 2001"; Richard D. Mahoney, *Getting Away with Murder,* Arcade Publishing, 2004; Tenet, *At the Center of the Storm.*

172: Some details of bin Laden at Tora Bora from the Tora Bora Report; Smucker, op. cit.; Peter Bergen, "The Battle for Tora Bora," *New Republic,* December 22, 2009.

173–174: Details of Katyal's testimony from transcript, Senate Judiciary Committee, "Preserving Freedom While Fighting Terrorism," November 28, 2001.

174–175: Some details of the capture of the Tipton Three from Shafiq Rasul, Asif Iqbal, and Ruhal Ahmed, "Composite Statement: Detention in Afghanistan and Guantanamo Bay"; Tania Branigan and Vikram Dodd, "Afghanistan to Guantanamo Bay—the Story of Three British Detainees," *Guardian,* August 4, 2004.

175: Some details of the opening volley in the Battle of Tora Bora from the Combined Arms Center Report and the Tora Bora Report. Also see OEF Handbook. The dialogue between Dailey and Berntsen was first reported in Gary Berntsen, *Jawbreaker: The Attack on Bin Laden and Al-Qaeda,* Broadway, 2005.

175–176: Details of the Soloway interview from Colin Soloway, "Tale of an American Talib," *Newsweek* online, December 1, 2001.

176: Campbell's interview with Hamdi from Matthew Campbell, "The Fort of Hell," *Sunday Times* (London), December 1, 2001.

177–178: The problems at Tora Bora from the Combined Arms Center Report; the response from the Pentagon from the Tora Bora Report.

178–179: Some details of the Bush-Ashcroft meeting from the White House press briefing by Ari Fleischer on December 12, 2001.

179, 180: The bombing halt is described in the Combined Arms Center Report; the experiences with Zaman were first reported in Dalton Fury, *Kill Bin Laden*, St. Martin's Griffin, 2008.

179–180: Some details about al-Libi's plan to engage in bogus "surrender" negotiations to allow for an escape—and his concern about younger fighters—from a June 20, 2008, memo from the Joint Task Force at Guantanamo to the Commander for United States Southern Command in Miami headed "Subject: Recommendations for Continued Detention Under DOD Control (CD) for Guantanamo Detainee, ISN US9YM-000549DO (S)" (*Detainee Assessment, Omar Ayden*).

181: The Ashcroft statements from a transcript of the press conference.

182–183: Dialogue from the Senate hearing from a transcript from Senate Armed Services Committee, "The President's Order on Trials by Military Tribunal," December 12, 2001.

183–184: Some details of Batarfi's experiences from official government transcripts of two Administrative Review Board proceedings for ISN 627 (Batarfi). The transcripts are undated.

184: Dialogue between Berntsen and Dailey was first reported in Berntsen, *Jawbreaker: The Attack on Bin Laden and Al-Qaeda*.

184–185: The journey out of Tora Bora by al-Libi and the young fighters from statements by al-Qaeda members, as well as innumerable government records. These include multiple memos from the Joint Task Force at Guantanamo to the Commander for United States Southern Command in Miami. They are a January 6, 2008, memo headed "Subject: Recommendations for Continued Detention Under DOD Control (CD) for Guantanamo Detainee, ISN US9YM-000549DO (S) (*Detainee Assessment, Hassan Said*); a December 16, 2006, memo headed "Subject: Recommendations for Transfer Out of DOD Control (TRO) for Guantanamo Detainee, ISN US9AF-000222DP (S)" (*Detainee Assessment, Umar al-Kunduzi*); a March 1, 2007, memo headed "Subject: Recommendations for Continued Detention Under DOD Control (CD) for Guantanamo Detainee, ISN US9SA-000268DP (S) (*Detainee Assessment, Abd al-Rahman al-Hataybi*); a June 20, 2008, memo headed "Subject: Recommendations for Continued Detention Under DOD Control (CD) for Guantanamo Detainee, ISN US9YM-000549DO (S)" (*Detainee Assessment, Omar Aden*); a December 1, 2005, memo headed "Subject: Recommendations for Continued Detention Under DOD Control (CD) for Guantanamo Detainee, ISN US9SA-000273DP (S)" (*Detainee Assessment, Abd al-Aziz al-Nasir*); and a March 31, 2007, memo headed "Subject: Recommendations for Continued Detention Under DOD Control (CD) for Guantanamo Detainee, ISN US9SA-000196DP (S)" (*Detainee Assessment, Musa al-Amri*).

185: Ivins's poem from the original e-mail, dated December 15, 2001. Also see the Dellafera affidavit.

185–186: Ivins's request for more spores from the original e-mail, dated December 17, 2001.

186: The exact date of bin Laden's departure from Tora Bora has been a matter of dispute; however, an American intelligence agency determined that it was December 16, and that information was shared with me. Other details from the Combined Arms Center Report and the Tora Bora Report and from "Summarized Detainee Sworn Statement" for detainee #801 at Guantanamo, unedited.

186–187: Descriptions of the terms of the Geneva Conventions from file folder, National Security Council Information, undated memo headed "For Attorney General Only: Legal Background"; Ray Murphy, "Prisoner of War Status and the Question of Guantanamo Detainess," *Human Rights Law Review* 3:2(2003); Judgment of the International Criminal Tribunal for the Former Yugoslavia, The Prosecutor Delatic et al. (IT-96-21) ("The Celebici case)," November 16, 1998; Task Force on National Security and the Rule of Law, New

York City Bar, "Reaffirming the U.S. Commitment to Common Article 3 of the Geneva Conventions," June, 2008; and "Sixty Years of the Geneva Conventions: Learning from the Past to Better Face the Future," *International Review of the Red Cross,* August 12, 2009. Also see March 6, 2003, letter from Kenneth Roth, executive director of Human Rights Watch, to Donald Rumsfeld.

188: Details of Taft's position from William J. Haynes memo to Rumsfeld, dated January 11, 2002, and headed "Detainee status." Also see memo from Taft to Gonzales, dated January 10, 2002, and headed "Draft memo from John Yoo (Taft memo)."

189: Leaflet quotes from a copy of one of the original documents.

189–191: Some of the details of the attempted shoe bombing from *United States v. Richard C. Reid,* crim. no. 02-10013-WGY, transcript of October 4, 2002. Also see criminal complaint, *United States v. Reid,* filed December 23, 2001; and Cathy Booth Thomas, "11 Lives: Courage in the Air," *Time,* September 1, 2002.

191–192: Seligman's background is described in Rob Hirtz, "Martin Seligman's Journey," *Pennsylvania Gazette,* January/February 1999. The meeting at his house was first described by Scott Shane and Mark Mazzetti, "In Adopting Harsh Tactics, No Inquiry into Past Use," *New York Times,* April 22, 2009.

192: Information about the SERE program from Department of the Army, "Code of Conduct, Survival, Evasion, Resistance, and Escape (SERE) Training," Army Regulation 350-30, December 10, 1985; U.S. Air Force, "Fact Sheet: U.S. Air Force Survival School," undated; Armed Services Report; and July 25, 2002, memorandum from the JPRA chief of staff for the Office of Defense General Counsel, "Subject: Exploitation." Also see January 15, 2003, memo from John F. Rankin and Christopher Ross to the officer in charge, FASOTRAGULANT (Fleet Aviation Specialized Operational Training Group Atlantic), "Subj: After Action Report Joint Task Force Guantanamo Bay (JTF-GTMO) Training Evolution" (*Rankin Ross memo*). Some of the details of the discussions to apply the techniques in Guantanamo from "JTF GITMO SERE Interrogation SOP," December 10, 2002; also see December 17, 2002, memo from Timothy James to JTF-GTMO/J2.

193: The earliest days of Mitchell and Jessen's involvement in the interrogation program, and the role and details of SERE training, from "Report of the Committee on Armed Services, United States Senate: Inquiry into the Treatment of Detainees in U.S. Custody," November 20, 2008 (*Armed Services Report*); Central Intelligence Agency Inspector General, "Special Review: Counterterrorism Detention and Interrogation Activities (September 2001–October 2003)," May 7, 2004 (*CIA Interrogation Report*); February 28, 2002, memo for Colonel Cooney, "Prisoner Handling Recommendations"; and September 24, 2007, testimony of Joseph Witsch before the Senate Committee on Armed Services in "Hearing to Receive Information Relating to the Treatment of Detainees." Also see Jim L. Cox, "Complaint: Dr. James Elmer Mitchell (License No. 23564)," submitted to the Texas State Board of Medical Examiners, 2007 (*Cox complaint*); and June 6, 2007, letter from Stephen Soldz et al. to Sharon Brehm, Ph.D., President, American Psychological Association (*Brehm letter*).

193: The lack of knowledge of Mitchell and Jessen on the subject of interrogation from the CIA Interrogation Report. Also see Cox complaint and Brehm letter.

193–194: The history of the Manchester Manual from the Behavioral Analysis Program, Operational Training Unit, Counterintelligence Division, FBI Headquarters, "Terrorist Training Manual," undated; Jason Lewis, "Lessons in Jihad as Secret Terror Manual Translated by MI5 Is Made Public by America," *Daily Mail,* March 15, 2008; and U.S. Army Training and Doctrine Command Deputy Chief of Staff for Intelligence Assistant Deputy Chief of Staff for Intelligence—Threats, "A Military Guide to Terrorism in the Twenty-first Century," August 2003.

194–195: Despite both public statements and court filings by the governments of the United States and Britain describing the Manchester Manual as an al-Qaeda document, it is not. Indeed, even a cursory reading makes that clear.

This is an enormously important fact. The Manchester Manual was at the center of some of the most sweeping and controversial decisions by the Bush administration. When detainees at Guantanamo launched hunger strikes and accusations of abuse, the Defense Department dismissed the actions and allegations as the false representations called for in the instructions of the manual, including directions that Islamists should falsely claim to have been tortured whenever they go to court. (No instructions to engage in such a deception exist in the document; I will explain below.)

Also, as the section in the main book text makes clear, the Manchester Manual was used to construct a psychological profile and analysis by James Mitchell and Bruce Jessen. The Defense Department wanted to use the document to assess "resistance strategies" employed by al-Qaeda members. But not only was the document unrelated to al-Qaeda; its "resistance measures" were irrelevant to anything either the Pentagon or Mitchell was looking for.

In other words, this mislabeling of the Manchester Manual as an al-Qaeda document was an error of massive proportions that fed false information about bin Laden's group to intelligence and law enforcement agencies in both the United States and Britain. Indeed, had someone analyzed the document correctly, at least some of the detainee abuse problems that occurred in the Bush administration could have been avoided.

Because I am contradicting the accepted version of this story, I will describe in detail both the evidence and the process that led to my conclusion that this document was not used by al-Qaeda. At one point early in my reporting, I was speaking with a foreign official and mentioned the Manchester Manual as an "al-Qaeda training manual." The official smiled at me and asked, "Have you ever read it?" I had to admit I had not—until then, I had relied solely on the representations in court documents and published reports. He suggested that I take the time to review it myself.

I did, and was astounded. Very quickly, it became obvious there were problems with the official representation; even a cursory reading made it clear that the Manchester Manual could not be an al-Qaeda document. Once I reached that conclusion, I spoke to two officials with a Middle Eastern intelligence service. Both agreed that their government had long known that the manual was not an al-Qaeda document, despite the representations of the American and British governments. One of the men called the idea that it had anything to do with al-Qaeda "absurd."

The evidence is overwhelming.

Starting with the basics: At no point does the manual mention al-Qaeda or bin Laden. It is not in digital format; instead, it was handwritten by at least two different people. Many have made the mistake of assuming it was written on a computer because the government translation came off a word processor; however, the Arabic version did not. The version found by the Manchester police on a computer was composed of digital scans of the original document.

That is important for several reasons. If this document was written in the middle to late 1990s (a best-case scenario, given that it was found in 2000) and was meant for widespread distribution, why was it not in a format that allowed for easy delivery? If the document was scanned at the time of its writing, someone must have had a computer. Yet it was not written on a computer.

This is part of why both the Middle Eastern intelligence service and I reached the same conclusion: that this document was written long before 2000.

Of course, those details about the format and structure of the document are merely suggestive. The information contained in the record is conclusive: The document was written between October 1990 and 1993. Those dates are critically important, as I'll explain below.

The evidence about the lack of connection between the Manchester Manual and al-Qaeda can be broken into numerous categories:

1. *Date of writing:* As I mentioned above, this document was written, at the latest, in the early 1990s. During that time period, al-Qaeda was just getting started and was flush with cash.

   Some of the proof about the date that the Manchester Manual was written comes from its references to technology. Digital cameras, cell phones, the Internet—none of these were in common usage at the time the document was written.

   Affordable digital cameras were widely available by 1994; the first mass-market version, the Apple QuickTake 100, manufactured by Kodak, could be purchased for less than $800. At that same time Fuji, Kodak, and Nikon all offered digital cameras for sale. By the following year, 1995, Canon introduced its Sure Shot 60 Zoom, which could be purchased for about $80.

   Why does that matter? Because only film cameras were available at the time the Manchester Manual was written.

   Whenever surveillance photographs are taken, the document says "the photographer should be experienced with film processing and developing." The reason, it says, is that the film cannot be taken to an outside film-processing service.

   Of course, many of the terrorists might be using film cameras. However, while the document is comprehensive in its description of how to use technologies, there is no mention and no description of digital cameras—where the photographs should be stored, whether they can be shipped online, etc. And, of course, there would be no need for all of the photographers to be proficient in film development unless they needed to develop film.

   Next, the document lays out specific details for how members of this group should communicate with each other. But it includes no instructions on the use of e-mail, which had become a popular means of communication by al-Qaeda in 1995. Mass-market e-mail services first became available in 1992, and exploded in usage the following year.

   More important is that the document describes a fax machine as a "modern" device. That technology was in wide usage by the mid-1980s, and by the mid-1990s, as Internet usage was booming, was hardly considered "modern."

   Then, phone booths. The Manchester Manual lays out instructions on how to use phone booths to escape detection when a member of the organization fears that his home line is tapped. The very description is, at least for the modern technological age, ancient history. There is no mention of cellular phones, which did not come into wide usage until the late 1990s.

   Historical references in the document make it clear that it was written sometime after October 1990. In a section giving descriptions of previous assassination attempts— both successful and unsuccessful—it mentions the terrorist killing of Rifaat El-Mahgoub, the speaker of the Egyptian parliament, who was murdered on October 12 of that year.

   All of these factors combined show that the document could have been written only between late 1990 and sometime in the middle of that decade. There is, however, another piece of data that the Middle Eastern intelligence agency officials I spoke with say has led to their conclusion that the manual was written no later than August 1993.

   The document mentions every assassination attempt of an Egyptian interior minister from 1987 through 1990. However, another took place in August 1993, in the unsuccessful attempt to kill Hassan al-Alfi. The intelligence officials' analysis is that, if written in 1994 or later, the document would not have ignored the most recent attempt on an Egyptian interior minister while exploring the earlier attempts in such detail.

All of that information—plus an estimate on the length of time it took to handwrite the almost two-hundred-page document—has led the foreign intelligence group to conclude that the manual was written in either 1991 or 1992. Those are the only dates that would account for both the timing of the 1990 assassination and the descriptions of the existing technology.

2. *The time line and al-Qaeda:* By the time of the October 1990 assassination of El-Mahgoub, al-Qaeda was in a shambles. Bin Laden had been in Saudi Arabia for months; while he still had his Arab fighters in numerous locations, most of his time was spent fomenting discord in Yemen, much to the dismay of the Saudi royal family. His relationship with Zawahiri and the Egyptians had unraveled, as each pursued different goals—a critical piece of information in the later analysis of the document.

Then, in April 1991, bin Laden moved to the Sudan and began reconstituting al-Qaeda. He was flush with cash, paying millions to help support the government there and to finance training camps. He remained wealthy until March 5, 1994, when he was cut off by his family. Again, the dates when he had wealth will be important in this analysis, as will be obvious below.

3. *The abilities of the group that composed the Manchester Manual:* Unlike al-Qaeda, the group that used the document had limited ability to obtain basic equipment that bin Laden had used for years, according to intelligence sources.

The evidence is again in the text of the document, when it refers to fax machines. Those would be unlikely to be used, the document says, because of the group's limitations. "Considering its modest capabilities and the pursuit by the security apparatus of its members and forces, the Islamic Military Organization cannot obtain these devices."

I do not have the original document, but an Arabic translator I consulted said that the term *capabilities* used behind the word *modest* is probably an English approximation. Most likely, the translator said, the correct translation would be more akin to *limited means,* a reference to financial condition. Of course, that translation cannot be offered as anything other than a probability, but even in English, it seems to be the most likely meaning. However, if the Arabic words are about a lack of an operational ability to obtain the technology, that would not change the fact that this is a description of a group that was different from al-Qaeda at that time. And again, al-Qaeda had fax machines by the time bin Laden traveled to the Sudan

There is one other indication that the group that wrote the manual was financially strapped: The document cautions that special operations (it specifies assassinations, kidnapping, bombings, and others) pose the risk of draining the group financially. This would not have been a challenge facing al-Qaeda before March 2004, long after the Manchester Manual appears to have been written. In other words, al-Qaeda was rich; the group that wrote the Manchester Manual was poor.

4. *The operations of the organization:* This is the most decisive evidence in establishing that the Manchester Manual has nothing to do with al-Qaeda: Not only does the operation of the group differ dramatically from that of al-Qaeda; it in fact does the *opposite* of what bin Laden called for in his organization.

Start with training. From its beginning, al-Qaeda maintained training camps, financed by bin Laden. Indeed, there were separate camps, some for early recruits and others for more advanced members. Nothing like this existed for the group that wrote the Manchester Manual. In fact, their training was conducted in places selected by lower-level individual trainers.

The Manchester Manual instructs individuals to set up their training facilities away from police stations and public establishments. (This was not a requirement for al-Qaeda camps; in Afghanistan, one was just off the main airport at Kabul. In the Sudan, no attempt was made to hide them from the police or government officials, whose operations were financed by bin Laden.) They are told that no one but the trainers and the trainees should know the location of the place, and that it should be suitable for the kind of training being provided. This also differs from al-Qaeda—with that group, individual trainers don't get to decide the methods of training. Instead, those techniques are established by a military council. Finally, the document says that all signs of training should be hidden once the lessons are completed. Al-Qaeda never made any serious attempt to hide its facilities; that is why they were so easy for the Americans to bomb.

The organization of the group that wrote the Manchester Manual also differs from al-Qaeda. There is no mention of the various committees that run bin Laden's network. Instead of a military committee of al-Qaeda, the entire group in the Manchester Manual is called the "military organization," which is run by commanders and an advisory council, a much looser structure.

The document also lists the requirements for someone to become a member of the organization. While they are similar to those listed in al-Qaeda's founding documents from 1988, they are not the same. There are no requirements that the member be recommended by a trusted aide, that he follow the rules without question, or that he has to be well mannered, as was contained in the original declarations prepared for al-Qaeda in 1988.

5. *Military training:* The organization that wrote the Manchester Manual was militarily unsophisticated; al-Qaeda was not. The document provides a written description about using weapons, but only the most basic—handguns, rifles, and small explosives—are described.

The first step described in the use of weapons is that the member needs to go buy one. But this would not be necessary for a member of al-Qaeda, which has long maintained weaponry that far exceeds those of some small armies. With bin Laden's group, the weapons are provided to the members, not the other way around. The purchaser described in the Manchester Manual also had to arrange for a place to store the weapons; al-Qaeda maintained its own weapons caches, including some dug into mountains.

The first weapon listed is a pistol. The manual offers a history of the pistol, and then discusses the benefits and disadvantages of both the automatic pistol and the revolver. Then, for several pages, it describes different ways to hold either a pistol or a revolver, the position a person should assume, where to place a finger, and so on. Alongside the descriptions are hand-drawn pictures.

The idea that al-Qaeda members would buy their own weapons and then learn how to use them by reading a manual would probably leave bin Laden laughing. Al-Qaeda trainees do not learn how to fire a gun by reading about it in a book; they attend the camps, are provided with the weapons, and then are guided through their usage one step at a time. They engage in practice against sophisticated targets, and then are taught how to use their weapons in raids.

The next weapon described in the manual is the rifle, and again, the document provides a history and step-by-step instructions on how to hold and fire it.

The next sets of weapons are the most basic: knives and blunt objects and poisons. All of the poisons mentioned come from beans, roots, and plants—there is nothing about cyanide, strychnine, or the other most deadly substances connected to al-Qaeda by American intelligence.

Then, bombs. The document provides a description of how to assemble a fuse with a blasting cap, but then says nothing about the actual explosives required or how the detonation device should be attached. It is as if the document gave instructions on how to turn a key in a car, but not how to drive.

Those are all the weapons described, and they are nothing like the al-Qaeda arsenal. There is no mention of how to use Stinger missiles, antiaircraft systems, grenade launchers, assault rifles, cluster bombs, Uzi machine guns, or any of the other deadly weapons that were possessed by al-Qaeda. Indeed, if this document was, against all evidence, written after 1993, at that point bin Laden was already paying millions of dollars in an attempt to purchase nuclear weapons; al-Qaeda had long ago passed the "gun, rifle, and fuse-explosive" stage.

6. *Goals of the organization:* By 1990, the United States had established operations in Saudi Arabia as part of the first Iraq War. Bin Laden's focus was on driving out the Americans; his goals were directed at outside enemies and remained that way for two decades.

The Manchester Manual says nothing about the situation in Saudi Arabia. Instead, its goals are quite different: to topple the "apostate rulers" of the Middle East and establish an orthodox caliphate. In other words, this group wanted to overthrow Arab governments that were not sufficiently Muslim and establish an Islamic regime.

This division of goals—fighting outside enemies or toppling Arab leaders—was the same issue that was splitting bin Laden and Zawahiri at that time. Bin Laden, as I mentioned, wanted to confront the Americans, Zawahiri wanted to overturn the Egyptian government. As a result of that disagreement, the two were not working together when this document was written. If this difference of opinion could divide Zawahiri and bin Laden, it is hard to understand how any government official could conclude that the al-Qaeda leader had suddenly adopted the goal he opposed.

Finally, there is one bit of information that is crippling to the idea that the Manchester Manual is an al-Qaeda document. The terror group maintained a vast collection of books and documents in its library based in Afghanistan; many of al-Qaeda's planners and fighters—the ones who would supposedly depend on the "tactics" in the Manchester Manual—consulted the information in that library. But according to two former al-Qaeda members I spoke with, the Manchester Manual was not included in the library. Indeed, that reality was made quite clear in the interrogations at Guantanamo of Abu al-Libi, the operations chief of al-Qaeda. The information is described in the detainee assessment of Abu al-Libi. The primary sources of information from the library that were used to teach guerrilla tactics, al-Libi told his interrogators, were translated military training manuals from the United States armed forces; in other words, the main reading material for learning fighting tactics came from America, not the Middle East. Other influential books from the library, al-Libi said, were translations of Mao Zedong's works on guerrilla warfare; these were widely used in al-Qaeda training camps. Indeed, excerpts from Mao's writings were distributed among al-Qaeda members in small pamphlets titled "The War of the Week."

If not al-Qaeda, then who wrote the document? While the specific identity will remain educated guesswork, it is relatively easy to narrow it down to a group of interrelated and, at times, contentious organizations.

The references in the Manchester Manual to an organization called the Ministry of Interior Affairs is significant in determining its provenance. Contrary to the statements of both American and British officials, the sections in the document about interrogation are not instructions on how to handle all official questioning. Instead, they are very specific about the method of dealing with questioning from the ministry. In the introduction to the section on interrogations, the manual says: "The agency that conducts the interrogation is the government's questioning apparatus that belongs to the Ministry of Interior Affairs. The officers of that apparatus graduate from the police academy."

The writers of the document then make it clear that they are discussing the security sector *in the country where they reside.* It states, "In *our country,* that apparatus has no values or code of ethics. It does not hesitate to use all kinds of torture" (emphasis added).

The name of the government agency—Ministry of Interior Affairs—helps to narrow down the possibilities of which country the writers are discussing. This type of agency goes by different names in different countries—Ministry of Interior, Ministry for the Interior and Public Health, Ministry of Home Affairs, Ministry of Internal Affairs, Department of Home Affairs, and so on. The Middle Eastern governments that name this group the Ministry of Interior Affairs are Egypt, Sudan, Afghanistan, and Saudi Arabia.

At the time the manual was written, Sudan had adopted an Islamic legal code and was tolerant, and even supportive, of fundamentalist groups; none of that matches the descriptions in the document. Afghanistan, of course, was in chaos and there was no settled "apostate ruler" to overthrow. Egypt and Saudi Arabia remain the only two nations that fit the depiction of the government and the name of its security agency.

But, as I mentioned before, there is nothing in the manual about Saudi Arabia or America, the focus of bin Laden's ire in the early 1990s. Instead, the focus of the manual is Egypt. Every terrorist attack it depicts involves that country and its officials.

The descriptions include mention of the groups involved, including the covert section of the Muslim Brotherhood and a fundamentalist organization called al-Najun min al-Nar (the government translates this to mean "[those who have] escaped the fire," but I am told the better translation is "rescued from the fire"). These are organizations that were working to replace the Egyptian regime with an Islamic state.

Only one of the examples listed in the Manchester Manual is given without naming any group as the perpetrator. This attack, the assassination of El-Mahgoub, is also by far the most detailed. For example, it describes the precise number of minutes that separated two convoys of cars, the attempts to flee on motorcycles, the actions of one of the terrorists when a motorcycle broke down, the circumstances surrounding the shooting of a police officer during the men's flight, and the fact that the identity of the officer was subsequently learned. In essence, the writers of this document had more direct information about the El-Mahgoub attack than about any other. By all appearances, the writers had personal or direct knowledge of the attack of the Egyptian official, additional evidence suggesting that this was written by an Islamist group in Egypt. Also, several individuals mentioned in the manual are cited as "brothers"—every one that I could gather information about was arrested or executed by Egyptian authorities.

The manual provides an extremely detailed description of the process of arrest and interrogation—what building a suspect is taken to, then where he is moved, and so on. The Middle Eastern intelligence officials said that those descriptions exactly match the process used in Egypt. For this and many of the reasons mentioned above, the officials said there is no doubt that this document is about Egypt.

The philosophy espoused by the writers also offers clues as to their identity. At the beginning of the manual's first chapter, the writers make reference to the "state of ignorance" subsuming Arabic society and how the young were lured into this state by the apostate rulers dangling community clubs, fancy clothes, and other Western amenities to persuade them to abandon fundamentalist Islam. This is, almost verbatim, the philosophy espoused by Sayyid Qutb, the Egyptian intellectual who served as the philosophical patron saint of the Muslim Brotherhood in that country. The document then cites Ibn Taymiyyah, the religious scholar from the Middle Ages who served as an intellectual foundation for the beliefs of the Muslim Brotherhood.

All of the attacks described in the document were committed by the military unit of the Muslim Brotherhood in the mid-twentieth century or by some of the violent offshoots of that organization that mostly took root in the late 1980s.

The organization refers to itself twice as Jemaah Islamiyah. The government correctly translates this to mean "the Islamic group," but apparently without recognizing that Jemaah Islamiyah is the name of an Egyptian terrorist organization. Jemaah has been in operation since the 1970s and is the largest militant Islamist group in Egypt. It is a radical offshoot of the Muslim Brotherhood, with its spiritual leader, Omar Abdel-Rahman, known in the United States as "the blind sheikh." Rahman is currently serving a life sentence in an American prison following his conviction on conspiracy charges involving terrorist plotting.

There is additional evidence suggesting the manual may be connected to Jemaah. The assassination of El-Mahgoub, which is the one described in the greatest detail, was linked to followers of Rahman. That would help to explain how the writers of the manual knew so much about that attack.

But there is another step to this identification. While the writers may be part of Jemaah, that organization worked with another terrorist group, Egyptian Islamic Jihad, run by Zawahiri. In 1991, Zawahiri took control of EIJ, and the organization lost many of its direct connections with other terrorist groups. The date, of course, closely coincides with the writing of the manual, and may have been produced as part of Zawahiri's new leadership.

This does *not*, however, link the manual to al-Qaeda. Once again, Zawahiri and bin Laden were heading in different directions at that time, and the document is focused on the government of Egypt, not something of particular interest to the al-Qaeda leader. Al-Qaeda began to significantly finance EIJ only in 1998, and only then did Egyptians begin to play a large role in the planning of attacks.

This is not, of course, a Sherlock Holmes mystery; whether the document was written by Jemaah, EIJ, or some other group, the significant point is that it could not have been an al-Qaeda manual. Beyond all of the factual issues, there is also the problem that the manual is amateurish. Again, contrary to the representations of various governments, there is virtually nothing in its pages that isn't basic. *Don't set up training near a police station, hold a gun like this, rent ground-floor apartments to allow for easy escape*—these are hardly the musings of a terrorist mastermind.

This analysis establishes four facts: that the Manchester Manual is not an al-Qaeda document, that it was written in the early 1990s, that the authors were part of a jihadist group looking to overthrow the government of Egypt, and that the goal was divergent from the aspirations of bin Laden at that time. Only by recognizing those points can the failures of the American and British governments in dealing with this document become clear.

Because this manual was written at a different time by a different group with different goals than Western officials believed, American and British policies were driven by a fiction. Challenges that did not exist were reviewed and countered with policies that were not necessary. False arguments were offered up to address criticisms. It was as if the Pittsburgh Steelers prepared for a game against the Dallas Cowboys by reviewing the playbook from Tuscaloosa High School; the meanings and threats were all misunderstood.

The majority of the problem came from the sections of the manual about interrogation, resistance, and responses. As the governments have said, the document *does* provide information about each of those areas. One of the points most often repeated by the Americans and the British is that the manual says Islamists who have been arrested should falsely proclaim in court that they had been tortured.

It says no such thing.

The interrogation section is not suggesting that captured members of the group make *false* allegations of torture, or employ *general* resistance measures—it is examining torture and resistance *in Egypt*. It is written by Islamists who, the writing shows, have been exposed to the torture inflicted universally by Egyptian security officers on suspected Muslim terrorists.

Again, this is made clear simply by reading the document. As mentioned above, in the interrogation and investigation section, it is discussing the "Ministry of Interior Affairs" in "our country." That is not some general reference to law enforcement and intelligence groups around the world.

It lists the forms of torture to expect: hanging by feet, beating with thick wires, pulling out nails, shocking with electric current, burning with fire, hitting the genitals, dragging over barbed wire, and eighteen other tactics. These are all cited by human rights groups as the tactics used by Egypt. Nothing like the torture of the Egyptians was ever inflicted by the Americans and the British.

The document provides specific examples of Islamists who were tortured—of course, all of them Egyptians (it does cite a book by an Iranian torture victim and instructs the members of the group to read it). And, as mentioned above, it provides a step-by-step description of the arrest and interrogation process, including an explanation of where torture would take place and when.

Eventually, if there are criminal charges brought, the suspect would be taken to court. And it is there that he is supposed to make his first public proclamation of having been tortured. "At the beginning of the trial . . . the brothers must insist on proving that torture was inflicted on them by State Security (investigators) to the judge . . . complain to the court of mistreatment in prison . . . the brother has to do his best to know the names of the state security officers who participated in the torture and mention their names to the judge . . . during the trial, the court has to be notified of any mistreatment of the brothers inside the prison. . . ."

This is not some arbitrary instruction intended to make the Egyptians squirm from false accusations; it is the best way to *make the torture stop*. Regardless of what investigators do, Egyptian courts are not tolerant of torture. Indeed, after the Islamists made repeated and vocal accusations of abuse to the court in the case arising from the assassination of El-Mahgoub, the court investigated and concluded that the men had been tortured. As a result, their confessions were tossed out as unreliable. So, by complaining of the torture to the courts, a detainee in Egypt is acting in the way most likely to make it stop. That is all the section on making public accusations of torture is about. That has nothing to do with the American and British interpretation about making false accusations, which simply does not match the text of the document.

In the end, the evidence is overwhelming that the Manchester Manual is not an al-Qaeda document and that its contents have been misinterpreted—or misrepresented—by Western officials. Moreover, while the document was found in the computer of a man associated with al-Qaeda, his strongest connection was to a Libyan terrorist group that, unlike al-Qaeda, is primarily focused on overthrowing that country's government. Unfortunately, the American and British governments fell into a common trap—assuming that all terrorists are al-Qaeda, when, at least at the time when the Manchester Manual was written, they were competitors for money, attention, and followers.

196–197: Some details of the White House meeting to discuss possible detention facilities from contemporaneous notes taken by one of the participants.

197: History of Guantanamo from Rear Admiral M. E. Murphy, *The History of Guantanamo Bay, 1494–1964,* an official government record written for the Department of the Navy and originally published in January 5, 1953. Also see Robert D. Heinl Jr., "How We Got Guantanamo," *American Heritage Magazine,* February 1962. Also see Admiral George Dewey,

"Our Navy for a Greater Navy," *Our Navy: The Standard Magazine for the U.S. Navy,* May 1913.

197: Some details of the contractor's experiences from his testimony of February 15, 2009, for the Center for the Study of Human Rights in the Americas.

BOOK TWO

Chapter 7

201–202: Some details of Blair's trip to meet Karzai from the Campbell diaries and from photographs of the event.

201: Details of the background and evolution of Hamid Karzai from the Combined Arms Center Report. Also see Nick B. Mills, *Karzai: The Failing American Intervention and the Struggle for Afghanistan,* Wiley, 2007.

203–204: Some details of the problems with intelligence distribution after 9/11 from an October 12, 2008, sworn declaration by Arthur Brown, former national intelligence officer for East Asia at the CIA, filed in Federal District Court in Washington, D.C., in the case of *Boumediene v. Bush.*

204–206: Some details of the January 8 meeting between Behmen and the Americans from sworn declarations of September 22, 2008, by the prime minister; Zlatko Lagumdžija, at the time the foreign minister and chairman of the Council of Ministers for Bosnia-Herzegovina; as well as the September 15, 2008, declaration of Wolfgang Petritsch, then the high representative of the European Union for Bosnia-Herzegovina. Petritsch is a member of the Austrian government, and subsequent to these events served as Austria's ambassador and permanent representative to the United Nations in Geneva. For background, see the Council of Europe's Parliamentary Assembly Report, "Lawfulness of Detentions by the United States in Guantanamo Bay," April 8, 2005; and United Nations Human Rights Council, "Joint Study on Global Practices in Relation to Secret Detention," advance unedited version, January 26, 2010 (*U.N. Detention Report*).

207–209: Some details of the FBI interrogation of al-Libi from Mayer, *The Dark Side;* Jason Vest, "Pray and Tell," *American Prospect,* June 19, 2005; "Off the Record: U.S. Responsibility for Enforced Disappearances in the 'War on Terror,' " a briefing paper published on June 6, 2007, and based on research conducted by Amnesty International; Cageprisoners; the Center for Constitutional Rights; the Center for Human Rights and Global Justice at NYU School of Law; Human Rights Watch; and Reprieve. Also see Open Society Foundations, "Confinement Conditions at a U.S. Screening Facility on Bagram Air Base," Policy Brief No. 3, October 14, 2010.

209–210: The arrival of the detainees was described in fascinating detail by Sue Anne Pressley, "Detainees Arrive in Cuba amid Tight Security," *Washington Post,* January 12, 2002. Also see Katharine Q. Seelye, "First 'Unlawful Combatants' Seized in Afghanistan Arrive at U.S. Base in Cuba," *New York Times,* January 12, 2002; and Agence France Presse, "Bound and Shackled Prisoners Unloaded at US Navy Base," January 11, 2002. Additional facts from Walter J. Boyne, *Beyond the Wild Blue: A History of the U.S. Air Force, 1947–2007,* Thomas Dunne Books. 2007.

211: Details of 374's condition from his medical records, entry dated January 12, 2002.

213: Details of the Circle Bar from direct observation. Also see Scott Aiges, "Circle Bar a Hangout for the Cool, the Hip and the Happening," *Times-Picayune,* April 7, 2000.

213–215: Some details of the debate over the draft Yoo-Delahunty memo from "Status of Legal Discussions re: Application of Geneva Convention to Taliban and al Qaeda," an undated and unsigned White House memo. Also see Tim Golden, "After Terror, a Secret Rewriting of Military Law," *New York Times,* October 24, 2004.

215–216: The description of the Sarajevo central prison from direct observation. Some details of the events there from the Behmen sworn statement. Also see the May 6, 2008, testimony of Stephen H. Oleskey of Wilmer Cutler Pickering Hale and Dorr, "City on a Hill or Prison on the Bay?" hearings before the House Committee on Foreign Affairs, Subcommittee on International Organizations, Human Rights, and Oversight.

216: Decision of Bosnian court from Decision, Municipal Court in Zenica, Kv9-2002, January 16, 2002. Also see Rjsenje, *"U Istraznom Premeto Protiv Belcasem Bansayah i. dr.,"* Vrhovni Sud Federacija Bosne i Hercegovine, Ki-101/01, 17.01.2002 (translation: Decision, "In the Investigation Case Against Belcasem Bansayah et al.," Supreme Court of the Federation of Bosnia and Herzegovina, Ki-101/01, January 1, 2002).

216: Some details of the Algerian Six's trip to Guantanamo from Oleskey testimony of May 6, 2008.

217: Some details about Gonzales's briefing of Bush and his decision from Alberto R. Gonzales, Memorandum for the President (draft), "Decision re: Application of the Geneva Convention on Prisoners of War to the Conflict with al Qaeda and the Taliban," January 25, 2002. Also see James P. Pfiffner, "Policy Making in the Bush White House," *Issues in Governance Studies,* Governance Studies at Brookings, October 2008.

217: Descriptions of the Common Article Three from Ray Murphy, "Prisoner of War Status and the Question of Guantanamo Detainees," *Human Rights Law Review* 3:2 (2003).

217–218: Details of the Rumsfeld memo and subsequent electronic communication from the original documents.

218–219: Some details of the CIA's interview of al-Libi from CIA operational cables dated February 4, February 5, and February 19, 2004; the Senate Postwar Report on Iraq; and the Senate Prewar Report on Iraq.

219: Details of the CIA files on Egypt were shared with the author.

220–221: Some details of the operations of Guantanamo from "Review of Department Compliance with President's Executive Order on Detainee Conditions of Confinement," an undated Department of Defense report (*DOD Guantanamo Report*).

221–222: Some details of the events leading to the pursuit of Sufaat from Detainee Assessment, Jamal Muhammad Alawi. Also see CIA Directorate of Intelligence, "Khalid Sheikh Mohammed: Preeminent Source on al Qaeda," July 13, 2004.

222–224: Some details about the interviews with Mazigh, and the subsequent call from Arar and Edelman, from a transit slip written by Buffam on January 5, 2003, and headed "Time Line Regarding Conversations with Maher Arar." Also see Royal Canadian Mounted Police Task Detail Report, Task ID 260, dated November 6, 2003, and headed "Re: Maher Arar"; and "Time Line—Maher ARAR, Project A-O Canada," March October 27, 2003. That is an official document that was prepared by the RCMP. Also see the Arar Report.

224–225: Details of the Yoo memorandum from the original document. Some details of the draft Gonzales memorandum from the original document.

225–227: Some details of Powell's reactions and his objections from the original memo of his comments on the Gonzales memo. Details of his letter from the original document. Also see William H. Taft IV, Memorandum to the Counsel to the President, "Subject: Comments on Your Paper on the Geneva Convention," February 2, 2002.

227: For the news article read by Gonzales see Rowan Scarborough, "Powell Wants Detainees to Be Declared POWs; Memo Shows Differences with White House," *Washington Times,* January 26, 2002.

227–228: Some details of El-Maati's experiences in Egypt from the Iacobucci Report and United Nations Human Rights Council, "Joint Study on Global Practices in Relation to Secret Detention," Advance Unedited Version, January 26, 2010 (*U.N. Detention Report*).

228: Some details of the Ivins interview on January 29, 2002, from the FBI 302 of that date for case no. 279A-WF-222936. Also see the 302 from the April 24, 2002, and April 25, 2002, interviews of Ivins for the same case.

228–229: Details of the State of the Union address from a video recording of the event.

229–230: A few details of the meeting about the Geneva Conventions from contemporaneous notes taken by a participant. The notes were only summarized to the author. Other details from participants in the meetings.

230: Details of the Ashcroft letter from the original document.

230–231: Information from the e-mail alerting the FBI to Ivins from the original document. Some details of the FBI's reaction, and its opinion of Ivins, from the Anthrax Panel Report.

231: Details of the request from the American Society of Microbiology from the original e-mail.

232: The quotes of Bush's order from the original document. As mentioned, these events are often depicted as a defeat for Powell; they were not. Most of those assertions are made in reference to the draft of the Gonzales memo, which was revised before going to the president. Powell also never told Bush that the Geneva Conventions should apply to al-Qaeda, or needed to be applied on a blanket basis to the Taliban. The results described in the narrative are what he was seeking. This was also confirmed by Jack Goldsmith, a subsequent head of the Office of Legal Counsel, in his book *The Terror Presidency,* W. W. Norton, 2007.

232–233: Ivins's manipulation of the sample submissions from the Anthrax Panel Report, the Amerithrax Report, and the first Arredondo affidavit. Also see FBI Electronic Communication from Washington Field Amerithrax 3, "Title: Amerithrax; Major Case 184," June 27, 2005.

233: Some details of the information provided by al-Libi from a CIA report, "Iraqi Support for Terrorism," January 29, 2003; another report of the same title, dated September 2002; a CIA report headed "Iraq and al-Qa'ida: Interpreting a Murky Relationship," June 21, 2003; a partially declassified report to the intelligence community from the Defense Intelligence Agency issued as DITSUM #044-02; DIA Special Analysis, February 28, 2002; the Senate Postwar Report on Iraq; CIA operational cables dated February 4, February 5, and February 19, 2004; and a May 24, 2007, letter from Edward J. Markey, William D. Delahunt, and Jerrold Nadler to President George Bush.

Chapter 8

235–236: Details of the *Rasul v. Bush* filing from the original document.

236: Details of the press conference from a transcript prepared by FDCH Political Transcripts, "News Conference Announcing the Filing of Petition of Habeas Corpus on Behalf of Detainees at Camp X-Ray," February 19, 2002. Other details of the press conference from the broadcast of *Channel 10* (Australia) *Late News,* February 20, 2002.

237: The man whose voice mail is quoted left virtually identical messages to habeas lawyers around the country, some of which were retained. His message was almost uniformly the same.

237–238: Some details of the meeting between Dunlavey and Rumsfeld from "Summarized Witness Statement of MG (Retired) Mike Dunlavey" (*Dunlavey statement*) prepared by Lieutenant General Randall M. Schmidt, the AR 15-6 investigating officer for what became the Schmidt-Furlow Report of April 1, 2005. The Dunlavey statement was exhibit 12 of seventy-six attached exhibits. Some details of Dunlavey's background from DOD press release no. 673-97, "Maj. Gen. Michael E. Dunlavey Appointed to Reserve Forces Policy Board," December 11, 1997. Also see the sworn August 24, 2005, testimony of Lieutenant General Randall Mark Schmidt, taken as part of an inquiry by the investigations division of the Army Inspector General's Office (*the Schmidt testimony*).

238–239: Some details of the "bitch" event at Guantanamo from an eyewitness account of Specialist Brandon Neely in a statement provided to the Center for the Study of Human Rights in America, December 4, 2008.

239–240: Descriptions of Chapri from Jason Burke, "Pathans Rule the Wild West," *Independent*, June 3, 1999. Some details of the events in Chapri from Tim McGirk, "Anatomy of a Raid," *Time*, April 15, 2002; Thành Tâm, *"Cuộc bố ráp o Faisalabad,"* November 7, 2003; and Detainee Assessment, Abu Zubaydah.

240: Some details of the events at the Jalalabad office of the CIA from John Kiriakou, *The Reluctant Spy*, Bantam, 2010.

240–241: Some details of the Rove steel meeting from Christopher Meyer, *D.C. Confidential*, Weidenfeld & Nicolson, 2005. Also see White House press release, "President Announces Temporary Safeguards for Steel Industry," March 5, 2002.

241: Details of Cheney's trip from the official itinerary.

241–242: Some details of the Cheney meeting with Blair from the January 18, 2010, testimony of Jonathan Powell, the former chief of staff for Blair, before the Chilcot Inquiry, an investigation by a British committee led by Sir John Chilcot, the former permanent secretary at the Northern Ireland office. Also see the briefing memorandum by Bill Burns to Colin Powell, "Principals' Committee Meeting on the Vice President's Trip," March 25, 2002; and the Campbell diaries.

242–243: Some details of the Hamdan expedition to Kandahar from the FBI 302 of March 13, 2002, chronicling the trip for file no. 265A-NY-259391 SUB AFG, prepared by Special Agents William W. Vincent and Robert Fuller.

244–245: Some details of the meeting between Manning and Rice from a David Manning memo to Blair, "Secret—Strictly Personal: Your Trip to the US," March 14, 2002. Also see Manning's testimony before the Chilcot Inquiry, November 30, 2009.

245: Details of the Manning memo from the original document.

245–246: Some details of the problems at Guantanamo from the Dunlavey statement. Also see Joseph Margulies, *Guantanamo and the Abuse of Presidential Power*, Simon & Schuster, 2006.

245: Some details of the structure of JTF 170 from United States General Accounting Office, *Combating Terrorism: Interagency Framework and Agency Programs to Address the Overseas Threat*, GAO-03-165, May 2003.

246: Details of the military commission rules contained in the black binder from the original document. Also see Office of the Chief Defense Counsel, "Desk Book," memos beginning on March 21, 2002.

246: Some details about Rumsfeld's formation of the council of wise men from a September 17, 2001, memo from Rumsfeld to Steve Cambone, subject line "Experts."

247–251: Some details of the capture and initial questioning of Abu Zubaydah from memo of Detainee Assessment, Abu Zubaydah; a January 6, 2008, memo headed "Subject: Recommendations for Continued Detention Under DOD Control (CD) for Guantanamo Detainee, ISN US9YM-000549DO (S)" (*Detainee Assessment, Hassan Said*); Oversight and Review Division, Department of Justice Office of the Inspector General, *A Review of the FBI's Involvement in and Observations of Detainee Interrogations in Guantanamo Bay, Afghanistan, and Iraq*, May 2008 (*FBI/OIG Report*); "Statement of Noor Uthman Muhammed," dated February 17, 2011, *United States v. Noor Uthman Muhammed*, filed with the Military Commissions Trial Judiciary—Guantanamo Bay; a CIA document titled "Psychological Assessment of Zain al-Abidin al-Abideen Muhammad Hassan, a.k.a. Abu Zubaydah," dated January 31, 2003; Tim McGirk, "Anatomy of a Raid," *Time*, April 8, 2002. Also see Kiriakou, *The Reluctant Spy*; John F. Burns, "In Pakistan's Interior, a Troubling Victory in Hunt for Al Qaeda," *New York Times*, April 9, 2002; Michael Isikoff, "We Could Have Done This the Right Way," *Newsweek*, April 25, 2009; Dan Eggen and Walter Pincus, "FBI,

CIA Debate Significance of Terror Suspect," *Washington Post,* December 18, 2007; David Johnston, "At Secret Interrogations, Dispute Flared over Tactics," *New York Times,* September 10, 2006; and Mayer, *The Dark Side.*

250: Details of the background of ear identification from A. J. Hoogstrate, "Ear Identification Based on Surveillance Camera's Images," Netherlands Forensic Institute, May 31, 2000.

251: Description of the Chilterns from direct observation.

251–253: Some details of the meeting at Chequers between Blair and his advisors from the Campbell diaries. Also see the December 4, 2009, testimony of Lieutenant General Sir Anthony Pigott before the Chilcot Inquiry.

253: Details about U-Tabao Air Base, although not in reference to its role as a location of a secret prison, from Jack Sikora and Larry Westin, *Batcats: The United States Air Force 553rd Reconnaissance Wing in Southeast Asia,* IUniverse, 2003. Also see Emma Chanlett-Avery, "Thailand: Background and U.S. Relations," Congressional Research Service, June 21, 2010. While Thailand has denied that any secret prison was located inside its borders, the United States publicly acknowledged that one of the facilities was there in documents filed in 2009 in the case of *American Civil Liberties Union v. Department of Defense,* 04 Civ. 4151, in Federal District Court for the Southern District of New York. Also see United Nations General Assembly Human Rights Council, "Joint Study on Global Practices in Relation to Secret Detention in the Context of Countering Terrorism," February 19, 2010, A/HRC/13/42; and U.N. Detention Report and Council of Europe, "Secret Detentions and Illegal Transfers of Detainees Involving Council of Europe Member States: Second Report," submitted by Dick Marty, June 11, 2007 (*Marty Report*). The location of the prison was conveyed by an official with connections to the Thai government.

254: The concept of "shock of capture" is described by Steven M. Kleinman, "KUBARK Counterintelligence Interrogation Review: Observations of an Interrogator," *Educing Information: Interrogation, Science and Art,* National Defense Intelligence College, December 2006. "Dislocation of expectation" is also described by Kleinman, in *Educing Information.*

254–255: Some details of the FBI interrogations of Zubaydah from FBI/OIG Report; the May 13, 2009, testimony of Ali Soufan before the Senate Committee on the Judiciary in the hearing entitled "What Went Wrong: Torture and the Office of Legal Counsel in the Bush Administration" (*the Soufan Senate testimony*); David Johnston, "At a Secret Interrogation, Disputes Flared over Tactics," *New York Times,* September 10, 2006; Peter Finn and Joby Warrick, "Detainee's Harsh Treatment Foiled No Plots," *Washington Post,* March 29, 2009; and Michael Isikoff, "We Could Have Done This the Right Way," *Newsweek,* April 25, 2009.

255–256: Some details of the CIA meetings, including Mitchell's "fear" comment, from Joby Warrick and Peter Finn, "Internal Rifts on Road to Torment," *Washington Post,* July 19, 2009. Also see CIA Interrogation Report.

256–257: The classified CIA report was written in the summer of 1958 by "Don Compos" (a pseudonym) and entitled "The Interrogation of Suspects Under Arrest."

257: Description of Al Jazeera's bureau from direct observation.

257–258: Some details of the contact with Fouda and his subsequent decision to travel to Islamabad from his book, *Masterminds of Terror,* Mainstream Publishing, 2003. The book recounted his experiences in the events leading up to and during his interviews with Khalid Sheikh Mohammed and bin al-shibh.

258–260: Some details of the discovery and movement of Hamdi from transcript, Defense Department Operational Update, April 4, 2002; Brief of Petitioners/Appellees, *Yaser Esam Hamdi et al. v. Donald Rumsfeld,* no. 027338, filed in the Federal District Court of Appeals for the Fourth Circuit, October 18, 2002; Matthew Dolan, "U.S.-Born Taliban Held in Norfolk," *Virginia-Pilot,* April 6, 2002; and Jennifer Elsea, "The Supreme Court and

Detainees in the War on Terrorism: Summary and Analysis," CRS Report for Congress, July 12, 2004.

260–262, 263–265: Some details of the Bush-Blair summit in Crawford from British government's FCO diplomatic telex, 101727Z, April 2002; the January 29, 2010, testimony of Blair before the Chilcot Inquiry, as well as the November 30, 2009, testimony of David Manning and the January 12, 2010, testimony of Alastair Campbell before the same body. Also see the Campbell diaries; and George Bush, *Decision Points,* Crown, 2010.

260: Information about "Operation Defensive Shield" from "Report of the Secretary-General Prepared Pursuant to General Assembly Resolution ES-10/10," Tenth Emergency Special Session of the United Nations, agenda item 5, July 30, 2002.

261, 263: The weather in Crawford—and the ongoing dry spell—from the National Weather Service Daily Summary, the hourly observations of the station in McGregor, Texas. Also see the transcript of the Bush-Blair news conference of April 6, 2002; and Laura Bush, *Spoken from the Heart,* Scribner, 2010.

262–263: Some details about Dunham and his response to the Hamdi case from Tim McGlone, "Frank Dunham Didn't Expect to Be Representing Terrorist Suspects," *Virginian-Pilot,* December 2, 2002. The newspaper quotes from Dolan, "U.S.-Born Taliban Held in Norfolk," *Virginian-Pilot,* April 6, 2002. Also see Jerry Markon, "Frank W. Dunham Jr.: Defended Terrorism Suspects' Rights," *Washington Post,* November 5, 2006.

265–266: Some details of Ivins's swabbing activities from "AR 15-6 Investigation: Anthrax Contamination of Building 1425, USAMRIID," dated May 15, 2002; the May 10, 2002, sworn statement provided by Ivins to the army on a DA Form 2823; a May 9 statement provided by a lab official listed only as "KS"; another statement from that same day provided by a contract lab technician listed only as "KA"; a May 6, 2002, e-mail written by Lieutenant Colonel David Hoover from the Walter Reed Army Institute of Research; an FBI 302 of a March 31, 2005, interview with Ivins for file no. 279A-WF-222936-BEI53; another 302 for Ivins interviews of April 24, 2002, and April 25, 2002; an FBI Electronic Communication from the Washington Field Office Amerithrax-3 Team to Inspection headed "Amerithrax; Major Case 184," dated May 24, 2005, for case no. 279A-WF-222936-USAMRIID; and the Amerithrax report. Other details of procedures from USAMRIID Regulation 385-69, "Biosafety Level Four Containment Area Safety Survey," March 1, 1995.

266: Details of the infections at USAMIIRD from Major General Lester Martinez, "MEMORANDUM FOR Commander, USAMRIID; " May 16, 2002; DA Form 2823, Sworn Statement of Ivins, Bruce,' May 6, 2002; DA Form 2823, Sworn Statement of undisclosed witness, May 10, 2002; Sworn Statement of undisclosed witness, May 9, 2002; Sworn Statement of undisclosed witness, May 10, 2002 (Number 2); Lt. Col. William D. Palmer, Findings, AR 15-16 Investigation, May 15, 2002.; David Hoover, "Summary of Genotype Positive Culture, Dates and Locations," May 9, 2002; Unnamed author, Bacteriology division, USAMIIRD, "Memorandum for Record," April 19, 2002; "Memorandum for Record, Subject: Area Surveys of USAMRIID for *B. anthracis* Conducted in Bacteriology Division 15-17 Apr 02," April 19, 2002. Also see Amerithrax Report.

266–267: Details of Dunham's letter and the military's response from a declassified e-mail, with sender and recipient removed, with the subject line "Weekly Update on the Care of Amcit Detainee," sent April 20, 2002, at 12:31 P.M. Also see Tim McGlone, "Defender Wants Meeting with Locally Held Taliban," *Virginian-Pilot,* April 27, 2002.

Chapter 9

267–269: Some details of Fouda's encounter from Fouda, *Masterminds of Terror.*

269–271: Quotes from the April 22, 2002, hearing for Moussaoui from that day's transcript in *United States v. Moussaoui.* Some other details from Philip Shenon, "Terror Suspect Says He

Wants U.S. Destroyed," *New York Times,* April 23, 2002; "The Moussaoui Case," Online *News-Hour,* April 22, 2002; and Brooke A. Masters, "Moussaoui Wants to Be Own Lawyer," *Washington Post,* April 23, 2002. Also see "Transcript of Arraignment," *United States v. Moussaoui.*

271–277: Some details of Almalki's experiences in Syria from the Iacobucci Report, the O'Connor Report, the Toope Report, and Pither, *Dark Days.* Also see "Abdullah Almalki: Chronology," a document created by Almalki and his lawyer, Paul Copeland; and Clifford Krauss, "Evidence Grows That Canada Aided in Having Terrorism Suspects Interrogated in Syria," *New York Times,* September 17, 2005. Also see State Department August 4 telex.

277–280: Some details of the continued FBI interrogations of Zubaydah, and the troubles with the CIA, from FBI/OIG Report; the Soufan Senate testimony; Steven G. Bradbury, "Memorandum for John Rizzo, Acting General Counsel for the Central Intelligence Agency: Re: Application of 18 U.S.C. §§2340–2340A to the Combined Use of Certain Techniques in the Interrogation of High Value al Qaeda Detainees," May 10, 2005; CIA Office of the Inspector General, "Memorandum for the Record," July 17, 2003 (*CIA/OIG Memorandum for the Record*); "Background Paper on CIA's Combined Use of Interrogation Techniques," official, undated CIA document (*CIA Interrogation Background Paper*); International Committee of the Red Cross, *ICRC Report on the Treatment of Fourteen "High Value Detainees in CIA Custody,"* February 2007 (*ICRC Report*); David Johnston, "At a Secret Interrogation, Disputes Flared over Tactics," *New York Times,* September 10, 2006; Peter Finn and Joby Warrick, "Detainee's Harsh Treatment Foiled No Plots," *Washington Post,* March 29, 2009; and Michael Isikoff, "We Could Have Done This the Right Way," *Newsweek,* April 25, 2009. Also see CIA/OIG Report; and the CIA Medical Guidelines.

279, 284: Some details of the confrontation between Soufan, Mitchell, and the CIA interrogators from the FBI/OIG Report; the Soufan Senate testimony; Isikoff, April 25, 2009. Also see "Amended Petition for Relief Under the Detainee Treatment Act of 2005, and, in the Alternative, for Writ of Habeas Corpus," *Zayn al-Abidin Muhammad Husayn v. Robert M. Gates,* filed in Federal District Court for the District of Columbia, case no. 07-1520.

280: The threat against Zubaydah's mother was disclosed in Department of Justice Office of Professional Responsibility Report, "Investigation into the Office of Legal Counsel's Memoranda Concerning Issues Relating to the Central Intelligence Agency's Use of 'Enhanced Interrogation Techniques' on Suspected Terrorists," July 29, 2009 (*the OLC Report*).

280–281: The timing of the initial days of the CIA interrogation program is particularly difficult to specify, primarily because so many of the records contradict each other.

A narrative of the events released on April 22, 2009, by Senator John D. Rockefeller IV (*Rockefeller narrative*) states that the CIA proposed the use of waterboarding at a meeting in mid-May 2002. The same document states that the CIA began discussions about the CIA interrogation plan in April. According to the FBI'S OIG report and Ali Soufan's congressional testimony, the agent witnessed the preparation for the use of cramped confinement on Zubaydah. Soon afterward, in late May, he left the prison where Zubaydah was held.

However, according to the July 29, 2009, report by the Office of Professional Responsibility for the Justice Department involving the Office of Legal Counsel's memo regarding aggressive interrogation, other records suggest that the first contact between the CIA and the DOJ was April 11, 2002, and that waterboarding was proposed at that point.

These, then, are the contradictions: CIA records says that the waterboarding issue was raised in mid-May; DOJ e-mails indicate it was raised in mid-April; the DOJ records also show that the oral approval for the techniques was not provided until July; however, the tactics were being used by CIA officers in mid-May, and one of the interrogators told Soufan they had been approved by Gonzales. Recollections of those involved are also contradictory.

I have placed events in the order that records seem to suggest they occurred, but I am not dating any of them. All of them occurred within a five-week period, however.

Some details of the application of the tactics from an undated, classified CIA document labeled "Chronology: Counterterrorism Detention and Interrogation Activities." Also see undated file folder, National Security Council Information, containing the undated memo "Proposed Enhanced Interrogation Techniques."

282–283: Some information about the meeting in the Situation Room from a September 12, 2008, document headed "Responses of Condoleezza Rice," submitted to the Senate Armed Services Committee.

284–285: Some details of the use of boxes for interrogation—and the decision to abandon them—from the CIA/OIG Report; Steven G. Bradbury, "Memorandum for John Rizzo, Acting General Counsel for the Central Intelligence Agency; Bradbury memo for Rizzo, "Re: Application of United States Obligations Under Article 16 of the Convention Against Torture to Certain Techniques That May Be Used in the Interrogation of High Value al Qaeda Detainees," May 30, 2005.

285–291, 293–294: Some details of the detention, interrogation, and arrest of Padilla from FBI 302 of the May 8, 2002, interview of José Padilla for case no. 265A-NY-259391, by Special Agents Russell Fincher and Craig Donnachie; the July 11, 2007, testimony of Fincher in *United States v. Hassoun et al.,* 04-60001-CR-Cooke, in the Federal District Court for the Southern District of Florida; "Report and Recommendation" of Magistrate Judge Stephen T. Brown, dated September 5, 2006; "Jose Padilla's Motion to Suppress Physical Evidence and Issue Writs Ad Testificandum," filed in the same case in May, 2006; Complaint, *Jose Padilla v. John Yoo,* CV-08-0035, filed January 4, 2008, in Federal District Court for the Northern District of California; and Donna R. Newman, "The Jose Padilla Story," *New York Law Review,* 48:39 (2003). Also see James Risen and Philip Shenon, "U.S. Says It Halted Qaeda Plot to Use Radioactive Bomb," *New York Times,* June 11, 2002; Transcript, State Department Regular News Briefing, June 11, 2002; "Remarks of Alberto R. Gonzales, Counsel to the President," American Bar Association, February 24, 2004; and "Declaration of Michael H. Mobbs, Special Advisor to the Under Secretary of Defense for Policy," August 27, 2002.

292: Description of the courthouse from personal observation.

293: Some details of the video teleconference from the FBI/OIG Report and the Armed Services Report.

Chapter 10

299: Details of the hearings before Magistrate Miller and his rulings from Tim McGlone, "U.S. Must Explain Why Man Is Being Held in Brig," *Virginian-Pilot,* May 15, 2002; and docket sheet, United States District Court for the Eastern District of Virginia (Norfolk) for civil case no. 2:02-cv-00439, *Hamdi et al. v. Rumsfeld et al.*

299–300: Some details of the analysis, preparation, and writing of the OLC memos on the CIA interrogation techniques from the OLC Report; the Rockefeller narrative; Jay S. Bybee, "Memorandum for John Rizzo, Acting General Counsel for the Central Intelligence Agency: Interrogation of al Qaeda Operative," August 1, 2002; Steven G. Bradbury, "Memorandum for John Rizzo, Acting General Counsel for the Central Intelligence Agency: Re: Application of 18 U.S.C. §§2340-2340A to the Combined Use of Certain Techniques in the Interrogation of High Value al Qaeda Detainees," May 10, 2005; an undated document in the White House Counsel's Office headed "Summary of Advice on Interrogations: Advice to the Counsel for the President"; undated file folder, National Security Council Information, containing the undated memo "Proposed Enhanced Interrogation Techniques"; April 28, 2003, document with a fax cover sheet, but which was not sent by fax, from Yoo to Scott W. Muller, Office of the General Counsel with the CIA, "Legal Principles Applicable to CIA Detention and Interrogation of Captured Al Qa'ida Personnel." Also see Captain Nikiforos

Mathews, "Beyond Interrogations: An Analysis of the Protections under the Military Commissions Act of 2006 of Technical Classified Sources, Methods and Activities Employed in the Global War on Terror," *Military Law Review* 192 (Summer, 2007).

300: Jennifer Koester's name was first disclosed in a footnote to the OLC Report.

300–301: The quotes from the government's Hamdi filing about the training of al-Qaeda members from the original document, "Respondents' Objections to Magistrate Judge's May 20, 2002 Order Regarding Access," filed with United States District Court for the Eastern District of Virginia (Norfolk) in the original docket for the case *Hamdi et al. v. Rumsfeld et al.*, civil case no. 2:02-cv-348. Dunham quote from Matthew Roy, "Judge Blocks Access to Detainee," *Virginian-Pilot,* May 25, 2002. Information about the Manchester Manual from the original document.

301–302: Some details of the hearing before Doumar from Bill Geroux, "Judge: Allow Meeting, Fundamental Right, He Says," *Richmond Times-Dispatch,* May 30, 2002; and Sonja Barisic, "Judge Says American-Born Prisoner from Afghanistan Can Meet with Attorney," Associated Press, May 29, 2002.

304–305: Some of the details about the administration's distress over the Lindh and Moussaoui cases from Jess Bravin, "More Terror Suspects May Sit in Limbo," *Wall Street Journal,* August 8, 2002. Also see Jane Mayer, "Lost in the Jihad," *New Yorker,* March 10, 2003; and Karen Breslau, "Why Did John Walker Lindh Make a Deal?" *Newsweek,* July 16, 2002.

305: Some details of the preparation for the recommendation package on Padilla from a February 24, 2004, speech of Alberto Gonzales before the American Bar Association Standing Committee on Law and National Security.

305–306: Some details about the movement of Padilla and the failure to notify Newman from Newman, "The Jose Padilla Story," *New York Law Review* 48:39 (2003).

306: The fact that the White House originally assigned Wolfowitz, Thompson, and Mueller to announce the Padilla case was first reported by John King, "DOJ Announcement of Padilla Arrest Criticized," CNNPolitics, June 12, 2002.

306: Details of Ashcroft's preparation for the Padilla announcement from the original feed to MSNBC. Also see Laura Sullivan, "Ashcroft's Faith, Persona Inspire Split Sentiments," *Baltimore Sun,* July 8, 2002.

307: Dialogue from Ashcroft's press conference from an official transcript.

307: Some details of the chaos surrounding Ashcroft's statement from Judy Keen and Kevin Johnson, "Dramatic Ashcroft Reads Lines Not in Script," *USA Today,* June 13, 2002; "The Padilla Announcement Blame Game," ABC News, June 13, 2002; Amanda Ripley, "The Case of the Dirty Bomber," *Time,* June 16, 2002; John King, "DOJ Announcement of Padilla Arrest Criticized," CNNPolitics, June 12, 2002; Dick Meyer, "John Ashcroft: Minister of Fear," CBSNews.com, June 12, 2002; and Sullivan, "Ashcroft's Faith, Persona Inspire Split Sentiments."

307, 308: Reaction of the stock market to Ashcroft's speech, and then the Justice Department press conference, from trading data of that day collected by Bloomberg L.P.

308: Some details of the Wolfowitz-Thompson-Mueller press conference from a transcript of the event.

308–309: Some details of Fouda's last weeks before broadcast from Fouda and Fielding, *Masterminds of Terror.* Also see Mayer, *The Dark Side.*

309–310: Some details of the government's argument in the Hamdi appeal from *Brief for Respondents-Appelants, Hamdi et al. v. Rumsfeld et al.,* no. 02-6895, filed with the United States Court of Appeals for the Fourth Circuit, June 2002; and Jennifer Elsea, "Detention of American Citizens as Enemy Combatants," *CRS Report for Congress,* as updated, March 31, 2005.

312: Details of the Ralpho case from the ruling handed down by the Federal District Court for the District of Columbia in *Ralpho v. Bell,* 569 F.2d 607 (D.C.Cir.1977).

314–315: Details of the Bush Middle East speech from "Remarks on the Middle East: June 24, 2002," *Public Papers of the Presidents: George W. Bush, 2002,* Vol. 1, United States Government Printing Office, 2004.

316–317: Quotes of the arguments before the Fourth Circuit from an audio recording of the hearing. Certain other details from Michael Buettner, "Court Hears Arguments over America-Born Prisoner's Detention," Associated Press, June 25, 2002.

317–318: Some details of the officer's conversation with Hamdi from a June 27, 2002, e-mail from the naval brig, subject line "Re: Care of USCIT Detainee."

318–319: Details of the hearing before Judge Kollar-Kotelly from an official transcript.

319–320: The quote defining an emergency medical condition from *Emergency Medical Treatment and Labor Act,* Title 42, Chapter 7, Subchapter XVIII, Part E, Section 1395dd. The use of such a law for the interrogation analysis from the final draft of the OLC memo from Jay S. Bybee, "Memorandum for John Rizzo, Acting General Counsel for the Central Intelligence Agency: Interrogation of al Qaeda Operative," August 1, 2002.

320: The decision of the OLC to revise the wording of the health care statutes in the memos on the CIA interrogation techniques from the OLC Report. Yoo acknowledged the variation in language in his interview with the OLC when he stated: "I don't think that was an effort to try to change it. I think that was just an effort to sort of, you know, sort of paraphrase what the statutory language was."

320–321: Some details about the specific intent analysis from a July 13, 2002, faxed letter from Yoo to Rizzo, which contains no subject line; and the final draft of the OLC memo from Bybee, "Memorandum for John Rizzo." Details of the medical supervision requirements from "Draft OMS Guidelines on Medical and Psychological Support to Detainee Interrogations," a CIA document dated September 4, 2003 (*CIA Medical Guidelines*). Also see an undated document in CIA files, "Legal Principles Applicable to CIA Detention and Interrogation of Captured Al Qa'ida Personnel"; and an undated document in the White House Counsel's Office headed "Summary of Advice on Interrogations: Advice to the Counsel for the President."

321: Details of the officer's e-mail about Hamdi from the original document.

321–322: Details of the Ministry of Defense–Pentagon meetings and the written advice given by Jack Straw from Jack Straw, Memo to the Prime Minister, "Iraq: Contingency Planning, PM/02/042," July 8, 2002. Also see the January 21, 2011, testimony of Tony Blair before the Chilcot Inquiry.

322: Information about Zubaydah's answers on July 10 from a CIA intelligence report of that date that was read to the author; I am not certain if I was read the entire document. Also see a July 13, 2002, letter from Yoo to Rizzo that contains no subject line.

322–323: Details of the appeals court ruling from a copy of the decision.

Chapter 11

324: Some details about the Criminal Justice Information Services Division from Peter Meyer, "26306: FBI," *National Geographic,* May 2005.

324–325: Some details of the discovery of Qahtani at Guantanamo from the FBI/OIG Report; "Case Study: FBI," an undated report by Cross Match Technologies; and Tim Golden and Don Van Natta Jr., "U.S. Said to Overstate Value of Guantanamo Detainees," *New York Times,* June 21, 2004.

324: Details of Qahtani at the airport from the Meléndez-Pérez testimony.

325: Details of the actions by Mohammed Atta at the Orlando Airport from Charge Sheet, "Name of Accused: Khalid Sheikh Mohammed et al.," filed on MC Form 458 for the Office of Military Commissions, February 11, 2008.

325: Some details about the concerns about an attack in the summer of 2002 from the June 17, 2008, testimony of William Haynes II before the Senate Armed Services Committee in the hearings headed "Origins of Aggressive Interrogation Techniques." The concerns are referenced in Eric Lichtblau, "FBI Braces for Possibility of July 4 Attacks," *Los Angeles Times*, June 19, 2002. In addition to information coming from a foreign intelligence service—which was at first dismissed as unreliable—information provided by Zubaydah reinforced those fears.

326–327: Details of the guilty plea of Lindh from a transcript of the hearing. Also see Bob Franken and John King, " 'I Plead Guilty,' Taliban American Says," CNN.com/Law Center, posted July 17, 2002; and Jane Mayer, "Lost in the Jihad," *New Yorker*, March 10, 2003.

327–328: Haynes discussed the disappointment with the information coming out of Guantanamo in his June 17, 2008, congressional testimony. Some details of the discussions between Haynes, Shiffrin, and Baumgartner from Shiffrin and Baumgartner's June 17, 2008, testimony before the House Armed Services Committee in the hearings headed "Origins of Aggressive Interrogation Techniques." Also see "Inquiry into the Treatment of Detainees in U.S. Custody," *Report of the Committee on Armed Services, United States Senate*, November 20, 2008 (*Armed Services Report*).

328–330: Some details of the beliefs of the Blair officials from the July 23, 2002, entry in the Campbell diaries. Also see the January 29, 2010, testimony of Tony Blair and the November 30, 2009, testimony of David Manning before the Chilcot Inquiry.

329–330: The battles between Doumar and the administration from *Hamdi v. Rumsfeld*, civil action no. 2:02cv439, filed in Federal District Court for the Eastern District of Virginia, Norfolk Division: "Order" of July 18, 2002; "Order" of July 22, 2002; "Respondents' Response to, and Motion to Dissmiss, the Petition for a Writ of Habeas Corpus" of July 25, 2002; "Respondents' Memorandum in Support of Motion for Relief from This Court's Order Requiring the Government to File Federal Rule of Criminal Procedure 26(a)(1) Initial Disclosures" of July 24, 2002. Also see Tim McGlone, "Norfolk Judge Insists He Be Told Why Hamdi Is Being Held," *Virginian-Pilot*, July 19, 2002; McGlone, "Judge Slams Government for Ignoring Order in Hamdi Case," *Virginian-Pilot*, July 24, 2002; McGlone, "Government Lawyers Object to Order for Summary by Judge in Hamdi Case," *Virginian-Pilot*, July 23, 2002.

329–330: Details of the Mobbs declaration from the original document.

330–331: Some details of Baumgartner's work and his conversations with Ogrisseg from the June 17, 2008, testimony before the Senate Armed Services Committee in the hearings headed "Origins of Aggressive Interrogation Techniques." Also see *Armed Services Report*. Background about the air force's concerns regarding the use of SERE techniques from a November 2, 2002, memo from USAF Colonel Ronald E. Richburg entitled "Memo for UN and Multilateral Affairs Division (J-5), Joint Staff (Attn. CDR Lippold); Subject: Counter-Resistance Techniques."

331–332: Details of the Baumgartner memos and their attachments from the original documents.

332: Some details of the "carotid" interrogation from Central Intelligence Agency Inspector General Special Review, *Counterterrorism Detention and Interrogation Activities (September 2001–October 2003)*, 2003-7123-IG, May 7, 2004 (*CIA IG Report*).

332–333: Some details of the initial interrogation of Qahtani from the FBI/OIG Report; "Summary of Administrative Board Proceedings for ISN 063," before an administrative review board at Guantanamo; and a partially unclassified FBI 302 of a September 10, 2004, interview with an unnamed agent for file no. 297-HQ-A1327699-A. Also see Golden and Van Natta, *New York Times*, June 21, 2004.

333–334: Some details of the issues discussed in the OLC meetings from the OLC Report.

334: Quotes from the final draft of the OLC Memo from Jay S. Bybee, "Memorandum for John Rizzo, Acting General Counsel for the Central Intelligence Agency: Interrogation of al Qaeda Operative," August 1, 2002.

335–336: Details of Kollar-Kotelly's decision from "Memorandum Opinion," in *Shafiq Rasul v. George Walker Bush,* civil action no. 02-299; and *Fawiz Khalid Abdullah Fahad al-Odah v. United States,* civil action no. 02-828, filed July 31, 2002, in the United States District Court for the District of Columbia. Also see "Brief for Plaintiffs-Appellants," *al-Odah v. United States,* filed with the Federal Court of Appeals for the District of Columbia Circuit, case no. 02-5251. Details of the Wilner e-mail from the original document.

336: Details of the Wilner–*al-Odah* e-mails from the original documents.

337–338: Some details from the CIA interrogation of Zubaydah from CIA/OIG Report; the CIA Medical Guidelines; Steven G. Bradbury, "Memorandum for John Rizzo, Acting General Counsel for the Central Intelligence Agency: Re: Application of 18 U.S.C. §§2340–2340A to the Combined Use of Certain Techniques in the Interrogation of High Value al Qaeda Detainees," May 10, 2005; the CIA/OIG Memorandum for the Record; and the ICRC Report.

338–339: Some details of the concerns of Powell, the dialogue of his conversations with Bush, and the Franks presentation from Bob Woodward, *Plan of Attack,* Simon & Schuster, 2004. Also see Christopher Meyer, *DC Confidential,* Weidenfeld & Nicolson, 2005.

339–340: Some details of the Soufan interrogation with Qahtani from the FBI/OIG Report. Also see Golden and Van Natta, *New York Times,* June 21, 2004; and Michael Isikoff, "We Could Have Done This the Right Way," *Newsweek,* April 25, 2009.

340: Some details of the removal of the Princeton mailbox from the first Arredondo affidavit; Center for Counterproliferation Research, *Working Paper: Anthrax in America,* November 2002; and Leslie Koren and Wendy Ruderman, "Anthrax Spores Found in Mailbox," *Record* (Bergen County), August 13, 2002.

341: Details of the August 13 hearing before Judge Doumar from a transcript of the event. Also see Tom Jackman, "Judge Skewers U.S. Curbs on Detainee," *Washington Post,* August 14, 2002.

342: Quotes from Doumar's ruling out of the original document filed August 16, 2002.

342–343: Some details of the Pasquale D'Amuro meetings from the FBI/OIG Report. Also see Isikoff, *Newsweek,* April 25, 2009.

344–345: Some details of the outcomes from Zubaydah's cooperation from Steven G. Bradbury, "Memorandum for John Rizzo"; Bradbury memo for Rizzo, "Re: Application of United States Obligations Under Article 16 of the Convention Against Torture to Certain Techniques That May Be Used in the Interrogation of High Value al Qaeda Detainees," May 30, 2005. Also see CIA Directorate of Intelligence, *Detainee Reporting Pivotal for the War Against Al-Qa'ida* (Secret/Noforn), June 3, 2005 (*CI/DI Report*); a partially declassified CIA Report numbered C05403863 (*CIA Numbered Report*). Also see Chitra Ragavan, "A Hunt for the Pilot," *U.S. News & World Report,* March 30, 2003.

345–346: Some details of the Lady-Pironi dinner from a formal statement given by Pironi on April 14, 2006, to the Milan district attorney. Also see "Decree for the Application of Coercive Measures," filed with the Judge Presiding of Preliminary Investigations in Milan, filed under article 292 c.p.p., no. 10838/05.

346–347: Some details of the robbery at the Toko Elita Indah jewelry store from Wayne Turnbull, "Bali: Developing the Tactical Plan," *Monterey Institute of International Studies,* July 31, 2003; Matt Cianflone et al., "Anatomy of a Terrorist Attack," a report prepared for the Matthew B. Ridgway Center for International Security Studies at the University of Pittsburgh, Spring 2007; and Eric Ellis, "Allah's Assassins," *Bulletin,* March 5, 2003.

349: Some details of the torture of Almalki from the Iacobucci Report, the Toope Report; the O'Connor Report; Paul Copeland, "Abdullah Almalki: Chronology"; and Kenny Pither, *Dark Days,* Viking Canada, 2008.

350–351: Some details about Black's writing of his statement from the September 26, 2002, document, "Unclassified Testimony of Cofer Black," delivered to Congress's Joint Select Committee on Intelligence that was investigating the 9/11 attacks.

351: Some details of the detection of bin al-Shibh's call from Jason Burke, "Brutal Gun-Battle That Crushed 9/11 Terrorists," *Observer,* September 15, 2002; and Mayer, *The Dark Side.*

352–353: The description of the stage at the VFW convention from photographs of the event. Quotes from Cheney's speech from "Full Text of Dick Cheney's Speech," *Guardian,* August 27, 2002.

353: Some details of the White House reaction to Cheney's speech from Julian Borger, "White House in Disarray over Cheney Speech," *Guardian,* September 2, 2002; Borger, "Daggers Drawn in the House of Bush," *Guardian,* August 28, 2002; and Meyer, *DC Confidential.*

353–354: Some details of Meyer's reaction to the Cheney speech and the call from the Clinton official from Meyer, *DC Confidential.*

354–357: Some details of the September 8 meetings between Blair and Bush from the Campbell diaries. Also see the January 29, 2010, testimony of Tony Blair; the November 30, 2009, testimony of David Manning; and the January 10, 2010, testimony of Jack Straw before the Chilcot Inquiry.

358–359: Details of the intelligence report, "Iraq: Status of WMD Programs," from the original document. Rumsfeld's e-mail to Myers from the original document.

BOOK THREE

Chapter 12

361–363: Some details of the capture of bin al-Shibh from the December 8, 2006, memo from Harry B. Harris Jr., "The Joint Task Force at Guantanamo to the Commander for United States Southern Command in Miami; Subject: Combatant Status Review Tribunal Input and Recommendations for Continued Detention Under DOD Control (CD) for Guantanamo Detainee, ISN US9YM-010013DP (S)" (*Detainee Assessment, Ramzi bin al-Shibh*); Jason Burke, "Brutal Gun-Battle That Crushed 9/11 Terrorists," *Observer,* September 15, 2002; and Michael Elliott, "Reeling in al-Qaeda," *Time,* September 15, 2002. Also see K. Alan Kronstadt and Bruce Vaughn, "Terrorism in South Asia," CRS Report for Congress, August 31, 2005; Laila Bokhari, "Paths to Global Jihad," FFI Rapport, Norwegian Defence Research Establishment, March 15, 2006; Fouda and Fielding, *Masterminds of Terror;* "Top al-Qaeda Suspect Captured," BBC News, September 14, 2002; and "Binalshibh to Go to Third Country for Questioning," CNN World News, September 17, 2002.

363: Details of the plot against Musharraf from the September 19, 2002, testimony of Richard Armitage before the Joint Hearing of the House and Senate Committees on Intelligence, "Events Surrounding the Terrorist Attacks of September 11, 2001."

364: Details of the atmosphere and events surrounding Bush's presentation at the U.N. from a videotape of the event. The words of his speech from a transcript in *Public Papers of the President, George W. Bush 2001,* Vol 2. Also see Senate Select Committee on Intelligence, "Report on the U.S. Intelligence Community's Prewar Intelligence Assessments on Iraq," July 7, 2004 (*the Senate Prewar Report on Iraq*); and Steven Metz, Army War College, "Decisionmaking in Operation Iraqi Freedom: Removing Saddam Hussein by Force," Operation Iraqi Freedom Key Decisions Monograph Series, February 2010 (*War College monograph*).

365–366: The troubles with Bush's teleprompter, and the subsequent calls to allies, were first disclosed in the November 30, 2009, testimony of David Manning before the Iraq inquiry.

366: Some details of the Hans Blix WMD effort from Hans Blix, *Disarming Iraq,* Pantheon, 2004; Sharon A. Squassoni, "Iraq: U.N. Inspections for Weapons of Mass Destruction," Congressional Research Service, Code RL31671, October 7, 2003 (*CRS WMD Report*); the September 26, 2006, Blix testimony before the House Committee on Government Reform, Subcommittee on National Security, Emerging Threats and International Relations, in a hearing entitled "Nuclear Nonproliferation (*Blix House testimony*); and Blix's testimony of July 27, 2010, before the Chilcot Inquiry (*Blix Chilcot testimony.*)

366: Details of the Sabri letter from the original document.

367: Some details of MI5's intelligence about the plotting of nightclub attacks from the report of the Intelligence and Security Committee (British Parliament), "Inquiry into Intelligence Assessment and Advice Prior to the Terrorist Bombings on Bali 12 October 2002," December 2002 (*British Bali Report*).

367–368: Some details of the visit to Guantanamo by the lawyers from Colonel Terrence Farrell, "Trip Report—DOD General Counsel Visit to GTM," September 27, 2002; "Inquiry into the Treatment of Detainees in U.S. Custody," *Report of the Committee on Armed Services, United States Senate,* November 20, 2008 (*Armed Services Report*); Barton Gellman, *Angler: The Cheney Vice Presidency,* Penguin, 2008; and Jack Goldsmith, *The Terror Presidency: Law and Judgment Inside the Bush Administration,* W. W. Norton, 2007.

367: The former Jordanian military official's role in the Qahtani interrogation from partially declassified handwritten notes of a September 10, 2004, FBI interview of an unnamed agent.

368–370: Some details of the hearings before the Joint Committees on Intelligence from a videotape and transcript of the event.

370–371: Details of the call to Callaghan from the O'Connor Report and records of the communication.

371–372: Some details of the flight, arrival, and encounters of Arar from Department of Homeland Security, Office of the Inspector General, "The Removal of a Canadian Citizen to Syria," Report OIG-08-18 (*OIG Arar Report*), March 2008, and its addendum dated March 20, 2010 (*OIG Arar Report addendum*). Also see the O'Connor Report; the State Department August 4 telex; and the transcript of Arar's statement to the press on November 4, 2003 (*Arar press statement*). Additional details from Arar's testimony of October 18, 2007, before the Subcommittee on International Organizations, Human Rights and Oversight with the Committee on the Judiciary, October 18, 2007; *Maher Arar v. Ashcroft,* Case number CV-040249 DGT VVP, Complaint and Demand for Jury Trial, filed with the United States District Court for the Eastern District of New York and dated January 22, 2004 (*Arar complaint*); from the same case, "Plaintiff Maher Arar's Memorandum of Law in Opposition to Defendant's Motions to Dismiss," filed January 14, 2005; from the same case, ruling of the District Court; from an appeal of the same case, February 16, 2006; from an appeal of the same case, Brief for Defendant-Appellee Edward J. McElroy filed with the United States Court of Appeals for the Second Circuit, February 27, 2007 (*McElroy brief*). Also see Maher Arar: Chronology of Events, available at www.maherarar.ca.

372–373: Details of the INS meeting about Arar were first disclosed in the OIG Arar Report.

372: Details of Ziglar's selection and troubled tenure as INS commissioner from Joe Cantlupe, "Bush's INS Pick Might Be a Shoo-In, but It's Said He's a 'Blank Page' on Immigration Policy," *San Diego Union Tribune,* July 19, 2001; Dan Eggen and Cheryl W. Thompson, "Angry Bush Orders Probe of 'Inexcusable' INS Action," *Washington Post,* March 14, 2002; Edward Walsh, "INS Shakeup Follows Criticism of Terrorists' Visas," *Washington Post,* March 16, 2002; and Susan Schmidt and Cheryl W. Thompson, "Commissioner of INS to Resign," *Washington Post,* August 17, 2002.

373, 375: Some details of Monia Mazigh's dreams and anxieties about her husband's disappearance from Monia Mazigh, *Hope and Despair,* McClelland & Stewart, 2008.

373, 374, 375: Some details of Arar's interrogation from the OIG Arar Report; the O'Connor Report; and State Department August 4 telex. Also see the Arar press statement and Pither, *Dark Days.*

374: The fact that the Joint Terrorism Task Force decided that there was no reason for a continued investigation of Arar from the OIG Arar Report addendum.

374: Blackman's decision from the original document.

374: Arar's inmate number from his intake form at the prison.

375, 379–380: Some details of Almalki's experiences in Syria related to Arar from the Iacobucci Report; the O'Connor Report; and the Toope Report. Also see "Abdullah Almalki: Chronology," a document created by Almalki and his lawyer, Paul Copeland; and Clifford Krauss, "Evidence Grows That Canada Aided in Having Terrorism Suspects Interrogated in Syria," *New York Times,* September 17, 2005. Also see State Department August 4 telex.

375–376: Details of Witsch's concerns from the original document to Wirts, headed "Concern with JPRA Involvement with Operation Enduring Freedom Exploitation of Detained Unlawful Combatants"; Wirts's response from the Armed Services Report.

376–377: Some details of Arar's call to his mother-in-law, and her subsequent call to her daughter, from Mazigh, *Hope and Despair;* and from the Arar press statement.

377: Details of the British travel advisory from the original document. The comparisons with other advisories and the failure to properly represent the threat from the British Bali Report.

377–379: Some details of the Guantanamo meeting from "Counter Resistance Strategy Meeting Minutes," dated October 2, 2002, and the Armed Services Report.

380–381: Some details of the meeting between Girvan and Arar from the O'Connor Report and a case note prepared by Girvan on October 3, 2002.

381, 384–385: Details of the contact with Flewelling from his August 22, 2005, testimony before the Arar Commission headed by O'Connor; and the O'Connor Report.

382: The call between Thompson and Armitage was first disclosed in the OIG Arar Report addendum.

382–383: Some details of the duct tape incident from the FBI/OIG Report; and multiple statements taken in the Schmidt-Furlow Inquiry: the Dunlavey statement; a partially declassified statement of the Interrogation Control Element Chief for Joint Task Force 170th/JTF-GTMO, taken March 3, 2005; a partially declassified statement of the second FBI witness taken the same day; a partially declassified statement of a former staff judge advocate with 170th JTF-GTMO, taken on January 21, 2005, and March 17, 2005.

383–384: Details of the National Intelligence Estimate from the original document, "Key Judgments: Iraq's Continuing Program for Weapons of Mass Destruction," October 2002. Also see Senate Select Committee on Intelligence, "Report on the U.S. Intelligence Community's Prewar Intelligence Assessments on Iraq," July 7, 2004.

385: Some details of Arar's meeting with Oummih from the OIG Arar Report; Pither, *Dark Days;* and Mozigh, *Hope and Despair.* Also see the Arar press statement.

385–386: Some details of the communication between INS headquarters and the asylum officers, the failure to appropriately contact his lawyers, and the subsequent hearing from the OIG Arar Report.

387: Details of the American findings about Syrian torture from U.S. Department of State, *2001 Country Reports on Human Rights Practices,* March 4, 2002.

387–388: Some details of the interview between Fuller and Khadr from Fuller's testimony of January 20–21, 2009, from the military commission hearing of *United States v. Omar Khadr;* Omar El Akkad and Colin Freeze, "Cracks Show in FBI Agent's Testimony on Khadr," *Globe and Mail,* January 21, 2009.

389, 390: Some details of Arar's removal to Jordan from the O'Connor Report and the OIG Arar Report. Also see State Department August 4 telex; the Arar press statement; and Pither, *Dark Days.*

389–390: Evidence cited in the removal order from the original document.

Chapter 13

391–394: Some details about the meeting between Blair and Putin from the Campbell diaries; Agence France Presse, "Blair, in Russia, Hopes to Sway Putin on Iraq," October 11, 2002; Fraser Nelson, "Blair Woos Russia to Back War," *Scotsman,* October 11, 2002; "Putin's Doubts over Iraq Weapons Dossier," *Birmingham Post,* October 12, 2002; and Graem Wilson, "Blair Humiliated as Putin Refuses Support on Iraq," *Daily Mail,* October 12, 2002.

394–401, 413–415: Some details of the Bali bombing and the subsequent investigation from assorted investigative files of the Balinese Police Region, from October 13 through November 23; dossier, "Re: Amrozi," submitted by Brigadier General Herman Hidayat to Wayan Pasek Suartha, January 6, 2003; Australian Federal Police, "Operation Alliance, Investigating the Bali Bombings of 12 October 2002," undated report. Also see Matt Cianflone et al., "Anatomy of a Terrorist Attack," Matthew B. Ridgway Center for International Security Studies; FBI 302 of interview of Mohammed Mansour Jabarah, August 21, 2002; Intelligence and Security Committee, "Inquiry into Intelligence, Assessments and Advice Prior to the Terrorist Bombings on Bali 12 October 2002," presented to Parliament by the Prime Minister, December 2002; Commonwealth of Australia, Information and Research Services for Parliament, "The Bali Bombing: What It Means for Indonesia," Current Issues Brief no. 4, November 4, 2002; Australian Department of Parliamentary Library, Research Note, "The Amrozi Bali Bombing Case: Is Indonesia's Anti-terrorism Law Unconstitutional?" no. 14, October 7, 2003; Nasir Abas, "Exposing Jemaah Islamiyah: Revelations of a Former JI Member," July 2005; Aratnan School of International Studies, "October 2002 Bali Bombings: A Case Study in Terrorist Financing," undated; Keith Moor, "Murder in Bali," *Herald Sun* (Melbourne), October 2, 2003; State Department Cable, "Ref: A) Jakarta 9857 B) Jakarta 10534 C) TD 314/47990-03," September 16, 2003; "Allah's Assassins," *Bulletin,* March 5, 2003; and Wayne Miller and Darren Goodsir, "The Laughing Bali Bomber Tells All," *Age,* November 14, 2002.

396: The identity of the Japanese couple from "Indonesia: Pain and Anger Linger in Bali 5 Years after Deadly Bombings," *South China Post,* October 13, 2007.

401: Details of the Australian reaction to the Bali bombings from press release, the Australian Greens, "Inexcusable Hate Behind Bali Horror," October 13, 2002; transcript of press conference by Prime Minister John Howard, October 13, 2002. Also see John Kerin and Matt Price, "Iraq and Bombers Linked," *Australian,* October 23, 2002.

401–402: Bush's statements from transcripts of the October 13 speeches in the *Public Papers of the President, George W. Bush 2001,* Vol 2. Also see Bob Dean, "President Suggests Bali Bombing Is Linked to Attacks in Kuwait; Bush Warns of Iraq Threat," *Austin American Statesman,* October 15, 2002.

402: The debate in Parliament from a transcript of Prime Minister's Questions session on October 15, 2002; and a video of the event. Also see Patrick Wintour, "Bali Bombing: Blair Denies That Iraq Focus Is Misguided," *Guardian,* October 15, 2002.

403–404: Information about the Phifer, Beaver, and Dunlavey memos from the original documents.

404–405: Some details about the videoconference from the FBI/OIG Report and the Armed Services Report. Also see December 17, 2002, memo from Timothy James, Special Agent in Charge, Criminal Investigative Task Force Guantanamo, to JTF-GTMO/J2, headed "Subject: JTF GTMO 'SERE' INTERROGATION SOP DTD 10 Dec 02."

405–407: Some details of the Lady-D'Ambrosio meeting from D'Ambrosio's formal statements to the Milan district attorney. Also see "Decree for the Application of Coercive Measures," filed with the Judge Presiding of Preliminary Investigations in Milan, filed under article 292 c.p.p., no. 10838/05.

407–408: Statements from Fallon's e-mail from the original document, "Re: Counter Resistance Strategy Meeting Minutes," October 28, 2002.

408–409: Some details of the appeals court hearing from a transcript of the event. Also see Katharine Q. Seelye, "Appeals Court Again Hears Case of American Held Without Charges or Counsel," *New York Times,* October 29, 2002; Tim McGlone, "Northfolk Detainee's Rights Are Concern of Appeals Court," *Virginian-Pilot,* October 29, 2002; and Tom Jackman, "Judges Wary of Interference in Hamdi Case," *Washington Post,* October 29, 2002.

409–411: Some details of Blix's visit to the White House from Hans Blix, *Disarming Iraq,* Pantheon, 2008.

411–412: Some details of the Lady-Mancini meeting from D'Ambrosio's formal statements to the Milan district attorney. Also see "Decree for the Application of Coercive Measures."

412–413: Details about Ivins's writings from the original documents.

415–417: Some details about the preparation of plans to interrogate Qahtani from the Armed Services Report; the Schmidt-Furlow Report; and the Schmidt testimony. Those spell out the different interpretations of what was communicated down the line by Rumsfeld. Also see memo of John F. Rankin to Captain Weis, "Subj: Physical and Psychological Pressures During Interrogation," January 3, 2003. Also see "Executive Summary," the Church Report re: Detainee Operations, March 2005.

417–419: Some details of the November 14 meeting between Powell and Graham from a telex from the American embassy in Ottawa to the secretary of state dated that same day and captioned "Secretary's November 14 meeting with Canadian Foreign Minister Bill Graham"; a Canadian government e-mail dated December 2, 2003, headed "Re: conversation between Secretary of State Colin Powell and Minister Graham"; the May 30, 2005, testimony of Graham before the Arar Commission; a June 16, 2005, document compiled for the Arar Commission headed "RCMP: Chronology of Public Information and Events"; the June 2, 2005, testimony of Graham before the Arar Commission; and the O'Connor Report. Also see "U.S. Asks What Canada Could Offer Iraq Attack," *North Bay Nugget* (Ontario), November 19, 2002; and Jim Fox, "U.S. Wants Canadian Cooperation," *St. Petersburg Times,* November 17, 2002.

419–420: Some details of the debate over the Qahtani interrogation plan from the FBI/OIG Report and the Armed Services Report.

420–421: Some details of the discussion in Prague between Graham and Powell in the Czech Republic from the June 2, 2005, testimony of Graham before the Arar Commission; and the O'Connor Report.

421–422: Some details of the meeting between Bush and Blair from a contemporaneous memo summarizing the discussions that was read to the author and the Campbell diaries.

422–426, 433–434, 436–437, 439–442: Some details of Qahtani's interrogations from "Interrogation Log, Detainee 063," recording questioning from November 23, 2002, through January 11, 2003; "Summary of Administrative Review Board Proceedings for ISN 063," conducted by an administrative review board at Guantanamo; a handwritten letter from Qahtani; and "Summarized Witness Statement of Major General Geoffrey D. Miller," taken on March 18, 2005, as part of the Schmidt-Furlow investigation. Also see Bob Woodward, "Detainee Tortured, Says U.S. Official," *Washington Post,* January 14, 2009.

426–427: Some details of the D'Ambrosio-Pignero meeting from D'Ambrosio's formal statements to the Milan district attorney. Also see "Decree for the Application of Coercive Measures."

427–429: Some details about the memo discussion and Rumsfeld's reaction, including the note he wrote, from the memo dated November 27, 2002, by William J. Haynes for the secretary of defense, headed "Action Memo," with the subject line "Counter-Resistance Techniques."

Chapter 14

430–433, 443: Some details about Mora's discovery of the interrogation issues from a memo stamped July 7, 2004, and written by Mora, headed "Memorandum for Inspector General, Department of the Navy; Subject: Statement for the Record: Office of General Counsel Involvement in Interrogation Issues" (*Mora memo*). The existence of the memo was first disclosed by Jane Mayer, "The Memo: How an Internal Effort to Ban the Abuse and Torture of Detainees Was Thwarted," *New Yorker*, February 27, 2006.

434–436: Some details of Mora's meeting with Morello, and his impression of the Beaver analysis, from the Mora memo and the Beaver analysis.

437–439, 444–445, 446–447, 450–451, 453, 475–476: Some details of Mora's meetings and contacts with Haynes from the Mora memo.

442–443: Some details of Leso's experiences and interactions with James were first reported in Larry C. James, *Fixing Hell: An Army Psychologist Confronts Abu Ghraib*, Grand Central Publishing, 2008.

445: Details of the Blix-ElBaradei presentations before the U.N. from a transcript of the event.

447–449: Some details of the interrogation experience from a partially declassified FBI 302, reflecting a September 7, 2004, interview with an unnamed agent for case file 297-HQ-1327669-A; handwritten notes of an FBI interview with an unidentified witness from an interview conducted on September 2, 2004; a partially declassified e-mail from an unidentified sender to an unidentified recipient, dated July 9, 2004, with subject line "GTMO"; and James, *Fixing Hell.*

451–453: Some details of Blair's meeting with his senior military officers and defense minister from "Record of the Meeting Between the Prime Minister and Chiefs of Staff to Discuss Op Telic: 15 Jan 03," MA/CIO, "Briefing to Prime Minister by CDS and DCJO (Ops)," January 15, 2003; Matthew Rycroft, letter headed "Iraq: Military Planning," January 15, 2003; and official record, "Brief to PM: 1715 Wed 15 Jan 03."

454–455: Some details of the meeting with Chirac from the Australian Iraq Report; Thomas Koenig and Katie MacMillan, Department of Social Sciences, Loughborough University, "The UN Weapons' Inspector Reports on Iraq in the US-American, British, and German Press," undated (*Loughborough Report*); and Blix, *Disarming Iraq.*

455: The order to set up the working group, and the details of how it should operate, were communicated by Rumsfeld to Haynes in "Memorandum for the General Counsel of the Department of Defense, Subject: Detainee Interrogations," dated January 15, 2003.

Chapter 15

460–461: Some details of Römer's role from *"George W. Bush et le Code Ezéchiel," Allez Savoir: Le magazine de l'Université de Lausanne* 39 (September 2007).

460: Information about "Gog and Magog" from Daniel Kretzmann, "Understanding the War of Gog and Magog," July 29, 2009; Sverre Bøe, *Gog and Magog: Ezekiel 38–39 as Pre-text for Revelation 19, 17–21 and 20, 7–10*, Mohr Siebeck, 2001; Book of Revelation, 20:1–6; Book of Ezekiel, 38–39; Douglas Berner, *The Silence Is Broken! God Hooks Ezekiel's Gog & Magog*, www.Lulu.com (self-published) 2006.

460: Reagan made his comment about Gog and Magog in 1971, as governor of California. The full quote is:

Ezekiel tells us that Gog, the nation that will lead all of the other powers of darkness against Israel, will come out of the north. Biblical scholars have been saying for generations that Gog must be Russia. What other powerful nation is to the north of Israel? None. But it didn't seem to make sense before the Russian revolution, when Russia was a Christian country. Now it does, now that Russia has become Communistic and atheistic, now that Russia has set itself against God. Now it fits the description of Gog perfectly.

461: Some details of the event at Versailles and the statements by Chirac and Schroeder from Dr. Daniela Schwarzer, *"France-Allemange: Si loin, si proche?"* Stifftung Wissenschaft und Politik, Berlin, December 2008; Lutz Rüstow et al., *"Festschrift zum 50-jährigen Jubiläum des Carolus-Magnus-Kreises 1954–2004,"* 2004; Jon Henley, "Europe's Big Two Unite for Versailles Lovefest: France and Germany Celebrate 40 Years Since Reconciliation Treaty," *Guardian,* January 23, 2003; Philip Delves Broughton, "France and Germany Are Friends Reunited: The 40th Anniversary of the Elysee Treaty Is Marked by Bonhomie and Back-slapping," *Independent,* January 23, 2003; John Leicester, "France, Germany Counter U.S. War Talk, Call for Peaceful Solution on Iraq," Associated Press, January 23, 2003. Some behind-the-scenes details of Chirac's opposition from a telex from the British embassy in France to David Manning headed "France: Iraq; From: Paris," and dated March 3, 2003; also see a March 13, 2003, letter from Peter Ricketts from Britain's Foreign and Commonwealth Office to Ambassador Sir John Holmes, headed "France and Iraq."

461–462: Bush's statements from a transcript in *Public Papers of the President, George W. Bush 2003,* Vol. 1, Government Printing Office.

462–463: Details of the Rumsfeld press conference from a transcript of the event. Details of the global response from John Hooper and Ian Black, "Anger at Rumsfeld Attack on 'Old Europe,' " *Guardian,* January 24, 2003; Lorne Cook, "France, Germany Fume over Rumsfeld's 'Old Europe' Remark," Agence France Presse, January 23, 2003; and Matthew Lee, "US Diplomats Cringe at Rumsfeld's 'Old Europe' Comment," Agence France Presse, January 23, 2003.

463: The final version of the Yoo memo, headed "Memorandum for William J. Haynes II, General Counsel of the Department of Defense; Re: Military Interrogation of Alien Unlawful Combatants Held Outside the United States," was dated March 14, 2003.

466: Details of the Blair note from excerpts reviewed by the author.

467–468: Blair and Frost's statements from a transcript of *BBC Breakfast with Frost,* in the program "Prime Minister Prepares for War," first broadcast on January 26, 2003.

468: Details of the confidential Goldsmith memo from Goldsmith, "Iraq: Interpretation of Resolution 1441," January 3, 2003, draft as handed to Blair on January 14, 2003. Blair spoke of his anxiety about the Goldsmith memo, and his decision to keep it secret, in his January 21, 2011, testimony before the Chilcot Inquiry.

468–469: The statements before the Security Council from Blix and ElBaradei's prepared statements of January 25, 2003. Also see Parliament of the Commonwealth of Australia, Parliamentary Joint Committee on ASIO, ASIS and DSD, "Intelligence on Iraq's Weapons of Mass Destruction," December 2003 (*Australian WMD Report*); CRS WMD Report; and Research Paper 03/22, "Iraq: Developments Since UN Security Council Resolution 1441," March 13, 2003 (*House of Commons Iraq Paper*).

470–472: Some details of the Bush-Blair meeting from contemporaneous notes taken during the discussion. Some details of the staff discussions from the Campbell diaries.

472–473: Some details about the Bush-Blair press conference from a transcript of the event.

473–474: Details of the Lovelace and Witsch e-mails from the original documents.

474–475: Some details about the draft working group report from "Working Group Report, Detainee Interrogations in the Global War on Terrorism: Assessment of Legal, Historical, Policy, and Operational Consideration," April 4, 2003; also see the same publication, but the earlier draft from March 6, 2003; the Armed Services Report; and the Mora memo. Also see "Memo from Air Force Office of the Judge Advocate General for the SAF/GC, Final Report and Recommendations of the Working Group to Assess the Legal, Policy and Operational Issues Relating to Interrogation of Detainees Held by the Armed Forces in the War on Terror," February 5, 2003.

475: Some details about the COBRA meeting from the Campbell diaries.

476–478: Some details of the Rice-Blix meeting from Blix, *Disarming Iraq;* Commonwealth of Australia, Information and Research Services for Parliament, " 'Disarming' Iraq Under International Law—February 2003 Update," Brief no. 16 2002-03 (*Australian Iraq Report*); the Loughborough Report.

477: The failure of the American intelligence agencies to share information with Blix from Senate Select Committee on Intelligence, "Report on the U.S. Intelligence Community's Prewar Intelligence Assessments on Iraq," July 7, 2004.

477–479, 480: Some details of the Abu Omar abduction from a formal statement given by Pironi on April 14, 2006, to the Milan district attorney. Also see "Decree for the Application of Coercive Measures," filed with the Judge Presiding of Preliminary Investigations in Milan, filed under article 292 c.p.p., no. 10838/05. Also see November 19, 2007, PowerPoint presented to European Parliament by Armando Spataro, Deputy Chief Prosecutor of Milan, "The Kidnapping of Nasr Osama Mostafa Hassan Alias Abu Omar."

479: Details of the Blix-ElBaradei presentation before the U.N. on February 12 from a transcript of the event. Also see the Australian WMD Report; the CRS WMD Report; and the Loughborough Report. Also see Ministry of Foreign Affairs of the Republic of Latvia, "Statement by the Foreign Secretary, Jack Straw, to the United Nations Security Council, New York, Friday 14 2003"; and Blix, *Disarming Iraq.*

480–481: Some details about the Blair-Blix conversation from Blair's testimony of January 21, 2011, and Blix's testimony of July 27, 2010, before the Chilcot Inquiry. Also see "Prime Minister's Statement of 25 February 2003 to the House of Commons"; the Australian WMD Report; and the CRS WMD Report.

Chapter 16

482–484: Some details of the capture and initial interrogation of KSM from "Verbatim Transcript of Combatant Status Review Tribunal, Hearing for ISN 10024," March 10, 2007 (*KSM hearing*); Indictment, *United States v. Khalid Sheikh Mohammed et al.,* (S14) 93 CR 180, filed in Federal District Court in Manhattan; KSM Charge Sheet; Detainee Assessment of KSM; Nick Fielding and Christina Lamb, "Natural Born Killer," *Sunday Times* (London), March 9, 2003; Oliver Burkeman, "How Mobile Phones and an £18m Bribe Trapped 9/11 Mastermind," *Guardian,* March 11, 2003; Rohan Gunaratna, "Khalid Sheikh Mohammed," *Playboy,* June 1, 2005.

484–485: The German, French, and Russian statement from an English translation of a copy of the original document.

485: Some details of the Blair government reaction from the January 21, 2010, testimony of Jack Straw and the January 29, 2010, testimony of Blair before the Chilcot Inquiry. Also see the Campbell diaries.

485–486: Details of the working group report from the original document.

486: Some details about the discussion of resignation by Blair from the Campbell diaries.

486–487: Some details of the flight taking Khalid Sheikh Mohammed to Poland from the Marty Report and the U.N. Detention Report. Some information about his treatment on arrival from undated report, "Background Paper on CIA's Combined Use of Interrogation Techniques."

487: While the Polish government has, at times, denied the existence of a secret prison inside the country, that statement has been proved false. For example, the head of Polish intelligence for 2002–2003, Zbigniew Siemiatkowski, confirmed the landing of CIA flights and the use of secret prisons in Adam Krzykowski, *"Politycy Przecza," Rzeczpospolita*, April 15, 2009. Also see Edyta Zemia and Mariusz Kowalewski, *"Polski wywiad w sluzbie CIA," Rzeczpospolita*, April 15, 2009; the December 17, 2010, letter from Danuta Przywara, president, Helsinska Fundacja Praw Czlowieka, to Andrzej Seremet from the Public Prosecutor's Office in Warsaw. Also see the application in *al-Nashiri v. Poland*, filed under Article 34 of the European Convention on Human Rights and Rules 45 and 47 of the Rules of the Court with the Cour Européenne des Droits de l'Homme, May 6, 2011; and Central Intelligence Agency, "Memo to DOJ Command Center—Background Paper on CIA's Combined Use of Interrogation Techniques," December 2004 (*CIA Rendition Background Paper*).

487–488: Some details of the issues surrounding the Blix-ElBaradei report from the Australian WMD Report and the CRS WMD Report. Also see House of Commons Iraq Paper.

488: Details of the State Department fact sheet from U.S. Department of State, "Fact Sheet on Unresolved Disarmament Issues," March 10, 2003; details of other attacks on Blix from Steven R. Weisman, "U.S. Says Blix Played Down Details of Banned Weapons," *New York Times*, March 11, 2003; John Donnelly and Elizabeth Neuffer, "U.S. Questions Blix Report; Omitted Examples of Banned Weapons," *Boston Globe*, March 11, 2003. Cheney's statements from a transcript of his March 16, 2003, appearance on *Meet the Press*. Also see the War College Monograph.

489: Some details of Goldsmith's partial—then full—reversal from David Brummell, "Iraq: Legal Basis for the Use of Force—Note of Discussion with Attorney General," March 13, 2003; Brummell letter to Matthew Rycroft at 10 Downing Street, "Iraq," March 14, 2003; Goldsmith's schedule book for March 13, 2003; Goldsmith, "Iraq: Interpretation of Resolution 1441," February 12, 2003; Simon McDonald, "Note for the Record; Iraq: Meeting with Attorney General," March 17, 2003; Jack Straw letter to Goldsmith headed "Iraq: Second Resolution," February 6, 2003; Chilcot Inquiry: Memorandum by the Right Honorable Jack Straw, MP, January 2010; and January 21, 2010, testimony of Straw and January 29, 2010, testimony of Blair before the Chilcot Inquiry.

489–490: Some details of the annual awards ceremony that honored Ivins from "Western Maryland in Brief," Associated Press, March 18, 2003; and photographs from the event.

490–491: Some details of the questioning techniques used on Sheikh Mohammed from CIA/OIG Report; the CIA Medical Guidelines; Steven G. Bradbury, "Memorandum for John Rizzo, Acting General Counsel for the Central Intelligence Agency: Re: Application of 18 U.S.C. §§2340-2340A to the Combined Use of Certain Techniques in the Interrogation of High Value al Qaeda Detainees," May 10, 2005; Bradbury memo for Rizzo, "Re: Application of United States Obligations Under Article 16 of the Convention Against Torture to Certain Techniques That May Be Used in the Interrogation of High Value al Qaeda Detainees," May 30, 2005; CIA/OIG Memorandum for the Record; CIA Numbered Report; CIA Interrogation Background Paper; and ICRC Report.

490–491: Details of Deuce Martinez's interrogation of and relationship with Khalid Sheikh Mohammed were first reported by Scott Shane, "Inside a 9/11 Mastermind's Interrogation," *New York Times*, June 22, 2008.

491–493: Some details of the information obtained from Sheikh Mohammed from CI/DI Report; partial version, CIA Directorate of Intelligence, "Khalid Sheikh Mohammed: Preeminent Source on al Qaeda," July 13, 2004; Bradbury memo for Rizzo, "Re: Application of United States Obligations Under Article 16 of the Convention Against Torture to Certain

Techniques That May Be Used in the Interrogation of High Value al Qaeda Detainees"; undated investigative summary for Mohd Farik bin Amin, alias Zubair; undated investigative summary for Riduan Isamuddin, alias Hambali; and "Classified Statement for the Record," General Michael V. Hayden, given April 17, 2007, before the Senate Select Committee on Intelligence. Also see CIA/OIG Memorandum for the Record.

493–495: Some details of the Azores meeting from contemporaneous notes of the events. Also see Raymond W. Copson, Congressional Research Service, "Iraq War: Background and Issues Overview," April 22, 2003; "Report in Connection with Presidential Determination Under Public Law 107–243"; the Campbell diaries; and Bush, *Decision Points.*

495: Bush's conversation with Campbell from the Campbell diaries.

495: Details of the press conference from a transcript of the event. Also see Bush, *Decision Points.*

496–497: Some details of the parliamentary debate from the official transcript headed "Iraq: 18 March 2003: House of Commons Debates."

497–500: Some details of the final hours before Bush's decision to strike Dora Farms from notes of a background briefing provided by a senior White House official, March 20, 2003; Bill Adair, "Last Hours Show Bush's Resolve," *St. Petersburg Times,* March 21, 2003; Rob Hotakainen, "Bush's Command: 'Let's Go,' " *Star Tribune* (Minneapolis), March 21, 2003.

501: Some details of the minutes before Bush's speech from a video feed of the event. Bush's statements from a transcript in *Public Papers of the Presidents of the United States: George W. Bush, 2003,* Book 1, Office of the Federal Register, United States National Archives and Records, 2006 (*Bush Public Papers, 2003, Book 1*).

Epilogue

503–504, 508: Some details of the second anniversary ceremony from "Ground Zero Readings," Associated Press, September 11, 2003; Ruth Padawer, "Dad Missing from Picture for 9/11 Victim's Son," *Record,* June 16, 2002; video summary, NBC News; Michael Powell and Dale Russakoff, "In New York, Roll of Names Is Part of Quiet Remembrance," *Washington Post,* September 12, 2003; "9/11 Commemorated at Ground Zero," *Life,* September 11, 2003; Andrea Elliott, "One More Chance to Say to Dad, 'I Love You,' " *New York Times,* September 12, 2003.

504: Bush's poll numbers from Richard Benedetto, "Bush's Approval Rating Plummets," *USA Today,* September 12, 2003.

504–505: Details of the reaction to the report about Blair from Glenn Frankel, "Panel Warned Blair of War Risk," *Washington Post,* September 12, 2003. Details of Blair's troubles and decision to step down from Sebastian Borger, "The End of the Tony Show," *Der Spiegel,* May 10, 2007; and Neal Lawson, "A Decade of Blair Has Left the Labour Party on Its Knees," *Guardian,* April 19, 2007.

505: Statistics regarding Bush's mention of bin Laden, Saddam, al-Qaeda, Afghanistan, and Iraq from an analysis of Bush Public Papers, 2003, Book 1.

505: Tenet made his accusation against Cheney in *At the Center of the Storm.*

505: Gallup poll on Cheney was conducted January 9–11, 2009.

505: Powell's call for the CIA and Pentagon to explain why they had not told him of Curveball's unreliability from Ed Pilkington, "Colin Powell Demands Answers over Curveball's WMD Lies," *Guardian,* February 16, 2011.

506: Wolfowitz's troubles at the World Bank stemming from his relationship with Shaha Ali Riza from Steven R. Weisman, "Wolfowitz Resigns, Ending Long Fight at World Bank," *New York Times,* May 18, 2007.

506: Jack Goldsmith described his hiring and subsequent withdrawal of the Yoo memos in *The Terror Presidency.*

506: Background of the OLC Report from the OLC Report.

507: The quote from Yoo's interview was cited in the OLC Report.

507–508: Goldsmith quotes from *The Terror Presidency.*

509: Details of Syria's level of cooperation from the November 9, 2005, testimony of Flynt Leverett, senior analyst with the CIA and senior director of Middle East Affairs at the NSC during the Bush administration, before the Arar Commission.

510: Quotes of Harper's letter of apology from the original document.

510: Graham disclosed Powell's complaint about having been misled in his May 30, 2005, testimony before the Arar Commission.

510–511: Details of the release of Almalki and El-Maati from the Iacobucci Report and the O'Connor Report.

511: The House of Commons vote to offer an apology and compensation to Almalki and El-Maati from "Bungling 'Terror' Cases," *Star,* June 21, 2009.

511: Details of the release of Abu Omar, and the convictions of Lady and the other CIA officers, from Rachel Donadio, "Italy Convicts 23 Americans, Most Working for C.I.A., of Abducting Muslim Cleric," *New York Times,* November 5, 2009.

511–513: The Supreme Court ruling for Rasul came in *Rasul v. Bush,* no. 03-334, decided June 28, 2004. For Hamdi, in *Hamdi v. Rumsfeld,* no. 03-6696, decided June 28, 2004. For Hamdan, in *Hamdan v. Rumsfeld,* no. 05-184, decided June 29, 2006. For the Algerian Six, in *Boumediene v. Bush,* no. 06-1195, decided June 12, 2008.

512: Details of the Military Commissions Act from Public Law 109-366, October 17, 2006, Military Commissions Act of 2006.

512: The results of the lie-detector test conducted on Ahmed and Rasul's decision not to participate from a videotape of the documentary *Lie Lab,* broadcast June 2, 2007.

512–513: The sentence of Hamdan in his military commission trial from a transcript of the sentencing hearing.

513: The changes in the case against the Algerian Six from Boudella CSRT Decision Report, Exhibits D(a) to D(jj), undated. Also see Craig Whitlock, "At Guantanamo, Caught in a Legal Trap," *Washington Post,* August 21, 2006.

513: The quote of Leon's ruling from Memorandum Order, *Boumediene v. Bush,* civil case no. 04-1166, in the United States District Court for the District of Columbia, November 20, 2008.

513: Details of the advancement in detecting anthrax mutations from press briefing by background official at the Justice Department, August 18, 2008; the Amerithrax Report; and the Anthrax Panel Report. Also see National Research Council of the National Academies of Sciences Independent Report Conducted for the FBI, "Review of the Scientific Approaches Used During the FBI's Investigation of the 2001 Anthrax Letters," prepublication copy, 2011.

513–514: Details of the FBI review of Ivins's decontamination effort in April 2002 from FBI Electronic Communication from Washington Field Office Amerithrax-3, "Title: Amerithrax; Major Case 184," May 24, 2005. Also see Amerithrax Report and Anthrax Panel Report.

514: Information about the codes from the Amerithrax Report and the Anthrax Panel Report. Some understanding of such codes can be learned from Douglas Hofstadter's astonishing book *Gödel, Escher, Bach: An Eternal Golden Braid,* Basic Books, 1979.

514: Findings in the search of Ivins's garbage from the Anthrax Panel Report.

515: Ivins's statements on his YouTube account from archived copies of the writings. Also see the Anthrax Panel Report; the Amerithrax Report; and "Application and Affidavit Search Warrant," signed by FBI special agent Marlo Arredondo, August 2, 2008, case no. 08-489-M-01, filed in the Federal District Court for the District of Columbia (*second Arredondo affidavit*).

515–517: Some details of Ivins's ravings during his group therapy session from Officer Reed Preece, Frederick Police Department, "Petition for Emergency Evaluation"; Protective Order filed by Jean C. Duley on July 24, 2008, from the FPD Victims' Services Unit; Loumis Gene Alston, Frederick Police Department, "Supplemental Report," OCA 2008044096, September 9, 2008. Also see the Anthrax Panel Report; the second Arredondo affidavit; and Application and Affidavit for Search Warrant, signed by Marlo Arredondo, August 7, 2008, case no. 08-497-M-01, filed in the Federal District Court for the District of Columbia (*third Arredondo affidavit*).

517: The list of items found inside Ivins's house from the Amerithrax Report.

517: Details of Ivins's purchases at Giant Eagle from the purchase log at the drugstore for July 24, 2008; and Alston, "Supplemental Report," August 13, 2008, entry, September 9, 2008.

517: Details of Ivins's trip to the library from the second and third Arredondo affidavits.

517: Quotes from the note left for Ivins by his wife, his reply, and her discovery of him unconscious from Alston, "Supplemental Report," entry of August 19, 2008.

518: Details of Ivins's emergency treatment and subsequent death from EMS Patient Care Report, Ambulance 18, Notes of Paramedic Jonathan Newman, July 27, 2008; Medical records from Frederick Memorial Hospital, first entry by Brooke Geranis at 1:55 A.M. on July 27, 2008. Also see Alston, "Supplemental Report," September 9, 2008; and Arredondo affidavits.

519–520: Some details of the conversation between Piro and Saddam from U.S. Department of Justice, Federal Bureau of Investigation, Baghdad Operations Center, a report by Piro on the casual conversation with Saddam, May 13, 2004. Also see several reports from U.S. Department of Justice, Federal Bureau of Investigation, Baghdad Operations Center: Interview Session No. 1, February 7, 2004; Interview Session No. 10, February 27, 2004; and Interview Session No. 12, March 5, 2004.

520–522: Some details of the pursuit and killing of Osama bin Laden from Press Briefing by Senior Administration Officials on the Killing of Osama Bin Laden, May 2, 2011; official transcript, "Remarks by the President on Osama Bin Laden," May 2, 2011; Nicholas Schmidle, "Getting Bin Laden," *New Yorker*, August 8, 2011; Mark Thompson, "Inside the Osama Bin Laden Strike: How America Got Its Man," *Time*, May 3, 2011; Associated Press, "The Man Who Hunted Osama Bin Laden," July 5, 2011; Jonathan Landy, "Bin Laden Raid Years in the Making, Minutes in Execution," McClatchy Newspapers, May 2, 2011; and Caren Bohan, Mark Hosenball, Tabassum Zakaria, and Missy Ryan, "The Kill Plan," Reuters, May 2011.

INDEX

Page numbers beginning with 525 refer to endnotes.

INDEX

INDEX

INDEX 581

INDEX   581

INDEX

INDEX

INDEX

INDEX

INDEX

INDEX

INDEX

INDEX

INDEX

Canadian authorities' suspicion of, 126, 222–24, 370, 419, 420–21, 509

Canadian restitution to, 509–10

El-Maati's relationship to, 163, 165, 227, 272, 370, 371, 389, 510

false al-Qaeda identification of, 387–88, 389

release of, 509

Syrian imprisonment of, 374, 381–82, 385, 386, 387, 388, 389, 390, 418–19, 420–21

U.S. detention of, 370–74, 376–77, 380–82, 384–87, 388–90, 418, 510

wife's search for, 375, 376

Armitage, Richard, 81, 381–82

Armstrong, Ann, 42

Army, U.S.:

in Afghanistan War, 140–41, 177, 181, 184

al-Libi's detention by, 207

anthrax vaccinations for, 115, 166

Construction Battalion 423 of, 245

Fourth Infantry Division's First Brigade Combat Team of, 518–19

and Guantanamo interrogation program, 434

202nd Military Intelligence Battalion of, 242

see also Special Forces, U.S.

Army, U.S., Special Operations Command of, Psychological Operations unit of, 189

Army Criminal Investigation Command (CID), 206, 242

Army Rangers, 140–41, 177, 181, 184, 361, 362–63

Ashcroft, John, 506

and anthrax attacks, 128

and CIA interrogation policy, 282, 283, 343

in detainee treatment policy position of, 230

in law enforcement power expansion, 78

in military commissions dispute, 145, 148, 149–50, 151, 152, 183

in Moussaoui indictment, 178, 181

on 9/11, 24, 46

in Padilla case, 305, 306–8

pre-9/11 warnings ignored by, 9–10, 528, 529, 530

in surveillance powers expansion, 106, 141–42

Ashkhabad, Turkmenistan, radioactive waste storage site in, 5

Atef, Mohammed (Abu Hafs), 6–7, 166, 243

Atif, Ahmed, 13

Atta, Mohammed, 269, 344, 441

9/11 preparations by, 12, 325

Attas, Hussein al-, 13

Atyani, Baker, 3, 4, 5–7

Australia, Iraq War opposition in, 401

Australian Federal Police, 413

Ayres, David, 529

Aznar, José Maria, 494

Azores, Iraq War summit in, 493–96

B

Bachelot, Roselyne, 463

Baghdad International Airport, 519

Bagram Air Base, 207, 378, 387, 484

Bakkali, Kacem, 15

Bali attacks, 394–401

bombs used in, 394

British travel advisory prior to, 367, 377

intelligence gathered on, 367

international response to, 401–2

investigation of, 413–15

KSM's intelligence on, 492

preparation for, 346–48

Bandar bin Sultan, Prince, 116

Bank of England, 53

Barksdale Air Force Base, 39

Barroso, José Manuel, 494

Bartlett, Andrew, 401

Bartlett, Dan, 471, 472

in 9/11 response efforts, 62–63
pre-9/11 concerns of, 8, 9
Blackman, J. Scott, 374, 389
Blair, Bob, 30
Blair, Cherie, 201, 391, 497
Blair, Tony:
  on 9/11, 40–41
  Afghanistan visit of, 201–2
  and Afghanistan War strategy, 137–38
  at Azores meeting, 493–95
  Blix's phone call with, 480–81
  British opposition to, 244, 328, 339,
    402, 422, 466, 471, 485, 486, 494,
    496–97
  Bush's relationship with, 54–55, 71–72,
    90–91, 137–38, 240, 244, 245,
    260–62, 263, 265, 322, 339, 353,
    354–57, 363–64, 421–22, 466, 468,
    470–71, 473, 485, 494, 495
  Cheney's meeting with, 241–42, 243
  Frost's interview of, 467–68
  in Heathrow plot response, 475
  Iraq first strike notification to, 499–500
  Iraq policy of, 72
  Iraq War legal analysis for, 468, 488–89
  in Iraq War parliamentary vote, 496–97
  Iraq War position of, 241–42, 244, 245,
    251–53, 260–62, 263, 316, 321, 322,
    328–29, 354, 355–56, 357, 363–64,
    365, 391, 393, 394, 402, 421–22,
    451–53, 466, 467–68, 470, 471,
    472–73, 480–81, 485, 486, 488–89,
    495, 496–97, 504–5
  Iraq War press conference misstep by,
    472–73
  9/11 response strategy of, 41, 53–55, 71,
    72, 90, 91
  political downfall of, 504
  Putin's meeting with, 391–94
Blee, Richard, 33
Blix, Hans, 366, 409–11, 421, 445, 454,
  467, 469, 471, 472, 476–77, 479,
  480, 481, 487, 488
Bolduc, John, 138
Bolten, Josh, 1, 3, 32
Bolton, Emily, 212

Bonk, Ben:
  on Iraq's al-Qaeda connection, 343–44
  in Libyan intelligence meeting, 116–18,
    123
  in 9/11 response efforts, 33, 62–63
  and Predator drone program, 57
  at pre-election intelligence briefing, 1–3,
    76
  Spann family notification by, 171–72
  and weapons of mass destruction report,
    383, 384
Border Patrol, U.S., 10
Bosnia-Herzegovina:
  counterterrorism operation in, 118–21,
    134–35, 204–6, 215–16, 229 see also
    Algerian Six
Bosnian War, 118, 135
Boston, Mass., 9/11 flight from, 16–17
botulism, 76
Boumediene, Lakhdar, 511, 512, 513
Bourke, Richard, 212, 213
Bovis Lend Lease, 164
Bowen, Stuart, 154
Boyce, Michael, 252, 451, 452
Brant, David, 430–31, 432, 433, 443
Breyer, Stephen, 310
briefcase bomb, 1, 2, 3
Brinkema, Leonie, 269, 270, 271
Brokaw, Tom, 88, 107, 110, 121, 122, 123,
  124, 126, 128
Brosnahan, James, 326
Brown, Bob, 401
Brown, Gordon, 504
Brown, Michael, 75
Buddhas of Bamiyan, 92
Buffam, Randy, 222–24
Burns, William, 116
burying alive, 333
Bush, George H. W., 60, 500
Bush, George W.:
  in Afghanistan War planning, 64–65, 73,
    74, 78, 79, 87, 137, 138, 180, 181
  in Algerian Six case, 205, 215, 216,
    229
  and anthrax attacks, 129
  at Azores meeting, 493–96

J

L

M

S

U